EXAMPLES & EXPLANATIONS

Corporations

EXAMPLES & EXPLANATIONS

Corporations

Seventh Edition

Alan R. Palmiter
Howard L. Oleck Professor of Business Law
Wake Forest University

Published by Wolters Kluwer Law & Business in New York.

Wolters Kluwer Law & Business serves customers worldwide with CCH, Aspen Publishers, and Kluwer Law International products. (www.wolterskluwerlb.com)

To contact Customer Service, e-mail customer.service@wolterskluwer.com, call 1-800-234-1660, fax 1-800-901-9075, or mail correspondence to:

Wolters Kluwer Law & Business
Attn: Order Department
PO Box 990
Frederick, MD 21705

Printed in the United States of America.

1 2 3 4 5 6 7 8 9 0

ISBN 978-1-4548-0247-1

Library of Congress Cataloging-in-Publication Data

Palmiter, Alan R.
Corporations : examples and explanations / Alan R. Palmiter.—7th ed.
p. cm.
ISBN 978-1-4548-0247-1 (alk. paper)
1. Corporation law—United States—Problems, exercises, etc. I. Title.
KF1414.85.P35 2012
346.73'066—dc23

2012012515

About Wolters Kluwer Law & Business

Wolters Kluwer Law & Business is a leading global provider of intelligent information and digital solutions for legal and business professionals in key specialty areas and respected educational resources for professors and law students. Wolters Kluwer Law & Business connects legal and business professionals as well as those in the education market with timely, specialized authoritative content and information-enabled solutions to support success through productivity, accuracy, and mobility.

Serving customers worldwide, Wolters Kluwer Law & Business products include those under the Aspen Publishers, CCH, Kluwer Law International, Loislaw, Best Case, ftwilliam.com, and MediRegs family of products.

CCH products have been a trusted resource since 1913 and are highly regarded resources for legal, securities, antitrust and trade regulation, government contracting, banking, pension, payroll, employment and labor, and healthcare reimbursement and compliance professionals.

Aspen Publishers products provide essential information to attorneys, business professionals, and law students. Written by preeminent authorities, the product line offers analytical and practical information in a range of specialty practice areas from securities law and intellectual property to mergers and acquisitions and pension/benefits. Aspen's trusted legal education resources provide professors and students with high-quality, up-to-date, and effective resources for successful instruction and study in all areas of the law.

Kluwer Law International products provide the global business community with reliable international legal information in English. Legal practitioners, corporate counsel, and business executives around the world rely on Kluwer Law journals, looseleafs, books, and electronic products for comprehensive information in many areas of international legal practice.

Loislaw is a comprehensive online legal research product providing legal content to law firm practitioners of various specializations. Loislaw provides attorneys with the ability to quickly and efficiently find the necessary legal information they need, when and where they need it, by facilitating access to primary law as well as state-specific law, records, forms, and treatises.

Best Case Solutions is the leading bankruptcy software product to the bankruptcy industry. It provides software and workflow tools to flawlessly streamline petition preparation and the electronic filing process, while timely incorporating ever-changing court requirements.

ftwilliam.com offers employee benefits professionals the highest quality plan documents (retirement, welfare, and nonqualified) and government forms (5500/PBGC, 1099 and IRS) software at highly competitive prices.

MediRegs products provide integrated health care compliance content and software solutions for professionals in healthcare, higher education, and life sciences, including professionals in accounting, law, and consulting.

Wolters Kluwer Law & Business, a division of Wolters Kluwer, is headquartered in New York. Wolters Kluwer is a market-leading global information services company focused on professionals.

For Fabiola, Andrés, and Erica

Summary of Contents

Contents

PART II. FORMATION OF THE CORPORATION

PART IV. CORPORATE FIDUCIARY DUTIES

PART V. SHAREHOLDER LIQUIDITY RIGHTS

Preface

For many students corporate law is an uninviting mystery. Notions such as debt/equity ratios, proxy contests, leveraged buyouts, and staggered boards cause many to freeze. Besides its unfamiliar business setting, corporate law uses a jumble of analytic methods. It mixes civil procedure, contracts and agency rules, tort concepts, constitutional and property principles, and even criminal law. In addition, statutory interpretation combines with case synthesis and regulatory analysis—flavored by federalism and policy debates.

But corporate law is actually coherent. An investment device for pooling money and labor, the corporation seeks to resolve the conflicts among money contributors (shareholders and creditors) and labor contributors (management). *Corporations: Examples and Explanations* presents a full and clear understanding of the legal rules that address the interests of the corporate participants. The book organizes these legal rules into eight different parts:

I—Introduction to Corporate Law introduces the history and attributes of the U.S. corporation and describes other noncorporate forms of business organization—such as partnerships, limited partnerships, and limited liability companies.

II—Formation of the Corporation explains the incorporation process, the financial rights in the corporation (corporate securities and the relation of debt and equity), and the information rights of shareholders.

III—Shareholder Voting Rights gives an overview of the role of shareholders in corporate governance. It describes the state rules on shareholder voting and judicial protection of the voting process, as well as the federal disclosure and antifraud regime that applies to voting in public corporations.

IV—Corporate Fiduciary Duties summarizes the rules on management accountability. It describes when judges review management decisions and oversight, and when they defer to management's business judgment, focusing on specific corporate activities: self-dealing transactions, executive compensation, indemnification, corporate opportunities, parent-subsidiary dealings. It also considers the procedures by which fiduciary duties are enforced.

V—Shareholder Liquidity Rights describes the shareholders' right to freely transfer their shares. It considers protections meant to facilitate this right (such as disclosure in securities trading markets) and exceptions to free transferability (such as insider trading restrictions).

VI—Closely Held Corporation discusses the dilemma of close corporations, which lack a market for their shares. It describes the special contractual arrangements, and sometimes judicial intervention, that substitute for stock markets.

VII—Corporate Creditors explains the rule of limited liability and its allocation of risks between corporate insiders and outsiders. It describes how limited liability arises during the incorporation process, when the corporation becomes bound in its outside dealings, and how insiders are constrained when corporate dealings affect outsiders.

VIII—Fundamental Corporate Changes considers how corporate rights and duties can be changed. It describes (and illustrates) amendments to the articles, corporate restructurings, and corporate combinations, as well as protections for shareholders. It summarizes federal regulation of takeovers and state regulation of takeover defenses.

In laying out these essential building blocks of the corporation, the book strives to be accessible to students who possess no background in business.

The book also gives you an opportunity to probe and test your understanding of corporate law. The textual discussion provides a framework for your understanding, and the follow-up examples and explanations reinforce the text. You will find that reading the relevant chapter and composing answers to the examples, before comparing them to my explanations, will go a long way in helping you prepare for class, the exam, and beyond.

Alan R. Palmiter

March 2012

Acknowledgments

Thank you to the many students whose insights and curiosity inspired this book. Your observations have helped me to organize the subject, your comments in class to focus my coverage, and your questions to frame my own.

I owe a special thanks to Caroline Igou ('12) and David Rugani ('13), whose research and editorial suggestions on this edition were particularly thoughtful and helpful. Caroline undertook a meticulous review of the leading Corporations casebooks, and identified recent cases, statutory materials and topics. Dave, before even taking the course in Business Organizations, suggested revisions to the book based on his review of other study books, as well as his perspective as a novice Corporations student.

Finally, I thank the many professors who have recommended this book to their students, and for their many helpful comments and kind words of encouragement.

Special Notice

To reduce the distraction of citations, this book departs from standard citation form:

1. **Dates.** References to statutory sources and SEC rules are usually undated. All such references are to compilations as of 2011, unless the book gives a different date.

2. ***State statutes.*** The book abbreviates the citations to corporation statutes:

MBCA §8.50	Model Business Corporation Act, Section 8.50 (as approved in 1984, with revisions through 2011)
Cal. Corp. §317	California Corporations Code, Section 317
Del. GCL §145	Delaware General Corporation Law, Section 145
N.Y. BCL §721	New York Business Corporation Law, Section 721

The American Law Institute's "Principles of Corporate Governance: Analysis and Recommendations" (as approved in 1993) is cited as "ALI Principles."

3. ***Case citations***. For state cases, the book cites only to the West regional reporters. An unadorned abbreviation of the state's name means the decision was by the state's highest court. For example,

> "493 A.2d 946 (Del. 1985)" cites to a decision of the Delaware Supreme Court,
> "316 A.2d 599 (Del. Ch. 1974)" cites to a decision of the Delaware Chancery Court.

The book usually does not indicate subsequent case histories, such as *certiorari denied* or *remanded on other grounds*. For cases decided by the U.S. Supreme Court, the book cites only to the "U.S." reports.

4. ***Federal securities law***. The book abbreviates references to the major federal securities acts by giving the section number of the act, but not the U.S. Code citation:

> Securities Act of 1933, compiled at 15 U.S.C. §77a et seq.,
> Securities Exchange Act of 1934, compiled at 15 U.S.C. §78a et seq.

For example, Section 10 of the Securities Exchange Act of 1934 is cited as "Exchange Act §10," without a cross-citation to 15 U.S.C. §78j.

Likewise, the references to rules of the Securities and Exchange Commission are abbreviated by giving the rule number, but not the Code of Federal Regulations citation.

> Rules promulgated under the Securities Act can be found at 17 C.F.R. §§230.___.
> Rules promulgated under the Exchange Act can be found at 17 C.F.R. §§240.___.

For example, Rule 10b-5 (the fifth rule promulgated pursuant to Exchange Act §10(b)) can be found at 17 C.F.R. §240.10b-5.

EXAMPLES & EXPLANATIONS

Corporations

PART I

Introduction to Corporate Law

CHAPTER 1

The Corporation—An Overview

What is a "corporation"? It is a framework by which people conduct modern business. It is a convenient legal entity that can enter into contracts, own property, and be a party in court. It comes in assorted sizes, from a publicly held multinational conglomerate to a one-person business.

The corporation is a creature of law—a legal construct. Nobody (not even your law professor) has ever seen one. The corporation's existence and attributes arise from state-enabling statutes, which give business participants significant freedom to choose their own customized relationships. But the statutory framework is incomplete, and judicial norms fill the many gaps left by the statutes. Other gaps, particularly those involving disclosure to investors, are filled by federal securities law.

Ultimately, the corporation is an investment vehicle for the pooling of money and labor—a grand capitalist tool. *Money capital* comes from shareholders and creditors; *human capital* comes from executives and employees. Both money and labor expect a return on their investment. The corporation defines their legal relationships and mediates their conflicting interests.

This chapter considers the principal attributes of the modern business corporation (§1.1); the history of the U.S. corporation and the sources of U.S. corporate law, including an overview of the Sarbanes-Oxley Act of 2002 (§1.2); and the status of the corporation as a "person" under the U.S. Constitution (§1.3). The corporation is not the only structuring device for modern business. Chapter 2 describes other business organizations, such as partnerships and LLCs, and compares their attributes. Like a corporation, these other forms resolve the basic issues that arise in every business organization.

§1.1 CORPORATION BASICS

§1.1.1 Five Basic Attributes

Suppose you are asked to make an investment. What would you ask? The paradigm corporation represents a set of answers to the five basic questions that arise in every investment relationship:

- **How long does the investment last?** The corporation has an independent, perpetual existence. It is an entity distinct from those who contribute capital (shareholders and creditors) and those who manage the business (directors and officers). The persons who constitute the corporation may come and go, but the corporation remains. It owns the business assets and is liable for any business debts.
- **Who manages the investment?** The locus of corporate power is the board of directors, which manages and supervises the business. (The board often delegates its power to officers to act for and bind the corporation.) In exercising their management powers, the directors are subject to fiduciary duties. Shareholders have only a limited governance role. They can vote to elect directors, approve fundamental corporate changes, and initiate limited reforms, but have no power to act on behalf of the corporation.
- **What is the return on the investment?** The corporation establishes a hierarchy to the financial returns generated by the business. Creditors (including bank lenders, bondholders, trade creditors, and employees) are first in line and receive a return based on their contracts. Shareholders are last in line and receive dividends as declared at the discretion of the board. If the business dissolves, creditors' claims have priority, and shareholders are residual claimants.
- **How can investors get out?** Ownership interests (shares) are freely transferable. Shareholders can realize the value of their investment by selling to other investors interested in acquiring their financial rights. The corporation, however, has no obligation to repurchase these ownership interests. Managers (directors and officers) cannot transfer their positions, but can resign at any time.
- **What are investors' responsibilities to others?** The corporation is liable for its own obligations, but otherwise creates a "nonrecourse" structure. Corporate insiders (directors, officers, shareholders) are not personally liable to outsiders on corporate obligations. Outsiders (such as contract creditors and tort victims) bear the risk of corporate insolvency. Corporate investors and managers risk only their investment.

In effect, the corporation combines five attributes: (1) separate, perpetual legal personality; (2) centralized management under a board structure; (3) shared ownership interests tied to residual earnings and assets; (4) transferability of ownership interests; and (5) limited liability for all participants.

Of course, there are exceptions. For example, shareholders in closely held corporations can agree to manage the business, pay themselves specified dividends, and limit their ability to transfer their shares. In some circumstances courts use equitable principles to hold shareholders personally liable for corporate debts beyond their investment, or lenders may require shareholders to guarantee personally the corporation's obligations. The corporation is mostly a malleable set of *default rules* that specifies the terms of the parties' relationship unless they agree otherwise. This places a premium on the lawyer's role as creative planner.

Note on Corporate Nomenclature

There is some confusion about what is meant by "private corporation" and "public corporation." A "private corporation" generally refers to a *nongovernmental, for-profit business* that has been incorporated under a state statute. A private corporation can be owned by a few shareholders—referred to as a "closely held corporation" or "close corporation." Or the private corporation can be owned by many shareholders whose shares trade on public trading markets such as the New York Stock Exchange—referred to as a "publicly held corporation" or "public corporation." See MBCA §1.40 (Definition 18A). Thus, Apple Inc. is a "private corporation" that is also a "public corporation." And Mom & Pop Grocery Corp. is a "private corporation" that is also a "close corporation." To keep things simple, this book avoids the term "private corporation."

Of course, there are some corporations that are *governmental*, such as the Federal Deposit Insurance Corporation. The FDIC, a government agency established to insure bank deposits, was created by an act of Congress and is governed by a board of governors whose members are appointed by the president. Although some people might call the FDIC a "public corporation," it's clearer to call it a "governmental agency."

Corporate Constituents

Many persons participate in the joint economic activities that constitute the corporation. Shareholders—whether individual investors or institutions that invest for their beneficiaries (pension funds, mutual funds, banks, insurance companies, endowments)—provide money capital. Managers (directors and officers) oversee the business and its employees. Lenders supply additional money capital as secured bank loans, unsecured bonds, short-term notes, and suppliers' trade credit. Suppliers provide inputs for the business under long-term contracts and in market transactions. For some, customers are the reason the business exists. Those injured by the business (whether as employees, customers, or strangers) have claims on the business directly or through governmental enforcement—antitrust, banking, environmental, health, product safety, and workplace safety. As an economic actor in society, the corporation pays federal, state, and local taxes.

Corporate law, however, focuses on the relationship between shareholders and managers—the two constituent groups understood to comprise the "internal" organization of the corporation. "Outside" relationships with creditors, suppliers, customers, employees, and government authorities usually are subject to legal norms that treat the corporation as a person—such as the laws of contract, debtor-creditor, antitrust, labor, and tax.

Note on "Share" Nomenclature

In this book, we use the term "shares" and "shareholders" to refer to the units of ownership interests in corporations and the persons (including entities) who own these units. See MBCA §1.40 (Definitions 21 and 22). You will notice that others, including the whole state of Delaware, refer to "stock" and "stockholders." They're referring to the same things, but they just sound more regal.

§1.1.2 Theory of the Firm

In the paradigm corporation, investors delegate control over their investment to managers. By separating the finance and management functions, the corporation creates an investment vehicle for raising large amounts of capital and operating large enterprises. This separation between shareholders and managers, however, makes the corporation a breeding ground for conflicting interests—and opportunism.

Ideally, shareholders and managers should want to maximize business returns, but they will have separate agendas. Once shareholders have invested, managers may become lazy, extract exorbitant perquisites (or worse), or be reluctant to take business risks that threaten their job security. Once managers have committed their human capital, shareholders may demand immediate returns, want managers to take high risks, or seek intrusive control powers. Despite these conflicts, the premise of the corporation is that neither shareholders nor managers can exist without the other—the corporation allows them to coexist.

Corporate law allocates risks between shareholders and managers in an attempt to minimize shareholder-manager conflicts and to maximize the firm's overall success. It creates a structure for business activities and devices to control conflicts of interest among corporate constituencies. These conflicts are often referred to as "agency problems" since they mimic the conflicts in the principal-agent relationship. In some contexts, corporate law assumes legal intervention is too costly and leaves risk with shareholders. For example, the judicially created business judgment rule gives directors broad discretion to run the business without judicial second-guessing (see §12.2). In other contexts, corporate law regulates conflicts. Shareholders, for example, must approve the board's decision to merge the corporation into another corporation (see §35.2.2).

Over the last few decades, some legal theorists have described the corporation as a "nexus of contracts." Contractarians view the corporation as a set of voluntary relationships among corporate constituents bound together by formal contracts, statutory norms, implicit understandings, and market constraints. The corporation serves as an organizing tool for their relationships. Corporate law, a collection of rules and mechanisms for specifying the roles of the corporate constituents, reflects the bargain the parties would have struck had they negotiated.

This vision of the corporation contrasts with the traditional notion of the corporation as a regulatory device. To traditionalists, the corporation creates dangerous opportunities for managers to exploit shareholders and other constituents. Traditionalists maintain that in public corporations active managers exercise "control" at the expense of passive shareholder "owners." In close corporations where no market exists for shareholder interests, the majority can unfairly exploit the minority. Corporate law, particularly corporate fiduciary duties, serves to protect shareholders.

Traditionalists thus place great emphasis on corporate law as a means to control manager opportunism. They urge greater shareholder voting powers, broad disclosure rights, and strong fiduciary protection. On the other hand, contractarians believe that corporate law embodies the terms the parties have chosen. Combined with market forces, these terms are enough to restrain manager opportunism. For example, contractarians argue that if managers act opportunistically, investors can sell their shares; falling market prices of corporate shares will make it harder for managers to raise capital and to compete in product and service markets; and, eventually, any corporation in which managers disregard shareholders will become a takeover target or go bankrupt.

Traditionalists	Contractarians
The corporation is a creature of law; no real bargaining occurs in the modern public corporation.	The corporation (like a contract) is a device, recognized by law, to organize specialized business activity.
Managers can use "control" to exploit shareholders and other constituents.	Managers cannot exploit "control" because market constraints align their interests with shareholders'.
Shareholders can be exploited because they are unsophisticated or uninformed.	Public shareholders act in sophisticated markets; close corporation participants can protect themselves by contract.
Capital (and other) markets are not always efficient; markets act slowly and unevenly to discipline poor managers.	Capital markets operate efficiently so stock prices of public corporations reflect all available public information.
Corporate law should mandate rules to promote fairness and efficiency.	Corporate law should seek to infer the parties' bargain, whether explicit or implicit.
Judges should actively enforce managers' fiduciary duties to shareholders.	Judges should intervene with caution, only to fill gaps in the parties' bargain and protect market constraints.
Managers will abuse incentives, such as by manipulating financials or taking excessive compensation.	Managers can be given incentives, such as stock options, to motivate them to make the business more productive.

§1.2 SOURCES OF CORPORATE LAW

§1.2.1 Historical Sketch of the Corporation

The modern corporation did not happen in one blazing moment of inspiration. Instead, we can trace its current attributes to various earlier times and forms. The idea of an amalgamation of persons forming a separate juridical personality moved from Greece, to Rome, to the Continent, and to England. Originally, perpetual separate existence in England was reserved for ecclesiastical, municipal, and charitable bodies whose existence was conferred by sovereign grant. The idea of common ownership by a body of passive investors originates from joint-stock trading companies, such as the East India Company (a monopoly franchise) in the early 1600s. A combination of continuity of life, centralized management, financial interests in profits, transferability of shares, and limited liability for private business existed in the 1700s in the form of complex deeds of settlement — an *unincorporated* association!

These concepts came to the American colonies. At first corporations, like political municipalities, had to receive a special charter from the state legislature. Legislatures granted charters on a case-by-case basis to noncommercial associations (such as churches, universities, and charities) that wanted the convenience of perpetual existence and to commercial associations (such as banks, navigation companies, canals, and turnpikes) with special public purposes and large capital needs. As the needs for capital (and thus incorporation) increased during the early 1800s, states began to enact general incorporation statutes for specified, usually capital-intensive, businesses. From the beginning, many feared the concentrated economic power inherent in the corporate device. Eventually, the U.S. corporation evolved in the mid-1800s into a legal form available to all, though subject to significant statutory restrictions.

During the late 1800s two major trends, leading in opposite directions, shaped modern U.S. corporate law. The first trend led to restraints on business activities. In the 1880s Congress created the Interstate Commerce Commission to regulate the railroad monopolies. In 1890 and 1916 Congress passed antitrust legislation (the Sherman and Clayton Acts) to combat concentrations of corporate economic power. In the early 1900s states enacted "blue sky" laws to deal with fraud in the sale of corporate securities. In the 1930s Congress passed a series of securities laws aimed at abusive management practices in national securities markets.

The other trend led to a liberalization of state corporation statutes. In the late 1800s, to attract incorporation revenues, some states amended their statutes to lift limits on the amount of capital that a corporation could raise, to permit corporate ownership of other corporations, and generally to increase the flexibility available to corporate management. Eventually Delaware won this race of laxity, which some have called a scurrilous "race to the bottom" and others an efficiency-producing "race to the top." Today most large, publicly traded U.S. corporations are incorporated in Delaware.

§1.2.2 Modern State Business Corporation Statutes

The corporation statutes of each state describe the basic corporate attributes. The MBCA is typical in that it details

- how to form a corporation (MBCA Chapters 1, 2, 3, 4, 5)
- the financial rights of shareholders (MBCA Chapter 6)
- the governance roles of shareholders, directors, and officers (MBCA Chapters 7, 8)
- the transferability rights of shareholders (MBCA §6.27)
- limited liability for shareholders (MBCA §6.22)
- structural changes such as charter amendments, mergers, and dissolution (MBCA Chapters 10, 11, 12, 13, 14)

Some of the statutory terms are mandatory, such as the annual election of directors and shareholder voting on dissolution. Others, such as the removal of directors without cause or shareholder action without a meeting, are default terms that apply unless the parties choose different terms. Contractarians often view corporate statutes as providing standardized "off-the-rack" terms that apply unless the parties (usually in the charter) choose different, firm-specific terms. Under the internal affairs doctrine, the law of the state of incorporation governs all shareholder-manager matters in multistate corporations (see §3.2.1).

Although no two state corporation statutes are identical, there has been a trend toward greater uniformity and modernization. In 1950 the American Bar Association's invitation-only committee on corporate laws published the first model business corporation act. This model act, and its many revisions, served as the basis for corporation statutes in most states. In 1984 the ABA committee substantially reorganized and rewrote the model act, which follows the enabling structure of Delaware's corporate statute. The model act has since been revised on a number of occasions. The 1984 revisions, first referred to as the Revised Model Business Corporation Act (RMBCA), have become simply the Model Business Corporation Act (MBCA). Significant revisions since 1984 include provisions on directors' conflicting interest transactions (1992), director standards of conduct and liability (1998), and shareholder rights in fundamental transactions (1999). A majority of states (32 as of 2011) have enacted corporate statutes based on the 1984 MBCA.

Not all states, however, have enacted a corporate statute based on the model act. In fact, the most prominent corporate law states — Delaware, California, and New York — have their own idiosyncratic corporation statutes. Delaware's statute is particularly important in U.S. corporate law because of the leadership of its legislature in being the first to enact corporate law reforms, the sophistication of the state's corporate bar, and the expertise and influence of its judiciary — and because most large, public corporations are incorporated in Delaware.

State corporation statutes generally treat all corporations the same. Corporations with numerous, widely dispersed shareholders (publicly held corporations) generally are subject to the same statutory rules as corporations with a small group of shareholders who do not have a public market for their shares (closely held corporations).

§1.2.3 Role of Judge-Made Law

Corporation statutes are not all-encompassing; court decisions clarify and fill in the gaps of the statutes and the corporation's constitutive documents. The most important judicial gap-filling involves the fiduciary duties of directors, officers, and controlling shareholders. Common-law fiduciary principles that regulate abuse by those who control the corporation's decision-making machinery lie at the heart of corporate law. See Chapter 11 (introduction to fiduciary duties). Lately, many fiduciary rules have turned on the disinterestedness and independence of outside (nonmanagement) directors in making corporate decisions.

§1.2.4 ALI Principles of Corporate Governance

In 1977 the American Law Institute embarked on a long-term project to describe and unify the basic standards of corporate governance and structure, particularly in those areas not addressed by state corporation statutes. The project was controversial, often pitting contractarians against traditionalists. In 1993, after more than 15 years, the project came to a conclusion when the ALI approved a final version of the Principles of Corporate Governance. The ALI Principles have not received the same reception as other ALI documents, such as the ALI restatements. Although some courts have embraced portions of the ALI Principles as useful statements of corporate law, other courts have given them little attention, and some have openly rejected them.

§1.2.5 Federal Law

There is no federal corporation statute, despite regular calls for a uniform national law applicable to some or all aspects of publicly traded corporations. Despite the absence of a federal law of corporations, federal statutes add a significant layer of corporate regulation. The Securities Act of 1933 regulates the disclosure when corporations raise capital in public markets, whether by selling stock or taking on debt (see Chapter 5). The Securities Exchange Act of 1934 imposes periodic reporting requirements (see §21.2) and proxy disclosure rules on corporations whose stock is publicly traded (see Chapter 9). In addition, the Exchange Act regulates the trading of securities in public and private markets, including insider trading—that is, the use of material, nonpublic corporate information to buy or sell stock (see Chapters 22 and 23).

Nonetheless, the landscape of corporate governance (the relationship between corporate managers and shareholders) has been significantly altered by two important pieces of federal legislation. In 2002, responding to a spate of corporate and accounting scandals, Congress passed the Sarbanes-Oxley Act—sweeping legislation that federalizes specific aspects of corporate law for public corporations. Among the Act's reforms are limits on corporations hiring their audit firms to do nonaudit work for the corporation, rules governing the composition and functions of the board's audit committee, provisions requiring forfeiture of executive pay when companies correct their financials, bars on individuals from holding corporate office if they have committed securities fraud, prohibitions on companies making personal loans to their executives, mandates for companies to institute and disclose systems of internal controls, and SEC rules governing professional conduct of corporate/securities lawyers. Sarbanes-Oxley is described more fully in §11.5.1.

In 2010, responding to the financial crisis of September 2008 and perceived gaps in financial regulation, Congress passed the Dodd-Frank Act — massive legislation principally concerned with banking reform and securities regulation, but also having major implications for public corporations. Among other things, the Act mandates that compensation committees be composed entirely of independent directors, requires that shareholders have a "say on executive pay," requires corporations to adopt "clawback" policies when executives profit on false financial disclosures, mandates a new SEC program for employees who report securities violations to receive "whistleblower" bounties, and authorizes the SEC to pass rules giving shareholders the ability (at corporate expense) to nominate directors to the board. Dodd-Frank is described more fully in §11.5.2.

Note on Securities Regulation

In keeping with the traditional demarcation of corporate law and securities regulation in the United States, this book considers the aspects of Sarbanes-Oxley and Dodd-Frank that deal primarily with corporate governance. Those reforms that address disclosure to investors — securities regulation — are left to other sources. See Alan R. Palmiter, *Securities Regulation: Examples & Explanations* (5th ed., Wolters Kluwer Law & Business 2011).

§1.3 CORPORATION AS A CONSTITUTIONAL PERSON

The corporation as "person" is a powerful metaphor. Corporate personality facilitates the aggregation of capital and labor with the attributes of a single entity capable of contracting, owning property, and being a party in court — just like a natural person. For commercial purposes, state and federal law largely respects the corporation-as-person metaphor. Most commercial statutes either specifically define corporations to be persons under the statute or have been so interpreted.

But there are many noncommercial contexts in which the law does not treat the corporation as a natural person, such as laws on intestacy, adoption, and political voting. This makes perfect sense. It would be ludicrous if a corporation could be an adoptive parent (except in the movies) or the political rule were "one corporation, one vote." When does the corporation have rights under the U.S. Constitution that normally are associated with natural persons?

§1.3.1 Broad Commercial Rights

According to the Supreme Court, the constitutional status of the corporation varies depending on the constitutional right at issue. The Supreme Court has had no trouble treating the corporation as a constitutional "person" when constitutional provisions can be seen as protecting *commercial interests* of the business.

Corporations are protected against state restrictions that burden interstate commerce. *Allenberg Cotton Co., Inc. v. Pittman*, 419 U.S. 20 (1974). Corporate property is protected against governmental deprivation under the Due Process Clauses of the Fifth and Fourteenth Amendments. *Oklahoma Press Publishing Co. v. Walling*, 327 U.S. 186 (1946). Corporations are "persons" entitled to equal protection under the Fourteenth Amendment, thus protecting them from state regulation aimed only at corporations. *Santa Clara County v. Southern Pac. Ry.*, 118 U.S. 394 (1886).

Corporations have First Amendment rights to express themselves as to commercial matters—such as advertising their products. *Virginia State Board of Pharmacy v. Virginia Citizens Consumer Council*, 425 U.S. 748 (1976). And corporations have a First Amendment right to *not* be associated with certain speech, thus permitting them to refuse to distribute state-mandated information to customers. *Pacific Gas & Electric Co. v. Public Utilities Commission*, 475 U.S. 1 (1986).

The one (and largely superceded) exception to the commercial-interest analysis was the Supreme Court's refusal to treat corporations as "citizens" protected by the Privileges and Immunities Clause of Article IV. *Paul v. Virginia*, 75 U.S. (8 Wall.) 168 (1868). In theory, this allows states to regulate "foreign" corporations (those incorporated in another state) doing in-state business differently from their own "domestic" corporations, though in practice the differences in regulation have been minor and the equal protection afforded corporations under the Fourteenth Amendment essentially ensures nondiscrimination.

§1.3.2 Limited Noncommercial Rights

As to the corporation's *noncommercial interests*, the Supreme Court has been less willing to extend constitutional protection. For example, corporations cannot claim a Fifth Amendment privilege against self-incrimination. *Bellis v. United States*, 417 U.S. 85 (1974). Yet when the corporation's interests are closely linked to an individual's interests—such as in a one-person corporation — some lower courts have suggested that the individual's privilege against self-incrimination may extend to the corporation. And corporations have only a limited Fourth Amendment right to be free from unreasonable searches and seizures, since business privacy is less compelling than personal privacy. *G.M. Leasing Corp. v. United States*, 429 U.S. 338 (1977).

Nonetheless, a corporation has significant free-speech protection under the First Amendment — even as to noncommercial political matters. For example, a state cannot forbid a corporation from expressing its views on a state referendum involving individual tax rates, even when the referendum did not materially affect the corporation's business. *First National Bank of Boston v. Bellotti*, 435 U.S. 765 (1978). Corporations can communicate with the legislative and executive branches by lobbying and commenting on proposed laws and rulemakings and can seek to sway the legislative branch in *amicus* briefs. Corporations can also set up their own political action committees (PACs) funded by voluntary contributions from their shareholders, managers, and employees — thus to speak on political issues and to contribute (subject to limits) to candidates and political parties.

More recently, the Supreme Court has held in a controversial 5-4 decision that a corporation cannot be prohibited from spending its own money to support or oppose a candidate for political office. *Citizens United v. Federal Election Comm'n*. 558 U.S. — (2010). Central to its analysis, the Court in *Citizens United* overruled an earlier 1990 decision that held a state could prohibit corporations from making campaign contributions to state candidates. *Austin v. Michigan Chamber of Commerce*, 494 U.S. 652 (1990). The Court in *Citizens United* rejected that there were compelling justifications to ban political expenditures by corporations that had "amassed" resources in the marketplace because wealthy individuals could not be banned from spending their money to speak out for or against candidates. Thus, although corporations (like individuals) can be limited with respect to their direct *contributions* to political candidates, corporations (like individuals) cannot be limited with respect to *expenditures* — on their own or through independent PACs — for speech that supports or opposes political candidates.

Note on Conception of "Corporation"

As you can see, the Supreme Court's conception of the corporation has different faces. The Court has variously viewed the corporation (1) as a creature of state law (a "concession" theory), (2) as a distinct legal entity separate from the incorporating state and its shareholders (a "natural rights" theory), and (3) as a set of voluntary relationships among its participants (an "aggregation" theory).

The "concession" theory is reflected in an early decision by the Supreme Court that disallowed states from unilaterally changing the corporate charter, viewing the corporation as

(continued)

a binding contract between two parties—the state and corporation. *Trustees of Dartmouth College v. Woodward*, 17 U.S. (4 Wheat.) 518 (1819). The "natural rights" theory, under which corporations are viewed as constitutional persons, was in vogue during the late 1800s when the Court protected corporate persons (and their economic interests) from discriminatory and burdensome state regulation. The "aggregate" theory has been used by the Court—most recently in *Citizens United*—to extend to the corporation the rights that individuals (and thus groups of individuals) have against government overreaching. In the end, though, the Court has never really articulated why the corporation is a "person" or the kind of "person" it is.

Examples

1. Alexa and George want to open a bank. They study the Uniform Partnership Act (UPA) and conclude that a partnership structure presents problems for them. According to the UPA, a partnership dissolves whenever any partner dies or withdraws (UPA §31(4)); each partner must contribute new capital (as needed) equally with other partners (UPA §18(a)); each partner is jointly liable for any business debts (UPA §15(b)); every partner votes on partnership matters (§18(e)); new partners can be added only by unanimous vote (UPA §18(g)). How does a corporation solve these problems?

2. Alexa and George incorporate their bank as First Bank of New Columbia, Inc. (FBNC). New Columbia has adopted a statute modeled on the MBCA. Alexa and George each become a director and officer of the corporation; to get the bank started, they raise money from a dispersed group of shareholders.
   a. First Bank accepts cash deposits from depositors, the principal source of capital for its lending business. The New Columbia statute mandates that holders of voting shares elect the board of directors annually. See MBCA §8.03(d). Can depositors, instead, elect the corporation's directors?
   b. New Columbia's corporate statute says directors must exercise their functions in good faith, in the best interests of the corporation, and with reasonable care. See MBCA §8.30. First Bank loses money because the directors approve construction loans in reliance on overly optimistic projections about the real estate market. Are the directors liable to the shareholders?
   c. After a series of New Columbia court decisions exonerating careless directors, New Columbia adopts a corporation statute that specifies that directors are liable to the corporation if they fail to inform themselves in making decisions. Which standard applies—the MBCA standard, the judicial standard, or the revised statutory standard?

3. The Federal Election Campaign Act (FECA) prohibits corporations from using general corporate funds to make any expenditure or contribution in connection with any election to federal office. 2 U.S.C. §441b. Comparable limits do not apply to individuals, who may spend their own money without limit for or against a federal candidate and may make campaign contributions to federal candidates subject to certain contribution caps.
   a. First Bank is faltering, and its managers contribute corporate funds to Save the Banks — a political action committee that contributes to federal candidates who support a bailout of frail financial institutions. Such a bailout would benefit First Bank's shareholders. Is FECA, which prohibits these contributions, constitutional under the First Amendment?
   b. New Columbia is in the middle of a heated federal senatorial race. One of the candidates, an outspoken critic of the banking industry, has proposed increasing criminal sanctions for bank managers who engage in "willful mismanagement." Alexa and George are aghast. They have First Bank fund a newspaper ad campaign to discredit this candidacy. Is FECA, as applied to First Bank's political advertising, constitutional under the First Amendment?
   c. Many of First Bank's shareholders actually prefer stronger bank regulation and support the pro-regulation candidate in the New Columbia race. How might they discipline the First Bank managers and prevent them from continuing to spend corporate funds opposing their preferred candidate?

Explanations

EXPLANATIONS

1. The corporation creates an immortal juridical entity that exists beyond the lives of its participants. Unlike a classic partnership, a corporation can have managers who need not contribute capital (directors and officers), and capital providers who have no direct role in the bank's management (shareholders). Shareholders expect financial returns based on bank earnings and can transfer their shares without first obtaining the approval of other participants — both greatly increase the liquidity of their investment (the ease with which their shares can be sold). None of the participants is liable for business debts except to the extent of their financial investment. Is a corporation necessary to accomplish these purposes? If banking law permitted banks to operate in partnership form, modern partnerships could be designed to have many of the attributes of a corporation. Most of the provisions of partnership law are not mandatory, but instead specify default rules as to which the parties can "agree otherwise." (See Chapter 2.) Thus, a partnership agreement could provide for

- *continuation* of the partnership after any partner's death or withdrawal
- *centralized management* in which some partners vote on how the business is run and others have only limited voting rights
- *partnership withdrawals* at specified intervals based on firm profitability
- *free transferability* of nonmanaging partners' interests

The one principal difficulty is that partners are jointly liable to third parties—a mandatory partnership rule of *personal liability*. Yet it may be possible to contract for a structure that resembles *limited liability*. Voluntary creditors—such as banks, customers, and suppliers—can be required to agree to indemnify partners (whether acting as managers or capital providers) and look only to partnership assets to satisfy their claims against the business. Liability to involuntary creditors—tort victims—can be minimized through insurance, as well as internal liability allocation (indemnification and contribution) among the partners.

But achieving all of this through the partnership form requires "custom tailoring." The advantage of a corporation is that all these attributes are "off the rack."

2. a. The depositors don't vote unless they own shares. As is true under most corporation statutes, the MBCA reserves voting power to shareholders. The theory is that depositors, and other contract providers of capital to the corporation, have rights fixed by their contract (to be paid interest, to make withdrawals, and to receive account information). Their contractual rights are senior to (come before) the shareholders' financial rights to dividends and payments on liquidation. Shareholders generally cannot withdraw their investment or receive specified periodic payments—their rights are residual. To protect their precarious position, shareholders receive voting rights.

   b. In general, corporate law and the famous "business judgment rule" say no. First Bank's losses can be seen as resulting from two kinds of risks: external risks beyond the control of the firm's managers (real estate market) and internal risks within their control (monitoring, evaluation, and reaction by management to external risks). Corporate law assumes that shareholders are more efficient bearers of risk. Efficient enterprise organization will be advanced if dispersed investors, each with a small stake in the firm, bear the risk of firm losses. Shareholders are better able than managers to diversify their investment, thus dampening the impact of a particular firm's loss, whether arising from external or internal risk. Rarely will a small group of managers, even if individually wealthy, be able to risk sufficient resources to provide the necessary capital for a large, modern business. Moreover, by having shareholders bear internal risks, corporate law facilitates management specialization and rational risk taking. If manager-specialists were required to bear the loss of their poor decisions, they might be reluctant to become managers in the first place (choosing a career in law instead) or they might become overly cautious (shunning positive net-value, high-risk projects).

But this does not mean that shareholders should (or do) bear all internal risks. There are some internal risks—such as embezzlement by managers—that if borne by shareholders would hardly encourage investment. But as to internal risks that turn on the honest and informed judgment of corporate managers, the business judgment rule places the burden of loss on shareholders.

c. The statutory standard applies. The MBCA is merely a model statute that a group of lawyers and law professors—members of an ABA committee—have recommended for adoption by state legislatures. No legislature has adopted a version of the model act wholesale without modifications. Corporate judge-made law, like all other state common law, is subject to statutory revision. New Columbia courts, after the statutory revision, will be bound by the statute, though they may use judge-made doctrines to interpret the statute's open-ended meaning.

3. a. *Citizens United* did not address the constitutionality of FECA's ban on corporate *contributions* to political campaigns or to nonindependent PACs that make such contributions. See *Buckley v. Valeo*, 424 U.S. 1 (1976) (permitting limitations on *contributions* to candidates to prevent the appearance of corruption, but not independent *expenditures* in support or opposition of candidates). The FECA ban on corporate campaign contributions may well depend on how we view the corporation. Is the corporation (1) a creature of state law—a "concession" theory? (2) an entity with rights arising by virtue of its existence—a "natural entity" theory? (3) a set of contractual relationships—a "nexus of contracts" theory?

If we regard the corporation as a "creature of law," regulation of corporate campaign contributions can be seen as an inherent consequence of the governmental concession. That is, "the state giveth and the state taketh away." This way of seeing the corporation, first articulated in the early 1800s, was at the heart of the Supreme Court's decision upholding a Michigan campaign finance law that prohibited corporations from using general funds to support specific candidates to state office. *Austin v. Michigan Chamber of Commerce* (see §1.3.2). The *Austin* Court found compelling the state's interest in preventing "the unique state-conferred corporate structure that facilitates the amassing of large treasuries" to obtain an "unfair advantage in the political marketplace." But this view was rejected by the majority in *Citizens United*, which concluded that banning the corporation from spending its own money to support or oppose a political candidate constituted an unconstitutional condition on the corporate form.

But if we regard the corporation as a natural entity whose rights extend beyond those conceded by the state, corporate rights (exercised by management) may approximate those of individuals. The Supreme Court adopted this viewpoint in *First National Bank of Boston v. Bellotti* (see §1.3.2) when it held Massachusetts could not interfere with corporate free-speech rights in a state referendum, absent a compelling interest. In a similar vein, the Court has viewed the corporation from management's perspective in cases that invalidate state regulation of management-written inserts accompanying monthly utility bills. *Consolidated Edison v. Public Service Commission of New York*, 447 U.S. 530 (1980) (state ban of such inserts); *Pacific Gas & Electric Co. v. Public Utilities Commission of California*, 475 U.S. 1 (1986) (plurality) (state requirement that management include messages by consumer group). Under this perspective, FECA's ban on direct contributions to candidates and their PACs—while such contributions are permitted for individuals, subject to caps—unconstitutionally infringes on the right of First Bank (really, management) to speak.

But if we regard the corporation as a "nexus of contracts," the rights of each constituent group that forms the nexus are relevant. The Supreme Court seemed to adopt this viewpoint when it invalidated FECA's application to a nonprofit corporation formed solely to promote political ideas. *FEC v. Massachusetts Citizens for Life, Inc. (MCFL)*, 479 U.S. 238 (1986). The Court held that the nonbusiness organization had "features more akin to a voluntary political association," and the First Amendment prohibited the burden imposed by the regulatory requirement that political expenditures come only from earmarked, segregated funds. Under this view, which the Court seemed to embrace in *Citizens United*, if First Bank's shareholders and other corporate constituents support management's contributions to Save the Banks, FECA interferes with the corporate constituents' collective First Amendment rights and cannot be justified as protecting them from becoming "captive political speakers."

b. This question would seem to be more difficult because the interests of shareholders and managers are not necessarily aligned, as they seemed to be in the previous question. The First Bank shareholders may not favor the use of corporate funds to oppose the Senate candidate or may support the candidate for other reasons.

Nonetheless, the Supreme Court in *Citizens United* made clear that a corporation (really, management) could not be prohibited from spending the corporation's own money to speak on a political issue, including to support or oppose a political candidate. The Court rejected the "creature of law" analysis in *Austin* and the notion that the accumulation of capital permitted by the corporate form justifies government regulation of corporate speech.

The *Citizens United* majority did not fully embrace a "natural entity" theory in finding FECA's ban on corporate political expenditures to be unconstitutional, given the majority's acceptance of a "compelling justifications" analysis for determining whether corporate expenditures could be banned. Thus, although the FECA ban singled out corporations for regulation not imposed on individuals, this alone was not enough to justify the heavier corporate regulation. Implicitly, the Court concluded the corporation was not fully a "person" under the First Amendment.

The *Citizens United* majority, however, seemed to accept a "nexus of contracts" approach that shareholders had delegated to managers the decision how to best advance corporate interests. Although the Court in *MCFL* (see §1.3.2) had suggested the First Amendment would not protect corporate speech that does not accurately reflect shareholders' political views, the Court in *Citizens United* chose to not raise this potential conflict to constitutional importance. Thus, even though First Bank shareholders might not agree with their managers' expenditure of corporate funds, the remedy — according to the Court majority — would come through "the procedures of corporate democracy," not a congressional ban infirm under the First Amendment.

c. Shareholders in public corporations have little control over corporate decision making on political spending for and against candidates. The shareholders of First Bank have limited options to protect themselves against management's political activism.

First, corporate political spending need not be separately disclosed under state corporate or federal securities law (see Chapter 21), and corporate donors to super-PACs can mask their identity by contributing to intermediaries. Lacking information, shareholders can't make investment choices based on such spending. Second, even if shareholders can identify the political spending of their corporation, the business judgment rule (see §12.2) precludes shareholders from challenging in court the spending choices of management (including political spending) if it is arguably beneficial to the corporation's business. Third, shareholders lack effective voting remedies. Although shareholders can pass resolutions condemning management's political spending, the resolutions are not binding but only advisory (see §9.4). And although shareholders can elect directors to the board who share their views on political spending, the significant costs of proposing an insurgent slate must be borne by the nominating shareholder (see §8.1.2).

Thus, the suggestion in *Citizens United* that any "abuses [in corporate political spending] could be corrected by shareholders through the procedures of corporate democracy" rings hollow. Although the Supreme Court held that corporations, like individuals and PACs, could be required to disclose their identities when communicating for or against a candidate, it is unclear whether current disclosure and shareholder input are enough. A recent study, for example, found that political spending by corporations in industries that are neither government dependent nor heavily regulated is correlated with poor corporate financial performance as well as lower shareholder rights and greater managerial abuse in the form of the use of corporate executive jets. The study further finds that corporate political lobbying and contributions to PACs increased after *Citizens United*, with the more politically active corporations experiencing greater losses in shareholder value. In short, the study suggests corporate political activity may not serve shareholder interests. See John C. Coates IV, *Corporate Politics, Governance and Value Before and After* Citizens United, SSRN Paper 1973771 (2011) (based on data of corporate contributions to PACs and voluntary disclosures).

Choice of Organizational Form

Given the advantages of incorporation, it is strange that corporate lawyers often advise their clients, "When in doubt, do not incorporate." There is a common lay perception that no business can be successful without the "corporation" mystique. But choosing what organizational form best suits the needs of the business and its participants is more complicated.

This chapter introduces the various investment vehicles—or business organizations—available for pooling money and labor (§2.1). We describe the basic attributes of the organizational choices (§2.2) and consider the tax implications of the choice (§2.3). The chart on page 38 describes the different organizational forms and how they differ from each other.

Note on Agency Law

The most basic business organization is the principal-agent relationship. Agency is the fiduciary relationship created when a "principal" manifests consent to another person (the "agent") to act on his behalf and under his general control, and the agent consents to this relationship. It is irrelevant whether the parties characterized their relationship as principal-agent. (The employer-employee relationship is a specialized principal-agent relationship, where the employer has the right to control the physical conduct of the employee's services.)

(continued)

The principal-agent relationship creates mutual duties. The agent must put the principal's interests ahead of her own; the principal must honor all obligations that arise between the agent and third parties in contract or tort.

The agent is bound by a duty of loyalty to her principal. She cannot compete directly with her principal on her own or as an agent of a rival company. She cannot misappropriate her principal's profits, property, or business opportunities. She cannot breach her principal's confidences. An agent who fails to act solely for the benefit of her principal is liable for the profits she earned in violation of her duties. No actual injury to the principal need be shown.

The agent may act on behalf of her principal with actual or apparent authority. *Actual authority* includes both express delegations of authority (the principal states to the agent that he wants something done) and implied delegations (past practice implies ongoing authority; general directions include implied authority to do all things proper, usual, and necessary). *Apparent authority* arises when the principal acts so as to lead a reasonably prudent third party to suppose the agent had authority, such as when an employee does those things usual and proper to the conduct of the employer's business. This depends on the employee's position, the reasonableness of the offered terms, and the employer's communications to the third party through the employee.

One important distinction is whether the principal is *disclosed* or *undisclosed*. An agent acting for a disclosed principal is normally not liable for obligations entered into on behalf of the principal; only the principal is liable. But an agent for an undisclosed principal is liable on such obligations, as is the principal who authorized the agent to act on his behalf.

Authority may also be created retroactively through *ratification*. This happens when the principal agrees (explicitly or implicitly) to be bound by the prior act of his agent, which was otherwise unauthorized. The principal then becomes bound as though he had authorized the act from the beginning.

An employer may become liable vicariously for tortious acts committed by its employees "acting within the scope of their employment." But a principal is generally not liable for the acts of a nonagent general contractor, unless the principal is negligent in hiring the contractor.

An agency relationship may generally be terminated at any time, for any reason.

§2.1 BUSINESS ORGANIZATION CHOICES

Suppose Bud and Rudy plan to open a flower shop. Bud will run the shop; Rudy will put in money. The organizational forms they can use to structure their for-profit business exist along a continuum. Each form can be manipulated to approximate the characteristics of the others. Keep in mind that whatever structure Rudy and Bud choose, it will not significantly affect how they conduct the business of selling flowers. The organizational form determines their legal relationship, their financial rights, their responsibilities for business debts, and their tax liability.

Today the organizational choices are mind-boggling.

Sole Proprietorship

A single individual, Rudy, owns the business assets and is liable for any business debts; Bud would be her employee. (Or Bud could be the proprietor and Rudy could lend him money.) Proprietorships usually are small, with modest capital needs that can be met from the owner's resources and from lenders.

General Partnership

Bud and Rudy arrange to carry on the business while agreeing to share control and profits, thus automatically creating a partnership. As partners, they are each individually liable for partnership obligations. The general partnership (GP) is prevalent in service industries—such as law, accounting, and medicine—where trust must exist among the participants and capital needs are not great. (All states, except Louisiana, have adopted a version of the Uniform Partnership Act (UPA 1914) or the more recent Revised Uniform Partnership Act (RUPA 1997); and in the last decade nearly all states have also adopted "limited liability partnership" (LLP) provisions to their partnership statutes.)

Limited Partnership

Bud or Rudy organizes a limited partnership (LP) in which so-called limited partners provide capital and are liable only to the extent of their investment. General partners run the business and are fully liable for partnership debts. Since limited partners need not be general partners, Bud could be the general partner and both of them limited partners. LPs combine tax advantages and limited liability. (Nearly all states have adopted the Uniform Limited Partnership Act (ULPA 1916) or the Revised Uniform Limited Partnership Act (RULPA 1985, revised in 2001); many states have also adopted "limited liability limited partnership" (LLLP) provisions in their LP statutes.)

Limited Liability Company

Bud and Rudy form a limited liability company (LLC)—a hybrid entity between a corporation and partnership. Like a GP, the members of the LLC provide capital and manage the business according to their agreement; their interests generally are not freely transferable. Like a corporation, members are not personally liable for debts of the LLC entity. (In 1977, Wyoming was the first state to adopt an LLC statute. Today all states have LLC statutes; a Uniform Limited Liability Company Act (ULLCA) was approved in 1996 and revised in 2006, but states have been slow in enacting the uniform acts.)

Corporation

Bud and Rudy form a legal entity called a corporation. Shareholders provide capital, and directors and officers manage the business. Corporate participants are not personally liable for corporate debts; only the corporation is liable. Corporations are the principal means of organizing businesses with complex organizational structures and large capital needs. The corporate form, however, works for any size business, including a one-person "incorporated proprietorship." (All states have corporation statutes, most based on the Model Business Corporation Act (1984); but some important states, notably Delaware, have their own idiosyncratic statutes.)

Other Choices

If this were not enough, there are other variants. A *joint venture* is basically a general partnership with a defined, limited-term objective. Examples include two law professors writing a casebook or three corporations developing a new chemical process. A *business trust* (or *Massachusetts trust*) involves the transfer of investors' property to a trustee who manages and controls the property for their benefit. The investors' beneficial interests are freely transferable, and the beneficiaries generally are not liable for trust debts. A *professional corporation* (as well as a *professional LLC* or *professional LLP*) allows specified professionals—doctors, lawyers, and accountants—to limit their vicarious liability without running afoul of ethical rules that prohibit professionals from practicing in the traditional corporate form.

§2.2 CHOOSING BETWEEN UNINCORPORATED AND INCORPORATED FIRM

If Bud and Rudy want to share in the control and profits of the flower shop, they would likely choose between an unincorporated firm (GP, LP, or LLC) and a corporation. Although a business planner can adapt each form to suit particular needs, some characteristics are relatively immutable—formation, liability, and tax treatment. Others involve default terms and require planning—duration, financial rights, management, and transferability of ownership interests.

Every business organization serves as an investment vehicle for the pooling of money and labor. Each organizational form must resolve five basic issues (see Chapter 1).

1. When does the investment begin and end?
2. What is the return on the investment?
3. Who manages the investment?
4. How can investors get out?
5. What are investors' responsibilities to others?

§2.2.1 Life Span—Formation and Duration

General Partnership

A GP is created when two or more persons associate to carry on a business as co-owners to share profits and control; it does not require legal documentation. UPA §6; RUPA §202(a). A profit-sharing arrangement creates a presumption of a GP even if the parties do not intend to be partners. UPA §7; RUPA §202(c)(3). A GP without a definite term (an at-will partnership) dissolves upon the withdrawal of any partner. UPA §31; RUPA §801(a). Absent an agreement, the withdrawing partner may demand that the business be liquidated and the net proceeds be distributed to the partners in cash. UPA §38(1); RUPA §807. Under RUPA, when a partner dies, the surviving partners may choose to continue the GP and buy out the deceased partner's interest, without a liquidation. RUPA §701 (buyout price is set at greater of liquidating or going concern value, taking into account discounts for lack of marketability or loss of key partner, but not for minority status).

A GP can obtain limited liability by filing a statement of qualification or registration with state officials as a limited liability partnership (LLP) and adopt a name that identifies its LLP status. RUPA §1001. The LLP statutes protect the personal assets of partners from the risk of negligence or malpractice by others in the firm. But LLP status does not protect partners from claims by co-partners that they have violated their partnership agreement. See *Ederer v. Gursky*, 881 N.E.2d 204 (N.Y. 2007) (holding partners liable for paying withdrawing partner's share, as specified in their agreement).

Limited Partnership

An LP arises when a certificate is filed with a state official. RULPA §201. An LP lasts as long as the parties agree or, absent agreement, until a general partner withdraws. RULPA §801.

Limited Liability Company

An LLC arises with the filing of a certificate or articles of organization with a state official. ULLCA §202. Many LLC statutes require there be at least two members, though increasingly one-member LLCs are possible. More recent statutes do not limit the duration of LLCs. ULLCA §203.

Corporation

A corporation arises when articles of incorporation are filed with a state official. MBCA §2.03. Corporate existence is perpetual, regardless of what happens to shareholders, directors, or officers. MBCA §3.02.

§2.2.2 Financial Rights — Claims on Income Stream and Firm Assets

General Partnership

Partners share equally in profits and losses, unless agreed otherwise. UPA §18(a); RUPA §401(b). A partner may enforce the right to profits in an action for an accounting. UPA §22; RUPA §405(b). Partners have no right to compensation for their services, unless provided by agreement. UPA §18(f); RUPA §401(h). On dissolution, after discharging partnership obligations, profits and losses are divided among the partners. UPA §40; RUPA §807.

Limited Partnership

Limited and general partners share profits, losses, and distributions according to their capital contributions, absent a contrary written agreement. RULPA §§503, 504. (Limited partners, however, are generally not liable to third parties for LP obligations. RULPA §303.) Pre-dissolution distributions are by agreement, as is compensation of the general partner. RULPA §601.

Limited Liability Company

Most LLC statutes allocate financial rights according to member contributions, though some provide for equal shares. ULLCA §405(a) (equal shares). Under many statutes, members can take share certificates to reflect their relative financial interests. Distributions must be approved by all the members. ULLCA §404(c). Absent agreement, members generally have no right to remuneration. ULLCA §403(d).

Corporation

Financial rights are allocated according to shares. MBCA §6.01. Distributions, from surplus or earnings, must be approved by the board of directors. MBCA §6.40. Directors and officers have no right to remuneration, except as fixed by contract.

§2.2.3 Firm Governance—Authority to Bind and Control the Firm

General Partnership

Each partner is an agent of all other partners and can bind the GP, either by transacting business as agreed by the partners (actual authority) or by appearing in the eyes of third parties to carry on partnership business (apparent authority). UPA §9; RUPA §301. Unless otherwise agreed, a majority vote of the partners decides ordinary partnership matters, but anything that is extraordinary or contravenes the agreement requires unanimity. UPA §18(h); RUPA §401(j).

With the broad powers come duties. See *Meinhard v. Salmon*, 164 N.E. 545 (N.Y. 1928) (managing co-venturer breached duty of loyalty, "the punctilio of an honor the most sensitive," to capitalist co-venturer by failing to disclose opportunity of expanded project after expiration of their venture, thus precluding capitalist from competing for project). Partners have fiduciary duties to each other to act in good faith with due care and undivided loyalty. RUPA §404. Among other things, partners must inform co-partners of material information affecting the GP and share in any benefits from transactions connected to the GP. UPA §20, 21; RUPA §404(b).

Partners can bring an action to enforce their fiduciary rights against co-partners. UPA §22 (accounting); RUPA §405(b) (legal or equitable relief, with or without an accounting). In keeping with its philosophy of promoting party autonomy, RUPA does not automatically prohibit partners from furthering their own interests so long as they do not violate their duty of loyalty. RUPA §404(e).

Limited Partnership

General partners have authority to bind the LP as to ordinary matters. RULPA §403. Limited partners have voting authority over specified matters, but cannot bind the LP. RULPA §302.

General partners have fiduciary duties akin to those of partners in a GP. RULPA §403 (liability to partnership and other partners). Limited partners may bring a derivative action to enforce fiduciary duties owed to the LP.

RULPA §1001 (if general partners have refused to bring action or effort to cause them to bring action "not likely to succeed").

Limited Liability Company

LLCs can be member-managed or manager-managed. ULLCA §203 (manager-managed must be specified). Under most statutes, members in a member-managed LLC have broad authority to bind the LLC in much the same way as partners. ULLCA §301(a). Members have no authority to bind the LLC in a manager-managed LLC. Generally, voting in a member-managed LLC is in proportion to the members' capital contributions, though some statutes specify equal management rights. ULLCA §404.

Members and managers of LLCs have fiduciary duties of care and loyalty, which vary depending on whether the LLC is member-managed or manager-managed. ULLCA §409. In a member-managed LLC, fiduciary duties parallel those in a GP. In a manager-managed LLC, only managers have fiduciary duties; a member who is not a manager is said not to owe fiduciary duties as a member.

Members may bring direct actions against the LLC and other members to enforce their rights as members under the operating agreement and the LLC statute. RULLCA §410 (legal or equitable relief, with or without an accounting). Members may also bring a derivative action on behalf of the LLC to enforce rights of the LLC, if the members or managers who could authorize such an action have refused to sue or an effort to cause them to sue is "not likely to succeed." RULLCA §1101.

Corporation

The corporation has a centralized management structure. Its business and affairs are under the management and supervision of the board of directors. MBCA §8.01. Officers carry out the policies formulated by the board. MBCA §8.41. Shareholders elect the board, MBCA §8.03, and decide specified fundamental matters; they cannot bind the corporation.

Corporate directors and officers owe fiduciary duties of care and loyalty to the corporation and, in some circumstances, to shareholders. These duties are the bedrock of corporate law. See Chapter 11. Controlling shareholders also have more limited fiduciary duties, principally in exercising their control when the corporation's business is sold. See Chapter 17.

Fiduciary duties may be enforced by the corporation or, more often, by shareholders suing on behalf of the corporation in a derivative suit. In many jurisdictions, shareholders must first demand that the board initiate a suit before the shareholder may sue on behalf of the corporation. See Chapter 18.

§2.2.4 Liquidity—Ownership Transferability and Withdrawal

General Partnership

A partner cannot transfer her interest in the GP unless all the remaining partners agree or the partnership agreement permits it. UPA §18(g); RUPA §401(i). A partner may transfer her financial interest in profits and distributions, entitling the transferee (such as a creditor of the partner) to a charging order. UPA §28; RUPA §502.

A partner may withdraw from the GP at any time. UPA §31 (dissolution of at-will partnership occurs upon "express will of any partner"); RUPA §601 (disassociation occurs upon "notice of partner's express will to withdraw"). If the withdrawal is not wrongful, the business is liquidated and the partner is entitled to payment in cash of his proportional share. UPA §38(1) (at-will partnership wound up and any surplus paid in cash to partners pro rata); RUPA §§801, 807 (same). Even if the partner's withdrawal is wrongful, the partner is entitled to a cash payment for his share, less any damages his withdrawal caused. See UPA §38 (without goodwill); RUPA §701 (including "going concern" value).

Notice that dissolution of a partnership (the same for other business organizations) does not necessarily mean the business comes to an end. Instead, partnership dissolution merely terminates the legal relationship among the partners, with the withdrawing partner paid his share of the partnership's value and (typically) the business continuing as a new partnership of the non-withdrawing partners.

Limited Partnership

A general partner cannot transfer his interest unless all the other general and limited partners agree or the partnership agreement permits it. RULPA §401. Limited partner interests are freely assignable. RULPA §702. Limited and general partners can assign their rights to profits and distributions. RULPA §703.

Limited Liability Company

Most LLC statutes provide that members cannot transfer their LLC interests unless all the members consent or transfer rights are established by agreement. ULLCA §503. Some LLC statutes permit the articles of organization to provide standing consent for new members. Many LLC statutes also permit transfer of financial rights to creditors, who can obtain a charging order against the member's interest. ULLCA §504.

Corporation

Corporate shares are freely transferable unless there are specific written restrictions. MBCA §6.27.

In a corporation, a minority shareholder cannot dissolve the corporation. Instead, dissolution requires board action and majority shareholder approval. See MBCA §14.02. Only if the minority shareholder obtained dissolution rights in a shareholders' agreement can he liquidate his investment using this route.

§2.2.5 Liability to Outsiders

General Partnership

General partners have unlimited personal liability for partnership obligations. Their personal assets are at risk for partnership obligations, whether contractual or from misconduct (torts) of the partners or partnership employees/agents. UPA §15; RUPA §306. Generally, partner liability is joint and several; but under some statutes, liability on partnership contracts is only joint so that partnership assets must first be exhausted before partners become individually liable. UPA §15(a) (joint for contract obligations); cf. RUPA §306(a) (joint and several liability).

Limited liability partnership (LLP) statutes graft limited liability onto the GP statutes. LLP partners thus avoid personal liability for partnership obligations, unless the partner's own conduct makes him personally liable or under some statutes the partner "supervised" the wrongful conduct of another partner or associate. See RUPA §306(c) (official comment states "partners remain personally liable for their personal misconduct").

Limited Partnership

At least one partner must be a general partner, with unlimited liability. Limited partners are liable only to the extent of their investment so long as they do not "participate in the control" of the business. RULPA §303. Older statutes did not define "participation," and courts construed the term broadly to cover limited partners who shared in operational decisions and retained control of financial matters. See *Holzman v. de Escamilla*, 195 P.2d 833 (Cal. App. 1948). Modern statutes clarify that some activities do not constitute participation in control. Limited partners do not lose their limited liability merely by being officers, directors, or shareholders of a corporate general partner, voting on major business matters, or advising the general partner. RULPA §303.

Limited liability limited partnership (LLLP) statutes limit the liability of the general partner—creating an LP with the essential attributes of a manager-managed LLC.

Limited Liability Company

LLC members, both in their capacity as capital contributors and managers, are not liable for LLC obligations. ULLCA §303. Nonetheless, courts have held that members can become individually liable if equity or justice so requires — so-called veil piercing.

Corporation

Shareholders have limited liability for corporate obligations. MBCA §6.22. This is also true for directors and officers acting on behalf of the corporation. Corporate participants can lose only what they invested unless there is fraud or an inequity that justifies "piercing the corporate veil." Often, large creditors of small corporations will demand that corporate participants personally guarantee the corporation's obligations, thus reducing the significance of corporate limited liability.

§2.3 TAXATION — CRITICAL ELEMENT IN THE CHOICE

Bud and Rudy are in business to make money, and their reasons for choosing an organizational form will be largely financial. Tax considerations will loom large. We provide a cursory introduction to this complex area, which is treated more fully in advanced tax courses.

§2.3.1 Tax Implications of Organizational Choice

Under current federal income tax law, a "corporation" is a separate tax-paying entity — but a "partnership" is disregarded. Consider three scenarios:

Scenario	Partnership	Corporation
(1) Business makes money and distributes it.	The partnership acts as a tax conduit. Its income flows through to its partners, who must pay	The corporation is taxed on its income when earned. If the corporation pays dividends to its

(continued)

Scenario	Partnership	Corporation
	tax—thus tax is paid only once. The partnership files an informational tax return disclosing relevant financial information.	shareholders, the shareholders must pay tax on the dividends—a double tax.
(2) Business makes money, but retains it.	The partnership's income flows through to the partners even if retained in the business. But it is taxed only once.	The corporation is taxed when it earns income. The tax on shareholders is deferred until the income is distributed or when they sell their shares after appreciation. Double tax is unavoidable.
(3) Business loses money.	The partnership's losses flow through to the partners, who can deduct them from other personal income (or "shelter" their income). (There are some limitations when the losses arise for a partner who is not active in the business—"passive" losses.)	The corporation can deduct ordinary business losses only against income the business generates. Sometimes, if there is insufficient income in a year, the losses can be carried forward or back to other tax years. Shareholders can deduct losses from personal income only by selling their shares at a loss and deducting capital losses.

As you can see, unless the firm plans on retaining earnings, taxation as a partnership has distinct advantages.

Flow-Through versus Entity Tax Treatment

To illustrate the basic structure of federal income taxation of business organizations, consider the following two cases. (We have used the tax rates for tax year 2011, disregarding the effect of exemptions and other deductions, as well as special tax rules for eligible dividends. As you will notice, individual and corporate tax rates are graduated based on taxable income. That is, taxpayers pay taxes at progressively higher rates as their taxable income increases.)

Case 1 (Low Income)

Bud and Rudy's flower shop generates $150,000 in revenues and $110,000 in tax-deductible expenses during the first year — generating $40,000 in taxable income. They share equally in after-tax earnings, they each are subject to tax rates for married individuals filing jointly, and they have no other income.

	Flow-Through Entity	Corporation
Taxable income	$40,000	$40,000
Entity tax	None	
entity rate		15% of taxable income
entity tax		$6,000
amount for distribution	$40,000	$34,000
Individual tax	Flow-through	Tax on dividends
distribution to each owner	$20,000	$17,000
individual rate	$1,700 + 15% of taxable income > $17,000	10% of taxable income
individual tax	$2,150	$1,700
after-tax income	$17,850	$15,300
Total tax (entity + individual)	$4,300	$9,400
Overall tax rates		
effective rate	10.9%	23.6%
marginal rate	15.0%	27.8%

Case 2 (High Income)

The same as Case 1, except the flower shop generates $1,300,000 in revenues and $900,000 in tax-deductible expenses — generating taxable income of $400,000.

	Flow-Through Entity	Corporation
Taxable income	$400,000	$400,000
Entity tax	None	
entity rate		$113,900 + 34% of taxable income > $335,000
entity tax		$136,000
amount for distribution	$400,000	$264,000
Individual tax	Flow-through	Tax on dividends
distribution to each owner	$200,000	$132,000
individual rate	$28,807 + 28% of taxable income > $139,350	$9,500 + 25% of taxable income > $69,000
individual tax	$45,070	$26,030
after-tax income	$154,931	$105,971
Total tax (entity + individual)	$90,139	$188,059
Overall tax rates		
effective rate	22.5%	47.0%
marginal rate	28.0%	52.5%

As these tables show, the impact of double taxation is substantial. There is a significant advantage in achieving "partnership" flow-through tax treatment and avoiding "corporation" status. In both cases a corporation generates greater tax costs compared to a flow-through entity, such as a partnership, LLC, or S corporation.

- Compare the *effective rates*—that is, the total tax bite stated as a percentage of taxable income. Whether taxable income is $40,000 or $400,000, the IRS takes about twice as much in taxes when the business is a corporation that distributes its dividends to shareholders as when there is flow-through tax treatment.
- Compare the *marginal rates*—that is, the tax bite on each additional $1 of taxable income. What happens if Bud and Rudy go to the trouble of earning another taxable dollar? In Case 2, only 28 percent of that dollar would be taxed if their business were a partnership, and 52.5 percent would be taxed if it were a corporation. Knowing the marginal rates helps them decide whether the trouble of earning an extra dollar is worth it.

§2.3.2 Characterizing the Firm: Corporation or Partnership?

For many years, the distinction between a taxable "corporation" and a flow-through "partnership" turned on a multi-factor test promulgated by the Internal Revenue Service, commonly known as the "Kintner regulations." Treas. Reg. §301.7701-2. The IRS looked at whether the firm exhibited three of four classic "corporate" characteristics—namely (1) continuity of life, (2) centralized management, (3) liability for business debts limited to corporate assets, and (4) free transferability of interests.

As the popularity of LLCs grew, the Kintner regulations proved to be a thorn in the side of this new hybrid entity. To avoid tax as a corporation, statutory drafters and business planners had to eliminate at least two corporate attributes—such as by providing for dissolution upon withdrawal (no continuity), restricting transferability of member interests (no free transferability), or establishing member-managed structures (no centralized management). As a result, the tax laws became the tail that wagged the dog, forcing LLC members to accept organizational relationships they would not otherwise have chosen.

All of this changed dramatically in 1996 when the IRS promulgated a bold "check the box" rule that allows any closely held domestic unincorporated firm to be taxed as a partnership, unless the parties elect corporate tax treatment. Treas. Reg. §301.7701-1. Unincorporated firms (GPs, LPs, LLCs) can choose whatever organizational attributes best suit the participants' needs, and flow-through tax status is assured.

§2.3.3 Avoiding Double Taxation

Before "check the box," business planners used various techniques to avoid double-tax without giving up limited liability. Some are still relevant for firms that prefer the corporate form.

Subchapter S Corporation

The Internal Revenue Code allows certain corporations to elect flow-through tax treatment. See I.R.C. §§1361–1378 (Subchapter S). An S corporation is one incorporated under state law and thus retains all its corporate attributes — including limited liability and centralized management. But it is not subject to an entity tax, and all corporate income, losses, deductions, and credits flow through to the shareholders. To be eligible, the S corporation

- must be a domestic corporation or LLC that chooses to be taxed as a corporation
- can have only one class of stock
- can have no more than 100 individual shareholders, though certain tax-exempt entities can be shareholders (such as employee stock ownership plans, pension plans, charities)
- can only have shareholders who are U.S. citizens or residents (thus precluding ownership by nonresident aliens or business entities)

When heavy losses are anticipated, the Subchapter S form may not be as desirable as an LLC or partnership. S corporation shareholders can only write off losses up to the amount of capital they invested (though the loss can be carried forward and recognized in future years).

Zeroing Out Shareholder Payments

Corporate tax in a small, closely held C corporation can be zeroed out by paying shareholders deductible compensation or interest. The effect is that tax is paid only at the shareholder level. For example:

- Shareholder-employees are paid salaries, bonuses, and contributions to profit-sharing plans. "Reasonable compensation" is deductible by the corporation from gross income in computing taxable income, while dividends are not. But there can be too much of a good thing. If compensation is not reasonable — that is, not related to the value of the services — the IRS can treat excess compensation as "constructive dividends," and the corporation loses its deduction.
- Shareholder-lenders are paid deductible interest, rather than nondeductible dividends. Again, there can be too much of a good thing. The IRS will recharacterize debt as equity if it appears the contributions were at "the risk of the business" (see §4.3.2).

Business Organizations (Basics)

	Formation	Financial	Mgmt	Voting	Liquidity	Liability	Tax	Change
Partnership								
General Partnership (GP)	association*	share profits	equal/ agent	equal	no	joint/several*	pass through	unanimous
Limited Liability Partnership (LLP)	association* + filing*	share profits	equal/ agent	equal	no	limited	pass through	unanimous
Limited Partnership (LP)	filing*	share profits	ltd P—no gen'l P—yes	contract	ltd P—yes gen'l P—no	ltd P—limited gen'l P—joint/ several*	pass through	majority
Corporation								
C Corporation (publicly held)	filing*	dividends	board*	directors*+ fundamental transaction*	yes	limited	entity*	majority*
S Corporation (closely held)	filing (and with IRS)*	dividends + salaries	board	directors + fundamental transaction	no (agree)	limited (PCV*)	pass through	majority
Limited Liability Company (LLC)								
Member-Managed	filing*	equal distribution	equal/ agent	equal	no	limited (PCV*)	pass through	majority
Manager-Managed	filing*	equal distribution	manager	equal	no	limited (PCV*)	pass through	majority

*mandatory term

Examples

1. Brigg has operated a landscaping business, Good Earth Landscaping, as a sole proprietorship. He has done most of the work himself and financed the business out of his own pocket. Brigg wants to expand by taking on regular employees and purchasing new equipment. His sister Pearl is willing to put up some money, but she wants to be sure she won't be at risk for more than what she invests.
   a. Pearl invests on the understanding that she will share in the profits, will help Brigg run the business, and will not be liable beyond her investment. Are her understandings valid?
   b. What forms of business organization might accommodate Pearl's multiple wishes?
   c. Is Pearl assured of limited liability if she is a limited partner? an LLC member? a corporate shareholder?
   d. For Pearl, what is the difference between being a partner in an LLP, a limited partner in an LP, a member in an LLC, or a shareholder in a corporation?
   e. Pearl will contribute cash, while Brigg will manage the business. If the business suffers losses, will Brigg have to bear them?

2. Brigg's friend Gravely is willing to invest in Good Earth Landscaping, but wants to help run the business. Gravely, naturally, is worried about personal liability for business obligations. Brigg and Gravely conclude that flow-through tax treatment will be advantageous.
   a. Will a corporation accomplish the parties' purposes?
   b. Brigg believes other wealthy investors (including his uncle in Germany) would be willing to invest. Given the favorable gift and estate tax rules for LP interests, will an LP accomplish the parties' purposes?
   c. Assuming that LLC interests also receive favorable gift and estate tax treatment, will an LLC have advantages over a corporation or LP?

Explanations

1. a. No. When Brigg and Pearl agreed to "carry on as co-owners of a business for profit" they formed a general partnership (GP) — whether they intended to or not. UPA §6; RUPA §202(a); cf. *Martin v. Peyton*, 246 N.Y. 213 1927) (finding creditor who shared in profits, but did not assume day-to-day control of business, was not partner for purposes of liability to third party). As a partner, Pearl is liable for the business's contractual debts, even if they exceed the amount of her investment. UPA §15; RUPA §306(a).
   b. Pearl wants limited liability. She can be
      - a partner in an LLP
      - a limited partner in an LP (or even a general partner in an LLLP)

- a member in an LLC
- a shareholder in a corporation

In each case, she will be shielded against personal liability if business debts exceed business assets. She will be "liable" only to the extent that the business suffers losses, in which case she may lose her investment. All limited-liability forms require a filing with state officials.

c. No. These organizational forms provide some, but not complete, assurance that participants can limit their losses to the amount they invested.

As a limited partner in an LP, Pearl would not be liable for business debts and obligations beyond her investment unless she "participates" in the management of the business. Although ULPA §7 provides little guidance as to when a limited partner participates in control, RULPA §303 offers a safe-harbor list of permissible activities. Pearl would risk becoming personally liable if she helps Brigg run the day-to-day business.

As an LLP partner, an LLC member, or a corporate shareholder, Pearl would not be liable for business debts or obligations beyond her investment unless the company or corporate veil is "pierced." Some LLC statutes suggest that LLC members may become personally liable "by reason of their own acts," a formulation similar to that found in corporate statutes. See MBCA §6.22(b). When and whether courts disregard corporate limited liability is an important (and vexing) question of corporate law and is dealt with in Chapter 32. Normally, Pearl would not become liable for corporate obligations merely by being active in the management of the business. Piercing typically happens only when a corporate participant defrauds or confuses creditors about limited liability or engages in activities that frustrate creditors' expectations to be paid ahead of shareholders.

d. As the previous answer illustrates, limited liability is somewhat similar in an LLP, LP (for limited partners), LLC, and corporation. But the tax implications can be markedly different.

Under a corporate structure, there may be double taxation that will reduce the amount of profits available to distribute to Pearl—the return on her investment. Unless the corporate participants can elect "Subchapter S" status, corporate earnings are taxed first at the corporate level and then a second time at the shareholder level when distributed as dividends.

Unless the parties have chosen to be taxed as a corporation, business earnings in a partnership (whether a GP, LLP, LP, or LLLP) or an LLC are taxed only once at the partner or member level, whether or not the earnings are distributed. This flow-through tax treatment leaves available more earnings to distribute to Pearl—a better return on her investment.

e. If they organize a limited liability entity (LLP, LP, LLLP, LLC, or corporation), neither participant will be liable for business losses. But if their agreement constitutes a GP, there is some question whether the capital partner and labor partner share losses equally. The plain text of the UPA assumes all partners, absent an agreement otherwise, share losses equally (including the capital partner's loss of capital). Yet some cases, recognizing the value of labor, suggest the labor partner loses only his labor and the capital partner his capital. *Kovacik v. Reed*, 315 P.2d 314 (1957).

2. a. Yes. A corporation can accomplish their purposes. Although a C corporation would be subject to double taxation, Brigg and Gravely can elect to have the corporation treated as an S corporation. This election affects only the corporation's tax treatment, not its nontax attributes. In this way Brigg and Gravely can obtain the limited liability afforded by the corporate form while enjoying the benefits of flow-through tax treatment. The corporation easily can be made to qualify: it must be incorporated in the United States, it must have fewer than 100 individual shareholders (none may be a nonresident of the United States), and it must have only one class of stock.

b. Perhaps. Although an LP's flow-through tax status is not affected by the number of investors or their nationality, limited liability would be jeopardized by Gravely's participation in the management of the business. In an LP, limited partners become liable as general partners if they take part in the control of the business. ULPA §7; RULPA §303.

Nonetheless it might be possible to form an LP with a corporate general partner, with Gravely and Brigg acting as shareholders, directors, and officers of the corporation. In their capacities as limited partners and participants in a corporation, they would enjoy limited liability for the LP's and general partner's liabilities. There is, however, some case law under ULPA §7 that limited partners who participate in the management of a corporate general partner are deemed to participate in the control of the LP — their limited liability is lost. RULPA §303, on the other hand, specifically allows such a structure without the limited partners becoming subject to partnership liabilities. The theory is that those dealing with the LP will be looking only to the credit of the corporate general partner unless they obtain personal guarantees.

c. Yes. An LLC avoids some of the pitfalls of the traditional LP and corporate forms. Unlike an LP, an LLC permits management roles to be specified in the articles of organization and the operating agreement without jeopardizing the parties' limited liability. Unlike a corporation, an LLC permits flow-through tax treatment, while permitting an unlimited number of investors (including nonresident investors). For these and other reasons, LLCs have become the entity of preference for many smaller businesses that seek limited liability, while maintaining flexibility as to ownership, management, and transferability.

PART II

Formation of the Corporation

CHAPTER 3

Incorporation — How, Where, and What

Forming a corporation under modern state corporation statutes is quick and straightforward. The process creates a public record of incorporation; it binds the parties (with rare exceptions) to the corporate law of the incorporating state; and it documents any optional terms the parties may have chosen. For the corporate planner, there are three significant questions:

- What provisions must be included in the articles of incorporation?
- What optional provisions can be included in the articles?
- In what state should the corporation be incorporated?

This chapter describes how the incorporation process works (§3.1), the choice of where to incorporate and the choice-of-law rules that apply to the incorporation decision (§3.2), and what powers the corporation has and what happens if the corporation exceeds its powers (§3.3).

Other chapters in this part discuss the financial rights of corporate investors (Chapter 4) and the informational rights of new investors when the corporation sells securities (Chapter 5).

§3.1 PROCESS OF INCORPORATION

Corporate existence and the attributes of "corporateness" begin with the filing of articles of incorporation. Forming a corporation involves three essential steps:

- preparing articles of incorporation (in some states called the charter or the certificate of incorporation) according to the requirements of state law, MBCA §2.02; Del. GCL §102
- signing of the articles by one or more incorporators, MBCA §1.20(f); Del. GCL §103(a)(1)
- submitting the signed articles to the state's secretary of state for filing, MBCA §2.01; Del. GCL §106

These steps are often carried out by a lawyer, who when acting for multiple parties acts as a "lawyer for the situation." Under professional ethics rules, a lawyer acting in such a capacity must consult with the parties about the pros and cons of multiple representation, including the loss of any attorney-client privilege among the parties, and must obtain each party's informed consent. See ABA Model Rule of Professional Conduct 1.13 (Organization as Client). A lawyer who helps organize a corporation may be seen as representing the corporate entity, not the individual investors. See *Jesse by Reineche v. Danforth*, 485 N.W.2d 63 (Wis. 1992) (holding that lawyer who organized a corporation for 20 physician-investors did not represent individual investors, thus permitting lawyer's firm to represent another client in a malpractice suit against two of the physicians).

§3.1.1 Articles of Incorporation

Modern corporate statutes prescribe the standard information the articles must contain.

Name of the Corporation

The articles must state the corporation's complete name and include a reference to its corporate status — a word such as "Corporation," "Incorporated," or "Inc." The name must also be different from other corporate names in the state. How different? Some statutes say it must be "distinguishable upon the records" of the secretary of state from other names already in use or reserved for use. MBCA §4.01; Del. GCL §102(a)(1). See *Trans-Americas Airlines, Inc. v. Kenton*, 491 A.2d 1139 (Del. 1985) (accepting "Transamerica Airlines, Inc." even though confusingly similar to existing "Trans-Americas Airlines, Inc." because both names were distinguishable). Some statutes require the name not be "deceptively similar" to existing names. See Cal. Code Reg. 21002. While the "distinguishable upon the records" test simply assures each corporate name will be unique and easy to identify, the "deceptively similar" test has a further aim to prevent deception or unfair competition.

Many states allow businesses to reserve a corporate name (for a fee) during the preincorporation process. MBCA §4.02 (nonrenewable reservation for 120 days); Del. GCL §102(e) (initial and renewable reservations for 120 days). In some states a corporation incorporated in another state (a "foreign corporation") may register its name with the secretary of state to keep local firms from using it. MBCA §4.03 (registration renewable annually); Del. GCL §102(e) (renewable every 120 days).

Registered Office and Agent

The articles must state the corporation's *registered office* for service of process and for sending official notices. MBCA §2.02; Del. GCL §102(a)(2). Often the articles also must name a *registered agent* at that office on whom process can be served. MBCA §§2.02, 5.01; Del. GCL §102(a)(2). Changes in the registered office or registered agent must be filed with the secretary of state. MBCA §5.02; Del. GCL §133.

Capital Structure of the Corporation

The articles must specify the securities (or shares) the corporation will have authority to issue. The corporation will raise capital by issuing its shares. The articles must describe the various classes of authorized shares, the number of shares of each class, and the privileges, rights, limitations, and preferences of each class. MBCA §§2.02(a)(2), 6.01; Del. GCL §§102(a)(4), 151(a). The corporation cannot issue more shares than are authorized, unless the articles are amended. No share price need be stated, and the requirement (once prevalent) of an initial minimum capitalization has virtually disappeared in the United States.

Purpose and Powers of the Corporation

The articles may (but need not) state the corporation's purposes and powers. With the decline of the ultra vires doctrine (see §3.2.1), a "purposes" clause is far less important than it once was. The modern presumption is that the corporation can engage in any lawful business. MBCA §3.01; Del. GCL §101(b). A limited purposes clause may be beneficial in a closely held corporation where an investor who lacks control wishes to restrict the corporation's lines of business. See Chapter 25.

Most state statutes also contain an all-inclusive list of the activities in which a corporation may engage. The articles need not state these powers. MBCA §3.02 (corporation has "same powers as an individual . . . to carry out its business and affairs"); Del. GCL § 122 (enumerated powers).

Size/Composition of Board of Directors

Many statutes no longer require that the articles name the initial directors. MBCA §2.02(b)(1) (permitting naming of initial directors); cf. Del. GCL §102(a)(6) (requiring names and addresses of initial directors, if power of incorporators terminates on filing certificate of incorporation). Likewise, most modern statutes have abandoned requirements that the board be composed of at least three directors or that the articles specify the number of directors. MBCA §8.03 (requiring board composed of "one or more individuals"); cf. Del. GCL §141(b) (one or more "natural persons").

Optional Provisions

The articles can contain a broad range of other provisions to "customize" the corporation. MBCA §2.02(b); Del. GCL §102(b). Such provisions are often important in closely held corporations where the participants want specific protections. "Opt in" provisions allow the parties to choose additional provisions defining their corporate relationship; "opt out" provisions allow the parties to avoid provisions that would otherwise apply:

- *voting provisions* that call for greater-than-majority approval of certain corporate actions, such as mergers or charter amendments (see §26.1.1)
- *membership requirements* that directors be shareholders or that shareholders in a professional corporation be members of a specified profession (see §26.3)
- *management provisions* that require that shareholders approve certain matters normally entrusted to the board, such as executive compensation (see §26.4)
- *indemnification provisions* that specify when the corporation will pay for the liability, settlement, or costs of defense if directors or officers are sued in their corporate capacity (see §15.1)

Corporate law is not fully enabling. In some situations, provisions that deviate too far from corporate norms may not be enforceable (see §§26.4, 39.3).

§3.1.2 Incorporators

The role of incorporators, as such, is purely mechanical. They can be an office assistant, a lawyer, an owner of the business — almost anyone. They sign the articles and arrange for their filing. If the articles do not name directors, the incorporators select them at an organizational meeting. After incorporation, the incorporators fade away and need not have any continuing interest in the corporation. Under some statutes the incorporators must be natural persons, though the trend is that a corporation may act as an incorporator of another corporation. MBCA §§2.01, 1.40(16); Del. GCL §101(a).

Comparison of Incorporators and Promoters

Incorporators, as such, carry no legal responsibilities. But when a person acts on behalf of a business during the incorporation process, such a "promoter" can become liable on preincorporation contracts. See §§29.1, 29.2.

§3.1.3 Filing Process

Filing the articles is today a simple task. Older statutes, reflecting a time when the legislature chartered corporations, gave the secretary of state significant discretion to reject articles of incorporation for technical or other perceived defects. Modern statutes, particularly the MBCA, remove much of that discretion. The MBCA *requires* state officials to accept articles for filing if

- they contain the minimal information required by the statute
- the document is typed or printed
- sufficient copies are submitted
- appropriate filing fees and franchise taxes are paid
- the corporate name is distinguishable on the secretary of state's records

MBCA §1.25; Del. GCL §103(c). In some states the filing fee is a flat amount; in other states (including Delaware, see Del. GCL §391) it depends on the number of authorized shares or the aggregate legal capital of the corporation (see §31.2.2).

Once the articles are filed, they become public documents. Those interested in confirming the corporation's existence can obtain a certificate of existence from the secretary of state (MBCA §1.28), a receipt returned by the secretary of state when the articles of incorporation are filed, a copy of the articles with an original acknowledgment stamp by the secretary of state (MBCA §1.25), or a certified copy of the original articles obtained from the secretary of state for a nominal fee (MBCA §1.27; Del. GCL §105) (certified copy of "certificate of incorporation").

§3.1.4 Organizational Meeting

Filing the articles merely brings the corporation into existence. It is the first step in its formation. For the corporation to function, the corporate planner must create a working structure. This is done at an organizational meeting of the incorporators or the board of directors named in the articles. The meeting, called upon written notice, usually follows a script already devised by the corporate planner.

The first item of business at the meeting — which need not take place in person, but instead by written consent — will be to elect directors unless the initial directors named in the articles are to remain in office. Once the board is constituted, other items on the agenda will include approving bylaws to govern the internal structure of the corporation, electing officers, adopting preincorporation promoters' contracts (including the lawyers' fees for setting up the corporation), designating a bank for the deposit of corporate funds, authorizing the issuance of shares, and setting the consideration for the shares. MBCA §2.05; Del. GCL §108.

Bylaws

As corporate articles have become more cursory and the statutes more open-ended, the bylaws have assumed greater importance under modern corporate practice. The bylaws typically describe such matters as the functions of each corporate office, how shareholders' and directors' meetings are called and conducted, the formalities of shareholder voting (including voting by proxy), the qualifications of directors, the functions of board committees (such as executive or audit committees), and procedures for and limits on issuing and transferring shares.

State law does not require the bylaws be filed. The bylaws must be consistent with the articles. MBCA §2.06; Del. GCL §109(b). Like the articles, the bylaws are not enforceable if they deviate too far from the traditional corporate model (see §§26.4, 39.3).

§3.2 CHOOSING WHERE TO INCORPORATE

In the United States a corporation can be formed in any state, no matter where it does business. That is, the parties can choose the governing law for their corporate relationship. The question of where to incorporate requires balancing the benefits of incorporating in a state that provides flexibility in managing the business against the costs of incorporating elsewhere and then qualifying to do business as a *foreign corporation* (see §3.2.2) in other states where business is to be conducted. The decision often comes down to a choice between the business's home state and Delaware.

The incorporation choice will determine how much in franchise taxes the corporation pays to the incorporating state. See Del. GCL §503 (based on authorized shares or capital). But business taxes will depend on where the corporation actually conducts business.

§3.2.1 Internal Affairs Doctrine

In the United States the law of the state of incorporation, with limited exceptions, governs the relationships among the parties in the corporation. This choice of law rule, known as the "internal affairs doctrine," permits the parties through the incorporation process to fix the law that applies to their corporate relationship, wherever litigation is brought. The corporation's "internal affairs" are those that relate to the legal relationships between the traditionally regarded corporate participants—including the rights of shareholders, the fiduciary duties of directors, and the procedures for corporate action.

Under the internal affairs doctrine, state courts are bound to accept the corporate law rules of the incorporating state, even when those rules are different or inconsistent with rules of the forum state. See *McDermott v. Lewis*, 531 A.2d 206 (Del. 1987) (applying Panamanian law that permitted parent corporation to vote shares of subsidiary, even though such voting is prohibited under corporate law of Delaware and all other U.S. states).

A few states have modified this choice of law rule and purport to regulate the internal affairs of corporations that have substantial operations in the state but are incorporated in another jurisdiction—sometimes called "pseudo-foreign" corporations. For example, California subjects foreign corporations to California corporate law if more than 50 percent of the corporation's property, sales, payroll, and outstanding voting shares are in the state. Cal. Corp. §2115; see also *Wilson v. Louisiana Pacific*, 187 Cal. Rptr. 852 (Cal. App. 1982) (applying California cumulative voting provisions to Utah corporation because majority of shareholders resided in California and California has "greater interest").

The validity of these statutes is questionable. The Supreme Court has suggested that the certainty fostered by the internal affairs doctrine may have constitutional dimensions for publicly held corporations. *CTS Corp. v. Dynamics Corp. of America*, 481 U.S. 69 (1987) (see §39.4.1). There the Court said, "No principle of corporation law and practice is more firmly established than a State's authority to regulate domestic corporations."

§3.2.2 Qualification of Foreign Corporations

A business incorporated in one state may conduct *intrastate* operations in another state (such as manufacturing or other regular business activities) if "qualified" to do business in the other state. To "qualify" the corporation must file a certified copy of its articles, pay a filing fee, and appoint a local agent to receive service of process in that state. MBCA §15.01; Del. GCL §371. But corporations that conduct only *interstate* business within other states (such as online-order companies) need not qualify because of the constitutional prohibition against interference with interstate commerce.

What are the penalties for doing business without being qualified? Some states fine the corporation and its officers for failing to qualify. Others treat the business as unincorporated, thus subjecting corporate officers to individual liability for contracts made in that state. Until a foreign corporation is qualified, it generally cannot bring lawsuits in local court. MBCA §15.02; cf. Del. GCL §383 (Court of Chancery can enjoin nonqualified foreign corporation from transacting business in state).

§3.2.3 Why Delaware for National Businesses?

Generally, a business that will operate locally will be incorporated locally because doing so is easier and less costly. If the business will operate throughout the United States, the corporation will be incorporated in one state and qualified as a foreign corporation elsewhere.

Most large publicly held corporations (and nearly three-fourths of companies that become public in an initial public offering) have chosen Delaware as their state of incorporation. There are a number of explanations for this:

- Delaware's statute is designed to give management flexibility in structuring and running the business
- the Delaware courts and corporate bar are highly experienced and sophisticated in corporate law matters
- a large body of case law interprets the Delaware statute, thus providing certainty to corporate planners
- the Delaware legislature is a leader in corporate law reform and regularly amends the Delaware corporations statute as new needs and problems arise

Some academics have criticized Delaware for having a pro-management slant and engaging in a chartering "race to the bottom." Cary, *Federalism and Corporate Law: Reflections upon Delaware*, 88 Yale L.J. 663 (1974). Others, observing the prevalence of Delaware corporations and the willingness of shareholders to invest in them, have argued that Delaware is engaged in a "race to the top." Winter, *State Law, Shareholder Protection, and the Theory of the Corporation*, 6 J. Legal Stud. 251 (1977). Empirical studies suggest that reincorporating in Delaware does not adversely affect (and may even raise) a corporation's stock prices. Moreover, the many Delaware court decisions favoring shareholder interests cast doubt on a "race to the bottom" thesis.

Nonetheless, the Cary/Winter debate continues—on new fronts. Recent scholarship has questioned whether a "market for corporate charters" produces optimal corporate law. Although nearly 60 percent of publicly traded U.S. corporations are incorporated in Delaware, whose antitakeover statutes are less protective of management than other states, many public corporations remain incorporated in their home states. This home-state protection suggests that states compete to insulate management from financially beneficial corporate takeovers, at the expense of shareholders. In fact, non-Delaware corporations are more likely to incorporate and remain incorporated in their home state when the state offers relatively greater antitakeover protections.

Examples

1. Xenon, Yentl, and Zeb want to incorporate their palm-reading business. They file articles in New Columbia, an MBCA jurisdiction:

ARTICLES OF INCORPORATION

First	The name of the corporation is XYZ, Inc.
Second	The corporation's registered address is 13 East-West Hwy, North Point, New Columbia; the registered agent at that address is Abner Zeb.
Third	The corporation is authorized to issue 3,000 shares of common stock.
Fourth	Any shareholder of the corporation must be a cosmologist certified by the Universal Association of Cosmologists.
Fifth	All voting by shareholders must be unanimous.
Sixth	The corporation will have a term of ten years.
Seventh	The incorporator is Abner Zeb, 13 East-West Hwy, North Point, New Columbia.

Abner Zeb

Abner Zeb, Incorporator

a. Are these articles sufficient?
b. The secretary of state's records show that two other New Columbia corporations have similar names: "XYZ Universal, Inc.," (a well-known health spa chain) and "X-Y-Z Palm Reading, Inc." Can the state official reject the articles?
c. Another "XYZ, Inc." operates a well-known chain of camera shops in an adjoining state. Can the New Columbia official reject the filing on this basis?

d. Xenon, Yentl, and Zeb have been sued for defrauding bereaved widows with promises they would communicate with their deceased spouses. Can state officials reject the filing on this basis?
e. New Columbia cases hold that requirements of unanimous shareholder approval (Article Fifth) are invalid. If the secretary of state's office accepts the XYZ articles for filing, does this affect Article Fifth's validity?
f. Can the XYZ, Inc., articles specify a term of ten years (Article Sixth)?

2. Xenon, Yentl, and Zeb want a bank loan for their business. The bank is willing to extend credit if a bank representative sits on the XYZ board and the shareholders pledge their shares to the bank. The bank does not want any public record that it holds pledged shares in a palm-reading business or that it has a representative on the XYZ board. Is this a problem?

3. New Columbia prohibits individuals (but not corporations) from charging usurious interest rates. Can XYZ, Inc., charge usurious interest to customers who are past due in paying their bills?

4. Suppose XYZ, Inc., is incorporated in Delaware even though it conducts its palm-reading business in New Columbia. New Columbia's corporation statute, unlike the MBCA, permits the removal of directors *only for cause*. Delaware's statute permits removal *with or without cause*. Del. GCL §141(k). Xenon and Zeb call a special shareholders' meeting and remove Yentl from the XYZ board.
   a. New Columbia's statute states: "This act does not authorize the state to regulate the organization or internal affairs of [an authorized] foreign corporation." See MBCA §15.05(c). Should Yentl sue in Delaware or New Columbia to get back his seat?
   b. Assume New Columbia has followed California's lead and regulates "pseudo-foreign" corporations under New Columbia corporate standards. Does New Columbia's "for cause only" standard apply?
   c. The XYZ articles state that directors cannot be removed for any reason during their term. Now which law governs: the articles, Delaware law, or New Columbia law?

Explanations

EXPLANATIONS

1. a. Yes. The articles are sufficient. MBCA §2.02 requires only a name for the corporation (Article First), a description of its capital structure (Article Third), a registered address and agent (Article Second), and the incorporator's address (Article Seventh). Further, the articles are signed by the incorporator, and one incorporator is enough. MBCA §1.20.
   b. Probably not. Under the MBCA, the articles can be rejected if they do not comply with statutory requirements. See MBCA §1.25. According to MBCA §2.02(a)(1), the articles must comply with MBCA §4.01, which requires that the corporate name be "distinguishable upon the

records of the secretary of state" from other names of corporations incorporated in the state. "XYZ Universal, Inc.," and "X-Y-Z Palm Reading, Inc.," are distinguishable from "XYZ, Inc.," for purposes of identifying the corporations and sending notice.

The similarity in names may work a deception, but this is a matter for the law of unfair competition or deceptive advertising.

c. No. Under the MBCA, the articles can be rejected only if the name "XYZ, Inc.," is (1) reserved or registered, (2) the name of a corporation incorporated or authorized to do business in the state, or (3) a fictitious name used by a qualified foreign corporation. MBCA §4.01.
d. No. Under the MBCA, state officials have no discretion to reject articles that comply with the technical filing requirements. MBCA §1.25. Even though Xenon, Yentl, and Zeb may be trying to create a corporate veil to limit their liability and may have a history of defrauding customers, this is not the concern of the secretary of state. Private plaintiffs may be able to pierce the corporate veil and hold the three swindlers individually liable (see Chapter 32) or the state's consumer affairs agency may close down the business. The MBCA's incorporation rules do not serve these functions.
e. No. Although accepting articles for filing is ministerial and not discretionary, the proper filing of a document does not affect its validity. MBCA §1.25.
f. Yes. Although MBCA §3.02 assumes the corporation will have perpetual duration, MBCA §2.02(b)(2)(iii) permits limitations on corporate powers, including duration. A limited duration acts as an agreement among the participants to dissolve the company after ten years.

2. No problem. The directors do not have to be named in the articles, the only corporate document that need be filed. MBCA §2.02. State law requires that the articles specify the types and number of authorized shares, but does not require disclosure about their ownership. The incorporators can elect directors (including the bank representative) in the organizational meeting. The board can then issue shares. The only record will be the minutes of the meeting, a nonpublic document. In a jurisdiction that requires that initial directors be named, the articles can name "dummy" directors who then elect replacements at the organizational meeting. The bank can condition extending a loan on the election of its representative.

3. Probably, but the articles should clarify. The MBCA specification that corporate powers are the "same powers as an individual" was meant to be as broad as possible. Official Comment, MBCA §3.02 (purpose to ensure that "corporate powers are broad enough to cover all reasonable business transactions"). But there may be instances, as here under the usury laws,

in which corporations have powers beyond those of individuals. XYZ's articles should be drafted to make clear the corporation can charge any lawful interest rate.

4. a. It should not matter because courts in either state will apply Delaware law. Even though New Columbia's "for cause" standard is more favorable to Yentl, the legal standard should be the same wherever suit is brought. Under the internal affairs doctrine, Delaware's "with or without cause" standard will apply. Both Delaware and New Columbia courts (federal and state) will apply the law of the state of incorporation to this shareholder-management dispute. See *Klaxon Co. v. Stentor Elec. Mfg. Co.*, 313 U.S. 487 (1941) (federal courts sitting in diversity must use choice of law rules of state in which they sit). This assures predictability and certainty in structuring internal corporate relationships.

   b. Perhaps. The choice of venue now may make a difference. A New Columbia court would seem bound to apply the New Columbia standard. Not surprisingly, Delaware courts have declared the virtual inviolacy of the internal affairs doctrine and would likely apply the law of Delaware, the state of incorporation. This means that two courts might answer the same corporate law question in two different ways. For example, the Second Circuit applied New York's broad statute on shareholder inspection rights to a Maryland corporation whose statute would not have required the inspection sought by a New York shareholder. *Sadler v. NCR*, 928 F.2d 48 (2d Cir. 1991).

   For public corporations, with dispersed shareholders for whom legal predictability is important in pricing their publicly traded shares, a choice of law rule that varies depending on where suit is brought may frustrate expectations and run afoul of the U.S. Constitution. This concern is less compelling for a closely held corporation, where private choice is now the rule.

   c. It may depend on the court where suit is brought. Would Delaware or New Columbia law permit the parties to choose an extra-statutory standard? Delaware courts have been jealous in applying Delaware law to Delaware corporations. For example, the Delaware Supreme Court applied Delaware law to a Delaware corporation, disregarding an agreement among the parties to be bound by New Jersey law. *Rosenmiller v. Bordes*, 607 A.2d 465 (Del. 1991). Non-Delaware courts have been more solicitous of party choice. For example, a Missouri court upheld the parties' agreement to waive application of the law of Delaware, the state of incorporation. *Yates v. Bridge Trading Co.*, 1992 Mo. App. Lexis 1629.

   Delaware, as the leading state for incorporation, has a vested interest in an all-encompassing internal affairs doctrine. That is, parties that incorporate in Delaware are bound exclusively by Delaware law and cannot choose to substitute other state or private provisions for their off-the-rack Delaware provisions. Non-Delaware courts may not feel so constrained and may deviate from the internal affairs doctrine to promote party choice or to remedy perceived gaps in Delaware law.

§3.3 CORPORATE POWERS AND THE ULTRA VIRES DOCTRINE

In the nineteenth century, state legislatures chartered corporations for narrow purposes and with limited powers. Likewise, early courts, concerned about the economic power of this capitalist invention, fashioned the "ultra vires doctrine" to invalidate corporate transactions beyond the powers stated in the corporation's charter.

As corporations became an accepted part of the economic landscape, state enabling statutes came to authorize "general purpose" clauses and virtually unlimited powers. See MBCA §§3.01, 3.02; Del. GCL §122 (see §3.1.1 above). Today the ultra vires doctrine applies only when

- the articles specifically restrict corporate activities
- the corporation engages in activities not directly related to profit seeking, such as excessive charitable giving
- the board of directors takes actions that undermine shareholder power (see §39.7)

§3.3.1 Early Common Law

Early corporations were formed to run capital-intensive businesses such as canals, railroads, and banks. To attract investors and obtain legislative approval, business promoters drafted the articles of incorporation to limit the scope of the business. Early courts applied the ultra vires doctrine with vigor. Whenever a transaction was beyond the corporation's limited purposes or powers, either party to the contract could disaffirm it, even after the other party's full or partial performance. The ultra vires doctrine thus invited parties to weasel out of contracts whenever a deal went sour—thus limiting the attractiveness of the corporate form.

§3.3.2 Erosion of Doctrine

Around the turn of the last century, courts recognized the commercial uncertainty created by the ultra vires doctrine and modified it in three respects.

First, courts permitted an ultra vires defense only if the contract was still *executory* and had not yet been performed. Second, courts interpreted charter provisions flexibly to authorize transactions reasonably incidental to the business. Third, most courts held that the ultra vires defense could be barred by unanimous shareholder approval, unless a creditor would be injured.

At about the same time, state legislatures passed "general incorporation" statutes that authorized a wide variety of corporate purposes and powers. Drafters of corporate articles accepted the invitation, enumerating multiple business purposes and specifying powers for virtually every imaginable business transaction.

Later, legislatures passed modern enabling statutes that authorized "general purpose" clauses and specified a long laundry list of corporate powers. Today detailed drafting is no longer necessary. In many jurisdictions, the articles need not recite even that the corporation has the purpose of engaging in any lawful business or the power to engage in any lawful transaction — both are implicit. MBCA §§3.01, 3.02; cf. Del. GCL §102(a)(3) (requiring articles to set forth "nature of the business or purposes to be conducted or promoted").

§3.3.3 Modern Ultra Vires Doctrine — Limited Planning Device

Modern statutes, including the MBCA, seek to eliminate the vestiges of inherent corporate incapacity. Neither the corporation nor any party doing business with the corporation can avoid its contractual commitments — whether executory or not — by claiming the corporation lacked capacity. MBCA §3.04(a); Del. GCL §124.

But if the articles state a limitation, the MBCA protects the expectations that arise from the limitation and specifies three *exclusive* means of enforcement:

- **Shareholder suit.** Shareholders can sue to enjoin the corporation from entering into or continuing in an unauthorized transaction. MBCA §3.04(b)(1); Del. GCL §124(1). A court can issue an injunction only if "equitable" and only if all of the parties, including the third party, are present in court. MBCA §3.04(c); Del. GCL §124(1). An injunction is equitable only if the third party knew about the corporate incapacity. See Official Comment, MBCA §3.04.
- **Corporate suit against directors and officers.** The corporation, on its own or by another on its behalf, can sue directors and officers (whether current or former) for taking unauthorized action. The officers and directors can be enjoined or held liable for damages. MBCA §3.04(b)(2); Del. GCL §124(2).

- **Suit by state attorney general.** The state attorney general can seek involuntary judicial dissolution if the corporation has engaged in unauthorized transactions. MBCA §§3.04(b)(3), 14.30; Del. GCL §124(3). This authority harkens back to the "state concession" theory of the corporation. See §1.3.

The modern ultra vires doctrine thus provides only limited assurance that charter restrictions on the scope of the corporation's business will work.

§3.3.4 Distinguishing Ultra Vires from Corporate Duties

The ultra vires doctrine, which concerns corporate *powers*, is sometimes confused with corporate *duties*—specifically, the corporation's duty not to engage in illegal conduct and managers' fiduciary duties. Consider a couple examples:

- **Illegality.** An incorporated manufacturing business dumps toxic wastes in violation of state and federal environmental law. If the corporation has a general purpose clause, has it acted ultra vires? Although courts once described illegal behavior as ultra vires, the doctrine is no longer used to enforce external norms. As a matter of modern corporate law, the corporation has the *power* to engage in business activities, including the dumping of toxic wastes, but as a matter of environmental law it has a *duty* not to. (Take note that directors who approve illegal corporate behavior may be liable for breaching their duty of good faith. See §12.3.1.)
- **Fiduciary breaches.** The corporation enters into a contract with a director on terms that significantly favor the director. Unless the articles disable the corporation from entering into self-dealing transactions, the corporation has the *power* to do this; the transaction is not ultra vires. The corporation, however, may avoid the transaction if its terms are unfair and the director has breached her fiduciary *duties*.

§3.3.5 Ultra Vires Doctrine and Corporate Largesse

A for-profit corporation's primary purpose is to make money for its constituents. Does such a corporation have the power to give away its profits by making charitable contributions? In particular, can the corporation give money to the founder's orphans or the chief executive's favorite art museum? Are these acts of largesse ultra vires?

Courts generally have accepted that corporations have implicit powers to make charitable gifts that in the long run may arguably benefit the corporation. See *Theodora Holding Corp. v. Henderson*, 257 A.2d 398, 405 (Del. Ch. 1969); but see Fisch, *Questioning Philanthropy from a Corporate Governance Perspective*, 41 N.Y.L. Sch. L. Rev. 1091 (1997) (studies fail to find a conclusive link between charitable giving and corporate profitability). Most state statutes specifically permit the corporation to make charitable donations. See MBCA §3.02(13); Del. GCL §122(9). Gifts cannot be for unreasonable amounts and must be for a proper purpose. In general, if the gift is tax deductible, corporate law treats it as a reasonable exercise of corporate powers. See I.R.C. §170(b)(2) (deduction for corporate giving limited to 10 percent of the corporation's taxable income).

If corporate largesse is demonstrably unrelated to corporate benefits — as when a gift is excessive — the transaction may be attacked as ultra vires. Such corporate altruism may also constitute corporate waste (see §12.3.2).

Examples

1. In 1965 Sam and Tom opened a small printing shop, which they incorporated as S-T Printing, Inc., in a jurisdiction that has now adopted the MBCA. When they incorporated, Tom worried that Sam's plans were too grandiose, so he insisted on the following provision in the articles:

   > The Corporation shall engage only in the business of printing unless all the shareholders agree otherwise.

   In 2000 both Sam and Tom retired, leaving all of their shares to their children, who continue to run the shop. The business has been dragging. Last month the board of directors decided to change direction. S-T Printing would enter into a ten-year joint venture agreement to sell computer printing systems to commercial customers. The board authorized president Sid to sign the agreement with DeskTop Corp.

   a. Sara, an S-T Printing shareholder, objects to the joint venture. She says the corporation has no power to be a joint venturer, and the charter forbids this particular agreement. Is either view tenable?
   b. If the articles can be construed to prohibit this particular venture, can Sara prevent Sid from signing the agreement?

2. Sara files suit, but after the joint venture agreement is signed.
   a. Assume DeskTop management did not know about the charter limitation, but could easily have found out. Can Sara prevent further performance?
   b. If DeskTop management's ignorance precludes a shareholders' suit, does Sara have any other recourse?
   c. Assume DeskTop management knew about the charter limitation, and the court enjoins the venture. Can DeskTop recover the profits it would have made had the venture gone forward?

3. The joint venture uses printing software it bought from a copyright pirate.
   a. When Sara learns of this, she wants to sue to enjoin the agreement as ultra vires. Can she?
   b. The state attorney general investigates the joint venture's use of pirated software. Can the state prevent S-T Printing's participation in the joint venture?

4. The computer printing business proves to be highly profitable.
   a. The S-T Printing board considers getting out of the joint venture to get into the business on its own. Can it use an ultra vires theory?
   b. DeskTop also considers abandoning the joint venture. Can it avoid the agreement as ultra vires?

5. The S-T Printing board authorizes a large cash "Christmas gift" to Sara. Maybe she will stop being so critical of the company! Is the gift ultra vires?

Explanations

EXPLANATIONS

1. a. Probably not. Corporations have broad, general powers under modern enabling statutes, including the power to be a joint venturer. MBCA §3.02(9). If nothing in S-T Printing's articles limits this power, Sara cannot attack the joint venture on this basis.

   The S-T charter, however, does limit the corporation to the "business of printing." How should this limitation be construed? Modern courts are reluctant to use the ultra vires doctrine to limit corporate flexibility. The provision could be construed broadly to encompass the business of selling printing equipment. The joint venture is a reaction to a change in market conditions in the printing industry. A modern court is unlikely to confine the corporate majority under an ambiguous charter limitation.

   b. Yes, but Sara must show an injunction would be equitable. MBCA §3.04(b)(1), (c). The S-T board could argue that enforcing the charter proviso would be inequitable because it impedes business adaptation and frustrates the majority will. The statutory requirement that any injunction be equitable provides a defense against unduly burdensome charter restrictions.

   At this pre-contractual stage, the third party DeskTop need not be made a party to the proceeding, and its awareness of the limitation on corporate powers would be irrelevant. Any injunction would affect only the S-T Printing board and Sid.

2. a. No. Under the MBCA, once the parties enter into the transaction, the third party DeskTop must be made a party to the proceeding and any

injunction must also be equitable as to it. MBCA §3.04(b)(1), (c). This means DeskTop must actually have been aware of the "printing business" limitation. The MBCA comments make clear that persons dealing with a corporation need not "inquire into limitations on its purposes or powers." Some state statutes go further in rejecting the vestiges of the ultra vires doctrine and only allow an injunction before the contract is signed.

b. Yes, but it won't be easy. Sara can sue the directors who approved the transaction in a derivative action. MBCA §3.04(b)(2) (see §18.1). A claim of fiduciary breach may be difficult. If there was no conflict of interest and if there was a rational business purpose for the transaction, the business judgment rule (see §12.2) may shield the directors from liability. It is unclear whether the directors' knowing disregard of a charter limitation would be tantamount to bad faith.

c. No. Although the MBCA allows a court to award damages for losses caused when an ultra vires transaction is enjoined, MBCA §3.04(b)(1), the damages are meant only to put the parties into the position they would have been in had the transaction not occurred. Anticipated profits are specifically disallowed. MBCA §3.04(c).

3. a. No. If entering into the joint venture agreement is within the corporation's lawful purposes and powers, it cannot be enjoined as ultra vires. The ultra vires doctrine only enforces limitations in the articles. Whether Sara can enjoin the venture on copyright grounds depends on whether she has standing under the copyright laws.

b. Yes. The modern ultra vires doctrine does not affect the legality of the corporate action under other laws. If the state can forbid participation in a copyright pirating, it makes no difference what the corporate articles say.

4. a. No. Modern statutes make clear the corporation cannot challenge the validity of corporate action on the theory it lacks power. MBCA §3.04(a). This evisceration of the ultra vires doctrine prevents precisely the kind of contractual weaseling that the S-T directors are contemplating.

Although the board might enlist a shareholder to seek to enjoin the corporation, the injunction would have to be equitable. Avoiding legitimate contracts through the artifice of a shareholder suit hardly seems equitable.

b. No. The third party can no more avoid its obligations on an ultra vires theory than can the corporation.

5. Probably not. Although some courts continue to frame the issue of corporate giving as one of corporate power, the real issue is one of fiduciary duty and corporate waste. If the payment involves a remote benefit to

the corporation, the business judgment rule shields it from review. A shareholder or creditor challenging this transaction would have to show extremely poor business judgment or a tainting conflict of interest.

Even if the gift were characterized as an unlawful distribution (that is, a dividend that was paid preferentially to only one shareholder), the challenge would not be of the corporation's power to distribute its assets to shareholders, but the failure to comply with the rules requiring pro rata distributions. See MBCA §§1.40(6), 6.40(a).

Financial Rights in Corporation

The corporation provides a structure for the financing of business operations and defining the financial rights that investors have to the firm's earnings and assets. Corporate financing comes from three sources:

- **Equity financing.** The corporation can issue shares of stock—equity financing. Shareholders pay the corporation for their shares, each of which represents an ownership interest in the corporation and gives the shareholder a bundle of rights and powers. Shareholders have financial rights to dividends when declared by the board and to a pro rata share of corporate assets on dissolution. To protect their financial interests, shareholders have voting rights to elect directors and approve fundamental corporate transactions (see §7.1) and liquidity rights to sell their interests (see §19.1). Equity securities fall into two general categories: common shares and preferred shares.
- **Debt financing.** The corporation can borrow money—debt financing. Corporate debt obligations (debt securities) are fixed by contract and can be issued to third persons (outside debt) or to shareholders (inside debt). Unlike equity, debt obligates the corporation to repay principal and interest according to an agreed-upon schedule. Unless provided by contract, debtholders do not acquire rights to share in earnings.
- **Corporate earnings.** The corporation can use funds generated internally by its business.

The financing mix varies depending on the business's stage of growth. During the start-up stage, entrepreneurs often rely on equity and inside debt financing. As the business becomes more established, it develops a credit history and outside debt financing becomes more available. For a business that has sold its equity shares to the public, there are often a wide variety of private and public sources for financing. Nonetheless, reinvested corporate earnings typically represent the largest source of corporate financing for publicly traded firms.

The financial rights given equity and debt investors constitute the "promises" the corporation makes to entice investors to voluntarily part with their money. The corporate planner can be seen as a chef putting together dishes (securities) for a menu (capital structure). In preparing each dish, the chef has many ingredients to choose from—the rights, powers, limitations, and preferences of which all securities are made. The ingredients usually are combined according to recipes, with an accepted nomenclature for each dish. But the chef can, and often does, add or vary the ingredients to give the dish its own alluring flavor. Moreover, each dish should complement the other dishes—in particular, the mix of equity and debt, expressed as the debt-equity ratio, should recognize the corporation's long- and short-term capital needs. Always on the chef's mind is whether the customers will buy.

This chapter describes the rights of equity shares (§4.1) and their issuance (§4.2). It then considers the attributes of debt securities (§4.3) and the considerations in choosing a debt-equity mix (§4.4).

§4.1 FINANCIAL RIGHTS OF EQUITY SHARES

§4.1.1 Creation of Equity Securities

The fountainhead of all equity securities is the articles of incorporation, which prescribe

- the classes (or types) of equity securities
- the number authorized for each class
- the preferences, limitations, and relative rights of each class

MBCA §§2.02, 6.01; Del. GCL §151. Equity securities (referred to as "shares" or "stock") are "authorized" when the articles permit the board to issue them; they are "issued" when sold to shareholders; and they are "outstanding" when held by shareholders. MBCA §6.03. Shares authorized and issued in accordance with the articles, usually by resolution of the board of directors, are "validly issued." Shares that are "issued but no longer outstanding" because they have been repurchased by the corporation are commonly known as "treasury stock." Cf. MBCA §6.31(a) (eliminating use of term).

To issue new shares, the corporation must have sufficient authorized, unissued shares. If not, the articles must be amended. MBCA §10.02; Del. GCL §241 (amendment by board, before shares issued); MBCA §10.03; Del. GCL §242 (amendment proposed by board and approved by shareholders). The MBCA also requires shareholder approval whenever a corporation issues shares for cash consideration if, after the issuance, shareholders will hold voting power equal to more than 20 percent of the voting power that existed prior to the issuance. MBCA §6.21(f) (similar to voting requirement imposed by stock exchanges for listed public companies). Shareholder approval of such "dilutive share issuances" is required regardless of how the issuance is structured, whether to raise capital or in a merger, sale of assets, or other restructuring.

Beyond the basic rule that one or more classes of shares "in whole or part" must have voting power and final liquidation rights—that is, a business corporation cannot be composed only of nonvoting shares or be unable to distribute its assets on dissolution to shareholders—modern statutes permit the rights and powers represented by equity securities to be mostly whatever the corporate planner decides. MBCA §6.01; Del. GCL §151(b).

§4.1.2 Basic Equity Ingredients

Equity securities have many recipes, though the ingredients are relatively standardized:

- **Dividends** are pro rata payments by the corporation to equity shareholders based on corporate earnings. Dividends can take many forms: cash, property, common shares, preferred shares, debt, even rights to whiskey during wartime liquor controls. Under U.S. corporate law, the declaration of dividends is within the discretion of the board of directors, limited by the corporation's financial and legal ability to pay (see §31.2).
- **Liquidation rights on dissolution** are pro rata distributions in cash or in kind by the corporation to equity shareholders based on corporate assets upon dissolution. The articles can specify the amount to be paid in liquidation and the priority of payment. "Senior" shares receive payment before "junior" shares.
- **Voting rights** empower shareholders to vote on governance matters, including the election of directors and the approval of significant corporate transactions proposed by the board, such as the amendment of the articles, the creation of new classes of shares, mergers, and sales of all the corporation's assets (see Chapters 35 and 36). Voting rights usually follow the rule "one-share/one-vote," though sometimes they are disproportionate or conditional. Voting rights can

be limited to specified matters, such as voting for only two of the corporation's five directors. MBCA §7.21; Del. GCL §151(a).

- **Conversion rights** give shareholders an option to convert their shares into another security of the corporation. The option, granted by the corporation, can be made exercisable only on certain events and during certain periods. MBCA §6.01(c)(2); Del. GCL §151(e). For example, conversion rights may be exercisable only for a short period after shares are issued or if the corporation does not pay dividends for a specified number of consecutive years.
- **Redemption rights** give shareholders an option to force the corporation to repurchase their shares. The right can be exercisable at the discretion of the option holder or only on certain events and during certain periods. The redemption price can be specified in the articles or set by the board if not in the articles. MBCA §6.01(c)(2); Del. GCL §151(b).
- **Preemptive rights** allow shareholders to acquire shares when the corporation issues new shares. This protects existing shareholders' proportional interest (voting and ownership) in the corporation's shares already issued and outstanding. For example, if a shareholder owns 300 of 1,000 outstanding common shares and the corporation proposes to issue 200 more common shares, a preemptive right would entitle the shareholder to acquire 60 more shares at the issue price, thus preserving the shareholder's 30 percent position.

  Preemptive rights were once viewed as an inherent aspect of share ownership. See *Stokes v. Continental Trust Co.*, 186 N.Y. 285 (1906) (treating preemptive rights as a matter of property). Over time this view became untenable, and preemptive rights are now generally a matter of statutory right. MBCA §6.30; Del. GCL §102(b)(3). In some states they exist automatically unless the articles specify otherwise ("opt out"). In others, including the MBCA, they do not exist unless the articles provide for them ("opt in"). Preemptive rights make issuing new shares cumbersome, particularly if the firm's shares are publicly held. Even when they do exist, preemptive rights do not arise in all situations. Common exceptions include when shares are issued for management services or for noncash property. MBCA §6.30(b)(3).

Other ingredients are possible—including special disclosure rights, limits on transferability, and the right to name directors to the board (see §§26.4, 26.6).

§4.1.3 Common Shares and Preferred Shares

The equity ingredients can be mixed in many ways. Recipes range from plain vanilla "common stock" to exotic "nonvoting, nonparticipating cumulative convertible redeemable preferred stock." Each dish, whose recipe is specified in the articles of incorporation, is known as a class of stock. Within a class, each share has the same rights and powers unless the class is divided into subclasses known as "series." Each series has a separate designation, their rights, limitations, and preference deviating from the class only as specified.

Often the articles will give the board of directors a "blank check" to specify the rights and powers of a series (or even a class) without further shareholder action. The board, in effect, fills in the blanks left by the articles. This provides the corporation flexibility to sell shares—particularly preferred shares—on prevailing market terms and rates without going through the lengthy process of amending the articles. MBCA §6.02; Del. GCL §151(g).

Generally, equity securities are either common shares or preferred shares, although many modern statutes do away with this categorization. MBCA §6.01.

Common Shares

Common shares represent the corporation's residual ownership interests—that is, what is left of the income stream after all other financial claims by creditors, employees, bondholders, and preferred shareholders have been satisfied. Common shareholders stand last in line. Dividends on common shares are not guaranteed. If the board does not declare them in a given year, there is no continuing right to receive them later. If the corporation is dissolved, common shareholders have *liquidation rights* only as to the assets remaining after "senior" claims of creditors, debtholders, and preferred shareholders have been satisfied.

Common shareholders—who are often described as the "owners" of the corporation—make up for their precarious "junior" position through *voting rights* (voice) and *liquidity rights* (exit), as well as the right to enforce *fiduciary duties* (loyalty). Some have described these basic attributes of ownership as the rights to vote, sell, or sue.

State statutes once limited *conversion rights* and *redemption rights* for common shares. The theory was that common shareholders, given their access to inside information and the corporate governance machinery, should not be allowed to leapfrog from the back of the line to the front. An "upstream" conversion into more senior securities or a corporate redemption of junior securities inverts the financial hierarchy. The MBCA eliminates these restrictions on the theory that fiduciary duties are sufficient protection. MBCA §6.01; Del. GCL §151(e).

Common shares can be issued in multiple classes. Classes can have special voting or dividend rights, such as the right to vote for a certain number of directors or to receive double dividends. *Nonvoting common* is possible, permitting financial participation without affecting the corporation's voting balance.

Common shares can be issued to insiders (the usual case in closely held corporations), to a few outside investors (a frequent phenomenon in start-up businesses), or to many outside investors who trade their shares on public trading markets (public corporations). Common shares can also be used as incentive compensation for company employees.

- **ESOPs.** Spurred by tax incentives, many firms have issued some of their common shares to *employee stock ownership plans* (ESOPs). Under an ESOP, the employer sets up a trust for the benefit of employees and then makes annual payments to the trust so the trust can purchase the company's shares. An ESOP gives employees a stake in the company, the employer's contributions to the ESOP are tax deductible, and the higher level of employee ownership may protect incumbent management from a takeover. It also means that employees may be overinvested in their employer.
- **Stock options.** Many firms, particularly in high-growth industries, have also granted employees *stock options*—a contractual right to purchase shares (usually common shares) at a specified date in the future at a specified price. Stock options create an incentive for employees to work so that the market price of the corporation's shares rises above the exercise price of the option. By exercising the option when the market price is above the exercise price (an *in the money* option), the optionholder acquires bargain shares and can instantly recognize a profit by selling at market. (Stock options also create incentives for corporate officials to focus on short-term gains over long-term growth and, as in the case of Enron, to manipulate company financial results so the market price rises and makes their options more valuable.)

Preferred Shares

Preferred shares are a hybrid between debt and common shares. They earn fixed dividends and are entitled to fixed liquidation rights. Preferred shares are "senior" to common shares as to dividends and liquidation rights, but "junior" to the claims of debtholders and creditors. The decision to pay dividends on preferred shares is within the board's discretion, and nonpayment is not an act of default.

The name given the preferred shares often reveals the *dividend preference*. For example, "$10 preferred" is entitled to a $10 payment per share each year before any dividends on the common shares are paid, and "15 percent preferred" means that 15 percent of the preferred shares' stated value or par value (described below) must be paid first. The *liquidation preference* is usually a fixed price per share (generally equal to stated or par value, though sometimes including a small liquidation premium) that must be paid in dissolution before any amounts are paid on the common shares.

Normally dividends on preferred shares, like common shares, are a matter of board discretion, though some cases have construed provisions in the articles to mandate payment of dividends. Even if dividends are not mandatory, preferred shareholders can have "carry-forward" rights to receive dividends if the board does not declare them in a given year. This depends on whether the preferred shares are *cumulative*—which means that if the board does not declare dividends, the corporation assumes a continuing, accumulating obligation to pay the unpaid dividends before it pays any future dividends. For example, if no dividends are paid on "$10 cumulative preferred" in Years 1 and 2, then no dividends (on preferred or common) can be paid in Year 3 or after, until the corporation first pays the accumulated $20 on the preferred.

Preferred shares can also have *participation rights*—that is, the right to participate with the common shares in any dividends declared on the common. Generally, preferred shares do not have *voting rights*, but these rights can be granted by statute or in the articles. Many state statutes grant preferred shares a right to vote on fundamental transactions—such as mergers or amendments to the articles that eliminate or dilute preferred shares' seniority. In addition, provisions creating preferred shares often vest voting rights in the preferred in adverse financial situations—for example, if the corporation fails to pay dividends for two consecutive years.

Preferred shares can have *conversion rights* that give preferred shareholders the option to convert their preferred into other shares of the corporation, usually common shares. In effect, preferred shareholders can exchange fixed dividend rights for voting and broad residual rights, which may become more valuable if the business has strong earnings. Besides specifying the ratio at which the conversion is to take place, the provisions setting up the preferred shares often will contain *antidilution* provisions to take into account changes that have occurred in the amount of common shares outstanding since the preferred shares were issued.

Preferred shares can allow for *redemption* at the option of either the corporation or the shareholder. The corporation often will retain the redemption option (a "call") when the corporate planner anticipates that dividends on preferred shares may become more expensive than other forms of financing. When the shareholder holds the redemption option (a "put"), the corporation often will secure its repurchase obligation by setting up a *sinking fund* into which the corporation sets aside earnings to redeem the shares and which may not be used to pay dividends or make other distributions. Most preferred shares are structured not to include a redemption right, though they are usually freely transferable giving preferred shareholders a "market out."

Examples

1. Bacchanalia Banquets, Inc., is in the catering business. Its articles authorize 100,000 shares of common stock. There are 20,000 shares issued and outstanding.
   a. Most Bacchanalia shares are owned by the firm's managers, who invested their life savings in the business. What are the advantages and disadvantages of their investment in the common stock?
   b. The Bacchanalia board declares a stock dividend that entitles each shareholder to receive one additional common share for every common share she holds. Are these new shares "validly issued"?
   c. An amendment to Bacchanalia's articles authorizes 50,000 shares of new convertible preferred, each share convertible into two shares of common stock. Are there any problems?
   d. Another amendment to Bacchanalia's articles authorizes a new class of nonvoting redeemable common shares under which holders can redeem their shares for $25 a share at any time. Any problems? Hint: The redemption right (a put option) will have much the same effect as a forced dividend payment.

2. Suppose Bacchanalia has two classes of stock outstanding: 100,000 shares of common stock and 6,000 shares of 10 percent cumulative preferred stock (stated value $100). In Year 1 Bacchanalia has sufficient earnings to pay only $100,000 in dividends.
   a. In Year 1 the board chooses not to pay dividends. Can it?
   b. The board does not declare dividends in Year 1 or Year 2. In Year 3 the board declares $10/share in dividends on the preferred for each of Years 1 and 2. It does not pay any interest on these arrearage payments. Any problems?
   c. In Year 1 the board declares a dividend of $5/share on the cumulative preferred. In Year 2 the board does not declare dividends. In Year 3 there are $100,000 in distributable assets, and the board declares a dividend of $10/share on the preferred and $0.40/share on the common stock. Can it?
   d. In Years 1 and 2 the board does not, and could not, declare a dividend on the cumulative preferred. In Year 3 Bacchanalia has $200,000 in distributable assets. The board declares a dividend of $30/share on the preferred and $0.20/share on the long-suffering common. Can it?
   e. In Year 3, with no earnings on the immediate horizon, Bacchanalia receives an offer from an outside investor interested in acquiring common shares—but on the condition the company engage in a recapitalization in which preferred shareholders agree to convert their shares to common shares. Can this be done?

3. All of Bacchanalia's 100,000 authorized common shares are family-owned. The family wants new investors but does not want to share in control. A venture capitalist firm is willing to invest. It wants a high fixed return on its investment, a share of profits if the business becomes successful, and control if the corporation stops paying a fixed return. The family agrees, but on the condition they can buy out the venture capital firm (at a premium) if the business becomes wildly successful. Draft an appropriate provision.

Explanations

EXPLANATIONS

1. a. Being a common shareholder has its pluses and minuses. As common shareholders, the Bacchanalia insiders are residual claimants of the firm's income stream. Any return on their investment comes only after the firm's creditors and senior shareholders are paid. They do not have a fixed right to dividends or other payments. As compensation for standing "last in line" behind the other holders of financial rights, shareholders receive broad participation, liquidity, and voting rights. If the firm succeeds, their rights to dividends and to distributions on liquidation can make their shares extremely valuable. To protect and maximize these rights, the shareholders elect the board and must approve any fundamental corporate changes.
   b. Yes. Shares are "validly issued" if the articles authorize them and the board approves their issuance. Cf. *Grimes v. Alteon Inc.*, 804 A.2d 256 (Del. 2002) (invalidating an oral promise by the company president to a 10 percent shareholder that if the company issued more shares the shareholder would have a preemptive right). Bacchanalia's articles of incorporation authorize the board to issue up to 100,000 shares. As a result of the stock dividend, the corporation will have 40,000 shares issued and outstanding, well within the limit.
   c. A problem. There are insufficient authorized common shares to handle all of the possible conversions, up to 100,000 common shares. Before issuing the new convertible preferred, the articles must be amended to authorize additional common shares.
   d. A problem. The statutory limits on dividends also cover the corporation's repurchase of its own shares (see §31.2). The redemption right must depend on meeting the relevant tests for corporate repurchases. Moreover, the possibility of a massive redemption makes business planning difficult. A sinking fund, into which the corporation makes regular contributions in anticipation of redemptions, would alleviate some of the uncertainty.
2. a. Yes. The declaration of dividends on common and preferred shares generally is within the discretion of the corporation's board of directors.

Equity securities, unlike debt, do not obligate the corporation to pay dividends, even if it is financially and legally able to pay.

b. No problem. Payments on preferred shares are largely a matter of contract. If the articles or the provisions setting up the preferred shares do not mandate the payment of interest on unpaid cumulative dividends, the corporation need not pay interest. This creates an incentive for the board not to pay preferred dividends and take in effect a no-interest loan, but preferred rights arise from the provisions setting up the shares. Preferred shareholders can protect against this opportunism by demanding interest, securing voting rights or representation on the board if dividends fall into arrears, or acquiring rights to resell their shares to the corporation (puts).
c. No. Before dividends can be paid on the common, the board must declare and pay the preferred a total of $150,000 in dividends—$30,000 accumulated from Year 1, plus $60,000 from Year 2, plus the current $60,000 preference. Thus, no dividends can be paid in Year 3 on the common shares.
d. Yes, unless the preferred is participating. After paying the preferred dividends, both in arrears and current, the board can declare up to $20,000 in dividends. If the preferred shares were participating, they would be entitled to participate in any additional dividends declared by the board in the proportion specified in the articles or the provisions setting up the preferred shares. This participation would be in addition to any regular dividends to which the preferred is entitled.
e. Yes. Even if the preferred shares do not carry conversion rights, the preferred shareholders can make a conversion by tendering their preferred shares and receiving common shares in exchange. If not all of the preferred shareholders undertake a voluntary exchange, the articles can be amended to effectuate a conversion, though the amendment must be approved by a majority of the preferred shares. See MBCA §10.04 (separate vote required by each class of shares subject to exchange); DGCL §242(b)(2) (class vote required by each class adversely affected by amendment).

3. Insert the following into the articles:

Article—. The corporation has authority to issue 10,000 shares of Preferred Shares ($100 face value). The Preferred Shares will have the following preferences, limitations, and relative rights:

A. *Dividends.* Holders of Preferred Shares are entitled annually to receive (1) cumulative dividends at the rate of no more than five

(continued)

> percent (5%) of face value [well above prevailing market rates], and (2) dividends equal share for share to any dividends paid on the Common Shares. Dividends will be paid only when, as, and if declared by the board of directors out of legally available funds. Cumulative dividends commence to accrue, whether or not earned or declared, from the date of issuance.
>
> B. *Dividend preference.* No dividend may be paid on the Common Shares, nor may any Common Shares be acquired by the Corporation, unless all dividends on any outstanding Preferred Shares are paid (or have been declared and set apart for payment).
>
> C. *Liquidation preference.* If there is a liquidation, dissolution, or winding up of the affairs of the Corporation, holders of Preferred Shares are entitled (1) to be paid in cash $150.00 per share, plus any unpaid dividends, and (2) to participate share for share with the Common Shares in any further distribution.
>
> D. *Voting rights.* Unless provided for by law, the Preferred Shares are nonvoting. If the Corporation fails to pay holders of Preferred Shares earned cumulative dividends for two consecutive years, the Preferred Shares may elect four directors [a majority of the board]. This voting right continues until all earned cumulative dividends have been fully paid.
>
> E. *Redemption.* The Corporation may at any time (in the discretion of the board of directors) redeem all or any part of the outstanding Preferred Shares by paying $150.00 per share, plus any accrued unpaid dividends. If less than all the Preferred Shares are redeemed, the Corporation will redeem the shares pro rata. Notice of redemption must be mailed, postage prepaid, to the holder of record at least fifteen (15) days but no more than sixty (60) days before the date of redemption.

Notice how this amendment accomplishes the family's and investors' purposes. It creates participation rights for the investors, yet the family retains voting control. Issuing common shares to the investors would not have done this. The preferred stock provisions give the investors contingent control rights and an incentive for the family to pay regular dividends. Yet the investors acquire voting rights only if dividends could have been paid, but were not, for two consecutive years. It caps the extent of investor participation by allowing the family to buy out the investors, though the buyout is at a 50 percent premium. The family can dissolve the corporation or redeem the preferred shares—the price is the same in either case. Although participation is "share for share," the significantly greater number of common shares (100,000 to 10,000 preferred shares) means that common participates in a 10:1 ratio.

§4.2 EQUITY FINANCING

Corporate statutes once mandated minimum initial financing for the corporation. Although a few state statutes continue to impose a minimum capital requirement (such as $1,000), the requirement provides little assurance the business will have enough assets to start or later to meet creditor claims. Most states do not require minimum capital.

Instead, the important question in issuing equity securities—a question on which new investors often seek a legal opinion to be sure they will not become liable for more than their investment—is whether the stock is "fully paid and nonassessable." The answer depends on the amount and quality of consideration paid for their shares.

§4.2.1 Amount of Consideration

Whether investors paid enough depends on whether their stock has "par value" or is no-par stock.

Par Value

Par value is an artificial dollar amount specified in the articles of incorporation; it has no relationship to the market value of the shares. Par value represents the amount that must be paid so the shares can be issued as "fully paid and nonassessable." Del. GCL §152. It is a concept that applies only when shares are originally issued, not when they are later traded. It is also a concept of diminishing importance.

The history of par value reveals its purposes. During the nineteenth century, the nascent period of the modern corporation, legislatures and judges grappled with how to best protect investors and creditors from free-riding insiders who issued themselves stock at prices below those paid by outside investors. The solution was par value—a price floor that in theory assured shareholders price parity and assured creditors an equity cushion that shareholders could not expropriate. The system placed aggregate par value (known as "stated capital") out of reach of shareholders through a system of primitive accounting rules. (In Chapter 31, as part of our discussion of creditor protection, we look at the limits on distributions to shareholders under this system of legal capital.)

Consider how par value theoretically worked to protect investors and creditors. Suppose Car Company issues 1,000 shares of common stock with a par value of $100. Under the par value system, every investor had to pay par—at least $100 per share. Creditors were assured that assets equal to the aggregated par ($100,000) could not be distributed to shareholders. See Del. GCL §163 (allowing board to demand payment for stock not paid in full).

Watered Stock Liability

What happens when stock is issued for consideration worth less than par (so-called *watered stock*)? Originally, courts required that the board valuation of the consideration reflect "true value," and courts imposed liability on any shareholder who paid for stock with consideration that a judge later decided had been overvalued. Although courts later relaxed this test to require that the board's valuation be made in "good faith" and reflect "reasonable prudence," it continued to create uncertainty for directors, investors, and corporate planners.

Today many statutes make the board's valuation conclusive "in the absence of fraud," though leaving open the question whether a challenger must show actual fraud (intentional deception) or merely constructive fraud (such as a breach of fiduciary duty). Cf. Del. GCL §152 (making the board's valuation conclusive absent "actual fraud"). Under the MBCA the board's valuation is "conclusive," though the statute purposefully does not address whether "fraud or bad faith" constitute grounds for canceling validly issued shares. See Official Comment, MBCA §6.21(c).

No-Par Stock

Par value is a thorn in the side of corporate planners, and its use is diminishing. Most modern statutes permit shares to be issued without par. MBCA §2.02(b)(2)(iv); Del. GCL §151(a). Although no-par stock avoids the problem of watered stock liability, limits on distributions to shareholders continue to apply (see Chapter 31).

When stock is issued without par, shareholders are liable to the corporation or its creditors only to the extent they have not paid "the consideration for which the shares were authorized to be issued . . . or specified in their subscription agreement." MBCA §6.22(a); see *Hanewald v. Bryan's Inc.*, 429 N.W.2d 414 (N.D. 1988) (holding insiders who failed to pay for their shares personally liable to corporation's creditors).

§4.2.2 Quality of Consideration

To be "fully paid and nonassessable," stock must also be issued for the proper kind of consideration. The MBCA broadly permits cash or any "tangible or intangible property or benefit to the corporation." MBCA §6.21(b); see also Del. GCL §152 (amended in 2004).

Many statutes (including Delaware's statute before 2004) require that stock be issued for money paid, services performed, or tangible or intangible property actually received—prohibiting the use of unsecured promissory notes or promises of future services. These statutes assume that consideration for stock should represent solid assets with realizable value, not mere promises of future value, to assure shareholder parity and to protect creditors.

Stock issued for ineligible consideration is treated either as voidable or as not being fully paid. If the latter, the shareholder can be assessed for the shortfall as in the case of watered or unpaid stock. Courts differ on whether the choice between cancellation and assessment belongs to the corporation or the shareholder.

These limitations severely restrict planning flexibility, and the MBCA eliminates them. For shares to be "fully paid and nonassessable," the MBCA requires that

- the board determine that the consideration is adequate (MBCA §6.21(c))
- shareholders be advised before the next shareholders' meeting if shares are issued for future services or promissory notes (MBCA §16.21(b))

Shareholders are left to their contractual and fiduciary remedies, and creditors are expected to evaluate the soundness of the corporation's business and assets in extending credit.

Examples

EXAMPLES

1. The articles of Bacchanalia Banquets specify that the common stock has par value of $5.00 per share. At the beginning of Year 1 the board approves the issuance of common stock for $10.00 per share. It issues shares as follows:

	# Shares	Consideration
Anna	1,000	$10,000
Benny	1,000	$ 7,000
Chris	1,000	$ 3,000

   a. After Year 1 the business is still solvent. Is any shareholder liable? To whom?
   b. After Year 2 the business is insolvent. Is any shareholder liable? To whom?

2. The Bacchanalia articles specify that the common stock has no par value. At the beginning of Year 1 the board issues 20,000 shares of common

stock to Anna and 10,000 to Benny. Anna pays $50,000 in cash. Benny agrees to work for the corporation for two years. The board values his agreement at $50,000.

a. Is Anna liable for having paid $2.50 per share while Benny paid $5.00 per share?
b. After Year 1 Anna and Benny have a falling out. Using her control, Anna has the corporation sue Benny to pay for his shares. Can the corporation recover?
c. In Year 2 Anna and Benny reconcile. Benny has not completed his two years of service. Can Benny nonetheless vote and receive dividends on his 10,000 shares?

3. Instead of promising future services, Benny offers a sketchy business plan for his 10,000 shares. He assures the board he will know how to carry it out. The board determines the plan has a value of $50,000, but does not seek an independent valuation. The board issues the shares to Benny. On the corporation's financial statements, the board carries Benny's business plan as an asset worth $50,000.
   a. In Year 1 Anna sells some of her shares to David, who later finds out how Benny got his shares. Can David sue to have Benny's shares canceled?
   b. David is also furious the board was so naive to think Benny's business plan was worth $50,000. Experts tell David the plan is worthless. Can David sue to have Benny's shares canceled?
   c. In Year 3 Benny's business plan flops and the business becomes insolvent. Creditors sue Benny to compel him to pay for his stock. Is Benny liable?

Explanations

1. a. Benny and Chris might be liable to the corporation. Anna, however, is in the clear because she paid an amount ($10.00 per share) greater than par and equal to the price set by the board, and she does not face watered stock liability.

   Benny bought stock ($7.00 per share) above par, but below the authorized price. Benny may be contractually liable if he agreed to pay the $10.00 price. Even if there was no contract, some statutes make Benny liable for the difference between the authorized price and the purchase price. See MBCA §6.22 ("consideration for which the shares were authorized to be issued"); Del. GCL §§162, 164 (corporation can collect whole of consideration not yet paid).

   Chris bought stock ($3.00 per share) below par and below the authorized price. In addition to any contract or statutory liability, Chris may be liable for the difference between the purchase price and par value. Although the MBCA abandons the notion, par value may have continuing vitality as a matter of charter interpretation. As in this example, par value serves to ensure shareholder parity. And a par value provision in the articles arguably prevents the board from issuing stock below the stated floor, unless the articles are amended to change the par value provisions.

Even though Anna overpaid for her stock, thus diluting her interest in the corporation, she cannot recover personally. The harm was to the corporation, and she must sue on behalf of the corporation in a derivative suit to recover any shortfall from Benny and Chris.

b. The liability and theories for recovery are the same as before, but on insolvency any corporate recovery is for the corporation's creditors.

2. a. Absent par value, there is no requirement that the board issue stock for a particular price. Even in a par value regime, the board can issue stock (so long as it is above par) for different prices and types of consideration.

   Benny may have some protection against the dilutive half-price issue to Anna under federal disclosure rules. Bacchanalia (and Anna) may not mislead Benny about the price or value of his shares, and the dilutive nature of the issuance to Anna might be considered a material omission entitling Benny to remedies under the antifraud provisions of the federal securities laws. See §§5.3, 22.2.

   b. It depends on the jurisdiction. Under the MBCA, Benny's contract for future services constitutes eligible consideration for his shares, and the board's valuation of the contract is conclusive. MBCA §6.21(b), (c). The MBCA recognizes that many other contingent assets (such as promissory notes given by others) are eligible, even though they may be equally illusory. If Benny is not performing his contract, any liability to pay unpaid consideration or to return the shares arises under contract law, not corporate law. And if he misled about the value of his services, fraud remedies apply.

   Under other statutes, Benny's promise of future services is considered too uncertain and is not eligible consideration. The corporation can seek to cancel his shares or assess him for any shortfall in consideration. Cases are split on whether Benny can choose to pay or to return the shares. Nonetheless, a good argument can be made that the choice should be the corporation's. If his original promised consideration was inadequate, giving him the option now to invest at the original price gives him an investment choice unavailable to the corporation's other investors.

   c. Yes. Benny is a full-fledged shareholder, though (depending on the jurisdiction) the validity of his shares may be subject to attack by the corporation or, on insolvency, by creditors. Even if Benny's consideration is statutorily ineligible, courts generally view such shares to be voidable, not void.

One way that corporate planners deal with Benny's contingent investment is to set up an escrow arrangement. The shares (and distributions made with respect to the shares) are released from escrow as services are performed under the employment contract. Failure to perform allows the corporation to cancel the shares. See MBCA §6.21(e).

3. a. Probably no. If David sues derivatively on behalf of the corporation to cancel Benny's shares, he will have to argue that the business plan is ineligible consideration under the statute. Under the MBCA the board can accept any "tangible or intangible property or benefit to the corporation." MBCA §6.21(b). In jurisdictions that limit eligible consideration, it will be difficult to argue that the business plan should be recharacterized as a promise for future services. Although this argument is plausible, courts increasingly permit greater flexibility in corporate financing. Cases read the prohibition against future services narrowly and have refused to void such transactions when all the shareholders had consented.

   b. No. The board's valuation of the business plan is conclusive under most statutes, absent fraud or bad faith. See Official Comment, MBCA §6.21(c). There is nothing to indicate that the valuation was meant to deceive investors or creditors. The board carried it on the company's books, which David could have asked for. Even if the consideration was paltry, the board's valuation should not be lightly disregarded. Only if the directors acted with tainted motives—such as if Benny had bribed them to buy stock for less than fair value—should a court question the board's valuation. Otherwise, it should be unassailable and conclusive.

   c. No. Although on insolvency creditors can enforce shareholder payment obligations, the creditors will run into the same problems as if the corporation were suing. Without more, the board's valuation is conclusive.

§4.3 DEBT FINANCING

While equity financing is infested with arbitrary and often archaic notions of par value and legal capital, debt financing—borrowing money to finance business operations—is a model of clarity. A debt security represents the corporation's promise to repay a loan made by the debtholder. The corporation is bound by contract to pay principal and interest on a fixed schedule. Corporations can borrow money in many ways—by issuing short-term commercial notes, making loans to shareholders, accepting bank lines of credit, taking trade creditors' extensions of credit, and issuing debt securities traded in public debt markets.

§4.3.1 Debt Securities

Debt securities include both short-term and long-term debt obligations. Short-term debt (to be paid within a year) usually consists of loans or notes to finance day-to-day operations of the business. Long-term debt is often freely transferable and a more permanent part of the capital structure. Common kinds of long-term debt securities are *bonds* (usually secured by specific corporate assets, such as a new hospital wing) and *debentures* (unsecured debts). The issuance of debt securities (like entering into any other contractual arrangement) is a matter within the board's discretionary power.

The terms of long-term debt are often contained in a contract or *indenture*, which sets forth the corporation's obligation to pay *interest* on a specified schedule and repay the *principal* on a specified date. These payment obligations are fixed, and the corporation must pay regardless of earnings. Failure to pay on schedule is a default, which often permits the debtholder to demand immediate payment of the principal and to pursue other remedies, including the right to initiate bankruptcy proceedings.

Debt securities do not have voting rights or, as a general matter, the participation, conversion, and redemption rights available for equity securities. See §4.1 above. But it is possible to incorporate these rights into a debt security. It is not uncommon for a corporation to issue bonds that are convertible at the holder's option into specified equity securities or that are redeemable at the holder's option ("put" bonds). These rights, however, are contractual. Significantly, the corporation's directors do not owe fiduciary duties to debtholders. See *Metropolitan Life Ins. Co. v. RJR Nabisco, Inc.*, 716 F. Supp. 1504 (S.D.N.Y. 1989) (upholding corporation's refinancing that increased bondholders' risk because bond indenture did not expressly forbid activity).

Given equity's right to elect the board and thus control corporate decision making, debtholders often protect their financial interests by contracting for *covenants* that require the borrowing corporation to refrain from certain actions that might jeopardize the debtholders' interests. For example, a bank lender might require that the corporation annually submit its budget and any changes to its business plan for approval by the bank. Or a bond indenture might specify that the corporation not pay dividends or repurchase its own shares unless certain solvency conditions are met.

Note on Credit Ratings

Issuers of debt securities—particularly corporations that issue publicly traded debt—are often rated by credit rating agencies so that investors can evaluate the creditworthiness of the issuer. The credit rating agencies (such as Moody's, S&P, and Fitch) grade debt securities from "AAA" (prime—almost no default risk) to "D" (in

(continued)

default). Investors use the ratings to decide whether to invest and what interest rate is appropriate for the risk of the investment. Credit rating agencies, which are paid by the very issuers that they rate, have been criticized for lack of objectivity. This conflict of interest, it has been argued, led credit rating agencies to give favorable ratings to debt obligations backed by subprime mortgages, contributing to the bubble in real estate prices in the mid-2000s. Under the Dodd-Frank Act of 2010, credit rating agencies are now subject to new responsibilities and liabilities. See §11.5.2.

§4.3.2 Leverage

Using debt to finance the corporation creates *leverage*—which simply means that debt financing is providing some of the firm's capital. The greater the ratio of debt to equity, the greater the leverage. High outside debt financing increases the potential for large returns (and losses) on the insiders' equity investment. Because the debt obligation is fixed, high earnings will produce a high return on equity; low earnings will do just the opposite.

The following two cases illustrate this. In each case, assume an investment of $100,000 and various earnings scenarios ($2,000, $10,000, $20,000). What is the return on equity in each case?

Case 1: Debt-Equity Ratio of 1:1

Debt (10% interest)	$ 50,000		
Equity	$ 50,000		
Total investment	$100,000		
	Scenario 1	**Scenario 2**	**Scenario 3**
Earnings	$ 2,000	$10,000	$20,000
Interest payments (10%)	$ 5,000	$ 5,000	$ 5,000
Net earnings	–$ 3,000	$ 5,000	$15,000
Return on equity	**–6%**	**+10%**	**+30%**

Case 2: Debt-Equity Ratio of 4:1

Debt (10% interest)	$ 80,000		
Equity	$ 20,000		
Total investment	$100,000		
	Scenario 1	**Scenario 2**	**Scenario 3**
Earnings	$ 2,000	$10,000	$20,000
Interest payments (10%)	$ 8,000	$ 8,000	$ 8,000
Net earnings	–$ 6,000	$ 2,000	$12,000
Return on equity	**–30%**	**+10%**	**+60%**

The two cases illustrate that *greater leverage accentuates the good and accentuates the bad* for equity, assuming the debt is from outsiders. Notice that if earnings are strong, the return on equity is twice as large when the debt-equity ratio is 4:1, compared to when it is 1:1. But if earnings are weak, the returns are much worse for the highly leveraged firm. (The financial advantages and dangers of leverage are created by outside debt financing. The effect of leverage is meaningless if the debt is held by insiders—that is, the same persons who hold the equity. Putting aside any tax effects or the higher priority in insolvency, the *overall* return to insiders who hold debt and equity will be simply the business's return on investment.)

Leverage also allows an equity investor to put up less money and still retain full control of the business. But greater leverage also increases the risk of loss for the debt investor because the equity cushion is proportionately thinner. A highly leveraged company is said to be "thinly capitalized."

§4.3.3 Tax Advantages of Debt

Interest payments by a corporation are tax deductible; dividend payments are not. I.R.C. §163. Interest deductions keep more money in the corporate treasury and hence out of the public treasury. For this reason, an investor considering whether to make a debt or equity investment will prefer debt, all other things equal.

The IRS is not blind to this tax-avoidance preference. Merely characterizing an investment as debt is not enough. The courts use a number of factors to distinguish real debt from equity masquerading as debt.

- **Payment schedule?** Debt must be paid when due; equity payments are never due. Failure to repay obligations as they mature is a sure way to risk losing debt characterization.
- **Fixed or variable return?** Debt is fixed; equity fluctuates. Variable payments are a sign of equity, not debt.
- **Payments from earnings?** Debt must be paid regardless of whether there are earnings; dividends on equity are paid from earnings.
- **Investor management?** Investments made by outsiders are easier to characterize as debt than those made by insiders. Inside debt will tend to be viewed as "at the risk of the business," particularly when the debt-equity ratio is high.
- **Thinly capitalized?** The higher the debt-equity ratio (particularly the ratio of inside debt to equity), the more likely it is that some of the debt will be recharacterized as equity.

The tax effect of recharacterizing debt as equity is twofold: (1) payments to the putative debtholder are not deductible by the corporation, often resulting in back-tax liability; and (2) that part of the payment to the putative debtholder characterized as a return of principal (normally not taxable when received) may be treated as a taxable dividend payment.

§4.3.4 Debt's Priority over Equity

When the corporation becomes insolvent or dissolves, creditors—that is, debtholders—are entitled to payment before equity shareholders. For this reason, investors prefer that their investment be characterized as debt rather than equity.

Courts do not always respect this preference. If the corporation has an insufficient equity cushion to satisfy all inside and outside creditor claims, outside creditors will seek to have the inside debt recharacterized as equity. This is essentially an equitable subordination question (see §7.2), which involves an inquiry into whether there was fraud or a fiduciary breach justifying the recharacterization. Courts also consider factors used in piercing the corporate veil (see §6.2), such as whether the corporation was undercapitalized, whether corporate formalities were followed, and whether the asserted debt was treated as such.

§4.4 DEBT-EQUITY MIX

Creating a capital structure—a debt-equity mix—is an art that balances the parties' relative desires:

- **Participation in profits.** Equity participates in earnings and with different preferences; debt generally receives fixed payments specified by contract.
- **Control rights.** Debt generally does not carry voting rights. Control over management provides protection for equity's last-in-line status.
- **Fixed payments.** Debt is "hard" and must be repaid, with interest. Equity is "soft" and need not be repaid, and dividend payments are discretionary and depend on earnings, subject to stated preferences.
- **Corporate-level taxes.** Interest payments, but not dividends, are deductible by the corporation. In a flow-through S corporation, shareholders are taxed on corporate earnings even if the earnings are not distributed.
- **Leverage.** Greater debt levels increase the risks for equity, as well as debt.
- **Priority in insolvency and on dissolution.** Debt and preferred equity have priority when the business is wound up.

Determining the proper mix of common and preferred stock—and their relative voting and participation rights—largely will be a matter of the parties' relative desires and bargaining strength. But if the mix is weighted too heavily toward debt (particularly inside debt), the advantages of tax deductibility of interest payments and debt's priority over equity may be jeopardized.

Examples

1. Lina and Maurice want to start a construction business. It will be incorporated. Lina has equipment (with an appraised value of $60,000) and some cash ($30,000). Maurice has a little cash ($10,000) and will manage the business with Lina. Each wants an equal voice in the company. To reflect her larger contribution, Lina wants a larger return and priority over Maurice. Lina also wants to get her investment back if the business fails, a common occurrence for construction firms.
   a. What financial arrangement would work for them?
   b. Assume Lina takes an $80,000 unsecured note from the corporation. Must this be authorized in the articles of incorporation?

2. The two agree. Lina and Maurice will each receive 10,000 shares of common stock at $1 per share. What financial instrument should be used to reflect the remaining $80,000 contributed by Lina? Consider the pros and cons of the following:
   a. Lina takes an unsecured note for $80,000. Consider the debt-equity ratio.
   b. Lina takes 8,000 shares of nonvoting common stock at $10 per share.
   c. Lina takes a combination of 300 shares of nonvoting preferred stock at $100 per share and a $50,000 unsecured note. Consider the debt-equity ratio.

Explanations

1. a. The two should receive an equal number of common (voting) shares to ensure an equal voice in electing the board and voting on other shareholder matters. Although some states permit debt securities to have voting rights, many do not. See MBCA §6.01(b) (articles must authorize one or more classes of "shares" that together have unlimited voting rights). Common shares have equal voting rights, unless different classes of common shares are specifically authorized in the articles. Lina's interests in larger returns and priority can be accomplished by giving her additional financial rights (such as preferred shares or debt securities) not given to Maurice.

b. No. Only equity securities need be authorized in the articles (see §4.1). The corporation's issuance of debt (its borrowing) is within the discretion of the board of directors.

2. a. **Pros:** Interest on notes is deductible by the corporation, and noteholders are not taxed on repayments of principal; noteholders share with other unsecured creditors on insolvency; debtholders have an enforceable contractual claim to payments of principal and interest; for Maurice, the note will be like outside debt, so that his equity investment will be subject to the up-side (and down-side) effects of leverage.

   Cons: The inside debt-equity ratio is 4:1, and it is possible the IRS might seek to recharacterize the note as a capital contribution, making interest on the note nondeductible and payments to Lina taxable dividends; Lina will not participate in profits to the same relative degree because her return under the note is fixed; Maurice's investment is at greater risk because of the company's heavy debt burden; outside lenders may be reluctant to lend money to a company so thinly capitalized; Lina's claim as an unsecured creditor may be equitably subordinated to those of other unsecured creditors because of the business's thin capitalization.

   b. **Pros:** Lenders will flock to such a well-capitalized company; if the corporation is successful, Lina will participate fully in the success (while she would not in the case of preferred stock or debt).

   Cons: Any payments to Lina will be subject to double taxation; Lina will have no assured return (as would be the case for debt); Lina will have no dividend or liquidation preference (as would be the case for preferred stock); Lina will have no priority with or over creditors on insolvency (as would be the case for debt).

   c. **Pros:** With an inside debt-equity ratio of 1:1, the IRS would probably not challenge interest deductibility on the note; Lina probably also would have unsecured creditor status on the note in a bankruptcy or insolvency proceeding; the note would provide Lina enforceable contract rights; Lina would have payment and liquidation preferences over Maurice on both the note and the preferred stock; Lina's assumption of debt gives Maurice some leverage; the capital structure provides lenders a pretty decent equity cushion.

   Cons: More debt would have been better for Lina, but then more debt would have been less likely to withstand tax and insolvency-priority scrutiny.

Federal Regulation of Securities Offerings

When a corporation issues its securities, it "promises" investors that future anticipated payments to the investors by the corporation justify the investment. Investors thus pay cash for the promise of future financial returns.

How can investors be sure the corporation will keep its promises—that its business plan is solid, that its management is able, that its earnings will cover principal and interest, and that its net earnings will be enough to pay dividends? In 1933 Congress created a complex "truth in securities" scheme for the issuance of securities to the public.

Much as food producers today must label their products and describe ingredients, calories, and fat content, the Securities Act of 1933 requires issuers of securities to provide investors with detailed information about the company, its management, its plans and finances, and the securities offered. The goal of the 1933 Act is disclosure, built on a philosophy that informed investors will not only have the confidence to invest, but will make better investment choices than would government bureaucrats.

This chapter provides an overview of the Securities Act's complex regulatory structure: Securities Act registration and disclosure requirements (§5.1), the principal exemptions from the registration requirements (§5.2), civil liability under the Act for violating the registration requirements and for making false or misleading statements in specified securities sales (§5.3), and the federal securities law's definition of a security—the linchpin of the Securities Act registration, disclosure, and liability provisions (§5.4).

Note on Difference between Securities Act and Exchange Act

The Securities Act of 1933 has a different focus than the Securities Exchange Act of 1934, which deals primarily with stock *trading*—that is, the buying and selling of securities after their original issuance—as well as the regulation of securities professionals and organized stock markets. Ongoing periodic disclosure is required under the Exchange Act by "public" or "reporting" companies—namely, companies whose stock is traded on a stock exchange or which have more than 500 shareholders and $10 million in assets (see §21.2.1).

§5.1 SECURITIES ACT DISCLOSURE MANDATES

The Securities Act of 1933 was an important part of the New Deal program to address the perceived causes of the Great Depression. Many believed that the stock market crash of 1929 and the ensuing collapse of the U.S. financial markets resulted from rampant speculation during the 1920s in new, financially unsound companies. Believing that state law was inadequate, Congress chose as the antidote a national system of mandatory disclosure to investors. In 1934 Congress created the Securities and Exchange Commission (SEC) to administer the federal securities laws.

§5.1.1 Public Offerings—Issuers, Underwriters, Dealers, and Investors

To understand the Securities Act's operation, you should understand the way securities are generally sold to the public. In a typical "firm commitment" offering, the marketing of securities occurs much as the marketing of other products to the public. The "issuer" (the company that creates the securities) sells the full issue to "underwriters" (wholesalers) who resell them to "dealers" (retailers) who sell them to "investors" (consumers). The process of getting securities from issuer to the investing public is known as a "public distribution." The issuer can be any person or entity selling an investment interest—usually a corporation raising capital by selling equity or debt securities. Underwriters and dealers are generally securities firms, which specialize in evaluating, recommending, buying, and selling securities. Well-known securities firms involved both in the business of underwriting (known as "investment banking") and the retail business include Merrill Lynch (part of Bank of America) and Goldman Sachs (mostly institutional customers). Investors come in many sizes and varieties. Some are unsophisticated retirees; others are enormous mutual fund groups with sophisticated investment advisers. See §19.2.

§5.1.2 Registration and Mandated Disclosure— §5 Prohibitions

The purpose of the Securities Act is full disclosure to investors in public offerings. The Act accomplishes this principally by requiring the filing and dissemination of disclosure documents. The regulatory centerpiece is §5, which broadly prohibits the sale of *any* security using the mails or other interstate means of communication unless (1) the issuer has filed a disclosure document ("registration statement") with the SEC, and (2) the registration statement has become effective.

Section 5 also requires that investors receive a disclosure document known as a "prospectus." The prospectus forms the main part of the registration statement and contains information about the company, its business, and its risks, its management, the securities being offered, the purpose of the offering, the company's capital structure, and its financial performance. The financial statements must be audited and certified by independent accountants. Registration statements are public documents and, once filed with the SEC, are available on the EDGAR database at *www.sec.gov*.

During the registration period, disclosure to investors and securities markets is strictly controlled and sometimes even prohibited. Before the registration statement is filed, marketing of the offering is significantly curtailed. After the registration statement is filed and before it becomes effective (the "waiting period"), marketing is mostly limited to oral communications and dissemination of the preliminary ("red herring") prospectus. (Recent rule changes give well-known, seasoned issuers greater freedom in their registration-period communications.) A violation of the disclosure rules during the registration period can force the issuer and underwriters to abandon the offering. Once the registration process is complete, the SEC permits the registration statement to become effective, and securities sales can commence. The SEC has no authority to stop an offering simply because of doubts about its merits, such as because the agency believes that the firm's business plan is flawed or its management is overcompensated. It is enough if these matters were disclosed in the prospectus for evaluation by investors.

SEC registration is time-consuming, expensive, and intrusive. The issuer's executives must gather information and ensure the accuracy of the prospectus. The issuer must also have its financial statements audited by an independent accounting firm. The issuer must retain legal counsel, typically a large, high-priced law firm. Printing costs of preliminary and final prospectuses are significant. The underwriters, who also retain separate legal counsel, charge commissions or fees. And once an issuer "goes public," it becomes subject to ongoing SEC disclosure requirements.

§5.1.3 State "Blue Sky" Laws

Originally, the Securities Act contemplated that securities offerings would also be subject to regulation under state securities laws—known as "blue sky" laws. These laws (which vary widely) contain a mix of three basic regulatory devices: (1) antifraud provisions that give state administrators authority to act against false or misleading statements in the sale of securities; (2) licensing of securities professionals to permit state supervision and disciplining; and (3) registration of securities prior to their sale or trading, which in some states requires administrative approval of the *merits* of a particular security.

In 1996, responding to claims that state "blue sky" laws impose more costs than benefits, Congress amended the Securities Act to preempt state regulation of many securities offerings. Specifically, §18 now prevents states from regulating offerings of "covered" securities, which include securities listed on the New York Stock Exchange or the NASDAQ National Market System, or securities exempt from registration under §4(2) (see §5.2 below).

The preemption, however, is not complete. States still can bring antifraud proceedings when securities are sold fraudulently and, for covered offerings not on an exchange or NASDAQ, states can collect fees and require filing of documents "substantially similar" to those filed with the SEC. States also can require full-blown registration of offerings subject to the intrastate exemption and the small-offering exemptions of Regulation A and Regulation D (see below).

§5.2 EXEMPTIONS—TEMPERING THE BREADTH OF §5

Broad exemptions temper the sweep of §5's prohibition against offerings of unregistered securities. Exempted from Securities Act registration and mandatory disclosure requirements are

- transactions in trading markets
- nonpublic (or private) offerings
- intrastate offerings by local issuers to local investors
- small offerings, as defined by SEC rules

Because SEC registration is expensive and intrusive, many securities lawyers devote a big part of their practice to helping clients gain an exemption from registration. In fact, most offerings of securities (particularly by smaller companies seeking to raise less than $20 million in capital) are structured as exempt offerings. Bear in mind, however, that none of the exemptions discussed below shields sellers from the antifraud provisions of the Securities Act or the Exchange Act (in particular, Rule 10b-5; see Chapter 22).

§5.2.1 Intrastate Offerings

To permit local offerings that are subject to state jurisdiction, the Securities Act exempts from its registration and disclosure requirements any offering made and sold only to residents within a single state. §3(a)(11). The exemption is narrow and strict, and relying on it is risky.

- **In-state issuer.** The issuer must reside and be doing business in the state of the offering. A corporation "resides" in the state of its incorporation. An issuer "does business" in a state if its revenues, assets, and principal office, as well as use of the proceeds of the offering, are principally in-state.
- **In-state offering.** The offering can be made only to in-state residents—actual residence and domiciliary intent controls. The statutory exemption is lost if any sale or offer (even one that does not result in a sale) is made to an out-of-state resident. The exemption is also lost if any in-state purchaser acts as a conduit and resells to out-of-state investors. The issuer cannot rely on representations by in-state purchasers.
- **Part of one issue.** The intrastate offering cannot be part of a larger offering in which there are out-of-state investors. Any other offers or sales that are part of the same offering must comply with the in-state restrictions.

The SEC has clarified and eased some of these requirements in a regulatory "safe harbor" rule. Under Rule 147 an issuer qualifies for the intrastate exemption if at least 80 percent of its revenues, assets, and proceeds are in-state; a purchaser's residence is determined without reference to domiciliary intent; resales to out-of-state investors are permitted beginning nine months after the initial offering; offers by in-state purchasers to out-of-state residents are forgiven so long as there is no actual sale during the nine-month holding period; other offerings conducted six months before or after the intrastate offering are separate. But, as with the statutory exemption, any sale or offer to an out-of-state investor by an issuer destroys the entire exemption.

§5.2.2 Nonpublic (Private) Offerings

The most important Securities Act exemption for issuers seeking to raise capital is the "private placement" exemption. §4(2) (any offering "by an issuer not involving any public offering"). Without it, virtually every effort to raise capital—regardless of who the investors are—would be subject to the expense and burden of the Act's registration and disclosure process.

The private placement exemption exists in two forms: (1) the §4(2) statutory exemption that provides a complete exemption from the disclosure and registration requirements of the Securities Act, and (2) a regulatory exemption (Rule 506 of Regulation D) created by the SEC to provide greater certainty to issuers, but conditioned on disclosure to certain investors.

Statutory Exemption

Courts have interpreted the §4(2) statutory exemption to be available if the offering meets the following criteria:

- **Qualified investors.** Each investor (as well as each person receiving an investment offer, "offeree") must meet a sliding-scale test that factors both her ability to evaluate the investment (given her business and investment sophistication) and the availability of information (based on both her access to it and its actual disclosure). The less sophisticated the investor, the more disclosure required; the more sophisticated, the less disclosure required.

  In *SEC v. Ralston Purina Co.*, 346 U.S. 119 (1953), the Supreme Court defined the scope of the §4(2) exemption. The case involved Ralston Purina's policy of selling company stock to employees who on their own initiative sought to invest. Hundreds of different employees (including chow loading foremen, stock clerks, and stenographers) had purchased unregistered stock from the company. The Court held that the exemption applies when offerees and investors, regardless of how many there are, are "able to fend for themselves." The Court gave as an example "executive personnel" with access to the same kind of information available in a registration statement. In the case, many of the Ralston Purina employees lacked this access, and the Court held that Securities Act registration was required.
- **Restricted securities.** The §4(2) exemption is lost if qualified investors resell to unqualified investors who cannot "fend for themselves." For this reason securities sold in a private placement are known as "restricted securities," and issuers will often seek to preserve their exemption by placing contractual restrictions on the transfer of the securities. Transfer limits are noted on the security certificates, and the issuer will instruct its transfer agent (usually a bank that keeps

records on share ownership) not to record any transfer unless it complies with or is exempt from the Act's registration requirements.

- **Strict compliance.** Private offerings under §4(2) can be made only to investors and offerees with the requisite sophistication and access to information. A sale or offer to just one unqualified investor (or to the public at large) causes the exemption to be lost for all.

There is no maximum either on the dollar size of a private offering or the number of offerees and investors. In fact, it is not uncommon for issuers to use the §4(2) statutory exemption for private placements that raise many millions of dollars and are sold to many institutional investors. Nonetheless, the larger the group to whom offers or sales are made, the more likely some will not be qualified, thus putting the entire offering at risk.

Regulation D — SEC Regulatory Exemption

In response to concerns from small business about the expense of Securities Act registration, the SEC has promulgated a set of rules, known as Reg D, that give detailed guidance on when an offering qualifies for the private placement exemption of §4(2). Rule 506. Reg D also exempts certain "small offerings" as authorized by §3(b) of the Securities Act. Rules 504, 505.

The three Reg D exemptions turn on (1) the dollar amount of the offering, (2) the number and kinds of investors (as opposed to offerees) who participate in the offering, (3) whether the Reg D offering is part of a larger offering, (4) the kind of advertisement used, and (5) the kind of information provided investors. Since their promulgation in 1982 the SEC has modified Reg D a number of times. The description below is as of 2008:

- **Rule 504—small offerings subject to state "blue sky" law.** Nonpublic companies can sell up to $1 million in securities in any 12-month year. There is no limit on the number or kinds of investors or any disclosure requirement. But general advertising and solicitations are not permitted, and the securities issued under the exemption are "restricted." To avoid these marketing and liquidity restrictions, small issuers can either (1) register the offering under a state blue sky law that requires public filing and delivery to investors of a disclosure document, or (2) limit the offering to "accredited investors" (see below) under any state exemption that allows general solicitations.
- **Rule 505—medium-sized offerings subject to SEC conditions.** Companies (except investment companies and those disqualified under the SEC's "bad boy" criteria) can sell up to $5 million in securities in any 12-month period. No general advertising or solicitations are permitted. The offering can be sold to an unlimited number of "accredited" investors, but there can be no more than 35 "nonaccredited"

investors. All nonaccredited investors must receive specified written disclosure and an opportunity to ask questions of the issuer. Securities acquired pursuant to Rule 505 become "restricted securities."

- **Rule 506—private offerings subject to SEC safe-harbor conditions.** Any company (provided it is not disqualified under the SEC's "bad boy" criteria) can sell an unlimited amount of securities under the same conditions as Rule 505, with one added condition. If any sale is made to nonaccredited investors, each of these investors (alone or with her purchaser representative) must have sufficient knowledge and experience in business and financial matters so she can evaluate the merits and risks of the investment. Rule 506 is a nonexclusive safe harbor; an offering that does not satisfy all the rule's conditions may still be exempt under §4(2).

Accredited Investors

The Reg D exemptions thus depend on whether particular investors are accredited. Rule 501 of Reg D defines various categories of accredited investors, which include:

Accredited Investors	
Institutional investors	banks, savings institutions, brokerage firms, insurance companies, mutual funds, and certain ERISA employee benefit plans
Big organizations	tax-exempt organizations and for-profit corporations with more than $5 million in assets
Key insiders	the directors, executive officers, and general partners of the issuer
Millionaires	individuals who have a net worth (along with spouses) of over $1 million, not counting the value of their primary residence
Fat cats	individuals who have had for two years, and expect to have, an annual income of at least $200,000 (or $300,000 with their spouse)
Venture-capital firms	firms that invest in start-up companies to which they then provide significant managerial assistance
Sophisticated trusts	trusts that have over $5 million in assets and are run by someone with the knowledge and experience to evaluate the merits and risks of the investment

Reg D assumes that investors that fall into these categories either have the sophistication to fend for themselves or the financial resources to seek the help of a sophisticated investment advisor.

SEC Filing and Noncompliance

The issuer must file an informational notice (describing itself and its Reg D offering) with the SEC within 15 days after the first sale. Rule 503(a) (now called Form D2). Even if an issuer fails to comply with Reg D, the exemption is not lost if the issuer shows that the failures were insignificant and noncompliance was immaterial to the particular investor seeking to avoid the exemption. Rule 508(a).

§5.2.3 Small Offering Exemptions

Under §3(b) of the Securities Act, the SEC has authority to exempt offerings of less than $5 million. In addition to the Reg D exemptions of Rules 504 and 505 (discussed above), the SEC has adopted Regulation A pursuant to this authority. Reg A exempts offerings by nonreporting companies of up to $5 million provided the issuer follows a simplified "mini-registration" process. See Rules 251–264. The exemption permits the use of a simplified question-and-answer disclosure document, and financial information need not be audited.

§5.2.4 Exemption for Postdistribution Market Trading

Ordinary trading — such as on stock exchanges or between investors — is exempt from the Securities Act's registration and disclosure requirements. Section 4(1) exempts any transaction by a person *other than* an issuer, an underwriter, or a dealer (during the initial distribution of an offering). The effect of the §4(1) exemption — along with the exemptions for postdistribution market transactions by dealers in §4(3) and for broker transactions in §4(4) — is that only transactions that are part of the *distribution* of securities are subject to the Act's registration and disclosure requirements.

Defining a Distribution

The §4(1) exemption has some hidden catches because of the way the Act defines a statutory "underwriter." An underwriter is defined under §2(11) to include any person (1) who purchases shares from an issuer "with a view to" their further distribution, or (2) who offers or sells shares "for an issuer" in connection with a distribution. In short, an underwriter is any person who acts as a conduit or agent for an issuer's securities into a public market.

As a result of this definition, the distribution of securities becomes a surprisingly broad concept. For example, a shareholder who owns *restricted securities* cannot resell them into a public trading market unless they are first registered. If the shareholder purchased the securities "with a view" to public distribution, their resale in a public trading market is known as a "secondary distribution," and the selling shareholder is deemed a statutory underwriter. This means that the holder of restricted securities must either have the issuer register the securities or wait until they have "come to rest" with him so their subsequent resale is not viewed as part of a distribution.

In addition, any person who acts as a conduit or agent for a *control person* is also defined to be an underwriter. (A control person is anyone who because of his position or shareholdings has access to confidential corporate information and the power to have the corporation register shares under the Securities Act.) For example, a brokerage firm that assists a control person to sell his shares on a public trading market is subject to the Act's registration requirements, just as if the assistance had been to the issuer. To prevent abuses by control persons, whose unregistered sales pose similar dangers as unregistered sales by an issuer, the §2(11) definition limits the ability of controlling shareholders and corporate executives to sell their shares in a public trading market.

Rule 144—Safe Harbor for Secondary Market Transactions

The SEC permits the resale of restricted shares and resales by control persons into public markets *without registration* under an important safe harbor—Rule 144. Under the rule (as revised in 2008), conditions for reselling securities vary depending on whether the seller is a noncontrol or control person, whether the resale is of restricted or nonrestricted shares, and whether the issuer is a reporting or nonreporting company.

Rule 144 Conditions

Resales by noncontrol persons of restricted securities	**Holding period:** 6 months for securities of reporting company, and 12 months for securities of nonreporting company **Issuer information:** current public information for reporting company, during 12 months before resale
Resales by control persons (restricted or nonrestricted securities)	**Holding period:** 6 months for securities of reporting company, and 12 months for securities of nonreporting company* **Trickle:** during 3-month period, resales of no more than 1% of outstanding equity securities or average weekly trading; resales of no more than 10% of tranche (class) of debt securities **Sale method:** brokers' transactions (can't solicit buyers) for equity securities **Issuer information:** current public information, whether reporting or nonreporting company **Notice:** must disclose on Form 144, if sell more than 5,000 securities or more than $40,000

*No holding period for resales by control persons of nonrestricted securities.

Thus, noncontrol persons can resell their restricted shares without limit after a 12-month holding period (and after a 6-month holding period, if the issuer is a reporting company current in its periodic filings). Control persons (whose informational advantages are presumed) must always abide by the various resale conditions, though no holding period applies to their resales of nonrestricted shares.

Examples

1. Adam, Boone, and Carver are friends, ardent outdoorsmen, and weekend chefs. They fix on a new concept in dining—a rustic outdoor restaurant offering a menu of muskrat steaks, squirrel sausage, and hickory ale. They form Outdoor Cafes, incorporated in the state of Mayflower, to operate the business in Mayflower. Each invests $100,000 and receives 100,000 shares of stock. Adam will manage the restaurant; Boone and Carver will be passive investors.
   a. Has Outdoor Cafes violated §5 of the Securities Act by issuing stock to Adam, Boone, and Carver?
   b. Adam and Boone are Mayflower residents; Carver lives in the adjoining state of New Columbia, though he covenants to be subject to Mayflower jurisdiction. Is Outdoor Cafes' issuance of stock exempted from registration by §3(a)(11)?
   c. After learning that Carver is from New Columbia, Adam and Boone decide that each will buy $150,000 of stock and later resell $50,000 to Carver. Is the intrastate offering exemption available, and does Rule 147 help?
   d. Adam has little wealth, though some experience running an eating establishment. Boone is a well-to-do physician who enjoys hunting and investing in start-up restaurants. Carver is a struggling securities lawyer with a modest investment portfolio. Is the issuance of Outdoor Cafes' stock to them exempted from registration by §4(2)?

2. After five years Outdoor Cafes becomes a success. Adam, Boone, and Carver plan to open new restaurants throughout New England. They will need about $3 million, which they can raise by selling 300,000 new shares at $10 to personal acquaintances and angel investors who look for these kinds of start-up companies. Many investors will be from outside Mayflower.
   a. Outdoor Cafes expects to raise the $3 million by selling to about 40 investors: Ten have net worths of over $1 million; another ten have incomes of over $200,000; another ten are intimately familiar with the restaurant business; the last ten are relatives of Adam, Boone, and Carver. Can Outdoor Cafes rely on Regulation D?
   b. Zach, who knows Adam because they have gone on hunting trips together, is a cross-country truck driver with minimal investment and business experience. He nonetheless has a net worth of $750,000. Can Outdoor Cafes sell stock to Zach under Rule 506?

3. Outdoor Cafes uses Rule 505 to avoid Securities Act registration.
   a. It places an advertisement in *Outdoor Life*, a national publication, soliciting interest in the company's offering. No sales are made through this advertisement except to accredited investors. Is this permitted?
   b. Adam, Boone, and Carver talk to Jane, who works for an investment firm that advises start-up businesses on how to raise money from angel investors. She agrees to help in the offering, and the investment firm's next mailing to its clients includes a reference to the Outdoor Cafes offering. Is this mailing permitted?
   c. Adam, Boone, and Carver send 60 letters to squirrel sausage-loving friends and acquaintances who have inquired about investing in their business. Of those who receive the letters, 50 do not satisfy the definition of an accredited investor. Is this mailing permitted?
   d. Adam, Boone, and Carver have identified exactly 35 nonaccredited friends and family members who are interested in buying stock. They also consider whether to sell to Michelle, a Hollywood producer, who has a current personal net worth of over $2 million but is squandering her fortune. Can they sell to Michelle?

4. The Outdoor Cafes issue took place under Rule 505 in August last year and was a complete (and legal) success.
   a. In January this year, Michelle, who purchased 10,000 shares, wants to resell 5,000 to her gardener George. Can Michelle sell?
   b. In January this year, Michelle wants to sell all her shares to Adam, who is still the Outdoor Cafes president. Can Michelle sell?
   c. In December this year, Michelle wants to resell all 10,000 shares to George, her still-unsophisticated gardener. Outdoor Cafes is still owned by only 50 shareholders and does not make public reports of its financial condition. Can Michelle sell?

5. In August this year, Outdoor Cafes registers and makes an initial public offering (IPO) of one million shares. After the IPO, a trading market in Outdoor Cafes stock develops, and the company becomes subject to and complies with the periodic reporting requirements of the Securities Exchange Act of 1934 (see §21.2.2). Two months after the $20 IPO, the price of Outdoor Cafes stock rises to $28.
   a. Adam, who acquired his stock ten years ago, wants to sell 20,000 of his 100,000 shares through his stockbroker at the current market price. Can he?
   b. Michelle, who purchased 10,000 shares 16 months ago pursuant to Rule 505, wants to immediately sell all her shares through her broker, who will actively solicit buyers. Can she?

Explanations

1. a. Possibly. It depends on (1) whether the mails or other interstate means of communication were used during the issuance, and (2) whether there is an exemption.

   It is virtually impossible to avoid using the mails in a securities transaction. If the parties transact a check, which will be cleared through the mails, §5 prohibits the sales to Adam, Boone, and Carver unless Outdoor Cafes registers the stock with the SEC or there is an exemption. To know if an exemption applies, we must know much more.

   b. No. The intrastate offering exemption requires that each investor be from the same state as the issuer, in this case Mayflower. Because Carver is a New Columbia resident, regardless of any representation or covenant to the contrary, the entire offering (including the sales to Adam and Boone) fail the intrastate offering exemption.

   c. No, under the statute; perhaps, under the safe-harbor rule. The statutory exemption is not available because Adam and Boone purchased their stock "with a view" to reselling to an out-of-state resident. See Securities Act §2(11) (definition of underwriter). They become statutory underwriters, and their resales to Carver — no matter when they occur — would be viewed as part of the original distribution, thus disqualifying the entire offering under the statutory §3(a)(11) exemption.

   If, despite their resale intention, Adam and Boone held on to their stock for nine months, Rule 147 would provide a safe harbor for their resales. But there is a twist. If Carver had agreed to this arrangement from the outset, it might be possible to characterize his original agreement as one to purchase from the company through Adam and Boone. If so, it would be an out-of-state sale, occurring during the nine-month holding period.

   d. Probably. The nonpublic offering exemption of §4(2) requires that each investor meet a sliding-scale test that factors both their ability to evaluate the investment and the availability of information (both their access to it and its actual disclosure). As manager of the business, Adam would seem to satisfy the test because his business knowledge and access to inside information enable him to fend for himself.

   Boone and Carver may also qualify. Their status as "weekend chefs," their personal relationship to Adam (and hence their indirect access to investment information), their investing experience, and their apparent wealth (and hence their ability to bear the risk and to afford sophisticated representation) indicate they can evaluate (or have someone else evaluate) the investment and its risks. Nonetheless, if either Boone or Carver fails the test, the private offering exemption is lost as to the whole issue.

2. a. Yes. Rule 505 allows for issues of up to $5 million each year; Rule 506 has no dollar limit. Because Outdoor Cafes plans to raise more than $1 million, Rule 504 is unavailable.

   Both Rules 505 and 506 allow for the sale to up to 35 nonaccredited investors. Twenty of the investors (the "millionaires" and $200,000 "fat cats") are accredited under Reg D and do not count against this limit. The other 20, on the facts, are nonaccredited. If any sales are made to these nonaccredited investors, they must be provided specified disclosure—in a Reg D offering typically called an "investment circular."

   b. Probably not, unless Zach has an investment representative. Zach is nonaccredited and would have to meet (alone or with an investment representative) the sophistication criteria of Rule 506. This presents a significant disadvantage compared to Rule 505. The issuer must reasonably believe that each nonaccredited investor (alone or with his purchaser representative) has knowledge and experience in business and financial matters so he can evaluate the merits and risks of the investment.

   Rule 505 has no such requirement because it derives from the small offering exemption of §3(b) of the Securities Act. On the other hand, Rule 506 is a safe-harbor rule for the private offering exemption of §4(2).

3. a. No. General advertising is not allowed under a Rule 505 or 506 offering. See Rule 502(c). The idea is that information about the offering should be limited to prevent the market from being softened or Reg D being used to sell speculative schemes, which generally depend on widespread advertising or solicitations.

   b. Yes. Inclusion in a mailing to angel investors *who are clients of the firm* is not a general solicitation. According to the SEC, if the issuer or its representative has a "preexisting relationship" with the solicited investors, it is not a general solicitation. Those who receive the mailing have shown an interest in such investments; Jane is not softening the market or widely touting a speculative scheme, and many of the recipients will probably qualify as accredited investors.

   c. Probably. This mailing does not seem to be a general solicitation because it is directed to those who had before expressed an interest in buying the company's stock—a "preexisting relationship." There seems little risk of creating a "speculative mania." Further, Rules 505 and 506, unlike the §4(2) statutory exemption, allow offers to nonaccredited investors as long as the final number of nonaccredited *purchasers* does not exceed 35. Unlike the statutory exemption, offers to nonaccredited investors (even if they have no investment representative when they receive the offer) do not undermine the Reg D exemption.

d. Yes. Rule 505 (like Rule 506) places no limit on the number of *accredited* investors who can purchase under the rule. Michelle satisfies the Reg D criteria for a "millionaire"—a person whose personal net worth exceeds $1 million. Even though she may not be able to appreciate the investment or its risks and would not meet the sophistication requirements of Rule 506 if she were nonaccredited, this makes no difference because she fits one of the "accredited investor" categories. Reg D is a safe harbor.

4. a. Almost certainly no. All securities acquired under Rule 505 are treated as restricted securities and cannot be sold unless their resale is itself registered or an exemption is available. See Rule 502(d). But no exemption seems to be available. The intrastate offering exemption of §3(a)(11) and the private placement exemption of §4(2) are available only to issuers—Michelle would not be selling for the issuer when she resells to George.

   The market trading exemption of §4(1), which at first blush seems it might apply, is unavailable because Michelle is probably a statutory underwriter. The definition of an underwriter includes anyone who buys stock "with a view" to its distribution to the public. Michelle, because of the short time she has held the securities, probably will be viewed as having purchased her shares with a view to reselling them. The sale to George is a public "distribution" because George does not appear to be an investor who can fend for himself.

   The safe harbor Rule 144 does not apply because Michelle has not held the shares for more than 6 months, the minimum holding period for noncontrol persons who wish to resell restricted shares.

b. Probably. The market trading exemption of §4(1) seems to apply. In her sale to Adam, Michelle fails the definition of a statutory underwriter. Although Michelle's quick resale to Adam might indicate that she purchased her shares with a view to their resale, the sale to Adam is not a *public* "distribution," which the Securities Act is meant to regulate. Adam qualifies as an investor who can fend for himself, and Michelle's sale to Adam would not be a "transaction by an issuer, underwriter, or dealer" and thus would be exempt under §4(1).

c. Perhaps. The market trading exemption of §4(1) depends on Michelle's intentions when she originally bought the stock. If Michelle originally purchased with "a view to" resell them, they remain restricted. Any sale to an unsophisticated investor (or in a public market) would be a prohibited public distribution, no matter how long Michelle holds on to the shares.

Nonetheless, original intentions are rarely clear. Michelle has held the stock for more than a year, negating a resale intention. Under the safe harbor Rule 144, she can resell without limitation because she satisfies the one-year holding period for resales by noncontrol persons of restricted shares. Securities lawyers would say that the stock had "come to rest" with Michelle, and she may now resell without being considered a statutory underwriter.

The resale conditions of Rule 144, such as the requirement that the issuer be a reporting company or that notice be given if more than 5,000 shares are sold, do not apply to resales by noncontrol persons who have held for more than 12 months.

5. a. Yes, but he must comply with the conditions of Rule 144. As a control person, Adam cannot sell into a public stock market using an intermediary unless he complies with the conditions of Rule 144. He must "trickle" his stock into the market—selling no more during any three-month period than 1 percent of Outdoor Cafes' outstanding shares or its average weekly trading volume. Adam must also provide notice to the SEC because he will sell more than 5,000 shares. Otherwise the conditions of Rule 144 appear to be met: current public information about Outdoor Cafes is available, and Adam has held his "restricted shares" for more than one year.

   b. Yes. Rule 144 permits noncontrol holders of "restricted shares" to resell without conditions if they have held their stock for more than one year (before 2008, this was two years). Michelle is not subject to any "trickle," public information, broker sales, or filing requirements.

§5.3 CIVIL LIABILITY UNDER SECURITIES ACT

Civil liability under the Securities Act is structured along three themes:

- **Statutory rescission for violations of §5.** To protect the integrity of the Act's mandatory disclosure system, investors can rescind their investment if there was any violation of the §5 registration and disclosure requirements. Securities Act §12(a)(1) (numbered §12(1) before 1995).
- **Antifraud liability for false registration statement.** Investors in a *registered* offering can recover any losses from specified participants if there are material misrepresentations or omissions in the registration statement (or prospectus). Securities Act §11.
- **Antifraud liability for falsehoods in public offering.** "Sellers" in public offerings are liable for material misrepresentations made in

the prospectus or orally. Securities Act §12(a)(2) (numbered §12(2) before 1995).

Sale of unregistered securities in violation of §5, or generally the deceptive sale of securities, is also subject to administrative and criminal sanctions.

§5.3.1 Section 12(a)(1)—Rescission for Violations of §5

Section 12(a)(1) is a simple and powerful provision that enforces the registration and prospectus dissemination requirements of §5. Whenever securities are offered or sold in violation of §5, any purchaser may rescind the transaction and get her money back with interest (or recover damages if she has resold the stock). Section 12(a)(1) thus imposes strict liability for violations of §5 and represents a significant private enforcement tool against the sale of unregistered securities for which no exemption applies.

§5.3.2 Section 11—Damages for Deceptive Registration Statements

Section 11 allows any purchaser of a *registered* security to recover damages from the issuer and others involved in the distribution if the registration statement contains any falsehoods or half-truths concerning any material fact—that is, one that a reasonable investor would consider important in deciding to invest.

Section 11 creates a complex liability scheme with

- specifically enumerated defendants
- convoluted nonculpability ("due diligence") defenses
- intricate formulas for computing damages
- allocation of liability among defendants
- tricky limitations period

Plaintiffs (purchasers in the offering) need only identify material untruths or omissions of material facts in the registration statement. Section 11 thus modifies the elements of common law fraud and equitable contract rescission. Plaintiffs need not prove the defendants' culpability, though each defendant (except the issuer) has a defense based on the defendant's diligence in checking the registration statement. Plaintiffs need not show actual reliance on the claimed untruths or omissions, or even that they read the prospectus—though there is a defense if the investor knew of the claimed untruths or omissions when she bought the securities. Plaintiffs need not prove the claimed misinformation caused their losses, though defendants have a "comparative causation" defense if the plaintiffs' losses were due to factors other than the misinformation.

Section 11 Defendants

As we have seen, a public offering is similar to the distribution of consumer products—from issuer through intermediaries to final purchaser. Just as modern products liability law cuts through old privity requirements, §11 specifies a list of potential defendants, most of whom are not in privity with investors:

- the issuer (who is strictly liable regardless of fault)
- the issuer's directors (whether or not they signed the registration statement)
- the issuer's senior executives who signed the registration statement
- the underwriters of the offering (though each is generally liable only to the extent of its relative participation in the offering)
- any expert whose opinion is used in the registration statement (such as the accounting firm that audits the company's financial statements)

To ensure full and honest disclosure for investors, §11 is purposefully designed to put fear in the hearts of potential defendants and create a diligent group of disclosure watchdogs.

"Due Diligence" Defenses

Very few litigated cases actually impose liability under §11. Instead, most cases are settled. Nonetheless, the section's staggering *potential* liability and its due diligence defenses mold the way in which participants in registered offerings behave.

What is "due diligence"—besides something often assigned to junior securities lawyers. Due diligence is the investigation by potential defendants of the information contained in the registration statement and prospectus—a task usually delegated to outside law firms and, within those firms, often to junior associates.

The level of diligence due varies according to who prepared (or certified) the information later attacked as false or misleading. It also depends on whether the false or misleading information arose in those portions of the registration statement certified by an expert, such as financial information audited by an accounting firm or legal opinions given by lawyers—the "expertised" portions. All other portions, most of the registration statement, are nonexpertised.

The due diligence defenses for experts and nonexperts are as follows:

Due Diligence Defenses		
	Expertised portion	**Nonexpertised portion**
Expert	Must investigate and believe information is true (*ignorance is no excuse*)	No liability
Nonexpert	No reasonable ground to believe information is false (*ignorance is excuse*)	Must investigate and believe information is true (*ignorance is no excuse*)

Although the statute does not explicitly create different standards for different defendants, courts have used a variable yardstick to judge when each defendant's investigation is sufficient.

Consider the leading case on §11 due diligence, *Escott v. BarChris Construction Co.*, 283 F. Supp. 643 (S.D.N.Y. 1968). The case involved a bowling alley construction company whose registration statement in a debt offering seriously misstated the company's financial position and its exposure to losses. The principal issue in the case was whether the nonissuer defendants had made out their §11 due diligence defenses. The court carefully analyzed each defendant's position with the company, his role in the offering, and his access to critical information. In the process, the court identified a continuum of "reasonable investigation" and "reasonable belief." Company insiders who had responsibilities that gave them broad access to company information were treated as virtual guarantors of the registration statement's accuracy. But nonemployee outsiders who did not have an advisory relationship were required only to read the registration statement and follow up on obvious discrepancies. See Rule 176 ("reasonable investigation" varies according to position and relationship to issuer).

§5.3.3 Section 12(a)(2)—Rescission for Misrepresentations

Section 12(a)(2) is an antifraud provision that picks up where §11 leaves off. Purchasers in an offering may seek rescission from "statutory sellers" if the offering is carried out "by means of a prospectus or oral communication" that is materially false or misleading. Reliance and causation are not elements of the claim, though sellers have a defense if they show the purchaser knew of the misstatement or if the claimed losses represent "other than the depreciation in value . . . resulting from" the challenged misstatements. See §12(b). In addition, defendants have a "reasonable care" defense if they show they did not know (and reasonably could not have known) of the misinformation.

Section 12(a)(2) does not require privity, but extends to those who actively solicit purchases and do so for gain—so-called statutory sellers. See

Pinter v. Dahl, 486 U.S. 622 (1988). This means that collateral participants in a securities offering, such as lawyers and investment advisers, who assist in the selling effort risk becoming liable.

The scope of §12(a)(2) has been significantly, though ambiguously, restricted by the Supreme Court. See *Gustafson v. Alloyd Co.*, 513 U.S. 561 (1995) (holding that misrepresentations in sales contract to outside investor group were not actionable under §12(a)(2) because the contract was not a "prospectus"). The decision, which surprised the securities community, stated that §12(a)(2) liability is limited to misrepresentations in prospectuses used in registered public offerings. The Court thus abandoned decades of uniform case law that §12(a)(2) also covers written misrepresentations made in exempt private sales, such as private placements under §4(2). Whether §12(a)(2) extends to exempt offerings that use "prospectus-like" offering circulars remains an open question.

Examples

1. Soon after Adam, Boone, and Carver form Outdoor Cafes—each investing $100,000—Carver becomes disenchanted with his investment. Adam (the restaurant manager) had given him an offering memorandum with pro forma income statements before he invested. The statement optimistically forecasted that the restaurant would have monthly revenues of $40,000. In fact, they have averaged only $15,000. Carver has come to you for some litigation advice.
   a. You conclude an exemption from registration was unavailable. Can Carver get his money back without having to litigate the accuracy of the income statement? From whom?
   b. You conclude a private offering exemption applied to the offering and the sale to Carver. Is there another route by which Carver can get his money back?
   c. Adam approaches Carver to purchase his shares. Adam knows that a national restaurant chain is about to offer to buy Outdoor Cafes at a significant premium, but does not tell Carver. Can Carver sue under the Securities Act?

2. Outdoor Cafes opens new restaurants in other states. To raise capital it sells its stock in a registered offering in compliance with §5. The prospectus states that the concept of a "rustic outdoor restaurant" has been tried successfully in other states besides Mayflower. The statement is false: the only such restaurants are in Mayflower. Michael buys some of the stock a couple months after the public issue. Within a year the price of the stock plummets.
   a. Can Michael sue Outdoor Cafes to recover damages? What must he show?

b. Joseph, Outdoor Cafes' outside counsel, had drafted the prospectus. Is he liable to Michael?

Explanations

1. a. Yes. Carver can seek rescission under §12(a)(1). If the sale was made using the mails or some means of interstate communication—a virtual certainty—the sale to Carver violated §5 because (1) no exemption was available, and (2) no registration statement was filed or became effective. Section 12(a)(1) provides for strict liability and rescission. He must bring his action within one year after the illegal sale. See Securities Act §13.

   Outdoor Cafes (the issuer) and Adam are both potential defendants under §12(a)(1). Outdoor Cafes was the privity seller, and Adam actively solicited Carver's investment and stood to gain by bringing in another investor. See *Pinter v. Dahl*, 486 U.S. 622 (1988).

   b. Probably not under the Securities Act. Although courts once allowed deceived securities purchasers to seek rescission under §12(a)(2), the Supreme Court has limited the remedy to "public offerings." In addition, there can be no liability under §11 because there was no registration statement.

   Nonetheless, Carver might sue under Rule 10b-5 of the Securities Exchange Act of 1934, though he would have to prove (among other things) that Adam knew projections were false or misleading and that Carver actually and reasonably relied on the projections. See §22.3.

   c. No. The Securities Act only regulates fraud in the *sale* of securities, not in the purchase of securities—as here. (Michael, however, can sue for this insider trading under Rule 10b-5; see Chapter 23.)

2. a. Perhaps. Michael could seek damages under §11 from Outdoor Cafes, which has no due diligence defense. Although some district courts have read *Gustafson* broadly to exclude Securities Act liability for aftermarket trading, denying §11 standing to plaintiffs who purchased their securities in the aftermarket of a registered offering, most circuit courts accept that §11 standing extends to aftermarket purchases "traceable" to the public offering. See *Hertzberg v. Dignity Partners, Inc.*, 191 F.3d 1076 (9th Cir. 1999).

   If Michael has standing, he would need only show the prospectus contained a materially false or misleading statement. The "other states" statement was false, and its materiality depends on whether a reasonable investor would consider it important in deciding whether to invest. Because the offering was meant to raise money to expand to other states, the success of a "rustic outdoor restaurant" outside Mayflower would seem significant to the expansion's success.

If the falsehood was material, the burden would switch to Outdoor Cafes to show that (1) Michael knew the "other states" statement was false—a reliance defense—or (2) some or all of Michael's loss was caused by factors other than the lack of non-Mayflower experience, such as a general decline in restaurant stocks—a comparative causation defense.

b. Probably not. Joseph is liable under §11 only if he falls in one of the categories of §11 defendants. As issuer's counsel in the offering, he can be liable under §11 for "other states" falsehood only if he was a company director or a statutory underwriter by actively soliciting investors. (For this reason, lawyers are well advised not to accept positions as directors of corporate clients or to assist in the solicitation of investors.) He cannot be liable as an expert because the "other states" statement did not constitute *expertised* information certified by him.

In addition, Joseph would be liable under §12(a)(2) for misstatements in the prospectus used in the registered offering only if he were a "statutory seller"—that is, only if he actively promoted the offering.

§5.4 DEFINITION OF SECURITY

All of the registration requirements and liability rules of the Securities Act turn on whether a transaction can be characterized as the sale of a security. What is a security?

§5.4.1 Statutory Definition

Section 2(a)(1) of the Securities Act, like the definitions of the other federal securities laws, contains a long list of financial instruments that qualify as securities: stock, bonds, debentures, notes, and transferable shares. See *Landreth Timber v. Landreth*, 471 U.S. 681 (1985) (holding that sale of a business, structured as a "stock" transaction, constituted sale of security). The section also contains some catch-all terms that qualify as securities: evidences of indebtedness, investment contracts, certificates of interest in profit-sharing agreements, and any instrument commonly known as a security.

In most cases, there is no question about whether a transaction involves the sale of a security. For example, a company's issuance of stock to new investors or the sale of limited partnership interests are unquestionably subject to the Act. The sale of real estate or the assets of a business are not. But many investment schemes fall in between. The borderline case often turns on whether the scheme involves an "investment contract."

§5.4.2 Definition of Investment Contract

The most important catch-all term in the statutory definition of securities is "investment contract." The Supreme Court has defined an *investment contract* as any transaction in which a person (1) invests money (2) in a common enterprise and (3) is led to expect profits (4) solely from the efforts of others. *SEC v. W. J. Howey Co.*, 328 U.S. 293 (1946). The Court's definition has taken on a quasi-statutory quality. Since it was first pronounced, lower courts have clarified the contours of the *Howey* test. Courts have accepted that the investment can take other forms besides money. Courts have also generally required that there be a number of investors in a common, managed pool (horizontal commonality), though some courts have held a single investor who allows another to manage his investment is enough (vertical commonality). The expected return must come from earnings and not merely additional contributions. Finally, the requirement that profits come "solely from the efforts of others" has been interpreted to mean that someone other than the investor has contributed the *predominant* managerial effort in the common enterprise.

Basically, the *Howey* test attempts to identify transactions in which investors are counting on others to manage an enterprise that will produce returns on their investment. This definition is consistent with the purpose of the Securities Act: to ensure that capital used in the production of goods and services in the U.S. economy goes to those ventures where a well-informed market dictates it should go.

The investment contract definition has been used in surprising ways. Courts have used the definition to hold that each of the following investment schemes involves the sale of a security:

- Visitors to Florida purchased rows of orange trees, and the seller promised to handle the cultivation, harvesting, and marketing of the fruit—the facts in the *Howey* case.
- Homeowners purchased earthworms, and the seller promised to buy back all of the worms (after they reproduced at geometric rates) for a guaranteed price and market them to fishermen.
- Internet users paid for shares in "virtual companies" on a "virtual stock exchange," and the website host promised price appreciation as other users bought into the pyramid "game."
- Vacationers bought beachfront condominiums, subject to limited occupancy rights, and the seller managed the condos and pooled rentals from many condo units.

In each case, people put money into a scheme in which the expected returns derived predominantly from the efforts of others. The enticement was not in the property ostensibly sold to the investor, but rather in a return on the investment created by others' management or marketing efforts.

Whether LLC interests, unknown when the Securities Act was enacted, constitute securities has led to different results under the *Howey* test. When LLC investors are passive and have only tangential involvement in the LLC's management, courts have found a security—that is, an investment in a common enterprise where profits arise primarily from the efforts of others. When LLC investors have significant management oversight, courts have refused to find a security. See *Great Lakes Chemical Corp. v. Monsanto Co.*, 96 F. Supp. 2d 376 (D. Del. 2000) (concluding that sale of 100 percent interest in LLC was not sale of a security because owner had complete authority to remove manager without cause and thus directly affect profits).

Examples

EXAMPLES

Outdoor Cafes is a smashing success. Adam, the company's president, decides to expand the business by selling "muskrat dogs" from pushcarts in downtown business districts throughout the Northeast.

Adam devises an ingenious way to finance the new pushcart venture. Under his plan, Outdoor Cafes will purchase the pushcarts and then sell them to pushcart owners who must agree to buy muskrat dogs and related supplies exclusively from Outdoor Cafes. The contract will specify that pushcart owners either can operate the carts themselves or enter into an operator's agreement with Outdoor Cafes. Under the operator's agreement, the company selects, trains, and supervises an operator hired by the owner to push the cart and the muskrat dogs. Outdoor Cafes advertises the sale of pushcart ownership interests in area newspapers, and Adam assures prospective purchasers they will earn significant returns.

1. Owen buys a muskrat cart from Outdoor Cafes, along with the services available under the operator's agreement. After a few months, Owen discovers his cart is losing money, and he wants his money back. How might he use the Securities Act?
2. Did Outdoor Cafes sell Owen a security?
3. Portia buys a muskrat cart from Outdoor Cafes, but decides to operate the cart herself. After a few months, Portia is losing money and wants her money back. Can she use the Securities Act?

EXPLANATIONS

Explanations

1. Owen can argue the sale of the cart *with the operator's agreement* was the sale of a security. If so, he can seek rescission under §12(a)(1), if the arrangement was an unregistered, nonexempt offering. (Owen could not seek rescission under §12(a)(2), even though Adam may have misrepresented the cart's profitability because the sale was not accomplished by a prospectus in a public offering.)
2. Most likely. The purchase of a pushcart, accompanied by an operator agreement, appears to satisfy the definition of an investment contract under the *Howey* test:
   - Owen invested money by purchasing the pushcart and agreeing to pay fees under the operator agreement
   - Outdoor Cafes contemplates a number of investors like Owen—horizontal commonality
   - Owen is led to expect profits from the sale of muskrat dogs
   - the return from Owen's investment comes predominantly (if not exclusively) from the efforts of Outdoor Cafes, which is responsible for selecting, training, and supervising the cart operator and producing the muskrat dogs

   Although Outdoor Cafes might argue Owen manages the investment by hiring the operator, this is only technically true. The Operator Agreement leaves to Outdoor Cafes all management decisions relating to running the business. Adam's promise of significant returns depends on Outdoor Cafes running the business successfully. Owen is counting on putting money into an arrangement (the pushcart purchase and Operator Agreement) in which others will manage an enterprise (the pushcart business) that will produce a return on his investment. The arrangement operates as though Outdoor Cafes had set up Pushcart Dogs, Inc. (which purchased carts and services from Outdoor Cafes) and Owen invested as a shareholder in this new corporation. In the end, disclosure about Outdoor Cafes and its management history and plans will be highly relevant to Owen's investment decision. Securities regulation is appropriate. See *SEC v. Edwards*, 540 U.S. 389 (2004) (finding sale-leaseback of pay phones to be a security, where investors were offered phones with a five-year arrangement for leaseback, management, and buyback by management company that selected sites for phones, installed equipment, arranged connections, collected coins, and maintained phones).
3. Standing alone, probably not. This is much more like a typical franchise arrangement, which generally has been held not to involve the sale of a security. Although the first three *Howey* factors are satisfied (Portia has

invested money, others have invested money, and they expect a profit from their investment), the critical element that these profits be derived solely or predominantly from the efforts of others is not met. Portia is not relying on Outdoor Cafes' management of her investment, and disclosure concerning Outdoor Cafes' history, performance, and plans as a supervisor of pushcart operators would have been largely irrelevant to her decision whether to buy the cart. Although Portia is expecting Outdoor Cafes' products will sell, her own efforts predominate in determining the cart's success or failure.

But if Portia had also been *offered* an Operator Agreement when she purchased the cart, the offer would have involved a security—as discussed above. As such, Portia might be able to seek rescission under §12(a)(1) of a transaction that included the unregistered, nonexempt *offering* of a security.

PART III

Shareholder Voting Rights

Shareholders' Role in Corporate Governance

More than 200 years ago Blackstone described the corporation as a "little republic." Conceptually, this description is still apt. The *statutory model* for the corporation prescribes a republican form of governance:

- **The shareholders (the corporation's *electorate*)** elect directors annually and vote on fundamental corporate transactions. Although they are nominal "owners" of the corporation, shareholders do not participate in managing the corporation's business or affairs. The shareholders, even a majority, cannot act on behalf of the corporation—this is left to the board of directors.
- **The board of directors (the corporation's *legislative organ*)** is the locus of corporate authority. "All corporate powers shall be exercised by or under the authority of, and the business and affairs of the corporation managed under the direction of, its board of directors." MBCA §8.01(b); see also Del. GCL §141(a). The board is not an agent for the shareholders, but has independent status. Directors have fiduciary duties to the corporation and the body of shareholders (see Chapter 11).
- **The officers (the corporation's *bureaucracy*)** are delegated the day-to-day management of the corporation and are answerable to the board. All authority to act for (and to bind) the corporation originates in the board of directors (see Chapter 30).

Corporate law protects shareholders' financial position through three principal mechanisms: voting rights, litigation rights to enforce management accountability, and liquidity rights to sell their shares. This part considers voting rights and the shareholders' role in corporate governance:

- the purposes of shareholder voting (§6.1) and its use in publicly traded corporations (§6.2) and closely held U.S. corporations (§6.3)
- the matters on which shareholders vote, the voting process, and the methods for electing directors (Chapter 7)
- judicial supervision of the voting process (Chapter 8)
- federal regulation of proxy voting in public corporations (Chapter 9)
- the liability for proxy fraud regime (Chapter 10)

Shareholder voting is a study in U.S. corporate federalism, as well as the division of labor between the legislative and judicial branches. *State corporate statutes* establish the structure of shareholder voting, including compulsory annual elections of directors and shareholder voting on fundamental corporate changes. *State courts* supervise the fairness of the voting process through judicially created fiduciary duties. *Federal regulations,* authorized by federal statute, fill a perceived gap in the state-enabled voting structure by mandating disclosure in connection with proxy voting in public corporations. *Federal and state courts* ensure the fairness of transactions on which public shareholders vote under judicial antifraud standards that assume voting by reasonable shareholders.

Note on Shareholders as "Owners"

Sometimes it is said (metaphorically) that shareholders "own" the corporation. But, as you study the role of shareholders in the corporation, you will notice the many things shareholders *cannot do* under the traditional model. They cannot act on the ordinary business and affairs of the corporation. Thus, they cannot bind the corporation contractually (see Chapter 30); they cannot select and remove *officers* (even for cause); they cannot fix employees' compensation; and they cannot have the corporation pay dividends (see §31.1). Furthermore, shareholders cannot compel or overturn particular board decisions, unless the board failed to comply with the corporate statute or the corporation's constitutive documents (see §3.3.3) or the directors breached their fiduciary duties (see Chapter 11).

§6.1 PURPOSES OF SHAREHOLDER VOTING

Shareholder voting has many functions. It gives self-help remedies to the shareholder majority to elect directors to the board, to pass on fundamental corporate changes, and to initiate limited changes to the governance structure. Voting gives shareholders the power to protect their position as last-in-line claimants of the corporation's profits. Majority voting prevents a minority from holding up useful change or extorting concessions from the majority. Although other corporate constituencies (such as employees, creditors, or bondholders) could in theory have voting rights, shareholders value these rights more highly than other constituents and pay for them when they invest.

Shareholder voting operates in tandem with shareholder litigation rights. The power of shareholders to replace lax or inept directors justifies deferential judicial review of directors' judgment in making business decisions. Likewise, shareholder approval of transactions involving managerial self-dealing or other conflicts of interest reduces the judicial scrutiny that would otherwise apply. When shareholders are prevented from exercising their voting right—as when the board changes the voting rules to thwart a shareholder insurgency to replace the board—judicial review is heightened.

Shareholder voting is critical to shareholder liquidity rights and the "market in corporate control." Because shares are sold with voting rights, buyers of a majority of shares acquire the power to install their own board and thus replace incumbent management. The availability in public trading markets of sufficient shares to constitute a voting majority creates strong incentives for managers to act consistently with shareholder interests.

§6.2 SHAREHOLDER VOTING IN PUBLIC CORPORATIONS

The reality of shareholder voting in modern public corporations diverges from the theoretical model. In public corporations, shareholders typically participate in the election of directors less fully than the model assumes. Historically, public shareholders have been mostly passive. They generally vote their proxies for the slate of directors and the transactions proposed by incumbent management. It is unusual for an insurgent to offer an alternative slate of candidates or for a management initiative to be defeated. Nonetheless, with the rise of institutional shareholders over the last two decades, shareholder initiatives in the form of nonbinding resolutions have become a prominent feature of U.S. corporate governance (see §9.4.2).

§6.2.1 Proxy Process

In the United States equity shares typically carry voting rights. In a public corporation, given the logistical difficulties and expense of assembling all of the corporation's shareholders, voting is mostly by proxy—in effect, absentee ballot. As a result, the process of soliciting and voting proxies effectively takes the place of the shareholders' meeting. The actual meeting is often a sparsely attended public relations event.

Proxy voting is usually an annual rite of spring that takes place after the company's management and its auditors have prepared financial statements for the previous year. (For the legal mechanics of shareholders' meetings, see §7.2.) The board of directors sets the date of the annual shareholders' meeting and then selects a "record date" used to identify which shareholders will be entitled to notice and to vote at the meeting. Under state law, only record shareholders vote. Beneficial owners must give their voting instructions to those who hold their shares in the company's records. The board (often by a nominating committee) then proposes director candidates, and the board decides which matters to submit for shareholder approval.

To solicit proxies, management sends to shareholders *at corporate expense* a voting package containing an annual report, a proxy disclosure document, a proxy card, and a return envelope. Since 2007, the SEC allows companies to send shareholders a notice that these materials are available online. Exchange Act Rel. No. 55,146 (2007) (permitting shareholders to always request printed materials). After receiving the notice by regular mail or email, shareholders can go online and vote their proxies electronically. This "notice and access" method reduces the costs of voting, which ultimately are borne by shareholders.

Dissemination of proxy materials is complicated by the situation that most public shareholders are beneficial owners, not record owners. This means shares are owned on the corporate books by a nominee, typically a brokerage firm, for the benefit of its investor-customers. Under SEC rules, the corporation must send proxy materials or notice of online access either (1) to the record owner for distribution to beneficial owners or (2) to beneficial owners who do not object to having their nominees furnish their names and addresses ("non-objecting beneficial owners" or "NOBOs"). Depending on brokerage firm practice, beneficial owners either complete the proxy card themselves or instruct the firm (the record holder) on how to complete it. A prior practice in which brokerage firms decided how to vote shares for which they had not received voting instructions is now prohibited under stock exchange rules mandated by the Dodd-Frank Act. See §11.5.2.

Shareholders receive their voting packages (whether by mail or online access) a few weeks before the scheduled meeting. The cover letter from the board chair invariably asks shareholders to vote promptly to avoid the expense of a second mailing. Few individual shareholders read the proxy materials, though many complete the proxy card or vote online as recommended by management. Institutional shareholders, which now hold more than 70 percent of voting shares in public corporations and often rely on proxy advisory firms, have become increasingly independent and activist.

The shareholders' meeting typically follows a script. Directors are nominated and other voting matters proposed. Votes, cast mostly by proxy holders, are taken. With the important business done, the company's senior executives describe company results and plans and respond to polite shareholder questions. If shareholders get unruly, the meeting chair can end the meeting. Although state law permits any shareholder to nominate her own slate of directors or to propose a proper shareholder resolution, the effort would be futile unless the shareholder has already solicited and obtained proxies. Many corporate bylaws also prohibit shareholder nominations or proposals if not submitted well in advance of the meeting. In the end, the shareholders' meeting is largely a formality, for the votes have already been "cast" in the proxy cards. In fact, to avoid surprises, the votes will often have been tabulated before the meeting.

§6.2.2 History of Public Shareholder Voting

Separation of Ownership and Control

In 1932 a Columbia law professor and an economics professor combined to write an influential book that systematically identified the separation of corporate ownership and management in U.S. public corporations. Berle and Means, *The Modern Corporation and Private Property*. The authors pointed out that when stock ownership is widely distributed and no group of shareholders has a sufficient interest to control the company's affairs, management becomes "a self-perpetuating body even though its share in the ownership is negligible." They found that 44 percent of the country's largest 200 companies were under "management control."

Central to the Berle and Means thesis of management control was the ineffectiveness of shareholder voting as a control device in public corporations. They found that when shareholders hand over their votes to individuals selected by existing management, the proxy mechanism leaves control in the hands of the board of directors, who "virtually dictate their own successors." Although shareholders can replace incumbent directors by soliciting proxies for an insurgent slate of candidates, they found proxy contests to be rare.

In reaction to the gloomy Berle and Means story of the separation of management and ownership in public corporations, Congress created the Securities and Exchange Commission in 1934 to (among other things) promulgate a federal regulatory regime for proxy voting. Despite SEC rules that mandate disclosure by management when soliciting proxies and compel shareholder access to the proxy machinery, shareholders in publicly traded corporations did not leap at the invitation to participate in corporate governance. During the 1950s and 1960s, proxy contests for board control were no more frequent than before the SEC rules. Management's candidates and initiatives won and insurgent's candidates and initiatives lost, each by wide margins. By the

1970s, many academics had come to accept shareholder apathy as insoluble, indeed "rational." Any shareholder dissatisfied with management had little choice but to exercise the "Wall Street rule" and sell his shares.

Institutional Shareholders

In the 1980s public shareholders began to use their powerful, latent control over managers despite the practical weaknesses in shareholder voting. Shareholders' power first arose not from voicing their views through voting, but from their ability to exit and sell their shares. During the takeover boom of the 1980s, the voting power that shares carry served as the linchpin for hostile stock acquisitions and takeovers. Public shareholders could sell to an acquirer, who consolidated the voting power of dispersed shareholders to replace the board and acquire control of the company. Takeovers—and their threat—provided the discipline that atomistic voting had not.

But as the era of hostile takeovers came to an end in the late 1980s, a new era in U.S. corporate governance began. In the 1990s institutional investors emerged as a powerful new corporate actor. As Berle and Means had noticed 60 years ago, large shareholders have relatively more incentives to become informed about management and proxy contests, and they are more likely to vote than other shareholders. The collectivization obstacles that discouraged any one shareholder from taking the initiative—because any gains would have to be shared among all shareholders—are overcome when a group of institutional investors organize against management.

Who are institutional investors? They take many forms, but are essentially financial intermediaries that hold large pools of investments for beneficiaries: pension funds (private and public), mutual funds, insurance companies, bank trust departments, hedge funds, endowments. As of 2009, institutional investors controlled 73 percent of the outstanding stock of the largest 1,000 U.S. public companies—up from 16 percent in 1965, 38 percent in 1980, 49 percent in 1990, and 61 percent in 2000. Institutional ownership is also increasingly concentrated. The ten largest institutional owners of each of the top 25 U.S. companies hold together on average 28.9 percent of the company's voting stock.

These trends are due to a combination of factors. Tax rules encourage employers and workers to contribute to retirement plans, which are invested in pension funds and mutual funds. And individual investors seeking diversification have moved from holding individual stocks to investing in mutual funds. As of 2006, mutual funds held 26.9 percent, and pension funds (both private and government) held 23.1 percent of U.S. public equities.

Institutional Activism

Institutional investors have fiduciary obligations to manage and vote their shares for the exclusive benefit of their beneficiaries. Although institutional investors have traditionally voted with management, often because they rely on management for investment business, this culture of acquiescence is changing. Pressure from regulators, such as the Department of Labor, which oversees private pension funds under ERISA, has led institutional investors to take their voting responsibilities more seriously. Disclosure of voting policies and actual votes, required by rule in 2003 for mutual funds, has exposed voting by institutional investors to greater scrutiny. Greater "indexation" (the diversification of investment portfolios to track the performance of whole markets) makes it difficult for institutional investors to follow the "Wall Street rule." An indexed institutional investor that disapproves of a company's management cannot simply sell its stock without defeating indexation—and so must become active in monitoring and voting.

Institutional investors have in some dramatic instances been successful in asserting their new power. For example, in the 1990s under pressure from institutional investors, corporate boards of prominent corporations (such as General Motors, Sears, American Express) ousted management, divested businesses, made structural governance changes, and revised dividend policies. Nonetheless, the corporate financial scandals of the early 2000s and the collapse of the largest U.S. investment banks in 2008 have led many to question the effectiveness of institutional investors in monitoring and disciplining wayward management. Moreover, diversification requirements (often imposed by law) prevent many institutional investors from holding a meaningful percentage of stock in a given company, thus diluting their effectiveness as monitors.

The story of institutional activism is still evolving. In the late 1980s and early 1990s, institutional investors used a strategy of confrontation. Insurgents in record numbers proposed alternative board slates and initiated proposals for structural reforms to enhance shareholder control. During the late 1990s, institutional investors turned to nonvoting strategies. Some larger institutions adopted policies of "relationship investing" to establish ongoing communications with company management. In the 2000s, many institutional investors have followed the voting recommendations of proxy advisory firms (such as Institutional Shareholder Services), which have assumed significant influence in the design of executive compensation packages and the terms of contested mergers. In addition, shareholder proposals on such governance matters as majority voting for directors and shareholder nomination of directors have received majority support, increasingly leading management to undertake reforms.

Lately hedge funds, which often buy positions in companies planning to sell after the company undertakes structural or governance changes, are becoming the most prominent shareholder activists. For some observers, hedge funds (with other institutional investors as their natural allies) realize the decades-old hope that institutional investors would be able to collectivize and serve as a disciplinary force for the benefit of all shareholders. Hedge funds seem particularly suited to their activist role for a couple reasons. First, hedge fund managers are highly compensated for making successful investments and thus have incentives to undertake short-term turnarounds of portfolio companies. Second, hedge funds are expected to focus on achieving high absolute returns rather than returns pegged to a benchmark.

§6.2.3 Voting Incentives for Public Shareholders

The greater activism of institutional investors in the governance of public corporations derives from the voting incentives large shareholders have compared to small shareholders. For a smaller shareholder who identifies value-producing reforms, there is little incentive to try to collectivize other shareholders. The insurgent must be prepared to commit significant time, money, and effort to overcome shareholder apathy. Expenses for an insurgent in a contested board election, for example, have been estimated to range between $5 million and $10 million.

If an insurgent loses, she absorbs the full costs of the contest; she cannot seek contribution from other shareholders or the corporation. If she wins, she may be able to obtain reimbursement from the firm, but any gains she creates will be shared with all other shareholders. Her portion of the gains is limited to her pro rata shareholding in the firm—usually quite small. In short, she must risk substantial amounts to create gains in which other shareholders will share even though they risked nothing. This "free rider" phenomenon leads rational small shareholders to do nothing to overcome voting "collective action" obstacles.

An insurgent's problems are compounded by the "rational apathy" of most small shareholders confronted with competing proxy solicitations. If an individual shareholder holds a small stake in a firm as part of a diversified portfolio, he has little incentive to spend time educating himself about the merits of any given proxy contest. Is management doing poorly? Will the insurgents improve the company's performance? Small investors will perceive (rationally) that the time spent becoming familiar with the contestants and the issues will not be worth any potential gains to his portfolio. It is not surprising, given the informational position of most small shareholders, they follow a general rule of thumb: vote for the incumbents. Small shareholders, it is said, awaken from their apathy only when presented with a premium bid in a takeover.

For larger investors, voting incentives are very different. Institutional shareholders have much larger stakes in individual companies, and there are fewer of them. It is not unusual in larger U.S. companies for the company's top ten institutional shareholders to hold 15–25 percent of its voting shares. Collective action by institutions is also easier under SEC rules that since 1992 have facilitated shareholder communications. In addition, for institutional shareholders it is not rational to be apathetic about the corporation's management and reform possibilities. Even though an institutional activist must share any gains it produces with all other shareholders, the institution's larger shareholding (and the greater ease in forming shareholder coalitions) may make its activism worth the effort. Finally, institutional investors (indexed or not) cannot easily exercise the "Wall Street rule" and sell their stock when they become dissatisfied with management. The very selling of a large block of stock drags down the stock's market price.

Hedge funds (largely unregulated investment pools for wealthy individual and institutional investors) have also changed the U.S. corporate governance landscape. Activist hedge funds make money for their investors by identifying under-performing public companies and then seeking, through proxy fights or litigation, to oust the company's incumbent management or change its business strategies. Hedge funds have enlisted the support of institutional investors, both through their voting and the lending of voting shares to the hedge funds. Activism by hedge funds has been controversial, with some asserting that they impose a useful discipline on management and others worrying that they force companies to focus on short-term results and not long-term value.

In addition to activism by hedge funds, voting recommendations by proxy advisory firms (particularly Institutional Shareholder Services) have been influential in how shareholders, especially institutional shareholders, vote on such matters as contested mergers, shareholder proposals on governance topics, "just say no" campaigns against individual directors, and lately "say on pay" proposals in which shareholders indicate their support (or opposition) to the company's executive pay practices. The ISS posts voting guidelines for how it will advise shareholders to vote—and corporate boards will often tailor their actions to conform to the guidelines.

§6.3 SHAREHOLDER VOTING IN CLOSE CORPORATIONS

In closely held corporations (those with few shareholders and no ready market for their shares), things are quite different. (See Chapter 25.) Shareholders who own a majority of the shares can exercise their voting power to elect the board, giving these owners virtually unfettered control of the business. Controlling shareholders, who often rely on the corporation as a source of livelihood, assume a far more active role in the corporation's governance than the statutory model contemplates.

For minority shareholders in a close corporation, voting rights are usually not a meaningful protection. Nor can these shareholders sell their shares in a public market if they become displeased with the majority's management. Instead, minority shareholders must negotiate for special voting rights (such as supermajority voting, see §26.1.1; cumulative voting, see §26.1.2; or class voting, see §26.2.2) or negotiate limits on the majority's discretion, specifying by agreement how the corporation is to be run (see §26.4). They may require that, as in a partnership, important decisions be made by unanimous consent (see §26.4), or they may negotiate for contractual withdrawal rights comparable to those of partners on dissolution (see §26.3).

CHAPTER 7

Voting Structure

Voting by shareholders is prescribed by corporate statutes. Modern statutes are mostly enabling, authorizing a wide variety of voting schemes as specified in the corporate articles and bylaws. Yet corporate law defines an immutable core. Shareholders must receive voting rights; elections of directors must occur with regularity; shareholders must approve any fundamental corporate transactions; shareholders must have access to specified corporate information; shareholders' meetings must comply with minimal procedures; and shareholders must be able to remove wayward directors.

This chapter describes the matters on which shareholders can vote and the information to which they are entitled (§7.1), the nature of shareholders' meetings and how shareholders vote (§7.2), and the methods by which shareholders select the board (§7.3). The next chapter (Chapter 8) describes judicial protection of shareholder voting, which builds from essential aspects of the statutory voting structure—such as the requirement of regular shareholder meetings or the prerogative of shareholders to choose the composition of the board. The following chapters describe federal proxy regulation, which piggybacks on the state-enabled voting scheme by overlaying a system of mandatory disclosure (Chapter 9) and proxy fraud rules that apply when shareholders exercise their voting rights (Chapter 10).

§7.1 SHAREHOLDERS' GOVERNANCE ROLE

The traditional corporate model gives shareholders—the "electorate" of the corporate republic—an oversight role in corporate governance. Shareholders can choose the board's composition, vote on fundamental corporate changes, and initiate (on a limited basis) corporate reforms. To protect these powers, corporate law gives shareholders access to specified information and judicial recourse.

Note on Voting Rights

Generally, common shares carry voting rights, though some classes of common shares are sometimes issued with limited or even no voting rights. Treasury shares (that is, common shares repurchased by the corporation) do not have voting rights. But common shares held by the corporation in a fiduciary capacity, such as in a pension plan, do have voting rights. Preferred shares sometimes have voting rights, though they may be conditioned on certain events (such as a longstanding failure to pay dividends) or limited to certain matters (such as charter amendments that negatively affect the rights of preferred shares). As a general matter, debt does not carry voting rights.

§7.1.1 Election and Removal of Directors

Shareholders have the power to elect directors at the first shareholders' meeting and thereafter annually. MBCA §8.03(d); Del. GCL §211(b). Shareholders can also remove directors before their term expires—for cause or without cause depending on the statute and the articles of incorporation. MBCA §8.08 (with or without cause). Control over the composition of the board is at the heart of the shareholders' governance role (see §7.3 below).

§7.1.2 Approval of Board-Initiated Transactions

Shareholders have the power to approve some transactions initiated by the board.

Fundamental Corporate Changes

Shareholders are entitled to vote on fundamental corporate changes initiated by the board of directors, including amendments to the articles of incorporation (MBCA §10.03; Del. GCL §242), mergers with other corporations

(MBCA §11.04; Del. GCL §251), sales of substantially all of the corporate assets not in the regular course of business (MBCA §12.02; Del. GCL §271), and voluntary dissolutions (MBCA §14.02; Del. GCL §275). (These voting rights are more fully described in Chapters 35 and 36.)

"Dilutive" Issuance of Shares

Shareholders are entitled to vote when the corporation issues shares that will significantly dilute existing shareholders. Under both the MBCA and stock exchange rules for listed companies, prior shareholder consent is required when the shares to be issued have voting power equal to 20 percent or more of the voting shares outstanding prior to the issuance. See MBCA §6.21(f); NYSE Rule 312.03(c); NASDAQ Rule 4350(i)(i)(D) (similar).

Conflicting Interest Transactions

Shareholders sometimes are permitted to vote (when the board permits it) on transactions with the corporation in which directors have a conflict of interest. MBCA §8.63; Del. GCL §144(a)(2). In addition, shareholders are permitted to vote to approve the indemnification of directors, officers, or others against whom claims have been brought because of their relationship to the corporation. MBCA §8.55(b)(4); Del. GCL §145(a) (see Chapter 15).

§7.1.3 Shareholder-Initiated Changes

Shareholders can initiate *on their own* changes in corporate governance and structure.

Amendment of Bylaws

Shareholders have the power to adopt, amend, and repeal the bylaws—the governance document that specifies the internal functioning of the corporation. See MBCA §10.20; Del. GCL §109 (board also has power, if in the articles). Even if the board shares the power to amend the bylaws, whether by statute or in the articles, the board's power is coterminous with the shareholders. See Official Comment to MBCA §10.20 ("shareholders always have the power to amend or repeal the bylaws"); Del. GCL §109(a) (board power does not divest or limit power of shareholders). Many states do not permit the board to amend bylaws approved by shareholders. MBCA §10.20(a)(2) (if shareholder-approved bylaw "expressly" so provides).

What is the scope of the shareholders' power to amend the bylaws? The question is an important one as institutional activism has increased. In a case of first impression, the Oklahoma Supreme Court held that Oklahoma law permits shareholders to adopt a bylaw that restricts board implementation of shareholder rights plans (see §39.2.3). *Int'l Brotherhood of Teamsters General Fund v. Fleming Cos.*, 975 P.2d 907 (Okla. 1999). Not finding any statutory or case law in Oklahoma that suggested rights plans were the exclusive province of the board of directors, the court concluded that a bylaw requiring any rights plan to be submitted to shareholders at the next annual meeting was within "the proper channels of corporate governance."

In a case with wide-ranging implications, the Delaware Supreme Court held that a bylaw that would require the reimbursement of election expenses (see §8.1.2) to shareholders who successfully propose a dissident "short slate" (fewer than half the directors on the board) would violate Delaware law. *CA, Inc. v. AFSCME Employees Pension Plan*, 953 A.2d 227 (Del. 2008) (issued in response to SEC certification of legal question). The court concluded that the bylaw would unlawfully prevent directors from exercising their full management discretion if their fiduciary duties required them to deny expense reimbursement for such a slate. That is, the power of shareholders to amend the bylaws under Del. GCL §109(a) must be consistent with the power of the board to manage the corporation under Del. GCL §141(a).

At the same time, the Delaware court stated that the proposed bylaw related to the process of director elections and was a proper subject for shareholder action under Delaware law. Thus, it would have been valid had it contained a "fiduciary out" that permitted the board to deny reimbursement if required by the directors' fiduciary duties. Although bylaws may not "mandate how the board should decide specific substantive business decisions," they may "define the process and procedures by which those decisions are made."

Amendment of Articles

A few statutes permit shareholders to initiate amendments to the articles of incorporation, and others describe the procedure for their adoption without specifying who initiates the amendment. Most statutes, however, vest the initiation power exclusively in the board. See MBCA §10.03(b); Del. GCL §242(b).

Most statutes do not permit shareholders to initiate other corporate actions even when they are entitled to approve the action. In most states the board must initiate mergers, sales of substantially all assets, and voluntary dissolution—the shareholders are entitled only to approve or reject the board's initiatives. MBCA §11.04, Del. GCL §251(a) (merger); MBCA §12.02, Del. GCL §271(a) (sale of all assets); MBCA §14.02, Del. GCL §275(a) (dissolution).

Nonbinding Recommendations

Shareholders can make nonbinding, precatory recommendations about governance structures and the management of the corporation, including matters entrusted exclusively to the board. In public corporations, such recommendations are often brought as shareholder proposals under the procedures of SEC Rule 14a-8 (see §9.4.2). Lately, the making of these proposals has moved management to undertake significant reforms, particularly in matters of corporate governance.

In the leading case on the subject, the court held that shareholders could properly make a nonbinding recommendation that the corporation's former president be reinstated, even though the recommendation had no binding effect on the board. *Auer v. Dressel*, 118 N.E.2d 590 (N.Y. 1954). The court reasoned that shareholders can express themselves on corporate matters, thus to put directors on notice—a kind of nonbinding poll.

§7.1.4 Informational Rights

To facilitate shareholders' voting powers, corporate law gives shareholders the right to receive information from the corporation.

Financial Reports

The MBCA, but not Delaware's corporate statute, requires the corporation to provide shareholders with annual financial information, including an end-year balance sheet, income statement, and statement of changes in shareholders' equity (see §31.2.2 for accounting description). MBCA §16.20. The financial information must be audited by a public accountant or include a statement by a corporate official either that the information was prepared on the basis of "generally accepted accounting principles" or that explains any deviations from GAAP.

For close corporations, these reports constitute the only periodic disclosure to shareholders mandated by law. (Federal securities law requires public corporations to prepare, file, and disseminate annual and quarterly reports. See §§9.3.1, 21.2.) Unlike the disclosures made by public corporations, which are available to the public after filing with the SEC, the financial information prepared by close corporations need not be publicly disclosed. The only requirement is the filing of an annual report with the state's secretary of state, which sets forth the name and address of the corporation (and registered agent), the names and business addresses of its directors and principal officers, a brief description of its business, and information on shares authorized and issued. MBCA §16.22; cf. Del. Corp. Franchise Law §502 (annual franchise tax report, requiring similar information but not business description or information on corporate officers, except one signing report).

Inspection of Corporate Books and Records

Corporate statutes codify shareholders' common law rights to inspect corporate books and records. MBCA §16.02; Del. GCL §220. Most statutes extend inspection rights to beneficial owners, not just record shareholders. MBCA §16.02(f); Del. GCL §220(a)(2). ("Record shareholders" appear as owners of shares on the company's records; "beneficial owners" have voting and investment power over shares held in record name by another person, typically a brokerage firm.)

The MBCA and Delaware's corporate statute specify somewhat different inspection rights. Delaware's statute makes shareholder lists available as of right 10 days before a shareholders' meeting. Del. GCL §219(a). Books and records (a broad category under Delaware law) and a shareholders' list more than 10 days before a shareholders' meeting are available for inspection upon a showing of a "proper purpose." Del. GCL §220(b).

The MBCA makes the articles of incorporation, bylaws, and minutes of shareholders' meetings available as of right. MBCA §§16.01(e), 16.02(a). The MBCA makes other records—such as board minutes, accounting records, and shareholder lists—available for inspection only upon a showing of a "proper purpose." MBCA §16.02(b), (c).

Courts have found a proper purpose if the shareholder's request for records relates to the shareholder's interest in his investment—such as to investigate corporate wrongdoing, to bring a shareholder lawsuit, or to initiate a takeover or a proxy contest. Thus, management must provide internal financial records to a shareholder seeking to value her investment or uncover mismanagement. See *Security First Corp. v. U.S. Die Casting and Dev. Co.*, 687 A.2d 563 (Del. 1997) (stating that shareholder has burden to show credible evidence of possible mismanagement to obtain inspection of books and records). But management need not provide records to a shareholder planning to give them to competitors or seeking to advance a political agenda unrelated to his investment. Cf. *Conservative Caucus v. Chevron Corp.*, 525 A.2d 569 (Del. Ch. 1987) (permitting inspection of shareholders' list by shareholder seeking shareholder support of a proposal that corporation stop doing business in communist Angola given alleged economic risks to corporation); *State ex rel. Pillsbury v. Honeywell, Inc.*, 191 N.W.2d 406 (Minn. 1971) (denying inspection of shareholders' list by shareholder seeking to communicate antiwar beliefs to other shareholders).

Lately, the right to inspect "books and records," particularly under Delaware's inspection statute, has proved an indispensable tool for shareholders seeking to file derivative suits or class actions. See *Brehm v. Eisner*, 746 A.2d 244 (Del. 2000) (suggesting that plaintiffs have "tools at hand" to develop necessary facts for pleading purposes in derivative suit challenging executive compensation). Inspection is all the more important because discovery is not available in defending a motion to dismiss on the grounds of demand futility in Delaware derivative litigation (see §18.3.3) or failure to allege particular facts creating a strong inference of scienter in a federal securities fraud class action (see §22.3.2).

In Delaware, the requesting shareholder must identify specific, already-existing documents and show how they are "essential" to the articulated purpose for the documents. See *Saito v. McKesson HBOC, Inc.*, 806 A.2d 113 (Del. 2002) (allowing inspection of third-party documents). A shareholder seeking to investigate corporate wrongdoing must present evidence establishing a "credible basis" of possible wrongdoing; a mere suspicion is not enough. See *Seinfeld v. Verizon Communications, Inc.*, 909 A.2d 117 (Del. 2006) (disallowing inspection of documents related to allegedly unauthorized and excessive executive compensation). In addition, shareholder-plaintiffs who bring derivative suits may seek inspection even during the course of the litigation, though it is "preferable" to file a suit for books and records before beginning derivative litigation. See *King v. VeriFone Holdings, Inc.*, 12 A.3d 1140 (Del. 2011).

The right to a shareholders' list, valuable to a proxy insurgent, creates some ambiguity. Most statutes specify a "shareholder list," without specifying whether it refers to the relatively useless "stock ledger" list of record shareholders or the more valuable computer-readable list of beneficial (or "street name") owners. Courts have generally not required that management create a list not already in existence.

Note on Inspection Rights in LLC

Most LLC statutes provide their members inspection rights similar to (and sometimes more extensive than) those provided shareholders. See ULLCA §408(a) (inspection for "proper purposes"). For example, Wisconsin LLCs must provide any member upon "reasonable request . . . true and full information of all things affecting the member." See *Kasten v. Doral Dental USA, LLC*, 733 N.W.2d 300 (Wis. 2007) (interpreting statute to be limited to "things" affecting financial interest of member). Whether an LLC member's request is reasonable (much like a shareholder request for inspection) depends on its scope, the reasons for the request, the importance of the information to the member, and whether the information could be obtained elsewhere. See *Sanders v. Ohmite Holding, LLC*, 17 A.3d 1186 (Del. Ch. 2011) (permitting LLC member to seek inspection of books and records for period before becoming member).

§7.1.5 Enforcement of Shareholder Rights

Shareholders can enforce their voting powers and informational rights in *direct* actions against the corporation or directors. In some situations, corporate statutes specify expedited judicial review and summary orders. See MBCA §7.03, Del. GCL §211(c) (summary order for failure to hold annual or special meeting); MBCA §16.04(a) (summary order for inspection of corporate information); MBCA §16.04(b) (expedited review of shareholder application for inspection of board records, accounting information, and shareholder lists); Del GCL §220(c).

§7.2 MECHANICS OF SHAREHOLDERS' MEETINGS

For the most part, shareholders act by voting at formal meetings. The statutory rules for shareholders' meetings are meant to assure informed, majority suffrage. They specify how meetings are called, the notice shareholders must receive, the number of shares that must be represented at a meeting, and the manner in which votes are counted.

§7.2.1 Annual and Special Meetings

There are two kinds of shareholders' meetings: annual (or regular) meetings at which directors are elected and other regular business is conducted (MBCA §7.01, Del. GCL §211(b)) and special meetings called in unusual circumstances where shareholder action is required. MBCA §7.02.

Usually, the bylaws specify the timing and location of the annual meeting. Cf. Del. GCL §211(c) (permitting board to hold meeting by "remote communication" without physical location). All corporate statutes require an annual meeting, and many permit shareholders to apply to a court to compel a meeting if one is not held within a specified period. See MBCA §7.03(a)(1) (within 6 months of end of fiscal year or 15 months of last annual meeting); Del. GCL §211(c) (within 30 days after designated date or 13 months after annual meeting).

Special meetings to vote on a merger or take other extraordinary action must be specially called by the board, the president (if allowed by statute or in the bylaws), shareholders who hold a requisite number of shares (as specified in the statute or bylaws), or other persons designated in the bylaws. See MBCA §7.02 (special meetings can be called by board, person authorized in articles or bylaws, or shareholders holding 10 percent of the voting shares); cf. Del. GCL §211(d) (special meeting can be called only by board or person authorized in certificate or bylaws).

The shareholders' meeting is conducted by a chair as designated in the bylaws or by the board. The chair has wide latitude to decide the order of business and the rules for conducting the meeting. See MBCA §7.08. The meeting need not be conducted according to Robert's Rules of Order, and the corporation can have bylaws that require advance notice of any shareholder nominations or resolutions.

§7.2.2 Notice

Shareholders entitled to vote must be given timely written notice of annual and special meetings.

Record Date

To determine which shareholders are entitled to vote, the board sets a *record date* before the shareholders' meeting. MBCA §7.07 (record date may not be more than 70 days before meeting); cf. Del. GCL §213(a) (no more than 60 days nor less than 10 days before meeting). Only shareholders "of record" whose holdings are reflected on the corporation's books as of that date—sometimes referred to as *record owners*—are entitled to notice and to vote.

Contents of Notice

In general, the notice requirements under state law are minimal. The notice describes the time and location of the meeting and sometimes summarizes the matters to be considered. MBCA §7.05; Del. GCL §222 (including for meeting by means of "remote communication"). For *annual* meetings at which only directors will be elected and other ordinary matters discussed, the notice need only state the date, time, and place of the meeting. MBCA §7.05; Del. GCL §222. Under some statutes, if any extraordinary matter will be discussed at an annual meeting, notice of the matter must be given. Notice of *special* meetings must specify the purposes of the meeting as well as time and location of the meeting. MBCA §7.05(c); Del. GCL §222(a).

State-required notice is perfunctory compared to the detailed federally mandated disclosure required in proxy statements in public corporations (see §9.3.1).

Timing of Notice

For both annual and special meetings, the notice must arrive in time for shareholders to consider the matters on which they will vote, but not so early that the notice becomes stale. Many statutes require that notice be given at least 10 days, but no more than 60 days, before a meeting. MBCA §7.05(a); Del. GCL §222(b).

Defective Notice

Shareholders can waive notice before, at, or after the meeting. MBCA §7.06; Del. GCL §229. Many statutes provide that a shareholder's attendance at a meeting (other than to object to improper notice) constitutes a waiver of notice. MBCA §7.06(b); Del. GCL §229. If notice is defective and the defect is not waived by all affected shareholders, the meeting is invalid and any action taken at the meeting is void.

§7.2.3 Quorum

For action at a shareholders' meeting to be valid, there must be a quorum. Statutes typically set the quorum as a majority of shares entitled to vote. MBCA §7.25(a); Del. GCL §216(a). Quorum requirements prevent a minority faction from acting at a shareholders' meeting without the presence of a majority. Some statutes allow the quorum to be reduced in the articles or bylaws to one-third. Del. GCL §216(a); but see MBCA §7.25(a) (allowing reduction in the articles without limitation).

Once there is a quorum at a meeting, most statutes provide that it cannot be broken if a shareholder faction walks out in the middle of the meeting. MBCA §7.25(b). Refusing to attend a meeting, however, may be a useful tactic for shareholders seeking to exercise their control rights. In close corporations a unanimous quorum requirement is sometimes used to ensure minority shareholders have a veto. See §26.1.1.

§7.2.4 Appearance in Person or by Proxy

Shareholders can appear at a shareholders' meeting, for purposes of a quorum and to cast their votes, either in person or by proxy. MBCA §7.22(a); Del. GCL §212. If voting is by proxy, state statutes require only that the proxy appointment be in writing and signed, including by electronic transmission. See MBCA §7.22; Del. GCL §212(b). The proxy, which creates an agency relationship in which the shareholder (the principal) grants the proxy holder (the agent) the power to vote her shares, can give the proxy holder full discretion or be subject to specific instructions. Unless irrevocable, the proxy can be revoked by the principal at any time by (1) submitting written notice with the corporation of an intent to revoke, (2) appointing another proxy holder in a subsequently dated proxy, or (3) appearing in person to vote. (The validity of irrevocable proxies and their use as a control device in close corporations is taken up in §26.2.3.)

In general, corporate statutes limit the duration of a proxy to 11 months—long enough for only one annual shareholders' meeting. MBCA §7.22(c); cf. Del. GCL §212(b) (three years).

§7.2.5 Voting at Shareholders' Meetings

Who Votes

Only shareholders of record actually cast votes. If shares are held by a nominee, as happens in most public corporations (see §19.2.1), the actual owners ("beneficial owners") must instruct the record owner how to vote their shares or to whom to give a proxy.

In general, each share is entitled to one vote. See MBCA §7.21 (each outstanding share, regardless of class); Del. GCL §212(a). The articles can specify multiple classes of shares with voting rights, including on a conditional or special basis. See MBCA §6.01(b) (requiring that articles authorize one or more classes of shares that together have unlimited voting rights). For example, preferred shares (see §4.1.3) often receive voting rights to elect a majority of the board whenever dividends on the preferred shares have not been paid for a given period. Some statutes even permit bondholders to have voting rights. See Del. GCL §221.

The articles can deviate from the one-share/one-vote standard and create, for example, supervoting shares or voting caps on any shareholder who holds a specified percentage of shares. See MBCA §6.01(c)(1) (permitting special, conditional, or limited voting rights, or no right to vote); *Providence & Worcester Co. v. Baker*, 378 A.2d 121 (Del. 1977) (upholding charter provision that reduced voting rights to one vote per 20 shares for any shareholder who owned more than 50 shares and capped voting rights for any shareholder who owned more than 25 percent of the company's shares).

In the late 1980s, the SEC attempted to federalize the one-share/one-vote rule by mandating that the U.S. stock exchanges delist any company that created different classes of voting shares, such as through a reclassification in which management holds supervoting shares and public shareholders low-voting shares. SEC Rule 19c-4 (1988). The SEC rule was struck down as an unauthorized federal intrusion into state corporate law. *Business Roundtable v. SEC*, 905 F.2d 406 (D.C. Cir. 1990). Nonetheless, bowing to congressional pressure, the stock exchanges voluntarily instituted a one-share/one-vote requirement for listed companies along the lines of the SEC rule.

Corporate statutes prohibit a majority-owned subsidiary (that is, a corporation whose voting shares are majority-owned by another corporation) from voting the shares of the parent corporation. See MBCA §7.21(b); Del.

GCL §160(c). This circular voting arrangement, if permissible, would enable a corporation's board to dilute the voting rights of the corporation's shareholders by placing the corporation's voting shares in a controlled subsidiary, which would vote them as directed by the corporation's board.

Majority Vote

Under many statutes, shareholder approval of board-initiated transactions—such as mergers, sale of assets, or dissolution—requires the favorable vote of an *absolute majority* of the outstanding shares entitled to vote. See Del. GCL §242(b) (charter amendment), §251(c) (merger), §271(a) (sale of assets), and §275(b) (dissolution). This means abstentions and no-shows effectively count as votes against the proposal. For example, if there are 1,000 voting shares outstanding and a quorum of 600 are represented at a meeting, a proposal must garner at least 501 votes to be approved.

Other statutes require shareholder approval only by a majority of shares represented at a meeting at which a quorum is present—a *simple majority.* See MBCA §7.25(c) (revised in 1999); Del. GCL §216(2) (unless specified otherwise). In the example above, a proposal would be approved if it received at least 301 votes. This means abstentions of shares represented at a meeting count as votes against the proposal, but shares not represented are neutral.

According to corporate statutes, voting for directors is not by majority vote, but instead by *plurality vote.* See MBCA §7.28(a); Del. GCL §216(3). This means that a director is elected if there are more votes for him than for other candidates. For example, if three board positions are open, the three candidates receiving the most votes are elected—even if none receives a majority. Unless the articles (or sometimes the bylaws) specify otherwise, abstentions or withheld votes (even if a majority) do not count against a director. See §7.3.2 below. In the past few years, however, many public companies (in fact, 99 of the 100 largest public companies) have abandoned plurality voting and have amended their articles or bylaws to adopt majority voting—with the result that no director can be seated without receiving a majority of shareholder votes. See Del. GCL §216 (shareholder-approved bylaw amendment specifying vote needed to elect directors may not be amended by board).

Election Inspectors

To determine the shares represented at a meeting, count votes, determine the validity of proxies, and resolve voting disputes, state statutes authorize the corporation to appoint inspectors to inspect proxies and votes. MBCA §7.24; Del. GCL §231. Often the corporation's accounting firm is chosen as election inspector.

The inspector's actions are subject to judicial review, though under standards deferential to the inspector's good faith judgment. Inspectors have broad latitude to accept facially valid proxies or reject those that raise reasonable doubts. Given their ministerial role, however, inspectors may not resort to extrinsic information (beyond the face of the proxy) to decide the validity of proxies. See *Salgo v. Matthews*, 497 S.W.2d 620 (Tex. App. 1974) (refusing to require the inspector to investigate beneficial ownership of bankrupt record owner); Del. GCL §231(d) (permitting the inspector to examine extrinsic information, but only to reconcile inconsistent proxies). The corporation and its election inspectors are not liable in damages for accepting or rejecting proxies in good faith. MBCA §7.24(d).

§7.2.6 Action by Consent

Under most statutes, shareholders can act without a meeting by giving their written consent. See Del. GCL §211(b) (permitting annual meeting by written consent). Action by consent has the same effect as action at a valid shareholders' meeting. Some statutes that allow the procedure require shareholder consent to be unanimous. MBCA §7.04(a). But most states, including Delaware, now require only that the consents represent the minimum number of shares that would be required to approve an action if the meeting were actually held. Del. GCL §228 (no prior notice required). Thus, for action requiring an absolute majority, consent by a majority of outstanding shares suffices.

To determine which shares are entitled to act by consent, the board must set a record date or, if not, the record date is the first date that written consents are delivered to the corporation.

§7.3 ELECTION OF DIRECTORS

§7.3.1 Qualifications and Number of Directors

Directors need not be shareholders, residents of the state of incorporation, or have any other special qualifications. MBCA §8.02; Del. GCL §141(b). The statutes require only that directors be individuals (sometimes at least 18 years old) who meet the qualifications (if any) prescribed in the articles or bylaws.

The number of directors on the board is specified in the articles or the bylaws. MBCA §8.03(c); Del. GCL §141(b). Frequently, the articles specify a variable range, with the actual number of directors fixed in the bylaws. The range can be changed only with shareholder approval, but the number of directors within the range can be set by the board. Many statutes once required a minimum of three directors, but most now permit a board of one director. MBCA §8.03(a); Del. GCL §141(b).

§7.3.2 Voting Methods

General Rule — Annual Election by Straight Voting

Generally, all directors face election at each annual shareholders' meeting. MBCA §8.03(d); Del. GCL §211(b). The general method for electing directors is by straight (plurality) voting — the top vote-getters for the open seats are elected. MBCA §7.28(a); Del. GCL §216(b). Under straight voting, shareholders vote their shares for each open directorship, which means a shareholder holding a majority of the shares can elect the entire board of directors.

To illustrate, suppose the articles of AB Corp. authorize five directors and there are two shareholders: Alphonse owns 51 shares and Byron owns 49 shares. Under straight voting, Alphonse and Byron would each cast their votes five times for five different candidates. Each of Alphonse's five candidates would receive 51 votes; each of Byron's five candidates would receive 49 votes. Alphonse's slate — the top five vote-getters — is elected.

Cumulative Voting

To ensure board representation for larger minority shareholders, some state statutes (and even some state constitutions) require cumulative voting. In the remaining states, cumulative voting is permissive and applies if adopted in the articles or sometimes the bylaws. See MBCA §7.28 (articles); Del. GCL §214 (certificate of incorporation).

Cumulative voting, unlike straight voting, allows minority shareholders to accumulate all of their votes and allocate them among a few or even one candidate. This increases the chances of board representation for minority shareholders. Cumulative voting, however, only applies to electing directors, not to shareholder voting on other matters.

The operation of cumulative voting can be tricky and involves some arithmetic. Suppose that Alphonse has 70 shares and Byron 30 shares. Under cumulative voting in an election of five directors, Alphonse would have a total of 350 (70 times 5) votes to distribute among his candidates as he chooses; Byron would have 150 (30 times 5) votes. If Byron votes intelligently, cumulative voting assures him at least one director. If Byron casts all of his 150 votes for his candidate, Alphonse cannot prevent the candidate's election. But Alphonse, if careful, can cast his 350 cumulative votes to elect the four other directors.

Cumulative voting has pitfalls for the unwary. If Alphonse spreads his votes unevenly or too thinly, he might elect only three or even fewer directors. Suppose Alphonse casts his votes and Byron responds as follows:

Alphonse (350 votes)		**Byron (150 votes)**	
Agatha	150	Bernice	50
Arthur	150	Bertrand	50
Alexis	20	Beatrice	50
Andrew	20		
Astor	10		

The top five vote-getters are Agatha, Arthur, Bernice, Bertrand, and Beatrice. By his inept voting, Alphonse placed only a minority of directors on the board despite owning 70 percent of the voting shares. To avoid such surprises, many statutes require advance notice of cumulative voting. Either the notice of the shareholders' meeting must state that cumulative voting is authorized or a shareholder planning to exercise her cumulative voting right must give notice before the meeting. MBCA §7.28(d) (notice to shareholders must be "conspicuous" or shareholder must give notice within 48 hours of meeting). How should Alphonse and Byron plan their strategies? There is a mathematical formula for determining how many shares assure the election of a director (or a given number of directors) and thus the optimal voting strategy under cumulative voting:

$$NS = \frac{ND \times TS}{TD + 1} + \text{some fraction (or 1)}$$

where

NS = number of shares needed to elect desired number of directors
ND = number of directors that shareholder desires to elect
TS = total number of shares authorized to vote
TD = total number of directors to be elected

The (ND × TS)/(TD + 1) part of the formula represents the equilibrium point where there would be a voting tie. To break the tie, a shareholder needs only a fraction more—hence the formula's requirement that something be added. Unless the corporation recognizes fractional voting, the needed shares must be pushed up to the next whole number, either by rounding up or adding one. In our example, where AB Corp. has 100 voting shares and five directors are to be elected, the formula produces the following results:

Number of directors you want to elect	Number of whole shares you need
1 director	100/6 + fraction = 16.67 + fraction = 17
2 directors	200/6 + fraction = 33.33 + fraction = 34
3 directors	300/6 + fraction = 50 + 1 = 51
4 directors	400/6 + fraction = 66.67 + fraction = 67
5 directors	500/6 + fraction = 83.33 + fraction = 84

According to this table, Alphonse's 70 shares assure him of electing at least four directors because he holds more than 67 shares but less than 84. If Alphonse casts all of his votes equally (or nearly so) for four candidates, he can elect four directors. Byron is assured of electing only one director because his 30 shares are greater than 17 but less than 34. Byron should cast all of his votes for one candidate to assure representation on the board.

Cumulative voting is not the only way to assure board representation. In close corporations with few shareholders, board representation can be assured by agreement (see §26.2) or classes of stock (see below). Cumulative voting is unusual in public corporations and is found most often in middle-sized corporations with approximately 50 to 500 shareholders.

Staggered Board

An exception to the one-year election cycle is a staggered or classified board, in which only some of the directors are elected at each annual meeting. A staggered board must be specified in the articles or, in some states, the bylaws. MBCA §8.06 (articles); Del. GCL §141(d) (charter, initial bylaws, shareholder-approved bylaws). A staggered board is classified into groups of directors, each group with a multiyear term. For example, on a twelve-person staggered board divided into three equal groups, only four directors are up for election each year, and each director's term is three years. To ensure a majority of the board is up for election at least every two years, many statutes specify that there be no more than three groups of directors. MBCA §8.06; Del. GCL §141d.

There are a number of reasons for a staggered board, some less laudable than others. First, a staggered board assures greater continuity in board membership from year to year because all of the directors are not subject to annual recall. Second, a staggered board reduces the number of directors up for election each year, and a majority of shareholders can effectively avoid minority representation on the board even if there is cumulative voting. For example, if Alphonse and Byron have a corporation with a staggered board with two classes in which two directors are elected one year and the remaining three the next year, Alphonse's 70 percent share will allow him to elect all of the directors each year. Third, it takes longer for shareholders (even those holding a majority of a company's stock) to replace the members of a staggered board because only part of the board is up for election each year. For this reason, staggered boards (along with limitations on removing directors without cause) often are used by incumbent management to discourage unwanted takeovers (see §34.2).

In the past few years, under pressure from activist shareholders who have submitted shareholder proposals urging that all directors stand for election each year (see §9.4.2), many public companies have dismantled their staggered boards. In fact, from 2002 to 2008, the proportion of the 1500 largest pubic U.S. companies with staggered boards fell from 62 percent to 47 percent, and among the 100 largest public companies the proportion fell from 44 percent to 16 percent.

Class Voting

Board representation can also be built into the corporation's capital structure. MBCA §6.10(a); Del. GCL §151(a). The articles can specify that certain classes of stock elect their own directors. For example, AB Corp.'s articles might specify that Class A common shareholders elect three directors and Class B common shareholders elect two directors. Classifying the board, whether in a close or public corporation, can distribute representation between different shareholder camps.

Majority shareholders can also use class voting to undermine a minority shareholder's cumulative voting rights. By amending the articles to create a new class of stock and assuming ownership of the new class, the majority can elect a greater proportion of directors than had been the case under cumulative voting. MBCA §8.04.

Holdovers

A director holds office until a successor is elected and qualified. MBCA §8.05(e); Del. GCL §141(b). This assures that the board remains intact and functional even if an annual shareholders' meeting is not held or there is a voting impropriety or a voting deadlock among shareholders. If a shareholder deadlock persists, some statutes permit a shareholder to petition a court for involuntary dissolution. See MBCA §14.30 (shareholder deadlock and failure to elect successor director for two consecutive annual meetings).

Enforcement

Shareholders may bring direct actions against the corporation for failure to seat a properly elected director. Procedural defects, such as election of the wrong number of directors or under an improper method, voids the election unless shareholders acquiesce in or ratify the results.

In addition, shareholders can sue the corporation if the board fails to observe procedural requirements intended to ensure full representation and board inclusiveness—such as notice, quorum, and voting rules at board meetings. See §7.1.5 above. Actions taken by the board that do not comply with these requirements are void, and shareholders can challenge them in a judicial proceeding.

§7.3.3 Removal of Directors

Built on the republican notion that legislators may remain in office during good behavior, the common law allowed shareholders to remove directors only for cause—such as fraud, criminal activity, gross mismanagement, or self-dealing. Most statutes today give shareholders greater latitude to remove directors during their term—with or without cause. MBCA §8.08(a) (removal with or without cause, unless articles specify otherwise); Del. GCL §141(k) (same). In addition, some states allow directors to be removed in a judicial proceeding brought by the corporation or by shareholders holding a specified percentage of shares. MBCA §8.09 (judicial removal for "fraudulent or dishonest conduct, or gross abuse of authority" when in the best interests of the corporation).

Procedures for Removal (Corporate "Due Process")

When a director is to be removed (whether for cause or without), shareholders must be given specific notice that removal will be considered at a meeting. MBCA §8.08(d). In addition, directors to be removed for cause have corporate "due process" rights (a vestige of corporate republicanism) to be informed of the reasons for removal and to answer the charges. See *Campbell v. Loew's, Inc.*, 134 A.2d 852 (Del. Ch. 1957) (requiring service of specific charges, adequate notice, and full opportunity for director to meet accusations by a statement in company's proxy solicitation).

Removal under Cumulative Voting

To prevent the majority from circumventing minority representation under cumulative voting, nearly all state statutes specify that a director elected under cumulative voting cannot be removed if any minority faction, with enough shares to have elected him by cumulative voting, votes against his removal. MBCA §8.08(c) (the Official Comment indicates that this restriction applies whether removal is with or without cause); Del. GCL §141(k) (only for removal without cause). For example, if 20 shares would have been enough to elect a director under cumulative voting, then he cannot be removed if 20 shares are voted against his removal. Delaware courts, however, have treated removal *for cause* as an absolute prerogative of the majority. See *Campbell v. Loew's, Inc.*, 134 A.2d 852 (Del. Ch. 1957) (holding that stockholders have inherent power to remove directors for cause even if elected under cumulative voting).

Filling Vacancies

In general, the board or the shareholders can fill board vacancies created by the removal, death, or resignation of directors or the creation of new directorships. MBCA §8.10. Shareholders can exercise this power, however, only at an annual or special shareholders' meeting. See MBCA §7.21. Under some statutes, any midterm replacement (even if filling for a director with a staggered term) must stand for election at the next annual shareholders' meeting. See MBCA §8.05(d). Some statutes limit the board's authority to fill vacancies, particularly when directors are removed or new directorships created, on the theory that the board cannot usurp the shareholders' power to elect directors. Delaware courts have stated that shareholders have the inherent right between annual meetings to fill newly created directorships. See *Campbell v. Loew's, Inc.*, 134 A.2d 852 (Del. Ch. 1957) (upholding proposal of minority faction to amend bylaws to increase size of board and fill vacancies with its candidates).

Examples

EXAMPLES

1. Graphic Designs, incorporated in an MBCA jurisdiction, designs and produces commercial art. Shirley is the majority shareholder and the board's dominant director. The company president is Buck. Shirley offers her friend Jenny, a highly qualified commercial artist, a job at Graphic Designs.
   a. If Jenny accepts the offer, is the corporation bound under the agreement?
   b. Shirley, as majority shareholder, instructs the board and Buck to hire Jenny, but they balk. How can Shirley force the board or Buck to follow her instructions?
2. Graphic's five-person board authorizes Buck to fire all of the company's commercial artists and replace them with a computer that would generate graphic designs. Shirley is upset about the board's action.
   a. As majority shareholder, she signs and submits a written consent that purports to remove all of the directors. Will this work?
   b. She calls a special shareholders' meeting to remove the incumbent directors and Buck. Will this work?
   c. She calls a shareholders' meeting to vote on a shareholder resolution requiring the board to reverse its decision. Will this work?

3. Graphic's articles specify a board of between three and seven directors, the exact number to be "fixed by the board of directors in the bylaws." The current bylaws call for five directors. Shirley wants to change the balance of power on the board at the next annual shareholders' meeting by proposing
   a. an amendment to the articles that would fix the number of directors at seven, with any vacancies to be filled by the shareholders. Is this proper?
   b. an amendment of the bylaws that would increase the number of directors from five to seven. Is this proper?
   c. an amendment to the bylaws that mandates that any shareholder must give notice of nominations to the board at least 60 days before the shareholders' meeting. Is this proper?

4. Mildred, a minority shareholder of Graphic, is convinced that Shirley's new directors—who dutifully rescinded the computer decision—were unduly influenced by the company's commercial artists. Mildred is considering a derivative suit against the directors.
   a. She wants to inspect minutes of last year's board meetings. Must the corporation provide the minutes?
   b. She wants to inspect Graphic's list of shareholders so she can contact them about joining her suit. Must the corporation provide the list?
   c. She wants the board to summarize its reasons for rescinding the computer decision. Must the board summarize its reasons?

5. Graphic's articles are silent on the question of how directors are elected. Nine directors sit on Graphic's board.
   a. How are Graphic's directors elected?
   b. Shirley owns 78 of Graphic's 100 shares. Mildred owns the remaining 22. How many directors can Mildred elect under a straight voting scheme?

6. Graphic's articles specify that the corporation's board is to be elected by cumulative voting. The bylaws specify a board of nine directors.
   a. With 22 of 100 shares, how many directors is Mildred assured of electing to the board?
   b. Shirley has heard that Mildred plans to cast her 198 cumulative votes in the following manner: Mary (66), Manny (66), Morton (66). Can Shirley take advantage of this information to increase her representation on the board?

7. Shirley becomes unhappy with the directors Mildred has elected to Graphic's board. With six of her nominees on the nine-person board, Shirley considers some strategies for the board to pursue. Consider the legality of
   a. an amendment to the articles that would eliminate cumulative voting.
   b. an amendment to the articles that would reduce the number of directors to three.

c. an amendment to the articles classifying the nine-person board into three groups, each group's members coming up for election once every three years.
d. an amendment to the bylaws to stagger the board in this way.

8. Milton, one of Graphic's directors elected by Mildred, has begun a competing graphic design business using secret customer lists he obtained as a director of Graphic.
   a. Before he does further damage, Shirley wants him removed from the board and calls a special meeting for that purpose. If Graphic's articles state that directors can only be removed for cause, can she remove Milton?
   b. At the meeting, Shirley votes her 78 shares to remove Milton, and Mildred votes her 22 shares against removal. Is Milton removed?
   c. Shirley considers other options to remove Milton. What other recourse does she have?
   d. Milton resigns. Graphic's articles state that "The board of directors shall have the authority to fill any midterm vacancies on the board." Shirley nonetheless calls a special shareholders' meeting to fill the vacancy left by Milton's resignation. Can she?

Explanations

EXPLANATIONS

1. a. No. As a shareholder Shirley has no authority either to act on behalf of the corporation or to bind the corporation contractually. Unless the corporation has special governance arrangements that permit shareholders to act as partners, which must be stated in the articles, such authority resides solely with the corporation's board of directors. MBCA §8.01(b).
   b. She cannot. Under the traditional corporate structure, Shirley is limited to electing directors and hoping they do as she wants. The board has the sole power to authorize Jenny's employment and delegate this authority to a corporate officer. If the current directors and officers fail to authorize Jenny's employment, Shirley has a couple of options. She can elect new directors at the next annual shareholders' meeting and hope they comply with her wishes. MBCA §8.03(d). Or, as a 10 percent shareholder, she can call a special shareholders' meeting to remove and replace the incumbent directors with others of her choosing. MBCA §8.08. The removal route, however, might be a problem if the articles of incorporation or the statute allow removal only for cause or if the articles only allow the board to fill midterm vacancies. MBCA §8.10.

2. a. No. The MBCA, like many state statutes that allow shareholder action by written consent instead of a vote at a meeting, requires that the consent be unanimous. MBCA §7.04; cf. Del. GCL §228.

b. In part. As the holder of more than 10 percent of Graphic's shares, she can demand a special shareholders' meeting. MBCA §7.02(a)(2) (demand on corporation's secretary). She must have a proper purpose for the meeting.

Removal of directors is a proper purpose, but removal of officers is not. The MBCA permits shareholders to remove directors with or without cause. MBCA §8.08(a). The removal and appointment of officers, however, is within the sole discretion of the board of directors. MBCA §8.40(a) (appointment by board), §8.43(b) (board can remove officers with or without cause).

c. No. Some courts have held that shareholders can approve nonbinding, precatory resolutions concerning the management of the corporation. (The SEC has adopted a similar view in its shareholder proposal rule, which requires that such resolutions be "significantly related" to the company's business and not related to "ordinary business operations." See §9.4.2.) Shirley's resolution, however, is not phrased as a request, but a demand. This shareholders cannot do.

If her resolution had "urged" the board to reconsider its decision, it would satisfy the proper purpose requirement. By linking the board's decision to employee morale and arguably company profitability, the resolution properly relates to the corporation's economic well-being.

3. a. No. Amendments to the articles must be recommended by the board of directors for approval by shareholders. MBCA §10.02.

b. Yes. Shareholders have an inherent power to amend the bylaws. MBCA §10.20. Even though the bylaws state the power to fix the size of the board rests with the directors, the MBCA makes the board's power at most coterminous. According to the courts, this is a mandatory right that cannot be waived.

An interesting question is whether the board could negate Shirley's bylaw amendment by amending the bylaws again to change the size of the board back to five. The MBCA explicitly provides that a shareholder-initiated bylaw amendment cannot be altered by the board, if the amendment expressly so provides. MBCA §10.20(a)(2). To protect her initiative from circumvention, the revised bylaw should state that it can be amended or rescinded only by the shareholders.

c. Probably. Courts have permitted shareholder-proposed bylaws to amend the procedures by which directors are elected. *CA, Inc. v. AFSCME Employees Pension Plan*, 953 A.2d 227 (Del. 2008) (indicating shareholder-proposed bylaw amendment to require reimbursement of reasonable expenses of shareholder nominating a "short slate" of directors is valid, so long as directors are not prevented from exercising their fiduciary duties). In fact, advance-notice bylaws are common, and their validity has not been questioned.

4. a. Perhaps not. The MBCA permits shareholders to demand "excerpts from minutes of board meetings" if the demand is made for a "proper purpose." MBCA §16.02(b)(1), (c). Bringing a derivative action—for the benefit of the corporation and the shareholders as a group—would seem to be such a purpose. Nonetheless, her request as currently formulated may be too broad in that it seeks all board minutes for the past year and thus goes beyond the shareholder's interest in challenging the board's rescission of its computer decision. The MBCA requires that the records be described with "reasonable particularity" and that they relate "directly" to the stated purpose. The board could refuse her demand on this basis.

   Support for a cautious understanding of the inspection right comes in a Delaware case where the court denied an inspection request by a public electronics company that had acquired a minority position in a family firm in the same line of business. *Thomas & Betts Corp. v. Leviton Mfg. Co.*, 681 A.2d 1026 (Del. 1996). The court found the minority shareholder's asserted purposes insufficient. First, the court found no "credible basis" for investigating possible waste and mismanagement. Second, the court concluded the public company had become a locked-in minority shareholder and had no reason to investigate the company's valuation.

   Nonetheless, more recent Delaware cases have encouraged shareholders to seek inspection before bringing a derivative suit. Some have even reformulated the shareholder's request to ensure its validity.

   b. Perhaps. A shareholder demand to inspect the shareholders' list must be for a proper purpose. MBCA §16.02(c). Courts have held that the burden to show an improper purpose is on the corporation. The corporation—that is, the board and current management—may argue that a shareholders' list is not relevant to bringing a derivative action. Courts, however, have interpreted the proper purpose test broadly. Unless Mildred seeks to use the list only to harass or advance her own personal interests, it would be enough if she argued that additional shareholder-plaintiffs will help defray the costs of the derivative litigation and add weight to the challenge of the directors' action.

   c. Probably not. Most courts have limited shareholder inspection requests to documents already in existence. See *Saito v. McKesson HBOC, Inc.*, 806 A.2d 113 (Del. 2002) (permitting inspection of documents prepared by third parties that predated the requesting shareholder's investment). To impose a duty to compile or assemble information would go well beyond the limited inspection rights provided by the statute.

5. a. Straight voting, each year. Under the MBCA, unless the articles specify otherwise, all directors are up for election at each annual shareholders' meeting. MBCA §8.05(b). Each Graphic shareholder may vote for nine director candidates, and the top nine vote-getters for the nine open

seats are elected. MBCA §7.28(a) (plurality voting). Cumulative voting and staggered terms apply only if specified in the articles. See MBCA §§7.28(c), 8.06.

b. None. Under straight voting, Shirley and Mildred each will cast their votes nine times for nine candidates. Each of Shirley's nine candidates will receive 78 votes, and each of Mildred's will receive 22 votes. The nine top vote-getters will be Shirley's slate; Mildred does not have the power to elect any directors.

6. a. Two directors. The cumulative-voting formula provides the answer:

$$NS = \frac{ND \times TS}{TD + 1} + \text{some fraction (or 1)}$$

where

NS = number of shares needed to elect desired number of directors
ND = number of directors that shareholder desires to elect
TS = total number of shares authorized to vote
TD = total number of directors to be elected

To assure herself seats on the board, Mildred needs the following:

Number of Directors	Number of Voting Shares
1 director	11 shares [1 × 100/(9 + 1) + 1]
2 directors	21 shares [2 × 100/(9 + 1) + 1]
3 directors	31 shares [3 × 100/(9 + 1) + 1]

Therefore, Mildred's 22 shares give her the power to elect at least two directors.

Under cumulative voting, Mildred will have a total of 198 votes (22 times 9) to distribute among her candidates. If she casts 99 votes for each of two candidates, there is no way Shirley can cast her 702 votes (78 times 9) so that *more* than seven of her candidates will receive more than 99 votes. At best, Shirley can cast 100 votes for each of seven of her candidates, but she will have only two votes left to cast for her eighth candidate.

b. Yes. Shirley can distribute her 702 votes among nine candidates, casting 78 votes for each. Shirley will elect all nine directors in this way—the top nine vote-getters will all be her candidates. By spreading her votes among three candidates, Mildred dilutes her cumulative voting power.

7. a. Legal. Assuming the board proposes the amendment and shareholders approve it, the articles may be amended to delete a provision not required in the articles. MBCA §10.01(a). Cumulative voting under

the MBCA is an opt-in right and can be removed by action of the board and majority approval of the shareholders.

To protect her right to minority representation from majority action, Mildred should have insisted on "anticircumvention" provisions in the articles. These provisions could have required, for example, that any changes to cumulative voting rights, the size of the board, the authorization and issuance of additional voting shares, or the staggering of directors' terms be approved by a supermajority vote. See §8.08(c) (director cannot be removed, if cumulative voting is authorized, if the votes sufficient to elect him voted against his removal).

b. Legal. As a practical matter, the reduction in board size will destroy the effectiveness of cumulative voting. Even though Mildred can continue to accumulate her votes, her 22 shares are no longer sufficient to elect a director. According to the cumulative-voting formula, a shareholder must have 26 voting shares to be assured of electing one director on a three-person board.

The effectiveness of cumulative voting is not assured under the MBCA. Nonetheless, the amendment would seem to "materially and adversely affect" Mildred's voting rights, and Mildred may have appraisal rights that allow her to dissent from the change and force the corporation in an appraisal proceeding to pay her the fair value of her shares. See MBCA §13.02(a)(4)(iv) (see Chapter 37).

c. Legal. The effect would be similar to reducing the size of the board. Mildred would no longer be assured the ability to elect a director despite her continuing right to cumulate her votes. Only three directors would come up for election each year, and Shirley could elect all of them. See *Humphreys v. Winous Co.*, 133 N.E.2d 780 (Ohio 1956) (upholding classification of board despite statute requiring cumulative voting).

d. Not legal. Shirley cannot adopt a classified board through a bylaw amendment. The MBCA requires that a staggered board be provided for in the articles. MBCA §8.06 (articles "may provide" for staggered terms); §8.05(b) (terms of "all directors" expire annually, unless terms are staggered under §8.06).

8. a. Yes. Milton's misappropriation of the company's trade secrets is not only illegal under state law, but also a breach of his fiduciary duties (see §16.2). There is cause for his removal.

b. No. Under the MBCA, Milton cannot be removed if the number of shares needed to elect him under cumulative voting are voted against his removal. MBCA §8.08(c). Eleven shares would have been sufficient to elect Milton [100/(9 + 1) + 1], and Milton cannot be removed if eleven (or more) votes are cast against his removal. See §7.3.2 (cumulative voting formula).

This means that Mildred can prevent his removal, even though there is cause. Mildred has the power to decide whether Milton's transgressions warrant removal, on the theory that she could reelect him if she so desired.

c. Shirley can seek to have Milton removed by judicial order. Under the MBCA, a 10 percent shareholder can have a director removed if the court finds the director engaged in "fraudulent or dishonest conduct" or "gross abuse of authority or discretion," and that his removal is in the corporation's best interests. MBCA §8.09. Milton's misappropriation of company trade secrets, particularly if it posed a continuing risk of damage to Graphic's business, would seem to easily meet this test.
d. Probably. Even though the provision might be read to give the board *exclusive* authority to fill vacancies, a strong argument can be made that shareholders nonetheless retain an inherent authority to fill vacancies. See *Campbell v. Loew's, Inc.*, 134 A.2d 852 (Del. Ch. 1957) (shareholders have inherent authority to fill board vacancies). The MBCA is ambiguous. It specifies that board vacancies can be filled by shareholders or directors, unless the articles provide otherwise. MBCA §8.10. Although it is possible to read this to permit waiver of shareholder authority to fill vacancies, the provision can also be read only to permit the waiver of board authority. This second reading is consistent with other MBCA provisions that, for example, give shareholders nonwaivable authority to remove directors for cause. See MBCA §8.08(a).

CHAPTER 8

Judicial Protection of Voting Rights

In theory, shareholder voting gives shareholders a role in corporate governance. In practice, shareholder voting creates the potential for opportunism. Insurgents who seek board control may have objectives at odds with the interests of the shareholder majority. And incumbent directors may seek to entrench themselves by manipulating voting procedures or by creating structures that diminish shareholder voting rights.

This chapter describes judicial protection of "corporate democracy"—judicial limits on insurgents, including restrictions on vote buying and reimbursement of election expenses (§8.1), judicial scrutiny of board manipulation of voting procedures and voting structures (§8.2). These protections complement other voting protections, such as the voting rules under state law (Chapter 7), the federal disclosure regulations for proxy voting (Chapter 9), and the proxy fraud rules (Chapter 10).

§8.1 LIMITS ON INSURGENT OPPORTUNISM

To protect shareholders in public corporations from their own rational passivity and their difficulties in collectivizing, courts have developed rules that minimize the risks of opportunistic insurgents.

§8.1.1 Vote Buying

Ownership and control are separated when a shareholder, for a price, agrees to vote his shares as directed. Early courts condemned corporate vote buying and declared it to be illegal per se. They doubted the incentives of vote buyers to maximize corporate value consistent with the interests of shareholders and creditors. Some courts reasoned that vote buying in the corporation is no different than in politics, and corporate legitimacy demands the independent judgment of each shareholder.

Yet few corporate statutes prohibit vote buying. See N.Y. BCL §609. Instead, courts have cautiously come to accept vote buying, just as corporate statutes have come to recognize other devices that separate voting and economic rights—voting trusts, dual-class voting structures, and irrevocable proxies. See §§7.2, 26.2.

Nonetheless, vote buying in public corporations presents special risks, including coerced changes in control or even looting. The leading vote-buying case is *Schreiber v. Carney*, 447 A.2d 17 (Del. Ch. 1982). There a large shareholder, facing a substantial tax liability if the company were reorganized, withdrew its opposition to a proposed reorganization after the corporation agreed to loan the shareholder sufficient funds to avoid the tax liability. Accepting the shareholder had sold his vote by ceding his discretionary voting power, the court concluded that transfers of voting rights without the underlying economic interest are not necessarily illegal "unless the object or purpose is to defraud or in some way disenfranchise the other stockholders." Because the reorganization was meant to benefit the shareholders and the tax-related loan was fully disclosed, the court decided there was no fraud or disenfranchisement. The court warned, however, that vote buying "is so easily susceptible of abuse it must be . . . subject to a test for intrinsic fairness."

Although modern courts have not yet decided a case of naked vote buying, they have permitted the transfer of voting rights when related to an otherwise legitimate corporate transaction:

- As part of an out-of-court settlement in which the corporation agrees to pay an insurgent's proxy expenses, the insurgent grants an irrevocable proxy to management. *Weinberger v. Bankston*, No. 6336 (Del. Ch. 1987).
- To facilitate a negotiated merger, corporate management convinces an institutional shareholder to support the merger by promising it new business as a co-manager of the deal. *Hewlett v. Hewlett-Packard Co.*, No. 19513 (Del. Ch. 2002) (noting that judicial suspicion of vote-buying agreements is "difficult to reconcile" with corporate statute's "explicit validation of shareholder agreements").
- To stave off an insurgent, corporate board agrees to add shareholder to its slate of nominees on promise the shareholder will support

board in proxy fight. *Portnoy v. Cryo-Cell Int'l, Inc.*, 940 A.2d 43 (Del. Ch. 2008) (but invalidating agreement that shareholder would buy more shares and vote with board, on promise board would add a new seat for shareholder's nominee).

The legitimacy of vote buying may depend on whether the buyer is a fellow shareholder or management. While shareholders may arguably be free to do whatever they want with their votes, management's use of corporate assets to buy votes is problematic and may require a showing there is no deleterious effect on the corporation or the corporate franchise.

Lately, hedge funds (investment pools that buy shares in companies and then seek to bring about company reforms) have developed ingenious ways to acquire corporate votes without also acquiring corporate shares—a decoupling of control and ownership. One technique is for hedge funds to borrow shares from institutional investors on the record date set for a voting contest, thus obtaining the right to vote without purchasing a financial interest. Another technique is for hedge funds to buy shares of a company, while at the same time buying "put" options that give the fund the right to sell the shares at a specified price. Thus, the fund acquires voting rights without bearing the usual financial risks of ownership. These techniques have been controversial, and academic critics have called for greater transparency and even regulation—but no case has yet addressed this form of vote buying.

§8.1.2 Payment and Reimbursement of Election Expenses

As Berle and Means observed more than half a century ago, management control over the voting machinery in public corporations arises from the board's control of the corporate purse strings. See §6.2.2. The rule on election-related expenses (such as preparing and mailing proxy materials to shareholders and placing advertisements in financial publications) is easily stated: the corporate treasury pays the expenses of incumbents, win or lose; insurgents can hope for reimbursement only by winning. The effect is to significantly discourage insurgents seeking board control through the voting process.

The few cases on election expenses grant the board wide discretion to authorize corporate payment of incumbents' voting-related expenses. They need only relate to corporate "policy," as opposed to a "purely personal" quest for power. See *Rosenfeld v. Fairchild Engine & Airplane Corp.*, 128 N.E.2d 291 (N.Y. 1955). Because any control or issue contest can be characterized as a question of how the corporation should be managed, not who should do it, all of the incumbents' expenses are payable by the corporation. Although courts have said these expenses must be "reasonable," no reported decision has denied incumbents less than complete payment.

The board has equally ample discretion to refuse reimbursement of voting expenses of outsiders. In practice, unsuccessful insurgents rarely receive payment. Only if an insurgent wins an election contest, installs a new board that approves reimbursement, and successfully solicits shareholder ratification of the board's action can the insurgent expect reimbursement. See *Rosenfeld* (permitting reimbursement of insurgent if proxy contest was over "policy" not "personality," and shareholders approved the payment). In that case, shareholders end up funding both sides in the campaign.

In an important recent case, the Delaware Supreme Court upheld the legality of a shareholder-proposed bylaw amendment that requires the reimbursement of reasonable election-related expenses by insurgents seeking to seat fewer than a majority of directors on the board. *CA, Inc. v. AFSCME Employees Pension Plan*, 953 A.2d 227 (Del. 2008). The court concluded that bylaw amendments that relate to the process of director elections (including expense reimbursement) are a proper subject for shareholder action under Delaware law, provided the bylaws allow directors to exercise their fiduciary duties, such as to deny reimbursement for a dissident slate inimical to corporate interests.

§8.2 REVIEW OF MANAGEMENT ACTIONS AFFECTING VOTING RIGHTS

§8.2.1 Board's Role in Shareholder Voting

Shareholder voting contemplates that the board of directors, like a legislature in political voting, administers the voting mechanism. The board oversees the *voting procedures*—choosing the location and date for the annual shareholders' meeting; calling special meetings; setting the record date that fixes which shareholders are entitled to vote; imposing advance notice requirements for nonmanagement candidates and proposals; conducting the shareholders' meeting through its choice of the meeting's chair; and tabulating votes, including proxies and consents.

In addition, the board can create voting structures that dilute the shareholders' franchise. The board establishes the corporate *voting agenda*—nominating its slate of candidates; setting the size of the board; proposing amendments to the articles of incorporation; recommending fundamental corporate changes, such as mergers and sales of assets; seeking approval of compensation plans and other corporate transactions; and deciding which shareholder proposals to censor.

As administrator and agenda-setter for shareholder voting, the board faces deep conflicts of interest. Incumbent directors can use the board's voting-related powers to preserve their incumbency by manipulating voting procedures or erecting structural barriers. Yet the board is the logical administrator of the voting mechanism and the natural locus of corporate innovation and change.

§8.2.2 Manipulation of Voting Process

Courts have strictly scrutinized board manipulation of the voting process during a pending voting contest. Such manipulation is treated as inequitable—a presumptive breach of fiduciary duty. *Schnell v. Chris-Craft Industries, Inc.*, 285 A.2d 437 (Del. 1971). Unless the board can articulate a "compelling justification" for its action, courts intervene to protect "established principles of corporate democracy." *Blasius Indus., Inc. v. Atlas Corp.*, 564 A.2d 651 (Del. Ch. 1988).

The following board manipulations of the voting process have been held invalid:

- advancing the annual meeting date in a way that burdened insurgents in a pending proxy contest. *Schnell v. Chris-Craft Industries, Inc.*, 285 A.2d 437 (Del. 1971).
- postponing the annual meeting date where opposing proxies already gathered by an insurgent would expire by the time of the rescheduled meeting. *Aprahamiam v. HBO & Co.*, 531 A.2d 1204 (Del. 1987).
- establishing bylaws that imposed waiting periods, advance-notice requirements, inspection, and record-date procedures for shareholder action by written consent when they unnecessarily delayed shareholder action. *Allen v. Prime Computer, Inc.*, 540 A.2d 417 (Del. 1988).
- adjourning a shareholders' meeting that prevented the defeat of a board-recommended proposal to increase the number of shares available for an executive compensation plan. *State of Wisconsin Investment Board v. Peerless Systems Corp.*, No. 17637 (Del. Ch. 2000).

The *Blasius* "compelling justification" standard, however, applies only when the "primary purpose" of the board's action is to impede the shareholders' opportunity to vote. Thus, if the board creates voting procedures when no voting contest is on the horizon, courts have shown remarkable deference. For example, the board may adopt an advance-notice bylaw that requires any shareholder to notify the corporation in advance of a shareholders' meeting of its intention to nominate a slate of directors or propose other action at the meeting. *Stroud v. Grace*, 606 A.2d 75 (Del. 1992). The board can even set a record date to impede a potential insurgency provided no meeting date had yet been set or proxies yet solicited. *Stahl v. Apple Bancorp*, 579 A.2d 1115 (Del. Ch. 1990).

Lately, many companies have amended their advance-notice bylaws to specify that shareholder activists seeking to place a nominee on the company board must disclose not only their holdings of company stock but also any derivatives (options and short positions) they may have in the stock. Companies have also specified that the submission of a nominee must comply with the advance-notice requirements, which are deemed exclusive. The greater specificity was spurred by a Delaware decision that ambiguous bylaw provisions are to be interpreted in favor of insurgent shareholders. See *Jana Master Fund, Ltd. v. CNET Networks*, 954 A.2d 355 (Del. Ch. 2008).

Nonetheless, there may be limits to the ability of shareholders to amend election-related bylaws to favor an insurgency. For example, when a bidder proposed a bylaw amendment that would accelerate the timing of the company's annual meeting, thus to circumvent the otherwise lengthy process of removing staggered board members, the court held that the bylaw would be inconsistent with the staggered board provisions in the articles and the Delaware statute. See *Airgas, Inc. v. Air Products and Chemicals, Inc.*, A.2d (Del. 2010) (concluding that word "annual" in company charter and Del. GCL §141(d) cannot mean four months).

§8.2.3 Interference with Voting Opportunities

The courts have been ambivalent about board actions that revise the corporation's voting structure either by shifting voting power to management-friendly shareholders or by adopting arrangements that make it more difficult for a shareholder majority to exercise control. Board actions *during a voting contest* that undermine shareholder voting rights, even though they do not manipulate or interfere with the voting process, have been invalidated as breaches of directors' fiduciary duty. But board actions *outside a voting contest* that reduce shareholder voting rights have been validated as within the board's prerogatives.

The following board actions have been invalidated for unilaterally undermining shareholder voting rights:

- issuing new stock to friendly shareholders to dilute an insurgent who has started or is threatening a proxy fight. *Condec Corp. v. Lunkenheimer Co.*, 230 A.2d 769 (Del. Ch. 1967).
- issuing high-voting preferred shares whose effect is to strip the relative voting power of common shares upon any transfer. *Unilever Acquisition Corp. v. Richardson Vicks*, 618 F. Supp. 407 (S.D.N.Y. 1985).
- increasing the board size, and then filling the resulting vacancies, to nullify an insurgent's pending consent solicitation to place its

nominees on the board. *Blasius Indus., Inc. v. Atlas Corp.*, 564 A.2d 651 (Del. Ch. 1988).

In addition, shareholders have a right to elect directors endowed with full powers to undertake corporate reforms. Thus, the board cannot adopt a poison pill plan (see §39.2.3—*Moran v. Household Int'l*) that can be rescinded only by incumbent directors or their chosen successors—a so-called dead hand or continuing director plan. Such plans deny to shareholders the right to choose directors with full decision-making authority and constrain directors in exercising their fiduciary duties. *Quickturn Design Systems, Inc. v. Shapiro*, 721 A.2d 1281 (Del. 1998) (invalidating delayed redemption "dead hand" plan); *Carmody v. Toll Brothers, Inc.*, 723 A.2d 1190 (Del. Ch. 1998) (invalidating "dead hand" plan as creating less equal directors and disenfranchising shareholders who elect directors committed to redeeming the poison pill).

Nonetheless, the courts have given boards significant latitude *outside a voting contest* to take preemptive actions that weaken shareholder voting. This is particularly true when an informed shareholder majority approves the defensive action. For example, courts have accepted the validity of "shark repellent" charter amendments that make voting insurgencies and hostile takeovers more difficult, even though studies show they diminish share value. Under the business judgment rule, courts have upheld such shark repellents as supermajority voting requirements, high-voting shares, staggered boards, aggregation caps on voting power, provisions dictating board size, and elimination of written consent procedures. See *Providence & Worcester Co. v. Baker*, 378 A.2d 121 (Del. 1977) (voting cap on any shareholder with more than 25 percent of company's shares); *eBay Domestic Holdings v. Newmark*, 16 A.3d 1 (Del. Ch. 2010) (applying business judgment rule to staggered board provision).

Judicial deference also increases when the board defends against a two-step proxy contest/tender offer (see §34.1), even if the defense dilutes shareholder voting power. For example, the board may engage in a repurchase program of company shares to increase the relative voting power of nonselling directors so long as a proxy contest remains a "viable alternative" for the insurgent/bidder after the repurchase. *Unitrin, Inc. v. American General Corp.*, 651 A.2d 1361 (Del. 1995) (applying *Unocal* test, see §39.2.3, to decide that repurchase program was proportionate response to "coercion" of low-price tender offer). But the board cannot amend the bylaws to require that any future bylaw changes be approved by a two-thirds supermajority, when the amendment would make it "mathematically impossible for an insurgent to prevail" and effectively give insiders an insurmountable blocking position. *Chesapeake Corp. v. Shore*, 771 A.2d 293 (Del. Ch. 2000) (invalidating amendment under both *Unocal* and *Blasius* standards of review).

§8.2.4 Deviations from One-Share/One-Vote

Adding nonvoting or multiple-vote shares to the voting structure can significantly alter shareholder voting power. If the board can convince shareholders to authorize a charter amendment or exchange their shares so that nonmanagement shareholders are left with low-voting shares and management with high-voting shares, the nonmanagement shareholders are effectively disenfranchised.

Corporate law once imposed a one-share/one-vote requirement, but modern corporate statutes permit deviations. MBCA §6.01(c)(1); Del. GCL §151(a). And courts have generally upheld dual-class recapitalizations in which common shares receive disparate voting rights so long as the plan is approved by shareholders after full disclosure. For example, in *Williams v. Geier*, 671 A.2d 1368 (Del. 1996), a control group proposed a recapitalization (amendment to the articles) that was then approved by a shareholder majority, which gave existing shareholders ten votes per share and any new shareholder only one vote for the first three years of ownership. The effect was to entrench management since any hostile acquirer would, by virtue of the plan, only be able to acquire low-voting shares. The Delaware court upheld the plan, approved by informed shareholders, under the business judgment rule—a presumption that directors act independently with due care and in good faith. See §12.2.

But if shareholder approval is coerced, courts have invalidated such recapitalizations. See *Lacos Land v. Arden Group, Inc.*, 517 A.2d 271 (Del. Ch. 1986) (invalidating issuance of new class of super-voting, nontransferable common shares likely to be taken only by company's CEO, since CEO publicly threatened he would block any future control transaction if shareholders did not approve the recapitalization).

Although deviations from the one-share/one-vote norm are common in close corporations, they are far less prevalent in public corporations. The stock exchanges, though permitting the issuance of low-voting shares to new investors, prohibit listed companies from engaging in dual-class recapitalizations or the issuance of super-voting shares. NYSE Listed Company Manual §313.00(A). This listing requirement was the result of pressure from Congress after the SEC sought to impose a one-share/one-vote standard by rule, which was successfully challenged as beyond the agency's authority and an encroachment on state corporate law. See *Business Roundtable v. SEC*, 905 F.2d 406 (D.C. Cir. 1990) (invalidating Rule 19c-4).

Examples

1. Conestoga Partners is an activist hedge fund—that is, a private investment firm that looks for companies whose assets are underutilized or mismanaged. Once it identifies a target, Conestoga buys a strategic stake in the company and then urges the company's management to make the business more profitable or face a takeover. Usually, management restructures the business as suggested; sometimes Conestoga replaces the board and sells the company. In any event, Conestoga usually garners a handsome profit. Recently Conestoga identified a target: Gillick Industries, a publicly traded corporation that manufactures shaving products.
   a. Conestoga and a couple other large shareholders form the Gillick Activist Shareholders Pact (GASP), open only to shareholders holding more than $1,000,000 of Gillick's shares. When they join, GASP members must agree to vote their shares as directed by the group. Is this secret arrangement valid?
   b. GASP contacts Ray King, Gillick's founder and largest shareholder. King has lately been displeased with Gillick management and agrees to vote for GASP's board candidates on the condition GASP pay him 10 percent of any spike in share prices before the election. Is this valid?
2. On April 1 Conestoga nominates four candidates to Gillick's 12-person staggered board. In its proxy solicitation Conestoga says its candidates are committed to putting the company up for sale. As the shareholders' meeting approaches, trading in Gillick stock intensifies.
   a. Gillick's bylaws specify that the annual shareholders' meeting will be held on the first Tuesday of May. The Gillick board, however, sets the record date to be March 1. As a result, recent purchasers (mostly arbitrageurs hoping the proxy contest succeeds) will not vote. Is the board action valid?
   b. Gillick's board follows through on a preexisting plan to place 25 percent of Gillick's stock in a newly created ESOP. A voting trustee will vote this stock according to employee instructions. Is the issuance to the ESOP valid?
   c. Gillick's board issues new zero-coupon debentures as a dividend on its common shares. Each debenture, which calls for interest and principal to be payable in five years, has a face value of $10—about one-fifth the current value of Gillick's common shares. The debentures, which can trade only with the common shares, contain a provision that adjusts the face value to $2 if any of Gillick's directors are replaced without management consent. Is this issuance valid?
3. Conestoga's candidates are defeated by a narrow margin.
   a. After the election Conestoga asks Gillick to reimburse it for its voting-related expenses, arguing that the election contest resolved a matter of corporate policy. Is Conestoga entitled to reimbursement?

b. During the campaign, Gillick's management placed numerous newspaper ads questioning the composition of Conestoga's investor group: "The Conestoga Dissidents—Who Are They Really?" The ads, paid for with company funds, say the group includes a shadowy foreign billionaire. In fact, the ads are false. Must Gillick's management reimburse the company for this deceptive advertising?

c. In a recount, Conestoga's slate of candidates is elected. Conestoga asks the new board to be reimbursed for its voting-related expenses. The board complies. Is this valid?

4. After the election the new Gillick board majority reviews the company's situation and comes to support incumbent management. The board authorizes the sale of some of Gillick's less profitable operations—not quite what Conestoga and GASP had in mind.

a. The proxy materials supporting the Conestoga candidates were clear. Their campaign was based on the company being sold. Can Conestoga and GASP demand the board sell the company as a majority of shareholders had wanted?

b. Anticipating that Conestoga might buy more shares and mount another proxy fight, Gillick's board adopts a poison pill plan. The plan calls for the dilution of any person who acquires more than 20 percent of Gillick's shares unless the board first redeems the poison pill rights. The plan specifies that only directors nominated by the board can make this redemption. The board explains that this ensures only directors independent of an insurgent/bidder will evaluate the merits of any outside bid. Is this poison pill valid?

c. Gillick's board also decides to concentrate voting rights in friendly hands. It issues a new class of super-voting shares with ten votes per share. If sold, the super-voting shares automatically convert to regular low-voting shares. The idea is that only long-term shareholders (loyal to management) will hold the super-voting shares. Assuming Gillick is listed on the NYSE, is this valid?

Explanations

1. a. Yes, under state law; no, under federal law. State corporate law—described in more detail in a later chapter, see §§26.1, 26.2—places no restrictions on the ability of shareholders (regardless of the size of their holding or their sophistication) to vote their shares as they please. So long as shareholders do not formally relinquish their votes to another, through an irrevocable proxy or voting trust or a vote-buying arrangement, a shareholders' voting agreement is valid. MBCA §7.31 (voting agreements are specifically enforceable); Del. GCL §218(c). The assumption of "corporate democracy" is that shareholders can decide what is in their best interests, including through secret mutual

action. In addition, by retaining control of their vote, shareholders who are parties to a voting agreement can readily protect themselves against a coparty's noncompliance or other opportunism.

Federal disclosure law—described in more detail in later chapters, see §§9.3, 10.2, 38.1—requires transparency in voting agreements among public shareholders. Conestoga and the other GASP members are a "group" for purposes of the shareholding disclosure requirements of federal securities laws. Because the GASP members (whose combined holdings exceed 5 percent) reached an understanding to affect control of a publicly traded corporation, they must disclose their identity and intentions to the remaining shareholders and management. See §13(d), Securities Exchange Act of 1934; see also §38.1. Form 13D may be required even if GASP's initial formation was exempt from the proxy rules' filing and distribution requirements for proxy-related discussions limited to fewer than 10 shareholders. See §9.3.5. In addition, when Conestoga and GASP solicit shareholder proxies, they will be obligated to disclose the nature of their agreement under the proxy rules (Form 14A, Item 4, see §9.2) and under judicial antifraud standards (see §10.2).

b. Perhaps valid. Although the agreement involves bald vote buying, recent courts have suggested that shareholders can do with their votes as they please. Nonetheless, perhaps drawn to the analogy of political vote buying, courts continue to scrutinize vote buying to be sure neither the corporation nor other shareholders are harmed. No harm is apparent.

2. a. Probably invalid. The MBCA, like other corporate statutes, contemplates that the board has the power to control the voting process, including the setting of a record date for determining which shareholders are entitled to notice and to vote. MBCA §7.07 (record date set in bylaws or by board, provided at least 70 days before the meeting); MBCA §10.20(a) (board has power to amend the bylaws). The board's setting of the record date is thus within its powers.

But the board's action, even if authorized, may violate the directors' fiduciary duties. The effect of the "backdated" record date is to dilute the voting power of recent purchasers, particularly the arbitrageurs. Because the shareholders' meeting date was already set (in the bylaws) and the board set a record date with no apparent business justification except to thwart the pending shareholder insurgency opposed by management, a court could find the directors acted inequitably. Cf. *Stahl v. Apple Bancorp*, 579 A.2d 1115 (Del. Ch. 1990) (accepting board's setting of record date to impede a potential insurgency, but where no meeting date had yet been set). Absent "compelling justifications," the action would constitute a breach of the directors' fiduciary duties. See *Schnell* and *Blasius* (see §8.2.2). Courts have found "compelling justifications" for board interference with the voting process only when the board was in the process of selling the corporation and the board concluded the shareholders needed more information. *Mercier v. Inter-Tel (Delaware), Inc.*, 929 A.2d 786 (Del. Ch. 2007) (board delayed a merger vote by 25 days to provide more information to shareholders).

b. Probably valid. Conestoga could argue that the ESOP is an entrenching device that dilutes the voting power of existing shareholders and makes the insurgency more difficult. In a similar case, a Delaware court assumed that employees as voters in an ESOP are likely to side with current management in any control contest, since faced with the choice of their jobs or a better return on their ESOP investment they would opt for job security. *Shamrock Holdings v. Polaroid*, 559 A.2d 257 (Del. Ch. 1989) (unsolicited insurgent with plans to sell company "will inevitably raise concerns about job security"). The ESOP issuance thus had an entrenching effect.

   Nonetheless, the ESOP's entrenching effect does not resolve the matter. The standard of review is determinative. In *Polaroid*, the court reviewed an ESOP issuance under a lower *Unocal*-proportionality standard (see §39.2.3) on the theory the ESOP responded to a pending hostile tender offer that was later withdrawn to be replaced by a proxy solicitation. The *Polaroid* court, finding the ESOP would increase employee morale and firm productivity, upheld the defense as proportional to the hostile tender offer. But another case held that an ESOP created during a pending two-step proxy contest/tender offer constituted a breach of the incumbent board's fiduciary duties under the heightened *Schnell-Blasius* standards. *AT&T v. NCR Corp.*, 761 F. Supp. 475 (S.D. Ohio 1991). Generally, ESOPs and other stock issuances that affect the allocation of voting power receive deferential business judgment review if the transaction is planned and implemented outside the context of a pending voting contest.

   In our example, the ESOP was already under consideration and not exclusively a defensive response. This strongly suggests that a court would use less scrutiny. The ESOP would easily pass muster as a business decision to increase employee productivity and loyalty. That it also realigned shareholder voting power would not be determinative.

c. Probably invalid. The debentures penalize shareholders for exercising their voting rights, apparently in the name of corporate stability. If incumbent directors (or their chosen successors) are maintained in office for five years, shareholders receive a significant cash dividend. If any are replaced, shareholders receive a much smaller dividend. Although any unpaid dividends would remain in the corporate treasury, retention by management of free cash flow generally hurts share prices. Shareholders will be leery of replacing management and jeopardizing share value.

   Courts have applied searching scrutiny of actions that dilute shareholder voting rights during a voting contest without commensurate business justifications. Although courts have accepted stock issuances that dilute shareholder power, the issuances have passed scrutiny when justified as legitimate corporate financing. Courts have also accepted temporary entrenchment measures designed to give incumbents time to accomplish a pending merger. When the board's business justifications are more tenuous, such as claims of amorphous corporate stability, entrenching action receives searching scrutiny. For example, a "dead hand" poison pill that provided for redemption only by incumbent directors or their chosen successors was invalidated for effectively precluding shareholders from voting for directors with full management power, including to approve a tender offer in a two-step takeover. See *Carmody v. Toll Brothers, Inc.* (Del. Ch. 1998) (see §8.2.3). In our case, the debenture issuance has little to recommend it. It came during a pending voting contest, it was not approved by shareholders, and it lacked substantial justification. Under the "corporate democracy" philosophy of *Schnell-Blasius*, the issuance violates the board's fiduciary duties.

3. a. No. An insurgent has no right to reimbursement unless the board authorizes it. As a practical matter, Conestoga can hope to be reimbursed only if it wins control of the board and the shareholders ratify the payment of the insurgent's voting-related expenses. See *Grodetsky v. McCrory Corp.*, 267 N.Y.S.2d 356 (Sup. Ct. 1966) (refusing to award reimbursement of dissident shareholder's election-related expenses even though dissident had successfully led voting campaign against wasteful corporate transaction). Although the proxy fight was over a policy issue—whether the company should be sold—reimbursement is not a matter of right. The matter lies in the discretion of the *incumbent* board. Otherwise, unsuccessful insurgents could claim reimbursement from the corporate treasury despite the shareholder majority's rejection of their position and failure to achieve board control.

   b. Perhaps. Management's false ads breached a duty of honesty owed shareholders during the voting contest. See §10.3. Like other manipulations of the voting process, management's *material* deceptions constitute a breach of fiduciary duties. Deceived shareholders could sue directly or derivatively, and an appropriate remedy for the manipulation might be to compel management to bear the costs of its false campaign.

   Is the composition of GASP's membership "material"? State courts have borrowed the formulaic test of materiality from federal proxy antifraud case law: whether it is substantially likely that a reasonable shareholder would consider the information important in deciding how to vote. See *TSC Industries, Inc. v. Northway, Inc.*, 426 U.S. 438 (1976) (§10.2.2). Arguably, reasonable shareholders would be less willing to support GASP if there were some indication of an international plot to plunder the company. On the other hand, reasonable shareholders might not care about GASP's makeup, instead focusing on the merits of GASP's desire to sell the company. Nonetheless, that Gillick management apparently believed shareholders would find GASP's composition relevant to their voting decision would seem to make it material.

In addition, the federal proxy rules prohibit any solicitation that is materially false or misleading. See §10.2.2. GASP and other Conestoga shareholders have a private cause of action. Although a new election would seem a logical corrective award, federal courts have broad discretion in formulating relief.

c. Perhaps not. Reimbursement of a successful insurgent's voting-related expenses is a conflict-of-interest transaction. The new directors have a self-interest in reimbursing themselves. For this reason, courts have required that reimbursement be ratified by a shareholder majority. *Rosenfeld* (see §8.1.2). Notice that this approach is more restrictive than that applicable in a derivative suit, where courts regularly authorize corporate payment of successful shareholder-plaintiffs' litigation-related expenses. See §18.1.2. Nonetheless, the reimbursement rule reflects the general judicial approach to corporate voting: shareholder sovereignty is paramount.

4. a. No. Victory in a proxy fight can be fleeting. Unless the insurgent places a majority on the board, the directors are under no obligation to institute the insurgent's "platform." Without winning a board majority, the most the insurgent can hope for is that the directors will exercise their business judgment to adopt the insurgent's agenda and that the increase in share value will justify the effort for the insurgent.

For this reason, insurgents rarely seek less than majority representation on the board. Further, to provide shareholders a tangible reason to vote for the insurgent, insurgents will often propose a recapitalization plan or tender offer that promises an immediate increase in share value. Although proxy fights in the 1960s and 1970s were often waged by former managers seeking to regain their positions, recent insurgents rarely wage proxy fights to gain merely a long-term management position.

b. Probably not. The poison pill plan dilutes the power of shareholders to elect a board fully empowered to undertake corporate reforms. Delaware courts have invalidated similar plans on the ground that they interfere with shareholder democracy and are not authorized by corporate statute. See Del. GCL §141(d) (permitting directors with greater voting powers, only if approved by shareholders). Board-created limits on the powers of directors—namely, successor directors who cannot redeem a poison pill—is inconsistent with directors' fiduciary duties and board powers. *Quickturn Design Systems, Inc. v. Shapiro* (see §8.2.3).

c. Probably not. The NYSE listing standards (see §7.2.5) adopt a flexible policy toward high-voting shares and recognize "the circumstances and needs of listed companies." The listing rules specifically permit issuances of high-voting shares issued in an initial public offering. But the NYSE policy states that existing public shareholders cannot have their voting rights "disparately reduced or restricted," including by the issuance of super-voting stock. NYSE Listed Company Manual §313.00(A).

   Thus, Gillick would have had to adopt this dual-class voting structure before it sold shares publicly, as Google did when it went public in 2004. Google's capital structure consists of two classes of shares. Class B shares have ten votes per share, and Class A shares have one vote per share. When Class B shares are sold, with few exceptions including transfers between the founders, they convert automatically to lower-voting Class A shares. In its 2004 IPO, Google sold only lower-voting Class A shares to the public. As Class B shareholders continue to sell, the Google founders' voting power only increases!

Federal Regulation of Proxy Voting

As we have seen, shareholders in public corporations vote primarily by proxy. But proxy voting creates opportunities for management abuse. If management obtains open-ended proxies from shareholders, management gets a "rubber stamp." If management does not inform shareholders how their proxies will be voted, management escapes accountability. And if management prevents shareholders from seeking proxies for their own initiatives, management's control becomes virtually airtight.

State law authorizes proxy voting, but does not significantly regulate its potential for abuse. See MBCA §7.22 (requiring writing and limiting duration to 11 months unless otherwise specified); cf. Del. GCL §212(b) (three years). To protect shareholders from management overreaching—common before federal regulation—federal rules promulgated under the Securities Exchange Act of 1934 ("Exchange Act") regulate proxy voting in public corporations.

This chapter describes federal proxy regulation of the content and process of proxy voting. It describes the nature and source of federal proxy regulation (§9.1), the scope of the federal proxy rules (§9.2), their formal requirements (§9.3), and the rules permitting shareholder-initiated proposals (§9.4). Chapter 10 describes the state and federal regimes that govern proxy fraud.

Note on Terminology

A "proxy" is the agency relationship where a shareholder grants the authority to vote her shares to another person, the "proxy holder." Sometimes the word "proxy" is used

(continued)

(ambiguously) to describe the signed writing by which this agency is created or the document that describes the powers of the proxy holder. But, for clarity's sake, the SEC rules refer to the writing as the "proxy card" and the disclosure document as the "proxy statement."

§9.1 FEDERAL PROXY REGULATION — AN OVERVIEW

Federal proxy regulation promotes fair corporate suffrage with a multi-pronged attack against proxy abuse:

- **SEC-mandated disclosure.** Rules of the Securities and Exchange Commission (SEC) require that anyone (including the board of directors) soliciting proxies from public shareholders must file with the SEC and distribute to shareholders specified information in a stylized "proxy statement."
- **No open-ended proxies.** The SEC proxy rules, beyond disclosure, prescribe the form of the proxy card and the scope of the proxy holder's power.
- **Shareholder access.** The SEC proxy rules equalize access to the proxy process in public companies by requiring management (1) to mail shareholders' material and bill for the cost or to provide a shareholder list and (2) to include "proper" shareholder proposals with company-paid proxy materials, subject to a number of conditions.
- **Private remedies.** Federal courts have inferred a private cause of action for shareholders to seek relief for violations of the SEC proxy rules, particularly the rule prohibiting false or misleading proxy solicitations.

Congress did not directly regulate shareholder voting. Instead, it delegated the task to the SEC, whose proxy rules derive from §14(a) of the Exchange Act:

> It shall be unlawful for any person, by use of the mails or by any means or instrumentality of interstate commerce or of any facility of a national securities exchange *or otherwise,* in contravention of such rules and regulations as the Commission may prescribe as necessary or appropriate in the public interest or for the protection of investors, to solicit or to permit the use of his name to solicit any proxy or consent or authorization in respect of any security (other than an exempted security) registered pursuant to section 12 of this title. (emphasis added)

Let's parse. First, the jurisdictional reach of §14(a) is effectively unlimited — the "or otherwise" language means Congress has gone as far as the Constitution permits. Second, §14(a)'s prohibition applies to proxy solicitations involving securities registered under §12 of the Exchange Act—this means publicly traded corporations (see §9.2.1 below). Third, the prohibition applies to "proxy solicitations"—a broad concept (see §9.2.2 below). Fourth, the proxy solicitation must comply with SEC rules on filing, disclosure, and distribution of proxy materials (see §9.2.3 below).

§9.2 REACH OF THE SEC PROXY RULES

§9.2.1 Public Corporations—Registration under the Exchange Act

The SEC proxy rules apply to companies whose securities are registered under §12 of the Exchange Act. Registration also compels the company to file periodic reports of business and financial information with the SEC. See §21.2. (Registration under the Exchange Act, which allows a company's securities to be publicly traded, is different from registration under the Securities Act of 1933, which allows securities to be sold to public investors.)

Registered (or *reporting*) companies fall into two categories:

- **Listed companies.** Companies whose securities (debt or equity) are listed on a national stock exchange. Exchange Act §12(a). Listing is voluntary. The New York Stock Exchange, for example, permits listing of companies with at least 2,200 U.S. shareholders and pretax earnings of at least $10 million for the past three years.
- **OTC companies.** Companies whose securities (equity) are traded on the over-the-counter (OTC, see §19.2) markets—specifically, any company with more than $10 million in assets *and* at least 500 equity shareholders of record at year's end. Exchange Act §12(g); SEC Rule 12g-1 (asset threshold increased to $10 million in 1996). Once *both* the asset and shareholder thresholds are surpassed, the company must register with the SEC within 120 days.

Once registered, a company may deregister only under specified circumstances. A company registered because its securities are listed on a stock exchange is no longer subject to the registration requirements once its securities are delisted. Exchange Act §12(d). Deregistration of an OTC company is more difficult. Deregistration is possible only when: (1) there are fewer than 300 shareholders of record; or (2) there are fewer than 500 shareholders of record and the company's total assets have not exceeded $10 million for its last three fiscal years. Rule 12g-4. The SEC takes the view that once an OTC company is registered, thus triggering the full range of federal protections for its shareholders, deregistration should not come easily.

§9.2.2 Definition of Proxy Solicitation

The federal proxy rules apply only to *proxy solicitations*. Although you might imagine a proxy solicitation refers to the formal document that accompanies management's request for shareholders to return a proxy card, the proxy rules are much broader. SEC Rule 14a-1(l) defines a "solicitation" to include: (1) *the obvious*—the informational document accompanying the proxy card; (2) *request to sign*—any request for a proxy even if a proxy card does not accompany it; (3) *request not to sign*—any request to not sign or to revoke a proxy; and (4) *the sly*—any other communication "under circumstances reasonably calculated to result in" shareholders signing, not signing, or revoking a proxy. The SEC also defines "proxy" broadly to include any action that gives or withholds authority concerning issues on which shareholders may decide—for example, when shareholders give written consents to an action taken without a shareholders' meeting (see §7.2.6). Rule 14a-1(f).

Federal courts construed these definitions liberally, leading to protests that the SEC was overregulating communications among shareholders. In 1992, the SEC responded to this criticism and amended its proxy rules to exempt a variety of shareholder communications from its filing and distribution requirements. We consider how the amended rules affect some leading cases.

Part of Solicitation Plan

In *Studebaker Corp. v. Gittlin*, 360 F.2d 692 (2d Cir. 1966), the court held that a proxy solicitation includes any communication to shareholders that asks for action that is *part of a "continuous plan" leading to the formal solicitation of proxies*—a broad notion, indeed. In the case, a shareholder who planned a proxy contest to elect a new board sought the company's shareholders' list under a state law that gave inspection rights only to shareholders holding at least 5 percent of the company's shares. When the dissident shareholder obtained authorizations to inspect the list from 42 other shareholders whose holdings totaled more than 5 percent, management sued to block the inspection on the theory the dissident's request for authorizations constituted an illegal proxy solicitation. The court agreed, pointing out that the definition of proxy includes "authorizations" and the dissident group's effort to obtain authorizations for an inspection was part of a "continuous plan" intended to end in a formal proxy solicitation. To ensure that shareholders are informed even in the preliminary stages of a voting contest, the court required the dissident group to start again with a proper proxy filing, distributed to all solicited shareholders.

The 1992 amendments to the SEC proxy rules explicitly reject the implications of this broad notion of solicitation when nonmanagement shareholders communicate with other shareholders. The shareholder communication rules permit shareholders to communicate so long as they do not seek to act as a proxy and do not furnish or ask for a proxy card. Rule 14a-2(b). Otherwise, such communications are not subject to the filing, disclosure, and distribution requirements of the proxy rules. The exemption, however, does not apply to communications by management, director nominees, or those already in a proxy fight with management. And exempt communications remain subject to Rule 14a-9, the rule that prohibits proxy fraud, if they qualify as a "solicitation" under the "continuous plan" test.

Under the current proxy rules, even though the dissident group in *Studebaker* would not be subject to the filing, disclosure, and distribution requirements—because the gathering of authorizations did not involve seeking proxies—the group might nonetheless be forced to disclose their intentions. The SEC rules applicable to control transactions require the filing of an SEC disclosure document (Schedule 13D) by any 5 percent group of shareholders who intend to act together to vote their shares. See Rule 13d-5(b) (see §38.1).

Public Criticism of Management

In *Long Island Lighting Co. v. Barbash*, 779 F.2d 793 (2d Cir. 1985), the court applied a "chain of communications" theory to hold that a newspaper ad could be a proxy solicitation if motivated to advance a pending shareholder insurgency. In the case, a public interest group had paid for a newspaper ad urging that LILCO be sold to a public power authority and accusing LILCO of mismanagement in raising rates to build an unnecessary nuclear power plant. Without mentioning him, the ad tended to support the position of a local political candidate (and LILCO shareholder) who had succeeded in having a special shareholders' meeting called to consider a sale of the company. The court held that a fact finder could conclude that the ad was "reasonably calculated" to influence shareholders' votes and was thus a "solicitation" under the proxy rules even though it did not mention proxies and purportedly addressed matters of "public interest" in a general publication.

To some, this result borders on a violation of First Amendment free speech rights. Read literally, the court's holding could turn every expression of opinion about a public corporation into a regulated proxy solicitation. If so, any person stating an opinion would be required to prepare a proxy statement and mail it to every shareholder being "solicited"—if a public opinion, this would mean all shareholders.

The current SEC rules, as amended in 1992, would exempt this kind of communication if the speaker neither seeks authority to act as a proxy nor requests a proxy card. See Rule 14a-2(b). Thus, a public interest group commenting on a shareholder vote—provided the group is not aligned with management or acting on behalf of a director nominee or someone seeking control—is under no filing, disclosure, or distribution obligations. The "solicitation," however, remains subject to the SEC proxy fraud rule. In addition, the amended rules go one step further to exclude from the definition of "solicitation" (and thus from the proxy fraud rule) a public announcement by an unaffiliated shareholder on how she intends to vote and her reasons. Rule 14a-1(l)(2).

§9.2.3 Mandatory Disclosure When Proxies Not Solicited

In some circumstances, as when a majority of a public corporation's shares are held by a parent company, it may be unnecessary to solicit proxies from minority shareholders. Nonetheless, the proxy rules require the company to file with the SEC and send shareholders, at least 20 days before the meeting, information similar to that required for a proxy solicitation. Exchange Act §14(c); Reg. 14C and Schedule 14C.

§9.3 FORMAL REQUIREMENTS OF SEC PROXY RULES

To enable shareholders to make an informed voting decision, the proxy rules

- specify the disclosure that must accompany (or precede) every proxy solicitation
- specify the form of the proxy card
- require the preliminary filing of the proxy statement and proxy cards for SEC staff review
- prohibit false or misleading proxy solicitations

§9.3.1 Mandatory Disclosure in Proxy Statement

Any time a shareholder's proxy is solicited, a "proxy statement" must accompany or precede every solicitation. Rule 14a-3(a). The proxy statement must contain information specified in Schedule 14A—a set of itemized instructions specifying the disclosures required in the proxy statement. The disclosure required depends on who is soliciting the proxy.

- **Management solicitation.** If management (or technically, the board of directors) solicits proxies, Schedule 14A requires information about the corporation, the background of all director nominees, the compensation of the company's CEO and four highest-paid employees and their stock holdings, and any other matters being voted on. It must also include a report by the board's compensation committee. If the solicitation is for the annual election of directors, management also must send to shareholders the corporation's annual report. Rule 14a-3(b). For many companies, this is the only requirement (state or federal) of periodic corporate communications to shareholders. Cf. MBCA §16.20 (requiring that shareholders be provided annual financial statements).
- **Nonmanagement solicitation.** If the solicitation is by someone other than management, such as a dissident shareholder or outside insurgent group, Schedule 14A requires that they tell about themselves, the background of their nominees, and any other matters on which they seek a proxy.

§9.3.2 Form of Proxy Card

So that shareholders do not give management (or anyone else) a carte blanche, the federal proxy rules specify the form of the proxy card. Rule 14a-4. The proxy card must state who is soliciting it and the matters to be acted on, and must leave a space for it to be dated. For the election of directors, the card must allow a shareholder to withhold a vote on directors as a group or individually. A nominee cannot be elected if he is not named in the proxy card. Rule 14a-4(d)(1). For other matters, shareholders must have a chance to vote for or against each matter to be acted on. A shareholder can give her proxy holder discretionary voting power if the proxy card states in **boldface** type how the proxy holder intends to vote. The proxy holder must then vote in accordance with the instructions.

Management can retain the authority to vote in its discretion on matters that it does not know, before the solicitation, are to be presented at the meeting. See Rule 14c-4(c)(1). Thus, the proxy statement need only mention those proposals that are reasonably likely to be submitted. Once a shareholder undertakes an independent solicitation for a proposal, however, the company must send shareholders a supplemental statement explaining clearly how it will exercise its discretionary authority, subject to contrary instructions from shareholders. *Union of Needletrades, Industrial and Textile Employees v. May Department Stores Co.*, 1997 WL 714886 (S.D.N.Y).

§9.3.3 Filing and Distribution of Proxy Statement

If proxies are solicited, each shareholder must be sent a copy of the proxy statement. Since 2007, this can be accomplished by sending shareholders a notice that the proxy statement (and other materials) is posted online for them to read and download. Exchange Act Rel. No. 55,146 (2007) (permitting shareholders to always request printed materials). The SEC has also specified the procedures for companies to allow their shareholders to vote their proxies online, something that has saved companies more than $140 million annually in printing and mailing expenses. Exchange Act Rel. No. 61,560 (2010).

Any person soliciting proxies must file *preliminary* copies of the proxy statement and the proxy card with the SEC at least ten days before they are sent to shareholders. Rule 14a-6. The SEC staff reviews and comments on these preliminary materials, giving filers a chance to make changes that conform to the staff's views on disclosure adequacy. Management need not make a preliminary filing if the solicitation is routine and relates to nothing more than the election of directors, selection of auditors, or shareholder proposals at an annual meeting.

All *final* proxy materials, whether or not filed preliminarily, must be filed with the SEC at or before the time they are sent to shareholders. (Like other SEC filings, proxy statements are available through EDGAR on the SEC's website *www.sec.gov.*)

Shareholders whose solicitations are exempt from the distribution and disclosure requirements because they do not seek proxy authority and do not have a substantial interest in the matter must nonetheless file a notice with the SEC that attaches all of their written soliciting materials. Such notice is required only of shareholders who own more than $5 million of the company's shares and is not required for oral solicitations, public speeches, press releases, or published or broadcast opinions. Rule 14a-6(g).

§9.3.4 Prohibition against Proxy Fraud

At the heart of the proxy rules is the prohibition against any solicitation (written or oral) that is false or misleading with respect to any material fact or that omits a material fact necessary to make statements in the solicitation not false or misleading. Rule 14a-9. Supplying the information specified in Schedule 14A is not enough. The proxy statement must also fully disclose all material information about the matters on which the shareholders are to vote.

Rule 14a-9 does not specifically authorize shareholders to sue for false or misleading proxy solicitations. Yet federal courts have inferred a private cause of action, which we discuss in Chapter 10.

§9.3.5 Exemptions from Proxy Rules

The proxy rules exempt some "proxy solicitations" from the filing, disclosure, and distribution requirements. Some exempt solicitations remain subject to Rule 14a-9, the proxy fraud rule:

- solicitations by persons not seeking proxy authority and without a substantial interest in the matter, Rule 14a-2(b)(1)
- nonmanagement solicitations to less than ten persons, Rule 14a-2(b)(2)
- advice by financial advisors in the ordinary course of their business, provided they disclose any interest in the proxy contest and receive no special fees from others for giving the advice, Rule 14a-2(b)(2)

Other solicitations are completely exempt from the proxy rules, including the proxy fraud provisions:

- communications by brokers to beneficial owners seeking instructions on how to vote the owners' shares, Rule 14a-2(a)(1)
- requests by beneficial owners to obtain proxy cards and other information from brokers that hold their shares, Rule 14a-2(a)(2)
- newspaper advertisements that identify the proposal and tell shareholders how to obtain proxy documents, Rule 14a-2(a)(6)

Examples

EXAMPLES

1. Video Palace, Inc. (VPI), owns and operates a video rental chain. VPI's management has solicited proxies for its slate of directors at the next annual shareholders' meeting. An insurgent, Garth, solicits proxies for his alternate slate of directors.
   a. Wayne, a VPI shareholder, first returns management's proxy card but then changes his mind and sends Garth's card. Who has Wayne's proxy?
   b. VPI management gives notice of the annual meeting but does not disclose that company earnings fell 60 percent last year. Is this information required under state law?
   c. The VPI board plans to issue already authorized stock to Jessica. The issue would bring her holdings to 35 percent, and VPI management would own 20 percent. Must VPI solicit proxies at the upcoming meeting?
2. The board does not issue shares to Jessica, and Garth's insurgency fails. As next year's annual meeting approaches, VPI management begins to plan its proxy solicitation. Consider whether VPI is subject to Exchange Act registration.

a. At the end of its last fiscal year, VPI had assets of $11 million and 650 shareholders of record. The shareholders acquired their shares in a public offering exempt from registration under §3(a)(11) of the Securities Act of 1933—the intrastate offering exemption.
b. At the end of its last fiscal year, VPI had assets of $11 million and 400 shareholders of record, though 650 beneficial owners of its shares. Also, last year VPI made a public offering of debt securities registered under the Securities Act.

3. VPI registers under the Exchange Act. Two years later, VPI struggles financially, and its assets fall below $8 million.
   a. VPI management does not want to bother with periodic disclosure and the SEC proxy rules. The company has 700 shareholders of record. Can it terminate its Exchange Act registration?
   b. VPI repurchases some of its stock, reducing the number of record shareholders to 450. Can VPI terminate its Exchange Act registration?
   c. VPI repurchases more stock, reducing the number of record shareholders to 100. Can VPI terminate its Exchange Act registration and avoid registration indefinitely?
   d. A few years after going private, VPI makes a large public offering. The company specifies that new stock must be held in street name with a specified list of qualified nominees. This keeps the number of record shareholders below 500. Can VPI avoid Exchange registration in this way?

4. The FBI is investigating several VPI directors and executives for conspiring to distribute "pirate" videos through local VPI outlets.
   a. Garth sends letters to 15 other shareholders suggesting they begin a derivative suit challenging the directors' actions as a breach of fiduciary duty. Are these letters a proxy solicitation?
   b. Garth appears on a financial talk show and says the directors should step down while the FBI concludes its investigation. Garth mentions he is thinking of running his own slate of directors at the next annual meeting. Are these statements proxy solicitations?
   c. Garth sends letters to 15 large VPI shareholders and suggests they discuss a special shareholders' meeting to remove the offending directors "for cause." Garth has enough shares under state law to call the meeting himself but will need the votes of the other shareholders in any proxy fight. Are these letters a proxy solicitation?

5. When VPI's management learns of Garth's activities, the company takes out newspaper ads claiming that "VPI only rents properly licensed videos" and suggests that "competitors jealous of VPI's success" have planted false accusations. The ads do not mention Garth or possible shareholder action.
   a. Are the ads proxy solicitations?

b. The ads are true. Can Garth seek to enjoin them?
c. Before placing the ads, the company had already distributed copies of its proxy statement to all shareholders. Do the ads violate the proxy rules?
d. After filing and distributing its proxy statement, management sends letters to its shareholders stating that Garth's accusations are false and Garth is "trying to tear down the company." Do these letters violate the proxy rules?

Explanations

1. a. Garth does. If the writing naming Garth bears a later date, the later-signed appointment revokes the earlier proxy. See §7.2.4. The election inspector will accept Garth's authority if the writing by Wayne on its face revokes his prior proxy to management. The only issue under state law would be whether Wayne granted management an irrevocable proxy "coupled with an interest." This is unlikely unless his proxy related to a pledge, purchase, loan, employment, or voting agreement. See MBCA §7.22; Del. GCL §212(e) ("interest in stock" or "interest in corporation generally").

   b. Generally, no. Most state statutes do not require more than notice of an annual meeting's location, time, and date. See MBCA §7.05; Del. GCL §222. If VPI is a public corporation, the "complete candor" duty of *Vickers v. Lynch* (see §10.3) may require management to disclose material adverse information with its notice and proxy statement.

   c. No proxy solicitation is necessary. Whether directors are elected by majority or plurality voting, management's slate will be elected if Jessica and management combined their votes.

   If VPI is a public corporation, even when proxies are not solicited, the federal proxy rules require management to file an information statement with the SEC and to distribute it to shareholders entitled to vote. Reg. 14C. This gives shareholders notice of any state rights they may have to challenge the election.

2. a. VPI must register under the Exchange Act and is subject to the proxy rules. VPI meets the conjunctive test of §12(g) of the Exchange Act: at year-end its assets exceeded $10 million, and it had at least 500 shareholders of record.

   The Securities Act exemption is irrelevant to the question of registration under the Exchange Act. The Exchange Act mandates periodic disclosure about reporting companies to facilitate trading in the stock of publicly traded companies; the Securities Act seeks to provide public investors information when they invest in a company's securities offerings.

b. VPI is not subject to the proxy rules. A company is subject to the proxy rules only if its securities are registered under §12 of the Exchange Act. Unless VPI's securities (debt or equity) are listed on a stock exchange, it is not subject to §12 registration because it has less than 500 *record* shareholders at year's end. Exchange Act §12(g). Beneficial shareholders are not counted for these purposes. This provides a readily determinable test for deciding whether registration is required.

Although VPI's public offering of debt securities makes it subject to the reporting requirements of the Exchange Act under §15(d) of the Exchange Act, it is not subject to the proxy rules except by registering under §12. Not all reporting companies are subject to the proxy rules.

3. a. No. Although the value of VPI's assets has fallen below the $10 million threshold for initial registration, SEC rules do not permit termination of registration if the number of shareholders of record exceeds 500, regardless of asset value. Rule 12g-4. The SEC takes the view that public shareholders come to rely on periodic disclosure and SEC proxy regulation, and its rules make "deregistration" difficult.

b. Perhaps. It depends on how long VPI's assets have remained below the $10 million mark. If the number of record shareholders remains below 500 (though above 300), SEC rules permit termination of registration only if year-end assets have not exceeded $10 million for the last three fiscal years.

c. Yes. If VPI goes private—whether by stock repurchase, engaging in an issuer self-tender, or structuring a squeeze-out merger—it can deregister. Once deregistered, the company is no longer subject to the periodic disclosure and proxy rules of federal securities law.

d. No. Under the literal terms of §12(g), it would seem an OTC company could avoid Exchange Act registration by using street-name registration to keep the number of record shareholders below 500. This ruse circumvents the purposes of the Exchange Act. Periodic disclosure and fair proxy voting are as important to beneficial owners as record shareholders. The SEC rules define record shareholders to include beneficial owners if the company has reason to know that the form in which securities are held is "used primarily to circumvent" the registration provisions of the Exchange Act. Rule 12g5-1(b)(3).

4. a. Probably not. It is difficult to characterize the letters as being part of a "continuous plan" leading to the formal solicitation of proxies. See *Studebaker Corp. v. Gittlin* (§9.2.2). A derivative suit, brought by a shareholder on behalf of the corporation to vindicate a corporate right, will not necessarily lead to a proxy contest.

Unless Garth's motives are to use the suit as part of a strategy leading to a proxy solicitation—for example, because the suit will provide free and damaging publicity about the directors—it is unlikely the letters will be deemed proxy solicitations. To do so would significantly hamper shareholder oversight of management abuse, undercutting the very purpose of the federal proxy rules.

b. Yes, but they are probably exempt solicitations. Garth's comments seem to be part of a plan leading to a proxy solicitation, and the proxy rules define them to be a proxy solicitation.

   Nonetheless, the 1992 amendments to the proxy rules exempt solicitations by those who do not seek power to act as a proxy *and* do not furnish or ask for a proxy card. Rule 14a-2(b). At this point, Garth is just testing the waters for an insurgency and is not asking for proxies. This exemption would not apply, however, if Garth is already a board candidate (or is paid by someone who is a candidate) or is a 5 percent shareholder who has declared a control intention.

c. Yes, but they may be exempt. Garth's letters to his 15 fellow shareholders seem to be part of a "continuous plan" leading to the formal solicitation of proxies, fitting the judicial definition of "proxy solicitation." These early communications, without an accompanying proxy statement, may "poison the well" and lead shareholders to join Garth's cause without full information. On the other hand, regulating preliminary steps to organize a proxy fight may discourage shareholders such as Garth from taking the first steps in exercising their control rights. Some courts have refused to treat preliminary organizational contacts as falling within the proxy rules. See *Calumet Industries, Inc. v. MacClure*, 464 F. Supp. 19 (N.D. Ill. 1978) (discussions among shareholders to organize a proxy fight not a "solicitation" because of the impracticality of preparing a preorganization proxy statement).

   Even if the letters are technically "proxy solicitations," the exemption for nonmanagement shareholder communications would apply unless Garth is "seeking the power to act as a proxy." See Rule 14a-2(b). If Garth is asking for shareholder "authorizations" to call a special meeting, the letters might constitute a nonexempt solicitation. But if he is simply asking for preliminary showings of interest—because he already holds enough shares to call the meeting himself—the letters are at most exempt solicitations. (Notice the exemption for communications to no more than ten shareholders does not apply.)

5. a. Probably, yes. Under a "chain of communications" theory, the ads seem "reasonably calculated" to influence shareholder voting on the removal of the accused directors. The decision to place the ads seems to have been related to Garth's threatened insurgency. No exemptions apply to these management communications.

   Nonetheless, a court might conclude the ads were primarily meant to answer pirating rumors that might have hurt business and to protect the reputations of the directors rather than to influence shareholder voting. After all, no shareholders' meeting involving the charges has yet been called. In the end, management's motives behind the ads are determinative. See *Long Island Lighting Co. v. Barbash* (§9.2.2).

b. Yes, if they are proxy solicitations. If management did not file a proxy statement and disseminate the statement to shareholders before placing the ads, they can be enjoined for failing to comply with the rule's filing and disclosure requirements. It makes no difference that the ads are absolutely truthful and well-meaning. As we will see, they can be enjoined either by the SEC or by a shareholder in a private action. See §10.1.
c. No, unless the ads were materially false or misleading. The proxy rules do not prohibit communications that affect shareholder voting, but mandate only that such communications be made after filing and distributing a proxy statement. This gets the essential information on the table.
d. Perhaps. The personal attack on Garth may violate Rule 14a-9's prohibition of false or misleading proxy solicitations. To prevent heated and not terribly informative shouting matches, the SEC treats as misleading under the rule "material which . . . impugns character, integrity or personal reputation."

§9.4 SHAREHOLDER INITIATIVES

In a public corporation, where shareholder voting happens by proxy, shareholder initiatives face large obstacles. Shareholders who identify value-producing ideas generally are unwilling or unable to commit the financial resources for mass mailings to other shareholders—their relatively small investment rarely justifies it. Even when they do, shareholders must overcome management's domination of the corporate-funded proxy mechanism.

The SEC proxy rules attempt to overcome these impediments in two ways. First, management can be compelled to help a shareholder communicate with fellow shareholders—but at the shareholder's expense. Second, in limited circumstances, management must include "proper" shareholder proposals in the company's proxy mailings to shareholders—at corporate expense.

§9.4.1 "Common Carrier" Obligation under Rule 14a-7

The federal proxy rules aid shareholders willing to pay for soliciting other shareholders. Rule 14a-7 requires management to mail, either separately or together with the corporation's proxy materials, any shareholder's soliciting materials if the shareholder agrees to pay the corporation's reasonable expenses. There is no limit on the length of the materials, nor does the SEC rule allow management to refuse if it objects to their contents.

Management can avoid this "common carrier" obligation by providing a list of shareholders, including intermediaries. This significantly expands the shareholder's rights under state law to obtain a list of shareholders for a "proper purpose" (see §7.1.4). As a practical matter, however, management is often reluctant to provide the shareholders' list because it can be used for personal solicitations or beyond a shareholder proxy solicitation—such as in a takeover contest.

§9.4.2 Shareholder Proposals under Rule 14a-8

The SEC shareholder proposal rule seeks to promote shareholder democracy by allowing shareholders to propose their own resolutions using the company-financed proxy machinery.

The shareholder proposal rule has gone through three stages. During its early history in the 1940s and 1950s, proponents used the rule to seek changes in corporate governance—proposing such things as mergers and more liberal dividend policies. In the 1970s and 1980s, many proponents used the rule to focus public attention on corporate social responsibility—proposing such actions as divestment from South Africa, environmental protection, and increases to (or reductions of) affirmative action plans. Since the mid-1980s, with the advent of institutional shareholder activism, many proponents have again focused on governance issues—proposing such things as greater board answerability, increased shareholder voting powers, and elimination of anti-takeover devices. At the same time, social policy issues (such as environmental matters) continue to be the subject of many proposals. Today approximately 300 to 400 public companies receive a total of about 900 shareholder proposals each year.

During the rule's first 40 years, shareholder proposals were uniformly unsuccessful. Of the thousands submitted for shareholder vote before 1985, only two were approved. Since 1985, however, proposals on governance issues have fared markedly better, regularly obtaining majority approval and increasingly leading management to make changes. Remarkably, labor unions have emerged as the most aggressive of all shareholder proponents, making proposals aimed at maximizing investment returns through such reforms as declassification of boards, caps on executive pay, and shareholder access to the nomination process.

The following tables illustrate the changing nature of the rule during three representative periods. The first table shows the kinds of proposals excluded by management, which the rule requires be submitted for SEC review. The second table shows the kinds of proposals that the SEC upon review found to be includable under its always-changing interpretation of Rule 14a-8.

Proposals Excluded by Management

*Type of Proposal**	*1981–1982*	*1991–1992*	*2001–2002*
Governance	26.5%	35.4%	47.3%
Operational	44.6%	30.2%	33.1%
Social/political	28.9%	34.4%	19.6%
Total	100.0%	100.0%	100.0%

Proposals Found Includable by SEC

*Type of Proposal**	*1981–1982*	*1991–1992*	*2001–2002*
Governance	18.2%	41.2%	55.7%
Operational	18.9%	3.4%	49.0%
Social/political	37.5%	18.2%	41.4%
Total	24.1%	21.9%	48.7%

*Categories:

Governance proposals: structure and composition of board, poison pills, shareholder voting
Operational: executive compensation, production/business matters, company communications
Social/political: environmental, political, consumer, labor

Notice that "governance" proposals over time have become more frequent and been treated more favorably by the SEC. Notice also that "social/political" proposals (though never the mainstay of shareholder proposal activity) have become less frequent, and the SEC has come to favor them less than the other types of proposals. (By the way, the reason for the very low inclusion rate for "operational" proposals in 1991–1992 is that the SEC then viewed any proposal dealing with executive compensation to be excludable; in the late 1990s the agency changed its view.)

Current SEC Rule

In 1998 the SEC responded to a congressional call to reappraise the shareholder proposal process. Exchange Act Rel. No. 40,018 (1998). While leaving the rule's structure largely intact, the SEC adopted some important policy changes and redrafted (and renumbered) the rule using a "Plain English" question-and-answer format. The revamped SEC rule begins as follows:

> Question 1: What is a proposal? A shareholder proposal is your recommendation or requirement that the company and/or its board of directors take action, which you intend to present at a meeting of the company's shareholders. Your proposal should state as clearly as possible the course of action that you believe the company should follow. [Rule 14a-8(a)].

Rule 14a-8 Procedures

Any shareholder who has owned (beneficially or of record) 1 percent or $2,000 worth of a public company's shares for at least one year may submit a proposal. Rule 14a-8(b)(1) (Question 2; dollar amount increased in 1998). The proposal must be in the form of a resolution (only one) that the shareholder intends to introduce at the shareholders' meeting. Rule 14a-8(c) (Question 3).

Shareholders must submit their proposals in a timely fashion. For an annual meeting, this will generally be at least 120 calendar days before the date proxy materials were sent for the last year's meeting. Rule 14a-8(e) (Question 5; information on submissions and deadlines can be found in last year's proxy statement). If the proposal is proper (see below), management must include it in the company's proxy mailing to shareholders. The proposal, along with a supporting statement, can be up to 500 words. Rule 14a-8(d) (Question 4). Management's proxy card must give shareholders a chance to vote for or against the proposal. Rule 14a-8(a) (Question 1).

If management decides to exclude a submitted proposal, it must give the submitting shareholder a chance to correct any deficiencies. Rule 14a-8(f) (Question 6; requiring management to give notice within 14 days of submission, and shareholder to respond within 14 days). If management intends to exclude the proposal, management must file its reasons (and a copy of the proposal) with the SEC for review. Rule 14a-8(j) (Question 10; reasons must include opinion of counsel if based on state or foreign law). The SEC staff issues a "no-action" letter if the staff agrees with management. Over time this procedure has created a body of SEC "common law" on the meaning of the rule.

Proper Proposals

Rule 14a-8 contains a dizzying list of 13 reasons for management to exclude a shareholder proposal. Rule 14a-8(i) (Question 9; formerly Rule 14a-8(c)). The list has undergone periodic changes, and the SEC's interpretation of its terms has ebbed and flowed. Management can exclude a proposal if it fits *any* of the categories specified in the rule. The SEC-created exclusions serve three central purposes.

(1) Proposals inconsistent with centralized management. Four of the exclusions aim at proposals that interfere with the traditional structure of corporate governance:

- **Not "proper subject."** Management can exclude proposals that are not a "proper subject" for shareholder action under state law. Rule 14a-8(i)(1). In *SEC v. Transamerica Corp.*, 163 F.2d 511 (3d Cir. 1947), the court upheld the propriety of proposals for shareholder election of independent public auditors, for changing procedures to amend the company's bylaws, and for requiring that a report of the annual meeting be sent to shareholders. Phrasing proposals to be precatory—that is, as advisory suggestions rather than as mandates—further assures their propriety under state law. See Note to Rule 14a-8(i)(1) (noting that "recommendations or requests" to the board are usually proper under state law); see also *Auer v. Dressel*, 118 N.E.2d 590 (N.Y. 1954) (see §7.1.3). Frequently, proposals will ask for management to conduct a study or issue a report, without compelling specific action.

Recently, an important question has been whether bylaw amendments that require specific action are proper subjects.

- **Not "significantly related."** Management can exclude proposals that are not "significantly related" to the company's business. Rule 14a-8(i)(5). To be significant, the proposal must relate to operations that account for at least 5 percent of total assets, net earnings, or gross sales. Or the proposal must be "otherwise significantly related" to the company's business. Beginning in the 1970s, the SEC has adopted a broad view of what is "otherwise significantly related." According to the SEC, matters relating to ethical issues, such as complying with the Arab boycott of Israel or carrying on business in South Africa, could be significant even though not from a purely financial standpoint. See also *Lovenheim v. Iroquois Brands, Ltd.*, 618 F. Supp. 554 (D.D.C. 1985) (holding to be "significantly related" a resolution calling for a report to shareholders on forced geese feeding even though the company lost money on goose pate sales, which accounted for less than .05 percent of revenues).
- **"Ordinary business operations."** Management can exclude proposals that relate to the company's "ordinary business operations." Rule 14a-8(i)(7). The SEC's interpretation of this exclusion has been checkered. In the 1970s and 1980s, the SEC accepted proposals dealing with such things as construction of nuclear power plants and employment discrimination on the theory they do not relate to "ordinary business" because of their economic, safety, and social impact. In 1992 the SEC reversed course and decided that proposals concerning employment policies (such as equal employment or affirmative action plans) can be excluded as "ordinary business." See *Cracker Barrel Old Country Store, Inc.*, SEC No-Action Letter (October 13, 1992). The Second Circuit ultimately agreed that the SEC could reinterpret the rule without a formal rulemaking proceeding. *New York City Employees' Retirement System v. SEC*, 45 F.3d 7 (2d Cir. 1995). But after widespread criticism the SEC announced in its 1998 rule revision a return to its pre-*Cracker Barrel* approach of case-by-case review into whether employee-related shareholder proposals raise significant social policy issues.

- **Related to dividend amount.** Management can exclude proposals that relate to the specific amount of dividends. Rule 14a-8(i)(13). This recognizes a fundamental feature of U.S. corporate law that the board has discretion to declare dividends, without shareholder initiative or approval.

(2) *Proposals that interfere with management's proxy solicitation.* The rule has four exclusions for proposals that threaten to interfere with orderly proxy voting:

- **Related to nomination or election to office.** Management can exclude proposals that relate to the nomination or election of directors. Rule 14a-8(i)(8) (amended in 2007). This exclusion prevents dissidents from "clogging" the company's proxy statement with their own candidates or views on management's nominees, as well as preventing shareholders from adopting procedures to nominate their own candidates to the board. Instead, a shareholder seeking to nominate its own slate to the board must undertake a proxy insurgency at its own expense.
- **Conflicts with management proposal.** Management can exclude proposals that "directly conflict" with management proposals. Rule 14a-8(i)(9) (amending previous exclusion of proposals "counter" to management submissions). Otherwise, the rule would create an open forum in which every shareholder could offer a proposal to undermine any management initiative subject to shareholder vote.
- **Duplicative.** Management can exclude proposals that duplicate another shareholder proposal for being included in the management's proxy materials. Rule 14a-8(i)(11).
- **"Recidivist."** Management can exclude "recidivist" proposals that had failed in the past. Rule 14a-8(i)(12). This exclusion covers any proposal dealing "with substantially the same subject matter" as a proposal submitted in the last five years that failed to get 3 percent on its first try, 6 percent on its second try, or 10 percent after three tries.

(3) *Proposals that are illegal, deceptive, or confused.* Five of the exclusions are meant to prevent spurious or scandalous proposals:

- **Violation of law.** Management can exclude proposals that would require the company to violate any law, including the SEC's proxy rules and in particular Rule 14a-9's proxy fraud prohibition. Rule 14a-8(i)(2), (i)(3). This allows management to exclude proposals it considers to be materially false or misleading.
- **Personal grievances.** Management can exclude proposals that relate to any personal grievance. Rule 14a-8(i)(4). This category covers the frequent phenomenon of proposals by disgruntled employees who

seek to have the body of shareholders recognize their talents and tribulations.

- **Beyond power.** Management can exclude proposals that deal with matters beyond the corporation's power to effectuate. Rule 14a-8(i)(6).
- **Moot.** Management can exclude proposals that are moot because the company is already doing what the shareholder proposes. Rule 14a-8(i)(10).

If a shareholder proposal dances through this minefield of procedural requirements and substantive exclusions, management must include it in the company's proxy statement and permit shareholders to vote in the proxy card—though management has a chance to recommend that shareholders vote against the proposal and give its reasons. Rule 14a-8(m) (Question 13).

If management fails to include a proposal that is not properly excludable, the proponent can seek an SEC determination that the proxy rules are being violated. Rule 14a-8(k) (Question 11). Alternatively, the shareholder can bring a private action in federal court to compel inclusion or enjoin management's proxy solicitation as a violation of the proxy rules. Shareholders who prevail in court may recover their attorneys' fees on the theory that "the litigation conferred a substantial benefit" on the body of shareholders. *Amalgamated Clothing and Textile Workers v. Wal-Mart Stores*, 54 F.3d 69 (2d Cir. 1995) (finding substantial benefit in proposal's communication to shareholders, even though proposal was defeated).

§9.4.3 Proxy Access

An interesting development in corporate governance has been the movement to open the board nomination process in U.S. public companies so that shareholder nominees are placed in the company's proxy materials *at company expense*. The history of "proxy access" has been convoluted and interesting. Nearly all the actors in modern corporate governance have played a role: activist and institutional shareholders, corporate management, the SEC, the federal courts, the U.S. Congress, the Delaware legislature, the Delaware courts, and even corporate law professors.

Proxy access began in 2003 when the SEC proposed a new Rule 14a-11 that would have permitted shareholders (or a group of shareholders) holding 5 percent of a company's voting shares to nominate directors to the company's board—provided a majority of shareholders had authorized such a vote in the previous election cycle or 35 percent had withheld their vote from a particular board nominee. See Exchange Act Rel. No. 48,626 (2003) (proposing release). The proposal met a firestorm of opposition from corporate management. At first the SEC dithered and then eventually decided not to pursue the rulemaking.

In response to the SEC's inaction, activist shareholders (supported by corporate law professors) began a company-by-company movement proposing amendments to company bylaws to create a process for shareholders to use the company's proxy mechanism to nominate a "short slate" constituting fewer than a majority of directors. At first the SEC took the position that such proposals were excludable under Rule 14a-8, but the Second Circuit held that Rule 14a-8 (as then worded) permitted shareholder proposals to create proxy access. See *AFSCME v. AIG, Inc.*, 462 F.3d 121 (2d. Cir. 2006). In response, the SEC revised Rule 14a-8 to overrule the court's decision, allowing companies to exclude such shareholder proposals. Exchange Act Rel. No. 56,914 (2007).

Thus, without a proxy access rule and faced with a revised Rule 14a-8 that limited shareholder-initiated proxy access, institutional shareholders turned to Congress. In 2010 Congress put proxy access back on the corporate governance agenda when it passed the Dodd-Frank Act and specifically authorized the SEC to promulgate a proxy access rule. Dodd-Frank §971. Within months, the SEC accepted the Dodd-Frank invitation and repromulgated Rule 14a-11 in even stronger form than before. Exchange Act Rel. No. 62,674 (2010) (permitting nomination of directors constituting at most one-fourth of the board by shareholders, or groups of shareholders, that had held 1, 3, or 5 percent of company's voting shares for at least three years, the percentage varying with company size).

The plot thickened, however, when corporate management (through the Business Roundtable and U.S. Chamber of Commerce) challenged the reincarnated Rule 14a-11 in federal court for failing to adequately consider the costs and benefits of the new governance rights granted to activist shareholders. The D.C. Circuit agreed and held that the SEC had failed to consider the rule's effect on "efficiency, competition and capital formation." *Business Roundtable v. SEC*, 647 F.3d 1144 (D.C. Cir. 2011) (vacating rule). Even though Dodd-Frank seemed to have authorized the SEC to make this cost-benefit determination, the SEC decided not to appeal the decision to the Supreme Court and not to propose the rule again, apparently worried it could not meet the (unusually) high standard of review set by the D.C. Circuit.

Despite the failure of proxy access to become an SEC rule, many shareholder activists decided to take matters into their own hands and returned to the company-by-company approach. The SEC had reopened this door in 2010 when it revised Rule 14a-8 (as part of its Rule 14a-11 rulemaking) to permit shareholders to propose bylaw changes to establish procedures for nominating directors in the company's proxy materials. Shareholder activists were further emboldened by changes to the Delaware corporate statute, added by the Delaware legislature in 2009, which made clear that shareholders can amend company bylaws to provide for proxy access as well as mandatory reimbursement of proxy expenses incurred by shareholders in director elections. See Del. GCL §§112, 113; see also MBCA §2.06(c).

As the 2012 proxy season begins, many companies with (allegedly) lackluster boards have been targeted with proposals to give shareholders access to the company's proxy mechanism. Under the proposals, shareholders would first vote on amending the company's bylaws to give nominating shareholders (with specified minimum holdings) access to the company's proxy materials. Then, the following year—if the bylaw amendment were approved—qualified shareholders (or a group of qualified shareholders) could nominate a short slate to the board.

You might wonder what all the fuss is about. At most, proxy access gives shareholders a chance to use the company's proxy materials to nominate and place a handful, but not a majority, of directors on the board. Why has corporate management fought this? For one, it's been argued that shareholder-nominated directors might make boards less collegial and more antagonistic. For another, proxy access by SEC rule would create a one-size-fits-all approach, away from the flexible private ordering permitted by state law. In the end, proxy access raises in stark relief the question of who defines shareholder voting rights—the SEC or Delaware. For now, it looks like Delaware retains its preeminence, with the SEC on the sidelines.

Examples

EXAMPLES

1. Two years ago Reba bought $2,000 worth of Video Palace (VPI) stock. She recently calculated that VPI's liquidation value exceeds its current stock price. Reba wants to bring this to the attention of other shareholders and to propose the company be liquidated—its assets sold for cash—and the cash distributed to shareholders.
   a. Reba plans to solicit proxies for a resolution she plans to present at the upcoming annual shareholders' meeting. The resolution will ask the board to take steps to liquidate VPI. Will the company reimburse her for her solicitation expenses?
   b. Reba notices that the company bylaws require that she give notice that she plans to submit her proposal at least 120 days before the next annual shareholders' meeting. She gives this notice. Must VPI provide information about the proposal in its proxy statement so the statement is not misleading.
   c. Reba wants management to include her proposal with the company's proxy mailing. When must Reba make this request?
   d. Reba plans to submit a four-page attachment to her resolution that explains the advantage of liquidation and gives financial details. In her attachment she blames VPI management for "destroying market confidence as reflected in the company's below-asset market price." Any problems?
   e. Reba corrects these problems and submits a resolution that calls for the board to liquidate the business, dissolve the corporation, and

distribute the proceeds to shareholders. Management objects. On what basis can management exclude this proposal from the company's proxy materials?

2. Reba's liquidation proposal is submitted for a shareholder vote and soundly defeated at the shareholders' annual meeting. Reba is relentless. Anticipating next year's shareholders' meeting, she wants to shake up the way VPI does business. Which of the following would be includable under the shareholder proposal rule?
   a. A proposal that shareholders elect Reba to the board.
   b. A resolution stating the shareholders' desire that management nominate at least two women as directors on the board.
   c. A resolution requiring the VPI board to prepare a report on affirmative action in the company's management training program.
   d. A proposal to amend the bylaws to permit shareholders holding more than 5 percent of the company's shares for two years to nominate up to two directors to the company's nine-person board.
   e. A proposal to amend the bylaws to require the corporation to reimburse the reasonable expenses of any shareholder that successfully nominates fewer than 50 percent of the directors to the board.

3. Management excludes Reba's proposal against "adult" videos, and the SEC issues a no-action letter accepting the proposal's exclusion. So Reba contacts some of VPI's larger individual shareholders, who say they agree with her proposal. She attends the shareholders' meeting and makes her proposal from the floor. VPI has no advance notice requirements for shareholder proposals.
   a. At the meeting Reba says her proposal is a proper subject for shareholders under the corporation's constitutive documents and state corporate law. If not, she explains, the shareholders can simply vote it down. Is the proposal proper?
   b. Reba's proposal is approved not counting the votes for which management has proxies. Management's proxy card gives management complete authority to vote in its discretion on "any other matters that might arise at the shareholders' meeting." The proxy materials, however, do not mention the possibility of shareholder proposals at the meeting. Does management have discretionary authority to vote its proxies against Reba's floor proposal?

4. VPI's management is tired of shareholder proposals. So are many VPI shareholders, who have never cast more than 20 percent of their votes for any shareholder proposal. The board proposes, and the shareholders approve, an amendment to the company's charter banning all non-management shareholder proposals unless by a shareholder (or group of shareholders) holding more than 20 percent of VPI's voting shares.

a. At the next shareholders' meeting, Reba proposes a resolution urging that no executive receive a salary greater than $1 million. Her ownership qualifies her to make the proposal under Rule 14a-8, but not the charter provision. Must management include the proposal?
b. Reba asks management to supply her with a list of shareholders or to send her proxy materials so she can solicit support for her executive pay proposal. Must management comply with her request under Rule 14a-7?
c. Why don't companies "opt out" of the shareholder proposal rule?

Explanations

EXPLANATIONS

1. a. Almost certainly no. Under state law, the board has no obligation to reimburse shareholders' solicitation expenses—and rarely does it happen. Only if a shareholder gains control of the board and gets other shareholders to ratify the reimbursement can the shareholder hope to be repaid. See §8.1.2.

   Neither Rule 14a-7 nor Rule 14a-8 of the federal proxy rules change this. Rule 14a-7 merely requires that management provide Reba with a shareholders' list or send her solicitation materials to other shareholders at her expense. Rule 14a-8 does not provide for reimbursement, only inclusion of proper proposals in the company-funded proxy statement by qualifying shareholders who comply with the rule's procedures.

   The only hope for a shareholder who undertakes her own proxy solicitation to be reimbursed is a shareholder-approved bylaw providing for corporate reimbursement of reasonable election-related expenses. See *CA, Inc. v. AFSCME Employees Pension Plan*, 953 A.2d 227 (Del. 2008) (finding such a bylaw to be proper under Delaware law, provided it includes a "fiduciary out" that allows the board to fulfill its fiduciary duties).

   b. No. A shareholder who announces an intention to make a proposal at an upcoming shareholders' meeting, but does not independently solicit proxies, cannot claim it would be false and misleading under Rule 14a-9 if the company omits mention of the proposal. *Union of Needletrades, Industrial and Textile Employees v. May Department Stores Co.*, 1997 WL 714886 (S.D.N.Y.) (requiring inclusion in the proxy statement would allow shareholders to "back door" their proposals "past the detailed requirements of Rule 14a-8"). This means that shareholders seeking to communicate with other shareholders using the company-financed proxy machinery must use Rule 14a-8.

   If Reba were to begin an independent solicitation seeking proxies for her proposal, however, the company would be required to provide shareholders specific disclosure of the proposal and management's intentions on how it would exercise its discretionary authority in voting proxies. The disclosure would be made either in the company's proxy statement or in a supplement. See Rule 14a-4(c)(1).

c. Under Rule 14a-8, to qualify for inclusion in management's proxy statement, Reba must mail her proposal so that management receives it at least 120 calendar days before the date on which proxy materials were sent out for last year's annual shareholders' meeting. This assumes this year's meeting is scheduled to fall within 30 days of the date of last year's meeting. Question 5, Rule 14a-8(e). To avoid any controversy, the SEC recommends proposals be sent by Certified Mail—Return Receipt Requested.

d. Reba's proposal is in trouble. First, her proposal probably exceeds the word limit for shareholder proposals. The rule limits proposals and supporting statements to 500 words—approximately two double-spaced, typewritten pages. See Question 4, Rule 14a-8(d). If so, management is obligated to point out this deficiency and give her 14 days to reduce the proposal's length. Rule 14a-8(f)(1).

Second, her statement impugning management's integrity may make the proposal excludable. Rule 14a-8(b)(1). Management can exclude proposals that are contrary to SEC rules, including the rule prohibiting proxy fraud. The SEC has said that fraud includes "material which impugns character, integrity or personal reputation." In the no-action process, SEC staff sometimes permits the proponent of an otherwise includable proposal to salvage the proposal by deleting any offending language.

e. A number of exclusions may apply. First, the proposal may not be a "proper subject" for action by shareholders under state law. Rule 14a-8(i)(1). Most state statutes require that sale of substantially all assets and voluntary corporate dissolution be initiated by directors (see §§36.1.2, 36.2.2). Although shareholder approval of the sale and dissolution may be necessary, the board generally has exclusive power to initiate these changes. Second, the proposal would require the company to violate state law regarding the process for approving a sale of all the company's assets and corporate dissolution. Rule 14a-8(i)(2). Third, the proposal may be seen as relating to "specific amounts of cash . . . dividends." Rule 14a-8(i)(13).

Reba should phrase the resolution to be precatory—a suggestion that the board consider a liquidation/dissolution. The resolution might also call on the board to prepare a report to shareholders on its decision. To make her proposal proper, Reba may have to make it toothless.

2. a. Excludable. The proposal improperly relates to an election to office. Rule 14a-8(i)(8). Although the election of directors is a proper subject

for shareholder action, the rule prevents shareholders from interfering with management's orderly operation of the proxy mechanism. If Reba or most other shareholders could propose their own nominees, management's proxy statement and proxy card would become unmanageable, jeopardizing proxy voting.

b. Probably excludable. This resolution is precatory and is a "proper subject" for shareholder action. Under current SEC interpretation, shareholders may make proposals under Rule 14a-8 that urge the board be composed of "outside" directors or "employee" directors. SEC staff has taken the view that such proposals do not relate to a particular election or nominee and do not "relate to an election" under the Rule 14a-8(i)(8) exclusion.

   Nonetheless, the proposal to nominate a specified number of women may be excludable on the ground it urges the company to run afoul of antidiscrimination laws. See Rule 14a-8(i)(2). Reba should have urged the board to consider women nominees to the board, without specifying a quota.

c. Includable. The resolution does not require specific board action, only a report. Further, it deals with a matter of substantial public importance, thus removing it from the "ordinary business" exclusion. Rule 14a-8(i)(7). The SEC once took the position that proposals dealing with a company's employment practices are within the company's "ordinary business," even when they raise "social policy" concerns. *Cracker Barrel Old Country Stores, Inc.*, SEC No-Action Letter (Oct. 13, 1992). The SEC, however, reversed this position in 1998.

d. Includable. Under the current Rule 14a-8, such "proxy access" proposals are permitted. See §9.4.3. The SEC staff once took the position that such proposals were not includable under the Rule 14a-8(i)(8) exclusion for proposals that "relate to an election." *Walt Disney Co.*, SEC No-Action Letter (Dec. 14, 2004) (reconsideration). But the SEC revised the rule in 2010 to permit such shareholder proposals as part of its rulemaking to create proxy access. As revised, Rule 14a-8(i)(8) now allows exclusion of proposals only if the proposal (i) would disqualify a director standing for election; (ii) remove a director from office; (iii) question the competence, judgment, or character of a director; (iv) seek to exclude a specific individual from being nominated; or (v) otherwise possibly affect the outcome of a board election.

   Furthermore, state law (including in Delaware) now permits shareholders to amend the bylaws to provide for a process of shareholder nomination of directors. See Del. GCL §112; see also MBCA §2.06(c).

e. Includable, though it might need to contain a "fiduciary out." The proposal dealing with a board election is permitted under revised

Rule 14a-8(i)(8) (see previous explanation). The only real question is whether it is excludable as invalid under state law. See Rule 14a-8(i)(1). This question turns on a recent Delaware case and subsequent statute.

In the case—which involved a similar proposal submitted by the SEC to the Delaware Supreme Court for the court's opinion—the Delaware court gave a mixed answer. *CA, Inc. v. AFSCME Employees Pension Plan*, 953 A.2d 227 (Del. 2008). The court first opined that the proposed bylaw related to the process of director elections and was a proper subject for shareholder action under Delaware law. The court then opined that the bylaw would unlawfully prevent directors from exercising their full management powers if their fiduciary duties required them to deny reimbursement for a dissident slate. The court explained that while bylaws may "define the process and procedures by which those decisions are made," they may not "mandate how the board should decide specific substantive business decisions."

Is a "fiduciary out" necessary so the board could deny reimbursement to a shareholder if required by the directors' fiduciary duties? Although the *CA* case seems to require such a "fiduciary out," a subsequent Delaware statute specifically permits bylaws that provide for reimbursement of shareholder proxy-related expenses without mentioning the need for a "fiduciary out." See Del. GCL §113; see also MBCA §2.06(c). The statute raises the interesting question of whether the legislature can remove the judicial power to decide when director fiduciary duties arise.

3. a. Perhaps. State corporate statutes do not specify what shareholder proposals are proper, which often presents a problem because Rule 14a-8(i)(1) excludes proposals that are "not proper" under the corporate law of the company's state of incorporation. State judicial decisions suggest that shareholders have broad powers to make nonbinding precatory proposals. See *Matter of Auer v. Dressel* (§7.1.3). This broad authority is supported by judicial interpretation in other contexts. For example, courts have permitted shareholders to inspect the shareholders' list (and other corporate documents) if the requesting shareholder articulates a purpose related to the financial interests of the company. See §7.1.4. In this case, the propriety of the proposal depends on what state law and state courts say, not on the independent views of the SEC.
   b. Perhaps. It depends on when management knew of Reba's proposal and how management phrased its proxy materials. In the 1990s many shareholders in public companies, to avoid the strictures of the Rule 14a-8 exclusions, made proposals from the floor of the shareholders' meeting. These shareholders then asserted that management lacked discretionary authority at the meeting to vote its proxies against the

proposal on the theory that management's proxy card did not create this authority.

In 1998 the SEC amended its proxy rules to permit management to create discretionary authority in the proxy card with respect to shareholder proposals at an annual meeting. The proxy card can create this discretionary authority if the proxy materials state either (1) management had not received timely notice of a shareholder proposal, or (2) management had received notice and stated how it planned to vote. Rule 14a-4(c). In general, notice is timely if received 45 days before the date of the prior year's proxy mailing. No discretionary authority arises, however, if the shareholder proponent is making his own proxy solicitation (and sending proxy materials to shareholders). The proponent's solicitation floats or sinks on its own.

In our example, management's failure to mention the possibility of a shareholder proposal—whether or not Reba's was received in a timely fashion under the rule—negates any discretionary authority. Although the grant of discretionary authority is valid under state law, the federal proxy rules deny management voting power when shareholders have not been informed how their proxies are likely to be voted.

4. a. Perhaps. It depends on whether the SEC proxy rules can be seen to create federal substantive rights or merely provide procedures to exercise rights under state law. Reba's proposal on executive compensation is includable under Rule 14a-8, but not under the company's amended articles.

   Many courts have justified Rule 14a-8 on a procedural theory. Without the rule it would be misleading for management not to disclose the shareholder proposals it expects shareholders will raise at an upcoming meeting. The rule provides a procedure for that disclosure. If a shareholder has no right to make a proposal, then presumably the rule does not require management to disclose it or include it on the proxy card. On the other hand, Rule 14a-8 has over time assumed a life of its own. Many of the exclusion categories—such as for proposals that have failed in the past or are counter to a management proposal or are not significantly related to the company's business—do not find any basis in state law. The SEC, arguably, has created a new substantive right, subject to the agency's list of exclusions. Under this view, companies cannot "opt out" of shareholder access pursuant to Rule 14a-8 any more than they could opt out of the other federal proxy rules.

   b. Perhaps not. Even if Reba were willing to pay for the solicitation under Rule 14a-7, management might argue that it need not act as a "common carrier" for proposals that are improper under state law. Unlike Rule 14a-8, however, the "common carrier" requirements of Rule 14a-7 do not offer management any explicit grounds for exclusion or for refusing to provide a shareholders' list. On its face, federal law supersedes state law.

c. Management may not be interested in opting out of the shareholder proposal rule for a number of reasons. First, opting out might be bad for shareholder relations (and stock prices) if management tried to insulate itself from shareholder proposals. Investors might lose confidence in a company whose management sought to cut itself off from shareholder input. Second, shareholder proposals have become an effective way for shareholders to express their views on a broad range of corporate matters (such as majority voting in director elections, shareholder access to the nomination process, and shareholder say on executive pay). Increasingly, management has chosen to adopt shareholder-approved resolutions, even when precatory. Without shareholder proposals, shareholders might turn to other protective devices, such as takeovers and litigation, that could be even more intrusive. Third, opting out might not be valid under state law. Just as shareholders have a basic right to amend the bylaws, courts could well hold that shareholders have an inviolable right to make proper proposals at shareholders' meetings. Finally, the shareholder proposal rule may provide a relatively painless way for activist shareholders to express their governance, economic, social, and political views short of seeking governmental intervention through the political process.

CHAPTER 10

Proxy Fraud

Corporate democracy depends on shareholders having full and honest information about the matters on which they vote. The federal proxy rules impose an *ex ante* disclosure regime specifying the information that public shareholders must receive when asked to vote by proxy. Federal courts, and lately state courts, have developed an *ex post* disclosure regime that enforces full and honest disclosure through private litigation. Courts, assuming the role of "reasonable shareholder," review the adequacy of disclosure and infer the likely outcome of a fully informed shareholder vote.

This chapter describes the private causes of action available to shareholders in public corporations to enforce their rights to honest disclosure (§10.1). In particular, it considers the implied proxy fraud action developed by federal courts under §14(a) of the Securities Exchange Act of 1934 (§10.2) and describes how state courts have borrowed elements of the federal action to create disclosure duties under state corporate fiduciary law (§10.3).

Note on Corporate Federalism

This chapter is a study in the interaction of state and federal law. You'll notice that the chapter begins by identifying the weakness of traditional state law in dealing with proxy fraud. It then describes the response by federal courts to create (and later weaken) a federal cause of action. Finally, it summarizes the emergence of a new state cause of action modeled on the federal one, though subject to some limitations. Today nearly all proxy fraud cases arise in state court in connection with challenges to corporate transactions.

§10.1 PRIVATE ACTIONS

State law traditionally provided limited redress for false or misleading proxy statements. Federal courts filled this gap by implying a private federal cause of action.

§10.1.1 Traditional State Remedies

Consider the traditional judicial remedies available to public shareholders unhappy with a corporate transaction procured by false information in a proxy statement. Using the *law of deceit*, the shareholders can sue those who fraudulently misrepresent material facts on which the shareholders relied to their detriment, which reliance was the cause of actual shareholder losses. The shareholders can sue directors who breached their *fiduciary duties* of care or loyalty by misrepresenting information to shareholders.

Each theory of liability has its pitfalls. Traditional state fraud law would require that the shareholders prove (1) the proxy statement contained an actual misrepresentation of fact, not just a deceptive opinion or an omission that made the statement misleading; (2) management actually knew of the falsity of the representations; (3) he and the other shareholders actually read the proxy disclosures and justifiably relied on them; and (4) the shareholders suffered losses because of their reliance, not because of extraneous factors. See *Kerbs v. California Easter Airways, Inc.*, 94 A.2d 217 (Del. Ch. 1953) (commenting that "verbal niceties" not always observed and puffing is permissible in corporate election campaigns).

Traditional corporate fiduciary law would also be problematic. If the disappointed shareholders brought a derivative suit on behalf of the corporation, assuming the deceit was viewed as harming the corporation, the suit would be subject to procedural obstacles such as demand on the board, security bond for expenses, and potential board dismissal. See §18.3. And if the deceit was viewed as directly harming the shareholders, a class action to enforce fiduciary duties would be unavailable if shareholder-plaintiffs have to prove they individually relied on the misrepresentations. See §10.3. In addition, shareholder-plaintiffs would have to overcome the powerful "business judgment rule" as well as liability exoneration provisions and the exclusivity of the appraisal remedy in control transactions. See §§12.2, 12.5, 37.3.

§10.1.2 Implied Federal Action

Federal securities law does not explicitly provide for private enforcement of its proxy rules. The Securities Exchange Act of 1934 simply prohibits proxy solicitations that do not comply with SEC rules. Exchange Act §14(a). The rules themselves do not mention private actions. The SEC's rule against proxy fraud merely prohibits any proxy solicitation "containing any statement which . . . is false or misleading with respect to any material fact." Rule 14a-9. Although §21(d) of the Exchange Act authorizes the SEC to enforce its rules in court, there is no explicit authority for a shareholder to seek relief for proxy fraud.

Can a shareholder make a claim under the federal proxy antifraud rule? In a famous (and conclusory) decision, the Supreme Court held that a shareholder has an implied cause of action to challenge a corporate transaction approved by a proxy solicitation that violates the SEC antifraud rule. *J.I. Case Co. v. Borak*, 377 U.S. 426 (1964). The Court used a broad theory that "where there is a wrong the law implies a remedy" and held an action for violations of §14(a) could be inferred under §27 of the Exchange Act. Section 27 is a remarkable source for the Court's implication. By its terms the provision merely gives federal district courts exclusive jurisdiction over actions "to enforce any liability or duty created" under the Exchange Act and prescribes service of process and venue requirements for these actions.

Borak's broad implied-remedy theory has since been rejected by the Supreme Court. Beginning with *Cort v. Ash*, 422 U.S. 66 (1975), a nonsecurities case, and in more recent cases arising under other provisions of the Exchange Act, the test has become whether Congress intended to imply a private action, taking into account the legislative history, the structure of the statute, and the availability of state remedies. See *Piper v. Chris-Craft Industries, Inc.*, 430 U.S. 1 (1977) (no standing for frustrated bidder that challenges tender offer disclosures under §14(e) of Exchange Act); *Touche Ross & Co. v. Redington*, 442 U.S. 560 (1979) (no private action for shareholders who claim violations of §17 of the Exchange Act, which requires annual informational filings by stockbrokers with SEC).

Nonetheless, despite its shaky underpinnings, the *Borak* holding that a federal private action exists for proxy fraud is now entrenched. See *Virginia Bankshares, Inc. v. Sandberg*, 501 U.S. 1083 (1991) (accepting *Borak* action).

§10.2 FEDERAL ACTION FOR PROXY FRAUD

The elements of the federal implied private action for proxy fraud are court-created. In fashioning the scope of action, federal courts have sought to ensure informed shareholder voting and to discipline management through the antiseptic of disclosure. Over the past decade, the federal proxy fraud action has fallen into disuse, but its elements and philosophy have formed the bedrock of a state-based duty of disclosure (see §10.3).

§10.2.1 Nature of Action

The proxy fraud action implied in *Borak* is federal. As such, a challenging shareholder can avoid the substantive and procedural impediments of a fiduciary challenge under state law.

Under *Borak* a private proxy fraud action can be brought by a solicited shareholder either in her own name (as an individual or class action) or in a derivative suit on behalf of the corporation. A *federal derivative action* provides a means for shareholder-plaintiffs to recover litigation expenses, including attorney fees, and to avoid state derivative suit procedures. *Borak* justified such an action on the tenuous ground that a federal derivative action would provide relief for damages to the corporation caused by deceptive proxy solicitations.

§10.2.2 Elements of Action

In the three decades following *Borak*, the Supreme Court gave shape to the federal proxy fraud action, opening the federal courthouse door in the 1960s and carefully leaving it ajar in the 1970s and 1980s.

Interestingly, the Court's proxy fraud cases all have the same factual pattern: a shareholder sues after management undertakes a merger or other control transaction accomplished with an allegedly false or misleading proxy statement. The following describes the elements of a federal proxy fraud action. (Notice how these elements both overlap with and are different from those for a securities fraud action under Rule 10b-5; see Chapter 22.)

Misrepresentation or Omission

Rule 14a-9 applies to any statement in a proxy solicitation that is "false or misleading . . . or which omits to state any material fact necessary in order to make the statements therein not false or misleading." This formulation, which represents an expansion of the traditional common-law view that silence is not actionable, invites disappointed shareholders to point to disclosure falsehoods and half-truths.

Statements of Opinions, Motives, or Reasons

Rule 14a-9 speaks of statements and omissions. Are statements of opinion, motives, or reasons concerning a transaction—though not actionable under the common law of deceit—actionable as proxy fraud? In *Virginia Bankshares, Inc. v. Sandberg*, 501 U.S. 1083 (1991), the Supreme Court held that a board's statement of reasons for approving a merger can be actionable. Shareholders rely on the board's expertise and the directors' fiduciary duties, and the board's opinions and reasons for a transaction "naturally" can be important to shareholders.

Virginia Bankshares, however, was reluctant to make actionable any misleading opinion or statement of reasons. Concerned that shareholder-plaintiffs could fabricate unstated board motives, the Court held that a statement of opinion, motives, or reasons is actionable only if the board both (1) misstates its true beliefs *and* (2) misleads about the subject matter of the statement, such as the value of the shares in a merger.

The *Virginia Bankshares* two-part test seeks to prevent shareholders from using the proxy rules to attack a transaction that, though accompanied by false or misleading information, may nonetheless be fair and thus beyond attack under state law. For example, a proxy statement that fails to explain that the company's majority shareholder was seeking a "quick sale" of the company to obtain cash to pay estate taxes is not materially misleading unless the plaintiffs can also show that the sale price was unfair. See *Mendell v. Greenberg*, 938 F.2d 1528 (2d Cir. 1991) (remanded in light of *Virginia Bankshares*).

Materiality

Rule 14a-9 requires that the challenged misrepresentation or omission be "with respect to a material fact." The materiality requirement serves to corroborate the complaining party's claim of reliance. Without it, information defects would be an easy pretext to escape bargains gone sour.

In *TSC Industries, Inc. v. Northway, Inc.*, 426 U.S. 438 (1976), the Court defined an omitted material fact as one as to which there is a "substantial likelihood that a reasonable shareholder *would* consider it important in deciding how to vote." The definition balances the Court's concern that trivial misinformation not be actionable and its concern that a complaining shareholder not have to prove with certainty that shareholders would have voted against the transaction had they been fully informed. The Court also stated the information must "significantly alter the total mix" of information available. That is, information is not material if it is redundant or otherwise available to shareholders. (This definition has been widely borrowed for actions alleging fraud under the federal securities laws, in particular fraud in connection with buying or selling securities under Rule 10b-5. See §22.3.1.)

The facts in *TSC v. Northway* illustrate the Court's materiality approach. A TSC shareholder complained that the proxy solicitation for a sale/liquidation of the company had not disclosed that National, the buyer of the assets, controlled the TSC board. The Court held that the omission was not material because the proxy statement had disclosed that National was a 34 percent shareholder and that five of TSC's ten directors were National nominees.

Further information about National's control was superfluous; it would not have altered the total mix of information.

Culpability

Rule 14a-9 is silent on the question of whether the defendant must have acted culpably, and the Supreme Court has not resolved the question. Most lower courts have not required a showing that the party making the misrepresentation knew it was false or misleading—that is, scienter is not required.

The Supreme Court has suggested the standard is negligence. *Aaron v. SEC*, 446 U.S. 680 (1980). Lower courts have agreed. See *Gerstle v. Gamble-Skogmo, Inc.*, 478 F.2d 1281 (2d Cir. 1973) (contrasting Rule 14a-9 with Rule 10b-5); *Gould v. American Hawaiian Steamship Co.*, 535 F.2d 761 (3d Cir. 1976) (analogizing to the liability in public securities offerings, outside directors' negligence is sufficient for liability under the proxy rules); *Shidler v. All American Life & Financial Corp.*, 775 F.2d 917 (8th Cir. 1985) (no strict liability for incorrectly opining on novel issue of state law).

Reliance

Rule 14a-9 does not address whether a shareholder must have relied on the defendant's misrepresentations—an element of common-law deceit. The issue raises difficult evidentiary questions. Must the complaining shareholders show they each actually read and relied on the alleged misstatements, or that the misstatements had a "decisive effect" on the voting outcome, or that the transaction was unfair and thus the shareholders would likely have voted it down?

In *Mills v. Electric Auto-Lite Co.*, 396 U.S. 375 (1970), the Court rejected these approaches and held it is enough if the alleged misstatements were *material*. In the case, public shareholders of a partially owned subsidiary challenged disclosures in a proxy statement for the merger between the subsidiary and its parent—specifically that the proxy statement had not mentioned that all the subsidiary's directors were nominees of the parent's controlling shareholder. The Court excused proof of actual reliance, thus eliminating it as an element in a proxy fraud case. The Court said that the materiality test, later refined in *TSC Industries*, embodies a conclusion that the misstatement would have been considered important by a "reasonable shareholder" and weeds out claims based on trivial or unrelated misstatements.

Causation

Rule 14a-9 does not mention whether the shareholders' reliance on the defendant's deception caused her loss—an element of common-law deceit.

Like the requirements of materiality and reliance, causation seeks to measure whether the plaintiff's loss is linked to the alleged misinformation.

In proxy fraud cases, federal courts have required that the challenged transaction have caused harm to the shareholders—*loss causation*. In a merger, loss causation is relatively easy to show if shareholders of the acquired company claim the merger price was less than what their shares were worth. If, however, shareholders in a merger receive stock in the surviving company and the stock price falls after the merger, shareholders would have to show that the loss in value happened because of the merger, not extraneous events.

Federal courts have also required that the proxy solicitation be "an essential link to the accomplishment of the transaction"—*transaction causation*. That is, there can be no recovery if the transaction did not depend on the shareholder vote. In *Mills*, for example, the Supreme Court concluded that transaction causation existed because a proxy solicitation of minority shareholders holding 46 percent of the company's stock was essential to getting the necessary two-thirds approval for the merger.

In *Virginia Bankshares*, the Supreme Court considered whether there can be transaction causation when the vote of minority shareholders is not necessary under state law to accomplish a squeeze-out merger. In the case, the board sought the proxies of minority shareholders even though the company's parent corporation held 85 percent of the shares and approval of the merger was assured. The plaintiff argued the board's solicitation of proxies was related to the transaction in two respects: (1) minority approval improved management's reputation among investors, and the omitted information, if revealed, would have shamed the board into acting differently—a "shame facts" theory of causation; and (2) minority approval insulated the merger from review under Virginia's corporate statute on conflict-of-interest transactions, and the omitted information made it less likely shareholders could sue to block the merger under state law—a "sue facts" theory of causation.

On the shame facts theory, the Court held that the board's desire for a cosmetic vote did not provide the essential link between the proxy solicitation and the merger. Otherwise, a judge would have to speculate about the board's timidity or boldness. The Court was unwilling to make presumptions about management behavior as it had about shareholder behavior in *Mills* when it excused proof of individual reliance.

On the sue facts theory, the Court held that even if the board had misled the minority into approving the merger, shareholders could still challenge it in state court, where a shareholder vote obtained through fraud would have no validating effect. The Court left open the possibility that disclosure defects might be actionable if they induced shareholders to forgo dissenters' appraisal rights or if they undermined their ability to challenge the transaction in state court. See *Wilson v. Great American Industries, Inc.*, 979 F.2d 924

(2d Cir. 1992) (finding causation when misstatements may have led shareholders to vote for merger, thus causing them to forgo appraisal remedy).

Prospective or Retrospective Relief

In *Borak* the Supreme Court held that relief for a violation of the proxy rules could be either prospective or retrospective. This gives federal courts a broad remedial arsenal: enjoin the voting of proxies obtained through proxy fraud, enjoin the shareholders' meeting, rescind the transaction, or award damages. In cases of mergers procured through proxy fraud, federal courts typically have awarded damages rather than unwind the merger because it's difficult to "unscramble eggs."

In *Mills* the Supreme Court stated that in fashioning relief the trial court should inquire into the transaction's fairness even though *Mills* purposefully rejected a fairness inquiry in deciding shareholder reliance. In *Mills*, despite a finding that a merger had been procured by fraud, the Seventh Circuit on remand decided the merger price was fair and denied the shareholders any relief.

Attorney Fees

In *Mills* the Supreme Court endorsed the awarding of attorney fees, even before a final remedy, to shareholders who successfully prosecute a proxy fraud case. The Court said attorney fees were available because shareholder-plaintiffs in a proxy fraud action, whether brought as a class action or derivative suit, are producing a benefit for the body of shareholders. This ruling creates an incentive for individual public shareholders with a relatively small stake to vindicate shareholder rights under the proxy rules.

§10.3 STATE ACTION FOR PROXY FRAUD

Other than the cursory notice required for shareholders' meetings, state corporate statutes do not specify the information that public shareholders are to receive when management solicits their proxies. Nonetheless, state courts (particularly in Delaware) have developed a body of case law that prohibits false and misleading statements in any management communication with public shareholders—whether in a proxy solicitation, tender offer, notice of a shareholders' meeting even when proxies are not solicited, or a notice of a short-form merger for which no meeting is required.

The seminal Delaware case, *Lynch v. Vickers Energy Corp.*, 383 A.2d 278 (Del. 1977), imposed on management a "complete candor" duty that explicitly borrows the framework of the federal proxy fraud action. See §10.2.2 above. Liability is premised on false or misleading information that "a reasonable shareholder would consider important in deciding whether to [vote]." As is true of federal proxy fraud litigation, challenging shareholders need not show the alleged misinformation would have changed the outcome of the shareholder vote; it is enough that the challenged disclosure was material.

In Delaware, shareholders have used the "complete candor" duty (which subsequent courts have labeled a "duty of disclosure") to successfully challenge mergers, reorganizations, and charter amendments. For many shareholder-plaintiffs, Delaware has become preferable to federal court. Delaware's standard for damages is based on rescissory damages (what the shares would have been worth at the time of judgment absent the challenged transaction) rather than the federal out-of-pocket or benefit-of-the-bargain standard (what the shares would have fetched at the time of the transaction absent the misinformation). Thus, shareholders can recover the loss of synergy value in a completed merger. In addition, attorney fees in Delaware are often computed on the basis of class action results, not the less generous federal "lodestar" method. In a variety of conflict-of-interest transactions involving shareholder voting—parent-subsidiary mergers, tender offers by controlling shareholders, and defensive recapitalizations—disclosure review has served as a substitute for fiduciary review on the merits.

In an expansion of the duty of disclosure, the Delaware Supreme Court extended the duty of disclosure to include all communications to shareholders, not just those seeking shareholder action. *Malone v. Brincat*, 722 A.2d 5 (Del. 1998). The case, brought as a class action, involved allegation of an ongoing financial fraud made in SEC filings. The court held that directors who knowingly disseminate false information that results in corporate or shareholder harm violate their fiduciary duty and should be held accountable. But given the existence of federal securities fraud liability (see §22.2), the court refused to adopt a "fraud on the market" theory—thus making individual shareholder reliance an element of the action. As a result, *Malone* has not been heavily used.

Examples

EXAMPLES

1. Global Paper, Inc. (GPI), is a multinational paper products company. Its stock is listed on the New York Stock Exchange. Sara, a GPI shareholder, is upset when she reads a newspaper account of the munificent pay package of GPI's chief executive officer. Sara claims the CEO's pay is a waste of corporate assets and the board failed to disclose fully the CEO's sizeable stock options in the company's most recent proxy statement.
   a. Sara sues in state court claiming federal proxy fraud, state fraudulent misrepresentation, and breach of fiduciary duty. Any problems with the suit?

b. SEC rules require that executive compensation be fully disclosed in the company's proxy statement. Schedule 14A, Items 8 and 10. Does Sara have standing to sue for violation of the SEC's line-item disclosure requirements?

2. Sara sells her GPI stock after reading in the company's proxy statement for the annual meeting that "management anticipates company earnings will remain flat for the next two years." At the time, GPI management is secretly buying GPI shares at depressed prices on the open market. In fact, earnings soon increase dramatically, a turn of events management was expecting.
   a. Does GPI management violate the proxy rules by making a misleading prediction?
   b. Sara sold her shares before she had a chance to vote. Does she have an implied right of action under the federal proxy rules?

3. GPI management is under investigation by the FBI for bribing environmental regulators with authority over the company's paper-processing operations. Although management is aware of the investigation, the company's proxy statement for the upcoming election of directors does not mention it.
   a. The FBI investigation is ongoing, and no charges have been brought against the company or its officials. Does failure to disclose the investigation violate the proxy rules?
   b. Sara sues under the proxy rules to enjoin the shareholders' meeting pending a corrected proxy statement. Assuming the investigation was material, does Sara have to show management intended to deceive?
   c. In her suit to enjoin the shareholders' meeting, does Sara have to prove that a majority of shareholders actually read the proxy statement and relied on it?
   d. After the election, the FBI concludes its investigation and turns the case over to the Justice Department, which seeks to fine the company for making the bribes. Sara wants the directors to reimburse the company for any fines. Will she succeed if she sues them on behalf of the company under the proxy rules?

4. GPI enters into a merger agreement with New Data Corporation (NDC), under which NDC will acquire GPI for $50 per share. GPI shareholders must approve the merger.
   a. GPI's proxy statement recommending the merger fails to disclose that NDC has been sued for price-fixing and faces potentially staggering civil liability. Sara sues to enjoin the merger under the federal proxy rules. Are NDC's problems material to GPI shareholders?
   b. NDC acquires 51 percent of GPI shares in a tender offer. Assured of the outcome of the shareholder vote, NDC then proceeds with a cash-out

merger. After the merger is approved, Sara claims the proxy statement seriously understated GPI's earnings for the last three quarters. Can Sara challenge the merger under the proxy rules?

c. After the merger, Sara claims that had she known about GPI's true earnings picture, she (and other GPI shareholders) would not have voted for the merger. Instead, she would have exercised her appraisal rights and sought payment of "fair value" for her shares—which she estimates to be $75 per share. Can she recover damages from GPI?

Explanations

1. a. Problems. Federal proxy claims cannot be brought in state court. Federal courts have exclusive jurisdiction over alleged violations of the Exchange Act, including the proxy regulations. Exchange Act §27. Sara must either drop her federal proxy claim from her state complaint or sue in federal court, where the state claims can be asserted under the court's pendent jurisdiction.

   In addition, the state fraud and fiduciary claims may face a number of procedural and substantive obstacles. To prove fraud, Sara will have to show that the board intentionally misrepresented the CEO's compensation, that shareholders collectively relied on the board representations, that the shareholders would have voted differently were it not for misrepresentations, and that the excessive compensation caused shareholders a loss. To maintain a derivative suit challenging the directors' fiduciary breach, Sara may have to make a demand on the board or offer an excuse for not making it and perhaps post a bond for defendants' litigation expenses, if her suit is unsuccessful. (See §18.3.) She will then have to overcome the business judgment rule that presumes disinterested directors act in good faith, with reasonable care, and in the corporation's best interests. (See §12.2.)

   b. Yes. Sara can bring an implied private cause of action to enforce any of the provisions of the SEC proxy rules. See *J.I. Case Co. v. Borak* (§10.1.2). Although most proxy cases are brought to enforce duties under Rule 14a-9, which prohibits proxy fraud, the same logic of protecting shareholder voting animates the other proxy rules and suggests implied causes of action for their violation. See *Haas v. Weibolt Stores Inc.*, 725 F.2d 71 (7th Cir. 1984) (implying action for violation of Rule 14a-7).

2. a. Yes. A prediction, like other forward-looking statements, can be misleading if the source is a speaker on whom shareholders rely. See *Virginia Bankshares, Inc. v. Sandberg*, 501 U.S. 1083 (1991). Although a prediction's veracity cannot be tested at the time it is made, the sincerity of the speaker and the existence of supporting facts (or the nonexistence of contradictory information) is implicit in a prediction. *Virginia Bankshares,*

however, requires both that (1) management not believe that the earnings would be flat, and (2) there was data that contradicted their view that earnings would be flat. That management was purchasing strongly suggests both. Management's purpose in issuing the misleading prediction seemed to be to manipulate the stock price, believing that earnings would not be flat and having information to support that view.

Nonetheless, the causal relationship between management's undue pessimism and the election of directors at the annual meeting may be lacking. See *Mills v. Electric Auto-Lite Co.* (§10.2.2). Although a company's earnings direction would normally be important to shareholders deciding how to vote, the pessimistic prediction actually hurts the incumbent directors' election chances. If the directors were reelected despite the false "bad news," it is improbable they would not have been reelected had the disclosure been more favorable. (Of course, investors who relied on the overly pessimistic forecast—such as by selling their stock—would have an action for securities fraud under Rule 10b-5. See Chapter 22.)

b. No. Sara lacks standing for two reasons. First, she did not vote and cannot claim that the misleading proxy statement influenced her vote. Although *J.I. Case v. Borak* speaks of shareholders as private attorney generals, the procedures applicable to both derivative suit and class actions require that the shareholder acting on behalf of others be a contemporaneous participant. See *Gaines v. Haughton*, 645 F.2d 761 (9th Cir. 1981) (denying standing to shareholder who had not himself granted a proxy to defendant).

Second, Sara was not harmed in her capacity as a corporate voter, but rather as a selling shareholder. The proxy rules are meant to preserve the integrity of the voting process, not stock trading. Other rules protect against deception when investors buy or sell stock. Under Rule 10b-5, Sara could claim the deceptive proxy statement was "in connection with the purchase or sale" of her shares. See §22.2. In addition, Sara could claim the proxy statement was a deceptive SEC filing on which she relied in the sale of her shares. Under Exchange Act §18, any person who purchases or sells securities in reliance on false or misleading statements in Exchange Act filings with the SEC, which statements affected the stock price, may sue any person who made the statement subject to a defense of good faith ignorance. It is unlikely the courts would expand the proxy fraud action beyond misinformed shareholder voting. See *Virginia Bankshares, Inc. v. Sandberg* (§10.2.2).

3. a. Not necessarily. Courts have not favored use of the proxy rules to embarrass management into compliance with other legal norms or to confess corporate wrongdoing. It is possible a court would decide the FBI investigation, which had not led to formal charges, was immaterial.

See Schedule 14A, Item 7, which refers to Regulation S-K, Item 401(f) (requiring disclosure only if person is actually convicted in criminal proceeding or named the subject of pending criminal proceeding). Nonetheless, some courts have required the disclosure of potential liabilities, particularly related to environmental compliance, under a probability/magnitude test that balances both the likelihood of the company's being liable and the significance of that liability. See *Grossman v. Waste Management, Inc.*, No. 83-C-2167 (N.D. Ill. 1983).

The investigation's immateriality is buttressed if the underlying bribery activities (even if they occurred) are not material. See *United States v. Mathews*, 787 F.2d 38 (2d Cir. 1986) (corporate officer who had not been charged need not disclose participation in bribery conspiracy because disclosure would be tantamount to admitting guilt to uncharged crime). To require management to disclose wrongdoing that might lead to criminal charges would put corporate insiders in the position of incriminating themselves. Nonetheless, some courts have mandated disclosure when a company engages in widespread criminal behavior even though the dollar amounts were relatively small. See *SEC v. Schlitz Brewing Co.*, 452 F. Supp. 824 (E.D. Wis. 1978) (requiring disclosure of $3 million in illegal kickbacks to beer retailers).

b. Probably not. Most courts have not treated scienter (or intentional deception) to be an element of proxy fraud. See *Gould v. American-Hawaiian Steamship Co.*, 535 F.2d 761 (3d Cir. 1976) (applying negligence standard on theory proxy rules impose a high standard of care on those responsible for informed shareholder voting). This heightened standard is particularly appropriate when the relief is sought against insiders and involves an injunction, rather than money damages. A scienter requirement in such circumstances would encourage careless disclosure practices, a result at odds with the §14(a) theory of informed shareholder voting.
c. No. The Supreme Court in *Mills* recognized that proof of individual reliance would be too burdensome. It is sufficient that the proxy statement contained omissions of material facts.
d. Probably not. Although *Borak* permits a shareholder to sue derivatively for violations of the proxy rules, Sara will *have* to articulate a theory that the corporation has been injured by the directors' fraud-tainted election. That is, there must be a causal link between the failure to disclose the directors' misdeeds and the bribes themselves. See *Abbey v. Control Data Corp.*, 603 F.2d 729 (8th Cir. 1979). The shareholders were never asked to approve the bribes, but instead to elect directors. If Sara were calling for new elections, a clearer causal link would exist. Instead, Sara is seeking to use a disclosure defect to enforce a duty of honorable management—a matter normally left to corporate fiduciary law. Disclosure that would have "shamed" directors to behave properly

has been rejected by the Supreme Court as establishing a causal relationship in a case of proxy fraud. See *Virginia Bankshares, Inc. v. Sandberg* (§10.2.2).

4. a. No. In the cash-out merger GPI's assets and liabilities will be absorbed into NDC, and GPI's shareholders will receive cash. (See §36.2.6.) GPI's shareholders, assuming they have received fair consideration for their shares, will have no continuing financial interest in the surviving company and should be indifferent to any contingent liabilities of the new joint business. NDC's problems are not material to GPI shareholders in this *cash-for-stock* merger.
   b. Yes, if the understatement adversely affects Sara's ability to exercise shareholder rights. Normally, shareholders whose vote is unnecessary—as it is in this transaction where NDC *holds* majority voting power—cannot establish the causal link between their vote and the transaction. *Virginia Bankshares* (finding lack of transaction causation when parent squeezed out minority of 85 percent–owned subsidiary) (§10.2.2). Nonetheless, if the deception was material and Sara voted for the merger, she will have lost her state appraisal rights that require her to have not voted for the transaction. See §37.2. In addition, if Sara was deceived into not pursuing state conflict-of-interest remedies, she can also claim a causal link between her vote and accomplishment of the transaction.
   c. Not GPI, but the surviving NDC. A damages award in a proxy fraud case involving a merger essentially rewrites the terms of the transaction. In this case, if Sara can show that disclosure of all material information would have led a "reasonable shareholder" to insist on a "fair" price, the court will award this as damages to all members of Sara's class action—that is, all shareholders who would have voted against the merger and exercised their appraisal rights. The judgment will be against NDC because it assumed the obligations of GPI in the merger. See §36.2.1.

PART IV

Corporate Fiduciary Duties

Chapter 11 Corporate Fiduciary Duties — An Introduction

At the heart of corporate law lie duties of trust and confidence — fiduciary duties — owed by those who control and operate the corporation's governance machinery to the body of constituents known as the "corporation." Directors, officers, and controlling shareholders are obligated to act in the corporation's best interests, which traditionally has meant primarily for the benefit of shareholders — the owners of the corporation's residual financial rights.

State courts, not legislatures, have been the primary shapers of corporate fiduciary duties. Judicial rules balance management flexibility and accountability, producing often vague and shifting standards. The American Law Institute has contributed the Principles of Corporate Governance (see §1.2.4) to articulate and provide guidance on corporate fiduciary duties and the standards of judicial review they entail. Fiduciary duties fuel the ongoing debate over the function and responsibility of the corporation in society.

This chapter introduces the theory and nature of corporate fiduciary duties (§11.1), gives an overview of the duties of care and loyalty (§11.2), and describes the reality of fiduciary duties in modern corporations (§11.3), particularly as they relate to independent directors (§11.4). The chapter also offers an overview of recent federal legislation — the Sarbanes-Oxley Act of 2002 and the Dodd-Frank Act of 2010 — that introduce a variety of corporate governance reforms in public corporations and thus federalize some corporate fiduciary duties (§11.5).

The other chapters in this part describe corporate fiduciary duties in specific contexts, as well as the procedures for their enforcement:

- duty of care of directors in making decisions and monitoring corporate affairs, as well as the operation of the business judgment rule and statutory exculpation provisions (Chapter 12)
- duty of loyalty of corporate officials when they enter into self-dealing transactions with the corporation and judicial review for fairness (Chapter 13)
- judicial review of executive compensation under corporate fiduciary law and federal restrictions and disclosure requirements (Chapter 14)
- indemnification of corporate officials under corporate statutes and by agreement and directors' and officers' insurance (Chapter 15)
- duty of loyalty of corporate officials who take business opportunities in which the corporation may be interested and who compete with the corporation (Chapter 16)
- duties in corporate groups, including dealings by parent corporations with partially owned subsidiaries and buyouts of minority shareholders (Chapter 17)
- enforcement of fiduciary duties in derivative suits, including procedural requirements and the board's role in litigation on behalf of the corporation (Chapter 18)

In short, this part focuses on fiduciary duties in the context of business operations. Other chapters focus on fiduciary duties in the context of shareholder voting (Chapter 8), disclosure to shareholders (Chapter 22), securities trading by corporate insiders (Chapter 23), and changes of control (Chapter 39).

§11.1 THE CORPORATE FIDUCIARY — A UNIQUE RELATIONSHIP

§11.1.1 Analogies to Trusts and Partnerships

What is the corporate fiduciary's relationship to the corporation? Early courts analogized the corporation to a trust, the directors to trustees, and the shareholders to trust beneficiaries. But modern courts recognize that the analogy is flawed because trustees have limited discretion compared to directors.

Sometimes the corporation, particularly when closely held, has also been analogized to a partnership. But corporate fiduciaries operate in a system that prizes corporate permanence as well as centralized management and the discretion specialization entails. Although some cases have implied partner-like duties for participants in close corporations (see §27.2.2), the cases are exceptions to the broad discretion afforded corporate directors.

In the end, the most that can be said is that directors have a unique relationship to the corporation. The relationship arises from the broad authority delegated directors to manage and supervise the corporation's business and affairs, subject to the rights of shareholders to elect directors.

Duties of Other Corporate Insiders

Courts have generally imposed on corporate officers and senior executives the same fiduciary duties imposed on directors. MBCA §8.41. Those employees who are officers in name but have no actual authority, as well as other employees, have traditional duties of care and loyalty as agents of the corporation. In addition, corporate officers and employees have a duty of candor that requires them to give the corporation (the board of directors or a supervisor) information relevant to their corporate position.

In general, persons retained by the corporation do not have corporate fiduciary duties. For example, an attorney who advises a majority shareholder in an unfair squeezeout of minority shareholders is not bound by fiduciary duties to the corporation, though the attorney can be liable for tortious aiding and abetting of a fiduciary breach by the majority shareholder.

§11.1.2 Theory of Corporate Fiduciary Duties

The genius of the U.S. corporation lies in its specialization of function. The corporation separates the risk taking of investors and the decision making of specialized managers. This separation creates an inevitable tension.

- **Management discretion.** The efficiency of specialized management suggests that managers should have broad discretion. Giving shareholders (and courts) significant oversight would undermine this premise of the corporate form. In cases of normal business decision making, judicial abstention is appropriate.
- **Management accountability.** Entrusting management to nonowners suggests a need for substantial accountability. As nonowners, managers have natural incentives to be lazy or faithless. Although shareholder voting constrains management abuse, voting is episodic. Without supplemental limits, management discretion would ultimately cause investors to lose confidence in the corporate form. In cases of management overreaching, judicial intervention is the norm.

Corporate fiduciary law must resolve this tension. Like much of corporate law, fiduciary rules aim to minimize "agency costs"—the losses of investor-owners dealing through manager-agents.

§11.1.3 To Whom Are Fiduciary Duties Owed?

Corporate directors are said to owe fiduciary duties to the "corporation," not the particular shareholders who elected them. Some courts and many commentators assert that fiduciary rules thus proceed from a theory of maximizing corporate financial well-being by focusing on *shareholder wealth maximization*. The theory posits that any fiduciary rule — whether governing boardroom behavior or use of inside information — must maximize the value of shareholders' interests in the corporation. As residual claimants of the corporation's income stream, shareholders are the most interested in effective management. Under this theory, the corporation's other constituents such as bondholders, creditors, employees, and communities where the business operates are limited to their contractual rights and other legal protections. See *Equity-Linked Investors, LP v. Adams*, 705 A.2d 1040 (Del. Ch. 1997) (finding that new borrowing by financially troubled firm did not violate rights of preferred shareholders, which "are contractual in nature"). To the extent other constituents have unprotected interests inconsistent with those of shareholders, the interests of shareholders prevail — a *shareholder primacy* approach.

In most instances, courts have said that corporate fiduciary duties run to equity shareholders. When the business is insolvent, however, these duties run to the corporation's creditors — who become the corporation's new residual claimants. See *Geyer v. Ingersoll Publications Co.*, 621 A.2d 784 (Del. Ch. 1992). When the corporation is on the verge of insolvency, the question arises whether directors should be allowed to take risks to return to solvency (for the benefit of shareholders) or avoid risks to preserve assets (for the benefit of creditors). Some cases suggest that the board's role shifts in such circumstances from being an "agent for the residual riskbearers" to owing a duty to the corporate enterprise. *Credit Lyonnais Bank Nederland N.V. v. Pathe Communciations Corp.*, No. 12150 (Del. Ch. 1991).

Dodge v. Ford Motor Co.

Despite its prevalence, the theory of shareholder wealth maximization has gaps. For example, the case most often cited as supporting the theory may actually have turned on nonshareholder concerns. In *Dodge v. Ford Motor Co.*, 170 N.W. 668 (Mich. 1919), the Michigan Supreme Court reviewed Ford Motor's decision to discontinue paying a special $10 million dividend, ostensibly to finance a new smelting plant while paying above-market wages and reducing the price of Ford cars. Minority shareholders claimed the decision was inconsistent with the fundamental purpose of the business corporation — to maximize the return to shareholders. The court agreed and faulted Henry Ford for reducing car prices and running Ford Motor as a "semi-eleemosynary institution and not as a business institution." The court ordered the special dividend, though curiously refused to enjoin Ford's expansion plans because "judges are not business experts."

At first blush, the case seemed to turn on Ford's stated view that his company "has made too much money, has had too large profits . . . and sharing them with the public, by reducing the price of the output of the company, ought to be undertaken." Nonetheless, more was below the surface. The plaintiff Dodge brothers (former suppliers of car chassis and motors to Ford Motor) hoped to use the special dividend to finance their own start-up car manufacturing company, and Henry Ford's dividend cutback was meant to forestall this competition, despite the attendant benefits of competition to the car-buying public and Michigan's auto industry. The court's decision to second-guess perhaps the most successful industrialist ever is at odds with the general judicial deference to management, as well as with the Michigan court's specific observation that Ford Motor's great success had resulted from its "capable management."

Using corporate law, the court advanced a social agenda. Fixing on snippets from Henry Ford's public relations posturing, the court labeled him an antishareholder altruist. This allowed the court to order Ford to fund the Dodge brothers' new car company, thus injecting some competitive balance into the expanding auto industry and ultimately into Michigan politics. Soon after, the Dodge brothers parlayed their court victory into a sizeable buyout of their Ford Motor holdings. (It is worth noting that no other minority shareholders participated in the case, though Henry Ford eventually bought them out, too.) Ironically, the case so often cited as declaring a philosophy of shareholder wealth maximization turns out — on closer examination — to have been about a squabble between two competitors where the stakes were consumer prices, product choice, employee wages, industry competition, and political pluralism.

"Other Constituency" Statutes

Some states have recently enacted "other constituency" statutes that permit, but do not require, directors to consider nonshareholder constituents (or stakeholders), particularly in the context of a corporate takeover. See Pa. BCL §1715 (directors may consider "shareholders, employees, suppliers, customers and creditors of the corporation . . . communities in which offices or other establishments of the corporation are located . . . short-term and long-term interests of the corporation"). The statutes have been controversial. Some commentators have praised them as signaling a new era of corporate social responsibility; others have criticized them as a ruse for incumbent entrenchment and fecklessness. By permitting directors to rationalize corporate decisions on such open-ended concepts as "long-term interests" and "communities where the corporation operates," the statutes appear to dilute director accountability.

Although no cases have confronted the meaning of the "other constituency" statutes, other cases give mixed signals about directorial deference to nonshareholder stakeholders. Some cases suggest directors can take stakeholders into account only if rationally related to promoting shareholder interests. See *Revlon v. MacAndrews & Forbes Holding*, 506 A.2d 173 (Del. 1986). Yet others suggest directors have significant latitude to consider "corporate culture," not just immediate shareholder returns, when responding to takeover threats. See *Paramount Communications, Inc. v. Time, Inc.*, 571 A.2d 1142 (Del. 1990).

Corporate Social Responsibility (CSR)

Over the past decade, many companies have recognized that the company's responsibilities extend beyond the legal duties toward shareholders and others with whom the company does business. Although not required by law, many companies (particular multinational companies) have voluntarily taken responsibility for their impact on customers, workers, communities, and other stakeholders, as well as the environment.

Companies tout their CSR activities—such as "green" initiatives or "fair labor" commitments—to bolster their reputations as corporate citizens. To show their commitment to CSR, many companies have agreed to reporting guidelines and operational standards developed by various nongovernmental organizations (NGOs). In addition, some institutional investors seek to take into account in their investment and voting decisions whether companies have implemented CSR programs.

Proponents see CSR as "applied business ethics" and a means more suited than regulatory compliance for companies and their decision makers to internalize externalities (the costs imposed by business on others). Critics claim that CSR is superficial window dressing that companies use to divert attention from the harms they cause and to forestall government regulation.

Recently, the CSR movement has received support from various quarters. In a nod to the growing relevance to investors of environmental concerns, the SEC has issued interpretive guidance to reporting companies on their disclosure regarding climate change. Guidance on Climate Change Disclosure, Securities Act Rel. No. 9106 (2010) (pointing out the insurance industry lists climate change as the number one risk facing the industry). While not taking a stance on the climate change debate, the SEC pointed out that under existing disclosure requirements (such as management's discussion of future contingencies) companies may have to disclose material information about (1) the impact on the company's business of existing (and even pending) climate change laws; (2) the impact of international accords on climate change; (3) the actual or indirect consequences of climate change trends (such as decreased demand for carbon-intensive products or higher demand for lower-emission products); and (4) actual and potential physical impacts of environmental changes to the company's business. As some have pointed out, "what gets measured gets managed."

In addition, nongovernmental organizations (such as Ceres) are organizing investor groups, environmental organizations, and other public interest groups to work with for-profit corporations to address sustainability challenges such as climate change, resource use, and water scarcity. Even as governments have been paralyzed to act, many investors and businesses in the private sector are moving ahead on sustainability initiatives. They understand that environmental and social sustainability presents risks (and opportunities) for their business and that sustainability considerations must be a part of their core business strategies if they are to achieve a competitive advantage—including corporate governance, stakeholder engagement, corporate disclosure, and performance. Some studies bear this out, finding a relationship between company sustainability performance and financial performance.

In a similar vein, the United Nations has reconceptualized the modern corporation as being quasi-governmental, with responsibilities not only to comply with law but also to respect human rights. For example, the U.N. Human Rights Council has adopted a set of guiding principles for business (known as the Ruggie Principles, for the professor who drafted them) that are designed to ensure that companies do not violate human rights in the course of their operations and provide redress when they do. The guiding principles—which place companies in the position of "private states"—lay out specific steps that companies should take to make sure they respect human rights. For example, companies are called on to undertake a "human rights due diligence," which includes an impact assessment, monitoring, community engagement, and a grievance mechanism, so people who have even minor complaints against a company have a place to go to have issues addressed. The assessment should cover not only potential for adverse human rights impacts of the company's activities but also the impacts of business partners. The guidelines call on companies to use leverage to prevent or mitigate human rights abuses by business partners or to end the business relationship.

§11.2 FIDUCIARY DUTIES OF CARE AND LOYALTY

According to traditional fiduciary analysis, corporate managers owe two duties to the corporation: care and loyalty. Each duty describes standards for judicial review of corporate decision-making and fiduciary activities.

Note on Duty of Good Faith

Delaware courts have recently articulated a duty of "good faith" that applies when directors act *intentionally* to violate positive law, with a purpose other than the corporation's best interests, or with a conscious disregard for their duties to act. *Walt Disney Co. Deriv. Litig.*, 906 A.2d 27 (2006). The courts have said that the duty of good faith is breached when directors fail to consider the financial ramifications of an executive's contingent pay package, when directors fail to establish an oversight system to monitor the corporation's legal compliance, or when directors act as "stooges" for a controlling shareholder. The courts have explained the good faith duty as a subset of the duty of loyalty and, as such, a duty that cannot be exculpated. See Del. GCL §102(b)(7) (see §15.1).

§11.2.1 Duty of Care

The duty of care addresses the attentiveness and prudence of managers in performing their decision-making and oversight functions. The famous "business judgment rule" presumes that directors (and officers) carry out their functions in good faith, after sufficient investigation, and for acceptable reasons. Unless this presumption is overcome, courts abstain from second-guessing well-meaning business decisions even when they are flops. This is a risk that shareholders take when they make a corporate investment. See Chapter 12.

To encourage directors to take business risks without fear of personal liability, corporate law protects well-meaning directors through exculpation provisions in the corporation's articles (see §12.5), statutory and contractual indemnification (see §15.1), and directors' and officers' insurance (see §15.2).

§11.2.2 Duty of Loyalty

The duty of loyalty addresses fiduciaries' conflicts of interest and requires fiduciaries to put the corporation's interests ahead of their own — that is, fiduciaries cannot serve two masters. Corporate fiduciaries breach their duty of loyalty when they divert corporate assets, business opportunities, or proprietary information for personal gain.

Flagrant Diversion

Diversion can be as simple, and as reprehensible, as a corporate official stealing tangible corporate assets. This is a plain breach of the fiduciary's duty of loyalty because the diversion was unauthorized and the corporation received no benefit in the transaction. Besides disaffirming the transaction as unauthorized (see §3.3.3), the corporation can sue for breach of fiduciary duty and in tort.

Self-Dealing

Diversion can be masked in a self-dealing transaction. When a fiduciary enters into a transaction with the corporation on unfair terms, the effect (from the corporation's standpoint) is the same as if he had appropriated the difference between the transaction's fair value and the transaction's price. Courts, as well as statutes, address when a self-dealing transaction is unfair. See Chapter 13.

A parent corporation that controls a partially owned subsidiary can breach its duty to the minority shareholders of the subsidiary if the parent prefers itself at the expense of the minority. See §17.2. The ultimate form of preferential dealing occurs when the parent squeezes out the minority (in a merger or other transaction) and forces the minority to accept unfair consideration for their shares. See §17.3.

Executive Compensation

When a director or officer sells his executive services to the corporation, diversion can occur if the executive's compensation exceeds the fair value of his services. See Chapter 14.

Usurping Corporate Opportunity

When a corporate fiduciary seizes for herself a desirable business opportunity that the corporation may have taken and profited from, diversion occurs if the fiduciary denies the corporation the opportunity to expand profitably. See Chapter 16.

Disclosure to Shareholders

Corporate officials who provide shareholders false or deceptive information, on which the shareholders rely to their detriment, not only undermine corporate credibility and transparency, but frustrate shareholders' expectations of fiduciary honesty and accountability. Duties of disclosure arise when directors seek a shareholder vote (see Chapter 8—state law; Chapter 10—federal proxy fraud) and when corporate officials communicate to stock trading markets (see §21.1—state law; Chapter 22—federal Rule 10b-5).

Trading on Inside Information

When a fiduciary is aware of confidential corporate information — such as the impending takeover of another company — and he buys the target's stock, diversion can occur if the fiduciary's trading interferes with the corporation's takeover plans. By the same logic, when the fiduciary trades with the company's shareholders using inside information, the fiduciary diverts to himself information belonging to the corporation. See Chapter 23.

Selling Out

A corporate official who accepts a bribe to sell her corporate office breaches a duty to the corporation. Likewise, a controlling shareholder who sells his controlling interest to a new owner who then diverts corporate assets to herself exposes the remaining shareholders to the new owner's looting. See §20.2.

Entrenchment

A manager who uses the corporate governance machinery to protect his incumbency effectively diverts control from the shareholders to himself. Besides preventing shareholders from exercising their control rights — whether by voting or selling to a new owner — management entrenchment undermines the disciplining effect on management of a robust market in corporate control. See Chapter 8 (voting manipulation); §39.2 (takeover defenses).

There is no uniform standard for judging these conflict-of-interest transactions. Some are flatly prohibited (insider trading), others receive searching judicial fairness review (squeezeouts), and others are subject to internal corporate safeguards (executive compensation).

§11.2.3 Judicial Enforcement of Fiduciary Duties

Fiduciary duties generally are said to be owed to the corporation and not to particular shareholders and must be enforced in the name of the corporation. This reflects the practical and conceptual danger of one shareholder purporting to speak for the body of shareholders. Rarely, however, are fiduciary breaches challenged by the corporation because those who abused their control are unlikely to sue themselves. Instead, fiduciary breaches usually are challenged by shareholders in derivative litigation brought on behalf of the corporation (see Chapter 18).

§11.3 FIDUCIARY DUTIES—CORPORATE AND MARKET REALITIES

§11.3.1 Fiduciary Duties in Closely Held Corporations

In closely held corporations (those that do not have a trading market for their shares) the corporate participants often have a relationship of special trust. No market exists for their shares. Some courts have implied a duty among participants akin to that of partners. Other courts have used statutory protections against "oppression" to intervene on behalf of minority shareholders. See Chapter 27.

A frequent issue in close corporations is whether fiduciary duties can be modified by agreement. Although modern partnership law permits partners to waive fiduciary rights, courts have been less willing to see corporate fiduciary duties as default terms. Compare RUPA §103(b) (permitting partners to waive duty of loyalty as to categories of activities, if not manifestly unreasonable, and to reduce duty of care if not unreasonable). Rather, corporate fiduciary duties have been viewed as immutable aspects of the corporate relationship.

§11.3.2 Fiduciary Duties in Modern Public Corporations

In public corporations, management has three principal functions. First, directors and senior executives make "enterprise" decisions concerning operational and business matters—such as where to locate a new facility or whether to discontinue a product line. The board establishes the strategic plan; senior executives carry it out. Directors rely on the senior executives for information in establishing and monitoring the business plan. Shareholder and management interests typically overlap as to these enterprise decisions, as reflected in the deferential business judgment rule.

Second, directors act on "ownership" issues—such as initiating a merger with another company or constructing takeover defenses. Outside directors (that is, directors who are not employed by the corporation) have assumed special prominence on these issues, as courts often defer to the independent judgment of outside directors when corporate control is at stake. Although directors in public corporations once were criticized for acting as "rubber stamps" for management, directors lately have become more forceful. Spurred by activist institutional investors and the clamor after Sarbanes-Oxley, outside directors have asserted themselves by replacing CEOs, negotiating takeovers, and making themselves more accountable. Outside directors, sometimes acting in special committees, often turn to their own legal and investment advisors.

Third, directors are responsible for "oversight" of the corporation—such as reviewing senior executives' performance and ensuring corporate compliance with legal norms. In public corporations the board often establishes compliance programs and receives regular management reports. As corporate responsibility has grown in such areas as regulatory compliance and foreign bribery, courts have increasingly insisted on higher levels of board oversight. In addition, disclosure by the company to public trading markets allows shareholders to gauge how well management is overseeing the corporation.

Management in public corporations lives under the watchful eye of the securities markets. When the market detects mismanagement, the trading price of the company's stock falls. This makes it attractive for outside bidders or shareholder insurgents to acquire control and oust the ineffective management. In extreme cases, a collapse in the stock price signals to creditors that the company is insolvent and should be put in the hands of a bankruptcy court. Fiduciary norms take these corrective mechanisms into account, relaxing scrutiny when control markets are available to discipline poor management and tightening scrutiny when the board attempts to insulate itself from these markets.

Note on "Imperial CEO"

In the United States *corporate management* in public corporations often refers to the Chief Executive Officer (CEO), whose vision and leadership make him (and sometimes her) the ultimate manager of the company. In most companies, investors focus on outside directors only when something goes wrong. The CEO puts together a management team — including a Chief Operating Officer (COO), Chief Financial Officer (CFO), and Chief Legal Officer (CLO or General Counsel) — to oversee and run the company's business. Generally, investors and employees look to the CEO as the symbol of ultimate authority for the company. This is not, of course, what the law says. But the reality is that outside directors, chosen through a nominating process often heavily influenced by the CEO, have few incentives to be suspicious or adversarial. They are mostly dependent on the CEO's management team for information and analysis. Strategy is typically developed by the management team in internal discussions and then presented to the board for approval.

§11.4 INDEPENDENT DIRECTORS

Over the last several years, directors who do not have an employment relationship with the corporation—so-called independent directors—have assumed increased prominence in U.S. public corporations. The accounting and financial scandals that came to light in the early 2000s focused attention on the failures of outside directors to monitor and oversee corporate management. Paradoxically, the response has been to assign even greater importance to independent directors. Empirical studies are mixed on whether outside directors increase company profitability and whether they have an effect on controlling management excesses.

Sarbanes-Oxley

The Sarbanes-Oxley Act of 2002 (described in §11.5.1 below) specifies the responsibilities of independent directors on the audit committees of public corporations. As required by Sarbanes-Oxley, stock exchanges have adopted listing standards that specify the composition and functions of the audit committees of listed companies (including foreign issuers and small business issuers). Under these standards, audit committees must be composed entirely of independent directors, as defined by the SEC.

In addition, all reporting companies must disclose whether at least one member of the audit committee is a financial expert. Sarbanes-Oxley §407, Reg. S-K, Item 401 (defining "audit committee financial expert" as one with significant auditing, accounting, financial, or comparable experience).

In addition, the exchanges' governance listing standards must also specify that the audit committee of listed companies be responsible for appointing, compensating, and overseeing the company's independent audit firm—a curtailment of the power of the full board and shareholders over outside accountants. The audit committee (not the board) must have the authority to hire independent counsel and other advisors, their fees to be paid by the listed company. Rule 10A-3; Exchange Act Rel. No. 47,654 (2003).

Dodd-Frank

The Dodd-Frank Act of 2010 (described in §11.5.2 below) also intrudes into the boardroom of public corporations, requiring the stock exchanges to adopt listing standards that require all the directors on the corporation's compensation committee to be independent. Dodd-Frank §952. The committee must also have the authority to hire independent compensation consultants.

Delaware

State courts, particularly in Delaware, have increasingly deferred to independent directors in various contexts. Delaware courts review deferentially corporate transactions in which management has a conflicting interest if a majority of the board is composed of directors who are *disinterested* (no conflicting financial interest in the transaction) and *independent* (neither beholden to interested party because of financial or business relationships, nor dominated by interested party through family or social relationships). See *Orman v. Cullman*, 794 A.2d 5 (Del. Ch. 2002) (distinguishing between "interest" and "independence" of directors).

Delaware courts focus on director independence in deciding whether

- to shift the burden to the challenging shareholder in transactions involving management conflicts. See §13.3.3 (director self-dealing transactions), §17.3.3 (squeeze-out mergers).
- to review executive pay under a waste standard, rather than the more burdensome fairness standard. See §14.2.3 (executive compensation).
- to indemnify corporate officials who become liable or settle claims arising from their corporate position. See §15.1.2 (permissive indemnification).
- to approve settlement of derivative litigation. See *Kahn v. Sullivan*, 594 A.2d 48 (Del. 1991) (approving settlement of claim that company had wasted corporate assets in donating money for art museum to house CEO's personal art collection).
- to dismiss shareholder derivative litigation, either on the basis of "demand futility" or recommendations of a special litigation committee. See §18.5.3 (demand requirement), §18.5.4 (special litigation committee).
- to uphold antitakeover measures (whether in anticipation of unwanted bids or in response to particular threats) and deal protection measures. See §8.2.2 (shark repellents), §39.2.3 (takeover defenses), §39.2.4 (deal protections).

Delaware courts have recently shown more willingness to inquire into the social and business relationships between outside directors and management — to test whether there exists implicit directorial bias. For example, the Delaware Chancery Court questioned the independence of a tenured Stanford law professor, who as a member of a special litigation committee was asked to determine whether suit should be brought against various corporate executives who allegedly had engaged in insider trading. The court concluded the professor's and executives' close and overlapping ties to Stanford — as large donors, fellow professors, and members of a university policy institute — suggested an institutional context in which motives of "friendship and collegiality" could not be ignored. *In re Oracle Corp. Derivative Litigation*, 824 A.2d 917 (Del. Ch. 2003). But the Delaware Supreme Court has stopped short of saying that social and business relationships alone undermine independence. See *Beam v. Stewart*, 845 A.2d 1040 (Del. 2004) (finding directors sufficiently "independent" in demand-futility case, despite longstanding personal friendships and close business relationships to CEO, who held 94 percent of company's voting power).

The MBCA goes one step further and makes lack of independence a basis for imposing liability on directors in an interested-party transaction. See MBCA §8.31(a)(2)(iii) (making director liable if director's judgment is affected because of a lack of objectivity due to director's familial, financial, or business relationship with interested person or a lack of independence due to director's domination or control by interested person). Upon such a showing, the director has the burden to prove that he reasonably believed the challenged conduct was in the best interests of the corporation. MBCA §8.31(a)(2)(iii)(B).

Corporate Governance in Stock Listing Standards

The New York Stock Exchange and the NASDAQ have adopted standards that compel listed companies to adopt corporate governance structures that emphasize "independent directors." In many instances, these listing standards are mandated by Sarbanes-Oxley and Dodd-Frank:

Governance Listing Standards (NYSE and NASDAQ)	
Independence of majority of directors	• Majority of directors must be "independent" and not have "material relationship" with company (NYSE only) • Majority of directors must be "independent" (NASDAQ only) • Determination of director qualifications disclosed in proxy statement (or annual report if company not subject to proxy rules)
"Independence" defined	Director not "independent" if • director is company employee or director's family member is company executive • director (or family member) receives payment from company (NYSE — more than $100,000; NASDAQ — more than $60,000) • director (or family member) affiliated with current or past auditor • company executives sit on compensation committee of outside director's company • company has significant dealings with outside director's company (NYSE — $1,000,000 or 2 percent of outside company's revenues; NASDAQ — $200,000 or 5 percent of outside company's revenues)
Executive sessions	• Independent directors must meet at regularly scheduled meetings without management • Company must have method for internal and shareholder communications to independent directors (NYSE only) *(continued)*

Governance Listing Standards (NYSE and NASDAQ)	
Committees	• **Audit committee** must be comprised solely of three or more independent directors who are "financially literate"; members must meet SEC standards on independence; at least one member must meet SEC "financial expert" standard • **Nominating committee** must be composed solely of three or more independent directors (with limited exception for one outside, nonindependent director); company must certify adoption of nomination process • **Compensation committee** must be composed only of independent directors (as defined by SEC rule) with exclusive power to hire independent compensation consultants
Code of conduct	• Company must adopt and disclose code of conduct that meets requirements of Sarbanes-Oxley • Any waivers for directors and officers must be approved by board and disclosed on Form 8-K
Corporate governance guidelines	• Company must adopt and disclose guidelines on director qualifications, compensation, education, responsibilities, succession, annual evaluation, access to management (NYSE only)
Audits	• Company must have internal audit function, cannot be outsourced to company's outside auditor (NYSE only) • Company must disclose receipt of audit opinion with "going concern" qualification (NASDAQ only)
Related party transaction	• Audit committee, or group of independent directors, must approve related party transactions (NASDAQ only)
Certification	• CEO must certify annually that company is in compliance with governance listing standards (NYSE only) • Company must notify NYSE or NASDAQ if company executives become aware of material noncompliance
Exceptions	• Independent director requirements not applicable to companies controlled 50 percent or more by individual, group, or another company • Investment companies generally not subject to governance listing standards • Foreign issuers listed on NYSE not subject to governance listing standards, except SEC standards on audit committee independence • Foreign issuers listed on NASDAQ may apply for exemptions from governance listing standards, except SEC standards on audit committee independence

§11.5 FEDERALIZATION OF CORPORATE GOVERNANCE

Although corporate fiduciary duties arise mostly under state law, federal law has come to play an important role in corporate governance of public corporations. Since the 1930s, federal securities regulation has imposed disclosure requirements that compel corporate fiduciaries in public corporations to reveal information about the operational and financial details of the business as well as the roles of the fiduciaries in the corporation. Thus, corporate fiduciaries in public companies must disclose information to new public shareholders (see Chapter 5) when shareholders vote (see Chapter 9) and when shareholders tender their shares (see Chapter 38). Corporate fiduciaries also face restrictions on their ability to trade in company shares while in the possession of nonpublic material information (see Chapter 23). But, with rare exceptions, the federal regulatory scheme has been premised on disclosure to shareholders.

Recently, federal law has expanded beyond requiring corporate disclosures. The corporate scandals of the early 2000s and the financial crisis of 2008 have caused Congress to rethink the place of federal law in corporate governance of public corporations. In 2002 Congress responded to the misdeeds at companies like Enron and WorldCom by enacting the Sarbanes-Oxley Act, which revamped the regulation of the accounting profession and imposed a variety of new rules on the boards of directors and officers of public companies. In 2010 Congress responded to the financial crisis in the banking sector by enacting the Dodd-Frank Act, not only to reregulate the financial markets but also to add new rules on corporate governance and executive compensation in all public companies.

Note on Securities Regulation

In keeping with the traditional demarcation of corporate law and securities regulation in the United States, this book considers the aspects of Sarbanes-Oxley that deal with corporate governance. Those reforms that address disclosure to investors — securities regulation — are left to other sources. See Alan R. Palmiter, *Securities Regulation: Examples & Explanations* (5th ed. Wolters Kluwer Law & Business 2011).

§11.5.1 Sarbanes-Oxley Act of 2002

Responding to the accounting and corporate scandals of the early 2000s, Congress passed sweeping legislation that departs in many instances from the disclosure-based philosophy of the federal securities laws. The Public

Company Accounting Reform and Investor Protection Act of 2002 (known as the Sarbanes-Oxley Act, after its congressional sponsors) seeks both to strengthen the integrity of the federal securities disclosure system and to federalize specific aspects of public corporation law.

Story of Enron

The story of Enron's rise and fall is an inextricable part of Sarbanes-Oxley. An energy trading company that started as a stodgy natural gas pipeline, Enron grew dramatically during the 1990s to become the seventh-largest corporation in the United States by market capitalization. Its innovative business model, widely lauded and studied, involved the creation of a freewheeling trading market in wholesale energy and transmission (with appurtenant risk management and financial hedging products).

At first the new market and Enron thrived. But as competitors imitated its model, Enron had to look for new ways to maintain its constantly growing profits. Its executives devised two main techniques: (1) Enron entered into paper transactions with special-purpose entities that created the appearance of revenues on Enron's financial statements, and (2) Enron financed these related entities with loans (secured by its high-priced stock) that were not reported as debt on Enron's balance sheet. In short, Enron began trading with itself and placing bets on its common stock.

Both the related-entity transactions (in which high-placed Enron executives held personal investments) and their accounting treatment received the blessing of the Enron board of directors, its auditing firm Arthur Andersen, and its outside law firm Vinson & Elkins. Also, securities firms that participated in financing Enron's related entities pressured their securities analysts to recommend the company's stock. Rather than question anomalies in its financial statements, the investment community awarded Enron with accolades and an ever-increasing stock price.

In 2001 Enron's stock price began to slip as investors became suspicious of its related-entity dealings. As federal investigators began their probes, Enron's auditor publicly vouched for the company's financial statements, while privately shredding incriminating documents. In late 2001, Enron restated its financials for the previous four years and, with a few pencil strokes, reduced its net income by $600 million and increased its debt by $628 million. Bankruptcy soon followed.

Although many in the financial (and political) community decried Enron as a "bad apple," the true impetus for legislative reform came from the almost weekly revelations in late 2001 and early 2002 of new financial scandals at other companies. Some had reported not actual earnings but predicted *pro forma* earnings. Some had treated payments for phone capacity as an investment, not a current expense — thus overstating both assets and net earnings. Some had engaged in paper buy-sell transactions to report immediate revenues while amortizing costs. The final straw came when WorldCom, the second-largest U.S. telecommunications company and operator of MCI, announced that $7 billion the company had reported as assets should have been treated as operating costs. Within weeks the company declared bankruptcy, and a few weeks later Congress passed Sarbanes-Oxley.

Pavlovian Response to Enron

Sarbanes-Oxley reads like a Pavlovian response to the stories of business and financial misconduct revealed in congressional hearings into the collapses at Enron, WorldCom, and a slew of other companies—most in the overbuilt telecom industry. Consider the list of corporate misconduct revealed to Congress and the regulatory responses in Sarbanes-Oxley:

Misconduct	Sarbanes-Oxley Response
Outside auditors failed to discover or report accounting fraud. Some attributed this failure to self-regulation of the accounting profession, which during the 1990s relied on technicalities to satisfy clients. In particular, the accounting firm Arthur Andersen (auditor for many scandal-ridden companies) was passive toward financial irregularities at many clients.	• **PCAOB.** Creates a self-regulatory, five-person Public Company Accounting Oversight Board to establish auditing standards and regulate accounting profession (Sarbanes-Oxley §101) • **Auditor registration.** Requires accounting firms that audit public companies to register with PCAOB (Sarbanes-Oxley §102) • **Audit standards.** Authorizes PCAOB to set standards for public company audits and to enforce its audit rules (Sarbanes-Oxley §§103, 104, 105) • **Auditor sanctions.** Authorizes SEC to sanction auditors for intentional, reckless, and highly negligent conduct (Sarbanes-Oxley §602)
Outside auditors performed nonaudit services that undermined their audit independence. For example, Arthur Andersen came to earn more from Enron for its nonaudit services than for its work as financial auditor.	• **Nonaudit services.** Bans auditors from providing certain types of nonaudit services and requires preapproval by the company's audit committee of permissible nonaudit services (Sarbanes-Oxley §§201, 202)
Outside auditors became too "cozy" with executives of audit clients. For example, many financial officers of Enron were former principals of Arthur Andersen, its auditor.	• **Auditor rotation.** Requires rotation of audit partner every five years (Sarbanes-Oxley §203) • **Revolving door.** Closes "revolving door" for members of audit team who within one year after engagement become financial/accounting officers of audit client (Sarbanes-Oxley §206) *(continued)*

Misconduct	Sarbanes-Oxley Response
Corporate boards (especially board audit committees) failed to supervise outside auditors and lacked expertise to understand the company's finances. The Enron board became a symbol of directorial inattention.	• **Audit committee composition.** Authorizes SEC to have stock exchanges change their listing requirements to require audit committees composed only of independent directors, with full authority over outside auditor (Sarbanes-Oxley §301 — see §11.4) • **Financial expert.** Requires disclosure whether company has at least one "financial expert" on audit committee (Sarbanes-Oxley §407 — see §12.3.5)
Corporate executives failed to ascertain the truthfulness of company filings and to supervise subordinates and pressured auditors to give "clean" reports.	• **Officer certification.** Requires SEC rules that CEO and CFO certify that SEC filings are true, complete, and fairly presented (Sarbanes-Oxley §302 — see §21.2.2) • **Internal controls.** Requires SEC rules on disclosure of internal controls, and requires top executives to certify them (Sarbanes-Oxley §404 — see §12.3.5) • **Auditor influence.** Prohibits company officials from improperly influencing outside auditors (Sarbanes-Oxley §303)
Companies failed to report (and the SEC failed to notice) their true financial condition, especially the potential effect of risky off-balance sheet arrangements.	• **Real-time disclosures.** Requires companies to make additional, real-time disclosures in "plain English" of current changes to financial condition (Sarbanes-Oxley §409 — see §21.2.2) • **Off-balance sheet transactions.** Mandates SEC rules requiring disclosure of all material off-balance sheet arrangements (Sarbanes-Oxley §401) • **SEC review.** Requires SEC to review filings by reporting companies at least every three years (Sarbanes-Oxley §408)
Corporate cultures encouraged irresponsible behavior, such as unauthorized or excessive loans to company executives. For example, at Adelphia the family of the company founder received $3.1 billion in loans and other benefits while the company was reporting large financial losses.	• **Code of ethics.** Requires disclosure whether the company has a code of ethics applicable to senior financial officers or justify why not (Sarbanes-Oxley §406 — see §12.3.5) • **Director and officer bans.** Authorizes SEC to remove "unfit" officers and directors from their positions and bar them from similar offices in other public companies (Sarbanes-Oxley §§305, 1105) • **Personal loans.** Forbids "personal loans" to company directors and officers, except in regular course of company's lending business (Sarbanes-Oxley §402–§14.4.2)

Corporate executives sold company stock while aware of accounting misinformation and while employees in the company's pension plan could not sell.	• **Clawbacks.** Requires forfeiture of executive pay and trading gains when company restates financials due to misconduct (Sarbanes-Oxley §304—see §§14.4.2, 23.4.2) • **Blackout periods.** Bars company executives from selling stock during any trading blackout period imposed on employees (Sarbanes-Oxley §306—see §23.4.1) • **Insider reports.** Requires corporate insiders to disclose their trading in company stock within two business days (Sarbanes-Oxley §403—see §24.2)
Outside securities lawyers "papered" illegal transactions or failed to intercede to stop company wrongdoing.	• **Up-the-ladder reporting.** Mandates SEC rules requiring lawyers working for public company to report securities violations and fiduciary breaches up the internal corporate ladder (Sarbanes-Oxley §307—see §12.3.5) • **Lawyer malpractice.** Authorizes SEC to bring enforcement actions against lawyers for malpractice (Sarbanes-Oxley §602)
Securities analysts prepared biased research reports for companies with whom their securities firms did business.	• **Analyst reports.** Mandates SEC to adopt rules on the independence and objectivity of securities analysts and protect them from retaliation for negative reports or ratings (Sarbanes-Oxley §501)
Many frauds only came to light because of courageous "whistle-blowers" inside the company.	• **Whistleblower protection.** Imposes criminal liability on those who retaliate against employees (whistleblowers) who provide evidence or assist in the investigation of business crimes (Sarbanes-Oxley §1107—see §12.3.5) • **Whistleblower action.** Creates an administrative redress for whistleblowers who experience retaliation to seek compensatory damages, reinstatement, back pay, litigation costs (Sarbanes-Oxley §806—see §12.3.5) • **Hotlines.** Requires audit committees to create procedures for handling (anonymous) complaints about accounting improprieties (Sarbanes-Oxley §301—see §12.3.5) • **Statute of limitations.** Extends statute of limitations in cases of securities fraud to two years from discovery or five years from violation (Sarbanes-Oxley §804—see §22.4.1) *(continued)*

Misconduct	Sarbanes-Oxley Response
Company officials and outside auditors destroyed documents to cover up wrongdoing. For example, Arthur Andersen employees destroyed Enron documents, hoping to hide the financial scandal.	• **Criminal sanctions.** Increases criminal sentences for destruction, alteration, or falsification of records in federal investigation and for violating rules on document retention (Sarbanes-Oxley §802) • **Obstruction crime.** Creates a new crime for obstructing a proceeding, including tampering with documents (Sarbanes-Oxley §1102)
Company officials did not take their oversight and disclosure responsibilities seriously.	• **Heavier sentences.** Increases criminal sentences for corporate officials who retaliate against whistleblowers, those who commit mail and wire fraud, and those who falsely certify financials (Sarbanes-Oxley §§806, 903, 906, 1107) • **New crime.** Creates a new crime of "knowing securities fraud," with maximum prison term of 25 years (Sarbanes-Oxley §807)

Disclosure versus Corporate Governance

Many of the congressional responses in Sarbanes-Oxley sought to strengthen disclosure — the heart of federal securities regulation. For example, the rules affecting auditors sought to revitalize auditor independence; the requirements for audit committees and certifications of SEC filings by company executives sought to focus corporate attention on proper disclosure; the requirements on internal controls, the encouragement of whistleblowers, and the "up-the-ladder" reporting by securities lawyers sought to deter and detect securities fraud. In each case, the ultimate goal was to improve the integrity of the disclosure system and to lower the risk of fraud.

Other congressional responses, however, ventured into waters previously uncharted by federal securities law. By specifying board functions and regulating specified corporate transactions, Sarbanes-Oxley moved into areas of corporate governance historically within the domain of state corporate law. For example, the provisions that specify the composition and responsibilities of board audit committees, the restrictions on loans to corporate executives, the forfeiture of executive pay after financial restatements, and limitations on trading by executives during blackout periods have traditionally been subjects of state corporate statutes and fiduciary law. The reforms aimed to reshape the corporate culture of public corporations.

Evaluation of Sarbanes-Oxley

How effective have the new accounting, internal controls, ethics codes, and compliance structures called for by Sarbanes-Oxley been? Many businesses, particularly smaller public companies, complained that the heavy compliance costs of the Act were not worth the marginal benefits. (And the Dodd-Frank Act codified the SEC approach to exempt small public companies from the Sarbanes-Oxley §404 requirement that an auditor attest to the company's internal controls. See Dodd-Frank §989G.) Others have commented on how Sarbanes-Oxley changed attitudes toward corporate governance, with both insiders and outside gatekeepers in public corporations more sensitive to their responsibilities.

Some public companies claimed that the costs of remaining public were too high after Sarbanes-Oxley and "went private" by using private capital to buy their public shares. The companies said that the costs of internal controls and other corporate governance mechanisms required by Sarbanes-Oxley made private financing less expensive than public financing. Nonetheless, many (if not most) of these companies continued to be subject to the reporting requirements of the federal securities laws (including Sarbanes-Oxley) when they issued publicly traded debt to repurchase their public equity. The claims about the excessive regulatory costs of Sarbanes-Oxley may have been political grandstanding.

Academic commentators have also debated the merits of the legislation. Some see it as part of the centuries-old cycle of capital market booms and busts, inevitably followed by a frenzy of regulation—in this case, perhaps unnecessary, ill-conceived, or even counterproductive. Others assert that except for the creation of a new regulatory structure for the accounting profession the legislation merely codified reforms already underway by the stock exchanges, the SEC, sentencing authorities, and state judges. Yet even if Sarbanes-Oxley was superfluous, some have found value in its signaling of the government's resolve to address improper corporate behavior.

Empirical studies indicate that investors have responded favorably to some of the Sarbanes-Oxley initiatives. According to one study, investors have shown greater confidence in the information contained in SEC filings certified by company officers (as mandated by Sarbanes-Oxley) compared to prior uncertified filings. Another study finds that questionable "management" of accounting earnings, which increased steadily from 1987 to 2001, decreased after the enactment of Sarbanes-Oxley, with a resulting greater reliance by investors on reported earnings. Most remarkable was the steady rise after the Act's enactment in corporate restatements of financial results, as corporate managers and accountants sought to correct errors large and small. More recently, corporate financial restatements by public companies (particularly larger companies) have been on the decline, suggesting that the audit function and internal controls may be working.

§11.5.2 Dodd-Frank Act of 2010

In the fall of 2008, the U.S. financial markets nearly collapsed. Banks stopped lending, investors dumped their securities, and the U.S. economy stumbled badly. The reasons for the collapse are still being debated, but the most popular culprit has been the "housing bubble" of the 2000s. Trillions of dollars went to finance unsustainable (subprime) mortgage loans, many of which ended up in the portfolios of the leading financial institutions in this country and abroad.

In response, Congress enacted the Wall Street Reform and Consumer Protection Act (known as the Dodd-Frank Act, after its principal congressional sponsors) to reform the U.S. financial system. Most of Dodd-Frank's reform agenda was focused on the systemic risks in the financial system, the stability of financial institutions, and the investment and lending practices of U.S. banks. But Dodd-Frank also took aim at corporate governance in public corporations—primarily by expanding the voting rights of shareholders and increasing the responsibilities in public companies regarding executive compensation.

Dodd-Frank is a massive piece of legislation, running 2,300 pages in length with 240 rulemaking directives to the SEC and other regulatory agencies (some of them new agencies) and 89 additional directives to these agencies to issue reports and conduct studies. Under Dodd-Frank, the SEC alone must adopt 95 new rules and prepare 22 reports—by comparison, Sarbanes-Oxley required only 14 new rules and 1 study by the SEC. The success of Dodd-Frank, as you can see, will depend on how the regulators carry out these directives.

Corporate Governance Reforms

Some of the corporate governance reforms introduced by Dodd-Frank sought to invigorate shareholder voting in public companies (eliminate broker voting and allow shareholders to nominate directors); others sought to foster further board independence (disclosure about separating chair and CEO positions and mandating independent directors on the board's compensation committee); and others sought to fine-tune the Sarbanes-Oxley reforms (exemption of small companies from internal controls and additional protection of whistleblowers). The Dodd-Frank corporate governance agenda, however, focused most of its attention on executive compensation in public corporations (expand disclosure, require independent compensation committees, mandate shareholder advisory votes on executive pay and golden parachutes).

Here is an overview of the Dodd-Frank corporate governance and executive compensation reforms, along with a notation of the status of their implementation as of the end of 2011:

Corporate Governance Reforms	
Shareholder voting reforms	• **Broker votes.** Requires national stock exchanges to prohibit voting by nonbeneficial owners (brokers), unless they have been specifically instructed to do so by the beneficial owner (Dodd-Frank §957 amending Exchange Act §6(b)—see §6.2.1) [partially implemented as of 2011] • **Proxy access.** Authorizes the SEC to issue rules that would specify the conditions for shareholders in public companies to access the company's proxy materials to nominate directors to the board (Dodd-Frank §971, amending Exchange Act §14(a)—see §9.4.3) [SEC rule withdrawn]
Oversight within corporation	• **Disclosure CEO/chairman role.** Mandates that the SEC adopt rules requiring public companies to disclose whether the CEO and board chair are the same person and, if so, the reasons for doing so (Dodd-Frank §972—see §9.4.2) [no proposed rules as of 2011] • **Internal controls exemption**. Exempts small business issuers (public companies with less than $75 million in market capitalization) from the Sarbanes-Oxley §404 requirement that an auditor attest to their internal financial controls and calls for the SEC to study how to reduce the compliance burden on companies with a market capitalizations of $75–$250 million (Dodd-Frank §989G—see §12.3.5) [fully implemented as of 2011]
Whistleblower protection	• **Increased protections.** Strengthens private action for whistleblowers against employers who retaliate against them, including remedies for reinstatement and double back pay (Dodd-Frank §924, amending Exchange Act 21F-1—see §12.3.5) • **Increased bounties**. Mandates new SEC program under which employees and others who report securities violations in a company can be rewarded between 10 and 30 percent of the funds recovered based on the information provided (Dodd-Frank §§922–924, amending Exchange Act 21F—see §12.3.5) [fully implemented as of 2011]
Executive Compensation Reforms	
Additional compensation disclosure	• **Pay for performance.** Mandates SEC rules requiring additional disclosure and charts comparing executive pay to stock performance over a five-year period (Dodd-Frank §953—see §14.4.4) • **Pay gap.** Mandates SEC rules comparing CEO pay and median pay of all of the company's employees (Dodd-Frank §953—see §14.4.4)

(continued)

Executive Compensation Reforms	
Internal governance reforms	• **Compensation committee independence.** Mandates that exchange listing standards require compensation committees of public companies be composed only of independent directors with the authority to hire independent compensation consultants (Dodd-Frank §952—see §30.1.3) [rulemaking underway as of 2011] • **Clawback policy.** Mandates that stock exchange listing standards require that companies have (and disclose) a policy that, whenever the company restates its financials because of misconduct, CEOs and CFOs must reimburse the company for any bonuses and other stock-based incentive compensation they received; provides that the SEC can bring an enforcement action to enforce this "clawback" obligation (Dodd-Frank §954—see §14.4.3) [not yet implemented as of 2011]
Increased shareholder role	• **"Say on pay."** Mandates nonbinding shareholder vote on the pay package given the company's top executives, as well as nonbinding shareholder vote on whether the "say on pay" vote will occur every one, two, or three years (Dodd-Frank §951(a), adding Exchange Act §14A(a)—see §14.4.4) [fully implemented as of 2011] • **"Say on golden parachutes."** Mandates nonbinding shareholder vote on compensation that executives receive in mergers and other extraordinary business transactions and requires disclosure on such compensation (Dodd-Frank §951(b), adding Exchange Act §14A(b)—see §14.4.4) [fully implemented as of 2011] • **Institutional reports of voting.** Requires institutional investors, such as pension funds and hedge funds, with more than $100 million under management to report annually their "say on pay" and "say on golden parachute" votes (Dodd-Frank §951(a), adding Exchange Act §14A(d)—see §14.4.4) [proposed rulemaking as of 2011]

As you can see, Dodd-Frank imposes significant regulatory requirements on public companies that intrude into areas once reserved to state law and company-by-company implementation. Some provisions, such as the creation of "clawback" policies, continue regulatory requirements first imposed by Sarbanes-Oxley. Others, such as shareholder voting on executive pay and nomination of directors through the company's proxy, are federal innovations. One of the more interesting aspects of these corporate governance reforms is that many of them came, for the first time, in response to the clamor of institutional investors, primarily activist pension funds.

Securities Regulation Reforms

The financial regulatory reforms of Dodd-Frank include many that affect traditional securities regulation. Some of the reforms create new regulation for financial intermediaries that had been only lightly regulated before (such as credit rating agencies, hedge funds, and private equity funds). Other reforms regulate new categories of financial instruments—such as credit-default swaps—forcing their trading on transparent exchanges.

Reflecting a concern that SEC regulation had been too lax, the agency received new enforcement powers and directives to provide greater protection to investors in private markets. The relationship between broker-dealers and their customers came under scrutiny, with a call for the SEC to consider subjecting broker-dealers to the same fiduciary standards as investment advisers and limiting the scope of predispute arbitration agreements in broker-customer disputes.

Here is a list of the more prominent Dodd-Frank reforms of securities regulation:

Securities Regulation Reforms	
New regulation of financial intermediaries	• **Credit rating agencies.** Subjects credit rating agencies to new duties—and accompanying liabilities—similar to those of securities firms that participate in securities offerings (Dodd-Frank §§932–939) • **OTC derivatives.** Authorizes SEC regulation of OTC derivatives such as credit-default swaps (Dodd-Frank §701–774) • **Private funds.** Requires that advisers of "private funds" (defined to include hedge funds and private equity funds) register with the SEC (Dodd-Frank §§402, 403)
New SEC enforcement powers	• **Aiding and abetting.** Increases aiding and abetting enforcement powers for the SEC under various securities laws not previously covered (Dodd-Frank §§929M, 929N) • **Subpoena powers.** Grants broader (nationwide) subpoena authority to the SEC (Dodd-Frank §929E) • **Extraterritorial enforcement.** Grants SEC enforcement powers over extraterritorial securities fraud (Dodd-Frank §929P) • **Collateral bars**. Grants SEC authority to bar directors and officers committing (or aiding and abetting) securities fraud from holding office in public companies (Dodd-Frank §925) *(continued)*

Securities Regulation Reforms	
Protection of sophisticated investors	• **"Bad boy" issuers under Reg D.** Mandates that the SEC preclude certain "bad boy" issuers from raising capital in private markets using Regulation D (Dodd-Frank §926 — see §5.2.2) • **Asset-backed securities disclosures.** Mandates that the SEC establish additional disclosures on asset-backed securities (such as debt obligations that are collateralized by mortgages — CDOs), even when offered to sophisticated investors in private markets (Dodd-Frank §943)
Broker-dealer regulation	• **Fiduciary duties on broker-dealers.** Requires the SEC to consider subjecting broker-dealers (securities firms), when they give investment advice to clients, to the same fiduciary "customer first" standards that apply to investment advisers (Dodd-Frank §913) • **Securities arbitration.** Mandates the SEC to prohibit or limit mandatory predispute arbitration in broker-customer disputes (Dodd-Frank §921)

CHAPTER 12 Duty of Care and the Business Judgment Rule

The board of directors manages and oversees the corporation's business and affairs. Judicial review of board decision making and oversight is governed by the duty of care, which in turn is confined by the business judgment rule.

This chapter considers the articulated standards of care (§12.1) and their actual application under the deferential business judgment rule (§12.2). It then explains how the presumption that directors act in good faith with due care in the best interests of the corporation can be overcome (§12.3) and summarizes the available remedies (§12.4). Finally, the chapter describes the protection from liability directors have under exculpation provisions that arise in corporate charters and by statute (§12.5).

As you will discover in this chapter and those that follow, directors are insulated from liability in many ways. The business judgment rule and the exculpation provisions described in this chapter are two of the legs of a four-legged stool on which directors sit. The other two are the indemnification available to directors under corporate statutes and internal corporate processes (see §15.1) and directors' and officers' (D&O) liability insurance (see §15.2).

§12.1 STANDARDS OF CARE—ASPIRATIONAL GUIDANCE

In performing their functions, directors (and senior executives) are subject to both statutory and common-law standards of care.

§12.1.1 Standards of Care

Statutory Standards

Many state statutes codify the standards for directorial behavior. Typical is MBCA §8.30 (as revised in 1998). Under the section, each *individual* director must discharge his duties in "good faith" and act "in a manner he reasonably believes to be in the best interests of the corporation." MBCA §8.30(a). In addition, members of the board must *collectively* become informed in performing their decision-making and oversight functions with "the care that a person in like position would reasonably believe appropriate under similar circumstances." MBCA §8.30(b) (replacing early, more stringent standard of "ordinarily prudent person"). Under many statutes, officers with discretionary authority are subject to similar standards. See MBCA §8.42(a).

Common-Law Standards

The articulated judicial standards follow much the same pattern as the statutory standards. The Delaware Supreme Court has stated that a party challenging a business decision must show the directors failed to act (1) in good faith, (2) in the honest belief that the action taken was in the best interest of the company, or (3) on an informed basis. *Aronson v. Lewis*, 473 A.2d 805 (Del. 1984). In general, these judicial standards also apply to officers. See *Gantler v. Stephens*, 965 A.2d 695 (Del. 2009) (confirming that officers have same fiduciary duties as directors, though without the possibility of exculpation available to directors).

§12.1.2 Facets of Duty of Care

Each of the *standards of care* articulated in the statutes and by the courts identifies a facet of the *duty of care*.

Good Faith

The "good faith" standard requires that directors (1) be honest, (2) not have a conflict of interest, and (3) not approve (or condone) wrongful or illegal activity. See *In re Walt Disney Co. Derivative Litigation*, 825 A.2d 275 (Del. Ch. 2003) (holding that attitude of "we don't care about risks" breaches duty of good faith, a subset of the duty of loyalty). Fraudulent or self-interested action is subject to scrutiny under the director's duty of loyalty. See §13.2. Conscious disregard of corporate duties and intentional violations of positive law violate the director's duty of good faith. See §12.3.1 below.

Best Interests

The "best interests" standard involves the *substance* of director decision making. The requirement that directors have a "reasonable belief" their decisions are in the corporation's best interests reflects both a subjective aspect (belief) and an objective one (reasonable). That is, directors must subjectively believe they are furthering the corporation's interests, and this belief must objectively be reasonable.

Under the "best interests" standard, a board decision must be related to furthering the corporation's interests. This standard embodies the "waste" standard, under which board action is invalid if it lacks any rational business purpose. See §12.3.2 below.

Informed Basis

The "informed basis" standard relates to the *process* of board decision making and oversight. Directors must be informed in making decisions (see §12.3.3 below) to monitor and supervise corporate activities (see §12.3.4 below). In both capacities, directors must have at least minimal levels of skill and expertise. The "like position" formulation is meant to establish an objective standard that recognizes that "risk-taking decisions are central to the director's role." See Official Comment, MBCA §8.30 (replacing "ordinarily prudent person" formulation to avoid suggestion that benchmark is negligence). The "under similar circumstances" language has been understood to allow a court to take into account the complexity and urgency of the board's decision-making and oversight functions.

§12.1.3 Careless Directors Rarely Held Liable

The articulated care standards have a familiar ring—they sound in negligence. Just as there is liability for negligent driving that causes a traffic accident, you might assume that directorial liability follows careless decision making that leads to business failure. But in the more than 150 years during which courts have articulated a directorial duty of care, there have been only a handful of cases in which directors and officers have been held liable for mere mismanagement uncomplicated by bad faith, illegality, fraud, or conflict of interest. What is really happening?

§12.2 BUSINESS JUDGMENT RULE

To understand a director's duty of care, one must understand the famous "business judgment rule." The rule, which is both procedural and substantive, reflects a judicial "hands off" philosophy—the golden rule of corporate law. As explained by the courts, the business judgment rule is a rebuttable presumption that directors in performing their functions are honest and well-meaning, and that their decisions are informed and rationally undertaken. In short, the business judgment rule presumes directors do not breach their duty of care.

Although the business judgment rule is not statutorily codified, courts have inferred its existence even in states with statutory care standards. As the Official Comment to MBCA §8.30 explains, the statutory standards of conduct for directors do "not try to codify the business judgment rule [which] continues to be developed by the courts." For this reason, some commentators have characterized the statutory standards as aspirational, their legal effect profoundly diluted by the business judgment rule.

§12.2.1 Operation of Business Judgment Rule

The business judgment rule shields *directors* from personal liability and insulates board *decisions* from judicial review—the latter sometimes referred to as the "business judgment doctrine." The business judgment rule also protects officers and their decisions. See ALI Principles §4.01.

The business rule has two aspects, one substantive and the other procedural. It describes the substantive *standard of review* to which director and board action should be submitted, and it creates a procedural *burden of proof* that requires the challenging party to rebut the presumption that directors act in good faith, in the best interests of the company, and with adequate information. Because of this burden and the procedural obstacles to overcoming the business judgment presumption (see §18.3, derivative suit procedures), claims that directors have breached their duty of care are often dismissed before trial.

§12.2.2 Justifications for the Business Judgment Presumption

The business judgment presumption has been justified on different grounds:

- **Encourages risk taking.** Shareholders expect the board to take business risks—the adage "nothing ventured, nothing gained" is at the core of why shareholders invest. Without the business judgment rule, directors might be too cautious. See *Gagliardi v. Trifoods Int'l Inc.*, 683 A.2d 1049 (Del. Ch. 1996) (explaining that shareholders can absorb risk by investing in many companies).

- **Avoids judicial meddling.** Judges are not business experts. Further, derivative suit plaintiffs (and their lawyers) have incentives that may be at odds with the interests of the corporation and the body of shareholders. Corporate statutes reflect this notion and uniformly specify that corporate management is entrusted to the board of directors.
- **Encourages directors to serve.** Business people detest liability exposure. The business judgment rule encourages qualified persons to serve as directors and take business risks without fear of being judged in hindsight.

Some commentators have even suggested that the business judgment presumption should be absolute and corporate law should not enforce care standards. Mismanagement would be subject only to shareholder voting and the markets. If directors and officers perform poorly, the business will suffer and the corporation's stock price will fall. This will make it harder to raise capital. It will also make management vulnerable to shareholder activism, a proxy contest, or even a takeover. Eventually, poor management will be replaced or the corporation will go bankrupt. Moreover, if the managers develop a reputation for poor judgment, they will become less attractive in the executive job market.

§12.2.3 Reliance Corollary

An offshoot of the business judgment presumption entitles directors to rely on information and advice from other directors (including committees of the board), competent officers and employees, and outsider experts (such as lawyers and accountants). In addition, directors can rely on others to whom the board has delegated its decision-making or oversight functions. This *reliance corollary* is contained in many statutes and widely accepted by the courts. See MBCA §8.30(c)(e) (revised in 1998). Under some statutes, it also extends to officers. See MBCA §8.42(b).

Particularly in public corporations, directors must rely on information from others. They cannot be expected to learn and know about the full range of the corporation's business. But to claim reliance, directors must have become familiar with the information or advice and must reasonably have believed that it merited confidence. In addition, directors can rely on each other. The "reasonable care" standard of the MBCA recognizes that directors typically perform their oversight and decision-making functions collegially. This means that directors in becoming informed can rely on each other's experience and wisdom. See Official Comment, MBCA §8.30 ("If the observance of directors' conduct is called into question, courts will typically evaluate the conduct of the entire board").

Directors, however, cannot hide their heads in the sand and claim reliance if they have knowledge or suspicions that make reliance unwarranted. Official Comment, MBCA §8.30 (directors remain subject to general standards of care in judging reliability and competence of source of information). For example, a director who knows that management has overstated earnings cannot rely on an auditor's opinion that earnings are properly stated. In addition, management directors (with greater familiarity with the corporation's business or expertise in a particular matter) have a correspondingly greater duty to independently verify information. See *In re Emerging Communications, Inc. Shareholder Litigation*, 2004 WL 1305745 (Del. Ch. 2004) (holding director with financial expertise liable for not recognizing that price in "going private" transaction was unfair to shareholders). In general, though, the reliance corollary is more protective than the due diligence and reasonable care defenses available to directors charged with securities fraud. See §§5.3.2, 5.3.3.

§12.3 OVERCOMING BUSINESS JUDGMENT PRESUMPTION

When a board decision is challenged, courts place the burden on the challenger to overcome the business judgment presumption by proving either (1) fraud, bad faith, illegality, or a conflict of interest (lack of good faith, see §12.3.1 below); (2) the lack of a rational business purpose (waste, see §12.3.2 below); (3) failure to become informed in decision making (gross negligence, see §12.3.3 below); or (4) failure to oversee the corporation's activities (inattention, see §12.3.4 below).

The MBCA (as revised in 1998) largely tracks these judicial categories and specifies *standards of liability*. A director can become liable for

- action not in good faith
- a decision the director did not reasonably believe to be in the corporation's best interests or as to which the director was not adequately informed
- conduct resulting from the director's lack of objectivity or independence, unless the director proves he believed the conduct was in the corporation's best interests
- a sustained failure to be informed in discharging the director's oversight functions
- receipt of an improper financial benefit

MBCA §8.31(a) (challenger must also show director not covered by charter exculpation provision, see §12.5, or the statutory safe harbor for conflict-of-interest transactions, see §13.4).

§12.3.1 Lack of Good Faith

A director loses the presumption that he was acting in good faith—and thus the protection of the business judgment rule—if the challenger shows fraud, the conscious disregard of duties, the condoning of illegality, or a conflict of interest.

Fraud

A director who acts fraudulently is liable, and any action tainted by the fraud can be invalidated, regardless of fairness. For example, directors who mislead shareholders in connection with shareholder voting cannot claim protection under the business judgment rule. See §10.3. Likewise, directors who knowingly disseminate false or misleading information to public trading markets breach a duty of disclosure, a subset of their duties of loyalty and good faith. *Malone v. Brincat*, 722 A.2d 5 (Del. 1998) (holding that misinformation in communications to shareholders, even though not requesting shareholder action, violates "duty to deal with shareholders honestly"). In addition, a director who knowingly or recklessly misrepresents a material fact to the board on which the other directors rely to the corporation's detriment can be held liable under a tort deceit theory.

Conscious Disregard

Directors who "consciously disregard" their responsibilities are liable for violating their duty of good faith. *Walt Disney Co. Deriv. Litig.*, 906 A.2d 27 (Del. 2006). For example, directors can be liable for failing to call board meetings and acting as "stooges" for a controlling shareholder. *ATR-Kim Eng Financial Corp. v. Araneta*, 2006 WL 3783520 (Del. Ch. 2006). According to the Delaware courts, the duty of good faith is a subset of the duty of loyalty—thus, violating the duty of good faith cannot be exculpated. See §12.5 below.

As you can imagine, the financial crisis of 2008 has spawned the argument that directors in financial firms "consciously disregarded" subprime-mortgage risks, thus violating their duties of good faith. The argument, however, has fallen on mostly deaf judicial ears, given the absolving power of the business judgment rule. For example, when shareholders of Citigroup alleged that the firm's directors had failed to notice "red flags" brewing in the real estate and credit markets when they approved various investments in subprime loans, which eventually resulted in losses for the firm of $55 billion, the court dismissed the case and held that the alleged warning signals did not evidence conscious disregard by the directors. At most, said the court, "they evidence that the directors made bad business decisions." *In re Citigroup Inc. Shareholder Deriv. Litig.*, 9643 A.2d 106 (Del. Ch. 2009) (pointing out that plaintiffs failed to allege board's risk management committee, charged with monitoring credit risk, had ignored the subprime risks).

Illegality

Directors who intentionally approve or consciously disregard illegal behavior by the corporation violate their duty of good faith, even if the directors were informed and the behavior benefited the corporation. Older cases described the duty of directors to abide by corporate and noncorporate norms as the "duty of obedience," a concept that continues to apply in nonprofit corporations.

For example, courts have said directors of for-profit corporations can be liable for approving

- bribery of state officials to protect an amusement park's illegal (and profitable) Sunday operations. *Roth v. Robertson*, 118 N.Y.S. 351 (Sup. Ct. 1909).
- bribery of foreign government officials, even though the practice was widespread. *Gall v. Exxon*, 418 F. Supp. 508 (S.D.N.Y. 1976).
- the dismantling of corporate plants and equipment to discipline unruly employees in violation of labor laws. *Abrams v. Allen*, 74 N.E.2d 305 (N.Y. 1947).
- a business plan that created strong incentives for employees to commit Medicare and Medicaid fraud to attract medical referrals. *McCall v. Scott*, 239 F.3d 808 (6th Cir. 2001).

Fiduciary rules against corporate illegality, however, produce a conundrum. By making scofflaw directors liable as a matter of *corporate* law, not the positive law that prohibits the behavior, corporate fiduciary duties become a fountainhead for the enforcement of business regulation. On the one hand, there may be many instances when approving illegal behavior maximizes profits for the corporation. On the other hand, condoning known corporate illegality would be an affront to noncorporate norms and could undermine the legitimacy of the corporation.

Modern courts have recognized this tension. In *Miller v. AT&T*, 507 F.2d 759 (3d Cir. 1974), shareholders brought a derivative suit challenging AT&T's failure to collect a $1.5 million debt owed by the Democratic National Committee, a failure the plaintiffs said violated federal campaign finance laws. The Third Circuit accepted that under corporate norms the directors' business decision to forgive a debt is normally immune from attack. But the court held AT&T's failure to collect the DNC debt could be actionable if the directors had no "legitimate" business justification, aside from illegally currying political favor, for forgiving the debt. In other words, an illegal purpose alone cannot be a rational business purpose sufficient to trigger the business judgment rule.

Miller illustrates the curious result when corporate law is used to enforce noncorporate legal norms. One year after *Miller* was decided, the Supreme Court held that shareholders had no implied federal cause of action to enforce federal campaign spending laws. *Cort v. Ash*, 422 U.S. 66 (1975). Thus, shareholders were able to use *state fiduciary law* to obtain relief based on a federal statute that the Supreme Court interpreted precludes *federal relief* for shareholders.

Conflict of Interest

A director who is personally interested in a corporate action because he stands to receive a personal or financial benefit loses the business judgment presumption. This is true whether the director is an inside corporate employee or an outside independent director. The director's liability and the validity of the action depend on fairness standards that apply to conflict-of-interest transactions. See §13.3.

In addition, a director may become liable if a corporate action is approved because he is beholden to another person interested in the action. See MBCA §8.31(a)(2)(iii) (liability of director who lacks objectivity due to director's familial, financial, or business relation with interested person).

§12.3.2 Waste

The presumption of the business judgment rule also can be overcome if the action of the directors lacked a "rational" business purpose. The focus is on the merits of the board action or inaction—a substantive review of the challenged decision. When the challenger claims a transaction wholly lacks consideration, the cases often speak of "waste" or "spoliation" of corporate assets. The absence of a rational business purpose powerfully suggests bad faith—that is, a conflicting personal interest, illegality, or deception.

Rational Basis

How much of a business justification is sufficient? Under the *rational purpose test*, even board decisions that in hindsight seem patently unwise or imprudent are protected from review and the directors shielded from liability so long as the business judgment was not "improvident beyond explanation." *Michelson v. Duncan*, 407 A.2d 121 (Del. 1979); see also ALI Principles §4.01(c) (comment) ("removed from the realm of reason").

Only when the board approves a transaction in which the corporation receives no benefit—such as the issuance of stock without consideration or the use of corporate funds to discharge personal obligations—have courts found corporate waste. See Official Comment, MBCA §8.31(a)(2)(ii) (stating that it is a rare case where corporation's best interest is "so removed from realm of reason" or director's belief "so unreasonable as to fall outside bounds of sound discretion"). The theme is to protect good-faith board decisions from judicial second-guessing.

Illustrative Cases

If it can be said that the corporation received some fair benefit, the matter is entrusted to the directors' judgment. As the following two famous cases illustrate, courts regularly forgive even glaring business folly:

- ***Shlensky v. Wrigley,*** 237 N.E.2d 776 (Ill. App. 1968). Before the Chicago Cubs joined the rest of the major leagues with night baseball games, Cubs' shareholders challenged the board's refusal to play night baseball at Wrigley Field. The shareholders alleged night baseball would increase profits and pointed to higher night attendance for the Chicago White Sox and other teams around the league. Phillip Wrigley, the Cubs' majority shareholder and dominant member of the board, thought "baseball is a daytime sport" and that night baseball might cause the neighborhood around Wrigley Field to deteriorate. The court dismissed the plaintiff's complaint, speculating that a deteriorated neighborhood might cause a decline in attendance or a drop in Wrigley Field's property value.
- ***Kamin v. American Express Co.,*** 383 N.Y.S.2d 807 (Sup. Ct. 1976). The directors of American Express faced the choice of liquidating a bad stock investment at the corporate level (taking a corporate tax deduction for the loss) or distributing the stock to the shareholders as a special dividend (a taxable event for the shareholders). Although the choice seemed obvious, the board opted for the stock dividend, and shareholders sued. The directors explained they were concerned liquidation at the company level would have adversely impacted the company's *accounting* net income figures. The court found the concern sufficient. That is, the court accepted that appearances could be more important than actual cash effects.

Safety-Valve Cases

Are actions by the board ever irrational? Only a small handful of cases have found good-faith board action so imprudent as to fall outside the business judgment presumption. But under closer inspection, even these few cases where courts have found waste may not reflect disinterested misjudgment, but rather judicial use of care standards when a conflict of interest could be inferred, but not proved—that is, "safety valve" cases.

Consider *Litwin v. Allen*, 25 N.Y.S.2d 667 (Sup. Ct. 1940), the most famous of these cases. The court imposed liability on the directors of Guaranty Trust, a bank affiliate of J. P. Morgan & Company, for approving stock repurchase agreements (repos) in the tenuous stock market after the 1929 crash. Under the repos, Allegheny Corp. sold Guaranty Trust convertible 5 1/2 percent debentures at $100 par at a below-market price. In return for this discount, Guaranty Trust gave an option to Allegheny to repurchase the debentures at par in six months—in effect, a call option. Although Guaranty Trust could have sold the bonds immediately, realizing the purchase discount, it took a gamble that prices would rise and it could sell higher. When prices continued to fall and Allegheny failed to exercise its option (to repurchase), Guaranty Trust was left holding the bonds. It had bought the bonds at a favorable price and guessed wrong that the panic of 1930 had reached bottom.

The court faulted the directors for approving a transaction "so improvident, so risky, so unusual and unnecessary to be contrary to fundamental conceptions of prudent banking practice"—precisely the kind of second-guessing precluded by the business judgment rule. Surely the Guaranty Trust directors, among the most experienced risk managers in banking, had not been inattentive to the repos' risk.

So what was really happening in *Litwin v. Allen*? Many commentators have explained the case as imposing a higher duty on directors of financial institutions, who frequently were defendants before the era of federal deposit insurance. But there may be another explanation. Allegheny was the holding company for the Van Sweringen empire in which J. P. Morgan & Company was deeply involved. Morgan's interest in buttressing Allegheny's sagging fortunes was surely not lost on the Guaranty Trust directors. Although the court agreed that there was no showing of conflict of interest, the court's use of a heightened care standard (a "safety valve") overcame this lack of proof.

§12.3.3 Gross Negligence

To claim the business judgment presumption in a decision-making context, directors must make reasonable efforts to inform themselves in making the decision. The focus is on procedure, and the courts assume diligent board deliberations ensure rational board action. Liability is generally based on "concepts of gross negligence." Compare MBCA §8.31(a)(2)(ii)(B) (director liable if not informed about decision "to an extent the director reasonably believed appropriate in the circumstances").

Trans Union

When are directors not adequately informed? The most famous and controversial answer comes from *Smith v. Van Gorkom (Trans Union)*, 488 A.2d 858 (Del. 1985). In a 3-2 decision, the Delaware Supreme Court held the directors of Trans Union Corporation could be personally liable for not informing themselves adequately when they approved the sale of the company in a negotiated merger.

The case involved a friendly cash-out merger. The sequence of events, described in great detail in the court's opinion, paints the picture of a CEO (Van Gorkom) who initiated, negotiated, and promoted a merger agreement whose terms may have favored the acquirer (Pritzker). Shareholders brought a class action challenging the board's failure to become sufficiently informed.

The court recited a litany of errors by a board composed of five management directors and five eminently qualified outside directors. According to the court, the directors had failed to inquire into Van Gorkom's role in setting the merger's terms; failed to review the merger documents; had not inquired into the fairness of the $55 price and the value of the company's significant, but unused, investment tax credits; accepted without inquiry the view of the company's chief financial officer (Romans) that the $55 price was within a fair range; had not sought an outside opinion from an investment banker on the fairness of the $55 price; and acted at a two-hour meeting without prior notice and without there being an emergency.

In response, the directors asserted they had been entitled to rely on Van Gorkom's oral presentation outlining the merger terms and on Romans's opinion. But the court held no reliance was warranted because Van Gorkom had not read the merger documents before the meeting and did not explain that he, not Pritzker, suggested the $55 price. In addition, the court pointed out that the directors had never questioned Romans about the basis for his opinion and had not asked about the views of senior management, who had strenuously objected to aspects of the agreement (including the price).

The *Trans Union* court rejected a number of arguments that normally would have carried the day under the business judgment rule. Consider the rational justifications given for the merger: the $55 merger price both reflected a significant premium over the then-$38 market price and was within internally calculated leveraged buyout ranges. The directors, who had significant business expertise and background knowledge of Trans Union's business, had no reason to doubt Van Gorkom's assertion of the merger's fairness. The board's approval was later conditioned on a "test market" during which other offers could be solicited. The board was operating under the time pressure of a Pritzker deadline. Outside counsel had advised the directors they might be sued for turning away an attractive offer.

What if the board had asked, read, and heard what it was charged with having failed to? At most, the directors would have learned that Van Gorkom had negotiated on his own initiative a deal with a personal and business acquaintance, had proffered a price during the negotiations at the low end of a credible range of fair value, and had agreed to a merger with some disadvantageous terms that senior management objected to. Even if the directors had been fully informed, as eventually happened at a later meeting when they reapproved the merger, there is little to suggest they might have extracted a better deal. The court's second-guessing of boardroom procedures has been harshly criticized.

Meaning of *Trans Union*

What are the *Trans Union* lessons? The case is among the few holding directors liable for a rational decision as to which there were no allegations of bad faith or self-dealing. Commentators have suggested various explanations:

- **Delaware reassertion.** The Delaware Supreme Court was giving teeth to Delaware fiduciary law, which during the 1970s and early 1980s had come under heavy criticism for being too lax. The Trans Union board's decisional failures provided a convenient target for the court to assert itself. Its emphasis on board processes also put a premium on good lawyering, presumably by the Delaware corporate bar.
- **Fast shuffle.** The case had self-dealing overtones. Van Gorkom was reaching retirement age, and the merger allowed him to realize an immediate $1.5 million increase in the value of his shareholding. As the *Trans Union* dissent pointed out, the majority seemed to believe the directors had been victims of a Van Gorkom-Pritzker "fast shuffle." In subsequent cases, the Delaware courts have readily faulted directors who approve transactions in which managers extract bribes from the acquiror as a condition for the transaction. See *Parnes v. Bally Entertainment Corp.*, 722 A.2d 1243 (Del. 1999) (finding breach of fiduciary duties when directors approved merger conditioned on CEO receiving special payments from acquiror).
- **End-period event.** A board's consideration of a cash-out merger deserves heightened review. When shareholders are cashed out in a merger, a faulty board decision cannot be corrected through the operation of product, securities, and control markets. For this reason, mergers and other "end period" decisions should be subject to more stringent review than typical operational decisions. See *Cede & Co. v. Technicolor, Inc.*, 634 A.2d 345 (Del. 1993) (*Cede II*) (finding care breach by directors who failed to inquire about negotiation and terms of merger); see also *In re Walt Disney Co. Derivative Litigation*, 825 A.2d 275 (Del. Ch. 2005) (explaining *Trans Union* as "sale of entire company" for which board approval required by statute).

- **Antitakeover implications.** Perhaps *Trans Union* was meant to promote board discretion in future takeover cases. After the case, directors who receive an unsolicited offer for their company can put off the unwanted buyer on the ground that Delaware law requires them to take their time to first become fully informed.

Despite its importance to corporate fiduciary law, the *Trans Union* puzzle has yet to be fully solved.

§12.3.4 Inattention

Directors have oversight functions that go beyond making decisions at board meetings. Particularly in public corporations, directors are expected to monitor management, to whom is delegated day-to-day business. To carry out their duties, directors are presumed to have unrestricted access to all corporate information. *Kortum v. Webasto Sunroofs, Inc.*, 769 A.2d 113 (Del. Ch. 2000) (corporation has burden to permit director's inspection of corporate information related to directorial role). The monitoring duty requires directors to inquire into managers' competence and loyalty. A director cannot passively sit by, for example, if she knows that the corporation's treasurer is embezzling money. Judicial review has varied depending on whether the director is inattentive to *mismanagement* or to *management abuse.*

Inattention to Mismanagement

Courts have been reluctant to hold directors liable for inattention to mismanagement. A classic case is *Barnes v. Andrews*, 298 F. 614 (S.D.N.Y. 1924) (Learned Hand, J.). There a director—whose "only attention to the affairs of the company consisted of talks with the president [who was a friend] as they met from time to time"—was sued after the business failed because of the president's poor business judgment. Learned Hand concluded the passive director, though he had technically breached his duty of care, could not be liable because nothing indicated he could have prevented the business failure. Learned Hand pointed out that it would be impossible to know if the director could have saved the business. Even if the inquiry were possible, the business judgment rule teaches it should not be conducted by judges.

Nonetheless, a few cases (perhaps confusedly) have imposed liability for mere inattention. See *Hoye v. Meek*, 795 F.2d 893 (10th Cir. 1986) (finding that bank director, whose family controlled the bank, violated duty of care under Oklahoma statute's "ordinarily prudent director" standard by not attending board meetings and not monitoring risky investment decisions of his son).

Inattention to Management Abuse

Courts have been less forgiving when a director fails to supervise management defalcations and deceit. In fact, most cases that impose liability on directors for care breaches—older bank cases and newer S&L cases—have involved directors who turned a blind eye to managers with their hands in the corporate till. Liability hinges on whether the director knew or had reason to know of the management abuse. Courts more readily infer knowledge of abuse in the case of management directors.

A modern (though not necessarily illustrative) example is *Francis v. United Jersey Bank*, 432 A.2d 814 (N.J. 1981). Mrs. Pritchard was the widow of the founder of Pritchard & Baird, a closely held reinsurance brokerage business. After her husband's death she became a director, but was inactive and knew virtually nothing about the business. She never read the firm's annual financial statements, which revealed that her sons were taking client funds in the guise of "shareholder loans." The court held her liable for failing to become informed and make inquiries and inferred that Mrs. Pritchard's laxity proximately caused the losses to the corporation. She could have brought her sons' illegal misappropriations to the attention of insurance officials.

Although *United Jersey Bank* seems to imply directors must inquire whenever management defalcation is possible, most modern cases do not go so far. Instead, inattentive directors are liable only if circumstances indicate they actually knew of or suspected management diversion. *United Jersey Bank* can be explained by its peculiar facts. The suit was brought by a bankruptcy trustee against the widow and her two sons, the only directors. After her husband died, Mrs. Pritchard had become listless and had started to drink heavily. During the proceedings she died, and the suit proceeded against her estate, whose beneficiaries were presumably her sons. The desire to add the estate's assets to the bankruptcy pool may explain the court's duty of care analysis.

Recent Delaware courts have used the duty of good faith to impose liability on directors who fail to adequately monitor management misbehavior. By couching the analysis in terms of lack of "good faith," rather than lack of "care," director liability is not subject to exculpation under Del. GCL §102(b)(7) (see §12.5 below).

Monitoring Illegality

The requirement that directors know of or suspect management abuse extends to the duty of directors to monitor corporate illegality. In *Graham v. Allis-Chalmers Manufacturing Co.*, 188 A.2d 125 (Del. 1963), the court held that the business judgment rule shields directors who had failed to detect antitrust violations (criminal bid-rigging) by mid-level executives. According to the court, unless the director knew of or suspected the bid-rigging, they were not obligated to install a monitoring system. The MBCA *standards of conduct* regarding directorial oversight functions also reflect this view. In matters of legal compliance, "the director may depend upon the presumption of regularity, absent knowledge or notice to the contrary." Official Comment, MBCA §8.30(b).

More recent Delaware cases suggest, however, that a board may have a duty to install corporate monitoring and reporting systems to detect illegal behavior—even in the absence of "red flags." See *In re Caremark Int'l Inc.*, 698 A.2d 959 (Del. Ch. 1996) (approving settlement of derivative suit challenging board's failure to create monitoring system, which allegedly would have revealed illegal kickbacks by company to get Medicare/Medicaid patients). Given the greater activism expected of corporate directors and the increased penalties under the federal sentencing guidelines for crimes committed by organizations without compliance programs, boards act at their peril by not instituting monitoring systems to assure accurate information about the corporation's compliance with law, financial reporting, and business performance.

In 2006 the Delaware Supreme Court clarified that director oversight is subject to review under the duty of good faith, which the court characterized as a subset of the duty of loyalty. See *Stone v. Ritter*, 911 A.2d 362 (Del. 2006). The case involved a derivative suit brought by shareholders against directors of AmSouth Bancorporation seeking personal liability for their failure to implement a monitoring system required by the federal Bank Secrecy Act. The shareholders claimed that better oversight would have revealed that bank employees had unwittingly allowed bank accounts to be used by a couple scoundrels running a Ponzi scheme (where returns to early investors are paid from investments by later investors). Federal banking authorities found that AmSouth's monitoring program was "materially deficient" and imposed record-setting fines and penalties of $50 million.

Nonetheless, the court held that the directors had not engaged in a *deliberate* failure to exercise oversight (or a *conscious disregard* of their responsibilities). The court found that the bank had implemented a monitoring system that was designed to present information on compliance with the Bank Secrecy Act requirements. That the system failed, according to the court, was not enough to establish "a sustained or systematic failure of the board to exercise oversight." The court pointed out that subjecting directors to personal liability for employee failures is "possiby the most difficult theory" in corporate law.

§12.3.5 Oversight under Sarbanes-Oxley and Dodd-Frank

In response to Enron and other accounting scandals, the Sarbanes-Oxley Act of 2002 (see § 11.5.1) mandated new corporate oversight mechanisms—in the process federalizing large swaths of corporate behavior previously within the board's discretion under the business judgment rule.. The Dodd-Frank Act of 2010 (see § 11.5.2) modified some of the Sarbanes-Oxley requirements.

Certification of SEC Filings and Internal Controls

As commanded by Sarbanes-Oxley, the SEC adopted rules requiring corporate officers of "reporting companies" (see §21.2.2) to certify the annual and quarterly reports filed with the SEC. Sarbanes-Oxley §302. Under SEC rules, the CEO and CFO each must certify that he reviewed the report and, based on his knowledge, that (1) it does not contain any material statements that are false or misleading, and (2) it "fairly presents" the financial condition and results of operation of the company—regardless of formal compliance with generally accepted accounting principles (GAAP). Exchange Act Rules 13a-14, 15d-14.

In addition, the officers must certify that they are responsible for establishing and maintaining "disclosure controls and procedures" that ensure material information is made known to them and that these internal controls were evaluated before making the report. Sarbanes-Oxley §302. If there are any significant deficiencies or changes in the internal controls or any fraud by those who operate them, the certifying officers must disclose this to the company's auditors and the board's audit committee. Exchange Act Rules 13a-15, 15d-15, 15d-14.

To impress upon certifying officers the gravity of these tasks, Sarbanes-Oxley enhanced the criminal sanctions for certifications that are knowingly or willfully false. Sarbanes-Oxley §906, 18 U.S.C. §1350 (requiring CEO and CFO to certify that periodic report "fully complies" with Exchange Act and "fairly presents" material financial condition and results). Knowing violations carry penalties up to $1 million and 10 years' imprisonment and willful violations up to $5 million and 20 years' imprisonment.

Internal Controls

In a significant expansion into state law, Sarbanes-Oxley increased the scope (and burden) of internal controls on reporting companies beyond financial accountability. Sarbanes-Oxley §404. (Internal controls are, as commanded by Sarbanes-Oxley, the SEC adopted rules requiring reporting companies to include in their annual report a statement of management's responsibility over internal controls, a statement of how those controls were evaluated and an assessment of their effectiveness (or weaknesses) over the past year, and a statement that the company's auditors attested to management's assessment. Items 307 and 308, Reg. S-K; Exchange Act Rel. No. 47,986 (2003).

From the beginning, the internal controls requirement was controversial. It was argued that such controls were not cost justified—particularly for smaller public companies. Responding to these arguments, the SEC permitted smaller public companies (with a market cap of less than $75 million) to delay until 2008 their implementation of internal controls and also exempted such companies from the auditor attestation requirement through 2010. In the Dodd-Frank Act of 2010, Congress made the attestation exemption permanent. Dodd-Frank §989G (adding §404(c) to Sarbanes-Oxley Act); Exchange Act Rel. No. 62,914 (2010). Thus, smaller public companies are only subject to the requirement that management certify the company's internal controls.

Whistleblower Protection

Sarbanes-Oxley gave whistleblowers in public companies special protections. The audit committee of listed companies must establish procedures to receive anonymous submissions from employees on "questionable accounting or auditing matters." Sarbanes-Oxley §301, Exchange Act §10A(m). In addition, whistleblowers in public companies who report securities fraud to a federal agency, Congress, or a company supervisor cannot be retaliated against. Sarbanes-Oxley §806; 18 U.S.C. §1514A (public company and specified individuals cannot "discharge, demote, suspend, threaten, harass, or in any other manner discriminate" because of lawful reporting). If there is retaliation, the whistleblower can file a complaint with the U.S. Department of Labor within 90 days. OSHA investigates the complaint, and civil penalties (back pay and attorney fees) can be imposed by the agency or in a court action against retaliating individuals and the company. Retaliation can also result in criminal penalties, including fines and prison terms up to ten years. Sarbanes-Oxley §1107; 18 U.S.C. §1513(e).

Enforcement of the Sarbanes-Oxley whistleblower provisions, however, has been mixed. In response, Dodd-Frank increased whistleblower protection by, among other things, providing whistleblower plaintiffs who claim retaliation a jury-trial right, double pay and reinstatement, as well as doubling the statute of limitations for whistleblower claims. Dodd-Frank §922 (adding new Exchange Act §21F). Dodd-Frank also sought to encourage whistleblowers by providing a monetary reward of between 10–30 percent of amounts recovered by the SEC in an enforcement action against the offending issuer, provided the recovery is above $1 million. Exchange Act Regulation 21F (implementing whistleblower reward program, which also creates incentives for employees to report company abuses internally; whistleblowers criminally convicted are not eligible for reward). See Exchange Act Rel. No. 54,545 (2011).

Audit Committee Regulation

Sarbanes-Oxley mandated that U.S. stock exchanges adopt standards on the composition and functions of the audit committee of listed companies. Sarbanes-Oxley §301, Exchange Act §10A(m). Under these standards, the audit committee of listed companies (including foreign issuers and small business issuers) must be composed entirely of independent directors, as defined by the SEC. In addition, companies must disclose whether at least one member of the committee is a financial expert. Sarbanes-Oxley §407, Reg. S-K, Item 401 (defining "audit committee financial expert" as one with significant auditing, accounting, financial, or comparable experience).

The audit committee must be responsible for appointing, compensating, and overseeing the company's independent audit firm—a curtailment of the power of the full board and shareholders over outside accountants. The audit committee (not the board) must have the authority to hire independent counsel and other advisors, their fees to be paid by the listed company. Rule 10A-3; Exchange Act Rel. No. 47,654 (2003).

Code of Ethics

Sarbanes-Oxley commanded the SEC to require reporting companies to disclose whether they have adopted a code of ethics applicable to their top financial and accounting officers—and if not, explain why. Sarbanes-Oxley §406; Item 406, Reg. S-K. Any changes or waivers of the ethics code for such officers must be promptly disclosed on Form 8-K. Exchange Act Rel. No. 47,235 (2003) (see §21.2.2).

"Up the Ladder" Reporting by Lawyers

As commanded by Sarbanes-Oxley, the SEC promulgated a rule requiring lawyers "appearing and practicing before" the SEC to report evidence of a material violation of securities law or breach of fiduciary duty (or similar violation) to the company's general counsel or CEO. Sarbanes-Oxley §307; 17 C.F.R. §205. Failing an appropriate response, the lawyer must then report to the company's audit committee, another committee composed exclusively of outside directors, or the full board. Although not free from doubt, this "up the ladder" reporting obligation applies both to inside and outside lawyers who represent the issuer before the SEC or advise on securities matters—whether the issuer is a reporting company or going public.

A securities lawyer's failure to report "up the ladder" can be the basis for SEC discipline and sanctions; no private right of action is created. This federalization of lawyer professional duties reminds corporate/securities lawyers that they work for the corporation and its shareholders, not corporate executives.

§12.4 REMEDIES FOR BREACHING THE DUTY OF CARE

If a challenger overcomes the business judgment presumption and shows the board's decision was uninformed or lacked a rational basis, any director who participated in the decision is liable for breaching a duty of care. The next question becomes what remedies the challenger can expect.

§12.4.1 Personal Liability of Directors

If board action violates the duty of care, courts have held that each director who voted for the action, acquiesced in it, or failed to object to it becomes *jointly and severally* liable for all damage that the decision proximately caused the corporation. Under most state statutes, a director who attends a meeting at which an action is approved is presumed to have agreed to the action, unless the minutes of the meeting reflect the director's dissent or abstention. MBCA §8.24(d). Some statutes allow a director who has not voted for the action to register her dissent or abstention by delivering written notice at or immediately after the meeting. MBCA §8.24(d).

Not every care breach, however, creates liability for damages. Some courts require the challenger to show the director's action (or inaction) proximately caused damage to the corporation. *Barnes v. Andrews,* 298 F. 614 (S.D.N.Y. 1924). Proximate cause is important in oversight cases. When directors disregard management abuse, courts readily find proximate cause. But when directors are inattentive to mere mismanagement, courts are less willing to make the causal finding. It would be anomalous to impose liability on a director for being inattentive to business mistakes that are themselves protected by the business judgment rule.

The MBCA's liability provisions state that directors who breach their care duties are liable in damages only if the violation proximately caused harm to the corporation or shareholders. MBCA §8.31(b)(1). Nonetheless, in a Delaware case involving uninformed board decision making, the court refused to make proximate cause an element of the plaintiff's case and shifted the burden to the careless defendants to prove the challenged transaction's "entire fairness." *Cede & Co. v. Technicolor, Inc.*, 634 A.2d 345 (Del. 1993) (*Cede* II). Under this approach, lack of proximate cause becomes an affirmative defense.

§12.4.2 Enjoining Flawed Decision

Courts can also enjoin or rescind board action unprotected by the business judgment doctrine. Some commentators have suggested that it should be easier to enjoin corporate action than to impose personal liability. Courts, nonetheless, have not explicitly distinguished between cases to impose personal liability and to enjoin board action.

§12.5 EXCULPATION OF DIRECTORS' CARE FAILURES

§12.5.1 Exculpation Statutes

After *Trans Union* a perception grew that service as a corporate director had become more risky. During the late 1980s, insurance premiums for directors' and officers' (D&O) insurance increased, and there were reports of directors who declined to serve for fear of liability exposure. In response, Delaware and most other states enacted exculpation statutes that authorize charter amendments shielding directors from personal liability for breaching their duty of care—a "raincoat" protecting directors from liability.

Delaware

No personal liability for breaches of duty, though director remains liable for

- breaches of duty of loyalty,
- acts or omissions not in good faith or that involve intentional misconduct or knowing illegality,
- approval of illegal distributions, and
- obtaining a personal benefit (such as by insider trading).

Del. GCL §102(b)(7).

MBCA

No liability for money damages to corporation or shareholders, except liability for

- financial benefits he received to which he is not entitled,
- intentional infliction of harm on the corporation or its shareholders,
- approving illegal distributions, or
- an intentional violation of criminal law.

MBCA §2.02(b)(4).

The exculpation provision can be included in the articles of a newly formed corporation or added by amendment with board and shareholder approval. None of the exculpation statutes affects the granting of equitable relief.

One important thing to notice is that exculpation provisions cannot cover officers, but only directors—on the theory that the promise of exculpation is necessary to attract directors to the board, but not officers to the corporation. Thus, officers are fully subject to the duty of care, their gross negligence not exculpable. See *Gantler v. Stephens*, 965 A.2d 695 (Del. 2009) (confirming that officers are subject to same fiduciary duties as directors).

§12.5.2 Effect of Exculpation

Exculpation provisions have been the subject of judicial interpretation, particularly in Delaware. Early cases focused on the meaning of the statutory exceptions. For example, exculpation provisions have been interpreted not to cover violations of disclosure duties, a theory of liability often used whenever a transaction involves shareholder voting. See *Zirn v. VLI Corp.*, 621 A.2d 773 (Del. 1993) ("equitable fraud" in a third-party merger). Left open are questions about the lines between care, loyalty, and good-faith violations. For example, when directors are sued for care violations, the real reason for liability (such as tacit approval of a managerial conflict of interest) suggests the statutory exceptions would not exculpate the directors from money damages. For example, if the Trans Union directors consciously acceded to Van Gorkom's "fast shuffle," their failure to become informed may have constituted "action not in good faith"—unprotected under a Delaware §102(b)(7) charter provision.

The Delaware courts have sought to explain the procedural effect of an exculpation provision in the corporate charter. In one case, the court held that plaintiffs challenging director conduct have the burden to allege well-pleaded facts that the conduct falls within the exceptions of the Delaware statute. *Malpiede v. Townson*, 780 A.2d 1073 (Del. 2001). But in another case, the court concluded that an exculpation provision is "in the nature of an affirmative defense," requiring directors to establish each of its elements, including good faith in a parent-subsidiary merger. *Emerald Partners v. Berlin*, 726 A.2d 1215 (Del. 1999) (*Emerald I*). Then in a second appeal in the same case, the court decided that when claims of care violations are mixed with claims of disloyalty and lack of good faith, the question of exculpation arises only *after* a finding that the transaction was not entirely fair. Only then can the trial court decide whether the unfairness arose from behavior challenged in the exculpated care claims or the nonexculpated loyalty or bad faith claims. *Emerald Partners v. Berlin*, 787 A.2d 85 (Del. 2001) (*Emerald II*).

Notice the effect of this procedural jumble. When a plaintiff adequately pleads conduct that falls within the statutory exceptions, directors charged with *both* care and loyalty/good-faith violations must go through a full trial on both claims before interposing their affirmative exculpation defense—which once presented presumably wipes clean any damages claims based only on care violations.

§12.5.3 Evaluation of Exculpation

Exculpation statutes and the charter provisions they have spawned raise troublesome questions. Is it good policy to allow directors to escape their care responsibilities? Does shareholder approval of an exculpation provision, particularly through proxy voting in a public corporation, provide meaningful assurances that shareholder interests are furthered?

One important study strongly suggests the shareholders (in stock trading markets) think exculpation statutes eviscerate care liability and disserve shareholders. The study found that share prices of companies incorporated in Delaware fell 2.96 percent compared to companies incorporated in other jurisdictions over the months surrounding the effective date of the Delaware "charter option" statute. The study also found that when particular Delaware corporations adopted a charter limitation their stock price experienced a second (somewhat smaller) drop. Bradley & Schiapani, *The Relevance of the Duty of Care Standard in Corporate Governance*, 75 Iowa L. Rev. 1 (1989).

Examples

1. EnTrade, a publicly traded company incorporated in an MBCA jurisdiction, is an energy trading firm that creates a marketplace for energy producers, carriers, and users. Offering an online system for buying and selling electricity and natural gas, along with energy transportation services, EnTrade is the largest energy broker in the country. In addition, to make participation in EnTrade's market more attractive, the company offers its customers "risk management" products that allow customers to buy financial contracts to protect themselves against price fluctuations. For example, an electric utility in California can use EnTrade to purchase electric power from a low-price industrial cogenerator in Louisiana, along with transmission services to get the power to California and a "hedging" contract that protects the utility if the market price falls. It is a brilliant business model that has won EnTrade recognition as the most innovative U.S. company by *Fortune Magazine*—for five years running. (These examples, drawn loosely from SEC filings of Enron Corp. and the February 2002 "Report of Investigation" by a special investigative committee of the Enron board, are wholly fictitious. For an excellent description and analysis of the Enron debacle, see William Bratton, *Enron and the Dark Side of Shareholder Value*, 76 Tul. L. Rev. 1275 (2002).)

   The success of EnTrade has attracted competitors offering similar energy trading systems, often at less cost. Even as EnTrade's revenues continue to grow impressively, its net income has grown more slowly—EnTrade's margins are shrinking. In response, EnTrade's management proposes a bold strategy. The company will expand its energy trading operations to other countries and begin to trade nonenergy commodities, as well. Although the company has no experience in these areas, the hope is that techniques used for energy trading in the United States can be used in other countries and in nonenergy markets such as pulp and paper, steel, and even telecommunications bandwidth. After some deliberations, the board approves the expansion plan.

   a. Sherron, an EnTrade shareholder, learns of the board's approval of the expansion and thinks it is a huge business mistake. Sherron wants to stop the expansion in court. How and on what theory?

b. The company spends $1.2 billion on a fiber optic network to run the company's expanded trading system. Sherron believes the money has been misspent and wants the directors to reimburse the corporation. On what theory?

c. Despite the state-of-the-art computer network and 1,700 new employees, the expansion project shows no signs of profitability. Six months after the expansion plan is put into effect, the company's stock has lost 40 percent of its value. Without knowing more, what chance does Sherron have of succeeding on either of these two claims?

2. As Sherron delves into the board's approval of EnTrade's expansion plan, she learns more. Which will support her challenge of the plan?

a. Online trading of telecommunications bandwidth (the biggest aspect of EnTrade's expansion plan) is not a new idea. Other companies have tried it and have uniformly discovered that the telecommunications market is not ready. In fact, finding that acting as a bandwidth broker is hugely unprofitable, these other companies have all withdrawn from the business.

b. When the EnTrade board met to approve the expansion plans, the company's CEO, Acosta, failed to tell the directors that telecommunications companies (some with more resources than EnTrade) had considered the idea of creating a bandwidth brokerage service and rejected it.

c. Acosta told the board that 40 percent of telecommunications companies in marketing surveys said they were interested in the concept of a bandwidth market. He failed to mention that 50 percent of the respondents who reviewed an online trading prototype said it did not fit their needs and they would never use it.

d. Acosta owns a majority interest in a company, Mastico, that will offer consulting services in EnTrade's bandwidth trading operations. Acosta reveals his interest in Mastico, and the board members are aware of EnTrade's plans to hire Mastico as part of the company's expansion into bandwidth trading.

e. Deere & Carbo, the company's outside lawyers, opined that the Mastico deal is fair to EnTrade, even though the lawyers failed to question or review the way in which EnTrade has guaranteed Mastico's obligations.

3. Problems for EnTrade mount. A key to EnTrade's online energy trading is its offering of risk management to traders through "hedge" contracts. Under these contracts EnTrade acts as principal, guaranteeing its online customers protection against the risks of shifting commodity prices, interest rates, foreign currencies, and even stock prices. Although EnTrade has assured its shareholders that it has instituted its own risk management programs to protect the company from exposure to sudden

price swings, EnTrade is not well hedged and lacks adequate reserves. The Commodity Futures Trading Commission, the federal regulator of commodities markets, investigates and threatens to sue EnTrade for "engaging in the business of commodity futures trading" without satisfying a host of regulations, including financial standards applicable to a "designated commodities futures market." At the next board meeting, CEO Acosta reports on the CFTC's position. Experienced, outside legal counsel opines there is a good chance a court would reverse the CFTC's jurisdictional grab, and the board authorizes a lawsuit against the CFTC.

a. The EnTrade board approves further steps in the company's expansion plan, including more aggressive, longer-term risk management programs that put the company at even greater risk if energy prices fall. The board does not seek authorization from the CFTC. If Sherron sues to enjoin the company's risk management program, is the board's decision to continue it protected by the business judgment rule?
b. The CFTC obtains a court injunction against EnTrade's continuing to offer risk management products, and the court imposes a substantial fine against EnTrade for marketing commodities futures without CFTC approval. Are the EnTrade directors liable to the corporation for approving the illegal conduct?
c. It turns out EnTrade's risk management practices were more aggressive than authorized by the board. EnTrade traders routinely understated the company's risk exposure by failing to "mark to market" their hedge contracts. This means the company's financial disclosure seriously misstates the company's contingent liabilities. The board, however, had never instituted a reporting system to keep track of the value (and exposure) of the company's proprietary risk management products. Are the EnTrade directors liable for not monitoring the company's risk management business?

4. The courts uphold the CFTC assertion of jurisdiction over EnTrade's risk management business, and Congress does not provide an exemption. All told, the company loses $150 million in business expenses, litigation costs, and regulatory penalties in its bid to be an unregulated commodity futures market. (This amount does not include the large losses the company eventually experiences when energy prices fall and it is forced to close its many "unhedged" positions.) Shareholders bring a derivative suit against the EnTrade board for failing to become adequately informed about the legality of the company's risk management business.
   a. The minutes of the meeting at which the board decided to continue in the risk management business despite the CFTC's position reveal the following: Director Nessum was not present; Director Rowland recused herself from the decision; Director Adams abstained from

voting; and the remaining six directors voted to approve continuing the business. Which directors can be held liable?

b. Director Rowland, who recused herself at the meeting, now claims that even if she had voted against the decision her dissent would not have changed the outcome. Does this affect her liability?
c. At the time of the board's decision, the EnTrade articles exculpated directors from personal liability to the corporation "to the full extent permitted by law." Does this provision insulate the EnTrade directors from liability?
d. Assuming the directors are not exculpated, are they liable for all of EnTrade's risk management losses?

5. EnTrade also owns natural gas utilities and pipelines—old-fashioned "hard assets." In addition to its aggressive risk management practices, the company uses its hard assets to create cash—adding even more luster to its soaring stock price. How? EnTrade moves hard assets worth billions into affiliated entities, many of them majority owned by EnTrade and most of them financed by borrowings from outside lenders (such as Citigroup and JP Morgan Chase) that take EnTrade stock as loan collateral. This means that EnTrade has leveraged its own stock to create cash in the affiliates, which cash then comes pouring into EnTrade. Only if EnTrade's stock price falls below preset thresholds will there be a problem. But as the stock market becomes concerned about EnTrade's investments and the risks in its core energy trading business, its stock price falls—triggering the collateral obligations that EnTrade owes to outside lenders of the affiliates. EnTrade's board was largely oblivious about the gravity of these contingent liabilities, which constitute nearly 40 percent of the company's net worth.
   a. To extricate itself from this potential mess, EnTrade negotiates a stock-for-stock merger with DuoNergy (see §36.2). Under the merger agreement, DuoNergy will infuse new cash into EnTrade's online trading business, and EnTrade's shareholders will exchange their shares for shares of DuoNergy. The EnTrade board approves the merger and recommends it to EnTrade shareholders, but fails to become fully informed about the contingent liabilities or to mention them to the shareholders. Is this a breach of the directors' fiduciary duties?
   b. The court finds that the EnTrade directors breached their fiduciary duties to become informed in the merger. Are the directors liable for the shareholders' losses when the contingent liabilities, which DuoNergy assumed in the merger, force the acquiring company into bankruptcy?

Explanations

1. a. Sherron might bring a derivative action on behalf of the corporation to enjoin the directors from carrying out their expansion plan. She might claim the directors violated their duty of care to the corporation in approving the risky plan. Absent any indication of dishonesty, illegality, or conflict of interest, she could claim the directors were not sufficiently informed in approving the plan or that they could not have believed it was a valid business risk. MBCA §8.30(a) requires that directors
   - act in a manner that the directors reasonably believe to be in the best interests of the corporation
   - become informed in their decision-making function with the care that a person in a like position would reasonably believe appropriate under similar circumstances

   Sherron might argue the plan is improvident and no reasonable director could believe it would maximize corporate returns. See MBCA §8.31(a)(2)(ii)(A). She might argue the directors did not have enough information concerning the costs and risks of the expansion. See MBCA §8.31(a)(2)(ii)(B).

   b. Sherron might claim, on the same grounds she sought to enjoin the plan, that the directors be held liable for any damages proximately caused by their duty of care violation. See MBCA §8.31(b)(1). If the directors breached their care duties—because the plan is wasteful or the directors were grossly negligent in approving it—each director who approved it or was at the meeting and failed to object can be held liable (jointly and severally) for any losses the plan causes the corporation. See §8.24(d) (directors present at meeting deemed to have assented to action taken, unless dissent or abstention from action entered in minutes or by written notice).

   c. Next to none. The board's approval of the expansion plan is protected by the presumptions of the business judgment rule, which applies despite the broadly worded standards of MBCA §8.30. The rule insulates the board's decision from attack and shields the directors from liability. Under the business judgment presumption, Sherron must show one of the following:
   - the decision was *not in good faith* (tainted by fraud, conscious disregard, illegality, or a conflict of interest)
   - the decision was *wasteful* (cannot rationally be said to be in the best interests of the corporation)
   - the directors were *grossly negligent* (failed to inform themselves about the plan)

That is, a showing of negligence is not enough. Instead, Sherron must show bad faith, an utter lack of business justification, or a collapse in the decision-making process. She thus faces dismal odds of proving a care breach. Although MBCA §8.31 seems to codify *standards of liability* that parallel the MBCA §8.30 *standards of conduct*, courts have continued to superimpose the business judgment presumption despite statutory standards. Fiduciary standards, largely a matter of judge-made law, build on the principles of delegated risk taking and centralized management embodied in the business judgment rule.

2. a. Probably not support. Sherron could argue the telecommunications industry's aversion to online trading of bandwidth suggests the EnTrade directors could not reasonably believe the project was in the best interests of the corporation. See Official Comment to MBCA §8.30(a)(2) ("reasonably believes" includes objective element). But the business judgment rule is a formidable shield. To impose on corporate directors industry-wide caution would kill corporate risk taking. Directors have broad latitude to experiment, and to fail, without being second-guessed or exposed to liability.

   b. Probably not support. Although this information might be relevant to "like position" directors, the business judgment rule teaches that courts should not second-guess the process of business decision making. Directors, of necessity, make decisions on incomplete information, often based on hunches and intuition. Lawyers can always dream up inquiries that the directors should have made, but the business judgment rule does not require courtroom-like thoroughness. The rule allows directors to act in an indeterminate business climate on imperfect information.

   The few cases that have faulted directors for not making sufficient inquiries have generally arisen in the context of hostile takeovers (where directors have ineluctable conflicts of interest) and negotiated mergers (where directors face fewer long-term incentives). In their function of deciding operational matters, directors have had wide latitude to take risks and rely on information from corporate subordinates. See MBCA §8.30(d) (absent knowledge that makes reliance unwarranted, director entitled to rely on corporate executives whom the director reasonably believes to be reliable and competent in the information provided).

   c. Probably not support. Even though Acosta's failure to mention the surveys may have been fraudulent—an intentional omission of a material fact—Sherron would have difficulty showing the board's reliance was unwarranted. See MBCA §8.30(d). She would have to argue that the board's approval of the expansion plan was tainted by fraud and unprotected by the business judgment presumption. If the board had reason to rely on Acosta (he had never been known to provide misleading information), then a shareholder challenge would be unavailing. See *Cede & Co. v. Technicolor, Inc.*, 634 A.2d 345 (Del. 1993) (*Cede II*) (concluding that a conflict of interest that affects one director does not necessarily remove board decision from business judgment rule). Of course, the board could later decide to fire or discipline Acosta—in fact, the possibility of such internal controls is at the heart of the business judgment presumption.

If, however, Sherron can show that reliance by the directors on Acosta's misleading presentation was unwarranted, the board action might be subject to attack. Personal liability of the directors, however, would be another matter. As in the cases involving directors' monitoring duties, directors making uninformed decisions are liable only if they should have known of management fraud.

In addition, consider Acosta's liability. Although the board decision might not be subject to attack, his misleading presentation might have violated his fiduciary duties as a corporate officer. See MBCA §8.42(a). If Acosta misled about the surveys for personal reasons, the business judgment rule would withdraw its protective presumption. Moreover, if it was obvious that the board would have wanted to know the full survey results, he could not have reasonably believed that withholding the information was in the corporation's best interests. Nonetheless, if there was some valid business reason for not describing the surveys fully or if it was a good-faith lapse, the business judgment rule would protect his actions.

d. Probably support. The business judgment rule does not protect a board decision if a director's conflict of interest may have tainted the decision-making process. See §13.2 (judicial suspicion of director self-dealing transactions). Although the board decision may be informed and the directors acted in good faith, where the transaction involves an interested director or senior officer, courts scrutinize the deliberative process and its outcome more closely. It would not be enough that the board merely knew of Acosta's conflicting interest. The board would also have to inquire into the fairness of the terms and price of Mastico's deal with EnTrade. See MBCA §8.60 (defining "required disclosure" in a director's conflicting interest transaction to include nature of conflict and facts respecting the subject matter of the transaction). The broad (and vague) care standards provide a convenient means for courts to adjust their scrutiny as the influence under which the board operates changes.

e. Probably support. The failure of outside counsel to fulfill its professional duties by conducting a slipshod investigation into a self-dealing transaction's terms and fairness can have repercussions on the transaction's validity. Not being informed on the critical issue of fairness can be the basis for invalidating the board's approval of the Mastico deal. See Official Comment to MBCA §8.62 (board approval of director's conflicting interest transaction "must be conducted in light of the overarching provisions of section 8.30(a)").

In addition, the Deere & Carbo lawyers may be subject to SEC discipline and sanctions under the new "up the ladder" reporting requirements. Under the rules, securities lawyers working for a reporting company (or one about to go public) must report "evidence of material violation" of the securities laws or breach of fiduciary duty by the company or its officials. 17 C.F.R. §§205.2, 205.3. The lawyer is first supposed to report the violation to the company's general counsel (or also the CEO) and, failing their response, to the board's audit committee or the board itself.

3. a. Perhaps. To overcome the business judgment presumption, a shareholder would have to show that the board's decision to expand the risk management program either was so improvident as to be beyond explanation or was grossly uninformed. The *possible* illegality of the test marketing, though a significant business risk, does not mean the directors violated a duty to the corporation. Directors are not guarantors of corporate legality.

   To show a breach of *substantive* care, Sherron would have to show the board proceeded without a rational business purpose. Any rational justification insulates the board's action from attack. For example, with energy trading increasing, the board could speculate that longer-term risk management products would fill an important market niche. These products would give the company a competitive advantage in the more competitive online energy trading market, and regulation is not certain. The CFTC's assertion of jurisdiction might be overturned on appeal. The CFTC might eventually authorize the product. And Congress might create a statutory exemption (which actually happened for Enron). A reasonable business person might conclude the *potential* benefits outweigh the risks—which is enough under the rational basis test.

   To show a breach of *procedural* care, Sherron would have to show the board knew so little it could not have acted rationally. This will be difficult. The EnTrade board knew of the CFTC determination and relied on the opinion of counsel that a court might reverse it. Under the business judgment rule, the directors have significant latitude to assess the risks and benefits of a course of action, even if only with sketchy information.

   b. Perhaps not. A shareholder could argue the directors are liable for not acting in good faith by approving illegal behavior. Earlier cases accepted this argument on the assumption corporate law should not shield those who disregard or flout the law. Imposing liability on directors promotes corporate responsibility. More recent cases recognize that directors act in an environment of legal uncertainty. At the time the directors approved the risk management expansion, it was not certain that CFTC approval was required to offer "hedge" contracts in its energy trading business. The directors could argue they reasonably relied on the advice of counsel that its risk management business would ultimately be found not to be subject to federal regulation.

Enforcing noncorporate norms (here financial capability laws) through corporate fiduciary law highlights the tension of making directors both agents of shareholder wealth maximization and guardians of legal compliance. This is particularly so if the CFTC regulations do not themselves penalize corporate decision makers for selling a risk management product while its legality is being tested in court. The business judgment presumption arguably is not overcome unless directors know or have reason to know their action is illegal. See *Graham v. Allis-Chalmers Manufacturing Co.*, 188 A.2d 125 (Del. 1963). From the *standpoint of shareholders*, the corporation (or shareholders in a derivative action) should not be asked to police noncorporate responsibilities. These responsibilities are more appropriately enforced under the regulatory regime, as happened in this case when the CFTC sought an injunction and penalties against the corporation. If this is insufficient to deter unwanted decisions, they can be increased—as has happened, for example, with penalties imposed on corporations and corporate actors under the federal sentencing guidelines. See Sarbanes-Oxley §§805, 807, 903, 904, 905 (increasing jail sentences for mail and wire fraud, securities fraud, and ERISA violations, and mandating review of federal sentencing guidelines on obstruction of justice and white-collar fraud).

c. Yes. A failure to be attentive to corporate illegality may breach a director's duty of good faith (a subset of the duty of loyalty). The EnTrade directors violated their duty of good faith by failing to implement a monitoring system to detect illegal behavior—something effectively required by the Delaware courts. See *In re Caremark Int'l, Inc.*, 698 A.2d 959 (Del. Ch. 1996) (suggesting current law requires monitoring systems to detect both corporate illegality and management irregularities); *Stone v. Ritter*, 911 A.2d 362 (Del. 2006 (accepting *Caremark* framework). The case for having a monitoring system is strong, as in EnTrade's situation, when there are indications corporate activities may be illegal.

4. a. Each director who was present at the meeting and failed to object or abstain from the action is assumed to have assented. MBCA §8.24(d). These directors may be held jointly and severally liable for the resulting loss suffered by the corporation. Consider the various excuses:

- Nessum, the absent director, is not liable under the MBCA, though some courts have imposed liability on absent directors who later acquiesced in wrongful board decisions.
- Adams, the abstaining director, is not liable so long as the minutes of the meeting reflect his abstention.
- Rowland, the nonparticipating director, is liable because she was present at the meeting. Unless during or immediately after the meeting she delivered written notice of an abstention or dissent, a procedure authorized by the MBCA, she is assumed to have acquiesced in the action.
- All directors who voted for the action are fully liable; there is no explicit right of contribution. Under the MBCA, they have no right to dissent or abstain once they have voted for the action.

b. Subject to an exculpation provision in the articles, the recused director is jointly and severally liable along with the other present, approving directors. Liability is to the corporation for all losses proximately caused by the board decision—namely the expansion of the risk management business. By failing to dissent, the nonparticipating director failed to register her views and perhaps remedy a mistaken decision.

c. Perhaps. Under MBCA §2.02(b)(4), in a corporation with an exculpation provision, a director can be liable for damages to the corporation or its shareholders only if his actions fit into one of four narrow categories. None seems to apply to the EnTrade directors in their approval of the expansion project:
   - The directors did not receive financial benefits to which they were not entitled. The only exception might be any benefits Acosta received in connection with his interests in Mastico, the bandwidth consulting firm.
   - The directors did not intentionally harm the corporation or its shareholders. On the assumption the directors believed that the risk management business would eventually be profitable and not subject to CFTC regulation, their approval represented good-faith business risk taking.
   - The directors did not approve illegal distributions, as defined in MBCA §6.40 (payments to shareholders). See MBCA §8.33 (liability for illegal distributions subject to standards of MBCA §8.30).
   - The directors, from appearances, did not intentionally violate criminal law. Although the directors understood there was a risk the company would violate CFTC regulations, there is no indication they or the corporation violated criminal law. Nonetheless, an argument could be made that an actual criminal conviction is not necessary and that engaging in risky financial arrangements is a criminal offense. This argument, however, would convert corporate fiduciary law into a prosecutor of criminal norms. See Official

Comment, MBCA §2.02 (exculpation does not extend to "improper conduct so clearly without any societal benefit that the law should not appear to endorse such conduct").

The exculpation clause is meant to insulate directors from liability for well-meaning business risk taking so long as the director does not enrich himself, does not carelessly approve unlawful distributions to shareholders (thus harming creditor interests), or consciously disregard potential harm to corporate interests or violation of noncorporate positive law. See *Stone v. Ritter*, 911 A.2d 362 (Del. 2006) (refusing to find breach of duty of good faith, on theory "bad outcome" cannot be equated with "bad faith").

d. Not necessarily. Even if the directors breached a duty for not inquiring sufficiently about the legality of the risk management business, their liability is not automatic. The MBCA places the burden on the challenging shareholder to show that the directors' inattention was a proximate cause of any corporate injury. See MBCA §8.31(b). This might be difficult if other causes, besides the lack of CFTC supervision, might explain the risk management losses. For example, if rogue traders caused the losses by having EnTrade assume unwarranted risks, the board's inattention to the CFTC issue might not be seen as the proximate cause of the losses. Moreover, a court might decide that even if the board had complete information about the CFTC jurisdictional issue, it would have reached the same decision. That is, the lack of information was not a proximate cause of the board's decision and the company's losses.

   Some courts, including now those of Delaware, would shift the burden to the inattentive directors to show their decision was nonetheless entirely fair to the corporation—that is, the board adequately informed itself that the risk management business was a good business risk.

5. a. Perhaps. At first blush, it might seem that the EnTrade board's approval of the merger without becoming informed about and disclosing "bad news" at the company actually produced a windfall for EnTrade shareholders, and a major headache for DuoNergy. Nonetheless, once these contingent liabilities are assumed by DuoNergy, they will have a negative effect on EnTrade shareholders, who (remember) acquired DuoNergy shares in the merger. That is, the board has a duty to inform itself about the company's business, including the contingent liabilities that DuoNergy is acquiring, because these liabilities will be material to EnTrade shareholders once they own DuoNergy shares. The board in a merger must ascertain both the value of the company's assets and liabilities, and the value of the consideration that the shareholders are receiving. On both counts, the EnTrade directors' failure to become informed

about such significant liabilities—and to tell the shareholders—would seem a breach of duty.

b. Not necessarily. Even though the EnTrade board should have become informed about EnTrade's liabilities when it sold the company, the shareholders' losses are not the result of the merger, but rather the earlier leveraging of the company's assets using company stock as collateral. In fact, bankruptcy would have been swifter and more certain had there not been a merger. Although the board should have become informed about this perilous leveraging of the company, and its failure may have violated the directors' fiduciary duties, this was not the failure that shareholders challenged. In fact, some Delaware cases hold that fiduciary breaches that existed before a corporate merger cannot be challenged by former shareholders—that is, the shareholders' fiduciary claims are lost in the merger. *Kramer v. Western Pacific Indus., Inc.*, 546 A.2d 348 (Del. 1988).

CHAPTER 13

Duty of Loyalty—Self-Dealing Transactions

A self-dealing transaction tests a fiduciary's loyalty to the corporation. When the fiduciary and the corporation are counterparties, the fiduciary plays two roles. She has a personal interest as a party to the transaction, and she participates in the corporate decision to approve the transaction.

This chapter discusses director self-dealing transactions—sometimes referred to as "director conflict-of-interest transactions." It describes self-dealing transactions (§13.1), the judicial approach to such transactions (§13.2), the various judicial fairness tests (§13.3), the statutory "safe harbors" (§13.4), and the remedies for self-dealing (§13.5).

Other chapters discuss other forms of self-dealing: the compensation of corporate executives (Chapter 14); parent-subsidiary dealings (Chapter 17); promoter's early dealings with the corporation (Chapter 29); and management buyouts and takeover defenses (Chapter 39). The taking of corporate opportunities and competing with the corporation, though also implicating the duty of loyalty, do not involve self-dealing with the corporation. See Chapter 16 (directors); Chapter 17 (controlling shareholders).

§13.1 NATURE OF SELF-DEALING

§13.1.1 Unfair Diversion of Corporate Assets

From the corporation's perspective, director self-dealing on unfair terms is like embezzlement. Little distinguishes the director who steals $100,000 from the company safe and the director who sells swampland to the corporation for $102,000 that is worth only $2,000. Although the land sale might seem like business as usual, the transaction effectively diverts to the transacting director corporate assets equal to the difference between the land's market value and its purchase price.

§13.1.2 Direct and Indirect Self-Interest

Self-dealing director transactions fall into two broad categories. In each instance, the director's conflicting interest risks that the transaction will be contrary to the corporation's best interests.

Direct Interest

In its classic form, self-dealing occurs when the corporation and the director herself are parties to the same transaction. MBCA §8.60(1)(i). Examples include

- sales and purchases of property, including the corporation's stock
- loans to and from the corporation
- the furnishing of services by a nonmanagement director (such as when the corporation's outside lawyer, accountant, or investment banker sits on the board)

Indirect Interest

Self-dealing also occurs when the corporate transaction is with another person or entity in which the director has a strong personal or financial interest. Courts generally look through the structure of the transaction to the substance of the director's interest. These include corporate transactions

- with the director's close relatives. See MBCA §8.60(1)(i), (3) (defining "related person" to include spouse, child, grandchild, sibling, parent, or family trust).
- with an entity in which the director has a significant financial interest. See MBCA §8.60(1)(i), (ii) (another entity in which director has

a significant financial interest or in which he is a director, partner, agent, or employee).

- between companies with interlocking directors. See MBCA §8.60(1)(ii). In the case of a parent-subsidiary relationship, the duties of interlocking directors are subsumed in the question of the duties of the controlling shareholder. See Chapter 17.

§13.2 JUDICIAL SUSPICION OF SELF-DEALING TRANSACTIONS

Corporate law's suspicion of director self dealing grows out of two assumptions. First, human nature tells us the self-dealing director will advance her own interests in the transaction to the detriment of the corporation. Second, the nature of group dynamics tells us the other directors will identify with their interested colleague even if they do not themselves have a financial interest in the transaction.

Nonetheless, transactions with insiders often make possible business deals that would otherwise be unavailable to the corporation from outsiders. Thus, modern corporate law allows self-dealing when "fair" to the corporation. Fairness is a multifaceted concept—a director satisfies her duty of loyalty if she is able to show the self-dealing transaction meets a mishmash of procedural and substantive tests.

§13.2.1 Early Rule of Voidability

Nineteenth-century courts, borrowing from the law of trusts, flatly prohibited self-dealing by directors. Self-dealing transactions, whether fair or not, were either *void* or *voidable* at the request of the corporation. The prohibition assumed that self-dealing rarely offers the corporation business opportunities not obtainable from other sources and that it is improbable that "disinterested" directors—those who do not have a direct or indirect interest in the transaction—will be immune to the actual and tacit influence of their interested colleagues.

§13.2.2 Substantive and Procedural Tests

The rule of voidability was abandoned at the turn of the century. See Marsh, *Are Directors Trustees?*, 22 Bus. Law. 35 (1966). Since then, courts have articulated a variety of substantive and procedural fairness tests. The substantive tests focus on the transaction's price and terms to measure whether the interested director advanced her interests at the expense of the corporation. The procedural tests focus on the board's decision-making process to measure whether the approving directors are disinterested in the transaction and independent of the influence of the interested director.

Over time, courts have articulated various review standards — with recent decisions focusing more on process than substance.

- **Substance plus process.** At first courts upheld self-dealing only if the transaction was fair on the merits *and* was approved by a majority of disinterested directors. See *Globe Woolen Co. v. Utica Gas & Electric Co.*, 121 N.E. 378 (N.Y. 1918) (invalidating one-sided supply contract entered with dominating director who failed to advise board of disadvantages).
- **Substance only.** By the 1950s, many courts upheld self-dealing if the court determined the transaction was fair on its merits. Approval by disinterested directors was not necessary.
- **Board process.** As the importance of outside directors grew in the 1980s, courts upheld director self-dealing provided disinterested, independent directors approved the transaction. See *Puma v. Marriott*, 283 A.2d 693 (Del. Ch. 1971) (upholding "independent business judgment" of disinterested directors who initiated and negotiated purchases from company's controlling family).
- **Shareholder process.** Courts have upheld self-dealing or shifted the burden to the challenger to prove unfairness — if disinterested shareholders (a majority or all) approved the transaction. Approval by disinterested directors has not been necessary.

The various tests ultimately turn on who decides whether the self-dealing transaction was in the corporation's best interests: a court, the board of directors, or the shareholders? See MBCA Chapter 8, Subchapter F, §§8.60-8.63 (comprehensive safe harbor for directors' conflicting interest transactions approved by appropriate action of directors or shareholders).

§13.2.3 Burden of Proof

Once a challenger shows the existence of a director's conflicting interest in a corporate transaction, the burden generally shifts to the party seeking to uphold it to prove the transaction's validity. See MBCA §8.61(b)(3) (absent disinterested approval by board or shareholders, transaction must be "established to have been fair to the corporation"); *Lewis v. S. L. & E., Inc.*, 629 F.2d 764 (2d Cir. 1980) (holding that interested defendants have burden of proving transaction between two affiliated corporations was fair and reasonable to the corporation).

Under the process-oriented approaches of the ALI Principles of Corporate Governance and Subchapter F of the MBCA, the challenger has the burden to prove the transaction's invalidity when disinterested directors or shareholders have approved the transaction. ALI §5.02(b); MBCA §8.61(b).

§13.2.4 No Business Judgment Presumption

The conflicts that permeate a self-dealing transaction rebut the business judgment presumption that directors act in good faith. See §12.3.1. Thus, for example, a company's sponsorship of a radio music program—normally subject to deferential review under the business judgment rule—becomes subject to intensive judicial review when the wife of the company's president was hired as a featured performer on the program. See *Bayer v. Beran*, 49 N.Y.S.2d 2 (Sup. Ct. 1944) (reviewing the process by which the board approved the program, the nature and quality of the program, and the wife's artistic competence and compensation).

Courts, however, have drawn a sharp distinction between directors who have an interest in the challenged transaction and "disinterested, independent directors"—that is, those directors who have neither a direct nor indirect interest in the transaction and are not dominated by the interested director. The business judgment rule protects from personal liability disinterested, independent directors who approve a self-dealing transaction in good faith. See §12.3.4.

One question that arises is whether self-dealing transactions can be sanitized by prior agreement or in the articles or bylaws. That is, can fiduciary duties be waived? "Fiduciary waivers" are recognized in LLCs, which are seen as more contractual than corporations. In fact, many LLC statutes permit the parties to agree to "specific types or categories of activities" that do not violate the duty of loyalty, provided the agreement is not "manifestly unreasonable." See ULLCA §103(b)(2). This is often given as a reason for choosing the LLC over the corporation. Courts, however, have been less willing to permit corporate agreements that waive the duty of loyalty in self-dealing transactions. See *Sutherland v. Sutherland*, 2009 WL 1177047 (Del. Ch. 2009) (agreement that placed corporate self-dealing transactions beyond judicial review would be "contrary to public policy"). Thus, the corporation remains less contractual, and more regulatory, than the upstart LLC form.

§13.2.5 Self-Dealing by Officers and Senior Executives

In general, officers and senior executives are subject to the same self-dealing standards as directors. See *Gantler v. Stephens*, 965 A.2d 695 (Del. 2009) (confirming that officers are subject to same fiduciary duties as directors); see also ALI §5.02(a), comment d. Nonetheless, because officers and senior executives generally will be expected to devote themselves primarily, if not exclusively, to the corporation, some cases indicate that such persons' transactions with the corporation are judged under more exacting standards.

§13.2.6 Aiding and Abetting Liability

Courts accept that an outsider who aids and abets a breach of fiduciary duty in a self-dealing transaction can also be liable. See *CDX Liquidating Trust v. Venrock Associates*, 640 F.3d 209 (7th Cir. 2011) (Posner, J.). Even though the outsider owes no fiduciary duties to the corporation, its "knowing participating" in the fiduciary's breach makes out a claim if the breach proximately results in damages to the corporation. See *Gatz v. Ponsoldt*, 925 A.2d 1265 (Del. 2007). But an outsider that merely negotiates with the board and seeks favorable terms for itself is not liable for aiding and abetting, but an outsider that attempts to exploit conflicts of interest on the board can become liable.

§13.3 JUDICIAL "FAIRNESS" TESTS

Under the traditional approach to self-dealing transactions, courts have applied both substantive and procedural standards of fairness.

§13.3.1 Substantive "Fairness"

A *substantive fairness* standard, first articulated by the courts in the 1940s, continues to be widely accepted. See *Remillard Brick Co. v. Remillard-Dandini Co.*, 241 P.2d 66 (Cal. App. 1952) (requiring that self-dealing transaction be "fair and reasonable"). Under this standard, which examines whether the director's interests won out over the corporation's interest, courts accept the fairness of self-dealing if the court concludes the transaction was in the corporation's best interests. Substantive fairness—sometimes called "intrinsic fairness"—has two aspects:

- **Objective test.** The self-dealing transaction must replicate an arm's-length market transaction by falling into a range of reasonableness. Courts carefully scrutinize the terms of the transaction—principally the price.
- **Value to corporation.** The transaction must be of particular value to the corporation, as judged by the corporation's needs and the scope of its business.

Both aspects of the fairness test involve significant judicial meddling in business matters and, ultimately, a judicial evaluation of the transaction's merits. See *Shlensky v. South Parkway Building Corp.*, 166 N.E.2d 793 (Ill. 1960); Official Comment to MBCA §8.61 ("Note on Fair Transactions").

Some cases and commentators suggest that substantive fairness is a flexible concept that varies with the degree of self-interest. That is, the level of scrutiny increases (or decreases) with the intensity of the director's self-interest. For example, courts impose less scrutiny on transactions between corporations with interlocking directors compared to transactions with directors in their personal capacity. The MBCA reflects this differential review and treats an interlocking-director transaction as a "director's conflicting interest transaction" only if so significant that it would normally require board approval. MBCA §§8.60(1)(ii), 8.61(a).

§13.3.2 Procedural "Fairness" — Process of Board Approval

Courts have also inquired into the process of board approval, showing various levels of deference if the transaction is approved by informed, disinterested, and independent directors. Courts sometimes refer to a combination of procedural and substantive fairness as "entire fairness."

Judicial review of corporate processes examines whether the directors who approved the transaction (even disinterested ones) lacked independence and acceded to their interested colleague. In reviewing the process, courts have focused on three procedural elements: (1) disclosure to the board, (2) composition of the board (or committee) that approved the transaction, and (3) role of the interested director in the transaction's initiation, negotiation, and approval.

Disclosure

Even when self-dealing may be fair on the merits, courts have invalidated the transaction if there was outright fraud in connection with its approval. Where there is no fraud, but only allegations of inadequate disclosure, courts have taken a variety of approaches. Some courts have said that full disclosure is a factor bearing on the transaction's fairness; others have required that there be disclosure only of the conflict of interest to put the board on guard; still others have required full disclosure of all material information, including the profit the interested director stood to make in the transaction. See *State ex rel. Hayes Oyster Co. v. Keypoint Oyster Co.*, 391 P.2d 979 (Wash. 1964) (invalidating transaction even though terms were fair on ground that director failed to disclose his interest). Each approach reflects different assumptions about whether full disclosure will give the board a meaningful opportunity to review the proposed transaction and to negotiate more favorable terms. See ALI Principles, comment to §5.02(a)(1).

Board (or Committee) Composition

Some courts have upheld self-dealing transactions approved by disinterested directors, applying a less exacting standard of review that approximates business judgment deference. See *Puma v. Marriott*, 283 A.2d 693 (Del. Ch. 1971) (without inquiring into fairness, accepting "independent business judgment" of disinterested directors who initiated and negotiated purchases from company's controlling family). Other courts, though while still reviewing the transaction's fairness, have shifted the burden of proving unfairness to the plaintiff—if the self-dealing is approved by a majority of disinterested directors. See *Cooke v. Ollie*, 1997 WL 367034 (Del. Ch. 1997) (upholding loans by insiders to corporation in desperate need of funds). The ALI Principles combine both a burden-shifting and modified fairness standard; Subchapter F of the MBCA makes disinterested approval conclusive.

The directors who approve the self-dealing transaction must be both "disinterested" and "independent." See *Orman v. Cullman*, 794 A.2d 5 (Del. Ch. 2002) (distinguishing "interest" and "independence" in case challenging fairness of merger involving company's management). A director is "disinterested" if he has no *direct* financial interest in the transaction, or *indirect* financial interest through close family ties or business relationships, that would affect his judgment. He is "independent" if he is neither beholden to nor dominated by the interested director. *Gries Sports Enterprises, Inc. v. Cleveland Browns Football Co.*, 496 N.E.2d 959 (Ohio 1986) (applying Delaware law, domination means more than being selected by the interested director to serve on the board, but acting as requested without independent judgment).

Sometimes these concepts are conflated. For example, Subchapter F of the MBCA defines a "qualified director" as one who is not a party to the transaction, does not have a beneficial financial interest that would influence the director's judgment, and has no familial, financial, professional, or employment relationship that would influence the director's vote on the transaction. MBCA §8.60.

Role of Interested Director

Although earlier cases held that the interested director's negotiation of a self-dealing transaction or her participation in the board's decision-making process invalidated the transaction, many modern statutes and recent cases allow the interested director to negotiate, participate, and vote without necessarily undermining the transaction's validity. See former MBCA §8.31 (replaced in 1989 by Subchapter F). An interested director's negotiation or participation, however, may evidence that the interested director dominated the other directors, undermining the advantage of disinterested approval.

Many modern statutes facilitate disinterested approval by easing quorum requirements for self-dealing transactions. Some statutes dispense with quorum requirements if the self-dealing transaction is approved by a majority of (but at least two) disinterested directors. See MBCA §8.62(c); former MBCA §8.31(c). These statutes overrule the early common-law rule that required disinterested directors to constitute a quorum of the full board. Other statutes allow interested directors to be counted for quorum purposes, even though they do not participate at the meeting.

What happens if an interested director discloses his conflict in a transaction with the corporation and then convinces his fellow directors that the transaction is nonetheless fair? At least one case holds that although disclosure may insulate the transaction from attack, the interested director remains liable for breaching his fiduciary duties. See *CDX Liquidating Trust v. Venrock Associates*, 640 F.3d 209 (7th Cir. 2011) (Posner, J.) (disinterested directors approved bridge loan in reliance on interested director, whose venture capital firm gave loan to company on terms highly favorable to firm). This approach seems a bit bizarre in that it would be possible for an interested transaction to be upheld because the conflict was fairly disclosed, while the interested director was held responsible for the transaction's unfairness. That is, the transaction could be both fair and unfair at the same time.

§13.3.3 Shareholder Ratification

Courts have shown substantial deference to self-dealing transactions approved or ratified by a majority of informed, disinterested shareholders.

Majority Ratification

Where a majority of the shares are cast by informed shareholders who neither have an interest in the transaction nor are dominated by those who do, most courts do not require that a defendant show "fairness." Instead, courts review the transaction under the business judgment rule and shift the burden to the plaintiff to show the transaction constituted waste—that is, no person of ordinary sound business judgment would say that the consideration was fair. See *Aronoff v. Albanese*, 446 N.Y.S.2d 368 (App. Div. 1982) (shareholder majority approved self-dealing rent reduction and rent-free lease modifications).

Delaware courts have followed this approach in cases where the self-dealing was by a *noncontrolling shareholder.* In such a case, approval by informed, disinterested shareholders of a transaction with the noncontrolling shareholder not only extinguishes any claim the board had acted without due care, but also leads disloyalty claims to be viewed under the business judgment rule. See *In re Wheelabrator Technologies Litigation,* 663 A.2d 1194 (Del. Ch. 1995) (merger with 22 percent shareholder). Disinterested shareholder ratification of transactions with *controlling shareholders,* however, is less cleansing and only shifts the burden to the challenger to show unfairness. See *Kahn v. Lynch Communication Systems,* 638 A.2d 1110 (Del. 1994). The different standards reflect the concern that controlling shareholders are in a better position to manipulate or unfairly influence the process of the shareholder vote.

Critical to shareholder ratification is complete and fair disclosure to the shareholders. Thus, when a board pursued a reclassification plan that assured the incumbency of the company's CEO and directors — rather than respond to an outside bid for the company — the Delaware Supreme Court held that shareholder approval of the reclassification plan was not sufficient to absolve the defendants. The shareholders had been misled, the court concluded, when they were told the board had conducted "careful deliberations" about the outside bid. Thus, the "entire fairness" standard applied to the interested transaction, not the business judgment rule or the proportionality *Unocal* standard (see §39.2.3). *Gantler v. Stephens,* 965 A.2d 695 (Del. 2009) (cleansing effect of ratification does not apply when shareholders approve charter amendment, but only when shareholders approve board action that "does not legally require shareholder approval to become effective").

Courts have been suspicious of self-dealing transactions if shareholder ratification is by a majority of shareholders interested in the transaction. *Remillard Brick Co. v. Remillard-Dandini Co.,* 241 P.2d 66 (Cal. App. 1952); *Fliegler v. Lawrence,* 361 A.2d 218 (Del. 1976) (leaving burden with defendants to show "intrinsic fairness" of transaction ratified by interested shareholders). Under some conflict-of-interest statutes, including the MBCA, shares voted by an interested shareholder are not counted for purposes of shareholder ratification. MBCA §8.63(b); former §8.31(d). Nonetheless, many statutes permit a majority of shares held by disinterested shareholders to constitute a quorum. MBCA §8.63(c); former §8.31(d).

Unanimous Ratification

If self-dealing is ratified unanimously by all of the shareholders or by a sole shareholder, courts agree that it cannot be set aside even under a waste standard so long as there is no injury to creditors. Effective ratification depends on full disclosure to shareholders of the director's conflicting interest.

§13.4 STATUTORY "SAFE HARBORS"

Because judicial self-dealing standards are often vague, there has been a movement toward adopting "safe harbor" tests that provide certainty to corporate planners seeking to ensure the validity of transactions between the corporation and its directors. Some courts, including Delaware's, have interpreted "interested director" statutes (which ostensibly remove the cloud of voidability from self-dealing transactions) as creating a safe harbor so that properly approved self-dealing transactions are subject only to business judgment review. Likewise, Subchapter F of the MBCA and the ALI Principles of Corporate Governance adopt safe harbors meant to assure the validity of self-dealing transactions if properly approved.

For each of the safe harbors, the initial question is whether there has been proper approval—that is, by qualified directors or qualified shareholders, at a meeting with the necessary quorum, and accompanied by adequate disclosure. If so, judicial review is muted or extinguished. If not, judicial review reverts to the common-law fairness standards described in §13.3.

§13.4.1 "Interested Director" Statutes

Many modern statutes codify the abandonment of the flat prohibition against self-dealing, though without explicitly specifying when self-dealing is valid. A good example is former MBCA §8.31(a) (rescinded in 1989), which states that a transaction *"shall not be void or voidable solely for the reason"* that a director (or an entity in which the director has an interest) is a party to a transaction with a corporation if

(1) the material facts are disclosed to the board, and a majority of disinterested directors authorized the transaction, or
(2) the material facts are disclosed to the shareholders, and the shareholders vote to approve the transaction (under some statutes the shareholders must be disinterested), or
(3) a court determines the transaction to be fair.

On their face, these "interested director" statutes are ambiguous. Do they merely reverse the common-law voidability rule for self-dealing transactions, leaving the *validity* of such transactions to judicial fairness review? Or do they create "safe harbors" that remove from judicial scrutiny properly approved transactions? Some courts have concluded the statutes do not displace judicial fairness review. See *Cookies Food Products v. Lakes Warehouse*, 430 N.W.2d 447 (Iowa 1988) (interpreting Iowa's "interested director" statute to still require judicial review of "good faith, honesty, and fairness" in self-dealing transaction);

Remillard Brick Co. v. Remillard-Dandini Co., 241 P.2d 66 (Cal. App. 1952) (interpreting California's "interested director" statute not to displace judicial role to ensure self-dealing transaction is "fair and reasonable").

Delaware courts have wrestled with the state's "interested director" statute. Del. GCL §144. At first, Delaware courts construed the statute as removing the shadow of automatic voidability, but without displacing the court's role to measure the transaction's entire fairness (both substance and procedure). See *Fliegler v. Lawrence*, 361 A.2d 218 (Del. 1976). Delaware courts treated disinterested director approval as merely shifting the burden to the plaintiff to prove the transaction was not entirely fair. See *Cinerama, Inc. v. Technicolor, Inc.*, 663 A.2d 1134 (Del. Ch. 1994), *citing Kahn v. Lynch Communication Systems*, 638 A.2d 1110 (Del. 1994).

But, as Delaware has relied more and more on disinterested directors to resolve corporate conflicts, Delaware courts have concluded the statute creates a safe harbor for self-dealing transactions, if approved by fully informed, disinterested, and independent directors. *Marciano v. Nakash*, 535 A.2d 400 (Del.1987) (suggesting in dicta that proper approval "permits invocation of the business judgment rule"); *Benihana of Tokyo, Inc. v. Benihana, Inc.*, 906 A.2d 114 (Del. 2006) (upholding issuance of preferred stock to director, which was approved by committee of disinterested directors that considered alternative financing plans and received fairness opinion on challenged issuance). In effect, the Delaware courts have decided that properly informed and qualified directors are superior at determining the value of a self-dealing transaction to the corporation than a reviewing judge.

§13.4.2 MBCA Subchapter F

MBCA §8.61(b)—the heart of Subchapter F—validates a director's conflict-of-interest transaction if it was

- disclosed to and approved by a majority (but not less than two) of qualified directors (MBCA §8.62), *or*
- disclosed to and approved by a majority of qualified shareholders (MBCA §8.63), *or*
- established to be fair, whether or not disclosed (MBCA §8.61(b)(3)).

Judicial review of board approval is thus limited to whether the directors were "qualified directors" and whether the disclosures were adequate. Official Comment, MBCA §8.61(b). Although an earlier version of Subchapter F suggested a court had the latitude to determine whether the self-dealing transaction was "manifestly unfavorable to the corporation," the current Subchapter F makes clear that judicial inquiry is foreclosed if the criteria of the safe harbor are met.

Judicial review of shareholder validation is similarly limited to whether a majority of disinterested shareholders approved or ratified the transaction after requisite notice and disclosure of the conflict. Neither the MBCA provisions nor the official comments suggest the court should engage in any substantive review—such as for waste—if the process satisfied the statutory safe harbor.

Some commentators have criticized Subchapter F for effectively removing self-dealing substantive review from the courts and placing it in the hands of disinterested directors or shareholders. The subchapter, first adopted in 1989, has not been well received in states adopting the MBCA. As of 2011, only 15 of the 38 MBCA jurisdictions have included the subchapter.

Only a few cases have interpreted the Subchapter F safe harbor, though they suggest a judicial willingness to defer to internal corporate processes. In *Fisher v. State Mut. Ins. Co.*, 290 F.3d 1256 (11th Cir. 2002), an insurance company sold one of its subsidiaries to a newly formed corporation owned by two of the company's directors. The insurance company's board created a special committee, which negotiated and approved the sale. When a shareholder challenged the transaction, the corporation argued the sale satisfied the safe harbor for "board action" under Subchapter F. Despite allegations that the interested directors had failed to disclose material information about the subsidiary, the court held the interested directors' fiduciary duties to the purchasing corporation (which they themselves had formed) barred their full disclosure to the special committee, and they thus met the terms of the safe harbor. See MBCA §8.62(b) (full disclosure not required if interested directors disclose their interest and play no part in the deliberations or vote on the transaction). Given the safe harbor, the court refused to consider the plaintiff's further allegations of waste and fraud.

§13.4.3 ALI Principles of Corporate Governance

The ALI Principles of Corporate Governance also adopt a safe harbor approach. The Principles recommend a disjunctive test under which director self-dealing is valid if *after full disclosure*

- a court finds the transaction was fair when entered into, or
- a majority of disinterested directors (not less than two) approved or ratified the transaction, or
- a majority of disinterested shares approved or ratified the transaction.

ALI Principles §5.02. By requiring full disclosure in every case, the focus of judicial review is on disclosure adequacy even when the transaction is substantively fair or approved by disinterested directors or shareholders.

The ALI Principles contemplate diluted judicial review of the substance of a self-dealing transaction validated by disinterested directors. The court must conclude the transaction "could reasonably be believed to be fair to the corporation." ALI Principles §5.02(a)(2)(B). The burden, however, is on the challenger to show disclosure was inadequate, the approving directors were not independent, or the transaction fails this watered-down fairness standard. The ALI Principles, unlike the MBCA, specify that self-dealing transactions validated by shareholders remain subject to judicial review under a substantive waste standard. Thus, minority shareholders who vote against the transaction can still complain if no reasonable business person would conclude the corporation received fair benefit.

The ALI Principles treat self-dealing standards as default rules. Disinterested directors or shareholders can authorize in advance specified types of self-dealing transactions that can be expected to recur in the company's ordinary course of business. ALI Principles §5.09(a). This standard must be stated in the articles or bylaws, or by board or shareholder resolution. ALI Principles §1.36.

§13.4.4 Summary Chart

The following chart summarizes the safe harbor approaches under the Delaware "interested director" statute, the MBCA Subchapter F, and the ALI Principles:

	Safe Harbor	Judicial Review
Delaware (§144)	Board: • material facts disclosed or known to directors • board or committee in good faith authorizes • majority of the disinterested directors • disinterested directors may be less than quorum	business judgment presumption
	Shareholders: • material facts disclosed or known to shareholders • specifically approved in good faith by vote of shareholders	waste (?)
	Court: • transaction fair to corporation • as of time approved	conclusive

(continued)

	Safe Harbor	Judicial Review
MBCA (Subchapter F)	Board: • after required disclosure • board or committee approves • majority (but not less than two) of qualified directors • majority of qualified directors constitutes quorum	"not manifestly unreasonable to corporation"
	Shareholders: • after required disclosure • approved by majority of qualified shareholders	conclusive
	Court: • established to be fair, whether or not disclosed	conclusive
ALI Principles (§5.02)	Board: • after full disclosure • approved or ratified by board or committee • majority of disinterested directors (not less than two)	"could [not] reasonably be believed to be fair"
	Shareholders: • after full disclosure • approved or ratified by majority of disinterested shares	waste
	Court: • transaction was fair when entered into	conclusive

Although all three follow a similar approach, there are subtle differences. The ALI Principles, for example, require full disclosure to the corporate decision-making body, even if neither of the procedural safe harbors applies. Delaware does not require actual disclosure, if the material information is already known to the directors or shareholders. Moreover, each approach leaves room for judicial review of board approval—"good faith" in Delaware, "manifestly unreasonable" under the MBCA, and "reasonable belief" under the ALI Principles.

Just as the judicial standards of review are not uniform, so too the statutory standards!

§13.5 REMEDIES FOR SELF-DEALING

§13.5.1 General Remedy — Rescission

As a general matter, an invalid self-dealing transaction is voidable at the election of the corporation — either in a direct action by the corporation or in a derivative suit. The general remedy is rescission, which returns the parties to their position before the transaction. Normally, the corporation cannot seek to "renegotiate" the terms of the transaction by retaining the transaction's benefits, but at a lower price. After all, a self-dealing transaction may provide value to the corporation, and a director who transacts with the corporation should not be exposed to the risk the corporation will use a fairness challenge to renegotiate the deal.

§13.5.2 Exceptions to Rescission

A rescission remedy does not always work — such as when self-dealing is also the usurpation of a corporate opportunity (that is, the taking of a valuable business opportunity in which the corporation has a preexisting interest or that is within its line of business), or when the property has been resold and is no longer held by the original party. In such cases, the corporation may be entitled to damages instead of rescission.

For example, in *New York Trust Co. v. American Realty Co.*, 155 N.E. 102 (N.Y. 1926), a director resold to the corporation at a significant profit timberland that he had purchased only a few months before. Although the transaction was voidable under the then-prevalent "fairness plus validation" test because the director dominated the board, the corporation chose not to rescind. The court, while stating that normally rescission is the exclusive self-dealing remedy, held the director could be liable for his profits on an "agency" (or "corporate opportunity") theory without the transaction being rescinded. The director was required to account for his profits and became liable as though he had acquired the timberland for the corporation.

Examples

1. Last year major league baseball approved an expansion team in Havana, Cuba — after the island's admission to the Union as the fifty-first state. The team (the "Cuba Libres") is incorporated in an MBCA jurisdiction that has adopted Subchapter F. The largest shareholder of the Libres is Silvio Garcia (40 percent); the remaining shares are held publicly, mostly by rabid Cuban baseball fans. Garcia, the board chair and company CEO, hand-picked the other four directors: Alejandro (his brother-in-law),

Bobby (a prominent Cuban politician), Camilo (a prominent Cuban businessman), and Duncan (the company's outside lawyer).

a. Salsa Services operates a successful food concession business on the East Coast and has bid to operate food and beverage concessions for the Libres. Alejandro is a director and 25 percent shareholder of Salsa. Any problem if the Libres accept the Salsa bid?
b. Garcia calls a board meeting to consider the Salsa bid. Only Camilo and Duncan attend the meeting. The Libres bylaws specify that three directors constitute a quorum at board meetings. Do the two constitute a board quorum?
c. Both Camilo and Duncan had been personally invited to join the Libres board by Garcia. Neither owns shares in the team. Are the two qualified to approve the Salsa contract?
d. The two directors adjourn their meeting to ask Garcia for information about other bidders seeking the concession business. Garcia attends their reconvened meeting, answers their questions, and joins Camilo and Duncan in approving the Salsa bid. Does Garcia's presence and participation affect the validity of the board's action?

2. Ibrahim, a Libres shareholder, has waited his whole lifetime for baseball in Cuba. When he learns of the Salsa contract, he shouts, "It's a sweetheart deal." Salsa's three-year contract calls for Salsa to make flat payments to the Libres of $20 million per year for the right to be the team's exclusive concessionaire.
   a. Ibrahim wants the Salsa contract invalidated. Assuming the bid was approved by the Camilo-Duncan committee, who should he sue and what will he have to show?
   b. Ibrahim discovers that Alejandro, though he disclosed his directorship and 25 percent interest, never disclosed to the committee his inside knowledge that Salsa would have agreed to pay $24 million per year. Does Alejandro's failure to disclose Salsa's reservation price nullify the committee's approval?
   c. Happieaux, another well-established food concessionaire and the only other bidder, had bid $14 million per year plus additional royalty payments of $4 for each fan who attends Libres games during the season. The committee, however, estimated annual attendance on the low end—1.4 million fans, producing for Libres $19.6 million in royalties. It chose the Salsa bid. Does this information indicate the Salsa contract is valid?
   d. Ibrahim discovers an internal Libres study that projects attendance of 2.6 million, 2.8 million, and 3.0 million during the first three seasons. Garcia failed to disclose this study to the Camilo-Duncan committee. Does this invalidate the Salsa contract?
   e. The Camilo-Duncan committee eventually became aware of the internal attendance study, though not from Garcia. The committee decided nonetheless to take the lower Salsa bid. Does this invalidate the Salsa contract?

3. At the next Libres shareholders' meeting, the board submits a shareholder resolution to ratify the Salsa contract. The company's proxy statement fully sets forth the terms of the contract, describes Alejandro's 25 percent interest in Salsa, and states the "Salsa contract assures the company a fixed payment not dependent on attendance figures."
   a. With Garcia (40 percent) voting for the resolution, it is approved by 55 percent of the outstanding shares. Most of the public shareholders vote against it. What effect does this shareholder ratification have on Ibrahim's challenge to the contract?
   b. The Libres articles of incorporation provide:

      > Any conflict-of-interest transaction between the Corporation and any director (or entity in which any director is interested) is conclusively valid if approved by a vote of a majority of the outstanding Shares. The Shares of any interested director may participate fully in such a vote.

      Does this affect the outcome of Ibrahim's challenge?
   c. Assume Garcia did not vote and a majority of public shareholders ratified the Salsa contract, though their shares did not constitute a majority. Would this vote affect Ibrahim's challenge to the contract?

4. The court rules that shareholder ratification was defective because the proxy statement failed to disclose the Happieaux bid, thus making the Salsa transaction unfair to the Libres.
   a. Ibrahim wants the court to modify the Salsa contract to conform to the payment schedule offered by Happieaux, which the court had found was fair. Will the court order Salsa to make these payments?
   b. Ibrahim had also sued Camilo and Duncan, the disinterested directors who approved the Salsa contract. Are they liable for the damages the Salsa contract caused the corporation?

Explanations

1. a. Yes. The concession could be rescinded as a director's self-dealing transaction because of Alejandro's and Garcia's conflicting interests. Alejandro's 25 percent shareholding in Salsa creates a "beneficial financial interest" that in all likelihood "would reasonably be expected to influence his judgment." See MBCA §8.60(1)(i). Moreover, even though nephews are not related persons under Subchapter F (see MBCA §8.60(3)), if Garcia's relationship with Alejandro is such that he would gain financially because of his Salsa holdings, he might have a "beneficial financial interest . . . of such financial significance" as to cloud his judgment. See MBCA §8.60(1)(i).

   Subchapter F, though it specifies when a director's conflicting interest transaction is valid, does not specify when the transaction is invalid. Nonetheless, courts have scrutinized director self-dealing and would impose a heavy burden on Alejandro and Garcia to prove the procedural and substantive fairness of the transaction.

b. Yes. Under Subchapter F, as under most modern statutes, a majority of disinterested directors (but not less than two) constitute a quorum for purposes of considering a self-dealing director transaction. MBCA §8.62(c). The MBCA and other modern statutes relax the quorum requirement for the approval of self-dealing transactions so these transactions can be considered without interested directors present, thus facilitating impartial review by the disinterested directors. If Camilo and Duncan are "qualified directors," they would constitute a quorum.

c. Perhaps. It depends on whether Camilo (the Cuban businessman) and Duncan (the company's outside lawyer) are sufficiently disinterested and independent. If they are, the two would be fully capable—as a majority of qualified directors—to approve the self-dealing transaction, despite the absence of the other directors. MBCA §8.62(a).

   If either Camilo or Duncan is interested or lacks independence, their action would fail under the MBCA safe harbor. MBCA §8.62(a) (at least two qualified directors). As the company's outside lawyer, Duncan might be disqualified in a variety of ways. If he or his law firm expects fees because of work connected to the Salsa deal, his financial interest in the transaction would constitute a "conflicting interest" under the statute. See MBCA §8.60(1). If Garcia "dominates" his activities as a director, perhaps because he feels beholden to him for continuing fees, his independence would be in doubt. This involves a factual assessment of motives and loyalties. As Justice Frankfurter once admonished judges, "[W]e should not be ignorant as judges of what we know as men." Nonetheless, Delaware courts have said that it is not conclusive merely because a director is selected by an interested director or controlling shareholder.

d. Yes, under the MBCA. The MBCA "safe harbor" for board action applies only if the qualified directors deliberate and vote "outside the presence of and without the participation by any other director." MBCA §8.62(a)(1). Other "interested director" statutes, however, are not as strict and specifically do not invalidate action by the board just because of the presence or participation of an interested director. See Del. GCL §144(a).

   Even though the safe harbor is not available because of Garcia's presence and vote at the meeting, a court would still have to review the transaction for procedural and substantive fairness. The MBCA Official Comments define "fairness" as encompassing both "consideration and other terms of the transaction" and "process of decision the director's conduct." Official Comment, MBCA §8.60 ("fair to the corporation"). Among the fair dealing factors is whether the director exerted "improper pressure" on the other directors, presumably by being present and participating in the meeting at which the self-dealing transaction is considered.

2. a. Ibrahim should bring a derivative action (see Chapter 31) on behalf of the corporation and name the interested directors, Garcia and Alejandro, and the approving directors, Camilo and Duncan. Under Subchapter F the challenger must prove the director's conflicting interest and must establish that board approval (or any shareholder approval) was flawed. If he does, the directors then bear the burden to show the transaction was fair. Failing this, the corporation can rescind the transaction. And the directors may be individually liable — the approving directors for their "lack of objectivity" under MBCA §8.31(a)(2)(iii), and the interested director for his "receipt of a financial benefit to which he was not entitled" under MBCA §8.31(2)(v). The business judgment rule would not apply, and there would be no presumption of validity.

   b. Probably not. The Subchapter F safe harbor for self-dealing approved by disinterested directors requires that the interested directors disclose the "existence and nature of their conflicting interest" and all facts known to them about the transaction that an "ordinarily prudent person would reasonably believe to be material" to whether or not to proceed. MBCA §8.60(4) ("required disclosure").

   The duty to disclose *material* information puts the director in the uncomfortable position of a fiduciary and a self-interested counterparty. In this case, the discomfort is even greater for Alejandro, who owes fiduciary duties to Salsa not to disclose confidential information. The Official Comments to Subchapter F recognize this and suggest the director need not disclose all material information, but only that information the corporation would normally ascertain in an arm's-length negotiation. Thus, the director need not "reveal personal or subjective information that bears on the director's negotiating position." For example, the director need not reveal "the lowest price he would be willing to accept."

   c. Probably. It may depend on the soundness of the committee's attendance estimates. The fixed Salsa price ($20 million) is slightly better than the variable Happieaux price ($19.6 million), if the committee's attendance estimates are valid.

   If the transaction was approved by a majority of qualified directors, there would be no further review under the current MBCA's safe harbor and the transaction could not be challenged. Instead, it would receive the business judgment presumption, requiring only that the decision was based on some rational business purpose. (An earlier version of the MBCA suggested that board approval of director self-dealing could be challenged if "manifestly unreasonable" — a standard less deferential than the business judgment rule, but more deferential than traditional fairness review.)

The current MBCA "safe harbor" approach is similar to that of Delaware under its nonvoidability statute. See *Benihana of Tokyo, Inc. v. Benihana, Inc.*, 906 A.2d 114 (Del. 2006) (holding that Del. GCL §144 creates safe harbor, and thus protection of business judgment rule, for self-dealing transaction approved by informed, disinterested directors). The challenger carries the heavy burden to show something akin to waste.

d. Probably. The information would seem material, as it reveals that the variable contract (producing royalties of $24.4 million, $25.2 million, and $26.0 million) is superior to the fixed $20 million Salsa bid. Even though the interested Garcia's failure to disclose this study renders the Salsa contract unprotected by the safe harbor for disinterested director approval, a court could nonetheless conclude the contract was fair. That is, the board-approval safe harbor is not exclusive.

The fairness safe harbor of the MBCA, like judicial fairness review, contemplates judicial inquiry into the process of approval. Note on Fair Transactions, MBCA §8.61 ("course of dealing—or process—is a key component to a 'fairness' determination under subsection (b)(3)"). For example, the *Weinberger* "fair dealing" standard requires that the process of negotiation and approval of the self-dealing transaction conform to what would be expected of an independent board. See §17.3.3. This means the interested director should disclose all *material* information, and the approving directors may not be influenced by the interested director. Note on Fair Transactions, MBCA §8.61 ("most obvious illustration of unfair dealing arises out of the director's failure to disclose fully . . . hidden defects known to him regarding the transaction"). If the undisclosed attendance study would have added to information the board had on attendance estimates, it could be expected that Garcia would have disclosed it if he were not interested. As such, it is material and the board's approval does not insulate the transaction from review.

e. Not necessarily. If the committee's approval otherwise complies with the board-approval safe harbor, "neither the transaction nor the director is legally vulnerable" because of the director's conflict. See Official Comment, MBCA §8.61(b).

Even if the committee's approval failed to comply with the board-approval safe harbor, the transaction might still be saved if shown to be "fair to the corporation." The burden would be on the interested directors to show not only that the terms of the deal are comparable to what would have been obtained in an arm's-length transaction, but also that the transaction was likely to yield favorable results for the corporation. The behavior of the interested director—such as incomplete disclosure, exertion of improper pressure, or an untoward role in negotiating the transaction — may also be relevant to the court's evaluation of the fairness to the corporation. See Official Comment, MBCA §8.60.

3. a. Very little. The resolution was not approved by a majority of shares held by disinterested shareholders. MBCA §8.62(a), (b) (safe harbor requires majority of "qualified" shares be cast for transaction; "qualified" shares are those not owned or controlled by the interested director). In fact, a majority of disinterested shares were cast against the resolution. The burden will fall on Garcia and the other defendants to show the transaction's fairness.

   b. Perhaps, but only mildly. The MBCA allows for the articles of incorporation to contain limits on the power of the board and shareholders. MBCA §2.02(b)(5). But the Libres provision would effectively gut judicial review of self-dealing if the interested director, as here, controls the proxy mechanism or holds a significant block of stock. Just as courts have been unwilling to read statutory provisions as displacing judicial review of self-dealing transactions, there should be judicial reluctance to give a broad exculpatory provision full effect. Perhaps, as has happened in some cases, the reviewing court would merely shift the burden of proof to the challenger to show unfairness.

   The ALI Principles permit corporate parties to preapprove self-dealing transactions in the articles, but this dangerous practice is limited to "specified types" of self-dealing transactions that "can be expected to recur in the company's ordinary course of business." ALI Principles §5.09(a). The carte blanche provision in the Libres articles would not be binding.

   c. Yes. Ibrahim would have to show some defect in the process of shareholder approval, such as a failure to disclose the terms of the competing Happieaux bid or to describe the internal study estimating large attendance figures in the first three years. Like the board-approval safe harbor, shareholder approval must be accompanied by "required disclosure" of all material facts known to the interested director. MBCA §8.63(a). Absent a showing of some process flaw, the MBCA safe harbor provision treats the shareholder ratification as conclusive, without further judicial inquiry into the transaction's merits. MBCA §8.63. This is a significant departure from the prevailing judicial approach in such cases to either shift the burden to the challenger to show unfairness or to show waste.

   The failure of the disinterested shareholders to constitute a quorum is not a problem. The MBCA, like many other statutes, requires only a majority of disinterested shares to constitute a quorum. MBCA §8.63(c).

4. a. Probably not. The usual remedy for unfair self-dealing is rescission of the transaction. This assures the self-dealing insider that the corporation cannot unilaterally revise the terms of the transaction in a judicial fairness challenge. If the royalties are indeed inadequate, the solution is to rescind the Salsa contract and for the corporation to find a better contract, presumably based on the Happieaux bid. In smaller corporations self-dealing transactions may be uniquely valuable, offering business opportunities to the corporation not otherwise available on the open market. The rescission-only rule keeps courts out of the business of reforming private arrangements.
   b. Probably not. Because they were not interested in the transaction, they are liable only if they violated their duties of care. If they rationally believed that they were acting in the corporation's best interests and sought to inform themselves about the Salsa contract, their liability for approving the contract is protected under the business judgment rule. See §12.3. They may also be shielded from personal liability under any exculpation provision in the corporate charter. See §12.5.

CHAPTER 14

Executive Compensation

Executive compensation is the most common form of corporate self-dealing. But the rendering of managerial services by corporate executives is also an indispensable corporate activity. For this reason, executive compensation receives special judicial deference. When approved by disinterested and independent directors, executive compensation is subject to business judgment review.

This chapter describes the various forms of executive compensation (§14.1), the different standards of judicial review (§14.2), the treatment of directors' fees (§14.3), and recent market and regulatory activities (§14.4).

§14.1 FORMS OF EXECUTIVE COMPENSATION

Modern corporate executives are compensated *directly* in a number of ways:

- **Salaries and bonuses.** Base salaries and bonuses, usually set annually, represent compensation for current services.
- **Stock plans.** Stock grants, stock options, and other plans based on stock value create incentives for executive performance; their purpose is to align management and shareholder interests by pegging compensation to the corporation's stock price.

A *stock grant* by the corporation provides the executive a shareholding stake in the business, but dilutes other shareholders' interests.

A *stock option* granted by the corporation gives the executive the option during a specified period (often in the future) to buy a specified amount of the company's stock at a fixed price (often set above the stock's current market price). If the market price for the company's stock rises above the option's exercise price ("in the money"), exercising the option becomes profitable. When the executive exercises a stock option, the executive receives company shares, thus diluting the shares held by other shareholders. If the market price does not rise above the exercise price ("out of the money"), no shares are issued and the corporation's capital is not diluted.

Phantom stock plans and *stock appreciation rights* provide similar incentives without the corporation having to issue any stock (or, for that matter, have any stock authorized in the articles). The executive is credited with units on the corporation's books, and the value of the units rises or falls with the market price of the company's stock (including dividends and stock splits). The units represent a form of deferred compensation, and their value is not paid until a specified date, such as retirement or death.

- **Pension plans.** Pension plans and other forms of deferred compensation provide executives' retirement income. Plans qualified under the Internal Revenue Code make it possible for the corporation to immediately deduct corporate contributions to the plan even though the executive is not taxed until later.

Executives also are compensated *indirectly* with fringe benefits (perks), such as expense accounts, company residences, contributions to charities designated by the executive, and the use of corporate jets.

Stock Options

Understanding the operation of stock options is basic to your understanding of modern executive compensation. Let's assume that ABC Corp. is a public corporation, its common shares trading at $15 per share. The corporation grants stock options to its CEO, Martha, that give her the right (the option) to buy 5,000 shares at $15 per share after two years, but not more than three years. This is like a lottery ticket for Martha; she wins if the stock price is above $15 in two years.

Let's say the stock price after two years is $25. Martha can exercise her options and buy 5,000 shares from the company at $15, immediately reselling them in the market at $25 for a gain of $10 per share, or

$50,000. Or Martha could hold on to the options (not exercise them) and hope the stock price rises even more before they expire in another year.

If, however, the stock price is only $12 after two years, Martha will not exercise the options, though they will still have value given the possibility that the stock price could go above $15 in the next year. But if the stock price stays flat, the options expire and she loses nothing—except her hopes for quick wealth.

Disclosure of Executive Pay in Public Companies

Under rules promulgated by the Securities and Exchange Commission (SEC), public companies must disclose in the company's annual proxy statement the compensation of their CEO, CFO, and three highest-paid executives. Exchange Act Schedule 14A (item 8), Reg. S-K, item 402 (see §§9.2, 9.3). Disclosure must be presented in tabular form covering the last three years of salary, bonuses, stock-based awards, nonstock incentive plan payments, retirement pensions, deferred pay, and perquisites. Any stock-based compensation must be presented as a dollar amount, reflecting the present value of any stock grants or stock options exercisable in the future, as well as amounts actually realized from stock-based awards. The table must then include a "total compensation" number.

In addition to disclosing this pay information, companies must discuss the objectives and implementation of their compensation programs (which the company's CEO and CFO must certify) and describe the process the board's compensation committee used to review and set the top executives' pay packages. Under the Dodd-Frank Act of 2010, public companies must also disclose the relationship between pay for the company's CEO and the company's financial performance. Dodd-Frank §953. Dodd-Frank also gives shareholders in public companies a "say on pay"—that is, the right to cast an advisory vote on the company's pay practices. Dodd-Frank §951. For example, shareholders can register their displeasure when there is a disconnect between pay and performance—such as when executive pay is going up at a company while the company's stock price is going down. See § 14.4.3 below.

These SEC-filed disclosures are carefully scrutinized by the business press, which uses them to report annually on the highest-paid executives and "grade" their relative value. Activist shareholders and proxy advisory firms also use the disclosures to identify companies where there is excessive pay or pay unrelated to performance. Companies failing to receive majority "say on pay" support from their shareholders have often changed their pay practices, sometimes even retroactively.

§14.2 JUDICIAL REVIEW

§14.2.1 Dilemma of Executive Compensation

Senior executives, particularly in public corporations, have significant sway over board decision making. As a result, the board's setting of executive compensation raises many of the same concerns as are raised in director self-dealing transactions: (1) the executive predictably will prefer his own interests, and (2) the board will predictably accede to the executive's wishes, at the expense of corporate interests.

But treating executive compensation like any other self-dealing transaction would force courts to *regularly* place a value on a particular executive's services to the corporation, often without a working knowledge of the corporation, the particular value of the executive to the corporation, or the executive's market value to other corporations. Some commentators argue that judicial deference is warranted because most large corporations link executive pay significantly to corporate performance. Others, however, have looked at multimillion-dollar executive compensation packages and questioned the sufficiency of internal process and market limits alone. Board compensation committees, each trying to give "above average" compensation to their "above average" executives, have set into motion a seemingly boundless upward spiral in executive pay.

The accounting scandals of the early 2000s and the failures of risk management in the financial crisis of 2008 also raise doubts about creating incentives for executives (and other employees) with stock-based compensation, particularly stock options whose value depends on the company's stock price rising above the options' exercise price. By linking compensation to a rising stock price, the corporation creates the perverse incentive for the executives to manipulate the stock price through accounting gimmicks or to engage in overly risky business strategies.

§14.2.2 Compensation Authorized

Executive employment contracts, like any other transaction with the corporation, must be properly authorized. The shares for stock-based compensation must be authorized in the articles. MBCA §2.02; Del. GCL §151(a). Transactions involving the corporation's stock (such as stock grants, options, or repurchases) require board approval. MBCA §6.24; Del. GCL §152. In addition, some statutes require that stock options be approved by shareholders when the options, if exercised, would result in a substantial dilution of existing shareholders. MBCA §6.21(f) (requiring shareholder approval if options can be exercised to acquire shares that will comprise 20 percent of the voting power of shares outstanding immediately before option grant); see also NYSE Listed Company Manual Rule 312.03 (same for companies listed on exchange).

The board, particularly in public corporations, often delegates the task of reviewing and approving executive pay to a compensation committee of outside directors. MBCA §8.25(d); Del. GCL §141(c). Whether a director interested in his own compensation can be counted for quorum purposes, or vote for his own compensation, raises the same questions as in other self-dealing transactions. Some statutes authorize approval by less than a quorum of directors if disinterested directors approve the compensation. See MBCA §8.62(a) (board action effective if director self-dealing transaction receives affirmative vote of majority (at least two) of qualified directors); Del. GCL §144(a)(1) (approval of director self-dealing transaction by disinterested directors, even less than quorum).

One recent practice that ran afoul of the requirement that stock-based compensation be properly approved was the backdating of options, where the exercise price was not set using the company's stock price on the grant date but instead an earlier date when the stock price was lower. Such "back-dated" options were thus immediately more valuable to those holding them because of their lower exercise price. Courts had little trouble concluding that the failure of compensation committees to follow the pricing rules of the company's stock option plans that had been approved by the board (and also the shareholders) was a violation of fiduciary duty, especially when the backdating was done in secret. See *Ryan v. Gifford*, 918 A.2d 341 (Del. Ch. 2007) (finding that deliberate violation of shareholder-approved stock option plan and false disclosures rebut the business judgment rule and constitute bad faith, thus violating duty of loyalty).

§14.2.3 Disinterested Approval

Executive compensation is not subject to fairness review so long as it is approved by directors who are informed, disinterested, and independent. Stock listing standards for public corporations require that a majority of directors be independent (see §11.4); the listing standards, as mandated by Dodd-Frank, also require that all directors on the compensation committee be independent (see §14.4.4 below).

The board must be aware of all material information related to the executive's compensation, and the interested executive cannot dominate the board's decision making. Courts have held that "back-scratching"—where officer-directors tacitly agree to approve each other's compensation, while each interested executive steps out of the meeting as his compensation is approved—does not satisfy the requirement of disinterested approval. *Stoiber v. Miller Brewing Co.*, 42 N.W.2d 144 (Wis. 1950). But courts consider approval to be disinterested if nonmanagement (outside) directors or a committee of outside directors make compensation recommendations to the full board, even if the outside directors or committee constitute less than a quorum of the board and the full board is composed of a majority of inside directors.

In general, it is easier to muster *disinterested* board approval in a public corporation, where outside directors have become the norm, compared to a closely held corporation, where a majority of the board (if not the whole board) may have an employment relationship with the corporation. For this reason, compensation in a close corporation often turns on the approval or ratification by a majority of informed, disinterested shareholders. ALI Principles §5.03 (placing burden of proof on challenger to show waste if compensation approved by informed, disinterested shareholders).

Effect of Ratification

Over time, courts have changed their views on whether (and to what extent) approval or ratification by a majority of informed, disinterested shareholders affects judicial review. Some earlier cases, reflecting doubts about the informational efficiency of shareholder voting in public corporations, suggest that approval by informed, disinterested shareholders merely "freshens the atmosphere," and the burden falls on the directors to disprove waste. *Gottlieb v. Heyden Chemical Corp.*, 90 A.2d 660 (Del. 1952) ("possible indifference, or sympathy with the Directors, of a majority of the stockholders"). More recent cases, however, have concluded that shareholder ratification cleanses the transaction and shifts the burden to the shareholder challenger to show waste. *Lewis v. Vogelstein*, 699 A.2d 327 (Del. Ch. 1997) (noting that in "this age in which institutional shareholders have grown strong," classic waste standard does afford some protection in egregious cases); *Harbor Finance Partners v. Huizenga*, 751 A.2d 879 (Del. Ch. 1999) (noting that if "fully informed, uncoerced, independent stockholders" approve compensation plan, "difficult to see the utility of allowing" plaintiff to prove compensation devoid of merit).

§14.2.4 Waste Standard

If executive compensation is approved by disinterested and independent directors, courts invoke the presumptions of the business judgment rule. One way the challenger can overcome the business judgment presumption is to show the compensation was a waste of corporate assets—that is, the compensation had *no relation* to the value of the services promised and was really a gift. See *Beard v. Elster*, 160 A.2d 731 (Del. 1960) (upholding approval by disinterested directors of stock options in "twilight zone where reasonable businessmen, fully informed, might differ"). Thus, for example, a post-death payment to an executive's widow not pursuant to any agreement lacks consideration and constitutes waste. *Adams v. Smith*, 153 So. 2d 221 (Ala. 1963).

The deference given disinterested and independent approval of executive compensation in a public corporation is illustrated by the much-litigated compensation paid the president and five vice presidents of American Tobacco during the Great Depression. *Rogers v. Hill*, 289 U.S. 582 (1933). Under a bylaw adopted by American Tobacco shareholders in 1912, the executives received annual bonuses based on a percentage of the corporation's net profits above a stated base. As the company prospered, so did the executives. By 1930, with the Depression deepening and America smoking more, the president's annual bonus under the bylaw grew to $842,000 and each vice president's to $409,000—at a time when the average U.S. household income was less than $2,000 per year. Shareholders challenged the compensation as excessive under federal common law (before *Erie*). Although the amounts were staggering at the time, the Supreme Court gave "much weight" to the shareholders' near-unanimous approval of the bylaw and held that the bonuses could be challenged only if they were shown to be wasteful—that is, only if there was no relation between the bonus amounts and the executive services.

Even as executive compensation has lately spiraled upward, courts have honed close to the waste standard, dismissing complaints that the courts admit describe "exceedingly lucrative" compensation. Nonetheless, some cases suggest that allegations of wasteful compensation may raise factual questions that require further evidence. See *Lewis v. Vogelstein*, 699 A.2d 327 (Del. Ch. 1997) (holding that "one time option grants to directors of this size" warrant the taking of evidence).

§14.2.5 Bad Faith Standard

Another way that a challenger can overcome the business judgment presumption—even when disinterested and independent directors have approved the compensation—is to show that the directors acted in bad faith. To show bad faith the challenger must show the directors "consciously disregarded" their duties in approving the compensation, either by not becoming informed or by engaging in a subterfuge or other deception of shareholders. For example, directors on a compensation committee violated their duty of good faith by approving executive stock options with an exercise price equal to the market price on the grant date when the directors knew that the company would be announcing favorable news soon after the grant date, causing the options to immediately rise in value. See *In re Tyson Foods, Inc.*, 919 A.2d 562 (Del Ch. 2007). The court held that such "spring-loaded" options are inherently unfair when concealed from shareholders.

Disney and Good Faith

The ongoing litigation over a $140 million severance package paid by the Walt Disney Company to Michael Ovitz, hired from Hollywood in 1995 to be the company's number two executive, illustrates the courts' deferential approach to executive compensation. The case, which was filed in 1998, was originally dismissed despite the "sheer magnitude of the severance package." *In re The Walt Disney Co. Derivative Litigation (Disney I)*, 731 A.2d 342 (Del. Ch. 1998). On appeal, the Delaware Supreme Court expressed concern about the "lavish" payout and the board's "casual, if not sloppy" review of the package, but affirmed the dismissal, with leave to amend. *Brehm v. Eisner*, 746 A.2d 244 (Del. 2000).

After the plaintiffs amended their complaint, based on new information gathered after a statutory inspection of the company's books and records, the Delaware Chancery Court took a different tack. Concluding that the allegations painted a picture of directors who "consciously and intentionally disregarded their responsibilities," the court set the case for trial. In a move that garnered much attention, the court suggested that the directors had breached their duty to "act honestly and in good faith"—leaving open the possibility that the company's exculpation provision under Del. GCL §102(b)(7) (see §12.5) would not shield the directors from personal liability. *In re Walt Disney Co. Derivative Litigation (Disney II)*, 825 A.2d 275 (Del. Ch. 2003).

After a protracted trial, the court concluded that the directors had not breached their fiduciary duties, even though their conduct "fell significantly short of the best practices of ideal corporate governance." *In re The Walt Disney Co. Derivative Litigation (Disney III)*, 907 A.2d 693 (Del. Ch. 2005), *aff'd*, 906 A.2d 27 (Del. 2006). The chancery court concluded that enticing Ovitz to leave his high-profile position in Hollywood required making significant financial assurances if he were ever terminated. The failure of the directors to analyze the full ramifications of the pay package was "at most ordinary negligence." The court, however, hinted that the result might be different for a present-day pay package approved in "an era that has included the Enron and WorldCom debacles, and the resulting legislative focus on corporate governance."

§14.2.6 Fair and Reasonable Standard

When compensation has not been approved by informed, disinterested, and independent directors, it is subject to fairness review—and judicial scrutiny is substantial. The court takes on the function of the board (or compensation committee) and assesses whether the challenged compensation is fair and reasonable to the corporation, taking into account

- the relation of the compensation to the executive's qualifications, ability, responsibilities, and time devoted
- the corporation's complexity, revenues, earnings, profits, and prospects
- the likelihood incentive compensation would fulfill its objectives
- the compensation paid similar executives in comparable companies.

Full-fledged fairness scrutiny arises mostly for compensation in close corporations where boards (or committees) of disinterested directors are the exception. *Wilderman v. Wilderman*, 315 A.2d 610 (Del. Ch. 1974) ("standard for fixing executive compensation is obviously more strict when it is fixed by the recipient himself"). The scrutiny parallels that given executive compensation when the IRS challenges the deductibility of salaries as an "ordinary and necessary business expense."

§14.3 DIRECTORS' COMPENSATION

§14.3.1 Directors' Fees

Originally, directors served without compensation. Their reward was the increased value of their shares. As public ownership of corporations grew and shareholdings of directors declined, directors came to be paid relatively modest fees for serving on the board and for each meeting they attended. Today, as outside directors have become more important, directors' fees have become significant—sometimes totaling up to $100,000 per year and often in the form of company stock, though not stock options given the excessive risk taking the latter induce. In addition, directors are compensated indirectly through expense reimbursement, directors' liability insurance (see §15.2), corporate travel, and even product discounts.

Directors' fees authorized by disinterested shareholders are reviewable only if they constitute waste. See Official Comment to MBCA §8.61 (noting that director compensation, though universally accepted in principle, must be fair to the corporation or favorably acted on by shareholders). Even when directors' fees are not approved by shareholders, courts have been reluctant to intervene. See *Marx v. Akers*, 666 N.E.2d 1034 (N.Y. 1996) (dismissing claim that outside directors' increase of their own annual retainer to $55,000, plus 100 shares of company stock, did not constitute waste or "call into question whether the compensation was fair to the corporation").

§14.3.2 Compensation for Outside Services

Services provided by outside directors (or their firms) to the corporation—such as by lawyers, accountants, and bankers—are treated as self-dealing transactions subject to fairness review. For instance, if a lawyer sits on the board and her law firm provides legal services to the corporation, legal fees must be what would be obtainable in an arm's-length relationship and must be for services for which the corporation has a need.

§14.4 REGULATORY AND MARKET PRESSURE

Over the last decade, executive compensation has been controversial. News stories and books have chronicled the exorbitant pay of many American CEOs. In the words of a corporate compensation expert hired by many large corporations, "CEOs get paid hugely in good years and, if not hugely, then merely wonderfully in bad years." Graef Crystal, *In Search of Excess: The Overcompensation of American Executives* (1991).

Over the past few decades, while inflation-adjusted pay for most workers has been stagnant, the pay for corporate CEOs has skyrocketed. In 2010 the median pay package for a CEO at an S&P 500 company was $7.5 million, compared to the average private sector employee's annual pay of $40,000. Thus, the ratio in 2010 between the pay of the average CEO and that of the average worker was about 185:1. This compares to a ratio of 24:1 in 1965, 125:1 in 1993, and 290:1 in 2001. This disparity in the sharing of the financial returns in large U.S. public corporations has been controversial—and various federal laws have been enacted in response.

§14.4.1 Securities and Tax Laws

During the 1990s, federal regulators responded to the public outcry against overpaid executives and sought to impose some discipline.

SEC Disclosure

In 1992 the SEC significantly revised its rules on disclosure of executive compensation in public companies. See §14.1. Although there was some hope that these disclosures would shame board compensation committees into reining in compensation excesses, the greater information fueled an upward spiral as companies sought to out-compensate each other.

The SEC has continued to tinker with its disclosure rules. See Exchange Act Rel. No. 54,302A (2006) (requiring new "Compensation Discussion and Analysis" section and summary compensation table, including a present dollar value for stock-based compensation). In addition, Dodd-Frank requires disclosure about the role of (and potential conflicts) involving executive pay consultants, as well as additional disclosures comparing CEO pay and the company's financial performance. See Dodd-Frank §§952, 953 (see §14.4.3 below).

Tax Deductibility

In 1993 Congress revised the tax laws to disallow corporate deductions for executive compensation to the CEO and four highest-paid executives in excess of $1 million per year. An exception is made for compensation based on performance goals (1) determined by a compensation committee composed solely of outside directors, (2) approved by shareholders after disclosure of material terms, and (3) certified by the compensation committee to have been met. See I.R.C. §162(m). The 1993 tax change induced companies to increase incentive compensation (particularly stock-based compensation) linked to the companies' market performance.

§14.4.2 Sarbanes-Oxley Act

In 2002, responding to stories of management abuse in companies hit by scandal, Congress took aim at abusive compensation practices.

Prohibition of Loans to Insiders

Sarbanes-Oxley prohibits public companies from giving "personal loans" to directors and executive officers. Sarbanes-Oxley §402; Exchange Act §13(k). A limited exception is available for loans to insiders made in the normal course of the company's business, such as credit cards offered by a bank to its executives on the same terms as offered to other customers.

The federal prohibition, which displaces state law, has forced companies to reassess such common practices as travel advances, personal use of company credit cards, retention bonuses (reimbursable if the executive leaves), indemnification advances by the company (reimbursable if the executive ultimately is not entitled to indemnification), loans from 401(k) plans, and cashless exercise of stock options (where the company or a broker gives the executive a short-term loan so the executive can exercise the options and then repay the loan once he sells the underlying shares).

Escrow during SEC Proceedings

Sarbanes-Oxley authorizes the SEC to seek a judicial order for the escrow of "extraordinary payments" made to corporate executives pending the outcome of an investigation and any charges against them. Sarbanes-Oxley §1103; Exchange Act §21C(c)(3). A recent case interpreted "extraordinary payments" to include "restructuring payments" of $37.6 million made to a company's CEO and CFO after they resigned their corporate offices to become "employees" of the company. *SEC v. Yuen*, 401 F.3d 1031 (9th Cir. 2005). The court determined the termination payments were "extraordinary" given both the unusual circumstances surrounding their approval (they were made after allegations that the company had overstated its revenues) and their relative size (they were five to six times larger than the executives' base salary in the previous year).

SEC Clawbacks of Incentive Pay

Under Sarbanes-Oxley, if a public company is required to restate its financial statements as a result of "misconduct," the company's CEO and CFO must reimburse the company for any incentive pay (such as bonuses or equity-based compensation) received from the company during the 12-month period after the misstated financials were issued or filed. Sarbanes-Oxley §304; 15 U.S.C. §7243. The provision raises a variety of uncertainties—not the least of which is whether the reimbursement action may be brought only directly by the company, or indirectly in a derivative suit, or through an enforcement action by the SEC. Also unclear is what constitutes misconduct and whether the CEO or CFO subject to reimbursement must have actually engaged in the misconduct.

Lower courts have held that §304 does not imply a private cause of action, but can be enforced only by the SEC. See *Cohen v. Viray*, 622 F.3d 188 (2d Cir. 2010). In the years following the adoption of §304, the SEC was criticized for not bringing any actions to enforce the clawback remedy. But beginning in 2009, the agency began to seek clawbacks from company executives under §304, including in cases where they were not personally involved in the misconduct that led to the financial restatements.

§14.4.3 Dodd-Frank Act

The Dodd-Frank Act again addressed the issues of executive compensation in public companies, responding especially to the public outcry against what was perceived as excessive executive pay at financial firms receiving government bailouts during the financial crisis of 2008. The Dodd-Frank reforms primarily focus on increased disclosure and greater shareholder input in pay practices.

"Say on Pay"

One of the most important contributions of Dodd-Frank is to provide shareholders an advisory (nonbinding) vote on executive pay in public companies. See Dodd-Frank §951(a) (adding Exchange Act §14A). Issuers must include on the proxy ballot a chance for shareholders to vote for or against the pay packages of the company CEO and the four other top-paid executives. The vote must take place at least every three years, though companies (as most have) can opt to make the vote annual.

In 2011, the first year of "say on pay," most companies received more than 90 percent support for their pay packages, but when companies received weaker support, especially when they received less than majority support, company boards often revised pay packages and even reduced pay retroactively. Many observers have commented that "say on pay" ushers in a new era in the shareholder-management dialogue.

Golden Parachutes

Dodd-Frank also gives shareholders an advisory vote on executive pay packages arising in mergers or other corporate acquisitions. Dodd-Frank §951(b) (adding Exchange Act §14A). Whenever shareholders are asked to approve an acquisition, the company must also provide full disclosure of any special pay arrangements for departing company executives, such as "golden parachutes" (see Chapter 34). Thus, shareholders have a chance to voice their displeasure if executives in a poorly performing company receive a windfall for having mismanaged the company.

Company Clawbacks of Incentive Pay

Seeking to strengthen and expand the clawback remedy adopted in Sarbanes-Oxley (see §14.4.2 above), Dodd-Frank mandates that exchanges require listed companies to adopt procedures to recover up to three years of incentive pay from the company's executives (both current and former) whenever the company is forced to restate its financials. Dodd-Frank §954 (adding Exchange Act §10D). The new approach covers more executives than just the CEO and CFO; it expands the clawback period from one year to three years; it applies to all restatements, not just those due to misconduct; but it requires a clawback only of incentive-based pay that exceeds what would have been paid under the restatement. If the company fails to seek a clawback, the SEC can bring an action against the corporation to enforce the recovery, though (as with §304) there is no express private cause of action.

Compensation Disclosure

Dodd-Frank adds new disclosures to the proxy statement. First, it requires that companies show "the relationship between executive compensation actually paid and the financial performance of the issuer." Dodd-Frank §953(a) (adding Exchange Act §14(i)). The disclosure of "pay versus performance" mirrors the growing view among shareholders that executives not reap rewards while their company fails. For example Kerry Killinger (the former CEO of Washington Mutual) was paid $25.1 million during 2008—the year that Washington Mutual collapsed under the weight of its ill-advised subprime mortgage exposure, was seized by the federal government and sold to JPMorgan for a fraction of its book value, and then filed for Chapter 11 bankruptcy.

Dodd-Frank also requires companies to determine and disclose (1) the total median compensation of all employees with the exception of the CEO, (2) the total compensation of the CEO, and (3) and the ratio of these two numbers. Dodd-Frank §953(b) (requiring the SEC to amend Item 402, Reg. S-K). The ratio, it has been said, can easily be manipulated by companies that outsource many low-level tasks, thus ensuring than non-CEO employee pay is relatively high and the ratio relatively low.

Finally, Dodd-Frank requires that the annual proxy statement include information on whether company officials are allowed to hedge any decrease in the company's securities—and thus bet against the company's financial performance. Dodd-Frank §955 (adding Exchange Act §14(j), requiring the SEC to issue rules).

§14.4.4 Market Pressure

Institutional shareholders also have targeted companies with high executive compensation compared to performance. Activist shareholders have used the SEC's shareholder proposal rule to urge compensation reforms (see §9.4.2), and institutional shareholders and proxy advisory firms have become increasingly involved in direct discussions with boards and compensation committees on pay issues. Proxy advisory firms, which advise institutional investors on exercising their voting rights, have created templates of acceptable terms in compensation plans—such as the ways that pay packages should ensure that executives are not paid for failure or the repricing of "out of the money" options. Compensation committees must be sure their plans satisfy these templates.

In addition, the advisory "say on pay" votes by shareholders—required by Dodd-Frank in all public companies beginning in 2011—have led companies, particularly those that have received negative votes for their pay practices, to amend their pay packages to match pay with performance and to provide clearer disclosure to shareholders on how pay is consistent with shareholder interests. Companies that have received negative votes have also been subject to shareholder suits against directors, alleging violations of fiduciary duties for approving (unpopular) pay packages.

Examples

1. More Parking Corp. (MPC), incorporated in Delaware, is in the glamorous business of owning and operating parking garages. Leonard More, the company's founder, is board chair, company president, and a 30 percent shareholder. The remaining shares are publicly held; no other shareholder holds more than 5 percent.
   a. More's three-year executive compensation contract is coming up for renewal. The MPC board is composed of seven directors: More, three company executives, and three nonmanagement outside directors. Advise the board on how approval of the contract should be handled.
   b. Would you recommend the board seek to have shareholders ratify the contract?

2. The MPC forms a compensation committee of three outside directors, who approve a five-year compensation package for More of $400,000 in annual salary and a bonus of 5 percent of net earnings. The committee knows the package is generous. At current earnings levels, More will make $650,000 each year, compared to the $200,000 per year that top executives in the parking garage industry are paid.
   a. Cheryl, a long-time MPC shareholder, is outraged and wants to challenge More's compensation. She brings a derivative suit. What must she allege?
   b. Is there other action she can take?

3. The compensation committee, at More's request, also provided for his retirement. After the three-year contract term, More can retire from the company and, by making himself available exclusively to the company, receive a guaranteed annual consulting fee of $400,000 a year, whether or not he actually performs consulting services.
   a. Cheryl is even more irritated when she learns of the consulting arrangement. Will she succeed if she challenges the consulting arrangement as a waste of corporate assets?
   b. The directors are worried about Cheryl's challenge. How might they change the consulting agreement to bolster its validity?

Explanations

1. a. Most lawyers advise the board to delegate the task of reviewing and negotiating the contract to a committee of directors, all of whom are nonemployee outside directors. This structure will avoid any claim that management directors set his compensation under a "back-scratching" arrangement where each director tacitly agrees to support each other's compensation. It will also avoid uncomfortable disclosure of committee conflicts under SEC disclosure rules. The committee should have access to all information about More and the company and should hire its own compensation consultant to provide pay information on comparable executives. It would be advisable that More not be present when the committee deliberates in order to avoid the appearance that he dominated or controlled the committee. If approved by directors who are informed, disinterested, and independent, More's compensation will be reviewable only under a forgiving waste standard.

   b. Probably. Under Delaware law, even if board approval is found to have been misinformed or tainted, shareholder ratification has a cleansing effect and shifts the burden to the plaintiffs to show waste. *Lewis v. Vogelstein*, 599 A.2d 2 (Del. Ch. 1997).

   Federal tax laws change the calculus for submitting pay packages for shareholder approval, particularly executive compensation above $1 million per year. Shareholder approval of performance goals is necessary for such compensation to be deductible. Although prior practice had been to submit only stock plans (authorization in the articles) for shareholder authorization, modern boards now regularly submit executive compensation plans for shareholder approval.

2. a. She must make allegations that rebut the business judgment presumption—a nearly insuperable standard. There are several possibilities suggested by the facts: (1) the directors failed to become informed, (2) the directors failed to act in good faith, (3) the directors were dominated by the interested director, or (4) the compensation was wasteful. If there were factual support, Cheryl might also allege that the compensation was specifically forbidden in the articles of incorporation or the compensation was illegal.

   Cheryl might first allege that the committee failed to become informed about comparable pay in violation of its duty of care. See *Smith v. Van Gorkom*, 488 A.2d 858 (Del. 1985) (see §12.3.3). Although a showing of gross negligence will support an injunction against the improperly approved pay, the committee members would not be individually liable for any damages to the corporation if the corporation has an exculpation proviso as provided by Del. GCL §102(b)(7) (see §12.5).

Next Cheryl might allege that the committee failed to act with good faith. If the committee approved the pay package, while consciously disregarding whether it was justified in light of comparable pay for comparable services, it would violate its duty of good faith. See *In re Walt Disney Co. Derivative Litigation (Disney II)*, 825 A.2d 275 (Del. Ch. 2003). Not only would the pay package be voidable, but the committee members could be individually liable because any exculpation cannot cover acts not in good faith. Del. GCL §102(b)(7) (see §12.5).

Next Cheryl might allege that More "dominates" the outside directors by virtue of his position as chairman and 30 percent stock owner—rendering the directors not independent and their approval a loyalty breach. "Domination" is a slippery and highly factual standard. Courts have held that generalized allegations of share ownership and position on the board are insufficient to establish domination. See *Aronson v. Lewis*, 473 A.2d 805 (Del. 1984) (essentially the facts of this example). Instead, Cheryl would have to show the directors acted as requested without independent judgment.

Finally, Cheryl might allege the compensation is a waste of corporate assets—that is, no reasonable business person would say that the compensation had any relation to the services received and that it was in reality a gift. *Lewis v. Vogelstein*, 599 A.2d 2 (Del. Ch. 1997). Mere allegations of a discrepancy between the compensation and pay to comparable executives, though sufficient under a fairness standard, would not be enough. The committee (and More) could defend the compensation by pointing to his experience with the company and other possibly unique attributes. Courts are reluctant to become involved in these matters of business judgment.

b. Cheryl might submit a shareholder proposal on executive compensation to be included in the company's proxy statement. Under Rule 14a-8, the proposal cannot demand the directors set a given pay, but can make precatory (advisory) recommendations or ask for the compensation committee to report on why More's compensation is more than three times higher than that of comparable executives. In 1992 the SEC changed course and now considers shareholder proposals on executive compensation to be includable under the rule.

3. a. Probably not. Cheryl would argue the consulting fee, by its terms, is unrelated to any services to the corporation. She could assert that there is no assurance More will actually provide the services; there is no indication the corporation will actually consult him; and whatever services he provides will be of little value and would be available from other sources for less money.

Despite these arguments, Cheryl will have an uphill fight. The directors (and More) can argue that his consulting services are unique and his *exclusive availability* will have great value to the corporation. Although outside consulting services can often be purchased for less than inside executive employment, courts have recognized the value of building up institutional knowledge and intuition. In addition, even if the consulting pay is argued to be unrelated to actual consulting services, it can be seen as deferred compensation for the five-year employment contract. Similar challenges to a comparable executive compensation package failed to impress the Delaware Supreme Court. See *Aronson v. Lewis*, 473 A.2d 805 (Del. 1984).

b. The compensation committee could provide that the consulting fee is contingent on More's agreement not to compete with the corporation. The committee should also make clear that the consulting fee is not necessarily related to future services, but rather to the noncompete agreement or the five-year contract. Courts have invalidated compensation tied to future services where there was no assurance the services would be performed.

CHAPTER 15

Indemnification and Insurance

In our litigious society, being a corporate official is risky business. Corporate directors and officers can be named in private lawsuits brought by shareholders, third parties, or in governmental proceedings challenging corporate behavior. To encourage qualified individuals to accept corporate positions and take good-faith risks for the corporation, corporate statutes permit (and sometimes mandate) the corporation to indemnify directors and officers against liability arising from their corporate position (§15.1). Directors' and officers' (D&O) insurance supplements this protection (§15.2).

Indemnification and insurance represent two of the legs of the four-legged stool on which directors sit. The other two are the protection under the business judgment rule (see §12.3) and liability exculpation authorized by corporate statutes, such as Del. GCL §102(b)(7) (see §12.5).

§15.1 INDEMNIFICATION — CORPORATE REIMBURSEMENT

What is corporate indemnification? It is simply the corporation's reimbursement of litigation expenses and personal liability of a director sued because she is or was a director. (Indemnification of officers and other corporate agents is similar and is discussed below.) In general, indemnification applies when the director is or was (or is threatened with being made) a defendant in any civil, criminal, administrative, or investigative proceeding. A director's indemnification rights continue even after she has left the corporation.

Open-ended corporate indemnification undermines directorial accountability under corporate law and other noncorporate regulatory schemes. For example, if directors could act with impunity to authorize the corporation to deceive investors or dump toxic chemicals, confident they would be held harmless if ever sued, the deterrent effect of personal liability under the securities and environmental laws would be undermined. Moreover, if the corporation indemnifies directors who breach their fiduciary duties to the corporation, the compensation and deterrence goals of fiduciary liability are effectively nullified.

Because of indemnification's potential to frustrate other goals and policies, a director's right to indemnification and the power of the corporation to indemnify depend on whether

- the director was successful in defending the action or
- the director, though unsuccessful in her defense, was justified in her actions (for example, by seeking in good faith to promote the corporation's interests in a legally ambiguous situation).

Generally, indemnification rights are fixed by contract or the corporation's constitutive documents (articles of incorporation or bylaws). See MBCA §2.02(b)(5) (permitting indemnification in articles of director's conduct to same extent corporation can exculpate liability for such conduct). Statutory indemnification provisions provide the framework for drafting, interpreting, and enforcing contractual indemnification rights. See MBCA Chapter 8, Subchapter E, §§8.50-8.59; Del. GCL §145.

Note on Indemnification of Nondirectors

In general, the corporation may indemnify nondirector officers, employees, and agents to the same extent as directors. MBCA §8.56 (official comment that corporation has power to indemnify employees and agents); Del. GCL §145(a). Indemnification of officers (though not others) is mandatory to the same extent as if the officers were directors.

§15.1.1 Mandatory Indemnification for Successful Defense

If a director is sued because of her corporate position (such as for approving a corporate decision or issuing a corporate statement) and she defends successfully, the corporation is *obligated* under all state statutes to indemnify the director for litigation expenses, including attorney fees. MBCA §8.52; Del. GCL §145(c). The right of the successful director to claim repayment of expenses is available whether the suit was brought on behalf of the corporation or by an outside party.

The right protects a director from the corporation's faithless refusal to indemnify a director who successfully defends a suit arising from her corporate position. Cf. Restatement (Second) of Agency §438 (requiring principal to indemnify agent whenever agent "suffers a loss which, because of their relation, it is fair that the principal should bear"); *New York Dock Co. v. McCollum*, 16 N.Y.S.2d 844 (Sup. Ct. 1939) (holding directors are not "agents" of corporation and thus not entitled to indemnification as would be the case for employee).

A director's statutory right to mandatory indemnification raises two issues: (1) When is a defense successful? (2) Can there be mandatory indemnification for a partially successful defense?

Success "on the Merits or Otherwise"

Corporate statutes uniformly require indemnification when the defendant is successful "on the merits," such as when the suit is dismissed for lack of evidence or on a finding of nonliability after trial. MBCA §8.52; Del. GCL §145(c). Under most statutes, success can also be on procedural grounds—success "otherwise"—such as when a suit is dismissed because the plaintiff lacks standing or the statute of limitations has run. MBCA §8.52; Del. GCL §145(c). A director, however, is not deemed successful if the claim is settled out of court.

Indemnification "to the Extent" Successful

Some statutes (including some in Delaware) require indemnification "to the extent" the director is successful, compelling the corporation to reimburse a partially successful director's litigation expenses related to those claims or charges she defends successfully. Del. GCL §145(c).

In *Merritt-Chapman & Scott Corp. v. Wolfson*, 321 A.2d 138 (Del. 1974), the Delaware Supreme Court interpreted a statute that required indemnification if the director was successful "in defense of any claim, issue or matter therein" as requiring indemnification for partial success. In the case, a director charged with five criminal offenses pleaded "no contest" to one on the condition the others were dropped. The court held he was entitled to indemnification as a matter of right for the litigation expenses related to the charges that were dropped. See also *Waltuch v. ContiCommodity Services, Inc.*, 88 F.3d 87 (2d Cir. 1996) (applying Delaware law to require indemnification of litigation expenses incurred by director charged with conspiring to corner silver market, after company (but not director) paid to settle private lawsuits brought by silver traders).

The *Merritt-Chapman* interpretation, it has been argued, permits undeserving directors to negotiate dismissals or plea bargain away most of the claims against them and become entitled to indemnification for the bulk of their litigation expenses. For this reason, some statutes make mandatory indemnification "all or nothing" and limit it to defendants who were "wholly successful." MBCA §8.52.

§15.1.2 Permissive (Discretionary) Indemnification for Unsuccessful Defense

Indemnification is not automatic when a director becomes liable because of his corporate role. Instead, corporate indemnification of an unsuccessful director's litigation expenses and liability is discretionary. The corporation may indemnify an unsuccessful director only if indemnification is approved by certain corporate actors or a court, under specified criteria. Under modern statutes the ability of the corporation to indemnify depends on whether the action was brought by a third party or was brought on behalf of the corporation.

Third-Party Actions

In an action brought by a third party—such as when the EPA sues for illegal dumping or investors claim securities fraud—the unsuccessful director must be deserving to be entitled to indemnification.

- **Indemnification criteria.** Many statutes permit corporate indemnification arising from third-party actions only if the director (1) acted in good faith (that is, the director did not know her conduct was illegal and did not act for improper personal gain), and (2) reasonably believed her actions were in the corporation's best interests. MBCA §8.51(a)(1) (or not opposed to corporation's best interests, if director acted in unofficial capacity, such as a representative to a trade association); Del. GCL §145(a). In a criminal proceeding, the director may have had no reasonable cause to believe that her actions were unlawful—a standard that goes beyond good faith. MBCA §8.51(a)(2); Del. GCL §145(a).

  Often the findings implicit in a final court judgment (or administrative order) against a director will be inconsistent with a finding that the director satisfied these criteria. A director increases her chances of permissive indemnification by settling or plea bargaining. Most statutes cooperate and state that a judgment, order, settlement, or no contest plea is not conclusive as to whether the director meets the criteria for indemnification. MBCA §8.51(c); Del. GCL §145(a).

- **Coverage.** A director sued in a third-party action may be indemnified for reasonable litigation expenses and any personal liability arising from a court judgment, an out-of-court settlement, or the imposition of penalties or fines. MBCA §§8.51, 8.50(4), (5); Del. GCL §145(a).
- **Procedures.** Statutes specify who must determine whether a director meets the criteria for permissive indemnification: directors who are not parties to the proceeding, a committee of nonparty directors, independent legal counsel appointed by nonparty directors, or disinterested shareholders. MBCA §8.55(b) (permitting legal counsel to determine if director meets criteria, but not actual amount of indemnification); Del. GCL §145(d). An internal finding that a director is entitled to indemnification is not conclusive, but is subject to judicial review. See *In re Landmark Land Co.*, 76 F.3d 553 (4th Cir. 1996) (applying California's indemnification statute to reverse decision by independent directors to indemnify directors because illegal avoidance of federal S&L regulation could not constitute "good faith").

Actions by or on Behalf of the Corporation

Most statutes do not allow the corporation to indemnify a director "adjudged liable" to the corporation if the action is brought by the corporation itself or by shareholders in a derivative action on behalf of the corporation. MBCA §8.51(d)(1); Del. GCL §145(b). Allowing indemnification would create the absurdity of the corporation receiving payment from a culpable director with one hand and reimbursing the director with the other. This circularity would gut the effectiveness of directorial accountability.

Nonetheless, the corporation can indemnify a director who *settles* a suit brought against her by or on behalf of the corporation for her *litigation expenses* if she meets the criteria for permissive indemnification. MBCA §8.51(d)(1); Del. GCL §145(b) (reasonable expenses indemnifiable if director meets standard of conduct). In addition, a court (as opposed to the corporation) can order indemnification of litigation expenses, if fair and reasonable, even though the director is found liable in a derivative suit. MBCA §8.54(a)(3); Del. GCL §145(b). The MBCA even permits a court to order indemnification of settlement amounts in a derivative suit, if fair and reasonable. MBCA §8.54(a)(3). In each situation, the idea is that well-meaning directors should be protected from the full brunt of their litigation exposure.

Court-Ordered Indemnification

Even if the corporation refuses to (or cannot) indemnify a director under its discretionary authority, some statutes allow a court to order indemnification (of expenses and liability) of an unsuccessful director who the corporation determines does not meet the criteria for permissive indemnification. MBCA §8.54(a). But if the director is adjudged liable to the corporation or is adjudged to have acted for personal gain, the court can only order indemnification of the director's litigation expenses. MBCA §8.54(a)(3).

§15.1.3 Advancement of Litigation Expenses

The promise of eventual indemnification of litigation expenses after a successful defense may be empty if the director cannot pay for a full defense out of his own pocket. For this reason most statutes allow the corporation to advance litigation expenses during the proceeding. MBCA §8.53; Del. GCL §145(e). When the advances are made, it will not be known whether the director ultimately will be successful or be entitled to permissive indemnification, and the statutes impose varying conditions for advancing expenses. In addition, there is some question under the Sarbanes-Oxley Act whether an advancement of expenses constitutes a prohibited executive loan. Exchange Act §13(k) (see §14.4).

For a director to receive an advancement, the MBCA requires the director to (1) affirm his good-faith belief that he would be entitled to permissive indemnification or indemnification under a charter provision, and (2) undertake to repay the advances if he is not entitled to indemnification. MBCA §8.53(a); cf. Del. GCL §145(e) (requiring only repayment undertaking). Under the MBCA, the corporation acting through disinterested directors or shareholders must then authorize the advancement of expenses, subject to the standards that apply to board action. Official Comment to MBCA §8.53 (board cannot authorize advance if there are "red flags" indicating director not entitled to indemnification); cf. Del. GCL §145(e) (no specification of who must authorize advancement).

Under the MBCA, a director need not give security for his repayment obligation. To avoid discriminatory treatment against directors of modest means, the corporation can accept the repayment obligation "without reference to the [director's] financial ability to make repayment." MBCA §8.53(b). In Delaware two factors are relevant for authorizing advancement: (1) the likelihood the defendant will reimburse the corporation if indemnification is determined to be inappropriate and (2) whether the advancement would serve the interests of the corporation. *Advanced Mining Systems v. Fricke*, 623 A.2d 82 (Del. Ch. 1992).

Advancement is discretionary. The corporation can bind itself by contract (in an agreement, the bylaws, or even the articles) to provide advancement, or can make an advancement on an ad hoc basis. Under the MBCA, a corporation that obligates itself to indemnify a director "to the fullest extent permitted by law" must advance expenses, including in derivative suits, unless the provision specifies a limitation. MBCA §8.58(a). But when the corporation has not bound itself to provide advancement, a corporation's decision not to advance expenses is discretionary and evaluated according to the business judgment rule.

§15.1.4 Exclusivity of Statutory Indemnification

Many statutes make the statutory indemnification provisions and procedures exclusive. Indemnification pursuant to the articles of incorporation, the bylaws, or an agreement is permitted only to the extent consistent with the statute. See MBCA §§8.58(a), 8.59. These statutes require a specific, case-by-case determination that the director is entitled to permissive indemnification or advancement of expenses. Official Comment to MBCA §8.58(a) (compliance with disinterested authorization "still required"). It is not enough that an employment agreement or the articles or bylaws contain a blanket indemnification clause.

Nonetheless, other statutes permit the corporation to indemnify directors under provisions in the bylaws or in a contract even though the statute does not contemplate it. Del. GCL §145(f). The indemnification procedures applicable under these extrastatutory provisions govern, provided they are consistent with "public policy." See *VonFeldt v. Stifel Fin. Corp.*, 1999 Del. Ch. Lexis 131 (interpreting Del. GCL §145(a) to require that director seeking indemnification under bylaw provision has acted in "good faith," though placing burden on corporation to show lack of "good faith"). Among other things, this means that the corporation cannot indemnify a director for liability to the corporation—because of the circularity problem.

§15.2 INSURANCE

Corporate statutes permit the corporation to buy insurance for itself to fund its own indemnification obligations and for directors to fill the gaps in corporate indemnification, principally when a director is liable to the corporation in a derivative suit.

§15.2.1 Insurance Covering Corporation's Obligations

Indemnification is a form of insurance provided by the corporation to its directors, officers, employees, and other agents. The corporation can meet its indemnification obligations, statutory or extrastatutory, either by acting as a self-insurer or by purchasing insurance from outside insurance companies.

§15.2.2 Insurance Covering Liability of Directors and Officers

To supplement indemnification and to cover liability to the corporation, the corporation also can purchase liability insurance for its directors and officers—*D&O insurance*. Premium payments for such policies constitute additional executive compensation and are authorized either as such or by specific statute. MBCA §8.57; Del. GCL §145(g). Many statutes authorize the purchase of insurance even if it covers expenses and liability the corporation could not indemnify. MBCA §8.57; Del. GCL §145(g). Although it might seem anomalous that the corporation can indemnify indirectly through insurance what it is prohibited from indemnifying directly, the theory is that the director herself could have bought insurance, and it should not make any difference that the corporation compensates her by paying the premiums.

Usually, the corporation submits the D&O application and pays the premiums in the name of the insured executives. D&O policies typically cover any liabilities or defense costs arising from the executive's position with the corporation. The policies typically exclude coverage for

- improper personal benefits (such as self-dealing)
- actions in bad faith (including dishonesty)
- illegal compensation
- libel or slander
- knowing violations of law
- bodily injury/property damage
- pollution
- other willful misconduct

Many policies also exclude coverage for fines and penalties (including punitive damages) regardless of the executive's intentions. The effect of the exclusions is to make D&O insurance sometimes less encompassing than indemnification by the corporation.

EXAMPLES

Examples

1. Jones, a shareholder of Trans Combo Corporation, sues the company's directors for failing to approve a merger for $55 per share with the Harmon Group, at a time the company's stock was trading at $38. Jones brings a derivative suit claiming the board failed to become informed about the Harmon bid and did not negotiate vigorously. Jones seeks damages from the directors. The Trans Combo board appoints a special committee composed of three directors who recently joined the board

and Jones did not sue. The committee is authorized to decide all indemnification issues. Assume Trans Combo is incorporated in an MBCA jurisdiction.

a. The director-defendants consider settling with Jones for $62 million—$5 per share. Must Trans Combo reimburse them for this settlement amount? Can Trans Combo reimburse them?
b. If the director-defendants settle, must Trans Combo reimburse them for their litigation expenses? Can Trans Combo reimburse them?
c. The defendant-directors reject the settlement offer, but ask the special committee to advance them money to pay for their mounting defense costs. Can Trans Combo pay the defendants' litigation expenses?
d. The special committee concludes the directors acted in good faith and with the best interests of the company in mind when they rejected the Harmon bid. The committee nonetheless decides not to advance the directors' litigation expenses. Can it?
e. The directors go to trial. The court decides the directors violated their duty of care by rejecting the merger without sufficient information, but are not liable for failing to negotiate vigorously. The defendant-directors seek repayment of their expenses related to their successful defense of the disclosure claim. Are they entitled?

2. Eventually, the directors settle with Jones and pay a significant settlement. Trans Combo has a typical directors' and officers' insurance policy with Concord Insurance Company. The policy period covers the claim brought by Jones.
   a. Does the D&O policy cover the settlement payments?
   b. Does the D&O policy cover the directors' litigation expenses?
   c. Orkin, Trans Combo's CEO, lied to the directors about the worth of the merger, which he wanted to avoid no matter what. Can Orkin seek indemnification under the D&O policy?

3. The Trans Combo directors get a second chance. The Harmon Group again offers $55 a share, and this time the directors accept. Trans Combo merges into New Trans Combo, a Harmon subsidiary. There is no pleasing Jones, who brings a class action in which he claims the directors were uninformed of the company's value, which he says is $65 per share.
   a. The directors again want to settle. Must New Trans Combo indemnify them for any settlement amounts? Can New Trans Combo indemnify?
   b. The bylaws of Old Trans Combo stated "each director is entitled to indemnification for losses because he is or was a director, if he acted in good faith and with a reasonable belief his conduct was in the best interests of the corporation." Is New Trans Combo obligated to pay for the directors' settlement?
   c. New Trans Combo makes significant payments to legal counsel to defend the directors. Must these payments be disclosed?

4. When the Harmon Group approached Trans Combo the first time about a merger, Orkin secretly bought Trans Combo stock on the market. He held on to the stock and eventually realized a hefty premium when the merger finally happened. The SEC sued him for insider trading (see §29.5), but was unable to show liability.
   a. Must New Trans Combo pay Orkin's defense costs?
   b. If New Trans Combo indemnifies Orkin, can it make a claim under Old Trans Combo's D&O insurance policy?

5. New Trans Combo hires Orkin to run the company. Orkin wants an indemnification agreement before he accepts. Draft one.

EXPLANATIONS

Explanations

1. a. Trans Combo is neither required nor permitted to indemnify directors for the amounts they pay in settling a derivative claim. Mandatory indemnification is available only for the expenses related to a successful defense. MBCA §8.52. Permissive indemnification is not available for amounts in settlement paid by directors. MBCA §8.51(d)(1). Otherwise, the corporation would be collecting from the directors in the suit and repaying them through indemnification, and the deterrent and compensation purposes of derivative litigation would be frustrated. See Official Comment, MBCA §8.51(d) ("permitting indemnification of settlements and judgments in derivative proceedings would give rise to a circularity").
   b. Trans Combo is not required, but is permitted, to reimburse litigation expenses in a derivative suit settlement. If the directors settle, they would not have been "wholly successful on the merits or otherwise," and there would be no mandatory indemnification. MBCA §8.52. Nonetheless, the directors may be entitled to indemnification of their litigation expenses—if they meet the statutory standards of conduct. MBCA §8.51(d)(1). Unlike a judgment of liability, a settlement leaves open the factual question of whether the directors acted in good faith and with a reasonable belief they were acting in the best interests of the corporation. See MBCA §8.51(c) (settlement is not determinative director did not meet standard of conduct). This means the corporation, to resolve derivative litigation, may end up paying both the shareholder-plaintiff's expenses (see §18.1.2) and the director-defendants' expenses.
   c. Probably. Under MBCA §8.53(a), the corporation may advance a director's litigation expenses if
      (1) He affirms his good-faith belief that he is entitled to permissive indemnification under the statutory standard of conduct. That is, that when he rejected the merger he acted in good faith (not

dishonestly or with a conflicting interest) and reasonably believing it was in the corporation's best interests.

(2) He undertakes to repay all advances if it turns out he is not entitled to indemnification. Even though some of the directors may never be able to repay these advances, the MBCA permits the committee to accept their undertaking "without reference to financial ability to make repayment." MBCA §8.53(b).

(3) A proper decision maker determines it knows of nothing that would preclude indemnification. Advancing expenses, like indemnification for liability, is a form of self-dealing. The MBCA requires that any discretionary decision to pay (or advance) expenses be made by directors (board or committee composed of at least two disinterested directors) or disinterested shareholders. MBCA §8.53(c) (unlike permissive indemnification, independent legal counsel cannot authorize advancement of expenses). If a quorum of the board consisting of nonparty directors cannot be obtained, the board may compose a committee of at least two nonparty directors—the case here. In approving the advance, the committee need not conduct a special investigation that the director would meet the standard of conduct. Official Comment to MBCA §8.53.

d. Yes. The advance of expenses is discretionary, and the corporation is under no statutory obligation. Unless the directors have nonstatutory rights in the corporation's articles or bylaws, or in an indemnification agreement, the statute limits mandatory indemnification to directors who are "wholly successful."

   Court-ordered indemnification, however, is available in some situations when the corporation has balked. See MBCA §8.54. The directors would have to show that it is "fair and reasonable" to advance the expenses. For example, the directors might show that the committee was acting out of spite and it was in the corporation's best interests for them to litigate the question of a director's duty to investigate merger proposals. The court can order the corporation to advance expenses even if the director was not entitled to this under the provisions of MBCA §8.53.

e. No. The MBCA requires that the directors be "wholly successful" to be entitled to payment of litigation expenses. MBCA §8.52. Even though the directors were successful in part of their defense, the MBCA seeks to prevent the result in *Merritt-Chapman & Scott Corp. v. Wolfson*, 321 A.2d 138 (Del. 1974), where an undeserving insider accepted criminal liability on one charge for the dismissal of others. Remember, though, that permissive indemnification may be available.

2. a. Yes. Typical D&O coverage extends to suits brought by or on behalf of the corporation. Typically, policies cover the directors for acts or

omissions in their capacities as directors or by reason of their status as directors. They exclude coverage for claims of personal profit, deliberate fraud, criminal acts, unauthorized compensation, short-swing trading profits, or failing to maintain insurance. That is, breaches of a director's duty of care are typically covered.

b. Yes. D&O policies typically cover defense costs. Some policies provide that the insurance company will conduct the defense and require that the insured directors turn over litigation to the insurance company.

c. No. D&O coverage, like nearly all other insurance, excludes coverage for willful, knowing, or fraudulent acts.

3. a. In this example, indemnification is not mandatory, but is permitted. In the merger the surviving corporation assumes all the liabilities of the Old Trans Combo, including any statutory indemnification obligations it would have had. See MBCA §11.07(a)(4).

There is no mandatory indemnification under the MBCA unless the directors are "wholly successful," which they would not be in the case of a settlement. Permissive indemnification, however, is possible in a class action. Here the settlement would be with Old Trans Combo shareholders, not the surviving corporation. New Trans Combo's payment to the directors will have the effect of the Harmon Group paying additional consideration for the merger. There is no problem of circularity.

b. Probably not. The MBCA, unlike Delaware's statute, does not permit extrastatutory indemnification unless it is consistent with the statute. The directors cannot enforce the indemnification bylaw against Old Trans Combo because it did not call for a determination that the directors had met their standard of conduct by a disinterested decision maker. MBCA §8.51(a).

It might be argued, nonetheless, that because a new set of shareholders (the Harmon Group) will bear the costs of any payments by New Trans Combo, this is not a self-dealing transaction and it would not be inconsistent with the statutory scheme for an *outsider* to reimburse the directors if the directors met the standard of conduct. This argument, curiously, would put the Old Trans Combo directors in the position of having greater indemnification rights after the merger.

c. Yes. The MBCA requires that indemnification payments be disclosed to shareholders in the corporation's annual report. See MBCA §16.21(a). Most corporate statutes (including Delaware's) do not require this disclosure.

4. a. Perhaps. New Trans Combo acquires the indemnification obligations of Old Trans Combo in the merger. See answer 3a above. The MBCA, however, is not entirely clear about whether a company's mandatory

indemnification obligations cover defense costs in an insider-trading case.

Mandatory indemnification applies to "any proceeding to which the director [or officer] was a party because he is or was a director [or officer]." MBCA §§8.52, 8.56(c) (officers have same mandatory indemnification rights as directors). Orkin could argue the SEC sued him for misusing inside information that he acquired "because" of his insider position. The statute's provisions on permissive indemnification, which allow indemnification in cases other than "conduct of official capacity," suggest that an insider's indemnification rights extend beyond corporate functions. See MBCA §8.51(a)(2); see also *University Savings Ass'n v. Burnap*, 786 S.W.2d 423 (Tex. App. 1990) (indemnification of director who successfully defended against tipping liability).

Some of the reasons for indemnification argue for finding the statute covers Orkin. Indemnification seeks to align the incentives of directors and officers with the risk-taking preferences of shareholders. So does stock ownership. Directors and officers may be reluctant to acquire shares if their service on the board may expose them to liability if they trade in the company's shares. To encourage share ownership by directors, an indemnification scheme allowing indemnification for trading in those shares makes sense.

b. Perhaps. Unless the D&O policy has a nonassignment clause, its coverage passes to New Trans Combo in the merger. Typically, D&O policies reimburse the company's indemnification of directors' liability or expenses pursuant to statute, contract, charter, or bylaw provision. D&O policies often exclude coverage for claims under §16(b) of the Securities Exchange Act of 1934, the provision for the disgorgement of short-swing profits. See §24.3. That is, insurance does not allow an insider to preserve his illegal trading profits. In this case, however, the director is not claiming a return of profits, and the exclusion would not seem to apply.

5. An indemnification contract might read as follows. Notice that the agreement calls for the corporation to pay fines, judgments, and settlements without a specific determination by disinterested directors or shareholders, as contemplated by the MBCA. In addition, the agreement does not require that the director seek advancement of expenses by making the good-faith affirmation and undertaking to repay if necessary, also as required by the MBCA. It is possible that a court might read these requirements into the agreement because the agreement is explicitly governed by the MBCA, including its requirements that permissive indemnification and advancement of expenses comply with statutory procedures. See MBCA §8.58(a).

Dear Mr. Orkin:

This confirms the agreement between you and New Trans Combo (Corporation) concerning indemnification.

1. *Indemnification.* The Corporation indemnifies you in your capacity as officer and director (or either) of the Corporation to the fullest extent permitted by law.
2. *Notice.* You will notify the Corporation in writing of any proceeding (whether threatened, pending, or completed) with respect to which the Corporation might be required to provide indemnity. You will provide this written notice within ten (10) business days after first becoming aware that you may be, are, or were a party to such a proceeding. The notice will describe the proceeding and your status in the proceeding and will attach any documents filed in the proceeding. If you fail to provide timely notice, the Corporation will not be obligated to indemnify you with respect to that proceeding.
3. *Defense and advancement of funds.* Unless independent counsel determines that the Corporation is not obligated to provide indemnity, the Corporation will: (a) defend and settle at the Corporation's expense any claims against you in your capacity as officer or director of the Corporation; and (b) pay any fines, judgments, and amounts in settlement in connection with claims against you in your capacity as officer or director of the Corporation. You will cooperate fully in any defense or settlement undertaken by the Corporation. If it is ultimately determined that you are not entitled to indemnity with respect to payments or expenses (including attorneys' fees) incurred by the Corporation, then you will reimburse the Corporation for these amounts.
4. *Insurance.* The Corporation will purchase and maintain director and officer liability insurance in the face amount of [typically $1 million] on your behalf under a standard such policy. If at any time after the first year of coverage you conclude that this coverage is inadequate, you will notify the Corporation. If the Corporation does not adjust coverage to your satisfaction, you may request that independent legal counsel (to be paid by the Corporation) review the adequacy of the coverage. Counsel's evaluation will be binding.
5. *Nonexclusivity and subrogation.* Your rights to indemnification and to advances under this agreement are not exclusive of any other rights to which you may be entitled. To the extent the Corporation has paid amounts under this agreement and you are also entitled to payment from any other person, the Corporation will be subrogated to any claim that you may have for such payment.

(continued)

6. *Duration, governing law, severability*. This agreement will terminate on the later of (a) ten (10) years after you cease to be a director or officer of the Corporation, or (b) the final disposition of any pending proceeding as to which you have a right of indemnification under this agreement. This agreement is governed by [MBCA jurisdiction] law. The provisions of this agreement are severable. This agreement is binding on and will inure to the benefit of the Corporation's and your heirs, personal representatives, successors, and assignees.

Accepted: New Trans Combo Corp.

By: ______________________ By: ______________________

CHAPTER 16

Corporate Opportunities and Unfair Competition

The duty of corporate managers to put corporate interests ahead of their own personal interests applies not only to dealings with the corporation but also to outside business dealings that affect the corporation. Financial harm to the corporation is just as real when a manager takes a profitable business opportunity from the corporation or sets up a competing business as when the manager enters into an unfair self-dealing transaction with the corporation.

But, just as self-dealing is not automatically void, corporate managers (directors and executives) are not flatly prohibited from taking outside business opportunities. Outside opportunities offer managers a means to diversify their own human capital, and a flat prohibition against outside business activities might well lead many managers to shun the corporate form. The *corporate opportunity doctrine*—a subset of the duty of loyalty—balances the corporation's expansion potential and the managers' entrepreneurial interests.

This chapter describes the corporate opportunity doctrine (§16.1), the definition of "corporate opportunity" (§16.2), the effect of corporate rejection or incapacity (§16.3), and competition with the corporation (§16.4).

§16.1 CORPORATE OPPORTUNITY DOCTRINE

§16.1.1 Prohibition against Usurping Corporate Opportunities

The corporate opportunity doctrine supplies corporate law a deceptively simple rule. A corporate manager (director or executive) cannot usurp corporate opportunities for his own benefit unless the corporation has rejected the opportunity. The plaintiff has the burden of proving the existence of a corporate opportunity.

The doctrine thus raises two issues:

- When does a business opportunity belong to the corporation and thus become a "corporate opportunity"? See §16.2 below.
- When can it be said the corporation has (or would have) rejected the opportunity, thus allowing the director to take it? See §16.3 below.

§16.1.2 Remedies for Usurping a Corporate Opportunity

A director who usurps a corporate opportunity without corporate rejection must share the fruits of the opportunity as though the corporation had originally taken it. Remedies include (1) liability for profits realized by the usurping manager, (2) liability for lost profits and damages suffered by the corporation, and (3) imposition of a constructive trust on the new business or the subject matter of the opportunity (such as land). *Farber v. Servan Land Co.*, 662 F.2d 371 (5th Cir. 1981) (requiring usurper to share profits with corporation after usurper resold business opportunity). Because an outside third party is on the other side of the opportunity, rescission is not available unless the third party had notice of the insider's wrongdoing.

The corporate opportunity doctrine thus gives the corporation an "option" to take for itself a business opportunity initially taken by a corporate manager. If the opportunity turns out well, the corporation can claim it for itself; if the opportunity flops, the corporation can choose not to pursue its rights.

§16.2 DEFINITION OF "CORPORATE OPPORTUNITY"

What is a corporate opportunity? The courts have articulated and applied a variety of definitions. Underlying these definitions are two conflicting premises:

- **Corporate expansion.** The corporation expects managers to devote themselves to expanding the corporation's business. This maximizes corporate profitability.
- **Manager entrepreneurialism.** Managers expect to have freedom to pursue outside business interests. This promotes entrepreneurial initiative.

It should not surprise you that the courts' attempts to accommodate these inconsistent premises have led to a variety of vague tests, which have evolved over time.

§16.2.1 Use of Diverted Corporate Assets

A fiduciary cannot develop a business opportunity using assets secretly diverted from the corporation. Requiring the fiduciary to share any profits derived from the misbegotten business simply enforces the prohibition against misappropriation.

This analysis is clearest when the assets are "hard" assets—such as when a director uses the corporation's cash, property, or employees to set up a business. In such cases the director is liable whether or not the corporation had an identifiable interest in taking the business opportunity itself and whether or not the business was related to that of the corporation. The real evil is not so much that the director took an opportunity for himself, but rather that he took something that belonged to the corporation to do it. *Guth v. Loft, Inc.*, 5 A.2d 503 (Del. 1939) (use of corporate funds).

Some courts, however, have refused to impose liability on directors who use corporate resources to develop an outside business if the opportunity was one in which the corporation did not have an interest or expectancy. See *Lincoln Stores v. Grant*, 34 N.E.2d 704 (Mass. 1941) (refusing to impose constructive trust on competing store that managers set up while still employed by corporation because "company had no interest in or thought of acquiring it").

§16.2.2 Existing Corporate Interest—Expectancy Test

Many courts employ an *expectancy test* to measure the corporation's expansion potential. If the corporation has an existing expectancy in a business opportunity, the manager must seek corporate consent before taking the opportunity.

Corporate expectancies need not rise to the level of an ownership interest. For instance, an expectancy exists if the corporation is negotiating to acquire a new business or an executive learns of a business offer directed to the corporation. See *Thorpe v. CERBO, Inc.*, 676 A.2d 436 (Del. 1996) (finding usurpation when controlling shareholders responded to an outside offer to purchase a corporate subsidiary with a counteroffer to sell the shareholders' controlling interest in the parent). In this regard, the manager's secrecy in taking an opportunity supports a finding of corporate expectancy, on the assumption the manager's concealment suggests the corporation had an interest. Courts have also interpreted the expectancy test to cover opportunities of special or unique importance to the corporation for which there is a presumed expectancy. For example, a corporation's avowed interest in finding a new headquarters site or in acquiring patents necessary for its business fall within the shadow of the corporation's expansion expectancies. See *Northeast Harbor Golf Club, Inc. v. Harris*, 661 A.2d 1146 (Me. 1995) (finding corporate opportunity when country club president acquired for herself property adjacent to club's golf course, which real estate agent had offered to her in capacity as president on assumption club would be interested).

Frequently, expectancies can be shown when the manager misappropriates "soft" assets of the corporation (such as confidential information or goodwill) to develop a new business. On the other hand, if the opportunity came to the manager in his individual (not corporate) capacity, courts are more likely to conclude the opportunity was not corporate. See *Broz v. Cellular Information Systems, Inc.*, 673 A.2d 148 (Del. 1996). It is important to note that the misappropriation of soft assets may also be subject to other prohibitions. For example, a director who uses customer lists or secret manufacturing processes of the corporation in developing his own business may be liable under state statutes prohibiting misappropriation of trade secrets.

§16.2.3 Corporation's Existing Business — Line-of-Business Test

Some courts apply a broad *line-of-business test* to measure the reach of the corporation's expansion potential. See *Guth v. Loft, Inc.*, 5 A.2d 503 (Del. 1939) (opportunity so closely associated with company's activities that it places insider in competition with company). Under the test, courts compare the new business with the corporation's existing operations. The corporation need not have an existing interest or a special need for the opportunity, or the manager need not learn of the opportunity in his corporate capacity. If the new project is functionally related to the corporation's existing or anticipated business, the manager must obtain corporate consent before exploiting it.

Under the line-of-business test a functional relation exists if there is a competitive or synergistic overlap that suggests that the corporation would have been interested in taking the opportunity itself. Consider *Miller v. Miller*, 222 N.W.2d 71 (Minn. 1974). Miller Waste, a closely held family corporation, was in the waste-reprocessing business. Rudolph Miller, one of Miller Waste's managers, developed a patented lubricator for diesel locomotives and set up his own company for their manufacture. Rudolph's company was supplied with waste products produced by Miller Waste's reprocessing business and competed with Miller Waste in the locomotive lubricator market. The court held that a fact finder could have found that Rudolph's business was in Miller Waste's line of business.

§16.2.4 Eclectic Approaches

ALI Principles

The ALI Principles of Corporate Governance lay out a comprehensive approach to corporate opportunities, one which goes beyond the case law. The ALI Principles begin with a definition that combines the narrower expectancy test and a broader line-of-business test. Under the ALI Principles *corporate executives* are subject to line-of-business and expectancy restrictions, while *outside directors* (who have no employment relationship with the corporation) are subject only to expectancy restrictions. See ALI Principles §5.05(b). The difference between corporate insiders and outsiders reflects a view that the corporation is able to demand greater loyalty of corporate insiders than of outsiders.

Fairness Test

Some courts go beyond the expectancy and line-of-business tests, and add (for good measure) an additional malleable fairness test. *Lewis v. Fuqua*, 502 A.2d 962 (Del. Ch. 1985). The fairness test in this context, unlike that for self-dealing, which focuses on the transaction's fairness to the corporation, focuses on the fairness of holding the manager accountable for his outside activities.

Again *Miller v. Miller*, 222 N.W.2d 71 (Minn. 1974), illustrates. Rudolph and Benjamin Miller had exploited a variety of opportunities for themselves that were closely related to Miller Waste's waste-reprocessing business. Rudolph had started a business that manufactured patented lubricators for diesel locomotives using waste filter elements; and together they had set up a packaging business and a plastics business that used waste cotton cuttings. The trial court found that none of the new businesses were within Miller Waste's line of business—a finding that seems factually questionable. On appeal the court, without upsetting the trial court's findings, held in addition that Rudolph's and Benjamin's taking of the new businesses was not unfair to Miller Waste. The new businesses had benefitted Miller Waste by supplying it with a captive market for selling its products; no corporate assets were diverted; there was no secrecy; and Rudolph and Benjamin had continued to work long hours at the waste mill. In the case, the fairness test recognized the managers' entrepreneurial interests and limited the breadth of the line-of-business test.

Multiple Boards

To which corporation does a director owe allegiance when he serves on multiple boards? Courts have shown sensitivity to the dilemma of a director with conflicting duties. For example, consider the situation of Richard F. Broz, an outside director of a cell phone company (Cellular Information Systems) and owner of his own cell phone company (RFB Cellular). CIS operated in the Midwest and RFB in the Upper Peninsula of Michigan. When a third company decided to sell its cellular license for the eastern tip of the Upper Peninsula, its broker contacted Broz but not CIS. Broz dutifully asked CIS's chief executive whether CIS would be interested in buying the license from the third party, and the CEO declined because CIS was strapped for money. So Broz went ahead on his own.

Soon afterward, CIS's financial fortunes turned when a large firm (PriCellular) agreed to buy the struggling company and inject it with new money. Then, before its purchase of CIS, PriCellular made a bid for the Mackinaw license, but Broz upped his bid and won. Had Broz violated his duties to CIS? Ultimately, the Delaware courts decided he had not. See *Broz v. Cellular Information Systems, Inc.*, 673 A.2d 148 (Del. 1996) (reversing a decision by Chancellor Allen). The court held that Broz had not taken a corporate opportunity of CIS. First, the court questioned whether CIS had a sufficient expectancy. The third-party license holder had not considered CIS a viable candidate for the license. At the time Broz bought the license CIS was in financial straits and was actually divesting its cellular license holdings. Although PriCellular had promised financial help, it had not yet acquired CIS. Second, the court noted Broz's duties to his own cell phone company, of which CIS was "wholly aware." That is, CIS knew that Broz had another master, which could well come first.

§16.3 CORPORATE REJECTION AND INCAPACITY

Even if a court determines that a business opportunity is a corporate opportunity under the applicable test, the corporation's interest is negated if the corporation either consents to the taking by a corporate manager or was unable to take the opportunity itself. By accepting that managers may engage in outside ventures under some circumstances, the corporate opportunity doctrine recognizes the entrepreneurial interests of managers.

Some courts have folded the question of corporate consent and incapacity into the question of whether the opportunity was a corporate opportunity, for example, placing the burden to show capacity on the corporation. Other cases separate the issues, treating them as defenses to be proved by the enterprising manager. The ALI Principles take the view that the corporation's capacity to take an opportunity is a matter to be decided by the corporation, not a court after the fact.

§16.3.1 Corporate Rejection

The corporation can voluntarily relinquish its interests in a corporate opportunity (for many reasons, such as financing difficulties or risk concerns) by generally renouncing any interest in categories of business opportunities or by rejecting a specific deal. Delaware's corporate statute permits a corporation to "renounce, in its certificate of incorporation or by action of its board of directors, any interest or expectancy of the corporation in . . . specified business opportunities or specified classes or categories of business opportunities" presented to the corporation. Del. GCL §122(17); see also MBCH §8.70 (permitting qualified directors or shareholders to disclaim corporation's interest in opportunity).

The corporation's rejection of a specific opportunity, however, may itself be a self-dealing transaction because of the possible conflict between the manager's and the corporation's interests. Some courts subject corporate rejection, like the approval of a self-dealing transaction, to fairness review and require rejection by informed, disinterested directors or shareholders. See *Telxon Corp. v. Meyerson*, 802 A.2d 257 (Del. 2002) (stating that board's informed, considered refusal of corporate opportunity creates safe harbor for interested director). Other courts have held that informal acquiescence to the taking (particularly in closely held corporations) constitutes rejection. Cf. *Farber v. Servan Land Co.*, 662 F.2d 371 (5th Cir. 1981) (finding shareholder inaction did not constitute acquiescence because shareholders relied on usurping insider to investigate business opportunities).

Sometimes courts have folded together the questions of corporate consent and the existence of a corporate opportunity. For example, in *Burg v. Horn*, 380 F.2d 897 (2d Cir. 1967), the part-time managers of a closely held real estate firm acquired other properties with the tacit consent of their co-shareholder. The co-shareholder knew from the start that the managers held and managed other similar properties. Further, the properties acquired by the managers (though in the same line of business as that of the corporation) had not been offered to or sought by the corporation. The co-shareholder's informal acquiescence to the managers' outside entrepreneurialism led the court to conclude they had not usurped a corporate opportunity.

§16.3.2 Corporate Incapacity

Many courts allow managers charged with usurping a corporate opportunity to defend that the corporation could not have taken the opportunity because it was financially incapable or otherwise unable to do so. See *Broz v. Cellular Information Systems, Inc.*, 673 A.2d 148 (Del. 1996) (refusing to find corporate financial capacity when director acquired cell phone license at time cash-strapped corporation was being acquired by another, better-financed company interested in the license). Under this approach, it is not determinative that the manager failed to inform the board. The question of incapacity is left to the court.

If the opportunity was never presented to the board or the shareholders, courts must speculate whether the corporation could have taken the opportunity. This leads to slippery arguments. Even if a manager shows the corporation lacked the funds to take the opportunity itself, it can always be argued that the corporation could have raised the funds by borrowing money or by issuing new stock. After all, the manager had sufficient access to capital to take the opportunity himself, and allowing a manager to later claim corporate incapacity may tempt the manager to not exercise his best efforts to bring the opportunity to the corporation.

Because of the vagaries of these after-the-fact inquiries, some courts have rejected the incapacity defense on the theory that the determination whether the corporation has the financial, legal, and institutional capacity to take the opportunity should be made by informed corporate decision makers, not the corporate fiduciary. See *Demoulas v. Demoulas Super Markets, Inc.*, 677 N.E.2d 159 (Mass. 1997) (whether out-of-state supermarket chain could legally acquire stores under New Hampshire liquor laws should be decided by informed board, not fiduciary). Delaware, however, has taken the view that formal presentation of an opportunity to disinterested corporate decision makers is not required. See *Broz v. Cellular Information Systems, Inc.*, 673 A.2d 148 (Del. 1996). Instead, the manager can decide the opportunity is one the corporation is incapable or unwilling to take—though at his risk.

§16.3.3 ALI Principles

The ALI Principles assume that the corporation's capacity to take an opportunity is for the corporation to decide, not the manager and later a judge in litigation. The ALI Principles thus take a disclosure-oriented approach that mandates informed corporate rejection before a manager can take a "corporate opportunity." Under this approach, (1) the manager must have offered the opportunity to the corporation and disclosed his conflicting interest, and (2) the board or shareholders must have rejected it. ALI §5.05(a). The manager's failure to offer and disclose the opportunity to the corporation thus creates automatic liability.

If disinterested directors have rejected the opportunity, the board's action is subject to review under the business judgment rule. If rejected by disinterested shareholders, review is under a waste standard. And if the rejection is not disinterested, or the challenger shows a lack of business judgment or shows waste, the defendant must then prove that the taking was fair to the corporation. ALI §5.05(a), (c).

In *Klinicki v. Lundgren*, 695 P.2d 906 (Or. 1985), the court applied this offer-rejection approach to the president of a closely held air transportation company who secretly took for himself a contract for a new air charter business. The court refused to consider the president's contention that the company lacked the financial ability to undertake the contract because the opportunity had never been presented to the other participant in the corporation. Under the ALI Principles, the offer-rejection "safe harbor" is exclusive.

§16.4 COMPETITION WITH THE CORPORATION

Competition with the corporation, although often the usurpation of a corporate opportunity, is subject to special treatment. In general, during their relationship with the corporation, managers may not compete with the corporation unless there is no foreseeable harm caused by the competition or disinterested directors (or shareholders) have authorized it. The prohibition applies whether the competing business is set up during the manager's tenure or was preexisting.

This noncompete duty goes beyond the duties of the corporate opportunity doctrine. A manager with an interest in a competing business that predates his joining the corporation usurps no corporate opportunity, but may be liable in damages for continuing to compete. Further, if the manager does not divert assets in setting up a competing business and if the corporation has no existing interest or need to expand, neither the misappropriation nor the expectancy theory prevents the manager from setting up the competing business.

A manager who violates the noncompete duty may be liable in damages for any competitive losses suffered by the corporation, but the manager need not share the competing business unless setting up the business usurped a corporate opportunity. See *Lincoln Stores v. Grant*, 34 N.E.2d 704 (Mass. 1941) (imposing damages, but no constructive trust, on managers who set up competing store while still employed by corporation).

Other theories of liability may also apply to a manager who competes with the corporation: (1) breach of contractual covenant not to compete,

(2) misappropriation of trade secrets (such as customer lists or confidential formulas), or (3) tortious interference with contractual relationships if the manager induces the corporation's customers or employees to follow him.

Examples

1. Atlantis Bottling, Inc., is the authorized bottler of Gusto Cola on the Atlantic seaboard. The corporation is owned and operated by the Garret family. A few years ago, Ruth Garret (Atlantis's founder and largest shareholder) brought her unemployed brother Percy into the business. He is now chief executive officer, and Percy often says, "I owe everything to Ruth." Recently, Percy set up his own chain of dessert shops, which has become highly profitable.
   a. Ruth is distressed and thinks Percy should be forced to share the chain's profits with Atlantis. Percy set up the dessert shops with loans that Atlantis guaranteed under Percy's unauthorized signature. Must Percy share his profits? Under what theory?
   b. As things turn out, Ruth got the facts wrong. Percy set up the dessert shops on his own time and with his own money without using the company's credit. Atlantis had no plans to diversify into the dessert business. Can Percy be forced to share his profits?
   c. Ruth points out that from the beginning the Garret family understood "everyone would pitch in and everyone would be taken care of." Does this understanding affect whether Percy must share his profits?

2. Atlantis managers have been considering installing new lighting at the company's dingy bottling plant. Sally Garret (Ruth's niece and supervisor of the plant) has drawn up a new lighting design, which she plans to submit to the board.
   a. Before Sally submits her plan, Percy receives a letter from DustriLite that it is going out of business and is liquidating its industrial lighting inventory. Without telling anyone, Percy uses his own money to buy a boxcar of DustriLite lighting fixtures—cheap! When the board approves Sally's plan, Percy resells the fixtures to Atlantis at the prevailing market price. Must Percy share his profits? Under what theory?
   b. Would it make any difference if Percy had originally disclosed the DustriLite offer to Atlantis's board and the board had at first turned down the offer?
   c. What if DustriLite had sold its inventory to Percy at a discount as a way to express its thanks for his steering Atlantis business to DustriLite. Must Percy share a personal gratuity?

3. Atlantis's sales have fallen recently and some of the company's bank lenders have expressed concern to Percy about the company's ability to repay its outstanding loans.

a. Percy, swimming in cash because of his successful dessert shops, wants to get the banks off Atlantis's back. He believes that Atlantis's credit is basically sound, and he buys Atlantis's loans from the banks at a deep discount. Can he be forced to share this discount with Atlantis?
b. Percy believes the banks would not have been willing, on principle, to allow Atlantis to renegotiate its debt. Does this affect Percy's duties?
c. Percy claims that everyone else at Atlantis knew about the banks' nervousness and did nothing. Does this affect Percy's duties?

4. Ofelia, a nationally known "beverage consultant" and an outside director on Atlantis's board, reads in the newspaper that Tanfa Beverages is going out of business. Tanfa is a bottler of fruit-flavored sodas in California, and Ofelia calls Tanfa's president, who confirms the company is for sale.
   a. Atlantis's board has never discussed expanding outside the Atlantic region, its traditional geographic niche. Ofelia figures Atlantis would not be interested in Tanfa. She wants to buy Tanfa for herself, but without disclosing her plans to Atlantis. Can she?
   b. Atlantis's board has lately had extensive discussions about the company's "cash flow difficulties." Ofelia figures Atlantis lacks the funds to buy Tanfa. Does this affect her duties?
   c. Ofelia buys Tanfa and convinces Jack Garret (Atlantis's promotional director) to leave Atlantis and work for Tanfa. Do you see any problems?

Explanations

EXPLANATIONS

1. a. Yes, under a misappropriation theory. Percy's unauthorized use of Atlantis's credit is as much a diversion of assets as if he had misappropriated money. His wrongful use of corporate resources imposes on him a duty not to take the opportunity whether or not Atlantis had any interest in opening dessert shops itself or whether the shops were related to Atlantis's existing soft drink business.

   Some courts, however, would limit Atlantis's recovery to the damages resulting from Percy's unauthorized use of the company's credit. See *Lincoln Stores v. Grant*, 34 N.E.2d 704 (Mass. 1941) (§16.2.1). If so, Percy would be liable for the value of Atlantis's guarantee.

   b. Unlikely. Percy's dessert business is not a "corporate opportunity" under any of the definitions applied by the courts.
      - Percy did not misappropriate corporate assets in setting up his business.
      - There is no indication Atlantis had any plans or need to enter the dessert business. Percy started the business on his own time and presumably with information he derived from outside Atlantis.

- The business opportunity is not within Atlantis's "line of business" because the dessert shops are not functionally related to the bottling business. There is no overlap in raw materials, production, and marketing. Even if Atlantis's charter permitted it and Atlantis had the financial means to expand into dessert shops, the line-of-business test does not treat every profitable business as within a corporation's expansion potential. In recognition of managers' entrepreneurial interests, the opportunity must be closely related to the company's existing or contemplated business.
- Percy's new business does not compete with Atlantis for customers, suppliers, employees, or assets.

c. Perhaps. Ruth could argue that Percy had a duty to share the opportunity because of the special expectations in this close corporation. The argument parallels the "reasonable expectations" argument that courts have increasingly come to accept in close corporation freezeout cases (see §27.2.1). If the participants in this family business had a "share and share alike" understanding—that a business opportunity available to any of them should be made available to the family corporation—a court might apply broader notions of corporate expectancy and line of business. Moreover, courts have frequently suggested that corporations can expect more of full-time managers (such as CEO Percy) than part-time managers or outside directors.

That is, the corporate opportunity doctrine provides a default rule that the parties have some leeway to contract around. The ALI Principles, for example, permit corporate participants to establish a "standard of the corporation" that permits the taking of specified corporate opportunities without further disinterested approval. ALI Principles §5.09. By the same token the corporation, just as it sometimes obtains noncompete promises, could expand the definition of what constitutes a corporate opportunity. Even if a court were to give significance to the family's "share and share alike" understanding, it should also consider Percy's entrepreneurial desire to diversify his human capital by branching into new businesses.

2. a. Yes, under an expectancy theory. The DustriLite opportunity was an existing expectancy of Atlantis because of Sally's plans for new lighting at the plant. It seems clear that Percy knew about her plans, given his secrecy and prescience to buy the right fixtures. If, for some reason, Percy did not know about the plans or that Atlantis might be interested in the fixtures, his *innocent* taking of a business opportunity would not be the breach of his fiduciary duties.

It makes no difference that the board had not yet approved Sally's plans or that Atlantis's interest was not based on preexisting rights (such as a DustriLite contract with Atlantis). Even though Atlantis could not legally preclude Percy or anyone else from purchasing the fixtures, Atlantis's plans were far enough along to impose on Percy a duty not to take the opportunity without allowing the corporation to consider it.

In these circumstances, a line-of-business theory would not work because buying lighting fixtures is not part of Atlantis's bottling business. The line-of-business test does not compel Percy to get permission to become a lighting-fixture marketer.

You might have noticed also that Atlantis could have sought damages from Percy on a self-dealing theory because he sold the fixtures to the corporation (see §13.1). Although the transaction's price might have been the fair market price, a court could characterize it as procedurally unfair—particularly if Percy failed to disclose how much he stood to profit when he made the sale. In such a case, the self-dealing remedy of rescission would be inadequate; courts have held that damages under a corporate opportunity theory are appropriate.

b. Yes, if the board had also known of Sally's lighting plans. Under most judicial approaches, the rejection of the opportunity by informed, independent, and disinterested directors of the Atlantis board relinquishes the corporation's claim to it, freeing Percy to take it for himself. Not only would Percy have to disclose the terms of the DustriLite offer, but also Sally's lighting plans and his intentions if the board turned down the offer. For the directors to be considered disinterested, they cannot have a financial interest in the lighting fixtures; and for them to be considered independent, Percy cannot dominate their decision making (§13.3.3).

c. Probably, because the gratuity was for past business with Atlantis, not with Percy. A similar question recently arose in the context of the allocation of IPO shares to corporate directors by an investment bank seeking to foster a relationship with the directors' company. See *In re eBAY, Inc. Shareholders Litigation*, 2004 WL 253521 (Del. Ch. 2004). When the directors turned around and sold the IPO shares for millions of dollars in profits, shareholders brought a derivative suit. Without deciding whether the allocations were a corporate opportunity, the court decided they constituted consideration for continued business with the company, and thus the directors had (at the least) breached their fiduciary duties of loyalty by taking something that belonged to the company.

3. a. Perhaps. Percy's purchase of the debt would mean that Atlantis would owe him 100 percent principal and interest under its loans even though Percy had paid less than 100 percent for these rights. Atlantis could use an expectancy theory to characterize Percy's purchase of its discounted debt as a corporate opportunity and compel Percy to share

the profits from his refinancing of the debt. Even if Atlantis had not expressed an interest in restructuring its debt, Atlantis could argue it (like any business) has an ongoing interest in repurchasing its own securities or obligations at a discount because of their "unique value" to the corporation.

On the other hand, Percy could argue that he was simply assuming Atlantis's credit risk from the bank and purchased the debt at market value. There is nothing to indicate Atlantis could have refinanced its debt with a lender other than Percy. It would be unfair to compel Percy to share any gains because his purchase of Atlantis's debt meant only he would bear any losses if Atlantis did not repay on schedule. His argument would be buttressed if Percy, not the banks, initiated the idea of refinancing or repurchase of the debt.

b. Perhaps. If the banks would have been unwilling to sell back their loans to Atlantis at a discount, Atlantis lacked the corporate capacity to take the opportunity itself. Some courts treat corporate capacity as an element of corporate opportunity. See *Broz v. Cellular Information Systems, Inc.*, 673 A.2d 148 (Del. 1996). If Percy could show that the banks would not have dealt with Atlantis, his loan purchase would not be treated as a corporate opportunity. This forces a court to speculate on what might have happened, placing the corporation at a disadvantage to rebut the banks' after-the-fact statements about not giving discounts to borrowers.

Because of this, a modern judicial trend (reflected in the ALI Principles, but rejected in Delaware) is to compel the manager to seek corporate rejection. If the banks are truly unwilling to deal with Atlantis, the company's disinterested participants presumably would have rejected even attempting the impossible opportunity. Under this approach, Percy would walk a dangerous line by not seeking formal corporate rejection.

c. Perhaps. Percy might be able to characterize the Atlantis inaction as an implied rejection of the opportunity to refinance its debt. Some courts, particularly in cases involving closely held corporations, have treated acquiescence as rejection of an opportunity.

Nonetheless, the approach of other courts, and of the ALI Principles, is to avoid speculation about corporate capacity. Under the ALI Principles, for example, the opportunity must be offered to the corporation and rejected by the board or shareholders. ALI Principles §5.05(a)(2). To meet the standards of the business judgment rule, the ALI Principles imply that rejection by the board must be by formal action; shareholder action must be taken at a meeting. This approach may not make much sense in a close corporation, such as Atlantis, where the corporate participants may act casually without corporate formalities.

4. a. Perhaps not. The Tanfa opportunity may be an opportunity within Atlantis's line-of-business expansion potential, but not necessarily one that outside director Ofelia must disclose or share. Although Atlantis has no present plans to expand into the West Coast market, the line-of-business test does not depend on actual expectancies. Tanfa is in the same business as Atlantis, though the two bottlers do not sell in the same markets. Atlantis's acquisition of Tanfa would create new opportunities for expanding Atlantis's existing business. It would provide new products for Atlantis's current markets and open a new market for its existing products.

   Some courts, however, would consider Ofelia's position as a non-executive outside director. Her entrepreneurial interests are presumably greater because she is not an employee of Atlantis, and her outside status diminishes the corporation's expectations in her exclusive loyalty. Under the ALI Principles, for example, a line-of-business opportunity is not considered a "corporate opportunity" when an outside director learns of it in a noncorporate capacity. See ALI Principles §5.05(b).

   b. Perhaps. If the opportunity were considered a corporate opportunity for Atlantis, Ofelia's incapacity defense depends on whether a court would require the board to make the call (after disclosure by Ofelia) or whether the court would decide the issue on its own. Some courts, particularly in Delaware, allow the defense even though the opportunity was never presented to the corporation. The burden of proving financial incapacity is difficult. Ofelia will have to show Atlantis could not have raised the money through new debt or equity financing. The argument that financing was unavailable will ring hollow because Ofelia seems able herself to afford the acquisition.

   Some courts, and the ALI Principles, have rejected the incapacity defense. Under their approach, corporate incapacity must be decided by fully informed, disinterested directors or shareholders. If the Tanfa opportunity were a corporate opportunity for Atlantis, the board would have to reject it. Under this approach, however, Ofelia need not offer to lend money to the corporation so it can make the acquisition.

   c. Yes, on three possible grounds.

   First, whether or not the acquisition of Tanfa is a corporate opportunity, Jack's continued employment with Atlantis might itself be seen as an opportunity. Atlantis could argue it has an expectancy that Jack will stay with Atlantis (particularly if he is under contract or is subject to a covenant not to compete) and that his services have special value to Atlantis. By hiring him away, Ofelia has usurped a corporate opportunity.

   Second, Tanfa is now competing with Atlantis, and Ofelia (as a fiduciary of Atlantis) is under a broad duty not to harm Atlantis competitively. (Notice that this may conflict with her duties to Tanfa and force her to cut her ties to one or the other. Ofelia can compete with Atlantis after she resigns from her board position.)

Third, if Jack is under contract and particularly if he is subject to a noncompete covenant, Ofelia may have tortiously interfered with Atlantis's contractual relationship by wooing Jack away.

Duties of Controlling Shareholders

Corporate fiduciary duties apply to those who control the corporate governance mechanisms. Not only are directors and officers accountable, but also any shareholder with voting control—a *controlling shareholder*. With the power to select the board and approve fundamental changes, a controlling shareholder can act to the detriment of minority shareholders. For this reason, courts impose fiduciary duties on controlling shareholders that generally parallel those of directors.

This chapter describes who are controlling shareholders (§17.1), how courts scrutinize transactions between controlling shareholders and the corporation—the duties in corporate groups (§17.2) and the special scrutiny given to squeeze-out transactions (§17.3). Our focus is on public corporations and parent-subsidiary dealings. The special duties of controlling shareholders in close corporations are discussed in Chapter 27.

§17.1 WHO ARE CONTROLLING SHAREHOLDERS?

A controlling shareholder, whether an individual or a parent corporation, has sufficient voting shares to determine the outcome of a shareholder vote. Directors are usually elected by plurality or majority vote, and any shareholder who can assemble a voting majority wields effective control of the board. In close corporations, effective control may require a shareholding of more than 50 percent—a majority shareholder. In a public corporation with widely dispersed shareholders, it may be enough to own as little as

20 percent and have the support of the incumbent board—a dominating shareholder. ALI §1.10(b) (presumption of control with 25 percent shareholding); but see *Williamson v. Cox Communications, Inc.*, 32 Del. J. Corp. L. 307 (Del. Ch. 2006) (concluding that shareholder with less than 50 percent interest not controlling, unless shareholder actually exercises control over subsidiary, beyond installing directors or exercising veto).

Why would shareholders ever invest in a business controlled by another shareholder? There are a number of reasons. A controlling shareholder has greater incentives and means to monitor management, a benefit shared by all shareholders. The controlling shareholder may also have other businesses, creating opportunities in the corporate group for economies of scale and captive markets.

§17.2 PARENT-SUBSIDIARY DEALINGS

In a public corporation setting, dealings between a controlling shareholder (the parent) and the corporation (the subsidiary) raise many of the same conflict-of-interest concerns as do dealings between a director and the corporation. For a parent and its subsidiary, multiple sources of conflict exist. Executives of the parent often serve on the board of the subsidiary; parent company executives often dictate (directly and indirectly) the subsidiary's operational policies and decisions; and the parent, by definition, has a controlling shareholding position.

§17.2.1 Dealings with Wholly Owned Subsidiaries

When a subsidiary is wholly owned and there are no minority shareholders, the parent has virtually unfettered discretion to do with the subsidiary corporation as it pleases. Duties exist only to corporate creditors and, to a limited extent, future minority shareholders. For example, promoters cannot enter into unfair self-dealing transactions to the detriment of future creditors or shareholders (see §29.3), and controlling shareholders are liable for siphoning corporate funds at the expense of creditors (see §32.1). But if these interests are not implicated, there is no conflict when a parent corporation deals with its wholly owned subsidiary.

§17.2.2 Dealings with Partially Owned Subsidiaries

Dealings between a parent and its partially owned subsidiary create risks of control abuse. Consider some examples:

- **Dividend policy.** The subsidiary declares dividends to a cash-strapped parent at the expense of internal expansion. Or the subsidiary adopts a no-dividend policy to force minority shareholders to sell to the parent.
- **Share transactions.** The subsidiary issues shares to the parent at less than fair value, thus diluting the minority's interests. The subsidiary purchases shares from the parent at more than fair value.
- **Parent-subsidiary transactions.** The subsidiary enters into contracts (with the parent or related affiliates) on terms unfavorable to the subsidiary, effectively withdrawing assets of the subsidiary at the expense of the minority.
- **Usurpation of opportunities.** The parent (or other affiliates) takes business opportunities away from the subsidiary.

When must the parent answer to the minority? Corporate statutes provide little guidance. Although conflict-of-interest statutes by their terms cover transactions when a director has a relationship to another corporation—the usual situation in parent-subsidiary dealings—the statutes either fail to provide conclusive standards of review for parent-subsidiary dealings or explicitly exclude such transactions from their reach. See Del. GCL §144 (declaring the nonvoidability of corporate transactions with director or entity in which director has an interest); Note on Parent Companies and Subsidiaries, MBCA §8.60(1) (stating that safe harbor provisions for director's conflicting interest transactions have "no relevance" to parent-subsidiary transactions, which in practice are dealt with "under the rubric of the duties of a majority shareholder").

§17.2.3 Judicial Review of Parent-Subsidiary Dealings

Courts have wavered on the degree of scrutiny applicable to parent-subsidiary dealings. Although using much of the terminology and analysis applicable to director dealings, courts have recognized the prerogatives that come from owning a controlling interest. See *Thorpe v. CERBO, Inc.*, 676 A.2d 436 (Del. 1996) (refusing to impose lost-profits liability on controlling shareholders who failed to make information on potential buyout of subsidiary available to subsidiary's board, since controlling shareholders could have used voting power to block the buyout).

Ordinary Business Dealings

Most courts, including in Delaware, view with sympathy the argument that a parent corporation should be able to exercise its control. Parent-subsidiary dealings in the ordinary course of business are subject to fairness review only if the minority shows the parent has preferred itself at the minority's expense. If so, the courts presume the parent dominates the subsidiary's board and places the burden on the parent to prove the transaction was "entirely fair" to the subsidiary. See ALI §5.10 (burden on parent unless approved by disinterested directors). But if there is no preference, the transaction is subject to business judgment review, and the minority must prove that the dealings lacked any business purpose or that their approval was grossly uninformed.

Sinclair Oil v. Levien

The dichotomous judicial treatment of parent-subsidiary dealings—scrutiny of preferential dealings and deference to nonpreferential dealings—is illustrated in *Sinclair Oil Co. v. Levien*, 280 A.2d 717 (Del. 1971). Minority shareholders of Sinven, a partially owned (97 percent) Venezuelan subsidiary of Sinclair Oil, challenged three sets of parent-subsidiary dealings:

- **Sub's high-dividend policy.** The minority alleged Sinclair had imposed on Sinven a dividend policy that depleted the subsidiary. The court held that the policy did not prefer Sinclair because Sinven's minority shareholders received their proportionate share of all dividends. In the absence of preferential treatment, the shareholders had the burden to show that the policy was not protected by the business judgment rule, which they failed to do.
- **Parent's allocation of projects to other affiliates.** The minority claimed Sinclair allocated industrial projects to its wholly owned subsidiaries, to the detriment of partially owned Sinven. The court held that the projects were not corporate opportunities of the subsidiary, and the parent was under no obligation to share them with Sinven.
- **Sub's failure to enforce contracts with other affiliates.** The minority claimed that Sinven's nonenforcement of contracts for the sale of oil products to other Sinclair affiliates preferred the affiliates to Sinven's detriment. The court treated the nonenforcement as self-dealing and held that Sinclair had failed to show that nonenforcement was fair to Sinven.

The key in each instance was whether the minority shareholders could show a clear parental preference detrimental to the subsidiary. The *Levien* test assumes the propriety of parent-subsidiary dealings, a departure from the traditional rule that fiduciaries have the burden to show the fairness of their self-interested dealings. See §13.2.3. The burden is on the minority shareholders to show the dealings were *not* those that might be expected in an arm's-length relationship, rather than on the parent to show that they were.

Exclusion of Minority

Some courts hold controlling shareholders to a higher standard when they use control in stock transactions to benefit themselves to the exclusion of minority shareholders. In the leading case, the court imposed on the controlling shareholder the burden to prove that a stock transaction that excluded minority shareholders was justified by a "compelling business purpose." *Jones v. H. F. Ahmanson & Co.*, 460 P.2d 464 (Cal. 1969). United Savings & Loan was controlled by Howard Ahmanson, who had made the S&L a great success. But the S&L's shareholders were unable to capitalize on the success because of a thin market for their shares. Although publicly held, the S&L had less than 7,000 outstanding shares, which traded at $2,400 per share. As a result, few investors were interested in buying even though S&Ls were then darlings of the stock markets.

To remedy this, Ahmanson set up a holding company (United Financial) that exchanged its stock for the S&L shares he and his friends owned—all told, 85 percent of the S&L shares outstanding. United Financial's shares became widely traded, creating a lucrative market for Ahmanson's majority interest in the S&L. The plaintiff, a minority shareholder who was not allowed to participate in the exchange, argued that Ahmanson should have created a market for all the S&L shareholders by splitting the S&L stock on a 250-for-1 basis. Ahmanson argued that he and the other favored shareholders had an unfettered right to do with their shares as they pleased, and that the exchange had not affected the plaintiff's legal interest in the S&L, which remained unchanged.

Writing for the court, Justice Traynor rejected Ahmanson's argument and held that controlling shareholders have fiduciary duties to minority shareholders. Even accepting (as the plaintiff conceded) that Ahmanson had caused no harm to the corporation, Traynor said that controlling shareholders cannot use their control to benefit themselves to the detriment of the minority. Ahmanson violated a duty to the minority by creating a market from which the minority shareholders were excluded without a compelling business purpose. The court required that the minority shareholders have an opportunity to exchange their S&L shares for a proportionate number of holding company shares.

Other courts have used this analysis to invalidate stock redemptions and conversions that prefer controlling shareholders. For example, in *Zahn v. Transamerica Corp.*, 162 F.2d 36 (3d Cir. 1947), a corporation had two classes of common shares, class A and class B. The class B shares held voting control. The class A shares, which were entitled to twice as much in liquidation as class B shares, could be redeemed by the corporation at any time for $60. The controlling shareholder had the corporation redeem all of the minority's class A shares and then liquidate the corporation's assets, which had recently tripled in value. The result was that the controlling shareholder received the lion's share of the company's liquidation value. The court stated there was "no reason" for the class A redemption except for the controlling class B shareholder to profit. In a subsequent opinion, the court upheld a recovery by the class A shareholders based on the liquidation value they would have received had they exercised their rights to convert their class B shares into class A shares. See *Speed v. Transamerica Corp.*, 235 F.2d 369 (3d Cir. 1956).

Approval by Disinterested Shareholders

Just as shareholder ratification insulates directorial self-dealing from review, approval by a majority of informed, disinterested shareholders of the controlled subsidiary insulates a parent-subsidiary transaction. If the parent discloses the conflict and the terms of the transaction, the transaction is subject to review only under a waste standard. That is, a challenger must show there was no rational business justification for the transaction. ALI §5.10(a)(2).

Remedies

Remedies for improper parent-subsidiary dealings are the same as those for self-dealing by directors (see §13.5). Rescission is the general remedy unless it is inadequate—such as when a parent usurps the subsidiary's corporate opportunities—or rescission is no longer possible. When a controlling shareholder transacts in the corporation's stock to the detriment of the minority, courts permit minority shareholders to sue directly and seek either equal treatment in the transaction or a recovery based on what the minority would have received absent the breach.

§17.3 SQUEEZE-OUT TRANSACTIONS—ELIMINATING MINORITY INTERESTS

Controlling shareholders often seek to buy out minority interests—particularly in corporate takeovers. Modern courts, though permitting controlling shareholders to structure transactions that eliminate minority interests, place significant restrictions on such transactions whose structure and terms are dictated by the controlling shareholder.

Note on Shift of Litigation Away from Delaware

Corporate takeovers—whether negotiated or hostile—usually end with a court challenge to the terms of the "squeeze-out" merger in which the acquiring company consolidates its

(continued)

control. Such challenges are typically brought by shareholders (and their law firms) looking to negotiate improved terms in the squeeze-out merger — and to collect attorneys' fees for their efforts. In the past several years, Delaware judges have become reluctant to readily grant requests for attorneys' fees to the lawyers bringing (or intervening in) such cases. As a result, many such cases have lately been filed in jurisdictions other than Delaware. Although Delaware corporate law still applies, the plaintiffs' lawyers have assumed that they will be treated more favorably by non-Delaware judges, whose experience with corporate litigation will typically be less extensive. See Armour, Black & Cheffins, *Is Delaware Losing Its Cases?* SSRN Paper 1578404 (2010).

§17.3.1 Squeeze-Out Mechanics

Consider the ways a controlling shareholder can force out minority shareholders and acquire 100 percent control:

- **Squeeze-out merger.** The parent and subsidiary agree to a merger under which the subsidiary's minority shareholders receive cash (a cash-out merger) or other consideration for their shares. The parent retains the subsidiary's shares and becomes its sole shareholder or the subsidiary merges into the parent as a new division. See §32.2.6 (description of mechanics of squeeze-out merger, including triangular merger).

  Squeeze-out mergers are common in leveraged corporate takeovers. After acquiring a voting majority, acquirers (whether in a friendly or unfriendly takeover) often use a squeeze-out merger to consolidate control, thus giving them unfettered access to corporate assets to repay their takeover debt.
- **Liquidation.** The subsidiary sells all of its assets to the parent (or an affiliate) and then dissolves and is liquidated. Minority shareholders receive a pro rata distribution of the sales price.
- **Stock split.** The subsidiary declares a reverse stock split (such as 1 for 2,000) that greatly reduces the number of outstanding shares. If no minority shareholder owns more than 2,000 shares, all minority shareholders come to hold fractional shares, which are then subject to mandatory redemption by the subsidiary as permitted under some state statutes.

These transactions (generically referred to as "squeezeouts" or "freezeouts") are all authorized by corporate statutes but present a clear conflict of interest. In each instance the parent will want to minimize its payment to the minority shareholders. The minority is particularly vulnerable because the parent both controls the subsidiary's board and has voting power to approve the transaction over the minority's opposition. Despite the potential for abuse, squeezeouts present the opportunity for important efficiencies. By eliminating minority shareholders, the parent can (1) use the subsidiary's assets as it pleases, (2) consolidate the businesses for tax and accounting purposes, (3) avoid reporting and disclosure costs under federal securities laws, and (4) resell the wholly owned subsidiary to another holding company. In short, depending on the price to minority shareholders, the subsidiary may be worth more to the parent if wholly owned.

§17.3.2 Business Purpose Test

A squeezeout terminates the minority shareholders' investment without their consent. Some courts require that the transaction not only be fair, but the parent also have some business purpose for the merger—other than eliminating the minority. See *Alpert v. 28 Williams Street Corp.*, 473 N.E.2d 19 (N.Y. 1984); *Coggins v. New England Patriots Football Club, Inc.*, 492 N.E.2d 1112 (Mass. 1986).

The business purpose test has been widely criticized as weak and easily manipulated. It imposes little substantive protection for minority shareholders because management can always create a record of avowed purposes for the squeezeout, such as greater operational or financial efficiencies, accounting simplicity, or tax advantages. At most, the business purpose requirement may sometimes distinguish between those squeeze-out mergers motivated by pique and those meant to create genuine gain.

Delaware has abandoned the business purpose requirement on the grounds it provides no meaningful protection beyond that afforded by the "entire fairness" test (see §17.3.3 below) and shareholder appraisal rights (see §17.3.4 below; Chapter 37). *Weinberger v. UOP, Inc.*, 457 A.2d 701 (Del. 1983), *overruling Singer v. Magnavox Co.*, 380 A.2d 969 (Del. 1977).

§17.3.3 "Entire Fairness" Test

Weinberger v. UOP

In Delaware squeeze-out mergers are subject to a two-prong *entire fairness* test. *Weinberger v. UOP, Inc.*, 457 A.2d 701 (Del. 1983). The test focuses on the fairness of both the transaction's price and the process of approval.

- **Fair price.** The *Weinberger* court characterized *fair price* as the preponderant consideration and liberalized Delaware's valuation methods for determining fair price in the context of a merger. It rejected the exclusivity of the *Delaware block method*, which gave a particular weight to historic earnings per share, asset value per share, and market price, and then added them together to produce a share price. Instead, the court held that valuation must take into account "all relevant factors," including discounted cash flow. The *discounted cash flow method*, generally used by the investment community to value companies, looks at the company's anticipated future cash stream and then, after making assumptions about risk-free interest rates and company risk, figures how much present cash would produce that future stream. The present cash value represents how much the business is worth.

- **Fair dealing.** The court described *fair dealing* as relating to "when the transaction was timed, how it was initiated, structured, negotiated, disclosed to the directors, and how the approvals of the directors and the stockholders were obtained." The court strongly recommended the subsidiary board form an independent negotiating committee of outside directors to act as a representative of the minority shareholders.

In *Weinberger*, minority shareholders of UOP challenged a cash-out merger at $21 per share that had been initiated by the parent Signal. The court faulted the procedures by which the merger had been initiated, negotiated, and approved—principally Signal's failure to disclose to UOP's outside directors or shareholders a feasibility study prepared by two of UOP's management directors, who were also executives of Signal. The study concluded that a price of $24 per share would have been a "good investment" for Signal. The court also found other deficiencies: Signal had initiated and structured the merger; there were no meaningful negotiations with UOP's outside directors; and the shareholders were not told that an investment banker's fairness opinion on the $21 price was based on a hurried and cursory review of the company. In all, the merger failed the fair dealing test, and the court remanded for the Chancery Court to reconsider whether the $21 price was fair and order appropriate relief in view of the procedural unfairness.

Post-*Weinberger* "Fair Dealing" Cases

Since *Weinberger* the Delaware Supreme Court has clarified some aspects of the "fair dealing" test and what constitutes procedural fairness. The Court has considered the independence of the subsidiary's negotiating committee, how the parent conducted the negotiations, and whether a majority of the subsidiary's minority shareholders approved the transaction.

Negotiation by a team or special committee of the subsidiary's independent directors significantly buttresses procedural fairness, particularly when the directors are well informed and negotiations are "adversarial." *Rosenblatt v.*

Getty Oil Co., 493 A.2d 929 (Del. 1985). This is so even though the outside, nonmanagement directors are chosen by the parent.

- **Shift of burden.** Negotiation and approval of the transaction by a committee composed of independent directors shifts the burden to the challenger to show lack of entire fairness. *Kahn v. Lynch Communication Sys., Inc. (Lynch I)*, 638 A.2d 1110 (Del. 1994) (rejecting business judgment review since controlling shareholder has inherent potential to coerce or unduly influence shareholder vote in merger). Merely initiating a merger or failing to obtain unanimous committee approval does not negate a finding of fair dealing.
- **Informed, independent committee.** The committee members must be independent and become fully informed, actively participate in deliberations, and appropriately simulate an arm's-length negotiation. *Kahn v. Tremont Corp.*, 694 A.2d 422 (Del. 1997) (faulting independence of committee members, who all received significant compensation or influential positions on parent's controlled companies; faulting failure to attend information meetings with committee advisors; faulting lack of independent analysis of company's market and reliance on parent projections); *Lynch I* (concluding that parent's threat to proceed with hostile tender offer if merger proposal not accepted compromised arm's-length negotiation with independent committee).

The parent must conduct the negotiations fairly, though at arm's length—remember that the parent's management also has fiduciary duties to the parent corporation and its shareholders.

- **Timing of transaction.** A squeeze-out merger, although its share price is within a range of fairness, may not purposely be timed by the parent to avoid an obligation to pay a higher contract price. *Rabkin v. Philip A. Hunt Chemical Corp.*, 498 A.2d 1099 (Del. 1985). The merger cannot blatantly advance the parent's interest at the expense of the minority shareholders'—a lingering business purpose analysis.
- **Disclosure during negotiations.** The parent need not disclose internally prepared valuations (its reservation price) unless directors or officers of the subsidiary prepare them. *Rosenblatt*. Only when executives have overlapping roles must the parent show its cards.

Approval by a majority of the subsidiary's minority shareholders, after full disclosure, buttresses (but does not guarantee) procedural fairness and shifts the burden to the challenger to show a lack of entire fairness. *Lynch I* (requiring court review of merger's procedural and price fairness to overcome perception of coercion in any squeeze-out merger). For this reason, it is advisable to condition the merger on approval by a specified "majority of the minority," even though such approval is not required.

Post-*Weinberger* "Fair Price" Cases

Although *Weinberger* held that appraisal (the post-merger procedure whereby the court sets a "fair value" payable in cash for the shares of dissenting shareholders, see Chapter 37) is normally the exclusive remedy for a challenge of the price in a squeeze-out merger (see §17.3.4 below), Delaware courts have clarified the "fair price" analysis:

- **DCF not exclusive.** The price paid minority shareholders, if supported by an outside fairness opinion and asset valuations by outside experts, can be calculated using the old Delaware block method. Valuation based on discounted cash value is not exclusive. *Rosenblatt.*
- **Range of fair value.** Fair value can be based on opinions of the parent's investment banker, even though the subsidiary's committee has received opinions of higher value from other investment bankers. *Kahn v. Lynch Communication Sys., Inc.* (Lynch II), 669 A.2d 79 (Del. 1995) (when parent bears burden of showing entire fairness, parent must come forward with credible, persuasive evidence of "fair value" under recognized valuation standards; holding that trial court properly found parent's valuation more persuasive than challenging shareholder's).
- **Post-transaction projections (sometimes) relevant.** Price fairness must take into account "all relevant factors." Although "speculative elements of value" arising from the merger are excluded, nonspeculative *pro forma* data and projections "susceptible of proof" as of the date of the merger may be considered. *Weinberger.* This means the parent must share with the minority shareholders any financial, operational, or tax gains expected in the merger. *Cede & Co. v. Technicolor, Inc.*, 684 A.2d 289 (Del. 1996) (accepting valuation in appraisal based on actual results of acquirer's partially implemented business plan, not limited to premerger strategy).

Short-Form Mergers

When a parent corporation eliminates minority shareholders using the procedure of a "short-form" merger (available to parents owning at least 90 percent of the subsidiary's shares), courts have limited complaining shareholders to an appraisal remedy. *Glassman v. Unocal Exploration Corp.*, 777 A.2d 242 (Del. 2001). It would defeat the summary nature of the short-form merger procedure (see §36.2.3) if the parent had to constitute a negotiating committee of subsidiary directors, hire independent financial and legal experts, and conduct an arm's-length negotiation. Nonetheless, minority shareholders who face the choice of accepting the merger terms or seeking an appraisal must receive full disclosure.

§17.3.4 Remedy in Squeezeouts

The traditional remedy for unfair self-dealing—rescission of the transaction—often is not possible in a squeezeout. A squeezeout fundamentally changes the corporate structure, and returning the corporation and its shareholders to their prior position may be impractical.

Appraisal (Sometimes) Exclusive

Even if minority shareholders prove the squeezeout is unfair, however, they are not necessarily entitled to recover damages. *Weinberger* held that dissenters' appraisal rights (see Chapter 37) are normally the exclusive remedy when a squeeze-out merger is challenged on the basis of price. But when a merger is challenged on the basis of fraud, misrepresentation, self-dealing, deliberate waste, or palpable overreaching—that is, a lack of *fair dealing*—the *Weinberger* court stated that appraisal would not be exclusive. See also Official Comment, MBCA §13.02 (appraisal is exclusive unless the transaction is "unlawful or fraudulent," which includes violation of corporate law on voting or of the articles, deception of shareholders, and fiduciary breach). Thus, appraisal is exclusive when only price is challenged, but not when procedural fairness or the adequacy of disclosure is challenged.

Consolidated Proceedings

What happens if shareholders bring an appraisal proceeding and during discovery learn for the first time of procedural irregularities in the merger? Is appraisal still the exclusive remedy? The Delaware courts have permitted shareholders in these circumstances to bring a separate, alternative claim challenging the merger on procedural grounds. See *Cede & Co. v. Technicolor, Inc.*, 542 A.2d 1182 (Del. 1988). That is, the election of remedies is not exclusive, and both a properly pleaded appraisal action and procedural fairness action can proceed simultaneously on a consolidated basis. But the plaintiff is limited to a single recovery, which can be based either on fair value in appraisal or rescissory damages in the fairness action.

Director Liability

Most challenges to parent-subsidiary mergers, though often couched in terms of director duties, rarely result in actual director liability. Instead, liability usually runs to the parent corporation—the beneficiary of unfair dealing or an unfair price. To the extent subsidiary directors fail in their negotiation duties, exculpation provisions in the subsidiary's charter typically insulate them from liability. See §12.5. A few cases, however, have imposed liability on directors. For example, a recent decision by the Delaware Chancery Court held directors of a partially owned subsidiary jointly and severally liable in a "going-private" transaction orchestrated by the company's 52 percent parent. *In re Emerging Communications, Inc. Shareholders Litigation*, 2004 WL 1305745 (Del. Ch. 2004). After determining the process and price in the transaction were seriously flawed, the court held three directors liable: the subsidiary's CEO (who was also a part owner of the parent company), the subsidiary's legal counsel (who was also the CEO's personal attorney), and an outside director (who had extensive experience as an investment advisor in the telecommunications sector).

The court concluded that the CEO had breached his duty of loyalty by being on both sides of the unfair transaction, the lawyer had breached his duty of loyalty and/or good faith by assisting the CEO in furthering his "antithetical" interests, and "with reluctance" concluded that the outside director who seemed to know the merger price was unfair had breached his duty of loyalty. Other directors on the board, though careless in relying on a flawed outside valuation opinion, were not held liable because of the subsidiary's exculpation clause under Del. GCL §102(b)(7).

The implication of *Emerging Communications* is that directors with conflicting financial interests act at their own peril when pursuing a transaction whose process or terms are later deemed unfair. More significant, the case suggests that directors with greater financial expertise bear a higher fiduciary duty to recognize and oppose a transaction that they "have strong reasons to believe" is financially unfair. In such circumstances, a director who seeks to ingratiate himself with conflicted insiders, who has "unique knowledge" that the transaction is unfair, and who "intentionally disregards" his responsibility to minority shareholders, violates his duty of good faith. See *Walt Disney Co. Deriv. Litig.*, 906 A.2d 27 (Del. 2006) (holding that directors who consciously disregard their responsibilities violate duty of good faith, a subset of duty of loyalty).

§17.3.5 Fairness in Parent Tender Offer

A parent corporation can also squeeze out minority shareholders of a partially controlled subsidiary through a two-step process: (1) a tender offer to bring the parent's holdings to more than 90 percent of the outstanding shares, and (2) a short-form merger in which the remaining minority shareholders are bought out and appraisal is their exclusive remedy. (A tender offer is a contractual offer to buy shares at a specified price, provided they are tendered for sale by a specified deadline. See §34.1.) Not only does this method (compared to a squeeze-out merger) avoid action by the subsidiary's board, but it also avoids questions of the fairness of the dealing and price for the shareholders who tender their shares in the first-stage tender offer.

Delaware courts have struggled with this anomaly. One view assumes shareholders (particularly institutional investors) can fend for themselves in a parent tender offer. If the tender offer provides minority shareholders a fully informed, voluntary choice, the Delaware courts have refused to impose any right "to receive a particular price." See *Solomon v. Pathe Communications Corp.*, 672 A.2d 35 (Del. 1996) (rejecting entire fairness review).

Another view is that the same "800-pound gorilla's retributive capabilities" that justify heightened judicial review in squeeze-out mergers, even when approved by a majority of the minority, argue for "some equitable reinforcement" in parent tender offers. According to the Delaware Chancery Court, for a parent tender offer not to be coercive, the offer must (1) be subject to a "majority of minority" tender condition, (2) include a promise to engage in a prompt back-end merger at the same price as the tender offer, and (3) not involve retributive threats. See *In re Pure Resources, Inc. Shareholders Litigation*, 808 A.2d 421 (Del. Ch. 2002) (imposing conditions to minimize distorting influence of tendering process on voluntary choice).

Examples

EXAMPLES

1. Yankee Holdings is a diversified conglomerate. One of its wholly owned subsidiaries, Yankee Air, operates a passenger and cargo airline with its main hub in Appleton. Holdings also owns Yankee Shipping, a commercial shipper in the United States and abroad. Under a contract with Yankee Shipping, Yankee Air provides air transportation services at rates significantly below those available from other airlines. All companies are incorporated in an MBCA jurisdiction.
   a. Most of Yankee Air's directors are officers of Holdings. Is the shipping contract subject to challenge?
   b. Yankee Air becomes insolvent because of the burdensome contract with Shipping. Can Yankee Air's creditors hold Holdings liable on a self-dealing theory?

2. To finance its expansion into new markets, Yankee Holdings issues common stock to public investors. After the public offering, public shareholders hold 20 percent of Yankee Air's outstanding stock. In its expansion, Yankee Air acquires new aircraft under long-term leases with Holdings. Under the arrangement, Holdings owns the aircraft and charges Yankee Air above-market rates for leasing them. Despite this financial burden, Yankee Air becomes highly profitable and issues a large stock dividend because Holdings needs cash.
   a. The Yankee Air board, composed mostly of Holdings' officers, remains unchanged after the public offering. Is the leasing arrangement subject to challenge?

b. The dividend is legally permissible, but weakens Yankee Air's ability to expand further. Is the dividend subject to challenge?

3. Holdings abandons its captive-lease strategy and allows Yankee Air to acquire aircraft from other companies. Yankee Air purchases aircraft and earns investment tax credits (ITCs) when it makes the purchases. (ITCs entitle their holder to reduce corporate income tax by the amount of the credit.) Holdings and Yankee Air agree to continue filing a consolidated tax return, which allows a parent corporation to include the income, deductions, and credits of any 80 percent subsidiary in a single consolidated return. Holdings files a consolidated return, and Yankee Air's ITCs reduce Holdings' total tax liability by $10 million. Yankee Air did not have any taxable income itself and, under the tax law, could not have used the ITCs.
   a. Under Delaware's approach to parent-subsidiary business dealings, must Holdings share this tax savings with Yankee Air?
   b. Under the judicial "equal treatment" approach, must Holdings share with the subsidiary shareholders the value of its tax savings?
   c. Under the MBCA's liability provisions, are the Yankee Air directors liable for approving a one-sided arrangement with Holdings?
   d. Yankee Air's prospectus had told investors that Holdings would continue to file a consolidated tax return after the public offering and that Holdings might use ITCs generated by Yankee Air in its consolidated return. Does this make any difference in deciding whether Holdings must share?

4. Francis, an outside director of Yankee Air, learns that Lone Star Airways is planning to sell its once profitable air routes at bargain prices. She suggests to Charles, the Holdings CEO, that the Yankee group buy the Lone Star routes. Charles agrees, confident the new routes will be highly profitable for Yankee Air. Holdings proposes a merger with Yankee Air in which minority shareholders will receive $50 per share, a 30 percent premium over market. Frances is the only Yankee Air director who knows the squeezeout will allow Holdings to profit fully once Yankee Air acquires the Lone Star routes. Which of the following insulates the merger from review in a challenge by a minority shareholder?
   a. Holdings does not disclose its interest in the Lone Star routes to the Yankee Air board or shareholders.
   b. The Yankee Air board forms a committee of outside directors (not including Frances) to consider the merger. The committee in turn hires its own outside lawyer and investment banker to advise it.
   c. The committee asks First Lynch Securities to opine whether $50 is a fair price for Yankee Air's shares, based on *current* earnings projections using a discounted cash flow analysis.

d. The committee concludes it will be easier for a combined Holdings–Yankee Air entity to attract financing than the current partially owned structure. The committee recommends the merger as proposed.
e. The Yankee Air board conditions the merger on the approval of a majority of the minority shares, though without disclosing the possibility that Yankee Air might buy the Lone Star routes.

5. Holdings and Yankee Air take all these actions, and the Yankee Air shareholders approve the merger. Mildred, a minority Yankee Air shareholder, sues on behalf of Yankee Air shareholders who voted for the merger and received the $50 merger price. (Many shareholders who did not vote for the merger have sought appraisal.)
   a. Who should be the defendants?
   b. What must the defendants show to withstand this challenge?
   c. Mildred seeks to have the merger rescinded. Is the court likely to rescind?
   d. Mildred claims the $50 merger price was unfair. She says that Yankee Air is today worth at least $65 per share after its acquisition of the Lone Star routes. Is the court likely to award $15 in damages? On what theory?

Explanations

EXPLANATIONS

1. a. No. Who is hurt and who would attack it? Yankee Air has no minority shareholders, and its board is controlled by its parent, Holdings. Although the shipping contract is self-dealing by Holdings and by the Yankee Air directors, it is not subject to fairness review. One of the benefits of complete ownership is the flexibility for the parent to choose profit centers—in this case Yankee Shipping.
   b. Perhaps. Under a theory that fiduciaries' duties to the corporation encompass duties to creditors that may be asserted on corporate insolvency, the creditors (or their representative) could claim a breach of Holdings' duty of loyalty to Yankee Air. In effect, the claim would be that Holdings was enriching itself at creditor expense through self-dealing. Whether the self-dealing was unfair may turn on whether Holdings disclosed to creditors its arrangements with Yankee Air (see §13.3.4). If the self-dealing was undisclosed to creditors, Holdings might also be held liable on a "piercing the corporate veil" theory (see §13.2.8).

2. a. Yes. Minority shareholders of Yankee Air could bring a derivative suit challenging the arrangement as a breach of Holdings' fiduciary duty to Yankee Air and its minority shareholders. See *Sinclair Oil Co. v. Levien*, 280 A.2d 717 (Del. 1971). The leasing arrangement is substantively unfair by being above market prices.

The arrangement is also nominally a "director's conflicting interest transaction" because of the interlocking position of some Yankee Air directors as officers of Holdings. See MBCA §8.60(1)(ii) (transaction brought before the board and director is employee of other party). Nonetheless, the MBCA safe harbor provisions are not meant to apply to this parent-subsidiary transaction. See Note on Parent Companies and Subsidiaries, MBCA §8.60 ("better approach" to deal with parent-subsidiary transactions under rubric of duties of controlling shareholder). As in Delaware, the MBCA focus is on the parent corporation's role in recognition that the subsidiary directors are unlikely to exercise meaningful independent judgment.

b. It depends. On its face, the declaration of dividends did not prefer Holdings since minority shareholders also received their pro rata share. Nonetheless, the parent may have put its cash needs ahead of the subsidiary's expansion potential. Were the dividends a parental preference or a business decision protected by the business judgment rule? The MBCA standards of liability for directors address this question by imposing liability on directors for a "lack of objectivity" due to the domination or control of an interested person. MBCA §8.31 (adopted 1997). The focus would be on whether the subsidiary directors' position as Holdings officers could reasonably be expected to affect their judgment and whether they can establish nonetheless that they reasonably believed the dividend was in the best interest of the subsidiary. That is, the MBCA's liability provisions look to director independence.

The prevailing judicial approach, reflected in Delaware cases, focuses on whether the parent was motivated to prefer itself at the expense of minority shareholders. In our example this would be a difficult showing since the minority shareholders shared pro rata, and any injury to the subsidiary's business was borne more heavily by Holdings than by minority shareholders. If the transaction were characterized as a preference, Holdings would have the burden to show a compelling business purpose for having the subsidiary declare the high dividends. This may be difficult because there are suggestions Yankee Air would have been better off with access to the internally generated capital. In the end, under the prevailing judicial approach, the minority faces a difficult burden to show the dividends preferred the parent.

3. a. Probably not. Holdings did not prefer itself to the detriment of minority shareholders, it could be argued, since the ITCs in Yankee Air's hands were of little or no value—Yankee Air did not have enough taxable income to have used them. Tested under the business judgment rule, the ITC-sharing by Yankee Air passes muster if the subsidiary received some

consideration for the ITCs. (The ITCs have some value since they could conceivably be used in the future under IRS carryforward rules—which allow credits that are unusable in one year to be used in future years when there exists taxable income—or if Yankee Air were sold to a company able to use the ITCs.) The calculation of a present value for this future, speculative value would be left to the discretion of the Yankee Air board. The prevailing judicial approach allows a parent corporation to exploit its control. But see *Case v. New York Central R. Co.*, 256 N.Y.S.2d 607 (N.Y. 1965) (requiring parent of partially owned subsidiary to share tax benefits realized through filing consolidated tax return).

b. Probably. Under the "equal treatment" analysis of *Ahmanson*, the court strictly protects the minority shareholders' interests and prevents the controlling shareholder from using its control to prefer itself. (There is some question whether *Ahmanson* applies to parent-subsidiary dealings not involving discrepant treatment of the minority's shares.) Under this approach, a court would require a showing of a "compelling business reason" for Yankee Air to give up the ITCs without receiving their value to Holdings. Unless the uncompensated sharing were shown to be necessary to Yankee Air—for instance, to keep Holdings as a source of future below-market financing—the court probably would require that Holdings pay the full value of the ITCs. This approach attaches little value to Holdings' control position or the prerogatives that come from control. In fact, rather than treat the subsidiary as an outside party in which negotiation would presumably lead to some sharing of the ITCs' value, the parent could be obligated to prefer the subsidiary.

c. Perhaps. The MBCA's new director liability provisions change the focus from the parent to the subsidiary's board. See MBCA §8.31(a)(2)(3) ("lack of objectivity" of controlled director). Although this new liability standard does not explicitly refer to parent-subsidiary dealings, it does contemplate that a director's employment by a related person triggers increased review. See Official Comment, MBCA §8.31(a). If shown to be nonindependent, the director must establish his reasonable belief in the transaction's *fairness to the corporation*. The giving to another of tax advantages, without negotiating some sharing of their value, would seem not to be an arm's-length transaction. This conclusion holds particularly for directors with special expertise. See *In re Emerging Communications, Inc. Shareholders Litigation*, 2004 WL 1305745 (Del. Ch. 2004) (see §17.3.4).

d. Yes. Under each approach, the disclosure of the ITC-sharing policy and the shareholders' awareness (or at least the pricing of their shares to reflect it) undermines any claim of unfairness to the minority. The knowing purchase (and pricing) of Yankee Air shares, both in the offering and in the trading market, arguably has the effect of implicit consent. Arguably, the policy is not even subject to waste review.

4. a. Does not insulate. In general, the parent need not disclose its motives and purposes. The management of the parent corporation has fiduciary duties to the parent's shareholders to achieve a favorable transaction.

   Nondisclosure in this case, however, creates two problems. First, Holdings will be responsible for any procedural unfairness on the Yankee Air board, including if Frances knows of the parent's interest in the Lone Star routes and fails to disclose this to the Yankee Air board and shareholders. *Weinberger*. Second, the parent cannot use control to prefer itself. Although it is unclear whether the Lone Star routes are corporate opportunities of Yankee Air, their possibility seems to be behind Holdings' desire to consolidate control. Holdings should be prepared to disclose this interest and pay for the potential value it creates for Yankee Air.

   b. Helps insulate. If Yankee Air's minority shareholders are represented by a board committee composed of outside and independent directors, a court might review the merger as an arm's-length transaction. See *Weinberger*. Not only should the committee members be outside directors — neither executives of Yankee Air nor directors or executives of Holdings — they should also be independent. Cases since *Weinberger* make clear that committee members should not have any current or past financial relationships with the controlling shareholder that would compromise their independence. *Kahn v. Tremont Corp.*, 694 A.2d 422 (Del. 1997) (finding lack of independence of committee members who had served as paid consultants to affiliates of controlling shareholder).

   Once properly composed, the committee should hire outside counsel and an investment banker, neither of whom should have any preexisting relationship with Holdings or Yankee Air. See *Kahn v. Tremont Corp.* (criticizing committee choice of lawyer recommended by inside counsel and investment advisor that had earned significant fees advising affiliates of controlling shareholder). The outside directors should be unhurried and fully inform themselves about, among other things, options for Yankee Air in the future — including adding new routes.

   A properly composed and advised committee, while assuring protection of minority shareholders' interests, may also benefit Holdings. The independent committee structure allows Holdings' management to negotiate aggressively, consistent with management's duties to the Holdings shareholders. Cf. *Kahn v. Lynch Communications Systems, Inc.*, 638 A.2d 1110 (Del. 1994) (criticizing controlling shareholder's threat of hostile tender offer).

   c. Might help insulate. The opinion gives the committee objective information on fair value. The discounted cash flow method provides a valuation of a company's cash-generating worth. It anticipates a future earnings stream and calculates how much cash today would be necessary (making some assumptions about future interest rates) to generate that same stream. The Delaware courts now accept this as a legitimate, though not exclusive, means of valuing a company.

Nonetheless, the opinion may not be as valuable if it does not include the future potential value of new air routes. The investment banker's failure to consider this potential future cash flow would undermine the reliability of the opinion.

d. Not help insulate. The committee should be considering the fairness to minority shareholders. It is not acting for Holdings. Whatever Holdings' business purposes, the committee must act as an arm's-length negotiator on behalf of Yankee Air's minority shareholders.

e. Not help insulate. In general, conditioning the merger on approval by a majority of the minority shareholders—that is, more than 50 percent of the public shareholders (20 percent)—bolsters the validity of the self-dealing transaction, *if the shareholders are fully informed*. See *Lynch I* (informed shareholder approval shifts burden to challenger to show transaction was not entirely fair). In this case, the failure to disclose the potential value to Yankee Air of possible new routes undermines the value of minority approval. Although Holdings need not discuss all its plans, it must describe plans that would have a material effect on price and that are known to the subsidiary's board. Holdings' interest in the squeeze-out suggests the possibility of obtaining the Lone Star routes is of actual importance to it. Frances's knowledge of the possibility compels her and the Yankee Air board to disclose this material information to the minority shareholders.

5. a. Holdings, as controlling shareholder, and the directors of Yankee Air. Until recently, the cases have placed principal responsibility with the controlling shareholder to ensure entire fairness to the minority shareholders. Although the corporation's board has significant responsibilities in protecting minority interests, liability has typically been assessed against only the parent. This may, however, be changing—particularly in view of the "good faith" analysis that forbids outside directors from "intentionally disregarding" minority interests. See *In re Emerging Communications, Inc. Shareholders Litigation*, 2004 WL 1305745 (Del. Ch. 2004) (§17.3.4).

b. The MBCA is unclear. A squeeze-out merger is a conflict-of-interest transaction in which minority shareholders are treated differently from the controlling shareholder. The minority receives the consideration (cash or other securities) specified in the merger agreement, and the controlling shareholder retains its equity ownership or acquires the subsidiary as a new division. The MBCA does not specify what standard applies to parent-subsidiary mergers. See Note on Parent Companies and Subsidiaries, MBCA §8.60(1) (stating that safe harbor provisions for director's conflicting interest transactions have "no relevance" to parent-subsidiary transactions).

Nonetheless, most courts permit such transactions provided they are fair to the minority. Under an entire fairness standard, the defendants would have to show both the price and the dealings were fair. This would be difficult if Frances failed to disclose her knowledge of Holdings' plans to acquire the Lone Star routes. Nondisclosure would affect price fairness and taint any negotiations if Frances withheld this information from Yankee Air.

c. No. Undoing the transaction would force shareholders to repurchase their shares at the merger price. The court would also have to rescind any postmerger transactions between Holdings and Yankee Air, and perhaps with third parties. Courts generally view postmerger rescission as unworkable.

d. Perhaps — on a disclosure theory. The MBCA states that appraisal is exclusive unless the merger was unlawful or fraudulent. MBCA §13.02 (see §37.3). If the court invalidates the merger as fraudulent, the usual remedy is rescissory damages — that is, what the shares would be worth if the merger had not happened. See *Weinberger*. This permits shareholders to recover the difference between the postmerger value of the company and the $50 merger price. In this case, if the shares are worth $65 because of postmerger events, whose possibility was improperly concealed in the merger, rescissory damages would be $15.

CHAPTER 18

Shareholder Litigation

Two litigation techniques are available to shareholders to vindicate their interests in the corporation. Shareholders can sue in their own capacity to enforce their rights as shareholders (a direct action, usually brought as a class action), or they can sue on behalf of the corporation to enforce corporate rights that affect them only indirectly (a derivative action). How one characterizes the suit affects a number of things: who pays for litigation expenses, who recovers, what procedures apply to the shareholder-plaintiff, and whether the suit can be dismissed by the corporation. Derivative litigation is the principal means by which shareholders enforce fiduciary duties.

This chapter describes the nature of a derivative suit (§18.1) and how it is distinguished from a direct suit (§18.2), the derivative-suit procedures applicable in state court (§18.3) and the special procedures in federal court (§18.4), and the dismissal of derivative suits, by the board or by a special board committee (§18.5).

§18.1 NATURE OF DERIVATIVE LITIGATION

The derivative suit is nineteenth-century equity jurisdiction's ingenious solution to the dilemma created by two inconsistent tenets of corporate law: (1) corporate fiduciaries owe their duties to the corporation as a whole, not individual shareholders, and (2) the board of directors manages the corporation's business, which includes authorizing lawsuits in the corporate name.

Derivative litigation breaks the stranglehold the board would otherwise have over fiduciary accountability.

In a derivative suit, a shareholder sues *on behalf of the corporation*. Without this procedure, management's fiduciary duties to the corporation would be virtually meaningless if the board's power extended to all litigation decisions. It would be the rare case that managers would choose to sue themselves.

Note on Derivative Litigation in LLCs

Derivative suits are also authorized in LLCs for members who want to vindicate the rights of the LLC, particularly based on claims that managers or other members have breached their fiduciary duties. See ULLCA §1101 (provided "members or managers having authority to do so have refused to commence the action"). Even when the LLC statute is silent, courts have permitted LLC members to bring derivative litigation on behalf of the LLC. See *Tzolis v. Wolff*, 884 N.E.2d 1005 (N.Y. 2008).

§18.1.1 Two Suits in One

In a derivative suit, shareholders sue on behalf of the corporation to enforce rights of the corporation. It is in effect two suits in one. In theory, the shareholder (1) sues the corporation in equity (2) to bring an action to enforce corporate rights, such as when there is a breach of fiduciary duties by corporate officials. Although the modern derivative suit is treated as one action, the historical notion of two suits survives. The corporation, an indispensable party, is made a nominal defendant. The corporation—that is, the board of directors and management—can compel the derivative suit plaintiff to comply with various procedural requirements (see §18.3 below).

The "two suits in one" notion spawns some procedural effects. For example, federal jury trial rights arise if they would have existed in a suit by the corporation, generally when the suit seeks damages. *Ross v. Bernhard*, 396 U.S. 531 (1970). (Many states have different jury trial systems; in Delaware, for example, the chancery court hears all corporate law actions, whether direct or derivative, without a jury.) In addition, the court must have personal jurisdiction over the individual defendants. See *Shaffer v. Heitner*, 433 U.S. 186 (1977) (holding *quasi in rem* action based on sequestration of defendant directors' shares in Delaware corporation insufficient to create personal jurisdiction). Many states, including Delaware, now have statutes that treat acceptance of a directorship as consent to jurisdiction in the state. See *Armstrong v. Pomerance*, 423 A.2d 174 (Del. 1980) (applying 10 Del. Code Ann. §3114).

One consequence of the "two suits in one" notion is that the corporation—in the articles of incorporation—can choose the forum in which derivative litigation must be brought on its behalf. See *In re Revlon, Inc.*

Shareholders Litigation, 990 A.2d 940 (Del. Ch. 2010) (holding that corporate charter can include forum-selection provision specifying exclusive forum for intracorporate disputes).

§18.1.2 All Recovery to Corporation

Derivative litigation enforces corporate rights. This means any recovery in derivative litigation generally runs to the corporation. The shareholder-plaintiff shares in the recovery only indirectly, to the extent her shares increase in value because of the corporate recovery. The shareholder-plaintiff also benefits indirectly by the deterrent value of an award or when equitable relief forbids or undoes harmful behavior.

Sometimes corporate liability is empty because the corporation is no longer in existence or because it would produce a windfall for new owners. Courts in these circumstances have allowed injured shareholders to recover directly in proportion to their holdings. See *Perlman v. Feldmann*, 219 F.2d 173 (2d Cir. 1955) (see §20.2.3); *Donahue v. Rodd Electrotype Co.*, 328 N.E.2d 505 (Mass. 1975) (see §27.2.2). The ALI Principles of Corporate Governance suggest that when derivative litigation involves a close corporation a court may exercise its discretion to allow direct shareholder recovery, provided the corporation is not exposed unfairly to multiple claims, creditors are not materially prejudiced, and the recovery can be fairly distributed. ALI Principles §7.01(d).

§18.1.3 Reimbursement of Successful Plaintiff's Expenses

Why would a shareholder, particularly a shareholder in a public corporation, undertake the effort and expense of a derivative suit? The answer is simple and troubling: the corporation reimburses the attorney fees of the successful plaintiff. Contrary to the prevailing American rule that each litigant bears his own litigation expenses, the universal rule in derivative litigation is that the court will order the corporation to pay the successful plaintiff's litigation expenses, including attorney fees. See MBCA §7.46(1) ("if . . . the proceeding has resulted in a substantial benefit to the corporation"). The theory is that the successful plaintiff (and her attorney) have produced a benefit to the corporation, and thus they should be reimbursed for their effort.

Effect of Rule

The engine driving the derivative suit in public corporations is the plaintiff's attorney—a "bounty hunter" for the corporation whose fees are contingent on an award by the court or in a settlement. Notice how the attorney is the real plaintiff in interest: The attorney often brings the possibility of a lawsuit to the shareholder-plaintiff's attention; the attorney usually runs the litigation; the attorney typically has the greatest stake in the outcome; and the attorney decides on when and whether to settle the litigation, often depending on the level of attorney fees provided in the settlement offer.

Corporate law deals with this alarming reversal of the client-attorney roles by regulating the bringing and settlement of derivative litigation (see §18.3.4 below).

Method of Fee Calculation

Attorney fees in derivative litigation generally have been calculated using either a *percentage-of-recovery* or a *lodestar* method. Under the percentage-of-recovery method, the attorney receives a percentage of the corporation's recovery, varying between 15 and 35 percent depending on the size of the recovery. Under the lodestar method, fees are based on the number of hours spent on the suit multiplied by the prevailing rate for similar legal work by an attorney of comparable experience and stature; this amount then may be adjusted upward or downward depending on the quality of work, the novelty of the issues, and the original likelihood of success. The lodestar method, unlike the increasingly used percentage-of-recovery method, creates an incentive for protracted litigation and discourages reasonable, prompt settlement.

§18.1.4 Derivative Suit Plaintiff— Self-Appointed Representative

In a derivative suit, the plaintiff-shareholder (with her attorney) chooses herself as a representative for the corporation. The possibility that the plaintiff will conduct the litigation for her own gain without serving the interests of the corporation or the shareholders as a group is evident. A shareholder (and her attorney) may bring a derivative suit solely as a nuisance to extract a settlement that primarily benefits themselves. For this reason, courts and statutes impose on the derivative suit plaintiffs a duty to be a faithful representative of the corporation's and the other shareholders' interests. See Fed. R. Civ. P. 23.1 (shareholder-plaintiff must "fairly and adequately represent the interests of the shareholders or members substantially similarly situated in enforcing the right of the corporation").

Shareholders are not the only parties who can bring a derivative suit. Creditors can bring derivative suits to enforce their claims against an insolvent corporation. *North American Catholic Educational Programming Foundation, Inc. v. Gheewalla*, 930 A.2d 92 (Del. 2007) (concluding that creditors cannot assert direct claim against insolvent corporation, but may assert derivative claims).

In addition, some statutes permit an officer or director to bring a derivative action. See N.Y. Bus. Corp. Law §720(b). But absent express statutory authorization, directors and officers lack standing to sue derivatively in their capacity as a director or officer. See *Schoon v. Smith*, 953 A.2d 196 (Del. 2008).

§18.1.5 Res Judicata—Preclusion of "Corporate" Relitigation

Because in a derivative suit the shareholder-plaintiff sues on behalf of the corporation, the corporation becomes bound by any judgment or settlement. This means neither the corporation nor a subsequent derivative suit plaintiff can bring a suit based on claims that were raised in the derivative suit. By the same token, if the corporation itself has already litigated or settled in court a claim in good faith, res judicata prevents a shareholder from bringing a derivative suit making the same claim. Given this preclusive effect, shareholders who were not parties in a derivative suit may have a right to appeal any settlement, even though they did not intervene and object in the trial court. See *Devlin v. Scardelletti*, 536 U.S. 1 (2002) (federal class action).

The res judicata effect of a settlement of shareholder claims can reach beyond the claims before the court. For example, the U.S. Supreme Court has held that a settlement of a class action approved by a Delaware court could preclude ongoing federal claims involving the same corporation brought in a federal court in California. *Matushita Elec. Indus. Co. v. Epstein*, 516 U.S. 367 (1996). In the case, the Delaware court approved a $2 million settlement that released all claims involving a tender offer in which the bidder had entered into side agreements to acquire shares of the target's officers. The Supreme Court held that if the Delaware court's approval of the settlement satisfied due process (particularly, adequacy of representation), the settlement could preclude federal claims (potentially worth $2 billion) even though the Delaware court could not have acquired jurisdiction over them.

§18.1.6 Time Limitation

Derivative claims typically involve claims of fiduciary breach. What is the applicable statute of limitations for such claims? Some courts view fiduciary breaches as sounding in tort and apply the relatively short two- or three-year limitations period applicable to tort actions. *Demoulas v. Demoulas Super Mkts.*, 677 N.E.2d 159 (Mass. 1997) (diversion of corporate opportunities and self-dealing). Other courts view the shareholder-corporation relationship as contractual and subject corporate fiduciary claims to the typically six-year statute of limitations applicable to contract claims. *Hanson v. Kake Tribal Corp.*, 939 P.2d 1320 (Alaska 1997) (discriminatory dividends).

In some states, claims of fiduciary breach are subject to specific statutes of limitations. See *Park City Mines Co. v. Greater Park City Co.*, 870 P.2d 880 (Utah 1993) (applying Utah statute that requires claims asserting liability against director or shareholder to be brought within three years). In Delaware, a three-year statute of limitations applies to damages actions arising from "an injury unaccompanied with force or resulting indirectly from the act of the defendant." Del. Code Ann. tit. 10, §8106. Delaware courts have interpreted the statute to apply to derivative actions seeking damages and to be tolled "until such time as a reasonably diligent and attentive stockholder knew or had reason to know of the facts alleged to constitute the wrong." *Kahn v. Seaboard Corp.*, 625 A.2d 269 (Del. Ch. 1993) (self-dealing). In derivative actions seeking equitable relief (such as a constructive trust or rescission of proxies), the Delaware courts have looked to the statutory period as "a presumptive time period for application of laches to bar a claim." *U.S. Cellular v. Bell Atlantic Mobile Systems, Inc.*, 677 A.2d 497 (Del. 1996).

§18.2 DISTINGUISHING BETWEEN DERIVATIVE, DIRECT, AND CLASS ACTION SUITS

A shareholder may also sue in her personal capacity to enforce her rights as a shareholder—a direct action. Unlike a derivative suit, a direct action is not brought on behalf of the corporation. To avoid the host of procedural requirements that apply to derivative suits, shareholders will often seek to characterize their suit as direct. For example, if state law requires a demand on the board (see §18.3.3 below), the characterization of the suit as derivative or direct may practically decide its viability.

§18.2.1 Examples of Direct Suits

In many cases, the characterization is straightforward. Direct suits are those in which shareholders seek to enforce rights arising from their share ownership, as opposed to rights of the corporation. Direct suits include suits to

- enjoin ultra vires actions (see §3.3.3)
- compel payment of dividends declared but not distributed (see §4.1.3)
- compel inspection of shareholders' lists, or corporate books and records (see §7.1.4)

- require the holding of a shareholders' meeting, whether the board has violated statutory or fiduciary duties (see §7.2.1)
- challenge fraud on shareholders in connection with their voting, sale, or purchase of securities (see §§10.3, 21.1, 22.5)
- challenge the sale of the corporation in a merger where directors violated their duties to become informed or structure a transaction that was entirely fair (see §§12.3.3, 17.3)
- challenge corporate restrictions on share transferability (see §26.6)
- compel dissolution of the corporation, such as for deadlock or oppression of minority shareholders (see §27.2.1)
- challenge the denial or dilution of voting rights, such as when substantially all the corporation's assets are sold without shareholder approval (see §36.3)

As you notice, direct suits generally vindicate individual shareholders' structural, financial, liquidity, and voting rights. See *Grimes v. Donald*, 673 A.2d 1207 (Del. 1996) (direct action when shareholder claimed directors abdicated statutory control to CEO under terms of employment agreement). Derivative suits, on the other hand, generally enforce fiduciary duties of directors, officers, or controlling shareholders—duties owed to the corporation. A suit claiming that fiduciary wrongdoing caused a loss in share value is usually derivative. For example, suits that ask directors to account for profits from a usurped corporate opportunity or that challenge executive compensation as corporate waste are derivative suits.

Under the *Grimes* approach, courts make the direct-derivative distinction by focusing on who was injured and who will receive the relief. *Tooley v. Donaldson, Lufkin, & Jenrette, Inc.*, 845 A.2d 1031 (Del. 2004) (characterizing a merger-delay claim as direct because delay of merger only harmed shareholders, not corporation, though dismissing direct claim on ground not yet ripe). In a direct suit, because damages are paid to shareholders and not the corporation, attorney fees are paid from the shareholders' recovery or in a class action from the common fund.

§18.2.2 Claims with Direct and Derivative Attributes

Some shareholder suits are difficult to characterize. For example, while most courts have characterized a suit to compel the payment of dividends as direct, some have characterized the suit as derivative. See *Cowin v. Bresler*, 741 F.2d 410 (D.C. Cir. 1984) (direct); *Gordon v. Elliman*, 119 N.E.2d 331 (N.Y. 1954) (derivative).

Sometimes, the facts suggest both a direct and a derivative claim. In such a case, the shareholder's pleading choice governs. For example, a wrongful refusal by management to provide a shareholders' list to a shareholder for a proxy fight may not only violate the shareholder's rights to inspection, but also management's duties of loyalty to the corporation. The shareholder may bring the claim as either a direct action to enforce inspection rights or as a derivative action to enjoin management's entrenchment, or both. See ALI Principles §7.01(c).

The shareholder's characterization of the suit, however, is not always controlling. A shareholder cannot escape the procedural restrictions of a derivative suit simply by claiming she was directly injured when the value of her shares fell as a result of a breach of a duty to the corporation. *Armstrong v. Frostie Co.*, 453 F.2d 914 (4th Cir. 1971).

But careful pleading can help. If a shareholder can characterize a transaction as diluting voting power, for example, even though the transaction may also be a fiduciary breach, the suit is direct. In *Eisenberg v. Flying Tiger Line, Inc.*, 451 F.2d 267 (2d Cir. 1971), a shareholder challenged a corporate reorganization in which shareholders of an operating company became, after a merger, shareholders of a holding company. The corporation sought to require the plaintiff to post security for expenses, a derivative suit requirement (see §18.3.2 below). The court, however, held that the action was direct because the reorganization deprived the shareholder of "any voice in the affairs of their previously existing operating company."

§18.2.3 Close Corporation Exception

Lately many courts permit participants in a close corporation to sidestep the derivative suit procedures and bring direct actions to vindicate their corporate rights, including claims of fiduciary breaches. See *Crosby v. Beam*, 548 N.E.2d 217 (Ohio 1989). On the theory that close corporation participants owe duties to each other similar to those of partners in a partnership, close corporation shareholder/managers can sue each other directly. See ALI Principles §7.01(d). In a close corporation, compared to a public corporation, there is less risk of multiplicity of suits, preferential recovery, or strike suits brought to coerce a settlement.

One effect of the exception is that recovery in a close corporation suit is to individual shareholder/managers, not the corporation. Direct recovery may disadvantage the corporation's third-party creditors, whose interests in the corporation's financial viability are unprotected when a fiduciary breach leads to direct recovery only by shareholder/managers. The ALI Principles address this potential problem by giving the court discretion to treat an action raising derivative claims as a direct action if to do so "will not materially prejudice the interest of creditors of the corporation." ALI Principles §7.01(d).

Another effect of the exception is that the complaining shareholder/manager need not make a pre-suit demand on the board (requirement that shareholder in a derivative suit first seek to have the board vindicate the corporate interests, see §18.3.3 below). This reflects the futility of demand in a typical suit involving close corporation participants. For example, when a minority shareholder challenges the majority's oppression or exclusion, a demand on the majority-controlled board would accomplish little except to delay judicial resolution. See *Barth v. Barth*, 659 N.E.2d 559 (Ind. 1995) (noting that direct action prevents dismissal by special committee).

§18.2.4 Class Actions — Direct Suits Brought by Representative

When a shareholder sues in his own capacity, as well as on behalf of other shareholders similarly situated, the suit is not a derivative action but a class action. In effect, all of the members of the class have banded together through a representative to bring their *individual direct actions* in one large direct action. Some of the most important suits enforcing fiduciary duties have been brought as direct class actions. See *Weinberger v. UOP, Inc.*, 457 A.2d 701 (Del. 1983) (class action challenging director actions and disclosure in squeeze-out merger); *Smith v. Van Gorkom*, 488 A.2d 858 (Del. 1985) (class action challenging director actions and disclosure in third-party merger).

Some procedural rules applicable to class actions — such as that the class action plaintiff be representative of the other shareholders' interests and that any settlement be approved by the court — also apply in derivative suits. See Fed. R. Civ. P. 23. They assure that shareholders are well represented and that the judicial process is not abused by nuisance plaintiffs.

A class action, however, does not interfere with the prerogatives of central corporate governance, and many requirements that apply to derivative suits do not apply to class actions. For example, in a class action the plaintiff need not make a demand on the board of directors before bringing suit (see §18.3.3 below). Class actions, however, have their own procedural hoops, such as that plaintiff-representatives bear the expense of providing notice to members of the class.

Examples

EXAMPLES

1. Ten years ago, Consolidated Engines acquired Digital Engineering in a merger. H. Russell Thoreau, Digital's principal shareholder, received 2 percent of Consolidated's common stock, and he was informally assured a seat on Consolidated's board for as long as he held the stock. Last year, Thoreau and Consolidated's chairman had a falling out. The board approved a repurchase of Thoreau's ten million shares for $90 a share,

at a time when the stock was trading on the NYSE at $80—a $100 million premium to Thoreau. Consolidated Engines' finances were seriously jeopardized by the purchase.

a. Abe Pomerantz, a corporate attorney with broad experience representing shareholders, brought the repurchase to the attention of Pam Walden, a long-time shareholder of Consolidated. Under what procedure can Walden seek to have the repurchase rescinded?
b. Walden (through her lawyer Pomerantz) sues to hold the directors liable for improvidently approving the repurchase of Thoreau's stock. Walden owns exactly $2,000 (.000004 percent) of Consolidated's stock. How much can she hope to recover?
c. Consolidated's directors offer to settle Walden's derivative suit by promising not to repurchase shares from other major shareholders without shareholder approval. The corporation, however, will recover nothing in cash. Can Pomerantz expect any fees?

2 Settlement negotiations fail and Walden's suit proceeds. Thoreau offers to repay 10 percent of the premium he received from Consolidated. The Consolidated board seizes the opportunity: It authorizes a suit against Thoreau, who then settles under the terms of his offer. The settlement is approved by the court.

a. Can Walden continue her suit?
b. Is there another course open to Walden?
c. When Pomerantz hears of Consolidated's settlement, he is outraged. He has spent a significant amount of time preparing Walden's derivative suit for trial. Can Pomerantz seek attorney fees?

3 Consolidated's senior executives propose a management buyout (see §34.2). Under the terms of the buyout merger, Walden and all other shareholders would receive $80 for their shares.

a. Walden thinks $80 is inadequate. The proxy materials seeking shareholder approval of the going-private transaction fail to disclose that Consolidated's board considered the company was worth at least $100 per share. Walden wants to enjoin the merger. What kind of suit would you advise?
b. Walden brings both direct and derivative claims. The board agrees to settle by amending its proxy materials and paying Walden $500,000 on the condition that she dismiss all her claims. Are there any problems if Walden accepts?
c. The shareholders approve the merger. Walden amends her complaint to claim damages. The court holds the directors liable for gross negligence in approving the merger at $80 per share. What is the appropriate remedy?

Explanations

1. a. Walden can model her suit to be derivative or direct:
   - **Derivative action.** Walden can sue on behalf of the corporation (derivative) alleging that Consolidated's directors breached their fiduciary duties to the corporation. The theory might be that the repurchase wasted corporate assets (see §12.3.2), lacked a reasonable relation to the threat of Thoreau launching a proxy fight or other takeover attempt (see §39.2.3), or constituted self-serving entrenchment (see §39.2.1). The suit would be subject to derivative suit requirements: demand on the board, possible shifting of fees, dismissal by the corporation.
   - **Direct action.** Walden might sue on her own behalf (direct) claiming the repurchases were an illegal distribution under an insolvency or balance sheet test (see §31.2). Otherwise, the transaction did not dilute Walden's voting rights (to the contrary, it concentrated them) or otherwise affect her financial or liquidity rights as a shareholder. Just because the corporation's assets are depleted, the indirect injury to Walden's interest does not allow her to sue in her own capacity.

   b. Nothing. This is a derivative suit because the allegation is that the directors violated their fiduciary duties to the corporation by approving the repurchase of Thoreau's stock and any recovery would go to the corporation. See *Tooley v. Donaldson, Lufkin, & Jenrette, Inc.*, 845 A.2d 1031 (Del. 2004) (§18.2.1). Walden can only hope to increase the value of her shares to the extent corporate recovery increases general share value. There are a few exceptions to this approach. Shareholders can recover directly if the corporation is closely held or no longer in existence, or recovery would not redound to the benefit of contemporaneous shareholders indirectly injured. None of these, however, applies to Consolidated.

   c. Yes. Pomerantz can expect attorney fees either as part of the settlement or as ordered by the court in its approval of the settlement even though the corporation recovered nothing. Studies show that attorneys in settlement of shareholder suits involving public companies receive fees 90 percent of the time even though only 55 percent of the settlements involve monetary recovery.

   Under a lodestar method for computing his fees, Pomerantz's billable hours would be multiplied by a reasonable hourly rate, which because of Pomerantz's stature would likely be at the upper end of the range. This amount then might be adjusted upward given Pomerantz's success in the face of the business judgment rule's teaching that courts normally defer to valuations by the board. The percentage-of-recovery method would not apply.

2. a. Probably not. Walden's derivative suit is brought on behalf of the corporation. If the corporation settles the subject matter of her claim, the corporate settlement is binding (res judicata) on Walden in her suit. The corporate suit resolves any corporate claims involving the Thoreau repurchase. Unless she can show fraud or a fiduciary breach that would justify vacating the judgment, she cannot continue her suit.
   b. A fiduciary challenge. Walden might be able to challenge the directors' decision to enter into the settlement as a breach of their duty of care or loyalty. This derivative claim may be difficult because of the business judgment rule. Unless Walden can show that the board was interested (because of an entrenchment motive) or failed to become informed about the settlement's terms, the board has discretion to make rational litigation decisions.
   c. Perhaps. Pomerantz might argue Walden's suit goaded the Consolidated board to act. In derivative litigation, shareholder-intervenors often recover their expenses and attorney fees if their efforts contributed to the recovery or settlement. Pomerantz could argue that Walden's suit brought the excessiveness of the repurchase price to the board's attention, and the board's out-of-court settlement (like a successful derivative suit settlement) should be seen as resulting from her suit and his efforts.

3. a. Walden can choose between a direct suit, a derivative suit, or a suit with both direct and derivative claims. She has a direct claim under the federal proxy rules and under the state "duty of disclosure" doctrine that the corporation failed to adequately disclose the terms of the merger. Rule 14a-9, Securities Exchange Act of 1934 (see §10.2); *Lynch v. Vickers Energy Corp.*, 429 A.2d 497 (Del. 1981) (see §10.3).

   Walden also has a derivative claim that the board's approval of this self-dealing, going-private merger and its deception about the merger price violate the executives' and the board's fiduciary duties (see §13.3.3). Walden maximizes her leverage by bringing both claims in one suit. If she brings a federal proxy fraud claim, she must sue in federal district court, which has exclusive jurisdiction over these claims. She could bring her state fiduciary claims as pendent claims.
   b. Yes. It is unclear why Consolidated is offering $500,000 to Walden. The payment does not seem to relate to her direct claim because the merger has not been approved and Walden has suffered no loss. Nor can the payment be tied to the derivative suit because any recovery in such a suit is to the corporation. Rather, the payment appears to be a bribe for her to dismiss the derivative claims. Although such a payment is perfectly acceptable in an individual direct action, it is not in a derivative suit. The court is unlikely to approve a settlement of the derivative claim in these circumstances (see §18.3.4 below).

c. Recovery by the shareholders, whether the claim is seen as derivative or direct. If the claim is direct, as was the case in *Smith v. Van Gorkom*, 488 A.2d 858 (Del. 1985) (see §12.3.4), the shareholder class members would recover in proportion to their shareholdings. The claim can be characterized as direct because the directors' approval of the merger led to the conversion of the shareholders' ownership interest to a cash payment right. To the extent the suit challenged the board's disclosure, it would also be direct. If the claim is seen as derivative, the normal rule is that defendant directors (or their insurers) would pay the corporation. In this case, this would result in payment to New Consolidated, the surviving corporation after the merger that acquired all the rights of Consolidated (see §36.2.1). But New Consolidated is controlled by new owners (the management team), and any corporate recovery would not remedy the injury to the body of shareholders who received an inadequate price for their shares. An exception to the rule of corporate recovery in derivative litigation is appropriate. Pro rata recovery by former Consolidated shareholders would produce a correct result.

§18.3 PROCEDURAL RESTRICTIONS ON DERIVATIVE LITIGATION

The derivative suit is an essential tool to enforce management accountability. It is also subject to abuse. To address the risk that the derivative suit plaintiffs may not represent corporate interests, various procedural requirements seek to filter out abusive or spurious derivative litigation.

§18.3.1 Distorted Incentives in Derivative Litigation

Derivative litigation allows self-appointed shareholders to become champions of corporate rights. But the incentives of the derivative suit parties may produce results at odds with corporate interests:

- The plaintiff may be indifferent to the outcome of the litigation. Any recovery will be to the corporation, and the plaintiff's financial interest in the corporation will often be insignificant.
- The plaintiff's attorney, whose fees are usually contingent on a settlement or court award, may be indifferent to the substantive outcome—so long as there are attorney fees.
- The individual defendants (typically directors or officers of the corporation) usually will prefer settlement rather than trial. Settlement

increases the chances their expenses, as well as amounts paid in settlement, will be indemnified by the corporation or covered by insurance (see §§15.1.2, 15.2.1).
- The corporation (the board of directors) often will be influenced by the interests of the individual defendants.

These realities of derivative litigation invite weak-willed and even evil-hearted plaintiffs. Some shareholders may be tempted to bring suit to coerce a settlement based on the suit's nuisance value—the infamous *strike suit*. The history of corporate law is spiced with colorful stories of "strike suit artists" with long and lucrative careers as gadfly plaintiffs. Derivative litigation also creates a potential for well-meaning but faint-hearted plaintiffs, unwilling to pursue a meritorious claim because of the incentives to settle.

Derivative litigation also threatens the integrity of the judicial process. By using the courts to bring vexatious litigation, strike suit plaintiffs waste and abuse judicial resources. Nonetheless, derivative litigation provides the means for enforcing fiduciary duties, and corporate statutes attempt to distinguish between the meritorious claim and the strike suit.

§18.3.2 Litigation Procedural Requirements

A variety of procedural requirements in litigation attempt to weed out strike suits.

Plaintiff's Verification of Complaint

Some statutes require that the plaintiff verify the complaint. See Fed. R. Civ. P. 23.1. The requirement provides a basis for applying sanctions for perjury against those who fabricate charges in a strike suit. It is not necessary, however, that the plaintiff have personal knowledge or comprehend the specific factual allegation in the complaint so long as the plaintiff reasonably relied on her lawyer's investigation and advice. *Surowitz v. Hilton Hotels Corp.*, 383 U.S. 363 (1966).

Equity Shareholder Standing

Most statutes give equity (common and preferred) shareholders standing to bring a derivative suit to protect their residual ownership interests in the corporation against management abuse. Some cases have also allowed holders of stock options or convertible securities and creditors of an insolvent corporation to protect their ownership interests and assert derivative claims. The MBCA limits derivative suit standing to equity shareholders and beneficial owners and excludes option holders and convertible debtholders. MBCA §7.40(2). Some statutes, however, require that the plaintiff be a record (not merely beneficial) owner. See Del. GCL §327.

Dismissal of Multiple Suits

Often multiple shareholder-plaintiffs (and lawyers) will bring more than one derivative suit concerning the same transaction. If each suit makes essentially the same claims, allowing all to proceed would produce a wasteful and potentially confusing overlap. Courts will want to choose which shareholder should be the leading representative. Toward this end, courts have broad discretion to dismiss redundant derivative suits, to consolidate derivative suits brought in the same court, to stay proceedings in one suit to await a board investigation or the outcome in another suit, and to transfer proceedings (in federal cases) to other courts. See ALI Principles §7.06 (stay pending board review or resolution of "related action").

Continuous and Continuing Ownership

Most statutes require the plaintiff to have been a shareholder when the wrong occurred—the *contemporaneous ownership* requirement. MBCA §7.41(1). The requirement is meant to assure that the shareholder did not buy shares to buy a lawsuit. The ALI Principles provide an exception to the requirement when an undisclosed wrong (such as a pattern of waste) was continuing when the plaintiff acquired her shares. See ALI Principles §7.02(a)(1).

A logical extension of the contemporaneous ownership rule is that the corporation itself cannot sue for wrongdoing that occurred before a change in ownership—the *vicarious incapacity* or *corporate incapacity* rule. If ownership changes, the corporation's new owners should not be able to cause the corporation to sue former managers (or shareholders) for wrongs committed before control changed hands. To allow the corporation to recover would produce a windfall for the new owners whose purchase price presumably took into account any losses caused by the earlier wrongs. See *Bangor Punta Operations, Inc. v. Bangor & Aroostook Railroad Co.*, 417 U.S. 703 (1974). The theory does not work as neatly when the recovery would benefit others besides the new owners–such as when the new owners hold less than 100 percent of the stock or when a corporate recovery would benefit creditors. Some jurisdictions, including Delaware, reject the vicarious incapacity rule and allow recovery by the surviving corporation. See *Lewis v. Anderson*, 477 A.2d 1040 (Del. 1983).

Another exception to the contemporaneous ownership rule arises when shareholders of a parent corporation complain about wrongdoing in a subsidiary. See *Brown v. Tenney*, 532 N.W.2d 230 (Ill. 1988) (finding "double derivative action" to be a longstanding doctrine of equity jurisprudence). In effect, a double derivative action permits the parent shareholders to claim that the parent has failed to take action against corporate wrongs occurring in the subsidiary.

In addition to the contemporaneous ownership rule, some statutes require that the plaintiff continue to be a shareholder when suit is brought and then through trial—the *continuing interest* requirement. Cf. MBCA §7.41 (no continuing ownership requirement, but plaintiff must "fairly and adequately" represent corporate interests). The continuing interest requirement tests the genuineness of the plaintiff's intentions. Delaware courts recognize a narrow exception when the plaintiff ceases to be a shareholder after a fraudulent or illegal merger. *Lewis v. Anderson*, 477 A.2d 1040 (Del. 1983). The ALI Principles broaden the exception to allow a plaintiff to continue her derivative action after a merger if the action was pending at the time of the merger or if the plaintiff is best able to vindicate the shareholders' interests. ALI Principles §7.02(a)(2).

Shifting Expenses to Plaintiff

Many statutes provide for shifting the defendants' litigation expenses, including attorney fees, to the plaintiff. This discourages unfounded derivative claims and compensates defendants who must defend strike suits. Under the MBCA, the court may order fee-shifting if the plaintiff commenced or maintained the suit "without reasonable cause or for an improper purpose." MBCA §7.46(2). This standard forces derivative suit plaintiffs to tread cautiously; the normal standard for recouping expenses based on a claim of frivolous prosecution is more demanding and requires a showing of malicious intent or fraud. Cf. MBCA §13.31 (in appraisal proceeding, expenses may be shifted to shareholder-dissenter who acted "arbitrarily, vexatiously, or not in good faith").

A once-common requirement in many states—though now very few—allowed the court to require the plaintiff to post security (pay a bond) for the defendants' litigation expenses as a condition of maintaining the action. The court would act on a motion of the corporation or the defendants. A security-for-expense requirement often had a lethal effect on derivative litigation. The cost of posting security and the risk of having to pay the amount that the bond secured usually outweighed any gain a shareholder-plaintiff might hope for in the suit. Most modern statutes reject this requirement as going too far in limiting fiduciary accountability. See ALI Principles §7.04(c).

Many of the security-for-expense statutes exempted shareholders with a specified percentage of ownership (such as 3 percent or 5 percent) or a minimum dollar amount ($25,000 or $50,000). The exemptions assumed that most strike suits are brought by shareholders with small holdings and presumably little real concern for the corporation's interests. Shareholder-plaintiffs would try to avoid the security-for-expense requirement by bringing direct actions (see §18.2) or actions under federal law, such as Rule 10b-5 (see §9.1).

§18.3.3 Demand Requirement—Exhaustion of Internal Remedies

Many statutes require that the derivative plaintiff's complaint state with particularity her efforts to make a demand on the board to resolve the dispute or the reasons she did not make demand. Del. Ch. Ct. R. 23.1; Fed. R. Civ. P. 23.1. By their terms, these statutes neither require the plaintiff to make a pre-suit demand on the board nor specify the effect that should be given the board's response. Nonetheless, many courts (including Delaware) have interpreted the statutes to make demand mandatory unless demand would be futile (see §18.5.3). The demand-pleading requirement allows the court to ascertain whether the board could have acted on the demand. *Aronson v. Lewis*, 473 A.2d 805 (Del. 1984).

A demand requirement has some advantages. It serves as a kind of alternative dispute mechanism that requires a challenging shareholder to first exhaust intracorporate remedies. If litigation is beneficial, it allows the corporation to control the proceedings.

But demand has a number of untoward effects. A pre-suit demand forewarns defendants of an impending suit, giving them an opportunity to take evasive actions. It delays litigation while the shareholder waits for the board to act on her demand. Making demand might be understood as the challenger's concession that the board is capable of addressing the problem. And if the shareholder brings suit without making demand, the court must resolve whether demand was excused—litigation within litigation.

Many recent statutes explicitly impose a demand requirement in all cases, thus forcing a shareholder contemplating a derivative suit to first make a demand on the board. Under the MBCA, the shareholder must wait for 90 days before filing suit unless the board rejects the demand or the corporation would be irreparably injured by waiting. MBCA §7.42. The demand requirement gives the board (even if the directors would be named defendants) a chance to take corrective action and avoids the difficult question whether demand is excused. See also ALI Principles §7.03(b) (recommending a universal demand requirement unless it would irreparably injure the corporation).

These different approaches do not answer what substantive effect should be given to the board's rejection of a demand or its refusal to bring a suit. Also unanswered is whether the board (or a committee of the board) can act on behalf of the corporation to dismiss the litigation. The demand-pleading requirement is inextricably linked to the question of who can decide the fate of derivative litigation. We discuss these issues and the dismissal of derivative litigation below. See §18.5.

§18.3.4 Court Approval of Settlement—A Clean Solution

The principal danger of derivative litigation is the potential for abusive settlements. Unlike normal litigation in which an arm's-length compromise agreed to by plaintiff and defendant provides the best measure of the suit's worth, derivative litigation provides no such assurance. In a derivative suit *none of the parties* may represent the interests of the corporation-on whose behalf suit is presumably brought.

Most statutes face this problem and require judicial approval before a derivative suit can be settled, discontinued, or dismissed. MBCA §7.45; Fed. R. Civ. P. 23.1. Proponents of the settlement have the burden to show it is fair and reasonable to the corporation. To decide whether to approve the settlement, the court has broad discretion to consider

- the terms of the settlement, including recovery by the corporation (or other relief) and any reimbursement of expenses (including attorney fees) to the shareholder-plaintiff and to the individual defendants
- the outcome that might have resulted from a trial, discounted by the inherent uncertainty of litigation, the costs caused by the delay of trial, additional litigation expenses that the corporation might be required to pay the plaintiff, additional indemnification payments to the defendants if they are successful or if indemnification is determined to be appropriate, disruption of business and possible negative publicity because of trial, and increased insurance premiums if recovery at trial is higher than in settlement

Because the proponents' reasons for supporting the settlement may diverge from general corporate and shareholder interests, many statutes require the court to notify nonparty shareholders and solicit their comments. MBCA §7.45; Fed. R. Civ. P. 23.1. In a public corporation, where such a notice-and-comment procedure would be tantamount to an expensive proxy solicitation, the court may request comments from a sampling of shareholders or solicit comments through published notice.

By their terms, these settlement procedures apply only to derivative litigation. An argument can be made, however, that they should apply whenever the corporation on its own (without a lawsuit being filed) settles claims out of court that might have been brought in a derivative suit. Such an out-of-court settlement by the corporation raises doubts about the parties' incentives much as an in-court settlement does. In *Wolf v. Barkes*, 348 F.2d 994 (2d Cir. 1965), the Second Circuit rejected this argument even though the corporation's out-of-court settlement purported to resolve fiduciary claims involving management stock options pending in a derivative suit. Judge Friendly explained that management flexibility should not be impeded in settling corporate claims and that the out-of-court settlement would not necessarily preclude the shareholder's continuing her derivative claims. The shareholder could still attack the settlement as unfair self-dealing, fraudulent, or wasteful. But under this analysis, a corporation's out-of-court settlement is subject to less stringent review than when the same claims are settled as part of a derivative suit.

§18.4 DERIVATIVE LITIGATION IN FEDERAL COURTS

§18.4.1 Diversity Jurisdiction

In federal diversity action, there are two principal issues: (1) Is the corporation a plaintiff or a defendant for assessing the parties' diversity of citizenship? (2) What procedural rules govern the action–state or federal?

Corporation Is a Defendant

The Supreme Court has held that even though shareholders technically bring derivative suits on behalf of the corporation, the corporation should be treated as a defendant for purposes of federal diversity jurisdiction if it (or, more precisely, its management) is antagonistic to the claim. *Smith v. Sperling*, 354 U.S. 91 (1957). (Recall from Civil Procedure that a corporation is considered both a citizen of its state of incorporation and its principal place of business. See 28 U.S.C. § 1332(c)(1).)

A further requirement under Fed. R. Civ. P. 23.1 is that the suit not be brought collusively to avoid "complete diversity" requirements. For example, if a North Carolina corporation wished to sue a North Carolina supplier for breach of contract (no diversity of citizenship), a Virginia shareholder of the corporation could not collude with management to bring a derivative action on behalf of the corporation based on diversity by naming the corporation as nominal defendant and the North Carolina supplier as real defendant.

State Derivative Suit Requirements Are "Substantive"

Courts have held that certain state procedural requirements (those that relate to the allocation of power between shareholders and management) are "substantive" under the *Erie* doctrine. This means that, even though not imposed by federal Rule 23.1, some state conditions such as the security-for-expense requirement apply in derivative actions brought under federal diversity jurisdiction actions. *Cohen v. Beneficial Industrial Loan Corp.*, 337 U.S. 541 (1949).

§18.4.2 Federal Actions

Actions brought in federal court on behalf of the corporation claiming violations of federal law are subject to federal, not state, procedures. The Supreme Court has held that derivative suits may be brought for alleged violations of Rule 10b-5 (the general securities trading antifraud rule) and Rule 14a-9 (the proxy antifraud rule) of the Securities Exchange Act of 1934 if the fraud was perpetrated on the corporation. *Superintendent of Insurance v. Bankers Life & Casualty Co.*, 404 U.S. 6 (1971) (Rule 10b-5); *J. I. Case Co. v. Borak*, 377 U.S. 426 (1964) (Rule 14a-9). In such derivative cases, the procedural requirements of Rule 23.1 apply, but state procedural requirements — such as state security-for-expense requirements — do not.

Even in a derivative suit brought under federal diversity jurisdiction, which generally adopts the substantive law of the state in which the federal court sits, federal procedural rules apply, such as the continuous ownership requirement of federal Rule 23.1. *Kona Enters. v. Estate of Bishop*, 179 F.3d 767 (9th Cir. 1999).

Nonetheless, the Supreme Court has said that when there are gaps in federal substantive law on the question of allocation of power in the corporation, federal law should refer to the law of the state of incorporation. *Kamen v. Kemper Financial Services, Inc.*, 500 U.S. 90 (1991). Thus, in a derivative suit brought under the federal Investment Company Act for the breach of fiduciary duties by a mutual fund's investment advisor, the Court held that demand on the board was to be determined by reference to state law, absent contrary federal policies. This is because the demand requirement serves to allocate corporate governance between the board and shareholders — traditionally a matter of state law. The Court rejected the lower court's conclusion that a universal demand requirement makes good policy sense and should be adopted as a matter of federal common law.

Examples

1. Protox Corporation, a public company incorporated in Delaware, issues options on 400,000 shares of its common stock to Paula, the outgoing CEO and chair of the board. The options entitle Paula to buy Protox shares at $30 (the current market price) at any time for the next five years.
   a. Lois, a longtime Protox shareholder, is outraged. She brings a derivative suit in federal district court in the State of New Columbia, claiming that the directors breached their fiduciary duties. Delaware does not have a security-for-expense requirement, but New Columbia does. Is Lois subject to New Columbia's procedures?
   b. Believing the security-for-expense requirement applies, Lois looks for other shareholders to join her so their aggregate shareholdings will exceed the New Columbia threshold of $50,000. Lois finds three such shareholders, but none owned their shares when the board granted Paula's stock options. New Columbia does not have a contemporaneous ownership requirement. Can Lois bring her federal diversity action?
   c. Is there any way for Lois to avoid this tangle of derivative suit requirements?

2. After discovery, Paula agrees to settle Lois's claims and to return half the stock options granted her.
   a. Lois's complaint had sought a return of all the options. Can the court approve the settlement?
   b. Under the terms of the settlement, the corporation agrees to pay Lois's attorney $500,000 for his representation. Is the court bound by the parties' agreement on attorney fees?

3. While the federal court in New Columbia is reviewing the settlement, shareholders file two more derivative actions challenging the stock options, one in state court in Virginia and the other in federal district court in California.
   a. What becomes of these later actions?
   b. What will be the effect on them of a court-approved settlement of Lois's claim?
   c. The plaintiff in the Virginia case filed his suit hoping that a successful resolution of the New Columbia suit would automatically allow him to claim attorney fees in his suit. Will this scheme work?

4. Protox has become the subject of takeover speculation, and the board approves contracts for top executives that promise three years' worth of compensation if forced to leave the company after a change in ownership (commonly known as "golden parachutes"). One year later, Protox is bought in a leveraged buyout by RKK Partners, which after a cash-out reverse subsidiary merger (see §36.2.5) becomes Protox's 100 percent parent.

a. The new Protox board fires many Protox executives, but RKK chafes at paying their golden parachutes. Can RKK bring a derivative suit on behalf of new Protox challenging the contracts?
b. RKK has the new Protox board initiate a suit against the old directors for awarding the golden parachutes. Can Protox assert these fiduciary claims?
c. Lois, who owned Protox shares when the board approved the golden parachutes, believes RKK paid less because of the contingent golden parachute liability. Can she bring a derivative suit challenging the golden parachutes?

Explanations

EXPLANATIONS

1. a. Perhaps not. Lois's action in New Columbia federal court is based on diversity jurisdiction. *Erie* requires that the district court apply the substantive rules of New Columbia, including its choice-of-law rules. In a case involving substantially the same facts, the Supreme Court has held that a security-for-expense requirement is substantive and must be applied in diversity actions. *Cohen v. Beneficial Industrial Loan Corp.*, 337 U.S. 541 (1949).

   Although this analysis would seem to require the court to impose New Columbia's security-for-expense requirement, closer analysis leads to the opposite conclusion. Remember the security-for-expense requirement (like other derivative suit requirements) has dual purposes, to protect corporate interests and prevent abuse of the judicial process. In this case, New Columbia has no reason to be concerned about either. Protox is a Delaware corporation, and to the extent the security-for-expense requirement assures that corporate interests are well represented in derivative litigation, this is a concern of Delaware corporate law, which does not impose such a requirement on its shareholder-litigants. Moreover, suit is brought in federal court, and to the extent the security-for-expense requirement protects courts from abuse of their process, that is a concern of the federal district court, whose rules (specifically Rule 23.1) do not impose a security-for-expense requirement. *Cohen* may have been wrongly decided.

   b. No. The three new shareholders, although their combined holdings exempt the plaintiffs from the security-for-expense requirement, are not contemporaneous owners. Rule 23.1 protects against abuse of judicial process in federal derivative suits and imposes this procedural requirement even though the state of incorporation, New Columbia, does not. Thus, Lois avoids the New Columbia obstacle but is now caught by the federal obstacle—a patchwork of federal and state rules.

   Also notice that in this diversity suit the plaintiff-shareholders must be from states completely different from that of the corporation (nominal defendant) and those of the other defendants (Paula and any named directors). The suit must also seek more than $75,000 in damages *to the corporation*, an amount unrelated to the shareholdings of the plaintiff-shareholders.

c. Perhaps, though she needs more facts. Lois can avoid the security-for-expense requirement by bringing a direct action against the corporation under state law. Direct claims are not subject to derivative suit procedural requirements (see §18.2 above). For example, she could make a direct claim if the options were not properly authorized or if they required shareholder approval.

In addition, Lois can avoid state derivative suit requirements by bringing a federal securities claim—whether direct or derivative. For example, she might bring a federal derivative suit claiming that Paula had violated her Rule 10b-5 duties of full disclosure to the corporation if she failed to disclose the options were without consideration (see §22.3).

2. a. Yes, if the court determines the settlement is fair and reasonable to the corporation. In making this determination, the court will weigh the terms of the settlement against the probable outcome of the case had it gone to trial, offset by the delay, expense, and inherent uncertainty of a trial, particularly when the board's grant may be protected by the business judgment rule.

b. No. Again the issue is whether this aspect of the settlement is "fair and reasonable." Whether the attorney fees are related to the outcome and represent a fair valuation of services is largely within the discretion of the court.

3. a. It depends on how the courts exercise their procedural discretion. Because derivative suit plaintiffs sue on behalf of the corporation, subsequent derivative suits may be dismissed, consolidated with the original suit, transferred to another court, or stayed pending the outcome of the original suit. Although the Virginia state court cannot consolidate or transfer the new case, it can dismiss or stay it. The federal court in California can dismiss or stay the case, or transfer it to the federal court in New Columbia for that court to decide its disposition.

b. The settlement would have a res judicata effect and bar the continuation of any other suit based on the same claims, provided the settlement satisfied due process (see §18.1.5). An important question would be whether the settlement advanced corporate/shareholder interests or merely benefited Lois's lawyers.

c. No. Many statutes permit the court to shift fees against derivative suit plaintiffs. Even if the New Columbia suit succeeds, the defendants in the Virginia suit could argue that the "me too" plaintiff brought it for an "improper purpose." See MBCA §7.46(2). Fee-shifting deters suits brought for their nuisance value.

4. a. Perhaps not. If RKK was not a shareholder when the directors awarded the golden parachutes, the contemporaneous ownership requirement would bar RKK from pursuing a derivative claim. Although RKK might argue the payments constitute a "continuing wrong" to the corporation, RKK in all likelihood discounted its purchase price to account for the contingent golden parachute obligations. If so, any recovery by RKK would be a windfall.

   Even if RKK owned some shares before the buyout and was a contemporaneous owner, a court might apply the same theory to deny a recovery to RKK or might decide the recovery should be shared pro rata with other pre-buyout shareholders. See ALI Principles §7.01(d) (applying this analysis in context of closely held corporation). It would be an important factual question whether RKK figured its potential golden parachute obligations in its buyout price.

   b. Perhaps not. Protox may be barred by the vicarious incapacity rule from bringing a suit that RKK, its only shareholder, could not bring derivatively. (See the previous answer.) Any recovery by Protox would produce a windfall for RKK if it had already discounted Protox's value to take into account the contingent golden parachute obligations. Nonetheless, some jurisdictions allow the surviving corporation (at the behest of new owners) to pursue existing fiduciary claims, and this contingent benefit is sometimes taken into account in deciding the purchase price.

   c. Perhaps, depending on the jurisdiction. If the jurisdiction does not have a continuing interest requirement, a former shareholder who was a contemporaneous owner would have standing if she fairly and adequately represented the corporation—or, here, all former shareholders after the merger. MBCA §7.41.

   If the jurisdiction has a continuing interest requirement, Lois could argue an exception to the requirement. Unless cashed-out shareholders could sue the former directors for premerger wrongdoing, their overreaching would go undeterred and the shareholders' loss uncompensated. See ALI Principles §7.02(a)(2) (allowing former shareholder to bring a postmerger derivative suit seeking pro rata recovery). The only question is whether Lois is best suited to represent the other former shareholders.

   Under Delaware's strict "continuing interest" rule, Lois could not maintain a derivative suit after the cash-out merger. At most, she could bring a direct action if the merger was illegal or accomplished by fraud. See *Lewis v. Anderson*, 477 A.2d 1040 (Del. 1983). The strict Delaware approach assumes the buyer has paid the former shareholders for the right to sue for management abuse. If RKK chooses not to pursue this claim, the claim would be lost.

§18.5 DISMISSAL OF DERIVATIVE LITIGATION—FINDING A COPORATE VOICE

In theory, a shareholder's derivative suit is brought on behalf of the corporation, and the "corporation" should have a voice in deciding whether the suit is brought, maintained, or settled. But who speaks for the corporation:

- the individual shareholder-plaintiff?
- the shareholders as a group?
- the board of directors?
- a committee of the board?
- the court?

As you review the variety of approaches to identifying a trustworthy corporate voice, consider the incentives of each speaker.

§18.5.1 Self-Appointed Derivative Suit Plaintiff

A derivative suit plaintiff, though purporting to step into the corporation's shoes and to represent general corporate interests, may in fact be representing his own inconsistent interests. To prevent abuse of the judicial process and protect the integrity of centralized corporate governance, derivative suit plaintiffs are subject to a variety of procedural rules (see §18.3 above). In addition, corporate law increasingly instructs judges to listen to other voices in deciding the fate of a shareholder's derivative suit.

§18.5.2 Unwieldy Body of Shareholders

In theory, allowing the body of shareholders to decide the fate of derivative litigation would overcome the problems of entrusting fiduciary litigation to individual shareholder-plaintiffs. But requiring a demand on all shareholders and permitting a shareholder majority to decide whether the suit should proceed would create its own problems:

- **Proxy contest.** In public corporations, a demand requirement would entail the shareholder-plaintiff initiating an expensive and burdensome proxy contest before suit could commence. It would effectively kill derivative litigation against all but the clearest and most costly fiduciary breaches.

- **Shareholder passivity.** Shareholders, particularly in a public corporation, might lack the incentives to evaluate the relative costs and benefits of derivative litigation. Shareholders might approve suits that are not in the corporation's best interests and disapprove others that are.
- **Illegitimate.** Allowing a shareholder majority to refuse to litigate would permit ratification of fraud, self-dealing, or waste. In a public corporation, management's control of the proxy machinery might make majority refusal of doubtful legitimacy. In a close corporation, majority refusal would predictably gut fiduciary protection for the minority.

Most statutes do not require a demand on shareholders. MBCA §7.42; ALI Principles §7.03(c); cf. Fed. R. Civ. P. 23.1 (pleading requirement). Moreover, in those states where shareholder demand is required, courts have excused it when the derivative plaintiff alleges a wrong (such as waste) that cannot be ratified by a majority of shareholders or when demand would be burdensome because of the number of shareholders. See *Mayer v. Adams*, 141 A.2d 458 (Del. 1958).

§18.5.3 Board of Directors — Voice of Centralized Corporate Governance

The board's power to speak for the corporation in a derivative suit is linked to whether shareholders must make a demand on the board.

Dilemma

Before we consider the various judicial and statutory approaches, consider the mixed signals from corporate law. On the one hand, the business judgment rule assumes the board has wide discretion to make business decisions, including litigation decisions. The directors, more than shareholders or judges, are better positioned to evaluate whether a claim has merit, whether it is consistent with corporate interests, and whether corporate resources (money and personnel) should be used to pursue it. If there is no conflict of interest, the board's incentives will predictably be closely aligned with general corporate interests.

On the other hand, if the claim involves charges of a fiduciary breach, corporate law doubts the board's impartiality. Even directors not involved in the alleged wrongdoing or not themselves named defendants may be solicitous of fellow directors (or other members of the control group) who are sued. *Structural bias* on the board because of personal, professional, and social ties may create pressures for directors to act in ways inconsistent with general corporate interests.

Despite this tension between board discretion and answerability, courts and statutes increasingly assume that disinterested directors may be a better voice for the corporation than self-appointed shareholder-plaintiffs.

Demand-Required (Futility Exception)

Under the prevailing *judicial* approach, the board of directors can decide the fate of derivative litigation if a pre-suit demand on the board is required. If the board receives a demand and refuses to act or settle the charges, its response (or nonresponse) receives deferential review under the business judgment rule. A shareholder-plaintiff must show the board's response to the demand was self-interested, dishonest, illegal, or insufficiently informed. Usually a demand-required claim is a lost claim.

But demand is excused if it would be futile to bring the matter to the board. When demand is excused, the directors cannot block a derivative suit. Their voice is silenced. The assumption in a demand-excused case is that the board is unlikely to be objective in considering the merits of the suit. Allowing a tainted board to make litigation decisions would be tantamount to allowing an accused to decide whether to prosecute himself.

The demand-excused approach produces the following results:

	Demand on Board
Demand required	Board decides fate of claim, subject to review under business judgment rule
Demand excused	Claim goes forward; board cannot dismiss

When is demand excused? The Delaware Supreme Court has adopted two tests for demand futility. *Aronson v. Lewis*, 473 A.2d 805 (Del. 1984). Demand is excused if the shareholder-plaintiff can allege *with particularity facts that create a reasonable doubt* on either of two scores—

- doubt that a majority of the current directors on whom demand would have been made are disinterested and independent, or
- doubt that the challenged transaction was protected by the business judgment rule—by showing a conflict of interest, bad faith, grossly uninformed decision making, or a significant failure of oversight.

To make this showing, the plaintiff must point to specific facts (before discovery) that tend to show *either* that the board is now untrustworthy to respond to the demand *or* that the underlying transaction was improper. (The *Aronson* decision states the trial court is to make both inquiries—a seeming conjunctive standard—but later cases make clear either showing is sufficient to establish demand futility.) See *Marx v. Akers*, 666 N.E.2d 1034 (N.Y. 1996) (adopting *Aronson* approach and excusing demand when (1) current board is "interested" in challenged transaction, or (2) board decision not appropriately informed, or (3) challenged transaction so egregious that it could not be product of sound business judgment).

As applied, the *Aronson* test places a heavy burden on derivative plaintiffs seeking review of board operational decisions. See *Brehm v. Eisner*, 746 A.2d 244 (Del. 2000 (refusing to excuse demand despite findings of "lavish" pay and "sloppy" review by board of directors) (see §14.2.4). In *Aronson*, for example, the plaintiff challenged a compensation package the board approved for the company's retiring chair and 47 percent shareholder. The court said that just because the defendant owned a controlling block of the company's stock and had selected all of the directors did not create a "reasonable doubt" concerning the directors' independence. Further, the court held the alleged facts failed to make out a claim of waste, even though the allegations included that the defendant performed "little or no service" and would be compensated whether or not he was able to perform.

In Delaware, once a shareholder makes a demand, she cannot bring a derivative suit unless she can show the board's rejection was wrongful—that is, it was not made in good faith after a reasonable investigation. *Spiegel v. Buntrock*, 571 A.2d 767 (Del. 1990). A shareholder who makes a demand cannot later assert that demand should have been excused. *Levine v. Smith*, 591 A.2d 194 (Del. 1991). Making a demand in Delaware effectively places the fate of the derivative suit in the hands of the board.

Universal Demand

The MBCA avoids the demand-required/demand-excused question (thus avoiding litigation within litigation) by making demand a universal precondition to derivative litigation. MBCA §7.42. A shareholder wishing to file suit must make a demand and then wait 90 days—unless the board rejects the demand or waiting would result in irreparable injury to the corporation. See also ALI Principles §7.03 (requiring demand in every case, except when "irreparable injury" would result).

After the 90-day waiting period, the shareholder may bring a derivative suit. If the board rejected the demand, the plaintiff must plead with particularity that either the board's rejection of the demand was not disinterested or the rejection was not in good faith or not informed. (This is similar to the Delaware *Aronson* approach.) After suit is brought, the board can move for dismissal if independent directors constitute a quorum (a majority of the board) and a majority of independent directors determine in "good faith" and after a "reasonable inquiry" that maintaining the suit is not in the corporation's best interests. MBCA §7.44(a), (b)(1). The statute defines independence much as have the courts. A director is not disqualified merely because he is named as a defendant, was nominated or elected to the board by defendants, or approved the challenged transaction. MBCA §7.44(c).

Demand and Dismissal in Federal Court

If a derivative claim is brought under federal law, the demand and dismissal rules are governed by the law of the incorporating state unless its application would be inconsistent with federal policy. *Burks v. Lasker*, 441 U.S. 471 (1984). The Supreme Court has rejected a federal universal demand standard in federal securities derivative litigation because the demand requirement bears on the allocation of power in the corporation, a matter federal law normally leaves to the law of the state of incorporation. *Kamen v. Kemper Financial Services, Inc.*, 500 U.S. 90 (1991).

State rules governing shareholder litigation, however, must also be consistent with federal policy. In *Daily Income Fund, Inc. v. Fox*, 464 U.S. 523 (1984), the Supreme Court concluded no pre-suit demand is required in a shareholder suit against a mutual fund's investment advisor under §36(b) of the Investment Company Act of 1940. The Court characterized the suit as not derivative, thus making Fed. R. Civ. P. 23.1 inapplicable. The Court pointed out that §36(b) is a remedial provision that allows mutual fund investors to challenge unfair compensation in investment advisory contracts, which are rife with conflicts of interest.

§18.5.4 Special Litigation Committee

During the 1970s, boards of directors responded to a spate of derivative litigation with an ingenious device. The board, whose members were usually named as defendants for various infractions, appointed a special litigation committee (SLC) of disinterested and often recently appointed directors with the exclusive power to decide whether the suit should go forward. The committee, often assisted by outside counsel, investigated the charges and prepared a (usually voluminous) report. The committee invariably recommended that the suit not be pursued further and then sought its dismissal.

During the 1980s, SLCs gained popularity. Typically, the board would give the committee full power to make litigation decisions for the corporation. See §30.1.3. The committee usually was comprised of directors who had not participated in the challenged transaction and hence could not be named as defendants. SLCs have shown a remarkable disposition for director defendants. In the vast majority of cases, SLCs refuse to continue the suit against a colleague.

Academic commentators doubted the trustworthiness of the SLC ruse and pointed to research on group dynamics suggesting committee members face unspoken pressure to dismiss charges against fellow directors—so-called structural bias. See *Lewis v. Fuqua*, 502 A.2d 962 (Del. Ch. 1985) (holding committee member not to be independent because he was director when the challenged actions took place, was named as defendant, had political and financial dealings with company's dominating CEO, and was president of university that had received significant contributions from the CEO and company).

Courts have responded to SLCs in a variety of ways.

Business Judgment Review

The first cases during the 1970s uniformly held that an SLC's recommendation to dismiss litigation was like any other corporate business decision, despite the self-interested taint of the board that had appointed the committee. Unless the plaintiff could show the committee's members were themselves interested or had not acted on an informed basis, the committee's recommendations were entitled to full judicial deference under the business judgment doctrine. *Gall v. Exxon Corp.*, 418 F. Supp. 508 (S.D.N.Y. 1976); *Auerbach v. Bennett*, 393 N.E.2d 994 (N.Y. 1979).

Under this approach, after a committee investigates the claims made by the plaintiff, it can recommend dismissal of the litigation on many grounds: The suit would undermine employee morale and waste employee time; litigation expenses would exceed any possible gain; the suit would create bad publicity for the company; the underlying claim lacks merit; the corporation might be required to indemnify a successful defendant; and so on. Some commentators criticized this business judgment deference as sounding the death knell for derivative litigation, and the approach has eroded. See *In re PSE&G Shareholder Litigation*, 801 A.2d 295 (N.J. 2002) (applying modified business judgment rule to require corporation to show SLC's independence, good faith, and reasonable decision).

Heightened Scrutiny (Demand-Excused Cases)

In Delaware, when demand on the board is excused as futile, the courts listen to the SLC—but with suspicion. In *Zapata Corp. v. Maldonado*, 430 A.2d 779 (Del. 1981), the Delaware Supreme Court agreed there might be "subconscious abuse" by members of the committee asked to pass judgment on fellow directors. The court established a two-part inquiry into whether an SLC's recommendation to dismiss would be respected:

- **Procedural inquiry.** The defendants must carry the burden of showing the committee members' independence from the defendants, their good faith, reasonable investigation, and the legal and factual bases for the committee's conclusions. If there is a genuine issue of material fact as to any of these counts, the derivative litigation proceeds. See *In re Oracle Corp. Derivative Litigation*, 824 A.2d 917 (Del. Ch. 2003) (finding lack of SLC independence, despite being composed of unnamed board members and its use of reputable outside law firm, because SLC members had long-standing professional/ academic relationships with principal defendants through Stanford University).

- **Substantive inquiry.** Even if the SLC's recommendation passes this first stage of inquiry, the trial judge may apply his own "independent business judgment" as to whether the suit should be dismissed. This second inquiry—which focuses on such matters as the strength of the fiduciary claims and the likelihood of recovery—is far more intrusive than even the fairness test applicable to self-dealing transactions. It recognizes that judges are particularly adept (in fact it is generally their job) to evaluate the merits of litigation and that judicial incentives to further the interests of the corporation are perhaps stronger than those of an SLC.

At first blush, the two-step *Zapata* inquiry seems to be a remarkable departure from cases that apply the business judgment presumption to SLC recommendations. But in Delaware, the *Zapata* test applies to SLC recommendations only in demand-excused cases. Three years after *Zapata*, the Delaware Supreme Court significantly limited the decision's importance by making demand a requirement in a large number of cases. *Aronson v. Lewis*, 473 A.2d 805 (Del. 1984) (see §18.5.3 above).

Heightened Scrutiny (Regardless of Demand)

Some courts have subjected SLC dismissal recommendations to heightened scrutiny whether demand is required or excused. Under this approach, the trial court independently evaluates the suit's merits, giving some (but not presumptive) weight to the SLC's recommendation. *Joy v. North*, 692 F.2d 880 (2d Cir. 1982); see also ALI Principles §7.08.

For example, in *Alford v. Shaw*, 358 S.E.2d 323 (N.C. 1987), the North Carolina Supreme Court focused on the court's supervisory function in derivative litigation under the state's demand-pleading statute. See §18.3.3. The court refused to read the statutory requirement that the plaintiff plead his demand efforts as requiring different levels of judicial scrutiny depending on whether demand was required or excused. Just as settlement of derivative litigation is subject to court review, so is dismissal. Under the statute, the court concluded, the trial judge could not disregard shareholder interests by relying blindly on the SLC's recommendations.

Measured Scrutiny (Universal Demand)

Under the MBCA, an SLC (of at least two independent directors) may seek dismissal of derivative litigation after a shareholder has made the obligatory pre-suit demand. If the committee was appointed by a majority of independent directors, the MBCA requires the court to dismiss the action under the same standards as board dismissal—namely that the SLC determines in "good faith" and after a "reasonable inquiry" that maintaining the suit is not in the corporation's best interests. MBCA §7.44(a), (b)(2). The same definition of independence applies for dismissal by the board. See *Einhorn v. Culea*, 612 N.W.2d 78 (Wis. 2000) (independence depends on whether committee member can decide "on merits of the issue rather than on extraneous considerations or influences"). A director is not disqualified merely because he is named as a defendant, was nominated or elected to the board by defendants, or approved the challenged transaction. MBCA §7.44(c).

Whether an SLC satisfies these standards requires a factual inquiry into the committee members' disinterestedness, assistance by outside advisors, preparation of a written report, adequacy of their investigation, and reasonable belief in their decision. See *Cuker v. Mikalauskas*, 692 A.2d 1042 (Pa. 1997) (adopting the procedures and deferential review standards of the ALI Principles, which the court noted is "a comprehensive, cohesive work more than a decade in preparation").

Federal Derivative Claims

When a derivative suit involves federal claims—such as under the federal securities laws—the Supreme Court has accepted as a matter of federal law that an SLC can dismiss the litigation provided dismissal is consistent with federal policy. In *Burks v. Lasker*, 441 U.S. 471 (1979), a shareholder brought a derivative action against several directors of a mutual fund and its investment advisor claiming violations of the Investment Company Act of 1940. The fund had purchased commercial paper of Penn Central Railroad just before it became insolvent. An SLC investigated the allegations that the directors and investment advisor had breached their duty of care. The SLC decided litigation was not in the fund's best interests and sought dismissal. The Supreme Court upheld the dismissal on the theory the suit on behalf of the fund was governed by the law of the state of the fund's incorporation, provided state law is not inconsistent with federal policy. In the case, the Court held that the 1940 Act did not forbid termination of nonfrivolous claims, and thus dismissal was not inconsistent with federal policy.

Examples

1. Owing-Indiana (O-I), a public company incorporated in an MBCA jurisdiction, manufactures glass containers. Last year O-I's board unanimously approved a $5 million loan to Glass Advocates Committee (GAC), a political action committee set up to stop a state referendum to ban disposable soda bottles. GAC was organized by Frank Jr., the son of O-I's CEO, Frank Sr. There were reports that GAC spent most of its funds paying its organizers. The GAC loan is now delinquent, and O-I has done nothing. Dottie, a long-time O-I shareholder, wants O-I to collect the loan. She asks you for litigation advice.
   a. Must Dottie first make a demand on the shareholders?
   b. Must Dottie first make a demand on the board?

2. Kerning International is a holding company incorporated in Delaware. Among its subsidiaries is wholly owned Kerning Glass, a glass container manufacturer, incorporated in Delaware. The Kerning Glass board also approved a loan to GAC, which is now delinquent. Phil, a long-time Kerning International shareholder, wants Kerning Glass to collect. He asks you for litigation advice.
   a. Must Phil first make a demand on shareholders?
   b. Must Phil first make a demand on the Kerning International or Kerning Glass board?
   c. What litigation strategy do you recommend to Phil?

3. Dottie and Phil do not make demands on the relevant boards, and each files a derivative suit naming the board's directors. In response, each board considers whether to request dismissal. After a cursory presentation by the company's inside attorney who says the suit is "no more than the machinations of another gadfly shareholder," each board moves the court to have the suit dismissed.
   a. Under the MBCA, how will the court respond to the O-I board's request?
   b. Under Delaware law, how will the court respond to the Kerning Glass board's request?

4. After Dottie files her complaint, the O-I board considers appointing an SLC to investigate the claims of the complaint. This will avoid any questions about the role of Frank Sr.
   a. What should the board do to maximize the effect of the committee recommendations?
   b. What should the committee do to maximize the chances that its recommendations will be listened to?
   c. The SLC issues a report recommending that Dottie's complaint be dismissed. Is the recommendation binding on the court?

Explanations

1. a. No. The MBCA has no requirement of a demand on shareholders.
   b. Probably. The MBCA requires a complaining shareholder to exhaust internal remedies by making a pre-suit demand on the board. MBCA §7.42. Dottie can avoid making demand if there would be irreparable injury by waiting for the board to act during the 90-day waiting period. Dottie might argue that the ongoing dissipation of funds by GAC makes time of the essence. Unless the suit proceeds immediately, the corporation may be unable to recover from GAC or its organizers.

      Demand on the board is required even though the GAC loans might be characterized as a director's conflicting-interest transaction. See MBCA Subchapter F (§13.4.1). The universal demand requirement gives even nonindependent directors an opportunity to reconsider their position and saves the time and expense of litigating the demand issue.

2. a. Probably not. Although the Delaware statute requires the plaintiff plead her efforts to make a demand on the shareholders or the reasons she did not, courts have largely read this demand requirement out of the statute in public corporations. If the shareholder can show such demand would be expensive or delay the action, or if the wrong is nonratifiable, courts have excused demand on shareholders. Making a demand on Kerning International's public shareholders would be burdensome; a demand on Kerning Glass's shareholder (the holding company) would be essentially a demand on the parent board.
   b. Not necessarily. Delaware case law permits a shareholder to bring a derivative suit and argue that demand was excused as futile. In a double derivative suit, such as this one, in which the shareholder seeks to have the parent exercise the subsidiary's litigation rights, the Delaware courts have focused their demand analysis on the *subsidiary's* board. See *Rales v. Blasband*, 634 A.2d 927 (Del. 1993) (look to subsidiary board because its decision is being challenged). Under *Aronson v. Lewis*, 473 A.2d 805 (Del. 1984) (see §18.5.3), Phil would have to plead particular facts that created reasonable doubts about either the lack of independence of the subsidiary's current directors, or the validity of the loan and its forgiveness. Although the sketchy pleadings are insufficient under Delaware case law to create doubts about the subsidiary directors' disinterestedness or independence, the subsidiary's forgiveness of a political loan may be illegal (see §12.3.1) and thus unprotected by the business judgment rule. Demand would be excused.
   c. Phil should file suit and not make demand. In Delaware, a shareholder who makes a demand concedes that a majority of the board has the requisite disinterest and independence to respond to the demand and decide the fate of the shareholder's claim. That is, a demand on the board shifts

the corporate voice to the board. If Phil makes a demand, he can continue his claim only if he shows the board's response to the demand—whether inaction or settlement of the claim—was not protected by the business judgment rule. That is, he would have to show the board was grossly uninformed or lacked any rational basis for its response. If Phil files suit and argues demand was excused, he must plead particular facts to create the doubts of *Aronson v. Lewis* (see previous answer).

3. a. Under the MBCA, assuming demand was excused because otherwise there would be irrevocable harm, the court must dismiss the suit if a majority of the board is independent and sought dismissal in good faith after a reasonable inquiry. MBCA §7.44. Under the doctrine of res judicata, the GAC loan controversy would then be precluded from further judicial review in any court. If the court determines a majority of the board was independent, judicial review approximates that under the business judgment rule. That the O-I directors were named by Frank Sr. or have been named as defendants does not necessarily cause them to not be independent. The burden will be on the shareholder to show the board acted insincerely or without sufficient information. The official comment clarifies that the board need not engage outside counsel or advisors if it has knowledge of the pertinent facts or reasonably relies on others. The board could dismiss if it honestly and reasonably believed Dottie was "another gadfly shareholder."

   b. If demand was required, the court will dismiss the action unless Phil can show that the board's decision to dismiss was grossly uninformed or irrational, thus not protected by the business judgment rule. If demand was excused, the board's dismissal request will have no effect. Demand excusal carries with it the assumption the board lacks the independence to make a dismissal request or the allegations are sufficiently serious that the board could not request dismissal in good faith.

   In Delaware, the board's capacity to entertain the demand depends on a lack of interest among a majority of current directors and their independence of interested directors. See *Rales v. Blasband*, 634 A.2d 927 (Del. 1993). A director is considered interested if he will receive a personal financial benefit from nonprosecution of the suit that is not equally shared with the shareholders. For example, a director facing a significant potential for personal liability is disqualified. A director lacks independence if he is "beholden" to interested persons. For example, an executive whose substantial salary depends on the favor of an interested person lacks independence.

4. a. The committee should be composed of directors who have no connection to the loan approval—either because they did not participate in the decision or were elected afterward. The committee should be given full power to hire outside advisors and to bind the

corporation. Its recommendations should not be subject to review or approval by the board.

b. The committee must create the appearance that it has fully investigated the charges of the plaintiff's complaint. It should conduct a discovery-like investigation: hire a prestigious unaffiliated special counsel (such as a retired judge or law professor), interview relevant people, review documents, and seek other knowledgeable and expert advice. The committee should carefully document its investigation and the basis for its recommendations.

c. Probably. If a majority of the whole board was independent when the SLC made its recommendation, Dottie would have the burden to overcome a business judgment presumption and show the SLC members acted insincerely or without adequate information. Even if a majority of the whole was not independent, but the committee members were, the SLC has the power to seek dismissal, but it would have the burden to show its recommendation is protected by the business judgment rule. See *Carlton Investments v. TLC Beatrice Int'l Holdings, Inc.*, No. 13,950 (Del. Ch. May 30, 1997) (approving settlement negotiated by SLC, intended to stop spiraling litigation costs and end distraction of lawsuit). The SLC need not achieve perfection so long as it demonstrates independence, good faith, and a studied process.

The MBCA's approach largely disregards the problems of structural bias on the board. Nonetheless, it is possible judges will review dismissal requests with greater scrutiny than under the normal business judgment rule. Just as a court has authority to consider the merits of the derivative suit when it approves a settlement, judges may feel inclined to delve into the SLC's "no sue" decision. See *Alford v. Shaw*, 358 S.E.2d 323 (N.C. 1987) (see §18.5.4). Judicial scrutiny of the SLC's independence or its deliberations would recognize the self-interested motives of the possible voices in a derivative suit. This would be consistent with the logic in demand-required cases of the two-step *Zapata* test (see §18.5.4) and the general judicial rejection of the *Auerbach v. Bennett* business judgment rule approach (see §18.5.4).

Judicial scrutiny of the SLC recommendations assumes, as does the second step of the *Zapata* test, that inevitably judges will exercise their own "business judgment" concerning the litigation's merits to the corporation. Although some have argued that such decisions are not significantly different from ordinary business decisions and should not be left to judges, a strong argument can be made that judges are particularly capable of making judgments about the expected value of litigation—a task at which they are expert. In any event, judges are often called on to make business judgments when considering the substantive fairness of self-dealing transactions.

PART

V

Shareholder Liquidity Rights

CHAPTER 19

Share Transferability— An Introduction

A fundamental aspect of the corporation is the right of shareholders to transfer their corporate shares. Share transferability—which actually predates corporate limited liability—has important ramifications:

1. Shareholders can liquidate their investment by selling their shares to new investors rather than drawing from the corporation—thus ensuring the continuity of corporate assets and permitting long-range business planning.
2. Trading markets in corporate shares allow investors to cash out their corporate investment with relative ease—thus increasing the value of corporate shares both for investors and when the corporation raises capital.
3. Trading in corporate shares establishes market prices for corporate ownership interests—thus signaling to management, as well as potential acquirers of corporate control, whether the corporate assets are well managed.

This chapter gives you an overview of shareholder transfer rights under state law (§19.1) and summarizes how public trading markets function (§19.2). Other chapters in this part describe various limitations and protections surrounding shareholder liquidity:

- state law limitations on the sale of control shares (Chapter 20)
- rights to disclosure, principally under federal law (Chapter 21)
- antifraud protection under federal Rule 10b-5 (Chapter 22)

- insider trading rules under state law and Rule 10b-5 (Chapter 23)
- federal liability for the disgorgement of insider trading profits (Chapter 24)

Share transferability also allows shareholders to sell their shares (and attached voting rights) to an acquirer in a corporate takeover. We discuss the techniques and the shareholder protections applicable to corporate takeovers in Chapters 34-39.

§19.1 SHARE TRANSFER RIGHTS

Corporate shares are freely transferable. So clear is this proposition that most state statutes omit the point, describing instead the limited circumstances when transfers may be restricted. See MBCA §6.27; cf. Del. GCL §159 (corporate shares deemed "personal property and transferable").

Transfer restrictions cannot be imposed by majority action. According to state corporate statutes, they apply only to shareholders who purchased subject to the restriction or who are parties to a restriction agreement. See MBCA §6.27(a) (transfer restriction "does not affect shares issued before the restriction"). And any restrictions on share transferability must be for "reasonable purposes." See *Goldberg v. United Parcel Serv.*, 605 F. Supp. 588 (E.D.N.Y. 1985); MBCA §6.27(c) (maintain close corporation status, preserve securities exemptions). In practice, transfer restrictions are found mostly in closely held corporations. See §26.6.

An important issue in corporate takeover cases is whether defensive actions taken by the board of directors illegally restrict share transferability. For example, in *Moran v. Household Int'l, Inc.*, 500 A.2d 1346 (Del. 1985), shareholders challenged a "poison pill" rights plan under which the board issued rights to existing shareholders that were designed to substantially dilute the financial interest of any acquirer of more than 20 percent of the corporation's shares, unless the board chose to accept the acquirer's bid and redeem the rights. (This convoluted antitakeover device is described more fully at §29.2.3.) The shareholders claimed the poison pill had the effect of discouraging an acquirer from making a tender offer, thus effectively preventing the shareholders from freely transferring their shares to such an acquirer. The Delaware Supreme Court assumed that a nonconsensual transfer restriction would be illegal but concluded that the particular poison pill challenged in the case would not necessarily prevent outside bids. The court pointed out that similar poison pills adopted by other companies had not stopped takeover bids and that a persistent bidder could always engage in a proxy contest to replace the incumbent board and then, after redeeming the poison pill rights, proceed with a tender offer. Nonetheless, the court accepted the premise that any corporate action that prevented share transferability would be beyond the board's powers.

§19.2 PUBLIC TRADING OF CORPORATE SECURITIES

The most significant characteristic of a public corporation is a market (or markets) in which shareholders can buy or sell the corporation's shares. The stock trading markets—sometimes known as "secondary markets"—account for about 99 percent of all share transactions. Only rarely do shareholders buy stock directly from a public corporation on what is known as the "primary market."

§19.2.1 Functioning of Public Stock Trading Markets

Suppose you have some money to invest. How does stock trading work? As an individual investor you will rely on securities intermediaries to match your "buy" interest with another investor's "sell" interest. You can contact a stockbroker (a salesperson at a brokerage firm such as Merrill Lynch, which is now owned by Bank of America) and place an order for your account, such as a "buy" order for 100 shares of General Electric stock at the market price—that is, a *market buy order*. Or, more likely, you can go online and place the same order on Merrill Lynch's website. Merrill Lynch can fill your order in several ways:

- **Exchange (auction) markets.** If the stock is "listed" on a stock exchange—the New York Stock Exchange in GE's case—Merrill Lynch (acting as your agent, or "broker") can relay the order to the "floor" of the exchange where trading occurs. Stock listed on an exchange is offered for sale and purchase by a single *specialist* in that particular stock, so there is always a seller to match every buyer. Your buy order will either be matched to another's sell order in a continuous auction or, if there is no matching order, the specialist will create a market by selling the stock himself at the then-prevailing price. Either way, you are assured of buying at the market price. The specialist's market-making role provides *continuity* and *liquidity*, thus preventing erratic price swings and assuring ready buyers and sellers. Along the line, Merrill Lynch and the specialist will charge you and the seller commissions for bringing you together.
- **Over-the-counter (dealer) markets.** If the stock is not listed on an exchange, Merrill Lynch can fill your buy order by using a

computerized system that quotes available prices from other brokerage firms that sell for their own account. The principal system, known as the NASDAQ (National Association of Securities Dealers Automated Quotations System), is an *over-the-counter market* (OTC). Many stocks available on NASDAQ are not listed on exchanges. Merrill Lynch (acting for its own account as a "dealer") can use NASDAQ to buy stock for its account and then resell it to you at a mark-up. Some dealers (on average eight for NASDAQ stocks) act as *market makers*, performing much the same role as specialists on exchanges. Orders on the OTC markets are placed between securities firms by computer, rather than being routed to a central exchange. Instead of receiving a commission, Merrill Lynch will earn the spread — that is, the difference between its purchase price and its price to you. Although less common, Merrill Lynch also can act as a broker on an OTC market by purchasing stock from another dealer on your behalf and charge a commission for acting as your agent. Merrill Lynch must tell you in which capacity it is acting.

- **Sell from inventory.** If Merrill Lynch owns GE stock, it can sell you the stock from its own "inventory." Whether it buys through NASDAQ or sells from its own account, however, the broker-dealer is supposed to execute at the best available price for the investor. If its sells from inventory, Merrill Lynch will make a profit or absorb a loss depending on the price at which it originally bought the stock. SEC rules require that the dealer's confirmation of the transaction disclose that it sold from inventory. Exchange Act Rule 10b-10.

Notice that these "buy" transactions take place in the secondary market, and do not involve General Electric. The only time you would buy directly from GE would be if the company issued stock in a public offering. In fact, some companies (including GE) now offer to their shareholders direct purchase programs in which shareholders can purchase shares (or reinvest dividends) without buying through a broker-dealer.

Electronic Trading

Today, individual investors can purchase securities with less reliance on securities intermediaries. For example, instead of calling a salesperson at your brokerage firm, you can place your order through E*Trade or other online brokers directly from your computer. In fact, all full-service brokerage firms like Merrill Lynch also offer online trading. Your order is then executed by the broker through an exchange, NASDAQ, or an electronic trading system.

Over the last several years, online electronic trading systems permit brokers, market makers, and fast-trading institutional investors to place large orders that the system automatically matches with other orders. These electronic communication networks (ECNs) have significantly lowered trading costs for investors and reduced the spread between buying offers (bids) and selling offers (asks).

Beneficial ("Street Name") Ownership

What record will you have that you own stock? Like most individual investors and more than 90 percent of all investors, you will not receive certificates for your stock. After your "buy" transaction closes—which now must occur within three days after the trade is executed—your account with Merrill Lynch will be debited the purchase price (plus any commissions) and reflect that you own 100 GE shares. You will be the *beneficial owner* of these shares—but will not receive stock certificates from the company. Even if you ask, most companies today do not issue certificates. Instead, your ownership will be reflected on the books of Merrill Lynch, which will act as your *nominee*. As nominee, Merrill Lynch owns your stock in "street name." Your *beneficial ownership* does not show up on GE's shareholder records (which are kept by a transfer agent, usually a bank) because Merrill Lynch is the record owner of your shares. (The SEC has been considering a proposal for a direct-registration system in which transfer agents would electronically register securities under investors' own names.)

The "street name" system, though seemingly cumbersome, means your transaction (and thousands of others like yours) need not be recorded on GE's books. Proponents of the system point out that it is more efficient to consolidate the records of ever-shifting investments by listing Merrill Lynch as the record owner. Individual investors, as beneficial owners, retain the power to decide how their stock is voted and whether it should be sold. Under SEC rules, GE must ensure that proxy materials (printed or online) are made available to you directly if you consented to Merrill Lynch informing GE of your beneficial ownership, or indirectly through Merrill Lynch. See §7.2.5. You will exercise your voting rights either by voting online or filling out a proxy card made available from Merrill Lynch or by instructing Merrill Lynch how to vote on your behalf.

§19.2.2 Efficiency of Public Stock Markets

It is often said that many U.S. public securities markets, such as the New York Stock Exchange, are efficient. Those who make this assertion usually mean that the markets are "informationally efficient" and that prices at any time "fully reflect" all information "available" to the public. Simply stated, efficiency means that particular information affects the market price of a company's stock as though everyone had the same information at the same time. New information gets impounded in the stock price as though all investors simultaneously discovered the information and reached a consensus on a new price. In an efficient market, there are no opportunities for super-profitable trading strategies.

Do securities markets impound all information into prices?

Weak-Form Efficiency

Many kinds of information can affect stock prices. When a stock market impounds information about historic trading patterns so that investors can't draw charts of past prices to extrapolate future prices, the market is said to have "weak form" efficiency. A French mathematician noticed at the turn of the last century that prices on the Paris stock market exhibited "weak form" efficiency because stock price patterns were completely random, like the Brownian motion of particles suspended in a liquid. There was no way to guess the next move in the price of stock based on past patterns. Studies of prices on U.S. stock markets show the same "random walk."

Semi-Strong Efficiency

When a stock market promptly impounds all publicly available information, the market is said to have "semi-strong" efficiency. This means that ordinary investors can't beat the market systematically by using public information that affects stock prices—such as information on a company's earnings, competitors' products, government tax policies, changes in interest rates—because the "market" will already have discerned the information and reacted to it. That is, the average investor cannot take advantage of information ahead of the market. In fact, a large body of evidence indicates public stock prices for widely followed companies in the United States change almost instantly and in an unbiased fashion (neither too much nor too little) in response to new public information. Often formal announcements of new developments, such as corporate earnings or new products, are already old news to public trading markets. "Semi-strong" markets behave like a herd of stampeding animals that instantly change course when just a few animals in the herd change direction—it is as though the herd has a single mind.

What are the trading mechanisms that rapidly transform new information into new prices to produce market efficiency? The answer lies in the activities of market professionals. A minority of knowledgeable traders who control a critical amount of trading volume can move stocks from "uninformed" to "informed" price levels. A critical mass of informed buyers and sellers (many advised by professional securities analysts), each trying to make money by outguessing the market, create a situation in which new information is almost instantly reflected in a new "consensus" on the stock price. Securities analysts follow the activities of larger public corporations, hoping to get an informational advantage. Once an analyst identifies an information nugget, such as a confirmed rumor that a company will pay a larger-than-expected dividend, the analyst will immediately have his firm or clients trade. Just a few well-placed analysts, with others following their lead, can drive market prices. Although analysts will beat the market a little over time, they will earn just enough to recompense their effort. The paradoxical effect of many analysts working assiduously to beat the market is that none can systematically beat it. The cap on trading profits is illustrated by the fact that managed equity mutual funds (which professionally invest in stocks for many small investors) on average only slightly outperform the market, but not enough to cover their fees.

Acceptance of semi-strong efficiency underlies important facets of U.S. corporate law. The business judgment rule, for example, assumes that if directors fail in their decision-making function, stock markets will impound this failure into the company's stock price—leading to discipline in the form of reduced executive pay, proxy contests, and takeover bids. See §12.2.2. The disclosure philosophy of the federal securities laws assumes that if some investors receive full and honest disclosure, the information will be impounded in the stock price—thus ensuring that all investors trade on the basis of a fair price. See §5.1 (disclosure in public offering), §21.2.2 (periodic disclosure by public companies). Even the Supreme Court has used the hypothesis of efficient capital markets to create a presumption that material misinformation to some (but not all) investors in a public stock market establishes that all investors who traded relied on the deception. See *Basic Inc. v. Levinson*, 485 U.S. 224 (1988) (see §22.3.3).

Despite some evidence of semi-strong efficiency in U.S. stock markets, there are disturbing incongruities. For example, studies show systematic mispricing over time of smaller or high-risk companies. In fact, studies suggest that stock markets (like the humans behind them) have a preternatural tendency to take risks even in the face of contrary information. For example, the "irrational exuberance" exhibited by U.S. investors (particularly in technology stocks) during the late 1990s and then the failure in the financial sector to recognize the risks of subprime mortgages, which led to the financial crisis of 2008, undermine the argument that stock markets always behave rationally. Sometimes stock markets seem unable to process obvious information.

Strong-Form Efficiency

One thing to bear in mind is that the public stock markets are not perfectly informationally efficient. That is, public stock markets do not impound *all* information that affects stock prices; they do not exhibit "strong form" efficiency. Evidence of this is that corporate insiders, who often have access to information not available to outside investors, can reap significant trading profits by exploiting market ignorance of their inside scoops.

Informational versus Fundamental Efficiency

Even if the public stock markets exhibit weak and even semi-strong efficiency for many U.S. public corporations, this does not mean stock markets and stock prices are efficient in allocating capital. Just because General Motors (an example used in an earlier edition of this book) is trading at $28 does not mean your future returns will justify spending $28 per share or that it is socially desirable that you pay $28 for General Motors shares as opposed to paying $28 for shares of Raleigh Bicycles. Informational efficiency does not translate into "fundamental efficiency"—that is, the optimal pricing and allocation of capital in society. It just means that the public stock markets act like a herd of stampeding animals so it is as though there is only one organism, not many individuals. Informational efficiency doesn't mean the herd isn't heading over a cliff.

CHAPTER 20

Limitations on Control Sales

Corporate control is a valuable commodity. A shareholder that holds a controlling interest can direct management of the business. But with control comes responsibility to other corporate constituents. This chapter considers the prohibition against the sale of a corporate office (§20.1) and the limitations on the transferability of control shares (§20.2).

§20.1 SALE OF OFFICE

Directors and officers are strictly prohibited from selling their offices for personal gain. *Rosenfeld v. Black*, 445 F.2d 1337 (2d Cir. 1971). Corporate offices do not belong to the incumbents. Officers are accountable to the board, and directors are accountable to the shareholders. As fiduciaries, corporate managers are bound to perform their functions under the terms of their appointment.

§20.2 LIMITATIONS ON SALE OF CONTROLLING SHARES

§20.2.1 Control Premium

The trading price of corporate shares does not always reflect fully their latent power (when combined with other shares) to exercise control. Normally, individual shares cannot alone affect control. But when a buyer accumulates enough shares for a voting majority, control value attaches to the shares. The difference between the value of latent control rights and the value of voting control is referred to as a "control premium."

What is a control premium? It is the additional value, above the financial value of a passive corporate investment, that comes with controlling the corporation's business. Suppose GenSys has 10 million shares outstanding and individual shares trade publicly at $50. Barbara, the largest shareholder, has 3 million shares. What is the value of her combined holding? Probably more than $50 per share because a 30 percent shareholder of a public company generally has effective control. If Kendall wants to buy Barbara's shares, Barbara will demand extra for her control block. Kendall will pay this premium because of the increased value to him of being able to extract greater returns from GenSys than if he owned a noncontrol interest. Suppose Kendall pays $240 million, or $80 per share—Barbara's control premium is the $90 million difference between the sales price and the prevailing market price of her shares, or a difference equal to $30 per share.

§20.2.2 No-Sharing Rule

Generally, shareholders can sell their shares at whatever price they can get—including at a premium not available to other shareholders. Controlling shareholders need not share the premium their control block commands. *Zetlin v. Hanson Holdings, Inc.*, 397 N.E.2d 387 (N.Y. 1979).

Some commentators have criticized this no-sharing rule. They have urged an "equal opportunity" rule under which all shareholders would share pro rata in any control premium. They argue that control should be viewed as a corporate "asset" in which each shareholder should share equally. See Berle, *The Price of Power: Sale of Corporate Control*, 50 Cornell L.Q. 628 (1965). Thus, a buyer willing to pay a premium for control (because the corporation's assets are more valuable in her hands) should be willing to pay the same premium for all the shares. See Andrews, *The Stockholder's Right to Equal Opportunity in the Sale of Shares*, 78 Harv. L. Rev. 505 (1965).

Opponents of an equal opportunity rule argue that it would result in fewer (beneficial) control transfers and leave inefficient management entrenched. A rule that would force a buyer to pay all shareholders a control premium would make the acquisition more expensive. Further, the buyer might be unable or unwilling to buy all the shares. Moreover, the rule would dilute the value of control held by existing controlling shareholders, for which they may have already paid a premium. These commentators argue that minority shareholders, on balance, would prefer a rule that resulted in efficient new management, even at the expense of not sharing in any control premium. Easterbrook & Fischel, *Corporate Control Transactions*, 91 Yale L.J. 737

(1982). Studies indicate that prices of minority shares in public corporations rise after the sale of control, even when the control buyer does not purchase minority shares. See ALI Principles §5.16, note 1.

Nearly all courts have rejected the equal opportunity rule—primarily because equal sharing would effectively require all control purchases to be by tender offer open to all shareholders and would discourage beneficial changes in control. Nonetheless, an equal opportunity rule of sorts now exists for acquiring control in *public corporations*. Under federal rules, *tender offers* in public corporations must be open to all shareholders—the "all holders" rule. Exchange Act Rule 14d-10(a)(1). In addition, each shareholder must be offered the highest price paid any other tendering shareholder—the "best price" rule. Exchange Act Rule 14d-10(a)(2). For tender offers in public corporations, these SEC rules preempt the state no-sharing rule. See §38.2.

Nonetheless, when the controlling shareholder is a parent corporation that seeks to sell a partially owned subsidiary, the subsidiary's board need not accept whatever terms the parent negotiates with the third-party buyer. Instead, the subsidiary's directors have duties to protect the interests of the minority shareholders—even though the shareholders have no ability to vote down the transaction or right to share in a control premium. See *McMullin v. Beran*, 765 A.2d 910 (Del. 2000) (requiring directors of subsidiary to reach "informed and deliberate judgment" that minority shareholders are receiving maximum value for their shares in merger with third-party acquirer, whether by tendering their shares in merger or seeking judicial appraisal based on subsidiary's going-concern value).

§20.2.3 Exceptions to No-Sharing Rule

To discourage harmful transfers of control, state courts recognize exceptions to the general rule of free transferability. See Elhauge, *Triggering Function of Sale of Control Doctrine*, 59 U. Chi. L. Rev. 1465 (1992). Controlling shareholders cannot sell their control block in three situations:

1. The sale is conditioned on the controlling shareholder improperly selling corporate offices to the buyer.
2. The buyer had proposed to acquire the whole company, and the controlling shareholder recast the transaction as a control block sale.
3. The controlling shareholder has reason to believe the seller will "loot" the corporation after acquiring control.

Sale of Office

Often the seller of a control block will promise, as part of the sale, to give the buyer working control of the board. This is accomplished by the seriatim resignation of the seller's directors, with each vacancy filled by the buyer's directors. Without such a promise, the buyer would have to conduct a special shareholders' meeting to elect his new board, or wait to buy until the next annual shareholders' meeting, or risk his investment until his board is seated.

Courts treat "board succession" promises as a prohibited sale of office if the challenger shows either: (1) the buyer did not acquire working control and could *not* have elected his own slate, *Essex Universal Corp. v. Yates*, 305 F.2d 572 (2d Cir. 1962), or (2) the sales price exceeds the premium the control block alone commands, suggesting the price included a prohibited sale of office, *Perlman v. Feldmann*, 219 F.2d 173 (2d Cir. 1955) (Swan, J., dissenting).

Usurpation of Corporate Opportunities

Some cases hold that a controlling shareholder cannot convert an offer made to the corporation into one to the shareholder alone. If the control buyer offers to deal with all shareholders on an equal basis, such as by proposing a merger or the purchase of all the corporation's assets, the controlling shareholder cannot divert this "corporate opportunity" to himself. Some courts focus on the seller's failure to disclose the offer to the corporation—that is, to disinterested directors. Others focus on how the buyer presented his offer. Cf. *Tryon v. Smith*, 229 P.2d 251 (Or. 1951) (upholding sale by 70 percent shareholder for twice that paid minority shareholders, even though buyer had first offered to deal with all shareholders equally).

Sale to "Looters"

A controlling shareholder may not sell control if the seller has reason to suspect the buyer will use control to "loot" the corporation and the shareholders (and other constituents) left behind. If the control seller has reason to suspect the buyer will steal corporate assets or engage in unfair self-dealing transactions, the seller becomes liable for any damages caused by the buyer, including any damage to the corporation's earnings power. Corporate recovery is not limited to the control premium the seller received.

When does a controlling shareholder have a reason to suspect a looter? Courts accept that too strict a duty discourages control transfers. The seller is not a guarantor of the probity of the buyer. Instead, the seller must investigate the buyer's intentions only when circumstances raise a reasonable suspicion that looting will follow the sale. See *Gerdes v. Reynolds*, 28 N.Y.S.2d 622 (Sup. Ct. 1941); *DeBaun v. First Western Bank & Trust Co.*, 120 Cal. Rptr. 354 (Cal. App. 1975). If circumstances surrounding the sale are suspicious and the seller fails to investigate or his investigation confirms the suspicions, the seller becomes liable for any losses to the corporation.

What factual circumstances create danger signals?

- **When price is too good.** Although a high price may merely reflect the buyer's view that the corporation is worth more in his hands than with the incumbents, an excessive premium should cause suspicion—particularly if the corporation has readily marketable assets. But courts give sellers a good deal of leeway. See *Clagett v. Hutchinson*, 583 F.2d 1259 (4th Cir. 1978) (holding that price of $43.75 per share, for shares that usually ranged from $7.50 to $10.00 per share, did not place the seller on notice of potential fraud on the corporation).
- **When buyer is dishonest or hurried.** If there is reason to believe the buyer is dishonest, the seller must make further inquiries. See *Harris v. Carter*, 582 A.2d 222 (Del. Ch. 1990) (even if the sellers themselves relied on misrepresentations by the buyer). In addition, if the buyer shows little interest in the company's business and urges that the transaction be closed quickly, the seller may be required to investigate the buyer's motives.
- **When buyer has bad business reputation.** If the seller knows the buyer has significant debts, outstanding liens against his other businesses, and fraud judgments against him, the seller should suspect that the buyer does not worry about how he makes his money. *DeBaun v. First Western Bank & Trust Co.*, 120 Cal. Rptr. 354 (Cal. App. 1975).

§20.2.4 Meaning of *Perlman v. Feldmann*

The overlapping sale-of-control limitations are illustrated by the famous, much-studied case of *Perlman v. Feldmann*, 219 F.2d 173 (2d Cir. 1955). Feldmann, who controlled 37 percent of the shares of Newport Steel, sold his shares for $20 per share—a two-thirds premium over the then-market price of $12. A minority shareholder brought a derivative suit on behalf of the corporation, claiming Feldmann had sold a corporate asset, namely Newport's steel supplies, during the Korean War's steel shortage when steel prices were controlled and access to steel commanded a premium. Feldmann had invented a way to skirt the price controls (known in the industry as the "Feldmann Plan") by having buyers make interest-free advances to obtain supply commitments. The buyer (Wilport), a syndicate of steel end-users, wanted Newport's steel supplies free of the Feldmann Plan.

The court held that Feldmann had breached a fiduciary duty to the corporation because his sale of control sacrificed the favorable cash flow to the corporation generated by the Feldmann Plan. The court held Feldmann accountable to the minority shareholders to share his premium.

What did Feldmann do wrong?

- **Sale of office?** After Wilport bought Feldmann's control shares, Feldmann and the rest of the board resigned and installed Wilport's nominees. The court agreed that the price Wilport paid for Feldmann's shares was a fair one, negating any inference that Wilport had paid Feldmann to sell his office.
- **Denial of "equal opportunity" to share the control premium?** Although the Second Circuit's opinion contains broad statements about the duties of fiduciaries, the court's focus on the loss to the corporation from discontinuing the Feldmann Plan undermines this broad reading of the case. Other courts, including state courts in Indiana whose law the Second Circuit was purporting to interpret, have rejected an equal opportunity rule.
- **Sale to looter?** Wilport wanted a supply of steel free of the Feldmann Plan prepayment terms—that is, it planned to engage in self-dealing at controlled (below-market) prices. Feldmann no doubt knew this. The Second Circuit rejected arguments that gray market pricing under the Feldmann Plan was unethical and concluded that Wilport had taken a corporate asset by discontinuing Newport's gray market profits. Nonetheless, Newport's minority shareholders on balance benefited from the sale, as measured by post-sale increases in their share prices. That is, the loss of gray market profits was offset by the vertical integration with Wilport or its more efficient management. Wilport was on balance a beneficent new owner, not a looter.
- **Taking of a corporate control opportunity?** There was evidence that another purchaser had originally approached Feldmann to merge with Newport, a transaction through which all of the shareholders would have shared in any control premium. Feldmann rejected this offer and soon after sold his shares to Wilport.

Although the minority shareholders sued derivatively on behalf of the corporation, the Second Circuit allowed them to recover in their own right. Recovery by the corporation of Feldmann's premium would have allowed Wilport to recoup part of the premium it paid Feldmann for control (see §18.1.2).

Why is *Perlman v. Feldmann* relevant? The case has not been followed by other courts; the real holding is obscure; and the court's conclusion that the corporation suffered harm is belied by the remedy ordered. Nonetheless, the case offers a chance to think about corporate control, who owns it, and the role of fiduciary duties in the corporation. Some law professors believe the case offers enough to teach a whole Corporations course—perhaps they're right, but it would be a stretch.

§20.2.5 Disclosure Duties

Sales of control in public corporations must be disclosed under SEC rules. The corporation must disclose any sale of control within four days after it happens. See Item 5.01, Form 8-K (if known to the company's board) (see §21.2). And any acquirer of more than 5 percent of the company's shares must disclose the size of its holdings, along with information about itself, the sources of its funding, and its plans with respect to the corporation. See Schedule 13D (must be filed within 10 days after acquirer passes 5 percent threshold) (see §38.1).

In addition, controlling shareholders may have disclosure duties to minority shareholders. Controlling shareholders who know of an impending control offer and buy shares from minority shareholders cannot misrepresent their reasons for buying. See §23.2.1. What if they say nothing? Under the "special facts" doctrine, controlling shareholders may have a fiduciary duty to reveal material information when they purchase shares from minority shareholders in a face-to-face transaction. See §23.2.2.

Rule 10b-5 (the famous federal rule prohibiting securities fraud) also imposes a disclose-or-abstain duty on controlling shareholders when trading on nonpublic confidential information in public and private markets. See §23.3.1. But a controlling shareholder who fails to tell minority shareholders that he is selling for a premium is not liable to them because they neither bought nor sold and thus lack standing to sue. See *Blue Chip Stamps v. Manor Drug Stores*, 421 U.S. 723 (1975); *Birnbaum v. Newport Steel Corp.*, 193 F.2d 461 (2d Cir. 1952), *cert. denied*, 343 U.S. 956 (1952) (same facts as *Perlman v. Feldmann* above).

EXAMPLES

Examples

1. Foamex Corp. makes foam for use in furniture. Stella, the firm's founder, owns 400,000 shares, representing 40 percent of Foamex's outstanding stock. Stella is getting on in years and has left management to her son-in-law Carl, the company's CEO and a 5 percent owner. There are 700 other shareholders for whom there exists a thin public trading market. Foamex stock has been trading at $20 a share.
   a. Boyer Inc., a large furniture manufacturer and Foamex's largest customer, wants to buy the company. Boyer offers to buy Carl's stock at $50 per share if he and the rest of the board resign and install Boyer's directors. Is this legal?
   b. Carl rebuffs Boyer, which then approaches Stella to buy her 40 percent block for $30 a share. What must Stella do before selling?

2. Boyer had originally approached Carl with a proposal that Boyer acquire Foamex in a $25 million merger—$25 per share. Carl told Stella about the offer, and she said the price was too low. Carl rejected Boyer's offer.
   a. Soon afterward, Stella suggested to Boyer that she would sell her 40 percent block for $12 million—$30 per share. Stella points out that this would be less expensive than Boyer acquiring control in a $25 million merger. Do you see any problems?
   b. Suppose Carl had informed the board of Boyer's merger offer, and the board had turned it down because the price was too low. Does this change things?
   c. A court holds Stella liable for selling her shares after Boyer's merger offer. Stella sold her shares for $12 million, at a time their aggregate market price was $8 million. In the merger she would have received $10 million. What is the appropriate remedy?

3. Soon after buying Stella's 40 percent block, Boyer buys Carl's 5 percent holding for $30 per share. Boyer bought on the condition that Carl use his best efforts to have the other board members resign and install Boyer's slate of directors.
   a. Shawn, a Foamex shareholder, challenges Carl's sale. On what theory?
   b. Evaluate the merits of Shawn's challenge.

4. After installing its own board, Boyer increases its foam purchases from Foamex and takes significant volume discounts not available to other Foamex customers or in the industry. This pattern is not new. Boyer has bought control positions in other suppliers to obtain supply discounts. Stella knew about Boyer's past practices.
   a. Shawn sues Stella. On what theory?
   b. Does Shawn have recourse against anyone else?
   c. A court finds Stella liable. To whom and for how much?

Explanations

1. a. No. Carl has sold his corporate office. Carl's 5 percent shareholding alone is insufficient to carry any meaningful control, particularly since Stella owns a controlling 40 percent block. The premium over market that Boyer is willing to pay can only be explained as consideration for Carl's promise to help install Boyer's slate of directors. A shareholder could challenge the validity of the board's filling of vacancies.
   b. Nothing, unless she suspects Boyer will loot the company. Shareholders have significant autonomy to decide whether or not to sell their shares, and a controlling shareholder's duty to investigate is triggered only when there is reason to be suspicious.

      Are there any apparent danger signals here? The 50 percent control premium hardly triggers suspicion—courts have approved control sales with premiums of up to 300 percent. Boyer's status as a Foamex customer does not necessarily imply future supply arrangements will be unfair. Unless Stella had some reason to suspect Boyer planned below-market arrangements—for example, because she knew Boyer needed to cut its foam costs significantly to stay competitive—Stella would be under no obligation to investigate or to refrain from selling her shares.

2. a. Perhaps. Stella's sale could be viewed as the usurpation of a corporate control opportunity. A merger would have meant equal sharing of any control premium. When the buyer (as here) is willing to deal with all the shareholders, a sharing rule would not prevent this control transaction from going forward.

   Nonetheless, an "equal opportunity" rule reallocates part of the control premium to the other shareholders and dilutes the value of the controlling shareholder's control block. The rule would put Stella in the untenable position of either rejecting the transaction or putting the merger to a shareholder vote and voting against it herself. Modern courts are not inclined to force sharing just because the buyer originally suggested a sharing transaction. Only if the seller fraudulently buys minority shares (a kind of insider trading) to resell them to the buyer do the courts impose a sharing obligation.

   b. Perhaps. Arguably, the board's rejection of the merger freed Stella to take the opportunity herself. But the board's rejection of the merger, like the rejection of a corporate opportunity in which a director has an interest, should be reviewed as a conflict-of-interest transaction under a fairness standard if Stella anticipated selling her control block. Was the board sufficiently disinterested, independent, and informed? See §16.3.1.

   c. Sharing of her control premium with the minority, even though the normal remedy for a fiduciary breach is recovery by the corporation. Requiring Stella to pay her control premium (or a portion of it) to the corporation would produce a windfall for Boyer—indirectly refunding it a portion of the control premium it had paid for Stella's shares.

   The failure to share breached a duty to the minority shareholders, and any remedy should be tailored to address the theory of liability. There are two possible theories, leading to different damage calculations—

   - Under an "equal sharing" theory—Stella improperly took a control premium—Stella would be liable for 60 percent of the premium to the other (60 percent) shareholders. This was the remedial approach in *Perlman v. Feldmann*. See §20.2.3. Stella's control premium was arguably \$4 million (the difference between her \$12 million sales price and her shares' \$8 million aggregate market price), suggesting a $2.4 million recovery for the other shareholders, who hold 600,000 shares—$4 per share.

- Under an "improper rejection" theory—Stella improperly blocked the merger—Stella is liable for the loss she caused minority shareholders. This is the difference between the proposed merger price ($25 per share) and the market price ($20 per share)—$5 per share.

3. a. Sale of office. Carl's sale is prohibited if Shawn can show Carl's premium ($10 per share over market) included a payment to relinquish his office. If so, Shawn can seek to have Carl share his premium.
   b. Shawn has a difficult challenge. Although a 5 percent block could not alone command a control premium, a 5 percent *incremental* block might have been of particular importance to Boyer, a 40 percent shareholder. The additional 5 percent would make it virtually impossible for the public shareholders to form an effective dissident block because it would take 91 percent of the public shareholders to outvote a 45 percent Boyer. On the other hand, the most significant impediment to Boyer exercising effective control is not Carl's 5 percent share ownership, but Carl's incumbency and the board's control of Foamex's proxy machinery. Nonetheless, courts are reluctant to accept the obvious: A "board succession" promise has value to a control buyer and forms part of the bargain. Only if there is some suggestion Boyer has bought the board's replacement to abuse its control should a court intervene.

4. a. Sale to a looter. There are two issues: (1) Did Boyer's self-dealing transactions constitute looting? (2) If so, did Stella have reason to suspect that Boyer would engage in them?

      Boyer's self-dealing purchasing appears to be on terms unfair to Foamex—the purchases do not fall into a range of what would be expected in arm's-length transactions (see §13.3.2). Yet overall Boyer's ownership may not cause losses to Foamex. Looting liability is limited to the losses the new owner causes the company.

      Even if Boyer is a looter, Stella is liable only if circumstances suggested Boyer planned to engage in unfair self-dealing. Although Stella should have known Boyer planned to increase its purchases from Foamex, Stella had no apparent reason to suspect the purchases would be on unfair terms. Stella was under no duty to investigate whether purchases from other Boyer-controlled companies were on unfair terms unless circumstances raised this suspicion.
   b. Yes. He can also sue Boyer, as controlling shareholder, on a self-dealing theory (see §17.2).
   c. Stella will be liable directly to the minority shareholders on a pro rata basis for their losses, not limited by the control premium she received. (Recovery in a derivative suit would indirectly reimburse

Boyer.) These losses could well exceed (and, if the looter does what it intended, should exceed) any control premium. Stella would be liable not only for the actual losses from the self-dealing (here $2 million a year) but also any losses to Foamex's earning power (consequential damages).

Disclosure in Securities Trading Markets

Information is the lifeblood of securities trading markets—and thus shareholders' transfer rights. State corporate law imposes minimal disclosure obligations on the corporation. Instead, shareholders' informational rights arise largely under federal securities law. The Securities Exchange Act of 1934 (Exchange Act) builds on the regulation of public securities offerings under the Securities Act of 1933 (Securities Act, see Chapter 5). While the Securities Act reflects a "truth in securities" philosophy, the Exchange Act reaches ambitiously for "integrity in stock markets."

This chapter describes the rules on corporate disclosure by publicly traded companies under state corporate law (§21.1) and under federal securities law (§21.2).

§21.1 STATE DISCLOSURE DUTIES

Statutory Disclosure

State corporate law imposes minimal disclosure duties on corporations. Besides requiring basic information in the articles of incorporation and bare-bones notice to shareholders when they vote, state corporate statutes generally do not require regular information to shareholders. An exception, adopted only in some states, is a requirement that shareholders receive an annual financial report. See MBCA §16.20.

Duty of Honesty

In 1998, the Delaware Supreme Court created a stir when it held that corporate managers have a state-based fiduciary duty not to knowingly disseminate false information to shareholders. *Malone v. Brincat*, 722 A.2d 5 (Del. 1998). The duty, the court held, arises whether or not the corporation is requesting shareholder action, and can be enforced by shareholders claiming individual losses or in a derivative action on behalf of the corporation. In the case, shareholders alleged that company directors (aided by the firm's outside accountants) had knowingly overstated the firm's financial position in SEC filings and public reports over a four-year period—causing a loss of virtually all of the company's value.

The chancery court dismissed the claim because the misinformation had not come in a "request for shareholder action," the usual context for Delaware's "duty of complete candor." See §10.3. Worried about duplicating or usurping federal securities law, the chancery court concluded that release of inaccurate information was not a "corporate governance issue." The supreme court rejected this formalistic line-drawing. The court held the alleged facts, if properly pleaded, could support a claim (either direct or derivative) that the directors had knowingly misinformed shareholders, a violation of their fiduciary duties.

Although some commentators have labeled *Malone v. Brincat* a "duty of disclosure" case, the label is misleading. The court created no general duty to disclose information, but simply held that *whenever* managers communicate they must be honest. This "duty of honesty" is triggered whether the communication involves a request for shareholder action, compliance with federal disclosure requirements, or a voluntary press release. Honest communications ensure that shareholders can exercise their voting and transfer rights, as well as their fiduciary rights to discipline management indolence or disloyalty.

What is the relationship of *Malone v. Brincat* to federal securities law? Under the Securities Litigation Uniform Standards Act of 1998 (SLUSA), any class action alleging fraud in publicly traded securities must be brought in federal court under federal law; state claims are preempted. Securities Act §16(c); Exchange Act §28(f)(2). The Delaware court interpreted SLUSA, passed after the case had commenced, to not apply. But as to future cases, the court pointed out that the federal legislation would not prevent "duty of honesty" litigation in state court. SLUSA excludes from its coverage derivative suits and state-based claims based on breaches of fiduciary disclosure obligations—the so-called Delaware carve-out. See §22.1.2. Nonetheless, a "duty of honesty" claim presented as a class action alleging merely management deception might not fit these exclusions.

Is a "duty of honesty" action more advantageous than a federal securities fraud action under Rule 10b-5? See Chapter 22. According to the Delaware court, a "duty of honesty" action (unlike a 10b-5 action) can be brought by shareholders who do not claim to have purchased or sold because of the false disclosure. But a "duty of honesty" action claiming loss in share value would require a showing of individual reliance on the alleged falsehoods—essentially foreclosing class actions using a "fraud on the market" theory permitted under Rule 10b-5. See §23.3.3.

A full comparison, however, is difficult because *Malone v. Brincat* left a number of questions unresolved. Although the court said directors cannot "knowingly" disseminate false information, it is unclear what level of culpability must be pled and proved. Must the plaintiff show actual knowledge of the falsehood or is it enough that the directors were negligent? In addition, does a breach of the "duty of honesty" constitute a breach of the duty of care or of loyalty? The answer could affect whether directors can be exculpated from individual liability (see §12.5). What "corporate damages," if any, must be shown in a derivative action? This might be problematic if corrective disclosure returns stock prices to "true value." What is the appropriate remedy? Damages that assume shareholders had bought or sold prior to the deception (rescissionary damages) might be more advantageous than the usual out-of-pocket damages under Rule 10b-5, which are based on the loss in market value caused by the dishonesty (see §22.3.4).

§21.2 FEDERAL DISCLOSURE REQUIREMENTS

The federal regime of ex ante *mandatory disclosure* applies to companies whose securities are traded in public stock markets. These companies become subject to a panoply of regulation, some of which is described in other chapters:

- **Periodic reporting.** Registered companies must file *periodic disclosure* documents with the Securities and Exchange Commission (SEC). These companies (including those that have made a public offering under the Securities Act) are known as "reporting companies." See §21.2.2 below.
- **Recordkeeping.** To carry out their periodic reporting obligations, registered companies must *keep records* and maintain a system of internal accounting controls. See §21.2.3 below.
- **Proxy disclosure.** Shareholders of registered companies must receive information under the SEC proxy rules when management (or others) *solicits proxies* on matters requiring shareholder voting. See §9.2. For annual shareholder meetings, shareholders must receive the company's annual report.
- **Takeover disclosure.** Any person or group that acquires more than 5 percent of a registered company's equity securities must disclose

its plans. See §38.1. Any person that makes a *tender offer* for the equity securities of a registered company is subject to substantive requirements and disclosure rules. See §38.2.

- **Insider trading disclosure/disgorgement.** Directors, officers, and 10 percent shareholders of registered companies must *disclose their trading* in the company's publicly traded *equity* securities and are liable to the company if they make profits (or avoid losses) from purchases and sales within any six-month window. See Chapter 24.

§21.2.1 SEC Registration

Companies must register with the SEC under the Exchange Act in two circumstances:

- **Exchange "listed" companies.** Companies whose *debt* or *equity* securities are listed on a stock exchange must register with the exchange, with copies to the SEC. Exchange Act §12(a) (prohibiting trading by broker-dealers on stock exchange in securities not registered). Stock exchange rules specify qualifications that issuers must satisfy to have their securities "listed" for trading on the exchange. The "listing" rules assure traders on the exchange that these companies meet certain sales, assets, and net worth thresholds.
- **OTC companies.** In 1964 Congress amended the Exchange Act to require registration of companies whose *equity* securities are publicly traded on the over-the-counter markets. A company must register if it has a class of equity securities held of record by more than 500 shareholders and has total assets exceeding $10 million. Exchange Act §12(g); Rule 12g-1 (asset threshold increased to $10 million in 1996).

Once registered, a company may deregister only under specified conditions. For a fuller treatment of this topic, see §9.2.1 (proxy regulation).

§21.2.2 Periodic Disclosure

Registered companies become "reporting companies" and must file annual, quarterly, and special reports with the SEC. Exchange Act §13(a). This ongoing stream of information is used extensively in securities trading markets. There are three important Exchange Act filings:

- **Annual report.** Reporting companies must file annually, within 60 to 90 days of the close of their fiscal year, an extensive disclosure document that contains much the same information as a Securities Act registration statement when a company goes public—including description of company's business, management's discussion of risks, and audited financial statements. Form 10-K (for smaller businesses, Form 10-KSB).

- **Quarterly report.** Reporting companies must file quarterly, within 35 to 45 days of the close of each of the company's first three fiscal quarters, a report that consists mostly of updated (and unaudited) financial information. Form 10-Q.
- **Special report.** Reporting companies must file a special report on specified, material developments. Form 8-K. Significantly expanded by the SEC in response to post-Enron concerns (see Sarbanes-Oxley §409), Form 8-K has moved closer to a continuous disclosure system. Exchange Act Rel. No. 49,424 (2004).

In theory, these mandatory disclosures represent a "public good" available to all securities market participants. Without a system of mandatory disclosure, management might not be inclined to provide *for free* such fulsome information, and traders would be reluctant to pay for it if others could observe trading patterns to "pirate" their information. To assure an adequate supply of company-specific information, the reporting system is mandatory and the information it produces is available to all.

Reporting by "Public Issuers"

In addition to companies that must register their securities for trading under the Exchange Act, companies that have made a registered securities offering (*debt or equity*) under the Securities Act are also subject to the Exchange Act reporting requirements. See Exchange Act §15(d); Rules 15d-1 to 15d-17. These companies must commence reporting once their Securities Act registration is effective even if their securities are not listed on a stock exchange and the company does not satisfy the size thresholds of OTC registration. Companies subject to reporting only by virtue of §15(d), however, escape other Exchange Act regulation applicable to other registered companies with respect to proxy solicitations, tender offers, insiders' short-swing profits, and takeover bids.

Certification of SEC Filings

As commanded by the Sarbanes-Oxley Act, the SEC has adopted rules requiring corporate officers of reporting companies to certify the annual and quarterly reports filed with the SEC. Sarbanes-Oxley §302. The CEO and CFO must each certify that he reviewed the report and, based on his knowledge, that (1) it does not contain any material statements that are false or misleading, and (2) it "fairly presents" the financial condition and results of operation of the company—regardless of formal compliance with accounting principles. Exchange Act Rules 13a-14, 15d-14 (certification not applicable to Form 8-K reports).

In addition, the CEO and CFO must certify they are responsible for establishing and maintaining "disclosure controls and procedures" that ensure material information is made known to them, and these internal controls must be evaluated before making their report. See §12.3.5.

Real-Time Disclosure

There is no requirement that reporting companies disclose all material information on a real-time basis. But there is a move in that direction. As revised in 2004, Form 8-K (special reports) requires filing and disclosure within four business days of the following events:

- **Operational events.** Entry into (or termination of) definitive material agreements, loss of significant customer, bankruptcy, or receivership
- **Financial events.** Acquisition or disposition of assets, results of operations and financial condition (such as interim earnings statements), direct financial obligations or obligations under off-balance sheet arrangements (or events triggering such obligations), restructuring charges, material impairments under existing agreements
- **Securities-related events.** Delisting or transfer of listing, unregistered sales of equity securities, changes in debt rating, material modifications to rights of securities holders
- **Financial-integrity events.** Changes in registrant's certifying accountant, nonreliability of previously issued financial statements or audit report
- **Governance events.** Changes in corporate control, changes affecting directors or principal officers (departure, resignation, removal, election, appointment), amendments to articles or bylaws, waivers of code of ethics
- **Executive pay.** Compensation agreements (attached to filing), compensation arrangements outside ordinary course of business

In addition, any voluntary company disclosure to some investors must be disclosed simultaneously to all investors, typically by simulcast or posting on the company's website. See Regulation FD (§23.3.4). Voluntary disclosures of interim financial data and press releases must also be "furnished" to the SEC on Form 8-K (by being furnished and not filed, the report does not trigger statutory fraud liability).

EDGAR

In the mid 1990s, the SEC computerized its filing and disclosure system. Today all disclosure documents must be filed electronically using the EDGAR system (Electronic Data Gathering, Analysis, and Retrieval). EDGAR filings are available on the Internet, going back to 1994 for most companies. Securities markets, as well as corporate and securities lawyers, have found EDGAR to be invaluable. You can find and play with it on the SEC's website at *www.sec.gov.*

§21.2.3 Recordkeeping and Foreign Bribes

In response to revelations in the 1970s of U.S. companies doctoring their books and setting up slush funds to bribe highly placed foreign government officials, Congress passed the Foreign Corrupt Practices Act of 1978. Cracking down on lax internal controls by publicly held corporations, the FCPA amended the Exchange Act to require reporting companies (1) to maintain financial records in "reasonable detail" to reflect company transactions accurately and (2) to put into place internal accounting controls sufficient to provide "reasonable assurances" of internal accountability and proper accounting. Exchange Act §13(b)(2).

The FCPA also prohibits reporting companies (or their officials) from paying bribes to foreign government officials to influence their official actions or decisions. Exchange Act §30A(a). In recognition of the way the world works, however, the FCPA excludes from its coverage "routine" payola to lower-level government officials to facilitate their performing their duties. Exchange Act §30A(b).

In 2002, responding to a wave of corporate and accounting scandals, the SEC adopted new rules that require reporting companies to establish and maintain an overall system of disclosure controls and procedures adequate to meet the company's Exchange Act reporting obligations. Exchange Act Rules 13a-15 and 15d-15.

Securities Fraud—Rule 10b-5

Rule 10b-5, the securities antifraud rule promulgated under the Securities Exchange Act of 1934, is a bedrock of U.S. securities regulation. Every securities transaction lives under its protective shade and its menacing shadow. For those who enter into securities transactions, the rule assures that relevant securities information is not purposefully false or misleading. For purveyors of securities information, it imposes standards of complete honesty that carry risks of heavy liability.

This chapter begins with an overview of Rule 10b-5 (§22.1) and then describes the nature of a private 10b-5 action: the persons and activities to which the rule applies (§22.2); the fraud elements that must be shown to establish liability (§22.3); the defenses that apply in a Rule 10b-5 action (§22.4); a comparison with other antifraud remedies (§22.5).

The next chapter covers the use of Rule 10b-5 as the principal regulatory tool against insider trading. Then Chapter 24 looks at the federal disclosure rules and short-swing disgorgement liability for market trading by specified insiders.

§22.1 OVERVIEW OF RULE 10b-5

§22.1.1 History of Rule 10b-5

Rule 10b-5 has been aptly described as "the judicial oak which has grown from little more than a legislative acorn." The rule's origins were humble.

In 1942, faced with reports that a company president was making unduly pessimistic statements about company earnings while at the same time buying his company's stock, the SEC filled a regulatory gap. The antifraud provisions of the Securities Act of 1933 prohibited fraudulent *sales* of securities, but there was no specific prohibition against fraudulent *purchases*.

Using its authority to promulgate rules that prohibit "manipulative or deceptive devices or contrivances . . . in connection with the purchase or sale of any security" under §10(b) of the Securities Exchange Act of 1934, the SEC filled the "purchase" gap with Rule 10b-5, which states:

> It shall be unlawful for any person, directly or indirectly, by the use of any means of instrumentality of interstate commerce, or of the mails or of any facility of any national securities exchange,
>
> (a) to employ any device, scheme, or artifice to defraud;
>
> (b) to make any untrue statement of a material fact or to omit to state a material fact necessary in order to make the statements made, in light of the circumstances under which they were made, not misleading; or
>
> (c) to engage in any act, practice, or course of business which operates or would operate as a fraud or deceit upon any person,
>
> in connection with the purchase or sale of any security.

The SEC approved the rule without debate, with one SEC commissioner asking rhetorically: "Well, we are against fraud, aren't we?"

The regulatory acorn sprouted in 1946 when a federal district court in Pennsylvania first inferred a private cause of action under Rule 10b-5. See *Kardon v. National Gypsum Co.*, 69 F. Supp. 512 (E.D. Pa. 1946). The implied 10b-5 action then grew and branched in the 1960s as federal courts used it aggressively to regulate not only securities fraud, but also negligent securities practices and corporate mismanagement. In the 1970s the Supreme Court pruned back this judicial activism and effectively limited the private 10b-5 action to securities deception. This pruning continued, though less dramatically, in the 1980s and 1990s as the Court dealt with issues of 10b-5 coverage and procedure.

Through all of this judicial shaping, the 10b-5 action has shown remarkable resiliency and has become a centerpiece of U.S. securities regulation. Its procedural advantages are many: nationwide service of process, liberal venue rules, and broad discovery tools. In 1995, however, Congress enacted the Private Securities Litigation Reform Act to limit perceived abuses in federal securities litigation, particularly 10b-5 class actions. While the number of securities class actions has remained stable (about 200 per year) since the PSLRA was enacted, the substantive and procedural rules introduced by the legislation have discouraged the filing of 10b-5 class actions. In 2002, responding to Enron and other accounting scandals, Congress enacted the Sarbanes-Oxley Act and signaled a renewed commitment to securities fraud liability. See §11.5.1. Then in 2010, responding to the financial crisis of 2008, Congress enacted the Dodd-Frank Act, expanding the SEC's enforcement powers, including in actions arising under Rule 10b-5. See §11.5.2.

§22.1.2 Private 10b-5 Actions and SEC Enforcement

Section 10(b), unlike other antimanipulation and antifraud sections of the Exchange Act, does not specify a private remedy for violations of its rules. Despite the absence of a statutory mandate, it is now beyond question that Rule 10b-5 implies a private cause of action. See *Kardon v. National Gypsum Co.*, 73 F. Supp. 798 (E.D. Pa. 1947) (first case to impose 10b-5 liability, holding corporate insider liable for misrepresenting that business would not be sold when in fact insider planned to sell it at substantial profit). See also *Superintendent of Insurance v. Bankers Life & Casualty Co.*, 404 U.S. 6 (1971) (confirming existence of private action). Such claims may be brought only in federal district courts, which have exclusive jurisdiction over actions arising under the Exchange Act. See Exchange Act §27.

Rule 10b-5 is also a potent tool in SEC enforcement. Section 21 of the Exchange Act gives the SEC broad enforcement powers to sue in federal court to enjoin violations of its rules, including Rule 10b-5. Using this authority, the SEC has sought injunctions and other equitable remedies. See *SEC v. Texas Gulf Sulphur Co.*, 401 F.2d 833 (2d Cir. 1968) (judicial order establishing a fund from which contemporaneous investors could recover lost profits from illegal insider trading). The SEC can also recommend that the U.S. Justice Department institute a 10b-5 criminal action, a common occurrence in insider trading cases. See §23.3.

Madoff Scandal

One of the most high-profile securities frauds—a Ponzi scheme orchestrated by Bernie Madoff in which he used new investor money to pay returns to old investors—illustrates the reach and limits of Rule 10b-5. Madoff was a stockbroker who promised his clients, mostly wealthy individuals and large charities, steady returns using sophisticated hedging techniques. The scheme lasted for nearly 20 years. All told, about $65 billion (including fabricated gains) was missing from client accounts when the fraud was revealed in 2008. Although the SEC had received complaints that Madoff's investment model was "too good to be true," the agency failed to unearth the fraud. Instead, it came to light only when Madofff himself told his sons that his investment funds were "one big lie."

Here is a partial list of the more than 250 cases spawned by the Madoff fraud (many as reported by "The D&O Diary" blog):

- Federal prosecutors brought a criminal case against Madoff, charging him with securities fraud (including under Rule 10b-5); Madoff pled guilty in 2009 and is serving a prison term of 150 years.
- Investors in the Madoff funds sued in federal court (including under Rule 10b-5), claiming fraud in their investments in the Madoff funds and seeking to recover a portion of their losses from the bankrupt funds.
- Investors in "feeder funds" that invested in the Madoff funds brought various federal class suits (including under Rule 10b-5) against the feeder funds, their advisers, and their accounting firms.
- Nonprofit institutions that invested their endowments in Madoff funds sued in federal court (including under Rule 10b-5) investment advisers who recklessly directed the investments to Madoff.
- Pension funds sued (under ERISA) investment advisory firms that, despite "red flags," had directed fund investments to the Madoff funds.
- Investors in the Madoff funds sued the SEC (under the Federal Tort Claims Act) for "sheer incompetence" in failing to investigate the Madoff scheme.
- Investors in feeder funds sued (under Florida law) the funds, along with their auditors, for investing in the Madoff funds.
- The Massachusetts secretary of state brought similar suits (under Massachusetts law) against different feeder funds, which had recorded phone calls from Madoff that began "This conversation never took place, okay?"
- Investors in variable annuity policies that invested in mutual funds that invested in Madoff funds sued in federal court (1) the insurance company offering the variable annuities and (2) the investment firm managing the mutual fund.
- Investors in the Madoff funds sued in federal court (under state law) to collect under their homeowners' insurance policy, which insures against "loss of money . . . resulting from fraud . . . perpetrated against the policy holder."
- A divorced man sued his former wife (under state law) to recover payments he made in their divorce to buy out her portion of their Madoff investments, now worthless.
- A pro se plaintiff, on behalf of Madoff, sued Britney Spears and Kevin Federline, alleging (under who knows what law) that Spears had "secret affairs with Madoff in return for Saks Fifth Avenue gift certificates."

Interestingly, although many of the claims involve fraud in connection with investments that ended up with Madoff, the claims often avoid Rule 10b-5. Why is this? You will discover that claims based on Rule 10b-5 face a number of impediments. There are procedural hurdles (such as discovery stays and limits on plaintiff representatives in 10b-5 class actions) and substantive impediments (such as proving the defendant's knowledge of the fraud and the victim's reliance on false information). In short, Rule 10b-5 casts a large shadow, but there are numerous ways to get at securities fraud.

§22.1.3 Some 10b-5 Pointers

In your study of Rule 10b-5, some preliminary pointers are in order.

Pointer	Elaboration
Look to the language of the statute, not the rule.	You will notice that the operative language of §10(b) is different from that of the rule. Over time, courts have interpreted the enabling statute and its phrase "manipulative or deceptive device or contrivance" as being narrower than the rule. The statute controls, and the phrasing of the rule's prohibitions has become largely irrelevant. The Supreme Court has repeatedly turned to the statutory language to fashion the 10b-5 action.
Identify a securities purchase or sale.	Both §10(b) and Rule 10b-5 apply to "the purchase or sale of any security." Thus, 10b-5 actions protect both investors who purchase and shareholders who sell. Rule 10b-5 also applies whether the securities are publicly traded or closely held and whether they are subject to registration or exempt. Securities exempt from registration under the Securities Act and the Exchange Act—significantly federal, state, and local government securities—are subject to the antifraud coverage of Rule 10b-5. See Exchange Act §3(a)(12) (definition of exempted securities).
Identify deception "in connection with" the securities transaction.	Both §10(b) and Rule 10b-5 apply to "any person" who engages in prohibited behavior "in connection with" a securities transaction. There is no requirement of privity. Rule 10b-5 applies to persons (such as companies that issue false or misleading press releases) even if they are not parties to securities transactions so long as their behavior affects the transactions.
Check (quickly) for the use of jurisdictional means.	Both §10(b) and Rule 10b-5 hinge on specified jurisdictional means: use of an instrumentality of interstate commerce, the mails, or a national securities exchange. In most situations, this raises essentially a nonissue. Almost always a securities transaction will involve the mails or interstate facilities at some point.

(continued)

Pointer	Elaboration
	If a check must clear or a letter confirms a transaction, the mail will be used. Further, the Exchange Act explicitly treats *intrastate* phone calls as involving the use of an instrumentality of interstate commerce. Exchange Act §3(a)(17). It is difficult to imagine, outside of a law school exam (such as a face-to-face transaction for cash), a securities purchase or sale not involving jurisdictional means at some point in its initiation, negotiation, or performance.
Check (with care) for procedural limitations imposed by the PSLRA.	Class actions claiming securities fraud under federal law (including Rule 10b-5) are a disfavored genre after the Private Securities Litigation Reform Act of 1995. The PSLRA seeks to discourage frivolous securities litigation. Among other things, it requires in a 10b-5 class action that the lead plaintiff be the "most adequate plaintiff," presumably the shareholder or investor with the largest financial stake in the class relief. The PSLRA imposes significant new burdens on lead plaintiffs and their counsel: heightened pleading requirements, stay of discovery while any dismissal motion is pending, shifting of attorneys' fees if the complaint lacks substantial legal or factual support, payment of a bond to cover any fees that may eventually be shifted, full and detailed disclosure of any settlement, and limits on the awarding of attorney fees.
Check whether the action is brought in federal or state court.	Actions claiming 10b-5 violations must be brought in federal district court. Exchange Act §27 (exclusive jurisdiction of "violations of this Act or the rules and regulations thereunder"). In addition, class actions alleging fraud involving publicly traded securities—whether under federal or state law—must be brought in federal court. Securities Act §16(c); Exchange Act §28(f)(2). This jurisdictional mandate was added by the Securities Litigation Uniform Standards Act of 1998 (SLUSA), which responded to a perceived loophole that allowed plaintiffs to avoid the PSLRA rules by bringing securities fraud class actions in state court, where state procedures and substantive law are less demanding. See §21.1. Under SLUSA, however, class actions that allege fiduciary breaches under state corporate law may still be brought in state court—the "Delaware carve-out." Securities Act §16(d); Exchange Act §28(f)(3)(A); *Gibson v. PS Group Holdings Inc.*, Fed. Sec. L. Rep. ¶90,921 (S.D. Cal. 2000) (permitting securities fraud class action that alleges state fiduciary breaches to be brought in state court, not limited to the company's state of incorporation).

§22.2 SCOPE OF PRIVATE 10b-5 ACTION

Although grounded in the elements and terminology of the law of deceit, the judge-made 10b-5 action varies from a garden-variety fraud action. Courts have interpreted §10(b) to impose limits on who can sue, who can be sued, and what counts as securities fraud (the subject of this subsection). Moreover, courts have conservatively honed the elements of a private 10b-5 action to resemble a decidedly old-fashioned action for deceit, except to relax significantly the normal requirement of reliance (see §22.3). Finally, courts have fashioned defenses to a private 10b-5 action that go beyond those of a typical fraud action (see §22.4).

Layered on this court-created 10b-5 profile are the provisions of the Private Securities Litigation Reform Act of 1995. Among other things, the PSLRA revamped 10b-5 class action procedures, called for the shifting of attorney fees as a sanction for baseless complaints, largely replaced joint and several liability with proportionate liability, and confirmed the elimination of aiding and abetting liability in private actions.

§22.2.1 Purchasers and Sellers: 10b-5 Standing

Birnbaum Doctrine

Only actual purchasers or sellers may recover damages in a private 10b-5 action. This standing requirement, often called the *Birnbaum* doctrine, avoids speculation about whether and how much a plaintiff might have traded. See *Birnbaum v. Newport Steel Corp.*, 193 F.2d 461 (2d Cir. 1952). Even if a false or misleading statement leads a person not to buy or sell, with results as damaging as actual trading, there is no 10b-5 liability.

In 1975 the Supreme Court affirmed the purchaser-seller requirement. *Blue Chip Stamps v. Manor Drug Stores*, 421 U.S. 723 (1975). The case—famous for the Court's virulent doubts about 10b-5 litigation and a precursor to the PSLRA restrictions on securities fraud actions—involved the unusual allegation that a corporate issuer had made overly pessimistic statements to discourage potential purchasers. Under an antitrust consent decree, the issuer (a trading stamp company) was required to offer its shares at a discount to retailers harmed by its prior anticompetitive activities. One of the retailers that did not buy sued to recover damages on the theory the prospectus offering the stock was pessimistic intentionally to discourage retailers from purchasing.

Speaking for the Court, Justice Rehnquist said the language of §10(b) and the Exchange Act's definitions did not cover offers to sell but only actual sales or purchases. He pointed out that for nearly 25 years Congress had let the *Birnbaum* rule stand. Justice Rehnquist then launched into a diatribe against potential abuse of 10b-5 litigation. He speculated that an indeterminate class of nonpurchasers would bring vexatious litigation to extract settlements, in the process disrupting business and abusing civil discovery. In addition, he argued liability would be staggering if nonpurchasers could base a claim on the speculative assertion they *would have purchased* had disclosure been less discouraging.

Securities Fraud Actions by "Holders" in State Court

The 10b-5 purchaser-seller requirement has led "holders" of securities to bring securities fraud class actions in state court alleging that false or misleading statements led them *not to sell* their shares. These "holder" cases ran into SLUSA, which requires that all class actions alleging fraud "in connection with the purchase or sale" of securities be brought in federal court. See §22.1.2.

In 2006 the Supreme Court held that "holder" class actions brought in state court are preempted by SLUSA, even though they are also barred in federal court under the *Birnbaum* doctrine. *Merrill Lynch, Pierce, Fenner & Smith, Inc. v. Dabit*, 547 U.S. 71 (2006). The principal issue was whether "holder" claims were "in connection with the purchase or sale" of securities. The Court, resolving a split in the circuits, decided they were. Noting that the *Blue Chip Stamps* policy against "vexatious" litigation also motivated the PSLRA restrictions on securities class actions, the Court concluded that SLUSA was intended to funnel such actions into federal court—and squelch them. The Court pointed out that "holder" claims (whether in federal or state court) raise factual issues of whether and how much the holders would have sold, the precise speculation *Blue Chip Stamps* had sought to avoid.

Lead Plaintiff (and Counsel) in 10b-5 Class Actions

The PSLRA, a successor to the *Blue Chip Stamps* antagonism toward private 10b-5 actions, sought to constrain 10b-5 class actions instituted by "professional plaintiffs" who own a nominal number of shares in many public companies and lend their names (for a bounty) to securities lawyers who sue whenever there are unexpected price swings in a company's stock. The PSLRA establishes procedures for the appointment of the lead plaintiff (and thus lead counsel) in securities fraud actions. After the filing of a securities fraud class action, the plaintiff must give public notice to potential class members inviting them to serve as lead plaintiff. The court then is to appoint as lead plaintiff the "most adequate plaintiff," which the statute presumes would be the investor with the largest financial interest in the action. Exchange Act §21D(a)(3).

These new provisions envision a prominent role for institutional shareholders, which typically will have the largest financial interest in securities litigation involving public companies. The provisions specifically exempt institutional shareholders from limits on the frequency a particular investor can serve as lead counsel. See Weiss & Beckerman, *Let the Money Do the Monitoring: How Institutional Investors Can Reduce Agency Costs in Securities Class Actions*, 104 Yale L.J. 2053 (1995) (cited prominently in PSLRA's legislative history).

§22.2.2 Primary Violators: 10b-5 Defendants

There is no privity requirement under Rule 10b-5. Any person who makes false or misleading statements and induces others to trade to their detriment can become liable—a *primary violator*. See *Central Bank of Denver v. First Interstate Bank of Denver*, 511 U.S. 164 (1994). Significantly, corporate officials who make statements about the corporation or its securities expose the corporation to 10b-5 liability, even though the corporation does not trade.

Control Persons

The Exchange Act imposes joint and several liability on any person who controls a primary violator—such as the parent corporation of a subsidiary that engages in illegal activity—unless the control person shows it "acted in good faith and did not . . . induce . . . the violation." Exchange Act §20(a). Courts have interpreted the "good faith" defense as requiring the showing of an affirmative effort by a control person to prevent subordinates from committing securities fraud.

Courts have wrestled with whether, aside from the control person liability of §20(a), the general rule of *respondeat superior* applies to a corporate defendant when an employee of the corporation commits securities fraud in the regular scope of her employment. See *Pugh v. Tribune Co.*, 521 F.3d 686 (7th Cir. 2008) (holding no *respondeat superior* liability under Rule 10b-5 when employee who gave false newspaper circulation figures was not executive officer and false figures were meant to deceive advertisers, not shareholders). The Exchange Act imposes liability on "persons," defined to include a corporation—an entity that can only become liable through its agents. Thus, as some courts have persuasively pointed out, the Act already makes corporate principals liable under traditional agency principles, regardless of the corporate defendant's "good faith" efforts to supervise its employees. Viewed in this light, §20(a) is an additional grounds for vicarious liability beyond traditional agency principles.

Aiders and Abettors

Until 1994 lower courts had uniformly upheld aiding and abetting liability in private Rule 10b-5 cases against secondary participants, such as accountants who certified a company's false financial statements or lawyers who advised and gave "substantial assistance" to securities swindlers. In *Central Bank of Denver*, 511 U.S. 164 (1994), the Court read the "manipulative or deceptive device or contrivance" language of §10(b) to require that 10b-5 defendants engage in actual fraudulent behavior, not merely provide collateral assistance—thus disallowing private actions based on a theory of aiding and abetting. The Court pointed out that none of the other express private causes of action under the Exchange Act impose aiding and abetting liability and that, in any event, such liability has never been widely accepted under tort law.

Even though lower courts had uniformly assumed the existence of 10b-5 aiding and abetting liability before *Central Bank*, the Court concluded Congress had never approved these cases and suggested Congress could remedy the problem if the Court's reading were in error. Congress accepted the Court's invitation in a limited way, permitting aiding and abetting liability in SEC enforcement actions. The PSLRA expressly authorizes the SEC to seek injunctive relief or money damages against those who aid and abet a 10b-5 violation by knowingly giving "substantial assistance" to the primary violator. Exchange Act §20(e).

The Dodd-Frank Act gives the SEC additional authority to challenge aiding and abetting. Responding to lower court decisions requiring a showing of "actual knowledge" for such liability, Dodd-Frank adopts a "recklessness" standard in SEC aiding and abetting actions. Dodd-Frank §929M. Thus, securities professionals (such as attorneys, investment banks, accountants, financial analysts, and credit rating agencies) that may not meet the definition of "primary violator" in a private action may be subject to liability in an SEC enforcement action. See §12.3.

Primary Violators (and "Scheme Liability")

Central Bank holds that peripheral actors who engage in fraudulent (or deceptive) conduct on which a purchaser or seller of securities relies may be liable as a primary violator. A recurring question has been whether the "primary violator" standard extends to those who facilitate the fraud. Some lower courts since *Central Bank* have held secondary participants (such as lawyers, accountants, and underwriters) liable as primary violators for their role in drafting and editing documents that contain misrepresentations, even though the participants were not mentioned and the documents were disseminated to investors by others. See *In re Software Toolworks, Inc. Securities Litigation*, 50 F.3d 615 (9th Cir. 1994). Other courts have held that primary violators must actually make the misstatement to investors or have it attributed to them. See *Wright v. Ernst & Young LLP*, 152 F.3d 169 (2d Cir. 1998) (refusing to hold liable an auditor that privately approved false press report because report stated financials were unaudited and did not mention auditor).

And what about 10b-5 liability for those who participate in fraudulent schemes by, for example, entering into sham transactions used to generate false financial results—so-called "scheme liability"? In 2008 the Supreme Court rejected scheme liability in private 10b-5 litigation. *Stoneridge Investment Partners LLC v. Scientific-Atlanta Inc.*, 552 U.S. 148 (2008). The Court held that the suppliers/customers who allegedly helped a cable TV company artificially inflate its earnings could not be liable as primary violators in a 10b-5 action brought by the company's investors. Even though the suppliers/customers had misled the issuer's auditors by documenting sham transactions with the issuer, their misdeeds were held not to be actionable in a private 10b-5 action.

The Court pointed out that the supplier/customers owed no duty to the company's investors, and the sham transactions were not disclosed to the public—and thus investors, could not have relied on the deception, a prerequisite for 10b-5 liability. Furthermore, the Court concluded that the suppliers'/customers' deception of the auditors was "too remote" from the issuer's fraudulent financial statements to support primary liability. In short, liability for the investors' full trading losses would have been disproportionate to their attenuated involvement in the company's fraud.

The *Stoneridge* Court noted that Congress, in the PSLRA, had placed various limits on private 10b-5 actions, including limiting aiding and abetting liability to SEC enforcement actions. Although the Court did not address whether private 10b-5 liability extends to "behind the scenes" lawyers and accountants who engineer securities deception without an attribution of their role, the case reflects the Court's misgivings about expanding the implied private 10b-5 action to cover additional parties and situations. Instead, *Stoneridge* puts pressure on the SEC and state regulators to investigate and bring enforcement actions against secondary participants.

Lower courts have followed the *Stoneridge* lead, denying secondary liability for lawyers and other professionals who created or facilitated fraudulent transactions—provided they were unknown to the victims of the fraud. See *Affco Investments 2001 LLC v. Proskauer Rose LLP*, 625 F.3d 185 (5th Cir. 2010) (refusing to hold law firm liable in disallowed tax avoidance scheme because investors did not allege investors' awareness of or reliance on firm); *Pac. Inv. Mgmt. LLC v. Mayer Brown LLP*, 603 F.3d 144 (2d Cir. 2010) ("behind the scenes" law firm not liable for facilitating fraudulent loan transactions and drafting false offering documents, where false statements were not attributed to firm). In short, lawyers can orchestrate a securities fraud and escape 10b-5 liability—so long as they hide themselves from view.

Securities Fraud in Mutual Funds

In a decision with potentially significant ramifications, the Supreme Court held in a 5-4 decision that a mutual fund's adviser cannot be held liable for securities fraud under Rule 10b-5 for false statements in the prospectus of a mutual fund that it advises. *Janus Capital Group, Inc. v. First Derivative Traders*, 564 U.S.—(2011) (fund investor claimed prospectus falsely stated fund adviser would implement policies to restrain abusive market timing practices). The Court concluded that only those with "ultimate control" over the statements in the prospectus (the mutual fund itself) could be liable.

In the case–in what was a somewhat unusual step in its 10b-5 jurisprudence–the Court focused on the language of Rule 10b-5, which makes it unlawful for "any person . . . to *make* any untrue statement of material fact" in connection with securities trading. The Court determined that the investment adviser had not "made" the untrue statements in the prospectus, even though it was "substantially involved" in its preparation. The Court said it was bound to interpret Rule 10b-5 with "narrow dimensions," likening the relationship of the fund and fund adviser to that of speaker and speechwriter.

The decision seemed not to understand that mutual funds themselves have no staff or employees, but outsource all of their operations to the fund adviser. It is the fund adviser, in turn, that makes all investment decisions for the fund and prepares all fund disclosures, including prospectuses. Nonetheless, the court concluded that "corporate formalities were observed" and that the investment adviser had a corporate board different from the board of trustees of the mutual fund, thus making them "separate legal entities." The Court stated that redistributing liability in securities cases based on a "close relationship" between investment advisers and the mutual funds they advise was not the responsibility of the courts, but rather Congress.

Despite what seems like a misguided result, the outcome might well have been different if the plaintiffs in the case had alleged that the fund adviser was the "control person" of the fund. Under Exchange Act §20(a) (described above), control persons assume the Exchange Act liability of the entities they control, which is the case in a typical mutual fund structure where the fund adviser controls all aspects of the fund's operations, including its drafting of disclosure documents. Any 10b-5 liability of the fund thus becomes the liability of the fund adviser, where the "good faith" defense would be unavailable if the fund adviser's actions satisfy the 10b-5 culpability standard.

§22.2.3 Fraud "in Connection with" Securities Transaction

Section 10(b) and Rule 10b-5 prohibit deception "in connection with" the sale or purchase of securities. How close must the deception be to the securities transaction?

No Privity Requirement

Courts have not required privity in 10b-5 actions. Thus, corporate misstatements in situations when the corporation itself is not trading are actionable—provided it is foreseeable that the misstatements will affect securities transactions.

Beyond Privity

Courts have had some difficulty interpreting the "in connection with" requirement when securities transactions are part of a scheme of corporate misdeeds or professional malpractice. If the securities transactions are tangential to the fraudulent scheme, some courts have assumed the matter is better left to traditional state fiduciary, corporate, agency, and contract law—a federalism concern. Nonetheless, on the three occasions that the Supreme Court has addressed the 10b-5 "in connection" requirement, it has construed it broadly and flexibly to further investor protection.

- **Stockbroker embezzlement.** Misstatements have been held to be actionable both as a breach of fiduciary duty and as a fraud "in connection with" securities transactions. *SEC v. Zandford*, 535 U.S. 813 (2002). In the case, the SEC brought an enforcement action against a stockbroker who had sold his customer's securities and pocketed the proceeds without the customer's knowledge or consent. The stockbroker argued that any deception of the customer lacked the requisite connection with the sales of securities from the customer's account because he had never misrepresented the value of the securities in the account. The Court rejected the sophistry and concluded the securities sales and the stockbroker's fraudulent practices coincided—with each sale furthering the stockbroker's fraudulent scheme.
- **Misappropriation of confidential information.** The fraudulent misappropriation of material, nonpublic information has been held to be "in connection with" securities trading based on that information. *United States v. O'Hagan*, 521 U.S. 642 (1997). In the case (discussed more fully in §23.3.1 and §23.3.3 below), a lawyer used information about a client's planned takeover bid and purchased stock in the target before the bid was announced. The Court concluded that the lawyer's unauthorized use of client confidences was deceptive and "in connection with" his securities trading. The fraud was consummated, according to the Court, when the lawyer traded on the information entrusted to him—thus, the securities transaction and the breach of duty coincided. Significantly, the Court commented that its interpretation furthered "an animating purpose of the Exchange Act: to insure honest securities markets and thereby promote investor confidence."

- **Fraudulent takeover scheme.** A complex scheme to acquire an insurance subsidiary by using the subsidiary's assets to finance the acquisition was held to state a 10b-5 claim. *Superintendent of Insurance v. Bankers Life & Casualty Co.*, 404 U.S. 6 (1971). In the case, the purchasers acquired the subsidiary's shares and then, to pay for them, had the subsidiary's board authorize the sale of approximately $5 million of U.S. Treasury bonds owned by the subsidiary. To cover their tracks, the purchasers engaged in an elaborate cover-up: they had the subsidiary purchase a $5 million bank certificate of deposit, which they then used in a series of transactions with other intermediaries as collateral to finance the CD's purchase. In short, the purchasers used the subsidiary's Treasury bonds to finance their acquisition and left a mortgaged CD on the subsidiary's books. The Court held the scheme, which effectively misappropriated reserved assets meant to cover the subsidiary's insurance obligations, to be "in connection with" a securities transaction—namely the sale of the Treasury bonds. Part of the fraudulent scheme, according to the Court, was the deception practiced on the subsidiary's board when it authorized the sale of the bonds without the subsidiary receiving compensation. The subsidiary "suffered an injury as a result of deceptive practices *touching* its sale of securities as an investor."

Sale of Business

The Supreme Court has held that Rule 10b-5 applies to stock transactions in the sale of a business even though the purchaser is not investing as a shareholder but buying the business outright. *Landreth Timber Co. v. Landreth*, 471 U.S. 681 (1985). The Court rejected a "sale of business" doctrine, adopted by some lower courts, that a securities transaction is not involved when a company is sold in a 100 percent stock sale. The Court read Rule 10b-5 literally to apply to any purchase or sale of securities, including the sale of a business structured as a stock sale.

§22.3 FRAUD ELEMENTS OF PRIVATE 10b-5 ACTION

Neither §10(b) nor Rule 10b-5 specifies the elements a plaintiff must show to be entitled to relief. Nonetheless, the Supreme Court has looked to the statutory language of §10(b) and insisted that Congress meant "fraud" when it said "any manipulative or deceptive device or contrivance." The plaintiff has the burden of showing the following elements, each of which tests whether the supplier of misinformation should bear another's investment losses:

10b-5 Elements	
Material misinformation	The defendant affirmatively misrepresented a material fact, omitted a material fact that made his statement misleading, or remained silent in the face of a fiduciary duty to disclose a material fact.
Scienter	The defendant knew (or was reckless in not knowing) the true state of affairs and recognized that the plaintiff might rely on the misinformation.
Reliance	The plaintiff relied on the misrepresentation. In 10b-5 cases involving a duty to speak, courts dispense with reliance if the undisclosed information was material. In 10b-5 cases involving transactions on impersonal trading markets, courts infer reliance from the dissemination of misinformation in the trading market.
Causation	The plaintiff suffered actual losses proximately caused by the misrepresentation.
Damages	The plaintiff suffered damages. Courts use a variety of theories to measure damages under Rule 10b-5. Punitive damages, though, are not available under Rule 10b-5.

The PSLRA modifies the court-made rule of joint and several liability in 10b-5 actions and specifies proportionate liability in some circumstances. Exchange Act §21D(g). Although "knowing" defendants remain jointly and severally liable for the plaintiff's full losses, "unknowing" (reckless) defendants are generally liable only for that portion of damages attributable to their share of responsibility.

§22.3.1 Material Deception

Rule 10b-5 prohibits false or misleading statements of material fact. Not only are outright lies prohibited, so are half-truths. This means a true, but incomplete, statement can be actionable if it omits material information that renders the statement misleading. Under the PSLRA, a 10b-5 complaint that alleges half-truths must specify which statements are misleading and why they are misleading. Exchange Act §21D(b)(1).

Deception in securities markets comes in many packages, encompassing far more than false or misleading statements. It includes securities trading that creates false impressions, as well as silence in the face of a duty to speak. Deception can also occur when a statement, though true when made, is superseded by new information that triggers a duty to update. Confirming the breadth of Rule 10b-5, the Supreme Court recently held that Rule 10b-5 covers deception in an oral contract for the sale of securities, despite the difficulties of proof. *Wharf (Holdings) Ltd. v. United International Holdings, Inc.*, 532

U.S. 588 (2001). In the case, the seller of a securities option who secretly intended not to honor the option argued that there had been no deception as to the option's value. The Court brushed aside the argument and held the seller's secret reservation was misleading because "the option was, unbeknownst to [the buyer], valueless."

Materiality

Not all deception is actionable. To prevent allegations of bad information from being used as a pretext for shifting trading losses, courts require that the misinformation be material. The Supreme Court has held that a fact is material for purposes of Rule 10b-5 if there is a substantial likelihood that a reasonable investor "would" (not "might") consider it as altering the "total mix" of information in deciding whether to buy or sell. *Basic, Inc. v. Levinson*, 485 U.S. 224 (1988) (adopting a "probability plus magnitude" test for disclosures pertaining to possible future events, such as merger negotiations, by considering probability that event might occur and the magnitude of its effect on stock price). In general, if disclosure of the information would affect the price of the company's stock, the information is material.

The PSLRA creates a safe harbor for forward-looking information (such as future plans, predictions or projections) if they are identified as forward-looking and accompanied by "meaningful cautionary statements identifying important factors that could cause actual results to differ materially from those projected in the forward-looking statement." Exchange Act §21E. The PSLRA safe harbor is in addition to a judicially created doctrine that disclosure that "bespeaks caution" (beyond boilerplate warnings) can negate the materiality of unduly optimistic predictions. See *Kaufman v. Trump's Castle Funding*, 7 F.3d 357 (3d Cir. 1993).

Duty to Speak

Normally, silence is not actionable under Rule 10b-5. Nonetheless, courts have imposed a duty to speak when defendants have a relationship of trust and confidence with the plaintiff. See *Chiarella v. United States*, 445 U.S. 222 (1980) (duty to disclose is predicate to 10b-5 insider trading liability). For example, bank employees who failed to tell shareholders that they could sell their shares for higher prices in a resale market, instead of the primary market offered through the bank, breached their duty to disclose. The bank, as transfer agent for the shareholders' corporation, had a relationship of trust that compelled it to speak fully about the shareholders' selling options. *Affiliated Ute Citizens v. United States*, 406 U.S. 128 (1972). A duty to speak also arises when a closely held corporation deals with its shareholder-employees. See *Jordan v. Duff & Phelps, Inc.*, 815 F.2d 429 (7th Cir. 1987) (holding securities firm liable for remaining silent when the firm repurchased the shares of an employee who resigned on the eve of a lucrative merger offer).

Silence is also actionable in connection with corporate activities in a limited number of circumstances: when the company itself is trading its own securities, when the company fails to correct misinformation it begot and that is actively circulating in the market, or when the company knows that insiders are trading based on information not available to the public. This means, for example, that a company need not comment on analysts' forecasts unless the company has become entangled with the analysts. See *Elkind v. Liggett & Myers, Inc.*, 635 F.2d 156 (2d Cir. 1980) (no duty to disclose projections by investment analysts if the company had not in some way created or validated them).

Duty to Update

In some situations, statements that were accurate when made become inaccurate or misleading because of subsequent events. Most federal circuits have held that there is a duty to update when forward-looking statements still "alive" in the market have become inaccurate. The notion is that a projection carries an ongoing assurance of validity and thus an implicit duty to supply new information as it becomes available. For example, the Second Circuit has held that the public announcement of a plan to find a financial partner to mend an over-leveraged capital structure triggered a duty to update when the company began to consider a dilutive stock offering as an alternative financing plan. *In re Time Warner Securities Litigation*, 9 F.3d 259 (2d Cir. 1993). In a similar vein, the Third Circuit has held that a company that had stated its policy to maintain a stable debt-equity ratio came under a duty to disclose negotiations of a merger that would have added significant new debt. *Weiner v. Quaker Oats Co.*, 129 F.3d 310 (3d Cir. 1997). But there is no duty to update periodic SEC filings, which speak only as of the date when made. See *Gallagher v. Abbott Laboratories*, 269 F.3d 806 (7th Cir. 2001) (no duty to update Form 10-K, which failed to mention FDA letter threatening compliance action when letter was dated eight days after filing of 10-K).

Corporate Mismanagement

Mismanagement by corporate officials can violate Rule 10b-5 if the mismanagement involves fraudulent securities transactions that can be said to injure the corporation. For example, when corporate insiders buy stock from the corporation and deceive those with whom they deal, a derivative suit can be used to enforce the corporation's 10b-5 rights.

But not every corporate fiduciary breach involving a securities transaction gives rise to a 10b-5 action. The Supreme Court has held that Rule 10b-5 only regulates deception, not unfair corporate transactions or breaches of fiduciary duties. *Santa Fe Industries, Inc. v. Green*, 430 U.S. 462 (1977). In the case, a parent company merged with its majority-owned subsidiary after giving minority shareholders notice of the merger and an information statement that explained their rights to a state appraisal remedy. The parent stated that a valuation of the subsidiary's assets indicated a $640 per share value, even though the parent was offering only $125 per share (which was slightly higher than a valuation of the subsidiary by the parent's investment banker). The Court held that unless the disclosure had been misleading, which plaintiffs did not claim was the case, no liability could result. An unfairly low price does not amount to fraud.

§22.3.2 Scienter— "Manipulative or Deceptive Device or Contrivance"

A plaintiff in a 10b-5 action must plead and prove the defendant's scienter, a "mental state embracing intent to deceive, manipulate, or defraud." *Ernst & Ernst v. Hochfelder*, 425 U.S. 185 (1976). In *Hochfelder*, an accounting firm negligently failed to audit a company's accounting practices, which would have revealed that the company president had induced investors to put money into nonexistent escrow accounts and pocketed the money himself. Defrauded investors claimed the accounting firm's negligence enabled the fraud. The Supreme Court rejected the argument, previously accepted by several lower courts, that negligence is actionable under Rule 10b-5. It based its holding not on the language of Rule 10b-5, which actually supports such a construction, but instead on the enabling "manipulative or deceptive device or contrivance" language of §10(b).

This culpability standard is the same whether the suit is brought by the SEC or a private plaintiff and whether the suit seeks injunctive relief or damages. *Aaron v. SEC*, 446 U.S. 680 (1980) (scienter required in SEC injunctive actions).

Meaning of Scienter

What is scienter in a securities fraud action? Scienter means the defendant was aware of the true state of affairs and appreciated the propensity of his misstatement or omission to mislead. Showing scienter, which requires evidence of the defendant's state of mind and intent to mislead, is often difficult.

The Supreme Court in *Hochfelder* left open the question whether a showing of recklessness can satisfy the 10b-5 culpability standard. Lower courts have uniformly concluded that recklessness is sufficient to establish scienter under Rule 10b-5, when misrepresentations were so obvious that the defendant must have been aware of them. See *Greebel v. FTP Software, Inc.*, 194 F.3d 185 (1st Cir. 1999) (summarizing approaches in various circuits). Under this view, recklessness exists when circumstantial evidence strongly suggests actual knowledge. Some courts have even said the plaintiff must show "deliberate recklessness." See *In re Silicon Graphics, Inc. Securities Litigation*, 183 F.3d 979 (9th Cir. 1999) (interpreting the PSLRA to compel 10b-5 plaintiffs to plead "facts that constitute circumstantial evidence of deliberately reckless or conscious misconduct").

The existence of liability for recklessness was implicitly acknowledged in the PSLRA, which creates different levels of liability for 10b-5 defendants. "Knowing" defendants are subject to joint and several liability, while "unknowing" defendants (presumably those who were only reckless) are subject to proportionate liability. Exchange Act §21D(g)(10) (see §22.3.5 below).

Pleading Scienter

Most 10b-5 actions are dismissed or settled. Frequently, dismissal turns on whether the plaintiff has adequately alleged scienter. In general, allegations of fraud must be pleaded "with particularity." Fed. R. Civ. P. 9(b). More specifically, the PSLRA requires a complaint alleging securities fraud to "state with particularity facts giving rise to a strong inference that the defendant acted with the required state of mind." Exchange Act §21D(b)(2).

The Supreme Court has interpreted "strong inference" to mean "more than merely plausible or reasonable—it must be cogent and at least as compelling as any opposing inference of nonfraudulent intent." *Tellabs Inc. v. Makor Issues & Rights Ltd.*, 551 U.S. 308 (2007). In the process the Court rejected a "middle ground" approach that looked at all the allegations collectively, without comparing them. The Court said that a comparison of "plausible inferences" (of both nonculpability and fraudulent intent) was necessary, and the inference of scienter must be "at least as likely as" any plausible opposing inference.

The Supreme Court thus concluded that the PSLRA pleading standard can be satisfied by pleading facts that create "cogent and compelling" inferences of scienter, provided these inferences are at least as strong as inferences of nonculpability. Significantly, the Court added that, as in any dismissal motion, the court must accept "all factual allegations in the complaint as true" and the complaint must be read as a whole. The Court majority also rejected the approach of two concurring justices who argued that the inference of culpability must be "more plausible" than the inference of innocence, or "more likely correct than not correct." That is, the Court decided that a tie goes to the plaintiff!

§22.3.3 Reliance and Causation

Reliance and causation, elements of traditional common-law deceit, are also elements of a private 10b-5 action—though not an SEC enforcement action. See *SEC v. Rana Research*, 8 F.3d 1358 (9th Cir. 1993). The reliance requirement tests the link between the alleged misinformation and the plaintiff's buy-sell decision—it weeds out claims where the misinformation had little or no impact on the plaintiff's decision to enter the transaction. The causation requirement, like proximate cause in tort law, tests the link between the misrepresentation and the plaintiff's loss—it weeds out claims where the securities fraud was not "responsible" for the investor's loss.

Reliance and causation are related. Each serves as a filter to ensure that the misrepresentations or omissions alleged by the plaintiff are causally linked to the plaintiff's actions and losses.

Reliance

Courts treat reliance as an element in all private 10b-5 cases, but relax the requirements of proof in a number of circumstances:

(1) Nondisclosure. When the defendant fails in a duty to speak—whether in a face-to-face transaction or an anonymous trading market—courts dispense with proof of reliance if the undisclosed facts were material. *Affiliated Ute Citizens v. United States*, 406 U.S. 128 (1972) (no reliance need be shown in face-to-face transactions when bank employees violated position of trust by failing to make material disclosures). The materiality of the undisclosed information indicates a reasonable investor would have considered it important, suggesting the plaintiff may have acted differently had he known the information. To require proof of reliance in a case of nondisclosure would impose a nearly insuperable burden on a plaintiff to prove reliance on something not said.

(2) Omitted Information. In cases of half-truths—omitted information that makes a statement misleading—courts are divided on whether reliance must be shown. The PSLRA, however, makes reasonable reliance an explicit condition for "knowing" securities violations and thus joint and several liability, whether the claim is based on a misrepresentation or an omission. Exchange Act §21D(g)(10)(A).

(3) Fraud on the Market. In cases of false or misleading representations on a public trading market—so-called fraud on the market—courts have created a rebuttable presumption of reliance. *Basic Inc. v. Levinson*, 485 U.S. 224 (1988) (plurality decision). The theory is that those who trade on public trading markets rely on the integrity of the stock's market price. In an open and developed stock market, the efficient capital market hypothesis (§19.2.2) posits that market prices reflect all publicly available information about a company's stock. On the assumption that material misinformation artificially distorts the market price, courts infer that investors have relied on the misinformation. This "fraud on the market" theory assumes that if the truth had been disclosed, investors would not have traded at the prevailing nondisclosure price.

A defendant can rebut the presumption of reliance and avoid the "fraud on the market" theory by showing either (1) the trading market was not efficient, such as by showing that the challenged misrepresentation did not in fact affect the stock's price, or (2) the particular plaintiff would have traded regardless of the misrepresentation. *Basic Inc. v. Levinson.*

Causation

Courts have required that 10b-5 plaintiffs show two kinds of causation to recover:

(1) Transaction causation. The plaintiff must show that "but for" the defendant's fraud, the plaintiff would not have entered the transaction or would have entered under different terms—a restated reliance requirement. Many courts equate transaction causation with reliance.

(2) Loss causation. The plaintiff must also show that the fraud produced the claimed losses to the plaintiff—a foreseeability or a proximate cause requirement. See *Bastian v. Petren Resources, Inc.*, 892 F.2d 680 (7th Cir. 1990) (no loss causation when losses attributable to market crash, not fraud). Normally, plaintiffs can establish loss causation by showing a change in stock prices when the misrepresentations were made and then an opposite change when disclosure corrects the false or misleading information. What if there is no price change when the corrective disclosure happens—is it enough to allege and prove that the purchase price was inflated? The Supreme Court has held that the plaintiff cannot simply allege losses caused by an artificially inflated price due to "fraud on the market," but must allege and prove actual economic loss proximately caused by the alleged misrepresentations. *Dura Pharmaceuticals, Inc. v. Broudo*, 544 U.S. 336 (2005). In the usual case, this will be done by showing a drop in price at the time of corrective disclosure, creating a logical link between the misrepresentation and the loss. If there is no price drop or the shareholder has sold before the corrective disclosure, the plaintiff may be out of luck!

§22.3.4 Damages

Private 10b-5 plaintiffs have a full range of equitable and legal remedies. The Exchange Act imposes only two limitations. Under §28 the plaintiff's recovery cannot exceed actual damages, implying that the goal of liability is compensation and effectively precluding punitive damages. Under §21D(e), added by the PSLRA, damages are capped according to a formula meant to disregard post-transaction price volatility unrelated to any misinformation.

Damages Formulas

Courts have adopted various damages formulas, though with no clear guidelines as to when each applies. Assume that a company issued a false press release at a time its stock was trading at $18. After the false statement, the stock rose to $25. When the company later corrected the false statement, the stock price fell to $15 and then continued to fall to $12. Consider how the following theories of damages might be used by a purchaser in the market at $25 who sells when the market price falls to $12.

- **Rescission.** Rescission allows the defrauded plaintiff to cancel the transaction. If the plaintiff sold, he gets his stock back; if he purchased, he returns the stock and the seller refunds the purchase price. Rescission is suited only to face-to-face transactions where the parties can be identified; this theory would not be applicable in our example.
- **Rescissionary (disgorgement) damages.** If rescission is not possible because the stock has been resold, rescissionary damages replicate a cancellation of the transaction. A defrauded seller recovers the purchaser's profits—the difference between the purchase and resale price. A defrauded purchaser recovers his losses—again, the difference between the purchase and resale price. Under this theory, the purchaser in our example would seek $13 in damages.
- **Cover (conversion) damages.** Cover damages, like those in a tort conversion action, assume the plaintiff mitigates her losses by selling or reinvesting. They are the difference between the price at which the plaintiff transacted and the price at which the plaintiff could have transacted once the fraud was revealed. Under this theory, the purchaser in our example would seek $10 in damages.
- **Out-of-pocket damages.** This is the most common measure of damages in 10b-5 cases. The plaintiff recovers the difference between the purchase price and the true "value" of the stock at the time of purchase. This measure does not take into account any post-transaction price changes. Valuing stock in the abstract is often speculative, and many courts (including the Supreme Court in *Dura Pharmaceuticals*, above, §22.3.3) look to the price at the time of corrective disclosure as a measure of the "but for" price. In our example, the purchaser might argue that the "true value" of the stock when he purchased was $12, with damages of $13; the defendant might argue the "true value" was $18, with damages of only $7.
- **Contract damages.** Contract damages compensate the plaintiff for the loss of the benefit of the bargain. They are the difference between the value received and the value promised. This theory would not be applicable in our example.

Courts have not developed a unified theory of 10b-5 damages except to say that the theory of damages should fit the facts of the case. In cases involving claims by customers against securities firms, courts often impose rescissory damages on the theory the customers would not have transacted had they known of the fraud. But in cases involving false corporate reports that affect trading in the company's shares, courts have been reluctant to use rescissory damages because it overpunishes the corporate defendant in a falling market. *Green v. Occidental Petroleum Corp.*, 541 F.2d 1335 (9th Cir. 1976) (Sneed, J., concurring in denial of class action certification). Moreover, even though out-of-pocket damages exclude the effects of extraneous price changes, aggregating such damages may result in a significant recovery that penalizes nontrading defendants and exceeds that necessary for deterrence.

Damages Cap

When recovery is based on the market price of the security—as with out-of-pocket and cover damages—the PSLRA imposes a damages cap. Congress created the cap on the assumption that damages are typically computed as the difference between the transaction price and the market price on the date of corrective disclosure—a rough out-of-pocket computation. Concerned that this "crash price" might substantially overstate plaintiffs' losses for a company with highly volatile stock, Congress required that courts consider a longer, 90-day window for determining the market price. In theory, prices during this longer window will more accurately impound the corrected disclosure. Under new §21D(e), damages are capped at the difference between the transacted price and the average of the daily prices during the 90-day period after corrective disclosure.

Circularity of Corporate Liability

When a corporation is made liable for damages in a 10b-5 class action, the effect will often be the subsidization of one group of shareholders (or investors) by current shareholders. For example, if the class action involves falsely optimistic statements by management, class members induced to purchase over-priced stock will receive compensation from the corporation. Rarely do managers themselves contribute significant amounts to the settlement of 10b-5 class action claims.

The result is that one group of investors (current shareholders) subsidizes another group of investors (purchasing shareholders)—net of the litigation expenses paid to class counsel and defense counsel. For investors who are diversified, as most individual and institutional investors are, 10b-5 class action litigation imposes costs, but no *net* financial gains for shareholders. Only to the extent that corporate managers (specifically and generally) respond to 10b-5 litigation by improving disclosure and corporate governance might the system be seen as cost-effective. Although studies indicate that companies that settle 10b-5 class actions subsequently undertake corporate governance reforms and then financially outperform their peers, it is unclear whether the benefits of class litigation are worth the costs.

Each year approximately 200 securities fraud class actions are filed in the United States, most of them "classic" cases of corporate misrepresentations that when revealed result in dramatic price swings. See Stanford Securities Class Action Clearinghouse, available at *securities.stanford.edu* (includes pleadings, court filings, dismissals, and settlement data in all post-PSLRA securities fraud class actions).

§22.3.5 Nature of 10b-5 Liability

Courts in 10b-5 cases have traditionally imposed liability on a joint and several basis—each culpable defendant becomes liable for all of the damages awarded. Joint and several liability serves to deter securities fraud and assures compensation for its victims. Potentially liable persons, facing the risk of full liability, feel compelled to guard against securities fraud. And plaintiffs are assured full recovery if they can identify at least one deep-pocket defendant.

The PSLRA, however, eliminates joint and several liability for defendants who do not "knowingly" commit violations of the securities laws. Exchange Act §21D(f)(2)(A). Instead, the Act creates a system of proportionate liability based on each "unknowing" defendant's proportion of responsibility. Exchange Act §21D(f)(2)(B). This liability scheme responds to concerns that tangential defendants in securities fraud cases (such as outside directors, lawyers, and accountants) with little or no responsibility for the fraud might be coerced by joint and several liability into settling out of fear that they might be found liable and forced to bear all the damages awarded the plaintiffs.

According to the PSLRA, a person commits "knowing" securities fraud when he makes an untrue statement or factual omission, on which others are likely to reasonably rely, with "actual knowledge" of the falsehood. Exchange Act §21D(g)(10)(A). Reckless conduct, by definition, does not constitute a knowing violation. Exchange Act §21D(g)(10)(B). In 10b-5 actions, the PSLRA liability system thus places significant importance on whether a defendant's scienter was knowing or merely reckless.

§22.4 DEFENSES IN PRIVATE 10b-5 ACTION

Not only do the procedures and elements of private 10b-5 actions reflect a judicial and legislative caution about permitting investors to shift their trading losses on the basis of claimed misinformation, but additional defenses (some of recent vintage) further limit the advantages of 10b-5 litigation.

§22.4.1 Limitations and Repose Periods

In 2002, Congress established a new statute of limitations for private 10b-5 actions. Sarbanes-Oxley §804. Under the new provision, "a private right of action that involves a claim of fraud, deceit, manipulation, or contrivance in contravention of a regulatory requirement concerning the securities laws" must be brought within two years after the discovery of facts constituting the violation (the limitations period), but no later than five years after such violation (the repose period). 28 U.S.C. §1658(b).

The statute extended the prior judicially imposed statute of limitations in 10b-5 actions—which had been one year after discovery of facts constituting the violation, but no later than three years after the violation. *Lampf, Pleva, Lipkind, Prupis & Petigrow v. Gilbertson*, 501 U.S. 350 (1991) (announcing a uniform federal limitations period for 10b-5 actions, which before had borrowed applicable state statutes of limitations).

So when is a plaintiff deemed to have discovered facts constituting the 10b-5 violation—thus beginning the §1658 two-year limitations period? Lower courts have been divided, some starting the clock when the plaintiff becomes "constructively aware" of possible fraud, with others waiting for the plaintiff to have specific evidence that establishes the elements of a 10b-5 claim. The Supreme Court resolved the divergent views among the lower courts in *Merck & Co. v. Reynolds*, 599 U.S.— (2010). The Court ruled that Merck shareholders could pursue a 10b-5 claim against the company for misrepresenting the safety and commercial viability of Vioxx, a pain reliever that the company ultimately withdrew from the market. The Court concluded that the two-year limitations period of §1658 accrues either (1) when the plaintiff actually discovers the 10b-5 violation or (2) when a reasonably diligent plaintiff would have discovered the facts constituting the violation—including the facts indicating scienter. The Court rejected the argument that the limitations period begins to run when the plaintiff was put on notice that something was amiss, requiring further inquiry. Thus, concerns about Vioxx's safety—based on a study showing troubling cardiovascular side effects, the filing of products liability suits, and an FDA warning letter—might have put the plaintiffs on notice that Merck's statements about the drug's safety were false, but not necessarily that they were made with an intent to deceive.

§22.4.2 Contribution and Indemnification

Securities fraud often implicates a number of actors. Contribution permits a defendant who becomes liable for more than his share to compel other responsible persons (whether or not they were sued) to pay their share of the total liability. Indemnification permits a defendant who has become liable to compel another person bound by contract to assume some or all of the defendant's liability. Both sharing mechanisms have the effect to encourage settlements with 10b-5 plaintiffs because they assure defendants there will be a later mechanism for them to "settle up," and thus expedite compensation to fraud victims.

Contribution

The PSLRA expressly authorizes contribution actions by parties jointly and severally liable under Rule 10b-5—typically "knowing" defendants. Contribution shares, like proportionate liability, are computed according to the percentage of responsibility. Exchange Act §21D(g)(8). The PSLRA also authorizes contribution by "unknowing" defendants who become subject to proportionate liability, but are forced to pay other parties' uncollectible shares. Exchange Act §21D(g)(5). Contribution may be sought from any person, whether or not joined in the original action, who would have been liable for the same damages. These statutory rights clarify a contribution right earlier recognized by the Supreme Court. *Musick, Peler, and Garrett v. Employers Insurance of Wausau*, 508 U.S. 286 (1993).

Under the PSLRA, contribution claims must be brought within six months after a final nonappealable judgment, though "unknowing" defendants who make additional payments beyond their proportionate share have six months after payment to seek contribution. Exchange Act §21D(g)(9).

Indemnification

Courts have recognized the right of indemnification by "passive" or "secondary" 10b-5 defendants against more culpable participants. Such indemnification, courts have pointed out, increases deterrence by shifting liability to deliberately deceptive participants.

§22.5 COMPARISON TO STATE LAW REMEDIES

State law provides several alternatives to a federal 10b-5 action. Shareholders can sue corporate managers for violating their "duty of honesty" if they knowingly disseminate false information that results in corporate injury or damage to individual shareholders. See *Malone v. Brincat*, 722 A.2d 5 (Del. 1998) (§21.1). Although the Delaware courts have yet to clarify the elements of a "duty of honesty" action, one apparent advantage is the absence of a "purchaser or seller" standing requirement.

In addition, many state "blue sky" laws (named after scams where farmers who were promised rain got nothing but blue skies) contain civil liability provisions modeled after §12(a)(2) of the Securities Act. See Uniform Securities Act §§410, 605 (see §5.1.3). For example, the civil liability scheme of §410 provides for rescission of both securities sales *and* securities offers made by means of false or misleading communications, whether written or oral, subject to a "due care" defense. Thus, the standing requirement and traditional 10b-5 elements of scienter, specific reliance, and causation are all relaxed. Moreover, state blue sky laws generally provide for recovery of attorney fees.

State common-law deceit, though its elements are similar to a 10b-5 action, offers some advantages over its federal counterpart. State statutes of limitations may be longer (particularly under the "inquiry notice" standard applied by federal courts); many states have relaxed scienter requirements; most states permit punitive damages in egregious cases; and none imposes the pleading and class action barriers of the PSLRA.

Although the Securities Litigation Uniform Standards Act of 1998 requires that any class action alleging fraud in publicly traded securities must be brought in federal court under federal law (see Securities Act §16(c); Exchange Act §28(f)(2)), not all state claims are preempted. Securities fraud in close corporations involving privately held securities can be brought under state law; "duty of honesty" claims may be brought as derivative actions; and state "blue sky" claims can be brought by individual investors.

Examples

EXAMPLES

1. Last year ITM Corp. (whose common stock is publicly traded) issued preferred stock to a group of institutional investors in a private placement exempt from registration under the Securities Act of 1933 (see §5.1.2). ITM is now experiencing financial problems—its annual revenues have dropped 25 percent, and it has discontinued paying dividends on the preferred. One of the investors, Lucre Life Insurance Company, thinks the offering circular accompanying the preferred issuance was misleading.
   a. Does Lucre Life have standing to bring an action under Rule 10b-5?
   b. Lucre Life is worried about delays in federal court. Can it sue in state court?

2. The offering circular stated: "ITM is committed to energy storage research and has spent over $200 million on this research in the last two years." Last year, ITM's total revenues were $25 billion.
   a. In fact, ITM had only spent $150 million on electrolysis research. Is there 10b-5 liability?
   b. The offering circular failed to mention that ITM's electrolysis research is a long shot and there is no assurance it will produce results having any commercial value. Is there 10b-5 liability?

c. The offering circular also states that "the company anticipates that sales of our energy storage technology in the next fiscal year will exceed research expenses." Senior management, however, has doubts whether this will happen. Is there 10b-5 liability?

3. ITM's offering circular falsely stated the company had been awarded a large military contract to create solar-powered electrolysis systems that would separate water into hydrogen and oxygen (a highly efficient method to produce and store energy). In fact, the company was hoping to receive the contract, but its bid lost. Jane, ITM's outside attorney who prepared the offering circular, had been told by Daniela (ITM's president) that it was a "done deal," though Jane had an inkling that ITM had not been awarded the contract.
   a. Assuming the offering circular was materially false, can Lucre Life sue Jane under Rule 10b-5?
   b. Lucre Life alleges that Jane, though she did not actually know about the status of the contract award, suspected the contract had not been awarded and was in a position to know. Is this sufficient?
   c. Nobody at Lucre Life actually read the portion of the offering circular mentioning the contract award. There is no organized market in ITM's preferred shares. Can Lucre Life recover against ITM under Rule 10b-5?
   d. Lucre Life bought its preferred shares at $100. After it learned ITM had lost the bid, it sold the shares to another institutional buyer at $85. Assuming liability, how much can Lucre Life recover?

4. Lucre Life settles its lawsuit. Soon afterward, ITM research scientists conduct preliminary tests on a cobalt/phosphate film that has efficient electrolytic properties at room temperatures. If the tests can be confirmed, the discovery would be an enormous breakthrough with great commercial value. It would mean that solar energy could be efficiently stored, potentially making every house or building its own power plant and filling station.
   a. Must ITM issue a press release disclosing the tests?
   b. In the week after the tests, there is an unusual amount of trading activity in ITM's common stock, which rises in price from $50 to $70. A *Wall Street Journal* reporter calls Daniela, ITM's president, and asks if she can explain the recent price rise. Daniela does not believe there has been insider trading, and doesn't want to say anything. What should she do?
   c. ITM's management wants to put an end to media speculation and issues a press release stating, "There are no corporate developments that would explain the unusual recent market activity in ITM's stock." Would this violate Rule 10b-5?
   d. How should the press release have been drafted?

5. Sharon sells her ITM stock when the price falls after the false press release. More than two years later, after many further tests by ITM scientists and much speculation among securities analysts, ITM files a report with the SEC announcing its invention of a low-cost, efficient electrolysis process using a cobalt/phosphate film. The company's stock price soars. But Sharon no longer owns ITM stock. What a disappointment!
   a. ITM never purchased or sold its stock in connection with the original false press release. Can Sharon sue ITM under Rule 10b-5?
   b. Sharon was not aware of the original false press release, and ITM argues her decision to sell was unrelated to it. Must Sharon show she acted in reliance on the press release?
   c. Sharon sold her ITM stock more than two years ago. Would a 10b-5 action now be timely?

Explanations

EXPLANATIONS

1. a. Yes. Lucre Life has standing as a purchaser of securities even though they are not traded on a public trading market. See *Blue Chip Stamps v. Manor Drug Stores*, 421 U.S. 723 (1975) ("purchaser" or "seller" standing requirement) (see §22.2.1).
   b. Not under Rule 10b-5. Jurisdiction over 10b-5 claims is exclusively in federal court. If the action were brought in federal court, any state fraud or blue sky claims could be brought as pendent claims. Many securities lawyers perceive federal judges to be more sophisticated in securities matters.

   Nonetheless, Lucre Life could sue in state court on a theory of common-law fraud or under state blue sky provisions whose elements are not as burdensome as those of Rule 10b-5. The preemption of the Securities Litigation Uniform Standards Act of 1998 does not apply because Lucre Life is not bringing a class action. See Exchange Act §28(f)(1) (preemption of "covered class actions").

2. a. Probably not. It is unlikely that the discrepancy was material. The $50 million difference between stated and actual research expenditures seems immaterial for a company with $25 billion in revenues. Lucre Life would have to show a substantial likelihood a reasonable investor would have considered the $50 million discrepancy important in its decision to invest at the offering price. For example, if the company's research activities were perceived to drive its stock value or if the company's stock price fell significantly when the discrepancy was revealed, materiality would be easier to argue.
   b. Probably not. It is unlikely that there was reliance. It seems unlikely a reasonable investor, particularly an institutional investor like Lucre Life, would have understood ITM's statement that it was "committed

to energy storage research" to suggest the company was sure of commercial success. The "no assurance" caveat would not have added to the overall mix of information available to the investors.

c. Perhaps. Scienter is an element of a 10b-5 action. A mere misstatement is not actionable, unless it was made with scienter. Even though it may be difficult to establish corporate awareness that the prediction of future revenues was not likely to occur, scienter can also be established by showing "recklessness." Here the lack of a basis for believing that energy-storage revenues would cover research expenses suggests that the falsity of the statement was "so obvious that the defendant must have been aware of them." See §22.3.1.

3. a. Perhaps. Even though she was not a party to the stock sale, privity is not required under Rule 10b-5. Jane may be liable as a "primary violator" if she made false or misleading statements on which investors relied. (She cannot be liable in a private action on an aiding or abetting theory.) Some lower courts have held collateral participants liable as primary violators for their role in drafting documents that contained misrepresentations, even though others disseminated the documents to investors.

   The Supreme Court's decision in *Stoneridge* (see §22.2.2) rejecting "scheme liability" under Rule 10b-5 suggests that investors must be aware of the alleged participant's role in the fraud. That is, merely preparing the disclosure documents—although necessary to carry out a fraudulent scheme—is not enough to establish private 10b-5 liability. This conclusion is reinforced in *Janus Capital* (see §22.2.2) where the Supreme Court held that merely drafting a false disclosure document did not subject a mutual fund adviser to liability where the document technically came from the fund itself. Thus, even if Lucre Life knew that Jane (and her law firm) had prepared the disclosure documents, it would seem Lucre Life cannot look to Jane, but only to ITM, for 10b-5 liability. And given that Jane (and her law firm) did not control their client, they would not be exposed to the client's 10b-5 violation as control persons.

   This, however, is not the end of the story for Jane. Although probably absolved of direct 10b-5 liability, Jane (and her law firm) might be subject to liability *to ITM* for professional malpractice arising from her knowing assistance in a securities fraud. She might also face liability in an SEC enforcement action for "aiding and abetting" ITM's 10b-5 violation, potentially resulting in an injunction and fines that could be as devastating as direct 10b-5 liability. See Exchange Act §20(e) (see §22.2.2).

b. Probably not. Even if Jane may be considered a "primary violator" (see previous explanation), Lucre Life must establish her culpability. She must have known or been reckless in not knowing the true status of the contract award. Negligence is not enough.

Are Lucre Life's allegations sufficient? The Supreme Court's decision in *Tellabs* (see §22.3.2) clarifies the PSLRA pleading standard for alleging scienter in a private 10b-5 action. The Court requires that the "plausible inferences" of nonculpability and fraudulent intent be compared, and the inference of scienter must be "at least as likely as" any plausible opposing inference. In this case, because Lucre Life is not alleging actual knowledge, it would have to show Jane's alleged *recklessness* is at least as likely as not.

Lucre Life's allegation that Jane suspected the disclosure was not true and was in a position to know the truth would seem to make out a claim of recklessness, at least as defined by the lower courts. Her suspicions would seem to create a "cogent and compelling" inference that the misrepresentations were so obvious she must have been aware of them. That is, circumstantial evidence strongly suggests Jane knew something was amiss and should have investigated, even if she did not actually know the true state of affairs. In a dismissal motion, the court must accept "all factual allegations in the complaint as true" and the complaint must be read as a whole.

The *Tellabs* approach effectively rejects the prior focus on the "motive and opportunity" of the defendant. Cf. *Novak v. Kasaks*, 216 F.3d 300 (2d Cir. 2000) (accepting pre-PSLRA pleading standard that strong inference of fraudulent intent can be established by alleging facts that show the defendant had both motive and opportunity to commit fraud). Thus, Lucre Life would not have to allege that Jane had a motive to deceive.

c. Perhaps. Reliance is an element of a 10b-5 action, and Lucre Life must show it acted on the basis of the circular's false statements concerning a government contract. This will be difficult because the plaintiff never read this part of the circular. Nor is there an open, developed, efficient market that sets the price for the preferred stock—undermining for the plaintiff a traditional "fraud on the market" theory of reliance.

   Nonetheless, Lucre Life might argue that it relied on the private placement market. Some courts have accepted the argument that a plaintiff establishes reliance if it can show a new offering would not have been marketed *at all* if the investors had known the true facts. That is, Lucre Life could argue it relied on the other institutional investors' decision to buy. This theory nearly excuses reliance in any issuance of stock, and some courts have limited the theory to fraud that was "so pervasive that it goes to the very existence" of the securities on the market. *Ross v. Bank South, N.A.*, 885 F.2d 723 (11th Cir. 1989).

d. Lucre Life has a number of remedial theories to choose from, depending on which defendant it seeks recovery from. If the plaintiff seeks recovery from ITM for selling its securities through a false selling document, a rescissory theory avoids issues of valuation and post-transaction losses. It prevents unfair enrichment by ITM and compensates Lucre Life for losses it would not have incurred but for the fraud—which matches its theory of liability. Lucre Life can support a rescission theory by pointing to §29(b) of the Exchange Act, which states that any "contract made in violation" of any rule under the statute is void. Rescissory damages in this case would be the difference between $100 (the purchase price) and $85 (the price at which Lucre Life later sold)—$15 per share.

A rescission theory does not fit as well for Jane, the arguably complicit attorney. Jane was not the seller and was not unjustly enriched; heavy damages might overdeter her conduct. A cover theory—which assumes the plaintiff sells once the fraud is revealed—does not fit the facts because there was no market into which the plaintiff could sell or to measure the effect on price when the fraud was revealed. An out-of-pocket theory, the traditional theory for fraud damages, would allow Lucre Life to recover the difference between the purchase price and what the price would have been had the disclosure been adequate. This will require Lucre Life to prove the "true" value of the preferred stock as of the time of its purchase. Recovery will probably be less than $15 per share, given that it might be difficult for Lucre Life to show the price drop was due entirely to the misinformation about the contract award.

According to the Supreme Court in *Dura Pharmaceuticals* (see §22.3.3) a plaintiff alleging "fraud on the market" (against a nonprivity defendant) must prove actual economic loss proximately caused by the alleged misrepresentations. Here the price drop is not clearly tied to misinformation in the offering circular. The burden is on the plaintiff to show proximate cause (loss causation).

In addition, damages will be capped by the difference between the $100 purchase price and the "average of the daily prices during the 90-day period after corrective disclosure." See Exchange Act §21D(e) (see §22.3.4—Damages Cap).

4. a. No. Rule 10b-5 does not require disclosure of all material information. Only if ITM has a duty to speak is silence actionable. A duty might arise in a few ways:
   1. ITM was buying or selling its own shares.
   2. ITM was aware of insider trading by others.
   3. ITM had a duty to update an earlier statement that had become inaccurate and that was still "alive" in the trading market.
   4. ITM had a fiduciary duty to its shareholders that required disclosure.

   None seems to apply here. There was no trading, and there was no "current" information about electrolysis research that the new tests contradicted. Finally, ITM's decision not to disclose the breakthrough is protected by the business judgment rule. Cf. *Malone v. Brincat*, 722 A.2d 5 (Del. 1998) (imposing a "duty of honesty" whenever corporate managers communicate with shareholders) (see §21.1). ITM's management could decide secrecy is in the corporation's best interests for competitive or any other business-related reason. An evaluation of ITM's disclosure duties turns on general, rather than individual, shareholder wealth maximization.

b. "No comment." The Supreme Court in *Basic, Inc. v. Levinson* (see §22.3.1) took the view that this would be tantamount to silence. Absent a duty to speak, silence is not actionable under Rule 10b-5—even when the company has highly material information.

   Although some might view a "no comment" answer to be tacit confirmation of undisclosed material information, the Supreme Court suggests companies can create a reputation for discretion, whether or not there are material developments. The president might well say, "We have a corporate policy not to comment on market trends or rumors."

c. Yes, if the preliminary tests were material. Whenever a company makes a statement about material information, it cannot be false or misleading. ITM's management might argue the press release is essentially true because management thinks the tests have been kept secret and does not know why there has been unusual trading activity. On similar facts, the Supreme Court in *Basic, Inc. v. Levinson* (see §22.3.1) rejected this sophistic argument. A "no developments" statement suggests management does not know of information that would be of interest to the market, which is misleading if the tests are material.

   To judge the materiality of the tests requires balancing the probability of an energy-storage breakthrough (which may be low because the tests were preliminary) and the breakthrough's significance to the corporation (which is extremely high). See *Basic, Inc. v. Levinson* (§22.3.1). The "probability plus magnitude" test suggests it is substantially likely that reasonable shareholders would consider the tests relevant to their buy-sell decisions. This conclusion is bolstered if the recent price increases were related to rumors about energy-storage research. They would indicate that energy-storage information is relevant to trading and pricing of ITM's stock.

d. The release should have made clear the tests are preliminary, have not been confirmed, and might never be confirmed:

   ITM's research scientists have conducted tests using a cobalt/phosphate film that results in high rates of electrolysis at room temperatures. The tests have not been confirmed by the company or by independent researchers. It is possible that they cannot be duplicated.

   The release must walk a fine line. If it is overly pessimistic, some shareholders may sell, be disappointed, and sue. If it is overly optimistic, some investors may buy, be disappointed, and sue.

5. a. Yes. A private purchaser (or seller) of securities has an implied right of action under Rule 10b-5. Further, there is no privity requirement if the challenged misstatements were made "in connection with" stock trading. ITM (even though it never transacted) should have known that shareholders and investors would rely on its press release.

   b. Yes, reliance is an element of a 10b-5 action. In a face-to-face transaction, Sharon would have to show that she actually knew of the press release and that she sold because of its bad news. When trading occurs in an impersonal stock market, courts relax the reliance requirement and accept a "fraud on the market" theory. *Basic, Inc. v. Levinson* (see §22.3.1). Under this theory, a public company's stock price is set by available public information and those who trade rely on the integrity of the market. If there is fraud, the stock price impounds the misinformation and those who trade rely on the misinformation as though they had known of it.

   Once Sharon had shown a developed trading market in ITM stock, ITM would have the burden to rebut the presumption of reliance by showing a break between the misinformation and Sharon's trading: (1) ITM's stock is not widely followed and misinformation is not necessarily reflected in its stock price; (2) securities traders already knew of the preliminary tests, the press release notwithstanding; (3) Sharon would have traded even if the price had been different or she had known the press release was false.

   c. Probably. Even though Sharon has sued more than two years after her purchase or sale of securities, the statute of limitations for federal securities fraud action permits a 10b-5 action to be brought within two years after "discovery of the facts constituting the violation," so long as the action is brought within five years after the violation. 28 U.S.C. §1658(b). Here the violation occurred when Sharon sold on the basis of the company's false press release. When should she have discovered the press release was false and the company had acted with scienter? See *Merck & Co. v. Reynolds* (see §9.4.1) (interpreting the two-year limitations period of §1658 to accrue either (1) when the plaintiff actually discovers the violation or (2) when a reasonably diligent plaintiff would have discovered the facts constituting the elements of the violation). Although there was much speculation about ITM's electrolysis research, the market seemed not to know for sure until the company's SEC filing, which also would have alerted Sharon to look into whether company officials knew that prior statements had been false. To expect Sharon to be more prescient than the market would seem inconsistent with Congress's purpose in lengthening the statute of limitations to protect defrauded investors against concealment.

CHAPTER 23

Insider Trading

Insider trading has captured the popular imagination. From press accounts, it would seem the most contemptible of corporate behaviors. Remarkably, state corporate law mostly accepts the principle of unfettered share liquidity and only narrowly regulates the trading of company stock by insiders. The real law of insider trading is federal—an offshoot of Rule 10b-5 under the Securities Exchange Act of 1934. See Chapter 22.

This chapter describes the nature of insider trading (§23.1), state corporate law of insider trading (§23.2), the federal "abstain or disclose" duties and enforcement under Rule 10b-5 (§23.3), and new rules on insider trading added by the Sarbanes-Oxley Act of 2002 and revised in the Dodd-Frank Act of 2010 (§23.4). Chapter 24 considers §16 of the Exchange Act, a remedial scheme applicable to short-swing trading profits by designated insiders.

§23.1 INSIDER TRADING—A PRIMER

§23.1.1 Classic Insider Trading

The paradigm case of insider trading arises when a corporate insider trades (buys or sells) shares of his corporation using material, nonpublic information obtained through the insider's corporate position. The insider exploits his informational advantage (a corporate asset) at the expense of the corporation's shareholders or others who deal in the corporation's stock.

The insider can exploit his advantage whether undisclosed information is good or bad. If *good news*, the insider can profit by buying stock from shareholders before the price rises on the favorable public disclosure. (An insider can garner an even greater profit on a smaller investment by purchasing "call options" on an options market that give him a right to buy the shares at a fixed price in the future.) If *bad news*, the insider can profit by selling to unknowing investors before the price falls on unfavorable disclosure. (An insider who does not own shares can also profit by borrowing shares and selling them for delivery in a few days when the price falls, known as "selling short," or by purchasing "put options," which give him the right to sell the shares at a fixed price in the future.)

§23.1.2 Misappropriation of Information— Outsider Trading

An insider can also exploit an informational advantage by trading in *other* companies' stock—"outsider trading." If the insider learns that his company will do something that affects the value of another company's stock, trading on this material, nonpublic information can also be profitable. The insider "misappropriates" this information at the expense of his firm. Although he trades with shareholders of the other company, he violates a confidence of his firm.

Many cases reported in the media as "insider trading" are actually cases of outsider trading on misappropriated information. Although classic insider trading and misappropriation often are grouped together under the rubric of "insider trading," it is useful to distinguish the two. The justifications for regulating each differ.

§23.1.3 Theories for Regulating Insider Trading

There are a number of theories for regulating trading by those with material, nonpublic information—whether insiders or outsiders.

Enhance Fairness

Insider trading is unfair to those who trade without access to the same information available to insiders and others "in the know"—a *fairness* rationale. The legislative history of the Exchange Act, for example, is replete with congressional concern about "abuses" in trading by insiders. This fairness notion, however, has not been generally accepted by state corporate law, which has steadfastly refused to infer a duty of candor by corporate insiders to shareholders in anonymous trading markets. See *Goodwin v. Agassiz*, 186 N.E. 659 (Mass. 1933) (rejecting duty of insiders to shareholders except in face-to-face dealings). Moreover, a fiduciary-fairness rationale cannot explain regulation of outsider trading based on misappropriated information.

Preserve Market Integrity

Insider trading undermines the integrity of stock trading markets, making investors leery of putting their money into a market in which they can be exploited — a *market integrity* rationale. A fair and informed securities trading market, essential to raising capital, was the purpose of the Exchange Act. Moreover, market intermediaries (such as stock exchange specialists or over-the-counter market makers) may increase the spread between their bid and ask prices if they fear being victimized by insider traders. Greater spreads increase trading costs and undermine market confidence. Yet a market integrity explanation may overstate the case for insider trading regulation. Many professional participants in the securities markets already trade on superior information; the efficient capital market hypothesis posits that stock prices will reflect this better-informed trading. See §1.2.

Reduce Cost of Capital

Insider trading leads investors to discount the stock prices of companies (individually or generally) where insider trading is permitted, thus making it more expensive for these companies to raise capital — a *cost of capital* rationale. In stock markets outside the United States, studies show that cost of equity decreases when the market introduces and enforces insider trading prohibitions. For this reason, most U.S. public companies have insider trading policies that permit insiders to buy or sell company stock only during "trading windows" — usually 7 to 30 days after important company announcements.

Protect Property Rights

Insider trading exploits confidential information of great value to its holder — a *business property* rationale. Those who trade on confidential information reap profits without paying for their gain and undermine incentives to engage in commercial activities that depend on confidentiality. Although in the information age a property rationale makes sense, theories of liability, enforcement, and private damages have grown in the United States out of the rhetoric of fiduciary fairness and market integrity

§23.1.4 Policing Insider Trading

Insider trading, cloaked as it is in secrecy, is difficult to track down. The stock exchanges have elaborate, much-used surveillance systems to alert officials if trading in a company's stock moves outside of preset ranges. When unusual trading patterns show up or trading occurs before major corporate announcements, exchange officials can ask brokerage firms to turn over records of who traded at any given time. The exchanges conduct computer cross-checks to spot "clusters" of trading—such as from a particular city or brokerage firm. An Automated Search and Match system, with data on thousands of companies and executives on such things as social affiliations and even college ties, assists the exchanges. If the exchanges see something suspicious, they turn the data over to the SEC for a formal investigation. The SEC can subpoena phone records and take depositions, and promise immunity to informants.

§23.2 STATE LAW ON INSIDER TRADING

In a relatively narrow range of cases, state law limits insiders' liquidity rights when they trade on material, nonpublic corporate information.

§23.2.1 Fraud or Deceit—Limited Tort Liability

The traditional law of deceit applies when

- the insider affirmatively misrepresents a material fact or omits a material fact that makes his statement misleading. (There is a duty to speak only in a relationship of trust and confidence.)
- the insider knows the statement is false or misleading or, under evolving notions, recklessly disregards its truthfulness.
- the other party actually and justifiably relies on the statement.
- the other party is harmed as a result.

Restatement (Second) of Torts, §§525, 526, 537, 538. Absent a duty to speak, the insider can avoid tort liability by remaining silent. In a public corporation, this is easy. For example, a company insider who knows of an impending special dividend can buy stock on an impersonal trading market. Even if subject to a special duty to speak, the absence of privity dissolves any causal link between the insider's purchases and particular shareholders' sales.

Early state courts, on the premise that corporate fiduciaries owe duties to the corporation and not to individual shareholders, regulated insider trading only on a showing of actual deceit. This is *caveat emptor*—the insider has no more duty than a used car salesperson owes her customers.

§23.2.2 State Fiduciary Rules

State corporate law has taken three approaches to insider trading: (1) a duty on insiders not to trade with corporate shareholders in face-to-face transactions while in the possession of highly material, nonpublic corporate information—the "special facts" rule (the majority rule); (2) a duty on insiders not to trade with corporate insiders in face-to-face transactions, regardless of the existence of special facts—the Kansas rule (the minority rule); (3) a duty on insiders *to the corporation* not to advance their own pecuniary position using corporate information, regardless of the harm to the corporation—the rule in New York.

Special Facts Doctrine

The traditional fraud rule fails to recognize an insider's fiduciary status. In recognition of this, state courts impose a diluted duty on individual shareholders to disclose their inside information or abstain from trading. In face-to-face transactions—as distinguished from transactions on stock trading markets between anonymous traders—courts have developed a *special facts rule* under which neither affirmative misrepresentations nor actual reliance need be established.

The special facts doctrine is limited as follows:

- The insider (an officer or director) must have purchased from an existing shareholder—sales by insiders to nonshareholder investors in the case of "bad news" are not covered.
- The insider must be in privity with the selling shareholder—there must be a face-to-face transaction or something approximating it (such as an insider using an agent to hide the insider's identity).
- The insider must know of highly material corporate information, such as the impending sale of significant corporate assets or the declaration of a special dividend.
- Secrecy is critically important to the sale—it must be clear the shareholder would not have traded had she known the information.

Special facts cases have often involved concealment of the insider's identity and sympathetic plaintiffs, such as widows.

The special facts rule arose in *Strong v. Repide*, 213 U.S. 419 (1909). The Supreme Court, applying general federal common law before *Erie Railroad v. Tompkins*, held a dominant insider could not trade surreptitiously with an unsuspecting shareholder when the insider possessed highly material, confidential corporate information. Repide (the company's majority shareholder and general manager) had finished negotiating the sale of a significant corporate property and sought to buy more corporate shares from a fellow shareholder. To hide his identity, Repide used an intermediary who bought the shares from the shareholder's agent. The Court agreed the agent would not have sold had he known Repide was the buyer. When the contract was finalized, the company's stock value increased tenfold. The Court held that Repide's position, along with his active concealment of highly material information, were "special facts" that supported rescission of the stock sale.

Strict (Kansas) Rule

A handful of state courts have expanded the special facts rule to impose a duty to disclose material nonpublic information in any face-to-face transaction. "Special facts" need not be present. This stricter approach, which originated in a Kansas case, is known as the "Kansas rule." In *Hotchkiss v. Fischer,* 16 P.2d 531 (Kan. 1932), the court said that in direct-negotiated purchases there is a "relation of scrupulous trust and confidence." A corporate president had told a widow, undecided whether to sell her shares or wait for a dividend, that he was unsure whether a dividend would be declared. The president bought the widow's shares for $1.25 per share, and a week later the board declared a $1.00 dividend—a possibility of which the president was aware. The court held the president liable. Although the case's facts fall in the "special facts" mainstream, the "scrupulous trust and confidence" rationale imposes a higher disclose-or-abstain duty. The "Kansas rule" has been rejected in some jurisdictions.

Limitations of Special Facts and Kansas Rules

The special facts and Kansas rules have two significant shortcomings. First, the rules assume purchases from existing shareholders on the basis of undisclosed "good news." A number of courts have refused to impose liability when an insider dumps stock on *nonshareholder investors* using inside "bad news." Second, the rules require privity. When insider trading occurs on an anonymous stock trading market, state courts have shown great reluctance to impose a disclose-or-abstain duty.

Consider *Goodwin v. Agassiz,* 186 N.E. 659 (Mass. 1933), where the court held that insiders who purchased their company's stock on the Boston Stock Exchange could not be held liable under a special facts test. The insiders had access to a geologist's theory that, if valid, indicated the possibility of valuable copper deposits on property owned by the company. The court found two problems with imposing liability. First, the insiders had a fiduciary duty to the corporation, not to individual shareholders. Assuming the insider trading did not harm the company, the insiders were not liable as fiduciaries. Second, privity between buyer and seller does not exist in anonymous trading on a stock exchange. There would be insurmountable practical problems of making disclosure to other traders, deciding when information (such as a geologist's theory) becomes material, and aligning sale and purchase transactions to determine which shareholders are entitled to recover and how much.

§23.2.3 Liability to Corporation

In an attempt to overcome these gaps in the common law, the New York Court of Appeals held more than 30 years ago that insider trading creates liability *to the corporation*, which liability can be enforced in a derivative suit. *Diamond v. Oreamuno*, 248 N.E.2d 910 (N.Y. 1969). The case involved insiders who had dumped their stock after learning nonpublic bad news about the company's earnings. To the objection that the corporation had not been harmed, the court had two responses. First, it held no harm need be shown. As between the insiders and the corporation—just as when an agent receives confidential information on behalf of his principal—the corporation "has a higher claim to the proceeds derived from the exploitation of the information." The insider cannot unjustly enrich himself. Second, the court inferred that the insider trading might have damaged the corporation's reputation and thus the marketability of its stock—though this need not be proved.

The *Diamond v. Oreamuno* court analogized its novel approach to §16(b) of the Exchange Act, which allows the corporation in a direct or derivative suit to recover short-swing trading profits from designated insiders (see §24.3). The court, however, pointed out the inadequacy of federal remedies. In the case, §16(b) offered no relief because trading had occurred outside the provision's six-month window. According to the court, Rule 10b-5 raised unresolved issues on the class entitled to recover, the measure of damages, and the allocation of recovery. (As we will see, these 10b-5 issues are today somewhat clearer. See §23.3 below).

The *Diamond v. Oreamuno* approach has not fared well outside New York. Some courts have rejected the approach outright. *Schein v. Chasen*, 313 So. 2d 739 (Fla. 1975). Other courts have said that corporate recovery for insider trading requires that the corporation "could have used the information to its own profit." *Freeman v. Decio*, 584 F.2d 186 (7th Cir. 1978). For example, if the corporation was about to repurchase its own stock in the market, insider purchases would directly compete and raise the price to the corporation. See *Brophy v. Cities Service Co.*, 70 A.2d 5 (Del. 1949).

In recent years, the Delaware courts have recognized the ability of shareholders to bring derivative claims on behalf of the corporation (so-called *Brophy* claims) when an insider uses material, nonpublic information to trade in the company's securities. See *In re Oracle Corp. Deriv. Litig.*, 867 A.2d 904 (Del. Ch. 2004). It is not necessary that the corporation suffered an actual harm; it is enough that the insider was unjustly enriched. The remedy in such cases is disgorgement of the insider's profits to the corporation. See *Kahn v. Kohlberg Kravis Roberts & Co.*, 23 A.3d 831 (Del. 2011) (holding that special litigation committee could not dismiss *Brophy* claim against insider who acquired company's preferred shares while in possession of material, nonpublic information).

Although liability to the corporation offers a practical solution to the limits of the traditional insider trading rules, it has some troubling and strange implications. First, shareholders who hold their shares during the insider trading receive a windfall in a corporate recovery. If the insider trading is on good news, the losers are the shareholders who sold their shares at deflated prices. They do not share in the corporate recovery at all. If the insider trading is on bad news, the losers are the investors who bought the stock at inflated prices. They recover only to the extent the corporate recovery increases the value of their stock—at most a partial recovery. Second, corporate recovery also creates the possibility of double liability. Besides being liable to the corporation, the insiders may be liable under Rule 10b-5 to contemporaneous traders (see §23.3.4). Although the *Diamond v. Oreamuno* court suggested this problem could be handled by interpleader, there will be jurisdictional, notification, and class certification difficulties.

Despite these deficiencies, the ALI Corporate Governance Principles adopted an unjust-enrichment approach similar to *Diamond v. Oreamuno* and the Delaware cases accepting *Brophy* claims, with the additional gloss that the corporation (or the shareholders as a group) can authorize or ratify insider trading if in the corporation's interest. ALI Principles §5.04 (prohibiting insiders from using material nonpublic information concerning the corporation to advance their pecuniary interests, whether or not this use harms the corporation). The ALI Principles views a rule of corporate recovery as better than no rule at all.

Outsider Trading under State Law

You may have noticed that, until now, we have talked only about insiders trading *in their company's shares*—classic insider trading. Very few state cases involve allegations of trading *in other companies' shares* using "misappropriated" information—outsider trading. At most, outsider trading may violate state trade secret laws and the antifraud provisions of state "blue sky" laws. See §5.1.3.

Examples

1. Elbert, a chemist of ITM Corp., has conducted tests on a cost-effective electrolysis process (separation of water into hydrogen and oxygen) using a cobalt/phosphate film at room temperatures. The results are a huge scientific breakthrough with enormous commercial potential. Daniela, ITM's president, learns of the tests and sends a memo to all who know of them urging complete secrecy. ITM's stock, which is publicly traded, doubles when ITM eventually confirms the tests and discloses the discovery. Assume the following happen before public disclosure:
   a. After Elbert's tests are confirmed, ITM's board offers Daniela options on the company's stock. Daniela accepts the options without telling the board of Elbert's tests. Is Daniela liable to the corporation under state law?
   b. Before Elbert's tests are confirmed, Daniela purchases ITM stock from Columbia Employees Pension Trust, one of ITM's major institutional shareholders. Daniela buys the stock from CEPT using a stockbroker, who does not disclose for whom the purchases are made. Is Daniela liable to CEPT?
   c. Daniela purchases ITM stock through her broker, who fills the order on a stock exchange. Shareholders who sold at about the time of Daniela's purchases seek to recover from her the profits they would have made if they had not sold. Can they under state common law?
   d. Elbert (who is neither a director nor officer of ITM) purchases ITM stock from fellow employees who do not know of the discovery. He says nothing to them, and they do not ask. Is Elbert liable to these shareholders under state common law?

2. Let's turn the tables. Assume ITM publicly announces Elbert's tests before they are confirmed. The price of ITM's stock rises dramatically. Elbert then tells Daniela the announcement was premature. The tests appear to have been a fluke and cannot be reproduced. When ITM issues a public disclaimer, the price of its stock plummets to preannouncement levels. Assume the following happen before ITM disavows the original announcement:
   a. Daniela sells her stock under a corporate stock repurchase program at current market prices. She does not tell the board or anyone else that the announcement has become misleading. Is Daniela liable to the corporation under state law?
   b. Daniela sells her entire shareholding to Mutual of Columbia, a major insurance company, through various brokers who do not disclose for whom they were selling. Is Daniela liable to MOC under state common law?
   c. Elbert (who is neither a director nor officer of ITM) buys put options as soon as he realizes the original tests are flukes. Can any of those on the other side of these transactions recover under state common law?

d. Elbert prepares the original announcement about the cobalt/phosphate electrolysis process, knowing that his preliminary tests are flukes. Elbert buys options, as above. Is he liable to the parties on the other side of these transactions under state common law?

Explanations

EXPLANATIONS

1. a. Probably, under both state fraud law and common law of insider trading. As the company's CEO, Daniela has a fiduciary duty *to the corporation* not to use her position to harm the corporation. Although she did not misrepresent anything, deceit law imposes a duty to speak on those in a relationship of trust and confidence. Further, her silence in the *face-to-face* negotiations fits the "special facts" test. The discovery had enormous potential value, and it is likely the board would have reconsidered its decision to approve the options.

   b. Perhaps under the strict Kansas rule. CEPT probably will be unable to show all the elements of fraud—there were no affirmative misrepresentations and CEPT did not actually rely on Daniela's silence. CEPT did not know it was buying from Daniela and thought it was selling at a good price. Although evolving fraud standards impose a duty to disclose in a confidential relationship—requiring disclosure to an employer or a client—state fraud law has not yet expanded to cover a corporate insider's relationship *to shareholders*.

   Both the strict Kansas rule and the more limited "special facts" doctrine cover insiders' trading outside of impersonal trading markets. Nonetheless, the "materiality" requirements under the tests are different. Under the "special facts" doctrine, Elbert's preliminary tests must have constituted unusual or extraordinary information that, if disclosed, would have caused a reasonable shareholder to have acted differently. This may be hard to show because the tests had to be confirmed, and a reasonable shareholder might have viewed the preliminary tests as flukes. The strict Kansas rule is less deferential. It is enough that the information would have been important to the shareholder's decision to sell. In view of the enormous potential revealed by the preliminary tests, Daniela's duty of "scrupulous trust and confidence" probably would have required her not to trade without first disclosing the tests and their potential implications.

   c. No. State fraud law requires some misrepresentation, absent in this case of impersonal market trading. Moreover, identifiable privity is required under the "special facts" doctrine and the strict Kansas rule. The absence of face-to-face dealings will preclude these shareholders from recovering from Daniela. Notice that the *Diamond v. Oreamuno* corporate recovery approach also leaves them in the cold because any recovery goes only to the corporation.

d. No. Although state fraud law prohibits silence by those in a confidential relationship, it is unlikely that Elbert's coworker relationship would be enough. Courts have applied the special facts and strict Kansas rules only to officers and directors. Thus, even though Elbert as an employee has a fiduciary relationship to the corporation, he may not have a corporate fiduciary relationship to fellow coworkers or shareholders under state law.

2. a. Probably. Just as a fiduciary cannot buy from the corporation on the basis of undisclosed "good news," the fiduciary cannot sell to the corporation on the basis of undisclosed "bad news." Elbert's inability to confirm the original tests would seem to be material under both a special facts and Kansas rule.

b. No. There was no affirmative misrepresentation or confidential relationship, and hence no fraud under state law. Further, liability under a special facts or strict Kansas rule is premised on the fiduciary's relationship to existing shareholders. Daniela's sale to a nonshareholder investor leaves MOC unprotected under traditional state law. Even if corporate recovery were available under a *Diamond v. Oreamuno* theory, ITM's recovery would only indirectly and partially compensate MOC to the extent the recovery increased the value of MOC's shares.

c. Probably not. Under a put option, Elbert receives a contractual right to sell ITM stock to the option sellers in the future at a predetermined price (the *strike price*). If the strike price is higher than the market price on the strike date—which will certainly be the case once the "bad news" is announced—Elbert will profit either by selling cheap stock or (as is more common) by simply having the other party buy back the commitment at the difference between the lower market price and the higher strike price. There are options markets on which these arrangements can be made.

There are a number of impediments for options sellers to recover. Fraud law requires some affirmative misrepresentation—there was none. Corporate fiduciary rules require that there have been some semblance of privity—there was none. Further, because options traders are not shareholders of the corporation, even *Diamond v. Oreamuno* recovery may be unavailable since the disappointed traders were not past or present shareholders.

d. Yes, under a fraud theory. Fraud law does not require privity; it is enough that Elbert knowingly made an affirmative misrepresentation intending that others rely, that the options sellers actually and justifiably relied, and that they were damaged as a result. Assuming the options sellers knew of the ITM announcement—which is likely—they have a good chance to recover. State corporate law, however, provides little help. None of the options sellers was trading in the capacity of an ITM shareholder.

§23.3 APPLICATION OF RULE 10b-5 TO INSIDER TRADING

Federal securities regulation of insider trading has developed in stages. It began with the novel scheme in the Exchange Act for the disgorgement of insider trading profits, a scheme aimed at discouraging stock price manipulation by corporate insiders (see Chapter 24). Later in the 1960s the SEC and federal courts used Rule 10b-5 to build an awkward "abstain or disclose" jurisprudence applicable to insiders who trade on material, nonpublic, confidential information. See *In re Cady, Roberts & Co.*, 40 SEC 907 (1961) (first case suggesting that trading on inside information might violate Rule 10b-5). In the 1980s Congress entered the fray and increased the penalties for insider trading, clarified the scope and mechanisms for private enforcement, and imposed additional surveillance duties on firms with access to inside information. In 2000 the SEC promulgated rules clarifying the state of mind that triggers liability and the persons who become subject to the "abstain or disclose" duty. In 2002 Congress sought to discourage insider trading by executives that came at the expense of employees or was based on falsified company financials. In 2010 Congress strengthened corporate "clawback" devices to discourage corporate executives from manipulating company financials to increase their stock-based pay.

The development of 10b-5 insider trading duties is a fascinating story of judicial activism and ingenuity in the face of a statutory lacuna. It also offers an insight into the operation of corporate federalism. Perceiving a failure by state corporate law to regulate insider trading, federal courts have used Rule 10b-5 to develop a theory of disclosure-based regulation that assumes the existence of fiduciary duties of confidentiality that state courts have been unwilling to infer.

§23.3.1 Federal Duty to "Abstain or Disclose"

Federal courts have interpreted Rule 10b-5 to prohibit securities fraud. See §22.1. No person may misrepresent material facts that are likely to affect others' trading decisions. This duty is meaningless to insider trading, which happens not by means of misrepresentations but rather silence. Over time, federal courts have developed rules against insider trading based on implied fiduciary duties of confidentiality.

Parity of Information

Early federal courts held that just as every securities trader is duty-bound not to lie about material facts, anyone "in possession of material, nonpublic information" must either abstain from trading or disclose to the investing public—a duty to *abstain or disclose*. See *SEC v. Texas Gulf Sulphur*, 401 F.2d 833 (2d Cir. 1968). But even the proponents of a "parity of information" (or "equal access") approach recognized that an absolute rule against trading when one has an informational advantage goes too far. Strategic silence is different from outright lying. To impose an abstain-or-disclose duty on everyone with material, nonpublic information—however obtained—would significantly dampen the enthusiasm for trading in the stock market. Capital formation might dry up if investors in trading markets were prohibited from exploiting their hard work, superior skill, acumen, or even their hunches. Investors would have little incentive to buy securities if they could not resell them using perceived informational advantages.

Fiduciary Duty of Confidentiality

In the early 1980s the Supreme Court provided a framework for the abstain-or-disclose duty. *Chiarella v. United States*, 445 U.S. 222 (1980); *Dirks v. SEC*, 463 U.S. 646 (1983). A decade later the Court brought "outsider trading" within this framework. *United States v. O'Hagan*, 521 U.S. 642 (1997). Reading Rule 10b-5 as an antifraud rule, the Court has held that any person in the possession of material, nonpublic information has a duty to disclose the information, or abstain from trading, if the person obtains the information in a relation of trust and confidence—a fiduciary relation. The Supreme Court thus anchors federal regulation of classic insider trading on a presumed fiduciary duty of corporate insiders to the corporation's shareholders—even though state corporate law has largely refused to infer such a duty in impersonal trading markets. See §23.2.2. Thus, the federal regulation of insider trading began largely as a judicial invention! The Court has extended this fiduciary-based regulation to cover trading by outsiders who breach fiduciary duty of confidentiality to persons or entities unrelated to the corporation in whose securities they trade.

Chiarella v. United States (classic insider trading)

Chiarella was employed in the composing room of a financial printer. Using his access to confidential takeover documents that his firm printed for corporate raiders, he figured out the identity of certain takeover targets. Chiarella then bought stock in the targets, contrary to explicit advisories by his employer. He later sold at a profit when the raiders announced their bids. The Supreme Court reversed Chiarella's criminal conviction under Rule 10b-5 and held that Rule 10b-5 did not impose a "parity of information" requirement. Merely trading on the basis of nonpublic material information, the Court held, could not trigger a duty to disclose or abstain. Chiarella had no duty to the shareholders with whom he traded because he had no fiduciary relationship to the *target companies or their shareholders.* (The Court decided that Chiarella could not be convicted for trading on information misappropriated from his employer since the theory was not presented to the jury.)

Dirks v. SEC (tipper-tippee)

Dirks was a securities analyst whose job was to follow the insurance industry. When he learned of an insurance company's massive fraud and imminent financial collapse from Secrist, a former company insider, Dirks passed on the information to his firm's clients. They dumped their holdings before the scandal became public. On appeal from SEC disciplinary sanctions for Dirks's tipping of confidential information, the Supreme Court held that Dirks did not violate Rule 10b-5 because Secrist's reasons for revealing the scandal to Dirks were not to obtain an advantage for himself. For Secrist to have tipped improperly "in connection with" the trading by Dirks's clients, the Court held, there had to have been a fiduciary breach. The Court took the view that a breach occurs when the insider gains some direct or indirect personal gain or a reputational benefit that can be cashed in later. In the case, Secrist had exposed the fraud with no expectation of personal benefit, and Dirks (whose liability depended on Secrist violating a fiduciary duty) could not be liable for passing on the information to his firm's clients.

United States v. O'Hagan (misappropriation)

O'Hagan was a partner in a law firm retained by a company planning to make a tender offer for a target company. He purchased common stock and call options on the target's stock before the bid. Both the bidder and law firm had taken precautions to protect the bid's secrecy. When the bid was announced, O'Hagan sold for a profit of more than $4.3 million. After an SEC investigation, the Justice Department brought an indictment against O'Hagan alleging securities fraud, mail fraud, and money laundering. He was convicted on all counts and sentenced to prison. The Eighth Circuit, however, reversed his conviction on the ground misappropriation did not violate Rule 10b-5. (The Eighth Circuit also held the SEC exceeded its authority in promulgating Rule 14e-3. See §23.3.3 below.) The Supreme Court reversed and validated the misappropriation theory. The Court concluded that the unauthorized use of confidential information is (1) the use of a "deceptive device" under §10(b) and (2) "in connection with" securities trading. First, the misappropriator "deceives" the source that entrusted to him the material, nonpublic information by not disclosing his evil intentions—a violation of fiduciary duty. Second, the "fiduciary's fraud is consummated, not when the fiduciary gains the confidential information, but when ... he uses the information to purchase or sell securities." Citing to the legislative history of the Exchange Act and to SEC releases, the Court concluded that misappropriation liability would "insure the maintenance of fair and honest markets [and] thereby promote investor confidence." O'Hagan's trading operated as a *fraud on the source* in connection with securities trading—a violation of Rule 10b-5.

Satisfying the Disclosure Duty

According to the logic of the 10b-5 "abstain or disclose" construct, a fiduciary may trade on confidential information by first disclosing the information to the person to whom she owes the fiduciary duty. See *SEC v. Texas Gulf Sulphur Co.*, 401 F.2d 833 (2d Cir. 1968) (suggesting that insiders wait 24 to 48 hours after information is publicly disclosed to give it time to be disseminated through wire services or publication in the financial press). In a similar vein, some companies have internal policies that permit corporate insiders to trade only during a one- or two-week period after the company files quarterly and annual reports. As a practical matter, the abstain-or-disclose duty is really a prohibition against trading, since any disclosure must be effective in eliminating any informational advantage to the person who has material, nonpublic information—thus eliminating any incentive to trade.

State of Mind

An unsettled issue in the cases has been the state of mind that triggers insider trading liability when a person purchases or sells securities. In *O'Hagan* the Supreme Court said that insider trading must be "on the basis" of material, nonpublic information. Lower courts have split on whether the trader must be in "knowing possession" of inside information or must actually consciously "use" the information in trading. Compare *United States v. Teicher*, 987 F.2d 112 (2d Cir. 1993) (accepting "knowing possession" standard, as simpler to apply and consistent with the expansive nature of Rule 10b-5, where a young attorney tipped inside information about transactions involving clients of his law firm); *United States v. Smith*, 155 F.3d 1051 (9th Cir. 1998) (requiring showing of "use" of inside information, particularly when a defendant's state of mind is at issue in criminal case).

In 2000 the SEC adopted a rule to clarify this aspect of insider trading liability. Rule 10b5-1. Under the rule, a person trades "on the basis" of material, nonpublic information if the trader is "aware" of the information when making the purchase or sale. Rule 10b5-1(b). In its release accompanying the rule, the SEC explained that "aware" is a commonly used English word, implying "conscious knowledge," with clearer meaning than "knowing possession." Does the SEC have rulemaking authority to define the elements of insider trading, which (until now) has been governed exclusively by judge-made rules? Arguably the agency that begot Rule 10b-5 can also change and define its contours.

Preexisting Trading Plans

The SEC has also sought to clarify when corporate insiders and others can trade in company stock even when aware of inside information. Individuals and entities who set up specific securities trading plans when unaware of inside information can avoid liability even if trading under the plan occurs later when they are aware of inside information. Rule 10b5-1(c). The person must demonstrate the following:

- She had entered in "good faith" into a binding contract to trade the security, instructed another person to execute the trade for her account, or adopted a written plan for trading securities—when unaware of inside information.
- This preexisting trading strategy either (1) expressly specified the amount, price, and date of the trade; (2) included a written formula for determining these inputs; or (3) disabled the person from influencing the trades, providing the actual trader was unaware of the inside information.
- The trade accorded with this preexisting strategy.

An entity (nonindividual) has an additional affirmative defense if the actual individual trading for the entity was unaware of inside information and the entity had policies and procedures to ensure its individual traders would not violate insider trading laws. Rule 10b5-1(c)(2).

In 2009 the SEC provided some interpretive guidance when Rule 10b5-2 plans are revised. First, although termination of a trading plan does not automatically trigger 10b-5 liability, a termination that "coincides" with insider trading may violate Rule 10b-5. Second, canceling and then replacing an existing plan may also run into problems if the actions are part of a "scheme to evade" the rule; such liability can be minimized with a "waiting period" between the cancellation and replacement.

§23.3.2 Insider Trading 10b-5 Primer

The linchpin of 10b-5 insider trading liability is the knowing misuse of material, nonpublic information entrusted to a person with duties of confidentiality. Attempting to provide a general definition, the SEC's Rule 10b5-1 offers a restatement of federal insider trading law:

> The "manipulative and deceptive devices" prohibited by Section 10(b) of the Act and Rule 10b-5 thereunder include, among other things, the purchase or sale of a security of any issuer, on the basis of material, nonpublic information about that security or issuer, in breach of a duty of trust and confidence that is owed directly, indirectly, or derivatively, to the issuer of that security or the shareholders of that issuer, or to any other person who is the source of the material, nonpublic information.

Although the Supreme Court has glossed over the provenance of these duties, its opinions lead to some clear guidance to persons who have material, nonpublic information:

Insiders	Insiders who obtain material, nonpublic information because of their corporate position — directors, officers, employees, and controlling shareholders — have the clearest 10b-5 duty not to trade in the securities of their company. See *Chiarella*.
Constructive (temporary) insiders	Constructive insiders who are retained temporarily by the company in whose securities they trade — such as accountants, lawyers, and investment bankers — are viewed as having the same 10b-5 duties as corporate insiders. See *Dirks* (dictum). Lower courts have also inferred status as constructive insider in family settings where there are expectations of confidentiality.
Outsiders (with duty to source of information)	Outsiders with no relationship to the company in whose securities they trade also have an abstain-or-disclose duty when aware of material, nonpublic information obtained in a relationship or trust and confidence with the company (or source) of that information. See *O'Hagan*. The outsider's breach of confidence to the information source is deemed a deception that occurs "in connection with" his securities trading.
Tippers	Those with a confidentiality duty — whether an insider or an outsider — who knowingly make improper tips are liable as participants in illegal insider trading. See *Dirks*. The tip is improper if the tipper expects the tippee will trade and anticipates reciprocal benefits — such as when she sells the tip, gives it to family or friends, or expects the tippee to return the favor. This liability extends to *subtippers* who know (or should know) a tip is confidential and came from someone who tipped improperly. The tipper or subtipper can be held liable even though she does not trade, so long as a tippee or subtippee down the line eventually does. *(continued)*

Tippees	Those without a confidentiality duty inherit a 10b-5 abstain-or-disclose duty if they knowingly trade on improper tips. *Dirks*. A tippee is liable for trading after obtaining material, nonpublic information that he knows (or has reason to know) came from a person who breached a confidentiality duty—whether an insider or an outsider. In addition, *subtippees* tipped by a tippee assume a duty not to trade if they know (or should know) the information came from a breach of duty.
Traders in derivative securities	The 10b-5 duty extends to trading with nonshareholders—such as options traders. *O'Hagan* (call options). The Insider Trading Sanctions Act of 1984 makes it unlawful to trade in any derivative instruments while in possession of material, nonpublic information if trading in the underlying securities is illegal. Exchange Act §20(d).
Strangers	A stranger with no relationship to the source of material, nonpublic information—whether from an insider or outsider—has no 10b-5 duty to disclose or abstain. *Chiarella*. Strangers who overhear the information or develop it on their own have no 10b-5 duties.

It is important to notice that corporate insiders (directors, officers, employees, and agents) often own stock in their companies. This is not illegal—in fact, it is sometimes highly desirable for corporate actors to have some "skin in the game." Nor is it illegal for these insiders to buy and sell their company stock. The only time there is a problem is when these insiders are aware of nonpublic, material information when they trade in their company's stock or the stock of another company—or improperly tip this information to others.

§23.3.3 Outsider Trading—Misappropriation Theory

The misappropriation theory is a bit tricky. Under the theory, 10b-5 liability arises when a person trades on confidential information in breach of a *duty owed to the source of the information*, even if the source is a complete stranger to the traded securities. *United States v. O'Hagan*, 521 U.S. 642 (1997). In effect, the deception is on the source and the trading with another party. This "fraud on the source" construct raises a number of issues: the basis for misappropriation liability, the scope of the duty of confidentiality, and the validity of the SEC's rule creating misappropriation liability for tender offer information.

Notice the difference between an *outsider* who misappropriates information from a source unrelated to the company in whose securities the outsider trades and a *tippee* who receives information from a fiduciary inside a company in whose securities the tippee (or subtippee) trades. The outsider's duty is to the "outside" source of the information; the tippee's duty is derived from the duty to the "insider" who tips improperly.

Misappropriation Theory

The *O'Hagan* decision was an important victory for the SEC, which ten years before had failed to convince the Supreme Court that Rule 10b-5 encompasses a misappropriation theory. *Carpenter v. United States*, 484 U.S. 19 (1987) (split 4-4 decision).

Although the ruling in *O'Hagan* removed any uncertainty about whether Rule 10b-5 regulates securities trading using misappropriated information, it exposed doctrinal rifts in the Court's 10b-5 jurisprudence. First, *O'Hagan* suggests that there can be no 10b-5 insider trading liability if there is no breach of trust and confidence. Thus, a person who gains access to material, nonpublic information by other wrongful means—such as outright theft—would seemingly not face 10b-5 sanctions. Moreover, a fiduciary who discloses his trading intentions or receives permission to trade from the information source would escape 10b-5 liability since there would arguably be no breach of his abstain-or-disclose duty. Cf. *SEC v. Rocklage*, 470 F.3d 1 (1st Cir. 2006) (upholding misappropriation claim against wife who "tricked" husband into revealing confidential company information and then tipped her brother who traded on the information, even though husband asked wife not to tip when she revealed her plans).

Second, *O'Hagan* leaves largely unanswered the question of who has duties of trust and confidence and when a duty of confidentiality attaches. For lawyer O'Hagan, it was easy to identify his duties to his law firm and thus to the bidder, but the inquiry becomes more difficult when a person overhears a conversation or has only a superficial relationship with the information source. See *SEC v. Switzer*, 590 F. Supp. 756 (W.D. Okla. 1984) (holding that eavesdropper is not liable for trading after overhearing CEO tell his wife company might be liquidated).

Duty of Confidentiality in Misappropriation Cases

The duty of trust and confidence in misappropriation cases is clearest when confidential information is misappropriated in breach of an established business relationship, such as investment banker—client or employer-employee. The duty is less clear in other business and personal settings.

In an attempt to provide clarity, the SEC has promulgated a rule that specifies when a recipient of material, nonpublic information is deemed to owe a duty of trust and confidence to the source for purposes of misappropriation liability. Rule 10b5-2(b):

- The recipient agreed to maintain the information in confidence.
- The persons involved in the communication have a history, pattern, or practice of sharing confidences (both business and nonbusiness confidences) so the recipient had reason to know the communicator expected the recipient to maintain the information's confidentiality.
- The communicator of the information was a spouse, parent, child, or sibling of the recipient, unless the recipient could show (based on the facts and circumstances of that family relationship) that there was no reasonable expectation of confidentiality.

Confidentiality Expectations outside the Family

By their terms, the rule's first two categories clarify when confidentiality expectations—and thus a duty of trust or confidence—arise in nonbusiness and business settings outside the family. Thus, a contractual relationship (though not necessarily creating a fiduciary relationship) could give rise to a duty not to use confidential information, if that is what the parties had agreed to or mutually understood. In addition, as the SEC stated in its preliminary note to the rule, the list is not exclusive, and a relationship of trust and confidence among family members or others can be established in other ways, as well.

Are confidentiality expectations, without a legal relationship of trust and confidence, enough to trigger a 10b-5 duty to "disclose or abstain"? That is, did the SEC overstep its rulemaking authority in Rule 10b5-2 by identifying duties of "trust and confidence" in the absence of a fiduciary relationship? Consider the case by the SEC against Mark Cuban, of Audionet and Dallas Mavericks fame. In 2004 Cuban had a phone conversation with the CEO of Mamma.com, a company in which Cuban was a 6.3 percent shareholder, and he learned that Mamma was planning to accept a new investor that would dilute existing shareholders. According to the SEC, Cuban said to the CEO he would keep the information confidential, but then he sold his Mamma shares and avoided losses of $750,000 in the process. When the SEC brought an insider case against him, Cuban argued that his relationship with the Mamma CEO and any confidentiality promise he made did not create a cognizable §10(b) duty. The trial court disagreed with Cuban, but dismissed the SEC's case on the theory that Cuban's oral promise of confidentiality encompassed only keeping the information confidential, but did not bar trading. On appeal, the Fifth Circuit did not address the lower court's novel parsing of Cuban's confidentiality promise or the validity of Rule 10b5-2, but instead held that the SEC's complaint laid a out a "more than a plausible" case of insider trading, and remanded for further proceedings. *SEC v. Cuban*, 634 F. Supp.2d 713 (N.D. Tex. 2009), *vacated and remanded*, 620 F.3d 551 (5th Cir. 2010). So the case continues.

Confidentiality Expectations inside the Family

Rule 10b5-2 was adopted largely in response to the anomaly in the case law that a family member who trades on material, nonpublic information obtained from a another family member violates Rule 10b-5 if the trading breached an *express promise* of confidentiality, but a family member does not violate Rule 10b-5 if there was only a *reasonable expectation* of confidentiality. The SEC rule treats trading by family members on the basis of inside information as undermining market and investor confidence, whether the expectation of confidentiality was express or implied. As the SEC explained, the trader's informational advantage in either case stems from "contrivance, not luck." Additionally, the SEC viewed its brighter-line approach as less intrusive than a case-by-case analysis into the nature of family relationships, as required by existing case law. See *United States v. Chestman*, 947 F.2d 551 (2d Cir.1991) (en banc) (holding that son-in-law owed no duty to in-laws who planned to sell their supermarket chain, when he and his broker traded on confidential information about impending sale).

Some courts have used this "expectation" analysis in cases of classic insider trading on the question whether family members qualify as "constructive insiders." In *SEC v. Yun*, 327 F.3d 1263 (11th Cir. 2003), a husband told his wife during divorce discussions that his stock options should be re-valued at a lower price because of a soon-to-be-made announcement of a drop in company earnings. The wife then told office mates about this impending news, who traded on the tip. The court held that spousal communications implicated a fiduciary duty when the communicating spouse has a "reasonable expectation of confidentiality"—given their history or practice of sharing business confidences. The court commented that Rule 10b5-2, which creates a presumption of spousal confidentiality in misappropriation cases, bolstered the conclusion that spouses should be understood to have expectations of confidentiality in cases of classic insider trading.

Tipping of Misappropriated Information

Not only is it illegal to trade on a tip from an insider, it is illegal to trade based on a tip from an outsider who passes on misappropriated information to obtain a personal benefit. That is, 10b-5 tipping liability described in *Dirks* applies to tips both from insiders and from outsiders. See *United States v. Falcone*, 257 F.3d 226 (2d. Cir. 2001) (finding 10b-5 liability when distributor of *Business Week*, before magazine went on sale to general public, passed on copies to neighbor/broker who traded on nonpublic information in magazine).

Rule 14e-3 — Misappropriation of Tender Offer Information

The SEC has used the misappropriation theory to adopt rules prohibiting trading based on material, nonpublic information about *unannounced tender offers*. Using its rulemaking authority under §14(e) of the Exchange Act—which allows rules aimed at "fraudulent, deceptive, or manipulative acts or practices, in connection with any tender offer"—the SEC prohibited trading by those with inside information about a tender offer. Exchange Act Rule 14e-3. The rule prohibits, during the course of a tender offer, trading by anybody (other than the bidder) who has material, nonpublic information about the offer that he knows (or has reason to know) was obtained from either the bidder or the target. Notice that there is no need under Rule 14e-3 to prove that a tipper breached a fiduciary duty for personal benefit. See *United States v. O'Hagan*, 521 U.S. 642 (1997) (upholding SEC's rulemaking authority to "define and prescribe means reasonably designed to prevent [fraudulent] acts" under §14(e) of the Exchange Act).

The Second Circuit has considered the difference between 10b-5 and 14e-3 liability. *United States v. Chestman*, 947 F.2d 551 (2d Cir. 1991) (en banc). In the case Chestman, a stock broker, learned of an impending tender offer from the husband of the niece of the company's controlling shareholder. The controlling shareholder had agreed to sell his control block as a prelude to the purchaser's tender offer. When Chestman traded on this information for himself and his clients, the government prosecuted him under Rules 10b-5 and 14e-3. The Second Circuit affirmed Chestman's 14e-3 conviction, for which no showing of duty was necessary. But the court held he could not be convicted under a 10b-5 misappropriation theory because the family tipper had no duty to his family to guard confidential information.

Mail and Wire Fraud — Criminal Liability for Misappropriation

Misappropriation of confidential information can also be the basis of non-securities criminal liability. In *Carpenter v. United States*, 484 U.S. 19 (1987), the Supreme Court had sidestepped the 10b-5 quagmire by affirming in an 8-0 decision a *Wall Street Journal* reporter's conviction under federal mail and wire fraud criminal statutes for misappropriating and tipping information before it appeared in a column he wrote. (The SEC cannot enforce the mail and wire fraud statutes, which can only be enforced by the Justice Department in a criminal prosecution.) The Court held that the newspaper had a "property" interest in keeping the column confidential prior to publication, and that the reporter's breach of his confidentiality obligation defrauded the newspaper. Although the Court's decision raises disquieting issues about criminal liability for breaching an employment stipulation, the case makes clear that trading on misappropriated securities-related information is subject to criminal penalties.

§23.3.4 Remedies for Insider Trading

Insider traders are subject to an imposing host of sanctions and liabilities. As the following list makes clear, it is no wonder that law firms tell new lawyers not to trade on clients' confidential information.

Civil Liability to Contemporaneous Traders

In an impersonal trading market, it is unclear who is hurt by insider trading and how much. Shareholders and investors who trade at the same time as an insider presumably would have traded even had the insider fulfilled his duty and abstained. If, however, the theory is that insider trading is unfair to traders, recovery should be equal to the traders' contemporaneous trading "losses"—typically significantly greater than the insider's gains. If the theory is that insider trading undermines the integrity of trading markets, recovery should be disgorgement of the insider's trading gains to the market as a whole. If the theory is that those who engage in insider trading pilfer valuable commercial information, recovery should be based on the losses to the owner of the confidential information.

Congress has addressed the issue and adopted a recovery scheme that borrows from both the unfairness and disgorgement rationales. The Insider Trading and Securities Fraud Enforcement Act of 1988 limits recovery to traders (shareholders or investors) whose trades were contemporaneous with the insider's. Recovery is based on the disgorgement of the insider's actual profits realized or losses avoided, reduced by any disgorgement obtained by the SEC under its broad authority to seek injunctive relief (see below). Exchange Act §20A.

Civil Recovery by "Defrauded" Source of Confidential Information

Owners of confidential information who purchase or sell securities can bring a private action under Rule 10b-5 against insider traders and tippees who adversely affect their trading prices. See *Blue Chip Stamps v. Manor Drug Stores*, 421 U.S. 723 (1975) (actual purchaser or seller standing requirement). A "defrauded" company may recover if it suffered trading losses or was forced to pay a higher price in a transaction because the insiders' trading artificially raised the stock price. *FMC Corp. v. Boesky*, 673 F.2d 272 (N.D. Ill. 1987), *remanded*, 852 F.2d 981 (7th Cir. 1988) (holding tippee not liable for trading on misappropriated information concerning company's impending recapitalization plan because company lost nothing in the recapitalization). Although some commentators proposed corporate recovery *on behalf of shareholders*, courts have insisted on a corporate (not shareholder) injury for there to be corporate recovery.

SEC Enforcement Action

The SEC can bring a judicial enforcement action seeking a court order that enjoins the inside trader or tippee from further insider trading (if likely to recur) and that compels the disgorgement of any trading profits. *SEC v. Texas Gulf Sulphur Co.*, 401 F.2d 833 (2d Cir. 1968) (ordering establishment of fund from which shareholders and other contemporaneous traders could recover from insider traders and tippers).

Civil Penalties

To add deterrence, the SEC can also seek a judicially imposed civil penalty against those who violate Rule 10b-5 or Rule 14e-3 of up to three times the profits realized (or losses avoided) by their insider trading. Exchange Act §21A (added by the Insider Trading Sanctions Act of 1984). The penalty, paid into the federal treasury, is in addition to other remedies. Thus, it is possible for an insider or tippee to disgorge her profits (in a private or SEC action) *and* pay the treble-damage penalty.

"Watchdog Penalties"

To create even more deterrence, the SEC can seek civil penalties against employers and others who "control" insider traders and tippers. Exchange Act §21A (added by Insider Trading and Securities Fraud Enforcement Act of 1988). Controlling persons are subject to additional penalties up to $1 million or three times the insider's profits (whichever is greater) if the controlling person knowingly or recklessly disregards the likelihood of insider trading by persons under its control. Broker-dealers that fail to maintain procedures protecting against such abuses may also be subject to these penalties if their laxity substantially contributed to the insider trading.

"Bounty Rewards"

To encourage informants, the SEC can pay bounties to anyone who provides information leading to civil penalties. The bounty can be up to 10 percent of the civil penalty collected. Exchange Act §21A(e) (added by Insider Trading and Securities Fraud Enforcement Act of 1988). This bounty program is in addition to the "whistleblower" bounty program created by Dodd-Frank. See Exchange Act §21F (see §12.3.5).

Criminal Sanctions

To punish those who engage in "willful" insider trading—that is, insider trading where the defendant knows that it is wrongful—the SEC can (and often does) refer cases to the U.S. Department of Justice for criminal prosecution. Exchange Act §32(a). Congress has twice increased the criminal penalties for violations of the Exchange Act and its rules. In the Insider Trading and Securities Fraud Enforcement Act of 1988, Congress increased the maximum criminal fines from $100,000 to $1,000,000 ($2,500,000 for nonindividuals) and jail sentences from five years to ten years. Then in the Sarbanes-Oxley Act of 2002, Congress upped the maximum fines to $5,000,000 ($25,000,000 for nonindividuals) and jail sentences to 20 years. Sarbanes-Oxley §1106, Exchange Act §32(a).

The Exchange Act's criminal provisions provide a curious defense against incarceration for violating an SEC rule if the defendant "proves he had no knowledge of such rule." Exchange Act §32(a). Courts have denied the defense if the defendant recognized he was engaged in deception.

§23.3.5 Regulation FD and Selective Disclosure

Inside information does not stay bottled up in companies forever. Sooner or later, companies communicate to securities markets. Formal disclosure in SEC filings is the soul of federal securities regulation. Informal disclosure, particularly by means of selective discussions with securities analysts and large investors, has been controversial—criticized as systematic tipping of valuable inside information and praised as an efficient way to reveal information to securities markets.

In 2000 the SEC took to heart the criticisms and adopted Regulation FD (Fair Disclosure) to forbid public companies from selectively disclosing material, nonpublic information. Exchange Act Rel. No. 43,154 (2000). The detailed rules on how companies may respond to analyst inquiries and engage in investor relations have altered how company information reaches securities markets. Disclosure practices once widespread, such as giving detailed financial projections to selected securities analysts or reviewing analyst reports before public release, are now regulated.

Regulation FD applies to issuer disclosures of material, nonpublic information to specified market professionals, as well as security holders who it is "reasonably foreseeable" will trade on the basis of the information. Rule 100(b)(1). When the disclosure is "intentional," issuers must disclose inside information to the investing public *simultaneously* with any disclosure to selected analysts or investors. Rule 100(a)(1). If the issuer discovers it has made an "unintentional" selective disclosure, the issuer must disclose the information to the public *promptly* (generally within 24 hours). Rule 100(a)(2). The information must be disseminated by methods "reasonably designed to achieve broad non-exclusionary distribution to the public"—such as through Internet postings or simulcasts, or by furnishing a Form 8-K to the SEC. Rule 101(e) (defining "public disclosure"). The restrictions apply to the issuer's senior officials and those who regularly communicate with analysts and investors, such as investor relations or public relations officers. Rule 101(f).

The "equal access" rules of Regulation FD have some important exclusions [Rule 100(b)]:

Context	Disclosure Allowed
Normal course of business	Disclosure may be made in the normal course of business, such as to professional advisers (attorneys, investment bankers, or accountants) or business partners in contract negotiations. Dodd-Frank calls on the SEC to eliminate the exclusion for credit rating agencies, unless the credit rating agency receives the information pursuant to a confidentiality or nondisclosure agreement. Dodd-Frank §939B.
Public disclosures	Disclosure may be made to media or government officials, such as by responding to newspaper inquiries or complying with regulatory investigations.
Public offerings	Disclosures may be made in securities offerings registered under the Securities Act, such as to analysts and institutional investors in going-public "road shows."
Foreign private issuers	Disclosure may be made by foreign private issuers (which, if they meet the jurisdictional requirements, remain subject to the securities antifraud provisions).

To take some of the sting out of these rules, Regulation FD is enforceable only through SEC enforcement actions and does not give rise to 10b-5 liability or private enforcement. Rule 102.

Regulation FD is an important step toward a systematic regulation of inside information. Rather than dealing with each selective disclosure as a possible instance of "tipping," the regime encourages wide dissemination of information—whenever the issuer decides to disclose. The rules encourage the release of information, not its suppression—consistent with the philosophy of securities regulation that all investors have access to the same company-provided information at the same time. The rules also avoid the potential conflicts that analysts once felt to report favorably on companies to protect the flow of selective disclosures and that company executives felt to delay public disclosure so as to curry favor with preferred analysts or institutional investors.

In 2002 the SEC brought its first enforcement actions under Regulation FD. In one case, a company CFO called a handful of analysts to explain that their reports had failed to note that company earnings usually were higher in the second half of the year. The SEC issued an administrative cease-and-desist order, pointing out the company should have publicly disclosed the seasonality of its earnings before calling the analysts. When the company balked and the agency brought a judicial enforcement action, however, the court concluded that the CFO's statements had already been disclosed (or were available) to the public, in the process chiding the SEC for being too linguistic and for chilling company disclosures. *SEC v. Seibel Systems*, 384 F.Supp.2d 694 (SDNY 2005). The court, however, did not address the fact that investors privy to the CFO's statements bought the company's shares, causing the stock price to surge. In short, the market's reaction to the private information suggested its materiality, even though the court's parsing of words led to a different conclusion.

§23.4 REGULATION OF INSIDER TRADING UNDER SARBANES-OXLEY (AND DODD-FRANK)

In response to the corporate scandals of the early 2000s, the Sarbanes-Oxley Act of 2002 regulates insider trading by company executives in two new situations: during pension fund blackouts and during the year before financials are restated. The Dodd-Frank Act of 2010 adds new "clawback" requirements for public companies.

§23.4.1 Insider Trading during Pension Plan Trading Blackout

Sarbanes-Oxley seeks to prevent insiders from "abandoning a sinking ship" while other employees are prevented from selling their stock. Sarbanes-Oxley §306(a). Directors and officers are prohibited from trading in their company's stock during any "trading blackout" in the company's pension plan—that is, when for more than three consecutive business days a majority of plan participants cannot obtain distributions or trade company stock held in the plan. ERISA §101, 29 U.S.C. §1021(h). The prohibition applies to any stock obtained by the director or officer in connection with his service or employment, whether or not held in the plan. The prohibition is meant to prevent company management from freezing trading in the company's pension plan for ordinary employees while dumping their own stock during a decline in the company's stock prices. Not only must the pension plan administrator notify plan participants (and the SEC) of the blackout, but the company must also notify directors and officers of the prohibition against trading in company stock. See Regulation BTR, Rule 104 (specifying contents and timing of notice).

Any trading profits realized by the director or officer during a trading blackout are recoverable by the company, regardless of intent—much like the strict liability scheme for short-swing profits under §16(b). See §24.3. The action to recover trading profits may be brought as a direct suit by the company or as a derivative suit by a shareholder after making demand on the company's board. The suit must be brought within two years after the profits are realized. See Regulation BTR, Rule 103 (specifying "profit recoverable" to be difference between the transaction price and the average market price after the end of the blackout).

Unlike short-swing trading, which only triggers reporting requirements and the possibility of disgorgement in private litigation, trading during a pension plan blackout is *prohibited*. Thus, directors or officers who trade during such a blackout may also be subject to SEC enforcement actions and even criminal sanctions.

§23.4.2 Reimbursement ("Clawback") of Incentive Pay When Financials Misstated

Sarbanes-Oxley "Clawback" Regime

Sarbanes-Oxley created a regime calling on corporate executives in public companies to reimburse the company for incentive pay when the company must restate its financials because of "misconduct." Sarbanes-Oxley §304 (adding 15 U.S.C. §7243). Specifically, the CEO and CFO are required to reimburse the company for any incentive pay (such as bonuses or equity-based compensation) received from the company during the 12-month period after the misstated financials were issued or filed. This "reimbursement" duty also applies to any profits on the sale of company stock by the CEO or CFO during the same period.

The Sarbanes-Oxley reimbursement provisions sought to prevent a company's top officers from profiting from false financials. The provisions, for which legislative history was scant, introduced numerous uncertainties: (1) Do voluntary restatements trigger a reimbursement duty? (2) What individuals are covered? (3) Are private actions (including derivative suits) available or only SEC enforcement? (4) Are negligent misstatements or only intentional ones considered misconduct? (5) How are trading profits calculated? (6) Can a company create its own definitions of misconduct and trading profits? (7) What is the statute of limitations?

There have been some answers to these questions, but only a few. Courts have uniformly interpreted §304 not to create a private cause of action, but only a basis for an SEC enforcement action. See *Neer v. Pelino*, 389 F. Supp.2d 648 (E.D. Pa. 2005) (plain language of Sarbanes-Oxley, buttressed by legislative history, precludes private right of action). The SEC, however, has brought few enforcement actions.

Dodd-Frank "Clawback" Regime

In response to the many weaknesses and unanswered questions of the §304 clawback regime, Dodd-Frank created a new one. Dodd-Frank §954. Under new §10D to the Exchange Act, the SEC is required to impose rules on the national stock exchanges that would compel listed companies to adopt "clawback" policies for the recovery of any incentive-based compensation (including stock options) from current or former executive officers for the prior three years in the event of a financial restatement due to material noncompliance with any financial reporting requirement under the securities laws. The amount to be recovered is set at the difference between the amount of incentive-based compensation received and the amount that should have been received under the restated financial results.

The §954 regime of Dodd-Frank is different from the §304 regime of Sarbanes-Oxley. First, the new clawback right is enforceable, not just by the SEC, but also in derivative actions whenever companies fail to seek such relief. Further, private plaintiffs may initiate litigation even when restatements did not occur, but should have occurred were it not for a conflict of interest by management. Second, while the §304 regime only allowed disgorgement from the company's CEO and CFO, the §954 regime covers the company's current and former "executive officers," which presumably includes all officers subject to §16 reporting. Third, the §954 regime lowers the trigger for clawbacks to instances of "material noncompliance with applicable accounting principles," while the §304 regime was limited to restatements resulting from "misconduct." Fourth, the §954 regime extends the look-back period from one year to three years.

Despite adding greater clarity—and increasing the likelihood of enforcement—the §954 regime leaves some important questions unanswered. First, if an executive and the company's board fight the clawback, it is unclear whether the usual corporate law rules on board demand and dismissal of derivative litigation would apply. In particular, it is unclear whether the board (or a special litigation committee) could argue that the benefits of any clawback are outweighed by the disadvantages. Second, it is unclear whether the SEC and stock exchanges would have any leeway in defining such terms as "executive officers" and "material noncompliance." Finally, Dodd-Frank imposes no deadline for the SEC to issue rules to the stock exchanges or for the exchanges to pass the new clawback standards.

Examples

1. ITM Corp. is a publicly traded company with an active research and development department. Elbert, an ITM chemist, has conducted preliminary tests on a cobalt/phosphate film that electrolyzes (separates water into hydrogen and oxygen) at room temperatures. If the test results can be confirmed, it would be a huge scientific breakthrough with enormous commercial potential in storing energy generated by solar panels. Daniela, ITM's president, learns of the tests and sends an intraoffice memo to all concerned urging complete secrecy.
   a. ITM's board grants ITM stock to Daniela, who accepts. She does not tell the board of Elbert's tests. Is Daniela liable to the corporation under Rule 10b-5?
   b. Daniela purchases "call" options (allowing her to buy ITM stock) on the options market. She does not trade with ITM shareholders. Is Daniela liable under Rule 10b-5?
   c. Elbert purchases ITM stock through a stockbroker under a written investment plan that calls for fixed, monthly purchases of ITM stock. Under the plan Elbert can choose to purchase more or fewer shares in any month, but he does not exercise this option. Is Elbert, who is neither a director nor officer of ITM, liable under Rule 10b-5?

2. After the test results are confirmed, but before public disclosure of the tests, Elbert tells Elsa (a fellow physicist who works for another research company) of the low-cost electrolysis breakthrough.
   a. Elsa buys ITM stock. Is she liable under Rule 10b-5?
   b. Elbert does not trade himself, but reveals the ITM test results to Elsa hoping to receive similar market-sensitive scoops from her. Assuming Elsa never reciprocates with information of her own, is Elbert liable under Rule 10b-5?
   c. Elbert and Elsa discuss the future of electrolysis and its impact on energy policy while riding in a limousine on their way to a scientific conference. Mickey, the limo driver, overhears their conversation and the next day purchases ITM stock. Is Mickey liable under Rule 10b-5?

3. Still before the electrolysis breakthrough is disclosed publicly, Daniela tells her husband Donald (from whom she is separated) that he should reconsider divorcing her since she stands to become wealthy because of

a "top secret breakthrough" at ITM. She asks him to keep the information confidential.

a. Instead, Donald buys ITM call options. Has he violated Rule 10b-5?
b. Donald also tells a colleague at his office that "Daniela tells me there's a breakthrough at ITM—you should buy." The colleague does. Has the colleague violated Rule 10b-5?
c. Donald and his good friend Martha have the same stockbroker, Merton. When Donald tells Merton to purchase ITM stock options, Merton assumes Donald knows from Daniela that something good is afoot at ITM. He calls Martha and says simply, "Donald's buying." Martha buys ITM stock. Has she violated Rule 10b-5?

4. Meanwhile, at company headquarters Daniela receives a phone call from Raymond, a securities analyst who follows high-tech companies. Daniela tells Raymond, "There have been significant developments in our energy-storage research." Daniela hopes to signal to the market the impending good news.
   a. Raymond tells his clients that ITM should be viewed as a "strong buy." Has Daniela violated any duties?
   b. Daniela calls you, the company's lawyer, and asks for your advice on how to handle disclosures about ITM's electrolysis research and results to securities analysts. Can she talk with you, and what would you advise?

5. Before public disclosure of the electrolysis breakthrough, Daniela discloses it to Wilbur (the president of Third Federal Bank) to obtain a loan for ITM to build a new manufacturing plant. Daniela asks Wilbur to keep the information secret.
   a. Wilbur calls his stockbroker and buys ITM stock. Is Wilbur liable under Rule 10b-5?
   b. Wilbur tells his wife Wanda over dinner that ITM's stock price is "probably going to go through the ceiling." Wanda asks no more but buys ITM stock. Is Wilbur or Wanda liable under Rule 10b-5?
   c. Tina, a corporate spy, breaks into Third Federal's offices and rifles the files to find the ITM loan application. She buys ITM stock. Is Tina liable under Rule 10b-5?

6. ITM's board decides it should be prepared to add manufacturing capacity to produce electrolysis machines using the company's cobalt/phosphate process. It decides to acquire Ovid Corporation, a publicly traded industrial builder, to build new manufacturing plants. ITM secretly negotiates an acquisition of Ovid.
   a. Before announcing the acquisition, ITM purchases a significant block of Ovid stock. Is ITM liable to Ovid shareholders under Rule 10b-5? Rule 14e-3?

b. ITM decides to proceed with a tender offer, but before announcing its bid the ITM board authorizes Daniela to purchase a limited amount of Ovid stock on the market. Is Daniela liable under Rule 10b-5? Rule 14e-3?

c. Ovid shareholders who sold during the period between Daniela's trading and eventual disclosure of the merger sue Daniela to recover the gains they would have made if they had not sold. Is Daniela liable to these shareholders under Rule 10b-5?

d. Daniela makes $100,000 in trading profits by buying Ovid stock. What is her maximum monetary exposure?

e. Daniela attends a stock analysts' meeting, which is simulcast on the company's website. She announces that ITM will manufacture its new electrolysis machines, but does not mention new manufacturing plants or the pending acquisition of Ovid. One of the analysts, Tom, figures out that ITM is likely to acquire Ovid. Tom tells his clients, who buy Ovid stock. Is Tom liable under Rule 10b-5?

Explanations

EXPLANATIONS

1. a. Yes, probably. Insider trading duties also apply to trading with one's corporation. As a corporate insider, Daniela has a fiduciary relationship to ITM and, under Rule 10b-5, a duty to abstain or disclose when trading *with the corporation* on the basis of material, nonpublic information. *Chiarella* (§23.3.1). An insider trading case under Rule 10b-5 must also satisfy the fraud elements of materiality and scienter:

   - *Materiality.* The information about the preliminary tests is material if a reasonable investor would consider it important to a buy-sell decision. Under the "probability plus magnitude" test of *Basic, Inc. v. Levinson,* 485 U.S. 224 (1988) (§22.3.1), the magnitude of discovering a low-cost electrolysis process would be demonstrated by a post-disclosure jump in ITM's stock price. The probability that the preliminary tests would confirm the process's effectiveness seem high.
   - *Scienter.* Daniela knew of the tests when she accepted the options and should have been aware of their propensity to affect the value of the company's stock. See §22.3.2. It is not necessary that she actually used this information, but that she was aware of it. Rule 10b5-1.

   When trading involves nondisclosure, the Supreme Court has presumed reliance upon a showing that the undisclosed information was material. *Affiliated Ute Citizens v. United States,* 406 U.S. 128 (1972) (§22.3.3). In this face-to-face transaction, Daniela might nonetheless rebut the assumption of reliance by showing that the corporation (acting through an independent board) would have offered the options anyway, even had it known of the inside information.

b. Yes, almost certainly. Daniela's abstain-or-disclose duty extends to shareholders and other investors in ITM's stock. *Chiarella* (§23.3.1). Does it extend to nonshareholder investors? Before 1984, some courts had held that option traders were owed no duty of disclosure. The Insider Trading Sanctions Act of 1984, however, closed this judge-made loophole by explicitly prohibiting trading in any derivative instrument if trading in the underlying securities would violate insider trading rules. See Exchange Act §20(d).

Although materiality would seem an issue, it rarely is in insider trading cases. If the insider considered the information important to her buy-sell decision, it is almost certain that a court will conclude that a "reasonable shareholder" would also consider the information important—and thus material.

c. Probably, because the trading plan left some discretion to Elbert. The 10b-5 insider trading rules apply to any corporate insider with a fiduciary (or agency) relationship to the corporation. Elbert, an employee-agent of ITM, is subject to the same duties as Daniela. His awareness of the test results would establish a culpable state of mind, subject to an affirmative defense that the trading plan was such that the stock purchases would have happened regardless of his inside knowledge. Elbert would have to show he entered into the written plan before he was aware of the low-cost electrolysis breakthrough and the plan specified the terms of purchases, contained a formula for these terms, or disabled him from influencing the broker. Rule 10b5-1(c). That Elbert retained the option to increase or decrease the purchases each month means the plan was not fixed, as required by the SEC safe harbor rule for plan purchases.

2. a. Perhaps, depending on Elbert's motives and expectations. If Elsa knows (or has reason to know) that the information was confidential and came from an insider who tipped for some personal or reputational benefit, Elsa is liable as a tippee. *Dirks*. A significant issue is whether Elbert disclosed the breakthrough for personal gain or for some nonpersonal corporate reason. If he expected reciprocal stock-trading tips or personal reputational gain, the tip violated Rule 10b-5 if Elsa had reason to know those were his motives. If, however, Elbert revealed the breakthrough for business reasons, such as to discuss the scientific aspects of the discovery, Elsa is under no confidentiality obligation. Elsa's liability thus hinges on Elbert's motives—a deficiency of the *Dirks* approach, but part of federal insider trading law.

In addition to his motives, Elbert's expectations of confidentiality might also be relevant. If Elsa and Elbert have exchanged confidential information in the past so that Elsa had reason to know that Elbert expected confidentiality, it might be argued she became a "temporary insider." In its recent Rule 10b5-2, the SEC has inferred a duty of trust and confidence in such circumstances. Although the rule by its terms applies only to misappropriation liability, its logic extends to identifying temporary insiders in cases of classic insider trading.

b. Yes. Elbert is liable as a tipper because he gave the tip in breach of his fiduciary duty for an improper personal benefit—the expectation of future reciprocal tips. Even though Elbert did not trade himself, a tipping insider is liable for placing confidential nonpublic material information in peril of abuse. *SEC v. Texas Gulf Sulphur* (see §23.2.1). Under this aiding and abetting theory, nontrading tippers are jointly and severally liable to the same extent as their trading tippees. See Exchange Act §20A(c).

c. Perhaps, though not as a tippee. If Elbert did not anticipate a personal gain from his discussion or there was an expectation of confidentiality, there was no breach of Elbert's duty and a tippee (or an eavesdropper) could not be liable on that basis.

Nonetheless, Mickey might be liable on a misappropriation theory. If Mickey worked for a limousine company that expected complete discretion of its employees, he could be liable for misappropriating the information in breach of *his employer's* expectation of confidentiality. See *United States v. O'Hagan* (§23.3.3). His trading would constitute a breach of duty owed to his employer if the employer expected that he would not divulge or use for personal purposes any information obtained on the job. The SEC confirmed this analysis by defining a relationship of "trust or confidence" to include a contractual relationship (though not necessarily creating a fiduciary relationship) in which there was an agreement of confidentiality. Rule 10b5-2(b).

One sticking point might be whether Mickey had the requisite state of mind. Although his awareness of the importance of the electrolysis breakthrough would appear to satisfy the general "awareness" standard for civil liability, see Rule 10b5-1(b), it may not be enough to establish the "willfulness" required for criminal liability. The *O'Hagan* court pointed out that under Exchange Act §32(a) a criminal 10b-5 defendant cannot be imprisoned if he "has no knowledge of the rule."

3. a. Probably. The question is whether Donald is a "constructive insider" who has a duty of confidentiality because of his relationship to Daniela. Although earlier courts held that within a family duties not to trade on material, nonpublic information arise only if there were *express* understandings of confidentiality, recent courts have followed the lead of the SEC (see Rule 10b5-2) and treated spousal communications as carrying a duty of confidentiality if the spouses had an *express* or *implied* understanding of confidentiality. See *SEC v. Yun* (§23.3.3). By

asking Donald to keep the information confidential, Daniela expected he would not use the information. Only if Donald could show her expectation was unfounded, perhaps because of his past indiscretions, would the presumption of spousal confidentiality be rebutted.

Notice that this is not a case of tipping. When Daniela told Donald of the breakthrough it was not in the belief he would trade on it—in fact, she asked him to keep it confidential. Much like the spouse in *SEC v. Yun*, who told his wife during divorce discussions about an impending drop in the company's stock, Daniela's revelation was meant to preserve the marriage, not facilitate advantageous stock trading. Spousal communications about work do not constitute a fiduciary breach if the communications are not intended as a stock tip.

b. Probably. The question here is whether the colleague is liable as a tippee. If Donald was a "constructive insider" (see previous answer), the issue becomes whether the colleague knew or had reason to know that Donald's tip violated his duty of confidentiality, which requires that Donald expected a personal benefit from the tip. See *SEC v. Musella*, 678 F. Supp. 1060 (S.D.N.Y. 1988) (holding two New York City police officers liable as tippees for receiving information from another officer, who had received it from an employee of a Wall Street law firm, on the grounds they "should have known" the original tip was a breach of fiduciary duty). Since the colleague knew that Donald had received the tip from Daniela, he should have (at the least) inquired whether Donald was expected to keep it secret. If the colleague had reason to know that Donald was not supposed to reveal the information, a personal benefit is virtually presumed—for example, it would be enough that Donald hoped for a good relationship with a workplace colleague. See *SEC v. Yun* (see §23.3.3). Courts have used the same broad analysis as to what constitutes a "personal benefit" in cases of classic insider trading and misappropriation. If the tipper wrongfully tips the information and anticipates the tip will result in some financial or reputational gain (however slight)—and the tippee should know this—liability is established.

c. Perhaps not. This is much like the trading in which Martha Stewart was said to have engaged. Merely knowing that an insider is trading does not establish that he is trading on material, nonpublic information. That is, in the normal case there is no reason to believe that the trading breached a fiduciary duty. Unless the tipper—here, the broker Merton—told Martha that Donald was trading on the basis of specific inside information, it may be difficult to establish the tippee's requisite state of mind. Under Rule 10b-5, trading must be with scienter to be actionable in an administrative or private lawsuit (§22.3.2), and must be "willful" to be criminal. Exchange Act §32(a). Perhaps for this reason, the SEC only brought an administrative action against Stewart seeking fines and disgorgement of her insider trading profits. In 2006, she settled these charges without admitting or denying any wrongdoing for $195,000, representing a trebling of the losses avoided plus interest. The criminal case against her was based not on her trading, but on false statements she made to SEC investigators about her reasons for selling her stock.

4. a. Probably. Daniela has clearly violated Regulation FD if her disclosure of the electrolysis breakthrough was to only one securities analyst. Senior officials of publicly traded companies are obligated to disclose material information *simultaneously* to the market when the disclosure is intentional. Here Daniela had already warned others in the company to keep the electrolysis test results secret—suggesting she understood the information was material and nonpublic. Rule 101(a) (definition of intentional). There does not appear to be any effort to disclose the information to other analysts or investors. Nor does any exception apply since Raymond was under no duty to maintain the information in confidence.

   Whether Daniela has violated the 10b-5 insider trading rules is not as clear. A violation of Regulation FD does not automatically create 10b-5 liability. Rule 102. And an argument can be made that Daniela is not liable under Rule 10b-5 since she was not a tipper under *Dirks*. She disclosed the information not for any personal gain but to inform the securities markets. Nonetheless, one must wonder why she told only Raymond. If it was because he has given favorable reports on ITM in the past (boosting the value of Daniela's stock options) and Daniela expects similar favors from him in the future, her disclosure might have violated her *Dirks* duties. At the least, Daniela risks being the target of an SEC investigation.

   b. Regulation FD forces companies to institute policies and procedures for dealing with market inquiries. Although conversations are permitted with company advisors, such as lawyers who have a duty of trust and confidence to the company client, senior company officials must be careful in disclosing material, nonpublic information to market professionals and investors who are likely to trade on the information.

   - *Materiality determinations.* Companies should have policies for determining what information is nonpublic and material—such as earnings information, important product or contract developments, and important acquisitions or extraordinary transactions. There should also be procedures for consulting with inside counsel and, when appropriate, outside counsel.
   - *Identify authorized officials.* Companies should limit analyst and investor contacts to specific company spokespersons—such as the CEO, the vice president of finance, and the head of investor relations. Private

meetings or phone calls between senior officials and securities professionals should be discouraged, particularly if material information may be discussed.

- *Coordinated disclosure.* Companies should have procedures for responding to both informal and formal contacts. There should be internal communications channels so that questions are directed to the right persons and responses are consistent. For example, responses to common queries could be posted on a company intranet, and scripts for analyst conferences should be prepared and reviewed in advance. There should be policies for prompt "debriefing" of informal contacts to cure unauthorized disclosures.
- *Wide dissemination.* Material disclosures should be disseminated by press release and accompanied by the filing of a Form 8-K. Any press conference or analyst calls should be conducted on the Internet to allow full media and investor access. These materials should also be archived for a set period, such as seven days. It may be useful to file a *procedural* Form 8-K to announce generally how the company will disseminate material, nonpublic information.
- *Forward-looking disclaimers.* Since many queries will ask for management's predictions and views about the future, the company should have policies for giving forward-looking statements that fit within the safe harbor rules. The speaker should identify the statement as predictive and refer the audience to risk disclosure in a readily available SEC filing. Exchange Act §21E(c)(2). These risk disclosures should be updated periodically.

5. a. Yes, under a misappropriation theory. Daniela provided Wilbur information on the electrolysis tests on the condition that the bank keep it confidential. Wilbur, in effect, misappropriated this information *from the bank.* If the bank had a policy against employees using confidential customer information—which seems nearly certain—he would be liable on a misappropriation theory. The theory protects confidential business information and assures stock trading markets that trading with information purloined in a relationship of trust and confidence is prohibited.

    Even if the bank did not have this policy, the new SEC rule defining the relationships that trigger misappropriation liability specifies that if there was a pattern of sharing confidences so Wilbur had reason to know Daniela expected confidential treatment, Wilbur would have a duty not to trade. Rule 10b5-2(b)(2). Although the bank was not an agent of ITM, since commercial lenders typically deal with borrowers on an arm's-length basis, the SEC rule stretches the notion of trust and confidence beyond that of state agency law. Compare *United States v. Chestman* (see §23.3.3).

    Notice, however, that Wilbur was not a tippee of ITM, since Daniela expected no personal gain from the disclosure and breached no duty when she provided it. She supplied the information so her company could get a loan, something permissible under the selective disclosure rules of Regulation FD. Rule 100(b)(2)(i).

b. Both are liable. Tipper and tippee liability work the same in an outsider misappropriation case as in an insider trading case. See *United States v. Falcone*, 257 F.3d 226 (2d. Cir. 2001) (see §23.3.3—Tipping of Misappropriated Information). If (as discussed in the prior answer) Wilbur is under an abstain-or-disclose duty because of his position at the bank or his taking of confidential information, he cannot tip the information. Wanda is liable as a tippee if she knew (or had reason to know) that Wilbur received the information in confidence and that Wilbur gained some personal benefit (such as a share of her trading profits) by disclosing it to her. She is liable as tippee, and he as tipper, for any trading gains.

c. No. Rule 10b-5 liability hinges on a relationship of trust and confidence, and there is none here. See *O'Hagan*. Tina does not have a relationship with and is not a fiduciary to either ITM or to Third Federal Bank. Nor has Tina agreed to maintain the information in confidence, nor is there any practice of sharing confidences with Tina from which an expectation of confidentiality might arise. See Rule 10b5-2(b). Although insider-trading prohibitions may be meant to protect confidential business information, 10b-5 liability is not so broad. Compare *SEC v. Cherif*, 933 F.2d 403 (7th Cir. 1991) (liability of *former employee* who used magnetic identification card to gain access to secret information on pending takeovers).

   Tina might, of course, be liable for mail and wire fraud. See §23.3.3—Mail and Wire Fraud. And, if any of the information she stole and traded on related to a tender offer, she would also be liable under Rule 14e-3. See § 23.3.3—Rule 14e-3. Neither of these "information protection" rules requires a relationship of trust and confidence.

6. a. No. The trading does not breach any duty of trust and confidence. *Chiarella* and *O'Hagan* (§23.3.1). ITM has not misappropriated any information, since any proprietary interest in the information concerning the Ovid acquisition belonged to ITM. The company is merely exploiting its informational advantage, based on its own plans, and has no abstain-or-disclose duty.

   This analysis is the same under Rule 14e-3, which applies to material, nonpublic information about a pending tender offer. Even if the Ovid acquisition were structured as a tender offer, the rule applies only to persons other than the "offering person." Rule 14e-3(a).

b. Probably not under Rule 10b-5, though perhaps under Rule 14e-3. Because Daniela had permission to trade on information about ITM's undisclosed plans, she did not misappropriate any information when she traded in Ovid's shares. See *O'Hagan*. In these circumstances, there was no deception *aimed at the source of the information*, a necessary element for liability under the Supreme Court's theory for liability in *O'Hagan*. Just as ITM's trading on its own information would not violate Rule 10b-5 (see previous answer), Daniela's trading could be seen as a form of additional, indirect trading by ITM itself. There might, however, be problems for ITM under federal line-item disclosure rules (or state corporate fiduciary law) if the company fails to disclose this implicit executive compensation, but not under Rule 10b-5.

Whatever Daniela's authorization, she violated the terms of Rule 14e-3, which regulates trading on confidential information about a *tender offer*. See §23.3.3. The rule prohibits trading by "any other person" (besides the bidder) who possesses material, nonpublic information she knows is nonpublic and came from the bidder. Rule 14e-3. By its terms, Rule 14e-3 is violated even if there is no breach of a duty of trust and confidence. Does the SEC have the rulemaking power to regulate trading not in breach of a duty? Although the Supreme Court in *O'Hagan* upheld Rule 14e-3 as applied to a lawyer who had breached his duties by trading on confidential client information, the Court reserved "for another day" the legitimacy of Rule 14e-3 as applied to "warehousing," the practice by bidders of leaking advance information of tender offers to allies and encouraging them to purchase target stock before the bid is announced. Like warehousing, Daniela's authorized trading breaches no duty. As applied to Daniela, Rule 14e-3 may go beyond the SEC's rulemaking power.

c. No, even if Daniela violated Rule 10b-5, only shareholders who traded "contemporaneously" with Daniela can recover. The Insider Trading and Securities Fraud Enforcement Act of 1988 provides an explicit private right of action to contemporaneous traders against misappropriators. Exchange Act §20A. At one time courts saw the misappropriation theory as protecting the confidences of the outside company, here ITM, and held that Rule 10b-5 did not protect trading shareholders, such as Ovid's. The 1988 Act rejects this view. Liability, however, is not tied to the period during which the misappropriator failed to disclose, but rather the period of the misappropriator's trading.
d. There is no cap, if she violated Rule 10b-5 or 14e-3. Daniela can be liable for her trading profits in a disgorgement proceeding by the SEC or in a restitution suit by contemporaneous traders—maximum $100,000. See Exchange Act §20A. In addition, she can be liable for additional civil penalties of up to three times her trading profits—maximum $300,000. Exchange Act §21A. She can also be subject to criminal fines—now up to $5 million. Exchange Act §32(a). Finally, she can be liable for any losses to ITM if it had to pay more

for the merger because of the signaling inherent in her trading—no maximum. All for a $100,000 trading gain!

e. No. Although Tom revealed nonpublic, confidential information to his clients (namely the likely ITM acquisition of Ovid), he ascertained it from public information and thus breached no duty. Nor did Tom have any duty to ITM (the source of the information) or Ovid (the company whose shares were traded).

   But didn't Tom misappropriate information about ITM's likely merger with Ovid from his own brokerage firm? Although the brokerage firm could have used this information to its advantage, it is unlikely the firm has a policy against analysts disclosing their analysis to clients. In fact, Tom's job is probably to do precisely what he did. The Supreme Court in *Dirks* recognized the crucial role securities analysts play in disseminating information to the market.

Section 16(b)—Disgorgement of Short-Swing Profits

The prohibitions of Rule 10b-5 are not the only federal limitations on share liquidity. To deter price manipulation by insiders in public corporations and encourage insiders to acquire long-term interests in their corporations, Section 16 of the Securities Exchange Act of 1934 requires specified insiders to report their trading in their company's securities, and authorizes the corporation to recover from these insiders any profits made on stock purchases and sales in a narrow six-month period—so-called short-swing trading profits.

This chapter describes the companies, trading, and persons subject to §16 (§24.1), the trading reports required of specified insiders (§24.2), and the rules on disgorgement of short-swing profits (§24.3). The previous chapter dealt with the state and federal rules against insider trading.

§24.1 COVERAGE OF §16

Section 16 only applies to trading in the *equity securities* of a corporation that has a class of equity stock registered under §12 of the Exchange Act—*registered* companies (see §21.2.1). Thus, §16 applies to trading in any equity securities of registered companies, whether or not the particular securities are subject to §12 registration. For example, if a company's common stock is subject to Exchange Act registration, but its preferred stock is not—because it is not listed on a stock exchange and is held by fewer than 500 shareholders (see §8.3.1)—trading by insiders in the unregistered preferred is subject to §16's reporting and disgorgement rules.

The SEC has broadened §16 coverage to include options, convertible securities, and other equity derivatives within the definition of "equity securities." Rule 16a-1(c), (d). Thus, insiders must also report their option trading and are subject to disgorgement of any profits on their short-swing option trading. The §16 short-swing trading provisions apply only to qualifying officers, directors, and shareholders who own (of record or beneficially) more than 10 percent of any class of the company's equity securities.

Exemptions for Executive Compensation

The SEC has created a complex set of rules that permit company executives to acquire and sell shares under company compensation plans. Recognizing the value of stock ownership in executive compensation plans, the SEC has exempted "tax conditioned" plans from the reporting rules and short-swing profit liability. These plans include those that are "qualified employee benefit plans" under the Internal Revenue Code (which allows tax deductions for the company and tax-deferral for the executive) and those that meet the requirements of a "qualified stock purchase plan" under the Internal Revenue Code. Rule 16b-3. This means that company executives can—worry-free—(1) acquire company stock or derivative securities with plan contributions; (2) purchase company stock in an employee stock ownership plan (ESOP); (3) dispose of company stock pursuant to domestic relation orders; and (4) receive distributions in company stock on death, disability, retirement, or termination. Company executives can even elect to transfer in and out of company stock funds, or receive cash withdrawals, if the election is made only once every six months.

Note on §16(b) Effect on Corporate Governance

The effect of the §16(b) short-swing trading provisions is effectively to discourage activist shareholders—particularly institutional shareholders—from taking a significant position in a company (more than 10 percent) or placing directors on the company's board. To do so would limit the activist shareholder's ability to buy and sell the shares it acquires in the company during any six-month window, forcing it to give up any trading profits while it holds a 10-percent position. Section 16(b) is regularly cited as one of the reasons that U.S. institutional shareholders do not take a more activist role in their portfolio companies.

§24.2 REPORTS

To facilitate the policing of insiders' short-swing trading, §16(a) requires reports by qualifying officers, directors, and 10-percent shareholders. Form 3 (initial reporting once insider status achieved); Form 4 (reporting of subsequent changes in beneficial ownership); Form 5 (annual report).

The reports, which must be filed electronically with the SEC and posted on the company's website, disclose the amount of securities *beneficially owned* by the insider and the price paid in any purchase or sale. Initial reports must be filed within ten days after a person becomes an insider, and updating reports must be filed within two business days after any change in the insider's holdings. Rule 16a-3; Securities Act Rel. No. 8230 (2003). Failure to file subjects the insider to penalties.

§24.3 DISGORGING SHORT-SWING PROFITS — MECHANICAL TEST

Section 16(b) imposes automatic, strict liability on qualifying officers, directors, and 10-percent shareholders who make a profit (as defined) in short-swing transactions within a six-month period. No proof of intent or scienter is required. Recovery is to the corporation, and suit may be brought either by the corporation or by a shareholder in a derivative suit.

The mechanical short-swing profit rules are both overly broad and overly narrow. They broadly cover innocent short-swing trading that occurs without the use of inside information or any wrongful intent, yet they fail to cover abusive insider trading that occurs outside the six-month window or by those who are not insiders specified under §16.

Short-Swing Algorithm

A two-part algorithm determines whether disgorgement is available (the examples at the end of this chapter reveal the many permutations involved in determining §16(b) liability):

(1) *Identify a qualifying insider, who under the statute is deemed to have access to insider information and the power to manipulate the company's stock price.*

- *Officer or director at either sale or purchase.* For qualifying officers or directors (but not 10-percent shareholders), official status at the time of either purchase or sale is sufficient — not necessarily both. The theory is that by trading when he was an officer or director, the insider had access to nonpublic information and was in a position to manipulate the price of the stock. Under Rule 16a-2, transactions occurring within six months before becoming a director or officer are not counted, though transactions occurring within six months of ceasing to be a director or officer are counted.

- *Shareholder (10 percent) "immediately before" both transactions.* For 10-percent shareholders, it is necessary that the person have held more than 10 percent *immediately before* both the purchase and sale to be matched. *Reliance Electric Co. v. Emerson Electric Co.*, 404 U.S. 418 (1972) (holding that shareholder must hold 10 percent or more before matching *sale*); *Foremost McKesson Inc. v. Provident Securities Co.*, 423 U.S. 232 (1976) (holding that shareholder must hold 10 percent or more before matching *purchase*). The different treatment of 10-percent shareholders comes from an exclusion in §16(b) of "any transaction where [the] beneficial owner was not such both at the time of the purchase and sale, or the sale and purchase, of the security involved." The rationale is that 10-percent shareholders are less likely to have access to inside information or to corporate control mechanisms than officers or directors. Thus, their insider status must exist at both ends of the matching transactions.

(2) *Match any transactions that produce a profit.* Section 16(b) liability is predicated on matching any *purchase* with any *sale* by a qualifying insider, regardless of order, that occurred during any six-month period in which the sale price was higher than the purchase price. There is no tracing of shares, and recovery is frequently measured by matching later lowest-cost purchases with earlier highest-cost sales. See *Smolowe v. Delendo Corp.*, 136 F.2d 231 (2d Cir. 1943) (establishing the "lowest price in, highest price out" method of calculating short-swing profits). There is no need to offset any losses—that is, any purchases and sales in which the sales price is *lower* than the purchase price need not be matched and can be disregarded.

Comparisons to Rule 10b-5

Section 16(b) is broader and narrower than the insider trading prohibitions of Rule 10b-5. Limited to trading in securities of registered companies during a six-month window, it is narrower than Rule 10b-5—which applies to all companies and regardless of holding periods. Yet, by covering any trading during a six-month period, whether or not based on inside information, §16(b) is also broader than Rule 10b-5—which requires a showing that trading was based on material, nonpublic information.

§24.3.1 Special Interpretive Issues

The literal terms of §16(b) are inflexible, sometimes too harsh, and other times too lenient. To accomplish the rule's purpose to discourage manipulative insider trading, courts have interpreted the section's significant terms — *officer* and *director*, *beneficial ownership*, and *purchase* and *sale* — to introduce policy analysis into the otherwise mechanical disgorgement rules.

Officer and Directors

Courts have interpreted §16(b) to reach persons and entities who do not fall within the literal definition of *officer* or *director*, but who are functionally equivalent for purposes of insider access

- **Functional officers.** For purposes of §16(b), a qualifying officer is any employee who has a position in the corporation that gives her access to confidential inside information that is not freely circulated. An official title may help identify these persons, but is not determinative. *Merrill, Lynch Pierce Fenner & Smith, Inc. v. Livingston*, 566 F.2d 1119 (9th Cir. 1978) (holding that a brokerage firm's "vice president" was not an officer for §16(b) purposes, because his title was merely honorary in recognition of sales accomplishments and did not reflect access to inside information). In 1991, as part of a comprehensive update of §16, the SEC defined "officer" to include those persons who perform policy-making functions. See Rule 16a-1(f) (definition based on title and policy-making functions).
- **Deputization.** Courts have developed a *deputization theory* for entities that hold stock in a corporation and are also represented on the corporation's board of directors. *Feder v. Martin Marietta Corp.*, 406 F.2d 260 (2d Cir. 1969). For example, suppose that Henrietta is a managing partner of Trout Brothers, an investment bank with a securities trading department, and that she also sits on the board of Bullseye Corporation, the subject of takeover speculation. If Trout Brothers purchases 5 percent of Bullseye's stock, §16(b) by its terms does not impose any short-swing trading liability: Trout Brothers is neither a 10-percent shareholder nor a director, and Henrietta is not the beneficial owner of Bullseye stock held by Trout Brothers. Nonetheless, there should be concern that Trout Brothers will use Henrietta as its conduit of inside information.

Under the deputization theory, Henrietta is treated as Trout Brothers' "deputy" and any Trout Brothers transactions in Bullseye stock are subject to the short-swing profit rules. The scope of the deputization theory is unclear. Under one view, Trout Brothers is treated under §16(b) as a "director" if

Henrietta (1) represents its interests on the Bullseye board and (2) actually passes along inside information to Trout Brothers. See *Blau v. Lehman*, 368 U.S. 403 (1962) (entire partnership not liable as an insider merely because one member was a director in a corporation in whose stock the partnership traded based on public information).

Beneficial Ownership

An important issue in many §16(b) cases is whether a person subject to the disgorgement rules beneficially owns securities that have been transacted. For example, if the spouse of an officer of Company X owns shares in the company, can transactions by the spouse be attributed to the officer? In 1991, the SEC promulgated a rule that defines beneficial ownership differently for 10-percent shareholders and officer/directors.

- **Ten-percent shareholders.** In general, beneficial ownership of securities under the Exchange Act depends on whether a shareholder has the power either to vote the securities or to dispose of them. Rule 13d-3(a). The SEC has adopted this definition for purposes of determining ownership by 10-percent shareholders. Rule 16a-1(a)(1). Under the SEC definition, this means that spouses and other family members (even if they share pecuniary benefits) are not the beneficial owners of each other's stock for §16(b) purposes unless they can control its voting or disposition.
- **Officers and directors.** Officers and directors are subject to a different rule of beneficial ownership that focuses on whether they have (or share) a "pecuniary interest" in the shares. Rule 16a-1(a)(2). The pecuniary interest can be direct or indirect, and does not depend on whether the officer or director has any voting or disposition power over the shares. It is enough if the officer or director stands to profit directly or indirectly from the transaction. This means that if the spouse of an officer of Company X sells her shares and the officer stands to profit indirectly, the sale is attributed to the officer.

Unorthodox Transactions (Purchases and Sales)

Usually whether a stock transaction constitutes a matchable purchase or sale under §16(b) is not an issue. But when the stock transaction is *unorthodox*—such as when shares are acquired in a merger or in an option transaction—the courts have been willing to inquire into whether the transaction should be treated as a matchable "sale" or "purchase" for purposes of §16(b). The SEC also has promulgated extensive (and very technical) rules that exempt certain transactions—such as redemptions, conversions, and transactions involving employee benefit plans—where the risk of insider abuse is minimal. Rules 16b-1 through 16b-11.

The Supreme Court has held that an unorthodox transaction by a hostile bidder (which became a 10-percent shareholder) in a takeover contest is not a matchable "sale" if there is no evidence of abuse of inside information. *Kern County Land Co. v. Occidental Petroleum Corp.*, 411 U.S. 582 (1973). In the case, Occidental successfully bid for 20 percent of Kern County's stock—a §16(b) "purchase." Concerned about Occidental's intentions, Kern County management found a white knight (Tenneco) that agreed to buy Kern County in a merger. Under the merger terms, "Old Kern" merged into a wholly owned Tenneco subsidiary and became "New Kern." Old Kern shareholders received Tenneco preferred stock in exchange for their stock. To buy Occidental's good will, Tenneco granted Occidental an option to sell its Tenneco preferred stock (after the merger) at a premium. Occidental agreed not to oppose or vote on the merger, and the remaining Old Kern shareholders approved. Occidental, along with the other Old Kern shareholders, then received Tenneco preferred stock for their Old Kern stock.

Was there a "sale" that could be matched with the tender offer "purchases"? The plaintiff argued there were two: (1) the option granted to Occidental—granted within six months of the original purchases, though exercisable after the six-month period; and (2) Occidental's exchange of New Kern stock for Tenneco preferred stock in the merger—which occurred within the six-month period. In other contexts, the receipt of consideration in a merger has been treated as a sale under the federal securities laws. See Securities Act Rule 145 (requiring prospectus disclosure for securities issued in a merger). Nonetheless, the Supreme Court decided that Occidental had not "sold" its Old Kern stock in the merger because the transaction was involuntary and the relationship between Occidental and Kern County's management was hostile. Likewise, there was no evidence of abuse of inside information in the granting of the option, which was granted to buy Occidental's acquiescence in the merger.

But when it is possible inside information has been abused, the granting of an option has been treated as a "sale." In *Bershad v. McDonough*, 428 F.2d 693 (7th Cir. 1970), McDonough and his wife had purchased more than 10 percent of Cudahy's stock, and McDonough became a director. Within six months of these purchases, the McDonoughs granted another company, Smelting Refining, an option to purchase the bulk of their Cudahy stock. McDonough then resigned from Cudahy's board, and Smelting Refining placed its representatives on the board. Under the option agreement, the McDonoughs placed their Cudahy shares in escrow. Smelting Refining exercised the option more than six months after their original purchase. The court held that the granting of the option was a matchable "sale" because it could lend itself to inside speculation.

§24.3.2 Section 16(b) Litigation

Compared to the factual and legal issues that surround 10b-5 insider trading litigation, §16(b) short-swing disgorgement litigation is a cinch. The statute specifies the elements of a disgorgement action:

- realization of profit
- by an officer, director, or 10-percent shareholders
- from matching purchases and sales during any six-month period
- of equity securities of a public company

Suit by the corporation or by a shareholder in a derivative suit must be brought within two years of the date the profit was realized.

In fact, the information to establish a §16(b) disgorgement case is available in public filings with the SEC. In such a case, there is no requirement that the plaintiff establish any of the elements normally required in a 10b-5 insider-trading private action, namely that the trading was based on material, nonpublic information; that the defendant acted with a culpable state of mind; that those who traded relied in some way; that the trading caused any losses; or that there were losses.

The only significant procedural issue in §16(b) disgorgement actions is whether the plaintiff has standing. Congress created a scheme of corporate enforcement and recovery. If the corporation fails to sue within 60 days of a demand, an "owner of any security of the issuer" may bring a derivative suit on behalf of the corporation. The statute does not specify any standing requirements for a derivative suit plaintiff, and courts have interpreted the statute broadly to be consistent with its remedial purposes. Thus, some of the standing requirements in a normal derivative suit, such as contemporaneous ownership (see §18.3.2), do not apply in a §16(b) suit. See *Gollust v. Mendell*, 501 U.S. 115 (1991) (holding that shareholder of corporation acquired in a merger had standing to continue a §16(b) action against former 10-percent shareholder, even though corporation was merged into a new entity).

Why would a shareholder or bondholder bring a §16(b) disgorgement suit if any recovery goes to the corporation? The holder's interest in the suit is limited to the increase in value (if any) of the holder's securities. This diluted incentive, it would seem, will rarely justify investigating a §16(b) violation and initiating the litigation. The real incentive for §16(b) litigation is that the attorneys' fees of a successful derivative-suit plaintiff are recoverable from the corporation. It is no defense that the §16(b) litigation was brought primarily to obtain attorneys' fees. See *Magida v. Continental Can Co.*, 231 F.2d 843 (2d Cir. 1956).

Examples

1. ITM Corp. has one class of common stock, which is registered under §12 of the Exchange Act. Dorothy is a director of ITM. For each of the following situations, what is Dorothy's disgorgement liability under §16(b)?
   a. Dorothy purchases 100 shares of ITM stock on February 1 at $10 per share, and sells on August 2 at $15 per share. ITM's stock price rose because it was awarded a large government contract on April 1, which Dorothy knew about when she bought.
   b. Dorothy buys 200 shares on July 1 at $5 per share, sells 200 shares on February 1 of the next year at $15 per share, and then purchases 300 shares on May 1 at $10 per share.
   c. Dorothy buys 100 shares at $10 per share on February 1, buys another 100 shares at $20 per share on March 1, sells 100 shares at $12 per share on April 1, and sells another 100 shares at $15 per share on May 1.
   d. Dorothy adds to her portfolio and buys 180 shares on February 1 at $10 per share, sells 150 shares on May 1 at $15 per share, and then sells another 100 shares at $18 per share on June 1.
   e. Dorothy became a director on March 1. Prior to this, on February 1, she had purchased 100 shares at $10 per share. She purchases 100 shares at $12 per share on April 1, and sells 100 shares at $15 per share on June 1.
   f. Dorothy purchases 100 shares at $10 per share on February 1. She becomes a director on March 1 and resigns as director on May 1. She sells 100 shares at $15 per share on May 2. Dorothy purchased in February at $10 per share knowing of confidential, nonpublic developments that would raise the price in May.

2. Cheryl is an investor with a keen interest in ITM. She is neither an officer nor a director of ITM.
   a. Over four years, Cheryl accumulates 9 million shares (9 percent) of ITM stock. On February 1 she buys 5 million additional shares at $15 per share, bringing her holdings to 14 percent. On May 1 she sells all of her 14 million shares at $20 per share. What is Cheryl's §16(b) liability?
   b. After selling all of her ITM stock last year, Cheryl decides to acquire control of the company by making open-market purchases and a tender offer. She is prepared, however, to sell her holdings if another bidder offers a good price. Advise Cheryl on how to purchase and, if the opportunity presents itself, sell her stock without becoming subject to §16(b) liability.

3. Cheryl does not take your advice. Instead, she buys 11 percent of ITM's stock in December and then buys an additional 9 percent on March 1, bringing her holdings to 20 percent. She then enters into negotiations with ITM's management and, on July 20, agrees to have the corporation repurchase all of her stock.

a. The repurchase agreement calls for closing on the repurchase to occur on October 1, outside the six-month window that opened on March 1. Under §16(b), can Cheryl's March purchases be matched with her July agreement?
b. If the closing had occurred on August 1—at a slightly lower price than the one negotiated for the October 1 closing—does your answer change?

4. After selling back her shares, Cheryl and her husband Charles each begin buying ITM stock. By November, each owns 6 percent of ITM's stock.
   a. In January, Charles purchases additional shares at $40 per share, bringing his holdings to 9 percent. In March of the same year, Cheryl sells some of her shares at $45 per share, bringing her holdings to 3 percent. Is either liable under §16(b)?
   b. In August, after Cheryl and Charles sell all of their remaining ITM stock, Cheryl joins the ITM board of directors. She purchases ITM stock as trustee for her child's college fund. In November of the same year, Cheryl sells at a profit all of this stock. Is she liable under §16(b)?
5. MACO Corp. decides to "greenmail" ITM. To do this, it will first buy a large stake in ITM on the open market, then threaten a hostile tender offer, and finally negotiate a sale of its stake to ITM at a premium.
   a. Otto, an officer of MACO, sits on ITM's board. Is there a possibility of §16(b) liability in MACO's plans?
   b. MACO has Otto resign from the ITM board. MACO then becomes a 10-percent shareholder in January and in February purchases 200,000 more shares. ITM management reacts by offering its shareholders a capital restructuring in which they will receive for their shares a package of cash and preferred stock. This will require an amendment to ITM's charter. MACO supports the restructuring, and its votes for the charter amendment prove decisive. After the June restructuring, MACO receives cash and preferred stock, producing a significant profit. Is MACO liable under §16(b)?

Explanations

1. a. No disgorgement liability. None of Dorothy's trades occurred within six months of each other. Under §16(b) it is irrelevant whether Dorothy had any confidential, nonpublic information about the government contract when she bought and sold. She may be liable, however, under Rule 10b-5 for insider trading (see §23.3).

Date	Transaction
February 1	Buy— 100 @ $10
April 1	Government contract
August 2	Sell— 100 @ $15

b. $1,000. Lower-priced purchases are matched with higher-priced sales occurring within six months. Only the February sale and May purchase can be matched; the July purchase is outside the six-month window. The disgorgement formula operates regardless of the order of the transactions as long as the sale price is higher than the purchase price. In this case, only 200 shares match, and Dorothy is liable to disgorge $1,000 in profits (200 shares times $5).

Date	Transaction
February 1	Sell—200 @ $15
May 1	Buy—300 @ $10

c. $500. Matching the February purchase and the May sale produces the highest gain—$500 (100 shares times $5). There is no need to offset any losses, so the $800 loss generated by matching the March purchase and the lower April sale can be disregarded. Even though Dorothy lost a net $300 during the six-month trading period—she purchased 200 shares for $3,000 and sold 200 shares for $2,700—she is subject to disgorgement liability. This crude rule of thumb assumes that her February and May transactions were based on inside information or short-swing market manipulations.

Date	Transaction
February 1	Buy—100 @ $10
March 1	Buy—100 @ $20
April 1	Sell—100 @ $12
May 1	Sell—100 @ $15

d. $1,200. First match the transactions that produce the greatest gains (100 shares—February and June) and then any other transactions that produce gains (80 shares—February and May). The combined recoverable profits are thus $1,200 (100 times $8 profits, matching the $18 June sale and the $10 February purchase, *plus* 80 times $5 profits, matching the $15 May sale and the $10 February purchase).

Date	Transaction
February 1	Buy—180 @ $10
May 1	Sell—150 @ $15
June 1	Sell—100 @ $18

e. $300. Although a February-June match produces a larger gain than an April-June gain, the February-June match is not available under §16(b) because Dorothy was not a director at the prior end of the match—the February transaction. Under Rule 16a-2(a), transactions *prior* to a person becoming director are exempt from §16(b) liability. The idea is that she could not have had inside information when she bought in February. Matching the April and June transactions, Dorothy's liability is $300 (100 shares times $3).

Date	Transaction
February 1	Buy— 100 @ $10
March 1	Becomes director
April 1	Buy— 100 @ $12
June 1	Sell— 100 @ $15

f. No disgorgement liability. There is no sale and purchase to match because Dorothy was not a director at the time of either trade. Nonetheless, Dorothy may be liable under Rule 10b-5 for trading on material, nonpublic information she received in her capacity as a director (see §23.3).

Date	Transaction
February 1	Buy— 100 @ $10
March 1	Becomes director
May 1	Resigns as director
May 2	Sell— 100 @ $15

2. a. Cheryl is not liable under §16(b). The February purchase cannot be matched because Cheryl was not a 10-percent shareholder *immediately prior* to it. (In fact, Cheryl would not have disclosed her February purchase on Form 3 because at the time of the purchase she was not a 10-percent shareholder.) Shareholders must have "inside" status—that is, hold more than 10 percent of the shares—immediately before each transaction to be matched. This differs from the rule for officers and directors and is based on an assumption that shareholders are less likely to have access to inside information or the ability to manipulate prices.

Date	Transaction
February 1	Buy—5MM @ $15
May 1	Sell— 14 MM @ $20

b. Cheryl should buy only 9.9 percent of ITM's outstanding shares on the open market. The purchase that brings her above 10 percent should be in one fell swoop—such as in a tender offer. In this way, none of her purchases will occur when she is a 10-percent shareholder, and none will be matchable. Cheryl can later sell without incurring any §16(b) liability. The assumption in *Kern County* (see §243.3), decided by the Supreme Court in 1973, that tender offer purchases that bring a shareholder's holdings above 10 percent are matchable was explicitly rejected by the Supreme Court in *Foremost McKesson* in 1976 (see §24.3).

If Cheryl makes any matchable purchases while a 10-percent shareholder, she should sell her stock in chunks, not all at once. In this way, only those sales that she makes while she is a 10-percent shareholder are matchable. Once her holdings fall to 10 percent or less, any further sales are not matchable. This limits her §16(b) exposure.

3. a. Probably not. Can the July 20 agreement be characterized as a "sale" for purposes of §16(b)? Management's apparent hostility to Cheryl suggests she had no access to corporate information or control, and there would be little purpose in imposing short-swing liability. Such liability would effectively allow the corporation to renegotiate the repurchase price.

b. Probably. There would then be a traditional purchase and sale within six months. Nothing in the language of §16(b) suggests that there are exceptions to the disgorgement rules if the evidence strongly suggests the absence of inside abuse. Although the August closing would seem for financial purposes to be equivalent to an October closing, §16(b) may elevate the form of the transaction over its substance.

4. a. Probably not. The critical issue is whether Cheryl and Charles are treated as a single beneficial owner. If so, their individual 6 percent holdings would be combined. As beneficial owners of more than 10 percent, the January purchases by Charles would be matched with the March sales by Cheryl to produce a recoverable profit. In each case, they beneficially owned more than 10 percent immediately before the transaction. If, however, they are not the beneficial owner of the other's shares, neither can be liable because neither individually surpassed the 10-percent threshold.

According to the SEC, holdings of shareholders' percents must be aggregated if one shareholder has voting or disposition control over the other's shares. Rule 16a-1(a)(1) (for purposes of determining whether shareholders own more than 10 percent, look to investment/voting control rule). In this case, unless Charles or Cheryl had control over the other's shares, there would be no beneficial ownership. This is an unusual result, which essentially permits family members to hold and trade outside the strictures of §16 so long as no family member holds more than 10 percent of the company's stock and they do not enter into any arrangement to vote or dispose of the others' stock. Rule 13d-3(a). This means that even if Cheryl and Charles share the financial benefits of ownership, they are not deemed to be beneficial owners of each other's shares, making their January and March transactions unmatchable.

b. Probably. The question of beneficial ownership also arises for a director whose family members trade in the company's stock. See Exchange Act §16(a) (requiring reports of "all shares of which [the officer/director] is a beneficial owner"). Normally, a director is subject to §16 for any trading by members of his immediate family. See Rule 16a-1(a)(2)(ii)(A) (defining "indirect pecuniary interest" in equity securities to include securities held by officer/director's "immediate family" sharing the same household). In §16(b) disgorgement actions, courts have attributed trading by a director's spouse to the director, treating profits realized as a result of the spouse's transactions as "profits realized by [the director]." See *Whiting v. Dow Chemical Co.*, 523 F.2d 680 (2d Cir. 1975).

In the case of securities held in trust for a family member, the SEC rules recognize the risk that a director may abuse her insider status in connection with the trading of securities as to which the director acts as trustee. See Rules 16a-1(a)(2), 16a-8(b)(2)(ii) (director who acts as a trustee is deemed to have "beneficial ownership" in trust securities if at least one beneficiary of the trust is a member of the director's immediate family). Nonetheless, some courts in §16(b) disgorgement cases have used a narrower understanding of beneficial interest than the SEC test. *CBI Industries, Inc. v. Horton*, 682 F.2d 643 (7th Cir. 1982) (Posner, J.) (director, acting as trustee for adult children, is subject to §16(b) liability for trading in trust only if director is able to use income or assets of trust). This different treatment, apparently in sympathy for the trading limitations otherwise placed on family members of a director, seems questionable in light of the §16(b) purpose to discourage insiders from manipulating company stock prices to benefit their own trading. A director, it would seem, would have as much incentive to manipulate her company's stock prices whether profits flow directly to her or whether they flow to her children's trust fund. That is, consistent with the statute's broad remedial purposes, there are "profits realized [by the director]" when her trading decisions enhance her (and her family's) overall financial position.

5. a. Yes. MACO might be treated as a Bullseye director under a "deputization" theory because Otto, an officer of MACO, sits on Bullseye's

board. If MACO is "deputized," any gains in its short-swing trading would be subject to §16(b) disgorgement.

To show deputization, Otto must have represented MACO on the board. In addition, it might be necessary to show some (or all) of the following: Otto was "controlled" by MACO; Otto was ultimately responsible for deciding about MACO's acquisitions of Bullseye stock; Otto had access to inside Bullseye information; and Otto actually passed such information on to MACO. Although requiring a showing of actual access or actual passing of inside information might seem inconsistent with §16(b) strict liability, deputization is meant to achieve the underlying §16(b) purposes of deterring and compensating for the abuse of inside information. A deputization test requires a showing of actual or probable abuse.

b. Perhaps, though it is hard to say. Although the February and June transactions are matchable because MACO was a 10-percent shareholder before each one, it could be argued that the June transaction was not a "sale" for purposes of §16(b). Arguably, the June restructuring was involuntary—that is, its timing was not of MACO's making—and MACO's relationship to ITM was such that it is unlikely any confidential information was passed to MACO. See *Kern County* (§24.3.1).

There are, however, two significant differences between this case and the situation in *Kern County*. First, MACO supported the restructuring. This should not make a difference if MACO was not involved in ITM's restructuring decision and there was no passing of inside information. Second, ITM's management may have had reasons to pass inside information to MACO. It is possible that the restructuring was negotiated with MACO—just as was the option in *Kern County*. If so, ITM's management might have found it useful to pass inside information to MACO to ensure the success of the restructuring. Nonetheless, even if ITM passed inside information, it may well have been "good news" to encourage MACO's support. Because all the MACO shareholders shared in the restructuring premium, the abuse would not have harmed them.

PART VI

Closely Held Corporation

Control Dilemma in Close Corporation

The word "corporation" brings to mind Exxon-Mobil or General Electric—business monoliths with far-ranging activities managed by gray-suited executives and funded by faceless investors through tumultuous stock markets. But the advantages of incorporation—limited liability and an "off the rack" governance structure—are just as attractive to less capital-intensive enterprises run by more comfortably dressed entrepreneurs. Small businesses with only a handful of owners, such as franchises and small retail or service centers, have taken advantage of the corporate form using the same enabling statutes used by publicly held corporations. But it is an awkward fit.

This part considers the special case of the closely held or "close" corporation and includes

- an introduction to the special problems in the close corporation (§25.1) and planning in the close corporation (§25.2)
- control devices that corporate planners use to deal with this dilemma (Chapter 26)
- dispute resolution and liquidity rights in close corporations (Chapter 27)

> **Note on State Statutes**
>
> Unlike other chapters in this book, the chapters on close corporations include references primarily to the MBCA, but not the Delaware corporate statutes. In the area of close corporation law, Delaware does not have the same prominence as it does for public
>
> *(continued)*

corporations. Most close corporations are incorporated in the state in which they do business, and most state statutes are modeled on the MBCA.

§25.1 SPECIAL PROBLEMS IN CLOSE CORPORATION

The close corporation presents a dilemma. On one hand, the *corporate statutes* call for majority control, centralized power in the board of directors, and a limited governance role for shareholders—a typical publicly held corporation. On the other hand, close corporation *participants* often want an "incorporated partnership" of shared governance and limited liability.

Consider the basic differences between a closely held and a publicly held corporation.

	Close Corporation	Public Corporation
Number of equity investors	Small, tightly knit group of equity investors (generally fewer than 30–75)—often family members or former partners	Large number of equity investors (more than 500)—no personal relationship between investors, besides their share ownership
Nature of management	Active, often informal management by nonspecialized investor/owners	Limited participation by shareholders through proxy voting; active, specialized management by business executives
Nature of investors	Undiversified investor/owners who often look to the corporation for livelihood through payment of salaries or dividends	Diversified investors (often financial intermediaries) that look for an investment return from dividend income and appreciation in market price
Liquidity of equity interests	No ready market for shareholders to dispose of their shares—sometimes contractual limits on transferability	Public trading markets (such as stock exchanges) for shareholders to easily dispose of freely transferable shares
Tax considerations	Corporation can be structured as a flow-through tax entity (see §2.3) so that business profits are taxed to shareholders even when dividends are not paid	Corporation is subject to entity-level income tax so that business profits are taxed at the corporate level and shareholders are taxed only when dividends are paid to them

For close corporation shareholders, options are few if they become disenchanted with their investment or are exploited by the controlling shareholders. In a public corporation, dissatisfied shareholders have access to stock markets where they can sell their shares at relatively low cost, based on prices established through widespread trading—a choice known as the "Wall Street rule."

Lacking a public trading market that offers liquidity and price discovery, a close corporation shareholder has few viable options. Finding an outside buyer is problematic since any potential buyer would have to undertake a costly study of the corporation's value and be willing to become stuck himself in the seller's unenviable position. If the disgruntled shareholder seeks to sell to the other shareholders, it will likely be at an unattractive price. If the shareholder seeks judicial protection, she can expect an expensive and drawn-out battle compounded by corporate law's traditional deference to majority control. Planning, through protection built into the corporate structure or a binding contract, becomes highly desirable.

§25.2 PLANNING IN CLOSE CORPORATION

The planner in a close corporation—often an attorney or accountant—creates control devices that adapt the statutory structure (subject to some limits) to accomplish the participants' purposes. These *ex ante* devices can be shareholder agreements, special provisions in the articles and bylaws, and dispute-resolution procedures. See ABA Section of Business Law, *Managing Closely Held Corporations: A Guidebook*, 58 Bus. Law. 1077 (2003). The planner must be familiar with the available devices and how corporate statutes and doctrines treat them.

In general, corporate statutes reflect a "unified" approach under which all corporations (both closely and publicly held) are governed by the same statutory provisions. Over the last few decades, however, corporate statutes have addressed the close corporation dilemma with special provisions that enable "boutique" close corporation structures. A few states have adopted special close corporation statutes. Del. GCL §§341-356 ("comprehensive" provisions for corporations that opt in to regime); ABA Model Close Corporation Supplement (drafters of MBCA include suggested supplemental provisions for use by close corporations.) Other states, such as California and New York, interweave these provisions throughout their corporate statutes. The MBCA includes provisions on shareholders' agreements and buyout remedies. Courts have also responded to the special needs of close corporation participants with *ex post* judicial doctrines that seek to protect minority shareholders from majority abuse. See §27.2.

In addition, planners can use organizational forms with many characteristics of close corporations—namely, the limited liability company (LLC), the limited liability partnership (LLP), and the limited liability limited partnership (LLLP). Each form offers limited liability and a structure that can be modified by agreement, much like a close corporation. See §2.2.

Although unincorporated business forms are growing in popularity, the close corporation has held its own. In part, planners are more familiar with corporate statutes and the accepted devices used to modify their structure. Recent judicial trends show greater tolerance for departures from the traditional corporate model. But recognition of the close corporation dilemma is not universal. The old rule that what is good for the public corporation "goose" is also good for the close corporation "gander" has remarkable staying power.

Examples

1. Three family members go into the pizza business. Bob has some pizzeria experience. His uncle Rich is willing to invest. Bob's cousin Sal has some spare cash and spare time. Rich, who knows nothing about pizza, puts up $80,000 and hopes for a steady 10 percent return on his investment. Bob contributes only $5,000, but he wants annual pay of at least $20,000. Sal invests $15,000 and agrees to be part-time bookkeeper. The three incorporate the business as Pizza Chateau, Inc.
   a. Is Pizza Chateau a close corporation?
   b. Who will run the business? Who will oversee it? What control arrangements will the three likely want?

2. The three participants agree to treat their business as a partnership and realign other corporate attributes to suit their needs. They want their financial interests to be proportionate to their capital contributions—Bob (5 percent), Rich (80 percent), and Sal (15 percent).
   a. Does incorporation assure them limited liability?
   b. Will the parties' objectives be accomplished if they take shares proportionate to their capital contributions?

Explanations

1. a. Yes. First, it is a corporation, organized under a state incorporation statute. Second, it has the defining characteristics of a close corporation: only a few shareholders (thus far only three) and shared illiquidity (as a practical matter, there is no organized market for their corporate shares).
   b. We can speculate. Rich, as an investor of money capital, will want to protect his investment. He probably will want some say over the significant financial and governance matters, though not day-to-day operations. Rich might want a veto over opening a new

restaurant, although he might not care if Bob adds anchovies to the menu—*modified centralized management*. Rich will want some assurances of steady dividends and salary caps for Bob and Sal—a further *constraint on centralized management*. Rich will want Bob to be the "working partner" and not transfer his role to another—*restrictions on transferability*. And Rich will want some way to liquidate his investment, perhaps by dissolving the corporation, if he wants out—*an exception to corporate perpetuity*.

Bob, as a manager investing his human capital, will have different expectations. He will worry that Rich might try to oust him or interfere with running the business. Bob will want assurances of incumbency and management discretion—*an exception to shareholder majority control*. He will want an assured salary, before dividends are paid—*modified centralized management*. Like Rich, he might not want the others to sell to other (unknown) investors—*a limit on transferability*. Bob probably also will want some way to sell his interest to the others if he decides to get out—*contractual liquidity rights*.

Sal, a hybrid capitalist-manager who invests both money and human capital, is a prototypical participant in a close corporation. Her expectations will be a mixture of Rich's and Bob's. She will want to adjust the traditional corporate attributes of centralized management, majority control, free share transferability, and perpetual corporate existence.

2. a. In theory, yes. Unless the corporate veil is pierced (see Chapter 32), neither contract nor tort creditors can hold any of them liable in their roles as shareholders, directors, or officers. Nonetheless, as a practical matter, contract creditors of a close corporation (such as banks) often will insist on personal guarantees from shareholders. Personal liability will often be contractual.

   b. No. Incorporating and receiving shares proportionate to capital contributions would be a grave mistake for Bob and Sal—who would become minority shareholders. Under the traditional corporate structure, Rich (as majority shareholder) would elect all the directors under straight voting. His directors would then have full power to decide all management matters—who is manager, who is bookkeeper, how much and when dividends are paid, and what are salaries and other benefits. Bob and Sal would be powerless. Bringing litigation would be expensive, and their claims of mismanagement would have to overcome the "business judgment rule." See §12.2. And without a market for their shares, there would be no mechanism for them to withdraw from the business by selling to other investors or to the corporation. Rich, on the other hand, could always look to sell his majority block (and control of the business) to another restaurant "owner." See §20.2.

CHAPTER 26

Planning in Close Corporation

Corporate planners have devised various solutions to the control dilemma in the close corporation. These control devices modify the traditional rules of majority rule and centralized management, and create contractual liquidity for close corporation shares.

Some control devices operate at *the shareholder level* and their validity is generally easy to assure: supermajority requirements and vote-pooling agreements (§26.1); voting trusts, multiple classes of shares, irrevocable proxies (§26.2); and transfer restrictions and buy-sell agreements (§26.3). Other devices—such as compensation guarantees, dissolution stipulations, limits on business operations, and dividend policies—operate at the *management or board level* and may conflict with the statutory norm of management discretion (§26.4). Throughout you will notice a tension between traditional corporate norms and the desire of incorporated partners to "contract out."

This chapter discusses the purposes, creation, and validity of the more common *ex ante* control devices used by corporate planners to anticipate problems in the close corporation before they arise. The next, Chapter 27, identifies *ex post* rules—such as fiduciary protection and statutory dissolution rights—that apply to situations where the planning failed.

§26.1 MINORITY CONTROL RIGHTS

§26.1.1 Supermajority Provisions

Supermajority quorum and voting requirements modify the usual rule of majority control. See §7.2.5 (shareholder voting); §30.1.2 (director voting).

Purpose

Supermajority requirements give minority participants a *veto power*. This power can cover specified matters—approving mergers, appointing officers, fixing dividends, or issuing new stock. Or it can exist for all matters coming before the shareholders or directors, though this risks deadlock.

Supermajority provisions also serve valuable anticircumvention functions by safeguarding carefully crafted minority rights. For example, if the articles specify a five-person board and cumulative voting—thus ensuring board representation for any 17 percent shareholder—the articles should also require an 84 percent vote for any charter changes. Otherwise, the promise of board representation for a minority shareholder (with more than 17 percent) could be eliminated by a simple majority-approved charter amendment.

Creation

Majority rule is the default. Under most statutes, the charter must specify supermajority quorum or voting requirements *for shareholder action*—either when originally drafted or by amendment. MBCA §7.25(a) and (c). In many jurisdictions, new supermajority provisions must receive supermajority approval. For amendment of articles, see MBCA §7.27(b) (same vote required to take action under voting requirements in effect or proposed to be adopted, whichever is greater); for shareholder amendment of bylaws, see MBCA §10.21(a) (same for board voting).

Supermajority requirements *for director voting* may be incorporated in the articles or sometimes in the bylaws if not inconsistent with the articles. See MBCA §8.24. In addition, if all the parties agree, supermajority requirements can be included in a shareholders' agreement. MBCA §7.32.

Validity

Corporate statutes generally permit supermajority requirements. See MBCA §7.27 (shareholder quorum and voting); MBCA §8.24 (director quorum and voting). Some statutes permit amendment of supermajority provisions only by supermajority vote. See N.Y. BCL §616(b) (requiring 2/3 vote to amend supermajority provision, unless certificate "specifically" states otherwise). Courts have read supermajority voting provisions expansively. See *Sutton v. Sutton*, 637 N.E.2d 260 (N.Y. 1994) (interpreting general unanimity provision in certificate, which did not "specifically" refer to amendment provisions, to declare ineffective 70 percent vote that sought to remove unanimity provision).

Notice that a supermajority *quorum* requirement allows a party to "cast" her veto by absenting herself. This leads to an obvious question. If the party shows up at a meeting and is counted for quorum purposes, can she break the quorum in mid-meeting? The MBCA gives two different answers. For shareholders' meetings, MBCA §7.25(b) states that once a share is represented at a shareholders' meeting, it is present for quorum purposes for the duration; for directors' meetings, the Official Comment to MBCA §8.24(c) states that the board cannot act if a director breaks the quorum by leaving during a meeting.

Some courts have refused to respect quorum requirements as a control device. In *Gearing v. Kelly*, 182 N.E.2d 391 (N.Y. 1962), the court said that a director who purposefully refused to attend a board meeting, thus preventing a quorum, could not complain when the remaining directors elected a new director without a quorum. The court held the absent director could not use the bylaw's quorum provision to deadlock the corporation. A well-reasoned dissent argued, however, that the court should not assist either side in their dispute. Other courts have understood that quorum requirements, though risking deadlock, can serve as a bargained-for "veto" and have invalidated actions taken without a quorum due to the complaining party's absence.

§26.1.2 Vote-Pooling Agreements

Sometimes in a close corporation, no one shareholder will have voting control. Rather, as in politics, there are often voting coalitions. Shareholders will agree formally or informally to vote as a voting block. For example, in a corporation with three equal shareholders, any two can join together to wield effective control.

Purpose

Vote-pooling agreements are important (and primarily used) in electing directors. Consider the workings of a pooling agreement under both straight and cumulative voting in the famous case of *Ringling Bros.-Barnum &*

Bailey Combined Shows, Inc. v. Ringling, 53 A.2d 441 (Del. 1947). The corporation had seven directors and three shareholders:

Mrs. Ringling	315 shares
Mrs. Haley	315 shares
Mr. North	370 shares
Total	1,000 shares

Under *straight voting*, candidates who obtain a plurality (the top vote-getters) for the open directorships are elected. North elects all the directors, assuming Ringling and Haley do not pool their votes. North's seven candidates each receive 370 votes and are the seven top vote-getters. But if Ringling and Haley pool their 630 votes, they can *elect all the directors*.

Under *cumulative voting*, the votes necessary to elect one or more directors is fixed by formula. See §7.2.5. To elect N directors under cumulative voting, a shareholder needs:

$$\frac{\text{N} \times (\text{total number of shares authorized to vote})}{(\text{number of directors} + 1)} + \text{fraction (or 1)}$$

In *Ringling Bros.*, 126 votes are needed to elect one director, 251 to elect two, and 376 to elect three. Each shareholder voting alone can elect at most two directors. (The seventh director will be elected depending on how the three shareholders split their votes.) But if Ringling and Haley vote their combined 630 shares together, they can *elect five directors*—it is more than coincidence that 5 times 126 equals 630.

Validity

In general, shareholder vote-pooling agreements are valid if they relate to a matter on which shareholders may vote. Most statutes require that they be in writing. See MBCA §7.31. Some statutes specify the maximum duration of the agreement, and a few require some notice of the agreement.

Vote-pooling agreements are governed by regular contracting rules. They must be supported by consideration beyond an "agreement to agree"; they may be of indefinite duration; they are subject to change only by agreement of all the parties; they may not be for some illegal end; and they may not be oppressive or fraudulent as to other shareholders or creditors (see §27.2.1).

If the agreement relates to matters beyond shareholder power—such as the board's management discretion—the agreement may be invalid. When does an agreement relate to nonshareholder matters? Consider the famous case of *McQuade v. Stoneham*, 189 N.E.2d 234 (N.Y. 1934). Three shareholders of the corporation that owned the New York Giants baseball team (when it still played at the Polo Grounds) agreed *as shareholders* to elect themselves as directors and then *as directors* to appoint themselves as officers at specified salaries. The New York Court of Appeals had no problem with the shareholder vote pooling per se. But it held the restrictions on directorial discretion were invalid as a matter of public policy and invalidated the entire agreement, including the nonseverable vote-pooling provisions.

Enforcement

Generally, vote-pooling agreements are specifically enforceable because of the difficulty in calculating money damages from a diminution of control if a coparty fails to vote as agreed. See Official Comment, MBCA §7.31(b). Sometimes vote-pooling agreements specify the remedy for failure to abide by the agreement. See *Ramos v. Estrada*, 10 Cal. Rprtr. 2d 833 (Cal. App. 1992) (upholding mandatory buy-sell provisions that were triggered when one group to vote-pooling agreement failed to vote for agreed-upon directors).

Drafting of vote-pooling agreements, however, should be approached with caution. The problem is illustrated by *Ringling Bros*. Two sisters, Mrs. Haley and Mrs. Ringling, each had sufficient shares to elect two directors. To enhance their voting power, they agreed to pool their votes and elect five of the board's seven directors. They also agreed to consult with each other before voting, and designated an arbitrator to resolve any differences. At a meeting to elect directors, Haley (through her husband) switched allegiances, abandoning her sister Ringling to join Mr. North, the third shareholder, who was not a party to the agreement. The arbitrator ruled how the sisters were to vote, but the Haleys refused to comply. When Ringling sued, the Chancery Court did not enforce the arbitrator's decision—which would have resulted in three Ringling directors and two Haley directors on the board of seven directors. Instead, the court ordered a new election and presumably a new arbitration.

On appeal, the Delaware Supreme Court went in another direction. Rather than enforce the arbitrator's decision or call for a new election, it disqualified the Haley shares. The effect was nonetheless disastrous for Ringling, who could not pool her votes with Haley. Since Ringling had only 315 shares to North's 370, North became the controlling shareholder. Eventually, Ringling was forced to sell.

Perhaps Ringling should have negotiated a different enforcement mechanism—for example, one in which the two shareholders would have agreed that the arbitrator would have full power over their combined votes in the case of disagreement. If the function of the arbitrator was merely to choose the fifth director, the agreement provided no protection against Haley shifting her allegiance to North. If the agreement was supposed to keep control from North—a plausible purpose given the parties' history—its enforcement mechanism was flawed. The Chancery Court's order of a new election may have been an attempt to correct this deficiency by making possible a new, more alert arbitration that would favor Ringling. But the Supreme Court was not as sympathetic to the drafter's carelessness.

EXAMPLES

Examples

1. After its incorporation, Pizza Chateau issues 500 shares to Rich and 250 shares each to Bob and Sal. The articles provide for three directors, and at the first meeting the three shareholders elect themselves.
   a. Rich assumes he will have a veto over any corporate matter. Is he right?
   b. Rich assumes he can replace any director who turns on him. Is he right?
   c. To assure each party a veto over management matters, Rich and Bob propose the following bylaw: "On any matter that comes before the board, the directors shall act only by unanimous vote." Does this accomplish their apparent objective?
   d. Bob and Sal distrust each other. Each worries that the other might join forces with Rich. Advise them on shareholder supermajority quorum or voting requirements.

2. Draft a provision so each Pizza Chateau director can veto any fundamental corporate change.

3. From the beginning, the parties follow the practice of voting each other to the board. After three years, Rich and Bob have a falling out with Sal. They sign an agreement to elect themselves and Rich's trusted friend Ruth to the board. At the next shareholders' meeting, Sal is voted off the board. She challenges the voting agreement on the ground it is precluded by their earlier practice. Is it?

4. The three shareholders patch up their differences and agree in writing to vote their shares to assure that each is elected as director. The agreement has no term. Soon after, Sal and Bob propose at a board meeting to open a second pizzeria. Rich objects, but is outvoted.
   a. At the next shareholders' meeting, Rich refuses to abide by the pooling agreement. The corporation has cumulative voting, and Rich divides his 1,500 votes between himself and his trusted friend Ruth. Bob and Sal cast their votes according to the agreement, 500 votes for Rich and 500 votes each for themselves. Absent the agreement, who is elected?
   b. Bob and Sal sue to enforce the agreement. Is it valid?
   c. If the agreement is valid, can Bob and Sal have the election set aside and compel Rich to comply with its voting provisions?

Explanations

1. a. No. As structured, Rich has a veto only at the *shareholder level*. No shareholder action can be taken without his shares being represented at a meeting and being voted. See MBCA §7.25(a) (majority quorum); §7.25(c) (voting majority at meeting). But at the *board level* Rich has no veto. The other two directors constitute a quorum and can outvote him. MBCA §8.24(a) (majority quorum); §8.24(c) (board acts by majority of directors present).

   b. No. If a schism develops on the board, Rich would be powerless. Although his 50 percent share ownership allows him to block shareholder action, he cannot elect a board majority. Under straight voting, there would be deadlock. Under cumulative voting, he can elect only one director. Rich needs some of Bob's or Sal's votes to choose the board.

   c. Perhaps not. At first blush the provision looks good. It seems to allow any objecting director to block any action by simply not voting, thus preventing unanimity. But the provision may be flawed:
   - The provision is in the bylaws and can be amended or deleted by a shareholder majority—that is, by Rich and Sal. MBCA §10.20. (Notice that the MBCA anticircumvention provision applies only to changes in quorum or voting requirements for *shareholders*. MBCA §10.21.)
   - Without a high quorum proviso, the unanimity requirement might be empty. If a quorum were a simple majority, two directors could then "unanimously" take board action at any meeting that the other failed to attend. The provision should specify that "unanimous" means a vote by "all directors in office."
   - Some courts have viewed unanimous voting requirements with disfavor because they risk deadlock. In some states, a unanimity requirement must be in the articles.
   - The provision gives a veto to Sal, thus diluting Rich's and Bob's power on the board. The two might be best served by a provision that permitted board action by the directors designated as Rich's and Bob's. (A classified board might accomplish this. See §26.2.2 below.)

   d. Bob and Sal each want their individual 25 percent voting interest to block any shareholder action. A high quorum requirement, such as 80 percent, theoretically would allow either simply not to show up and block any action by the others. But it has two defects. First, once a shareholders' meeting with a proper quorum has started, Bob or Sal might be unable to break the quorum and could then be outvoted. Second, some courts might not enforce the quorum requirement on the theory that a shareholder cannot challenge a quorum defect of her own making.

A high voting requirement may be preferable. To avoid questions under earlier cases about the validity of a unanimous voting requirement, a voting requirement of 80 percent of the *outstanding* shares would act as a unanimity requirement. (Notice that if the quorum were a majority, and the voting requirement were 80 percent of the *voting shares present*, it would be possible for Rich and Sal to meet and take action without Bob being able to exercise his veto.)

2. Insert in the articles of incorporation:

> **Article XX.** Besides any shareholder approval that may be required, the following corporate actions must be approved by the affirmative vote of at least three-fourths (75 percent) of the directors of the corporation in office: amendments to the articles of incorporation; amendments to the bylaws; dissolution of the corporation; merger or consolidation of the corporation; forced share exchange; sale, lease, mortgage, or transfer of all or substantially all of the corporation's assets; issuance of stock; purchase, redemption, or retirement of the corporation's stock.

This provision operates as a unanimity requirement. It cannot be circumvented because at least three directors must approve any change to the provision or to the number of directors on the board (which is specified in the articles). MBCA §10.03(b).

3. Probably not. Although the parties' vote-pooling practice may have reflected an implicit prior agreement, the agreement was not in writing—a requirement of many statutes authorizing vote-pooling agreements. See MBCA §7.31(a). Nonetheless, even if the prior practice did not create a binding agreement, it might have created "reasonable expectations" enforceable as fiduciary duties or in an action based on oppression. See §27.2.1.

4. a. The three top vote-getters are elected: Rich—1,250 votes, Ruth—750 votes, either Sal or Bob—500 votes.
   b. Yes. Vote-pooling agreements for the election of directors are generally valid. The agreement would be invalid in only two circumstances—if it were subject to a statute imposing specific requirements, such as a maximum term or a notice requirement, or if it included illegal management restrictions.
   c. Yes. Vote-pooling agreements are specifically enforceable. See MBCA §7.31(b). The election can be set aside. By virtue of the agreement, Rich is in a minority on the board, and he cannot extricate himself during the term of the agreement.

§26.2 SELF-ENFORCING CONTROL STRUCTURES

§26.2.1 Voting Trusts

Vote-pooling agreements are not self-enforcing. A *voting trust* overcomes this disadvantage. Under a voting trust agreement, shareholders transfer legal title to their shares to a voting trustee. The trustee, for a defined period and according to specified instructions, has the exclusive voting power over the transferred shares. Other attributes of ownership (such as rights to dividends and other distributions) remain with the beneficiaries of the trust—usually the former shareholders. The beneficiaries often take voting trust certificates as evidence of their equitable ownership interest.

Purpose

A voting trust, compared to a vote-pooling agreement, avoids the need for court-ordered specific performance, a stability often sought by creditors—for example, when a corporation is coming out of bankruptcy or receivership. A voting trust also permits transferability of *ownership interests* without giving up control. This may be desirable, for example, when a shareholder wants to give her children a financial interest in the company without giving them voting power.

Creation

The requirements for creating a voting trust are straightforward. MBCA §7.30 is typical:

- Shareholders enter into a written trust agreement setting out the trustee's obligations.
- The shareholders transfer some or all their shares to the trustee. The transfer is normally reflected on the corporation's stock transfer ledger, which shows the trustee as the registered holder of the transferred shares.
- The trust agreement specifies a term not to exceed ten years. The shareholders can extend the trust by later agreement; the extension binds only those who sign it.
- The trustee prepares a list of trust beneficiaries (who may be different from the shareholders who transferred their shares), together with a description of the shares transferred to the trust. The trustee delivers a copy of this list and the trust agreement to the corporation's principal office.

Generally, a shareholder cannot revoke his transfer to a voting trust. Only the vote of all the trust beneficiaries can terminate or amend the trust during its life. In general, the powers of the voting trustee are set by contract and depend on the authorizing language of the trust agreement. Where the trust agreement is silent or unclear, courts impose equitable limitations on the trustee's powers if they might damage the corporation's business.

Validity

Early courts were suspicious of voting trusts and invalidated them because they separated shareholders' voting power and economic ownership interests. Today statutes specifically authorize voting trusts in virtually all jurisdictions. Nonetheless, reflecting the early antipathy, a voting trust that fails to comply with all of the statutory requirements risks invalidity.

Unlike a vote-pooling agreement, which in many jurisdictions can be of indefinite duration and may be kept secret, a voting trust must be on file in the corporation's main office and must be for a limited (usually ten-year) term, subject to periodic extension. The voting trust statutes are intended "to avoid secret, uncontrolled combinations formed to acquire control of the corporation to the possible detriment of non-participating shareholders." See *Oceanic Exploration Co. v. Grynberg*, 428 A.2d 1 (Del. 1981).

Voting trusts must also be for a "proper purpose," which means the trust instrument cannot call on the trustee to do things that would be fraudulent, illegal, or detrimental to nonbeneficiaries. In most instances, the trustee's fiduciary duties are coextensive with the "proper purpose" doctrine.

De Facto Voting Trusts

Litigants have sometimes ingeniously turned the rules on voting trusts to challenge other control devices. A device (particularly a novel one) that locks the parties into a control arrangement in which a third party has decision-making authority—thus resembling a voting trust—can be argued to be a de facto voting trust. If it fails to comply with the duration or publicity requirements, it is invalid. See Del. GCL §218 (former provision imposed ten-year limit). Three Delaware Supreme Court cases illustrate:

- ***Ringling Bros.-Barnum & Bailey Combined Shows, Inc. v. Ringling***, 53 A.2d 441 (Del. 1947): Two shareholders in a three-shareholder corporation entered into a vote-pooling agreement in which an arbitrator was to resolve any voting disagreements. When after a disagreement one of the parties refused to comply with the arbitrator's instructions, the other party sued. The noncomplying shareholder argued that the arbitration procedure operated as a voting trust by separating voting from ownership. The court sidestepped the argument since the agreement technically had not transferred any voting rights to the arbitrator, who had not been given formal power to vote the shares.

- ***Abercrombie v. Davies,*** 130 A.2d 338 (Del. 1957): A group of shareholders together holding a voting majority agreed that eight designated agents would vote their shares under proxies granted for ten years. Voting was to be determined by agreement of seven agents or, if seven could not agree, by arbitration. To enforce the agreement the parties endorsed their share certificates and deposited them with the agents. The court held the agreement was a de facto voting trust because (1) it separated ownership and voting; (2) it transferred voting power irrevocably for a definite period; and (3) its principal purpose was to provide for voting control of the corporation. As a voting trust, it was invalid for not complying with statutory requirements.
- ***Lehrman v. Cohen,*** 222 A.2d 800 (Del. 1966): The corporation, owned equally by two families, had two classes of stock that entitled each family to elect two directors to a four-person board. To avoid board deadlock, a third class of stock—consisting of one share with $10 par value—elected a fifth director, but had no financial rights beyond its $10 value. This share was issued to the company's counsel, who eventually joined one of the family camps and was elected as president with a long-term executive employment contract. Unhappy about the internal coup, the other family challenged the third class as a de facto voting trust and illegal because of the Delaware statute's then ten-year limit. The court applied the *Abercrombie* three-factor test and concluded the first factor had not been shown since voting rights of the *original* classes of stock had not been separated from ownership even though the new class had diluted voting power—as usually happens when new stock is issued.

§26.2.2 Classes of Stock (Classified Board)

As you may have noticed, many control devices allocate voting power *disproportionately* to financial interests. A straightforward way to do this is with different classes of shares, each class entitled to elect a specified number of directors.

Purpose

Suppose one shareholder in a three-shareholder corporation contributes 80 percent of the start-up capital and wants commensurate financial rights, but is willing to share control. This desire can be effectuated by creating two classes of shares: Class A elects one director and Class B two directors; Class A participates on a 4:1 ratio with Class B in all corporate distributions. The

80 percent contributor gets Class A shares (80 percent financial rights, and one-third voting rights); the other shareholders get Class B shares (20 percent financial rights, and two-thirds voting rights). The problem is solved.

Different classes of shares can serve many purposes:

- Board representation—Class A elects two directors, and Class B elects three directors.
- Protection in fundamental changes—Class A and Class B must separately approve any charter amendment.
- Modified control structures—nonvoting common has financial rights equal to voting common, but does not affect control balance.
- Limitation on board discretion—the company's president and vice president must be Class B shareholders.

Creation

Different classes of shares, like any equity securities, must be authorized in the articles. MBCA §6.01(c).

Class voting has its pitfalls. Notice that a majority shareholder can circumvent the expectations of class voting if she can remove minority directors. This possibility becomes all the more real if the majority shareholder can remove them with *or without* cause (see §13.2). To avoid this, the articles or bylaws should specify that Class B directors can be removed only by Class B shareholders, or only by other shareholders for cause.

Validity

Besides its simplicity and ease of enforcement, class voting is subject to few (if any) of the statutory and common-law limitations that dog other control devices. Most states set no limits on classes that elect a specified number of directors, that vote only on specified matters, that have limited financial rights, or that have multiple or fractional voting rights or no voting rights at all. MBCA §6.01.

For example, in *Lehrman v. Cohen*, 222 A.2d 800 (Del. 1966), the Delaware Supreme Court upheld the validity of a class of stock entitled to elect one director where two existing classes of stock each elected two directors. The deadlock-breaking class consisted of one share, $10 par value, with no right to dividends or distributions on liquidation beyond its $10 value. The court accepted that this class "became a part of the capitalization" of the corporation, even though its purpose was not to raise capital, but rather to resolve control disputes.

Classes of equity interests can also be employed in an LLC to ensure protection of minority members. For example, when Class A members of an

LLC sought to refinance their faltering business and Class B members refused to relinquish their "put" rights to sell their interests back to the LLC (which if exercised would have prevented the refinancing), the Delaware court held that Class B members had no duty to facilitate the refinancing sought by the Class A members. Instead, the LLC operating agreement specifically required 75 percent approval for financing decisions, a provision that empowered Class B members to block financing proposals they opposed. See *Fisk Ventures, LLC v. Segal*, 2008 WL 1961156 (Del. Ch. 2008).

§26.2.3 Irrevocable Proxies

Shareholders in close corporations can also structure control by giving another person (or each other) binding authority to vote their shares—*irrevocable proxies*. Unlike a regular proxy, the shareholder-principal cannot change her mind and withdraw the proxy holder's authority to vote her shares.

Purpose

An irrevocable proxy provides a "self-executing" means (thus avoiding litigation) to protect those who have an interest in the corporation. Pledgees, prospective shareholders, and shareholders who have entered into voting agreements—to give some examples—may want an irrevocable proxy to ensure that the shares in which they have an interest are voted as they want.

Creation

Irrevocable proxies raise the "separation of voting and ownership" concerns that fueled the attack on voting trusts. The modern trend, reflected in corporate statutes, is to recognize irrevocable proxies "coupled with an interest." See MBCA §7.22.

What kind of "interest" supports an irrevocable proxy?

- **Interest in stock.** The most widely recognized interest is when the proxy holder himself has an interest in the stock—for example, when the proxy holder has an option to buy the stock or lends money to the shareholder who pledges the stock as collateral. MBCA §7.22(d)(1), (2).
- **Economic interest in corporation.** Increasingly, it is sufficient if the proxy holder has an economic interest in the corporation, though not an interest in the stock itself. Del. GCL §212(c). For example, the holder has agreed to lend money to the corporation or has become

a shareholder (or an employee) in reliance on the other shareholders' granting him an irrevocable proxy. MBCA §7.22(d)(3), (4). The proxy holder's economic interest in the corporation provides an incentive to vote to further the corporation's best interests. See *Haft v. Haft*, 671 A.2d 413 (Del. Ch. 1995) (finding that interest in employment could support irrevocable proxy).

- **Designated by shareholders.** The hardest case is when the proxy holder has no direct interest in the stock or the corporation but has been designated to hold proxies pursuant to a shareholders' agreement or other control arrangement. See MBCA §7.22(d)(5) ("party" to a shareholders' voting agreement has sufficient interest). In this situation, the proxy holder may have little incentive to vote the proxies to further the corporation's best interests. Nonetheless, irrevocability in a shareholders' agreement facilitates corporate contracting, and presumably the shareholders sought to protect their financial interests by agreement.

An irrevocable proxy terminates or becomes revocable when the qualifying interest is extinguished. MBCA §7.22(f).

The "coupled with an interest" requirement may preclude control devices that call for compulsory voting of shares. The most famous case is *Ringling Bros.* (see §26.2.1 above), where the Delaware courts considered the validity of a vote-pooling agreement that set up an arbitration procedure to resolve voting disputes between two parties. When the two parties reached an impasse and one refused to vote according to the arbitrator's decision, the noncomplying party argued the agreement gave the arbitrator an implied proxy, which she could revoke because it was not supported by an interest. The Delaware Supreme Court held that the agreement did not call on the arbitrator to actually vote the shares and thus the parties had not granted a proxy, revocable or irrevocable.

EXAMPLES

Examples

1. Pizza Chateau is a success, and Rich is delighted with Bob's able management. Rich suggests that he and Bob consolidate their voting power. Rich owns 500 common shares, Sal 250, and Bob 250. They consider a voting trust under which Bob would have full voting authority over their 750 shares. Each would retain a beneficial interest in all dividends and distributions. The agreement would have a term of ten years, automatically renewable for another ten years unless either objects in writing. Bob would send a copy of the agreement to Sal.
   a. Do you see any problems?
   b. Rich, although he trusts Bob, is cautious. He wants a provision that he can remove and replace Bob as trustee upon the "majority vote of

the beneficial interests represented by the voting trust certificates outstanding." Do you see any problems?

2. Rich goes to Europe for a few years. Bob wants to make sure things will run smoothly while Rich is gone and asks for a proxy to vote his shares. Rich agrees and hands over his share certificates. Two days later Rich has misgivings and signs a three-year proxy appointment form naming attorney Conley as his proxy holder.
   a. Who has Rich's proxy?
   b. Upon hearing about this turn of events, Bob implores Rich not to leave the fate of the business in the hands of a lawyer. Rich understands and signs a proxy naming Bob his proxy holder during his absence. Who can vote Rich's shares?
   c. Besides appointing Conley as his proxy holder before he left for Europe, Rich also authorized Conley to sell his shares, with Conley to earn a 15 percent commission of the sales price. Further, the proxy naming Conley provided that it was irrevocable until Rich returned or the shares were sold. Is Conley's proxy irrevocable?

3. Rich returns from Europe and all proxies end. Rich says that he wants "fluidity." Neither Bob nor Sal knows what he means, and they wonder about Rich's intentions and mental acuity. Rich still controls 500 shares, and each of them controls 250. Worried about deadlocks, the two propose that each shareholder turn over a nominal number of shares to attorney Conley. Rich will transfer two shares, and Sal and Bob one each.
   a. The corporation has four directors, elected by cumulative voting. What will be the effect of this arrangement?
   b. Can Conley be a deadlock-breaker at both the shareholder and board level, without any ownership interest?

Explanations

EXPLANATIONS

1. a. Yes. Rich and Bob may not have complied with the voting trust statute. Disclosure to Sal may not satisfy the requirement of disclosure to the "corporation's principal office." See MBCA §7.30(a). Such disclosure provides notice not only to other shareholders, but directors and officers, and possibly creditors, of the special control arrangement.

   In addition, the automatic extension provision may violate the spirit of the statutory provisions allowing extension after reexamination and voluntary consent by the parties. The MBCA's requirement that the extension "binds only those parties who sign it" implies that the extension must be accomplished with an additional formality and cannot be automatic. Some statutes make this explicit. Cal. Corp. §706 (extension must be agreed to within two years prior to expiration of original term); Del. GCL §218 (same); N.Y. BCL §621(d) (six months).

b. No. This provision would undermine some of the certainty for Bob, but there is nothing that prevents the trust agreement from specifying the responsibilities or term of the trustee. Except for limitations imposed by statute, a voting trust agreement can contain any provisions to which the parties agree.

2. a. Most probably Conley. Bob's assertion of a proxy has two problems. First, his authority was not in writing and most statutes require a proxy, whether or not revocable, be in writing. See MBCA §7.22(b); cf. Del. GCL §212 (writing not explicitly required). Second, even if an oral proxy were possible, Rich's handing over of the share certificates does not necessarily imply irrevocability. The subsequent written authorization to Conley is a proxy, even though it covers more than one shareholders' meeting. See MBCA §7.22(c). A subsequent proxy revokes any prior revocable proxies.

b. Probably Bob. Rich revoked Conley's revocable proxy when he named Bob in writing. Conley's proxy was not irrevocable for two reasons. First, Rich did not intend it to be irrevocable. Many statutes, including the MBCA, require that the proxy's irrevocability be conspicuously stated on the appointment form. Second, Conley's proxy could not be irrevocable because it was not coupled with an interest. From the facts, Conley has no interest in the corporation, its shares, or any agreement of the shareholders. There is no assurance that his voting will be consistent with the corporation's interests since he has no economic or contractual incentive to maximize corporate welfare. It is conceivable, for example, that Conley might vote his proxy to create situations that will generate attorney fees from the corporation. Although such conduct might violate his duties as Rich's agent, corporate law does not yet recognize this interest as sufficient to support an irrevocable proxy.

c. Probably. Conley's interest is probably sufficient under modern views supporting irrevocability. This would mean Rich's attempt to give Bob his proxy was probably a nullity.

Conley's authorization to sell Rich's shares (for a commission) aligns Conley's interests with the corporation's. Although this interest is not enumerated in MBCA §7.22(d), the MBCA list is meant to be illustrative, not exhaustive. Official Comment to MBCA §7.22 (illustration 3). Conley can be expected to vote to further the corporation's interests because his commission is tied to the sales price and thus to the corporation's fortunes. On the other hand, he receives only a percentage of the selling price, and countervailing interests (such as creating opportunities for attorney fees) might weigh more heavily in Conley's voting. Nonetheless, the MBCA recognizes that others (such as creditors and employees) with potentially mixed interests in the corporation can nonetheless have a sufficient interest to support irrevocability. Arguably, Conley would be just as interested in protecting his commission as a creditor would be in protecting the corporation's solvency or an employee in assuring the corporation's viability. Cf. *State ex rel. Breger v. Rusche*, 39 N.E.2d 433 (Ind. 1942) (holding that attorney, given proxy and authority to sell shareholders' stock, did not have irrevocable proxy even though he had a right to reimbursement for selling expenses).

3. a. Transferring the shares to a new shareholder has the effect of a new class of shares with the power to break *shareholder* deadlocks between the Rich camp and the Bob-Sal camp. But unlike a nonparticipating class of shares, Conley will participate in any dividends and distributions in proportion to his shares. If the corporation is successful, this ownership interest may exceed the value of Conley's services as a stand-by deadlock breaker. The arrangement will not work to break deadlocks at the board level. Rich, even with 498 of 1,000 shares, will still have the power to elect two directors. Deadlocks among the directors remain possible.

   b. Yes. The parties could create a new class of shares that would have one vote on general shareholder matters and the power to elect a new fifth director. If the new class of shares—"Class D" (for deadlock-breaker)—were made voting, but nonparticipating (no rights to dividends), the parties' purpose would be accomplished. The articles of incorporation would have to be amended to provide for and specify the powers and rights of this new class.

   Although the validity of such a class of shares may have been questionable once, the ability to create such an arrangement is now generally recognized. See MBCA §6.01(c).

§26.3 TRANSFER RESTRICTIONS AND CONTRACTUAL LIQUIDITY RIGHTS

A significant attribute of many close corporations is closely knit ownership. To exclude unwanted outsiders, the owners often agree not to transfer their shares. But change is inevitable, and absolute restraints on transferability would produce hardships. Transfer limits are usually combined with contractual "outs," such as purchase options or mandatory purchase obligations. These provisions create a "private market," a substitute for the liquidity available to public shareholders.

Transfer restrictions (1) ensure stability in the control and management of the corporation; (2) maintain proportionate ownership interests among shareholders and guard against internal coups (by also applying to transfers between insiders); (3) ensure that the corporation will satisfy the Subchapter S requirement that it have no more than 100 shareholders (see §2.3.3); (4) ensure compliance with professional corporation statutes, such as the requirement that only licensed physicians can be shareholders in a professional medical corporation; and (5) preserve exemptions under federal (and state) securities laws that prohibit the sale of unregistered restricted securities (see §5.2.2).

Just as important, transfer restrictions are usually tied to buy-sell agreements that create liquidity rights in the close corporation.

§26.3.1 Creating Transfer Restrictions and Liquidity Rights

Transfer restrictions and liquidity agreements typically cover stock sales, transfers in trust, gifts, and stock pledges. They can be placed in the articles, the bylaws, a shareholders' agreement, or an agreement between the corporation and its shareholders. In some states, any agreement creating transfer restrictions must be filed with the corporation and be available for inspection.

Notice

To bind putative transferees—and avoid a "bona fide" purchaser avoidance—the *certificates* must note conspicuously that the shares are subject to transfer restrictions. MBCA §6.27(b); UCC §8-204(a). A stock legend is conspicuous if printed in *italics*, **boldface,** or contrasting color, or typed in CAPITALS, or <u>underlined</u> MBCA §1.40(3). Even if not conspicuous, transfer restrictions are enforceable against any transferee with knowledge. MBCA §6.27(b).

Drafting Issues

In creating transfer restrictions and buy-sell rights, the planner must address a host of issues:

- What are the restrictions, and who is subject to them?
- What triggers the buy-sell provisions?
- Who has the option (or obligation) to purchase—the corporation, the shareholders, or both?

- If the corporation purchases, who participates in the decision?
- If more than one party is to purchase, in what proportion and order do the purchases take place?
- How is the price for the shares determined (perhaps the thorniest issue)—book value, outside offer, mutual agreement with periodic revision, capitalization of earnings, a formula combining these methods, or an independent appraisal?
- What if the corporation cannot repurchase the shares because of legal capital or solvency impediments (see §31.2)?
- If funding comes from death or disability insurance policies, who pays the premiums?

The planner should keep in mind that shareholders generally will not know beforehand whether they will be "sellers" or "buyers" under the liquidity provisions. Each party usually will consider symmetry to be in his best interests.

§26.3.2 Validity of Transfer Restrictions

The general rule, and a significant advantage of the corporate form, is that shares are freely transferable. Even though share transfer restrictions are at odds with the rule, most state statutes recognize their validity. MBCA §6.27. Transfer restrictions must be *reasonable under the circumstances*, an approach that balances two conflicting corporate tenets: free alienability of corporate ownership interests and private corporate structuring to meet the participants' needs.

The treatment of various transfer restrictions illustrates this balance.

- **Flat prohibition.** An outright prohibition against *any transfer to any person* likely would be invalid even in a jurisdiction that had a statute authorizing transfer restrictions. But a limited restriction related to some legitimate purpose—such as a restriction in a professional medical corporation limiting transfers only to licensed physicians—would be enforceable. MBCA §6.27(d)(4) (restriction limited to designated persons permissible if "not manifestly unreasonable").
- **Prior approval.** Prior-approval restrictions require a shareholder to first obtain approval of the board or other shareholders. Although some cases have invalidated prior approval procedures when obtaining consent would be practically impossible or when consent is arbitrarily withheld, many corporate statutes allow this procedure if "not manifestly unreasonable." MBCA §6.27(d)(3).
- **Purchase option.** First-option provisions require the shareholder (or the shareholder's estate) to first offer her shares to the corporation or the other shareholders *at a specified option price*. Courts have enforced first

options. See MBCA §6.27(d)(1). The corporation's decision to refuse a first offer, so that a controlling shareholder can purchase, is a self-dealing transaction subject to fairness review. See *Cash v. Cash Furniture Co.*, 296 A.2d 207 (Vt. 1972).

- **First refusal.** First-refusal rights obligate the shareholder to first offer her shares to the corporation (or the other shareholders) *at the price and on the terms offered by the outsider*. The difference between a purchase option and a first-refusal right is that the option price is set by agreement while the first-refusal price is whatever price is offered by the outsider. The outside offer provides significant assurances that the first-refusal price is fair, and courts readily uphold their validity.
- **Mandatory buy-sell.** On death, withdrawal, deadlock, or other specified contingencies, the shareholder (or the shareholder's estate) is obligated to sell to the corporation or to other shareholders, who in turn must purchase the shares at a specified price. See *Concord Auto Auction, Inc. v. Rustin*, 627 F. Supp. 1526 (D. Mass. 1986) (enforcing buy-sell agreement against deceased shareholder's estate, even though parties had failed to update price under repricing procedure in agreement). A mandatory buy-sell agreement has advantages for both sides. It assures the shareholder a market for her shares and, if the price is established in good faith to reflect actual value, it helps fix the value of the shares for federal estate tax purposes. It assures the corporation's closed status and provides a way to buy out fractious shareholders. Buy-sell arrangements are valid, provided the corporation has sufficient legal capital to redeem the shares. See §31.2.

In general, the failure of the corporation (or other shareholders) to purchase frees the shareholder to transfer the shares.

There are no statutory or judicial limits on how long transfer restrictions can last. Regular contract rules apply, and shareholders can forsake transfer restrictions by express agreement or by a course of conduct. For example, implied abandonment might be shown if shareholders have failed to object to noncomplying sales by previous shareholders.

Fiduciary Duties in Buy-Sell Agreements

A recurring issue is whether the majority has fiduciary duties to act fairly in exercising its rights under a buy-sell agreement. For example, can the majority fire an at-will employee-shareholder in order to purchase his shares at low "book value" as provided under their buy-sell agreement? Or does the majority owe a fiduciary duty not to act opportunistically?

Some courts have strictly enforced the terms of the contract—on a theory of *caveat emptor*—in the belief that close corporation participants can negotiate protections and should be bound by their agreement. See *Gallagher v. Lambert*, 549 N.E.2d 139 (N.Y. 1989) ("These agreements define the scope of the relevant fiduciary duty and supply certainty of obligations to each side"). Other courts, particularly when the buy-sell agreement produces an unexpected hardship, have inferred fiduciary duties that compel the majority to justify its actions. *Pedro v. Pedro*, 489 N.W.2d 798 (Minn. App. 1992) ("depleting a corporation's value is not the exclusive method of breaching one's fiduciary duties").

Examples

1. When they incorporated Pizza Chateau, Rich, Bob, and Sal agreed not to sell their shares to any outsider unless the others first approved the sale. But they did not put their agreement in writing.
   a. Rich takes out a bank loan and pledges his Pizza Chateau stock as collateral. If he defaults on his loan, can the bank foreclose on the pledged shares?
   b. If the restriction satisfied the formal requirements, would it be valid?
2. The three parties amend Pizza Chateau's articles to provide: "Any shareholder may withdraw from the Corporation by giving the Corporation ninety (90) days written notice. The Corporation shall be obligated to purchase all of the shareholder's shares." What price provision would you recommend?
3. The parties do not want the buy-sell arrangement to be the exclusive means by which shareholders can sell their shares. Any shareholder can sell his or her shares to outsiders if the remaining shareholders agree.
   a. How should the parties implement this restriction?
   b. Draft a legend for the share certificates reflecting this transfer restriction.
4. The parties abandon the buy-sell arrangement, but agree to forced redemption by the corporation upon any shareholder's death. Draft a provision.

Explanations

1. a. Probably. The restriction suffers from two defects. First, it should have been noted conspicuously *in writing* on the share certificates—a so-called stock legend. Second, even if the "legending" defect is excused because the bank had notice of the restriction, the restriction (which only covered "sales") does not cover pledges of stock as collateral for a loan. Some courts strictly construe transfer restrictions on the theory they are restraints on alienation. For this reason, transfer restrictions are typically written to cover "sales, exchanges, assignments, pledges, gifts, bequests, or other transfers."

b. Perhaps not. The restriction should probably have been less absolute. Allowing any shareholder to veto a transfer threatens stock liquidity, and some courts have invalidated prior-approval restrictions where consent can be arbitrarily withheld. The parties should have specified that prior approval "cannot be unreasonably withheld." Objecting shareholders thus would bear the burden of showing some legitimate business purpose, such as stability in management or preventing opportunistic realignments in share ownership.

2. Any buy-sell price should reflect fair value. At the time the parties agree to a buy-sell agreement, it is unlikely that any will know who will be the selling shareholder and who will be the buyers. The provision should strike a balance between assuring fair value and assuring that the corporation's value as a going concern is not depleted.

   There are a number of possibilities, each with advantages and defects:

   - *A stipulated price subject to periodic revision* has the advantage of mutuality (each party should have the same incentives to change the price and thus for it to be fair) and relatively low cost. But it is always possible that the price will not be updated through oversight or an inability to agree.
   - *A best-offer price* may reflect an open market valuation of the shares. But it assumes that there has been a best offer and that the offer was made in good faith.
   - *Book value of the shares*—that is, the per share value of assets minus liabilities—is tantalizingly popular and readily capable of calculation by established accounting methods. It is, however, probably the least accurate measure of the business's value as a going concern. It will reflect fixed (historic) value of assets, not the earnings potential (and goodwill) of the business as a going concern.
   - *Capitalization of earnings* measures the earnings potential of the business—presumably what a rational investor would want to know. It depends on defining earnings and determining a capitalization rate (or multiplier) based on similar businesses. Choosing how earnings are defined and what capitalization rate to use is an "art form" requiring experience in such matters and is often practiced by professional business valuators.
   - *Discounted cash flows* (DCF) is a more sophisticated way of determining the present value of the business as a going concern—focusing not on "earnings" (an accounting term), but instead estimates of how much "cash" the business will generate in the future. These future cash flows are then "discounted" to present value to determine the

overall business value. Estimating future cash flows and choosing a discount rate (which reflects the time value of money and future risk) is fraught with potential error. Professional business valuators (sometimes investment banks) are expensive, with fees for valuing a business using a DCF analysis starting at $50,000.

3. a. The articles of incorporation, bylaws, or a shareholders' agreement must specify the procedures for prior approval by the other shareholders. In addition, the share certificates must reflect the transfer restriction.
   b. The following legend should be placed conspicuously on all share certificates:

> **TAKE NOTICE that the sale, assignment, transfer, or pledge of the shares represented by this Certificate is subject to restrictions contained in the Articles of Incorporation. The Articles permit the transfer of stock only with the permission of the Corporation's board of directors.**

For the legend to be conspicuous, the MBCA requires that a reasonable person against whom it is to operate should have noticed it. The MBCA suggests some visual devices, such as printing in italics, boldface or contrasting color, typing in capitals, or underlining. MBCA §1.40(3).

4. A redemption provision in the articles or bylaws, or in an agreement between the shareholders and corporation, would bind the corporation and the shareholders:

> **Redemption upon death.** Upon the death of any shareholder, the Corporation shall redeem, to the extent it is legally able, all of the Corporation's shares owned by the deceased shareholder at the time of his death. The deceased shareholder's estate shall surrender the certificates representing the shares to be redeemed. The Corporation shall redeem the shares at the value fixed by this provision, using insurance proceeds and current liquid assets, and if necessary by liquidating assets or borrowing funds to the extent permitted by law.
>
> (1) *Life insurance*. The Corporation will acquire, maintain, and become the owner of a renewable-term life insurance policy on the life of each shareholder in a face amount equal to $______, which coverage is subject to change as described below. Each shareholder agrees to cooperate fully in causing such a policy (and any amendment) to be issued and maintained.
>
> *(continued)*

(2) *Payment of premiums*. The Corporation will pay the premiums on these life insurance policies, and will provide proof of payment to the insured shareholders within twenty (20) days before the due date of each premium. If the Corporation fails to pay a premium twenty (20) days before it becomes due, the shareholder may pay the premium and will be reimbursed by the Corporation.

(3) *Share valuation*. The shareholders and the Corporation have valued each of the one thousand (1,000) outstanding shares of the Corporation as of the date of this agreement at $______. Each March 1, the Corporation, acting through its board of directors, will recalculate the value of each share. This recalculated value will be reflected in the board minutes. If the board of directors fails to recalculate a value, the last fixed value will remain in effect.

(4) *Insurance coverage*. If in any year the share valuation reflects more than a 20 percent increase in value over the last fixed value, the Corporation will purchase a proportional amount of additional insurance coverage to reflect the increase in the shares' value. If any shareholder is not insurable at standard rates, the Corporation need not purchase additional coverage.

As with any liquidity right, this redemption provision addresses the trigger (death of shareholder), to whom it applies (the shareholder's estate and the corporation), the limits on the corporation's obligation (legal capital rules), the repurchase procedures (surrender of certificates), the repurchase price (set under a revaluation procedure), the source for payments (insurance proceeds), and assurance of payments (the premium-payment obligations).

§26.4 RESTRAINTS ON DIRECTORS' DISCRETION

Up to this point we have focused on control devices that affect *shareholders'* discretion to vote their shares. These devices do not guarantee control over *board* decisions, such as appointing officers, setting salaries, declaring dividends, issuing or repurchasing shares, dissolving the corporation, or limiting the scope of the business. Planners beware!

For parties to effectively control the management of a close corporation, restraints must be placed on the discretion of the board. These restraints can take many forms:

- contractual agreements by parties (sometimes in shareholders' agreements) to act in specified ways in their capacity as directors;
- contracts with the corporation that effectively disempower the board, such as employment contracts granting an employee significant management discretion; and

- agreements that the shareholders will assume some or all of the powers of the board of directors.

These restraints allow "incorporated partners" to conduct their business as they please. But, as salubrious as they may seem, the restraints run into the corporate tenet and statutory mandate that the corporation's business be managed by (or under the supervision of) the board of directors. MBCA §8.01(b). Any arrangement that restrains directors' discretion is inconsistent with this norm and may undermine expectations of others (nonparty shareholders and creditors) that directors will act flexibly and independently in the best interests of the corporation. Absent statutory authorization, management restraints are problematic control devices.

§26.4.1 Validity of Management Agreements

Modern Statutes

The validity of management agreements depends on the corporate statute. Although older statutes mandated exclusive board management, many modern statutes have special close corporation provisions that specifically authorize agreements limiting directorial discretion. Cal. Corp. §§158, 300(b) (corporations with no more than ten shareholders); N.Y. BCL §620 (nonpublic corporations); Del. GCL §351 (corporations that file articles of incorporation adopting "close corporation" status).

The MBCA authorizes shareholders' agreements that govern "the exercise of corporate powers or the management of the business and affairs of the corporation or the relationship among the shareholders, the directors and the corporation." MBCA §7.32 (revised in 1991). An agreement is authorized if approved by all of the shareholders, whether in the articles or bylaws, or in an agreement signed by all then-current shareholders and "made known" to the corporation. MBCA §7.32(b). The section validates agreements that create alternative governance structures and any others "not contrary to public policy." MBCA §7.32(a). An agreement may run ten years, unless specified otherwise, and any amendment must be approved by all existing shareholders.

Common Law

In those jurisdictions that do not have special statutory provisions or where the parties have not properly used them, the validity of restraints on directors' discretion is a matter of common law. Early common-law decisions imposed a strict rule that any restraint on the board violates public policy and is unenforceable. Over time cases have adopted an increasingly more relaxed approach, allowing such restraints if the agreement (1) relates to a close corporation, (2) does not adversely affect interests of nonparty shareholders or of creditors, (3) deviates only slightly from the statutory norm that directors "manage the business of the corporation."

This evolution and the operation of the relaxed rules are illustrated in four New York Court of Appeals cases dealing with agreements restraining board discretion.

- **Manson v. Curtis,** 119 N.E. 559 (N.Y. 1918): A majority of the shareholders (though not all) agreed that one of the parties was to be general manager for a year, managing the corporation's business and setting its policy. The court invalidated the provision, along with the rest of the agreement, because by vesting management authority in a single manager it "sterilized the board."
- **McQuade v. Stoneham,** 189 N.E. 234 (N.Y. 1934): The majority shareholder and two other shareholders (though less than all) agreed to keep one another in office as directors and officers and specified their positions and salaries. The court invalidated the entire agreement because its provisions on appointment and compensation usurped the board's function.
- **Clark v. Dodge,** 199 N.E. 641 (N.Y. 1936): The corporation's only two shareholders, Clark and Dodge, agreed that Clark would be general manager with compensation pegged to the corporation's "net income." The court held that the agreement was valid since Clark's promised tenure as long as he "proved faithful, efficient and competent" could harm nobody. The court interpreted Clark's remuneration set at one-fourth of "net income" to mean he could receive only distributable amounts as determined by the board in its "good faith" discretion. The agreement was viewed as only a slight infringement on the statutory authority of the board.
- **Long Park, Inc. v. Trenton-New Brunswick Theaters Co.,** 77 N.E.2d 633 (N.Y. 1948): All the shareholders designated one of themselves as manager with full authority to run the business. The court invalidated the agreement because the directors completely surrendered their powers to the manager.

§26.4.2 Effect of Invalidity and Enforcement

An illegal restraint of board discretion is invalid and unenforceable. But what if the restraint is part of an agreement that includes other provisions that, standing alone, are perfectly valid? Early cases, reflecting the judicial antipathy toward limits on the board, applied a strict rule against severability, and the whole agreement stood or fell with the provisions restraining directorial discretion.

Reflecting the trend toward greater contracting freedom, modern courts often sever or rewrite troublesome provisions. *Triggs v. Triggs*, 385 N.E.2d 1254 (N.Y. 1978) (refusing to invalidate stock purchase provisions contained in an agreement among less than all shareholders that contained illegal provisions—which the corporation had largely ignored—limiting board discretion); *Galler v. Galler*, 203 N.E.2d 577 (Ill. 1964) (saving an agreement without an express term of duration by inferring that the agreement would operate only as long as one of the parties was living).

Courts have also specifically enforced contractual restraints on directorial discretion. Many of the same arguments supporting specific enforcement of pooling agreements apply since control expectations generally are vindicated by money damages. Some courts have even specifically enforced employment contracts in close corporations. See *Collins v. Collins Fruit Co.*, 189 So. 2d 262 (Fla. App. 1966). At the same time, courts have held parties to the terms of their agreements, including when poorly drafted provisions permitted the majority to amend (and undo) unanimity requirements. See *Blount v. Taft*, 246 S.E.2d 763 (N.C. 1978) (upholding majority-approved amendment of bylaw establishing minority veto, since bylaws explicitly permitted amendment by majority vote).

§26.5 CLOSE CORPORATION STATUTES

Some states, rather than trying to fit "round-shaped" close corporations into the "square" public corporation hole, have adopted special "comprehensive" close corporation statutes. These statutes recognize the special control needs of "incorporated partnerships" and create a special statutory regime for corporations that opt in. Cal. Corp. §§158, 300-303; Del. GCL §§341-355. The MBCA's provisions on shareholder agreements follow the lead of these statutes.

Compare Delaware's close corporation statute to the MBCA:

Opting In	
Delaware. A close corporation is one that has fewer than 30 shareholders of record, whose stock is subject to transfer restrictions, and that has not publicly issued any stock. Del. GCL §342. To elect close corporation status, the articles must originally state (or be amended to state) that the corporation is a close corporation. Del. GCL §§341, 342, 343. In Delaware, an amendment opting into close corporation status requires a two-thirds majority vote. Del. GCL §344.	**MBCA.** There is no "close corporation" category and opt-in is not necessary. Nonetheless, any shareholder agreement modifying the control structure must be conspicuously noted on share certificates, much as transfer restrictions. See MBCA §7.32(c). In addition, to ensure validity, this shareholder agreement must be approved by all shareholders. MBCA §7.32(b).

Getting Out	
Delaware. An amendment to the articles voluntarily terminates close corporation status; it must be approved by a two-thirds majority vote. Del. GCL §346. Close corporation status terminates when the corporation files the charter amendment or if any condition of close corporation status is breached. Del. GCL §345.	**MBCA.** All shareholders must agree to any amendment to the shareholder agreement. MBCA §7.32(b)(2). Further, the agreement ends automatically after ten years, unless the parties agreed otherwise, or if the corporation's shares are traded in a national stock market. MBCA §7.32(b) (2), (d).
Agreements Restraining Directors' Discretion	
Delaware. Shareholders holding a majority of voting shares can enter into written agreements that "restrict or interfere with the discretion or powers of the board of directors." Del. GCL §350. In addition, the certificate of incorporation can provide that the business will be managed by the shareholders rather than by a board of directors. Del. GCL §351.	**MBCA.** The statute provides a comprehensive list of the kinds of provisions permitted to shareholder agreements, but requires that all the shareholders approve the agreement. MBCA §7.32(a), (b).
Resolving Deadlocks	
Delaware. If the shareholders manage the business and become deadlocked, or if they have the right under the articles to dissolve the corporation, a shareholder may petition the court for the appointment of a custodian—a court-appointed manager. Del. GCL §352. The court also may appoint a provisional director—who is neither a shareholder nor creditor of the corporation—if the corporation is deadlocked. Del. GCL §353.	**MBCA.** Shareholders are left to their regular statutory deadlock remedies. See §27.3.2.
Opting In Shareholder Responsibility	
Delaware. If the shareholders take over management functions as the statute allows, they assume the duties (including fiduciary duties) of directors. Del. GCL §357(2), (3); *Graczykiowski v. Ramppen*, 477 N.Y.S.2d 454 (App. Div. 1984) (applying Delaware's close corporation statute to challenge of asset transfer by a managing shareholder).	**MBCA.** Those vested with management responsibilities are liable for "acts or omissions imposed by law on directors." MBCA §7.32(e).

Examples

1. How should Pizza Chateau, originally incorporated in an MBCA jurisdiction, reincorporate as a close corporation in Delaware?

2. Pizza Chateau has three shareholders: Rich has 500 common shares, Bob has 250, and Sal has 250. Rich and Bob agree that each will vote to assure that each is elected as director and, as directors, they will appoint Bob as general manager at a guaranteed annual salary of $30,000. The agreement has no term.
   a. Is the agreement valid under traditional case law?
   b. Is it valid under the MBCA?
   c. Is it valid under Delaware's close corporation statute?

3. All three shareholders enter into a new agreement. They agree to elect themselves to the board and, as directors, to appoint Bob as general manager so long as he "faithfully performs his duties." In addition, Bob will receive an annual salary of $30,000, and annual bonuses equal to 50 percent of profits.
   a. Is this agreement valid under the common law?
   b. Is it valid under the MBCA?
   c. Is it valid under Delaware's close corporation provisions?

4. Bob worries about the enforceability of the agreement's employment provisions. He proposes a long-term employment contract with the corporation on the same terms as the shareholder agreement.
   a. Would this employment contract be valid under the MBCA?
   b. Pizza Chateau hires a nonshareholder, Sam, to manage the business with the same salary and bonus arrangement and subject to the same "faithful performance" provision as applied to Bob. Is this contract valid?

5. The three shareholders want to do as they please. They revise the articles to do away with the board and set up a partnership-type governance structure in which each shareholder can veto any fundamental business changes.
   a. Is the arrangement enforceable under the MBCA?
   b. Pizza Chateau reincorporates in Delaware, but the new articles inadvertently do not choose close corporation status. Bob plans to lease a new store, and Rich vetoes his action as the articles permit. Is the veto provision enforceable?
   c. After a couple years, Sal and Rich are chagrined at how often Bob uses his veto. They vote to amend the articles and delete the veto provision. Can they?

Explanations

1. There are two common techniques for reincorporation: merger and sale/dissolution.
   - In a merger, the parties form a new Delaware close corporation and merge the existing corporation into it (see §35.2). On merger, the corporate assets and liabilities automatically pass to the new Delaware close corporation, and the original shares are converted into shares of the new Delaware corporation. The MBCA permits the merger if approved by a majority of the board and of the shares. See §36.2.2.
   - In a sale/dissolution, the parties form a new Delaware close corporation and transfer the existing corporation's assets and liabilities by agreement (see §34.2). The original corporation, which receives as consideration shares of the new Delaware close corporation, then dissolves and distributes the Delaware corporation shares to its shareholders. The MBCA permits the sale and dissolution if approved by a majority of the board and of the shares. See §§35.2.2, 36.3.2.

2. a. Probably not. There are two aspects to this agreement. The first, the agreement among shareholders to elect an agreed-upon slate to the board, is a perfectly valid vote-pooling agreement standing alone. It affects *who* will be on the board, but not *what* the board must decide.

   The other, the agreement among directors to appoint Bob as general manager at a specified salary, is of dubious validity even under modern common-law rules. The agreement among less than all shareholders governs the discretion of Rich and Bob as directors, binding them to place management in Bob's compensated hands. Who's hurt? Nonparty Sal and creditors may be hurt since the board would be powerless to do anything if Bob turns out to be a lousy manager. There are no limits on Bob's discretion or on whether the board can act if he becomes incompetent or faithless—the board is "sterilized."

   b. Probably not. Although the vote-pooling agreement is valid, see MBCA §7.31, the management agreement may not be. The MBCA safe harbor for special management arrangements requires agreement among *all* current shareholders. See MBCA §7.32(b). Although this defect does not render the agreement invalid, the agreement becomes subject to the common-law rules on management agreements. As discussed above, the agreement has a number of faults. Nonetheless, if Sal were aware of the agreement before she invested and there is no showing of harm to creditors, modern courts may be reluctant to invalidate the agreement.

   c. Probably yes. If the corporation opted in to close corporation status, the shareholders who hold a majority of the shares can agree in writing to take action that "restricts or interferes with the discretion or powers of the board." Del. GCL §350. The agreement is valid "as between parties to the agreement," suggesting that Sal could seek to invalidate it—if it adversely affected her interests.

3. a. It's now a close question. The vote-pooling agreement is perfectly valid. The management agreement has a number of merits: (1) all shareholders of the close corporation are parties, thus avoiding the problem of injury to nonparty shareholders; (2) the condition requiring Bob's "faithful performance" gives the board some flexibility to deal with Bob's bad management; and (3) the deviation could be characterized as "slight" because the board structure remains and management discretion appears to relate only to a narrow range of issues—the board is not completely sterilized.

    But the management agreement has some demerits. There is no assurance that the salary and bonus specified in the agreement will continue to be appropriate under changing circumstances. The board, for example, might at some future time be compelled to abide by the agreement despite outstanding creditor claims or future plans for growth that should get first priority. Cf. *Galler v. Galler* (§26.4.2). In addition, the agreement is indefinite, conceivably tying up the corporation beyond the parties' original expectations, although a court might read in an implied duration. Cf. *Galler v. Galler*. On balance, particularly in a jurisdiction with case law or statutory recognition of close corporation flexibility, the agreement probably would be enforceable.

   b. Yes. The MBCA specifically permits an agreement among all shareholders that "restricts the discretion . . . of the board," "governs the . . . making of distributions," "establishes the terms . . . of any agreement for . . . services," or "transfers to one or more shareholders . . . authority . . . to manage the business." MBCA §7.32(a). The agreement must be "made known" to the corporation and conspicuously noted on share certificates.

    The agreement does not bind nonparties. See Official Comment, MBCA §7.32. Its validity as to creditors and other third parties may depend on making the salary and bonus contingent on the availability of funds. To the extent the board's hands are tied, those persons "in whom such discretion or powers are vested" assume the fiduciary responsibilities of directors. Presumably, Bob acquires fiduciary duties to moderate his compensation if it interferes with others' corporate claims.

   c. Yes. The shareholders of a statutory "close corporation" can "restrict . . . the discretion or powers of the board." Del. GCL §350. The agreement is valid "as between parties to the agreement."

    The shareholders assume fiduciary duties by usurping the board's management functions. Under a scheme broader than the MBCA,

Delaware's statute imposes "upon *the stockholders* who are parties to the agreement the liability for managerial acts or omissions which is imposed on directors." Del. GCL §350. The shareholders could be liable in a suit by a trustee in bankruptcy acting for the corporation on behalf of creditors.

4. a. Yes, if signed by all the shareholders. A long-term employment contract can raise the same problems as a shareholder agreement that restricts management discretion. Some courts have held that employment contracts of unusually long duration, such as lifetime contracts, are invalid as infringements on the board's discretion. Nonetheless, the MBCA permits arrangements that restrict board discretion if signed by all the shareholders. MBCA §7.32(a), (b).

   If the shareholders did not all sign, the MBCA suggests the agreement should be subject to judicial scrutiny since agreements described in §7.32 "can effect material organic changes in the corporation's operation and structure, and in the rights and obligations of shareholders." Official Comment to MBCA §7.32(b).

   b. Yes, if signed by all the shareholders. Long-term management contracts with third parties suffer the same problem as agreements among shareholders designating one as a manager, if not more so. Such an arrangement locks the board out of management, and the nonshareholder manager (who has no equity position in the corporation) may have less incentive than a shareholder manager to further its best interests. Courts have invalidated long-term management contracts that do not give the board any power of review even if for cause. *Sherman & Ellis, Inc. v. Indiana Mutual Casualty Co.*, 41 F.2d 588 (7th Cir. 1930); *Kennerson v. Burbank Amusement Co.*, 260 P.2d 823 (Cal. App. 1953).

   If all the shareholders signed the contract, it becomes a valid shareholder agreement under MBCA §7.32(a). If they did not all sign, the issue becomes whether the board retained sufficient supervisory authority. The "faithful performance" provision and an implied term, such as periodic review every five years, would suggest the contract's validity.

5. a. Yes. All three approved the change to the articles, which the MBCA authorizes as an agreement that "governs the exercise of the corporate powers or the management of the business." MBCA §7.32(a)(8).

   b. Perhaps. The articles' failure to elect close corporation status is not necessarily fatal to the veto provision's enforceability *as against Bob*. Requiring election in the articles provides notice to all interested parties (shareholders and creditors) of the possibility of special management arrangements. Although Rich's veto rights cannot undermine the third-party lessor's expectations, Bob is bound by them. The statute's publicity requirement was not meant to protect Bob, and he should not be able to hide behind his own failure to properly elect close corporation status.

A similar issue arose in *Zion v. Kurtz*, 405 N.E.2d 681 (N.Y. 1980). There the New York Court of Appeals in a 4-3 decision enforced a shareholders' agreement in a Delaware corporation that gave both shareholders veto power over any new business, even though the corporation had not elected close corporation status under Delaware law. The agreement could be read to have required this, and the court enforced the veto provision against the party who had failed to effectuate the election. The dissenters argued that the veto provision was unenforceable because it restrained board discretion without public notice in the articles, as required by the statute.

c. Yes, unless the articles had a supermajority voting requirement. Special management arrangements, like any other contract, are subject to amendment according to the amendment provisions of the contract. See *Blount v. Taft*, 246 S.E.2d 763 (N.C. 1978) (upholding majority-approved amendment to bylaws that eliminated power of minority to veto employment nepotism, even though veto had been agreed to unanimously, since bylaw permitted amendment by board majority). In our example, the amendment rules are supplied by the corporate statute, which permits majority-approved changes unless the parties specified otherwise. See Del. GCL §242 (see §35.1.2). To prevent circumvention, the articles should have specified a supermajority voting requirement for any amendment to the veto provision. Corporate planners must think strategically!

Dispute Resolution in Close Corporations

The close corporation is a breeding ground for internal squabbles. Without a market into which to sell their interests, minority shareholders are at the mercy of the majority. This chapter discusses how close corporation disputes arise (§27.1), how corporate law protects minority shareholders and creates liquidity rights (§27.2), and how corporate law resolves deadlocks in close corporations (§27.3).

§27.1 CLOSE CORPORATION DISPUTES

§27.1.1 Freezeouts and Forceouts

Majority owners can abuse their control in two ways. They can consolidate control openly—a *forceout*. Or they can engage in a strategy of attrition—a *freezeout*. Together these strategies are sometimes referred to generically as *squeezeouts*.

- **Forceouts** are bolder. The majority can manipulate the fundamental structure of the corporation and forcibly eliminate minority interests. For example, the majority can have the corporation sell its assets to (or merge with) another corporation controlled by the majority. Or the majority can recapitalize the corporation and amend the articles to eliminate minority shares. See §35.1.

- **Freezeouts,** as we use the term, isolate minority shareholders from corporate participation, forcing the minority to sell to (or buy from) the majority on unfavorable terms. To work this coercion, the majority can remove minority participants from office, deny them compensation, impose a no-dividend policy, and exclude them from new stock issues or stock redemptions.

§ 27.1.2 Squeeze-Out Dilemma

Squeezeouts expose the close corporation dilemma—namely, how should corporate law treat a "partnership" in corporate clothing. The partnership principles of liquidity and coequality run smack into the close corporation reality of non-liquidity and the legal rules of perpetual existence and majority control.

The traditional corporate model gives the majority discretion to elect directors. In turn, the board appoints officers, sets salaries, declares dividends, repurchases shares, and proposes fundamental changes. Shareholders can freely sell their shares to other investors, but the corporation has no obligation to buy them. Although majority control and perpetual existence may be efficient in a public corporation, they frustrate expectations in a close corporation. Minority shareholders often count on the close corporation for their livelihood, and they usually have nobody to whom to sell their shares.

§27.1.3 Minority Shareholder's Options

Imagine a close corporation with three equal shareholders. What if two join together to remove the third from office, stop her salary, discontinue paying dividends, and refuse to redeem her shares? What can she do?

Market Out

In a close corporation, by definition, the option to sell into a liquid trading market is unavailable. Any purchaser of close corporation shares would not only have to incur costs to value the investment, but would be in the same exploitable position as the seller. For public shareholders the stock trading markets perform the pricing and liquidity functions, and the threat of public shareholders joining together in a takeover or proxy fight disciplines management.

Usually, the only viable "market" for minority shareholders in a close corporation is fellow shareholders of the corporation. But a minority shareholder cannot force the majority (or the corporation) to repurchase her shares at a fair price. Corporate law does not create liquidity rights for shareholders unless they enter into a contractual buyout arrangement (see §26.3.2) or unless a state statute provides a special buyout right. (The shareholder should have planned.)

Dissolution

If the minority shareholder were a partner in a partnership, she could withdraw from the partnership. RUPA §601 (disassociation occurs upon "notice of partner's express will to withdraw"); UPA §31 (partnership dissolution occurs upon "express will of any partner"). If her withdrawal were not wrongful, she would be entitled to liquidation of the business and payment in cash of her proportional share. RUPA §§801, 807 (at-will partnership wound up and any surplus paid in cash to partners pro rata); UPA §38(1) (same). Even if her withdrawal were wrongful, she would receive payment for her share, less any damages her dissolution caused. See RUPA §701 (including "going concern" value); UPA §38 (without goodwill).

In a corporation, a minority shareholder cannot dissolve the corporation. This requires a board proposal and majority shareholder approval. See MBCA §14.02 (for description of dissolution process, see §35.2). Only if the minority shareholder obtained dissolution rights in a shareholders' agreement can she liquidate her investment using this route.

Involuntary Dissolution

Modern corporate statutes provide a minority shareholder one other option—involuntary dissolution. The minority shareholder can ask a court to dissolve the corporation, and she would receive a final distribution after the corporation's assets are liquidated and its affairs wound up. A court in its discretion may order involuntary dissolution if the shareholder shows one of the statutory grounds:

- *Board deadlock.* Management is deadlocked—that is, the directors cannot agree and the shareholders have been unable to break the impasse on the board—and the corporation's business is suffering as a result. See MBCA §14.30(2)(i); Cal. Corp. §1800(b)(2); N.Y. BCL §1104.
- *Shareholder deadlock.* The shareholders are deadlocked—that is, the shareholders have been unable to elect new directors for a specified period, such as two consecutive annual meetings. MBCA §14.30 (2)(iii); Cal. Corp. §1800(b)(3); N.Y. BCL §1104.
- *Misconduct.* The majority group has engaged in misconduct. The statutes express this in various ways:

(1) Those in control have acted in a way that is "illegal, oppressive, or fraudulent." See MBCA §14.30(2)(ii).
(2) The corporate assets are being "misapplied or wasted." See MBCA §14.30(2)(iv); Cal. Corp. §1800(b)(4); N.Y. BCL §1104-a.
(3) Dissolution is "reasonably necessary for the protection" of the complaining shareholder. See Cal. Corp. §1800(b)(5); N.C. GS §55-14-30.

In a minority of states, deadlock is the exclusive ground for involuntary dissolution. In some states, nondeadlock grounds are available only in close corporations. See N.Y. BCL §1104-a.

Note on Involuntary Dissolution in LLC

Many LLC statutes also permit members of an LLC to petition a court for involuntary dissolution of the LLC. See ULLCA §801(4) (permitting application for judicial decree when, among other things, controlling members are acting in manner that is "illegal, oppressive, fraudulent, or unfairly prejudicial"). In Delaware, though, in recognition of the contractual freedom available in an LLC, the LLC members can contractually waive their right to petition for judicial dissolution. See *R&R Capital, LLC v. Buck & Doe Run Valley Farms, LLC*, 2008 WL 3846318 (Del. Ch. 2008).

Fiduciary Challenge

The minority shareholder can also challenge the majority's use of control as a breach of fiduciary duty. Over the last three decades, courts have become more sympathetic to the plight of minority shareholders in close corporations. Recognizing the "incorporated partnership" nature of close corporations and the absence of a market out, some courts have inferred heightened fiduciary duties in the close corporation.

§27.2 JUDICIAL PROTECTION OF MINORITY SHAREHOLDERS

Judicial protection for the minority against majority abuse comes in two related forms: involuntary dissolution and fiduciary review.

§27.2.1 Involuntary Dissolution

Effect

Before considering this important option, we should define some terms.

- **Dissolution** is the formal extinguishment of the corporation's legal life.
- **Liquidation** is the process of reducing the corporation's assets to cash or liquid assets, after which the corporation becomes a liquid shell.
- **Winding up** is the process of liquidating the assets, paying off creditors, and distributing what remains to shareholders. See §35.2.3.

Courts once viewed involuntary dissolution as a drastic remedy. In fact, the Official Comment to MBCA §14.30 advises courts to be "cautious" in granting dissolution in nondeadlock situations and to distinguish between "genuine abuse" and "acceptable tactics in a power struggle." Nonetheless, the usual effect of dissolution on the corporation's business rarely is fatal. Most often a dissolution order acts as a powerful negotiating chip for the minority and forces the majority to buy out the minority (or make other accommodations) on terms favorable to the minority. If the majority fails to offer a fair price or make other concessions, it will lose significant "going concern" value if the corporation is actually liquidated. In other words, a dissolution order usually does not terminate the business, but simply advises the majority to be more accommodating in its negotiations with the minority.

"Oppression" Doctrine

Many recent cases have made involuntary dissolution easier by interpreting the "oppression" and "reasonably necessary for the protection" conditions of the statutes to refer to the *reasonable expectations* of shareholders in the corporation. For example, in *Matter of Kemp & Beatley, Inc.*, 473 N.E.2d 1173 (N.Y. 1984), the court ordered involuntary dissolution on behalf of minority shareholders who had been long-time employees. The court found oppressive the majority shareholders' decision to increase their own executive compensation, while discontinuing the long-standing practice of distributing earnings as dividends or extra compensation.

Other courts have referred to the parties' original (and sometimes evolving) understandings about salaries, bonuses, dividends, and employment, saying that consideration must be given to whether dissolution is a feasible means of protecting those expectations. *Meiselman v. Meiselman*, 307 S.E.2d 551 (N.C. 1983). In effect, courts have used the dissolution remedy to enforce unwritten agreements by close corporation participants who may have been ignorant of how to formalize their relationship. In this sense the oppression doctrine may be more protective than the contractual protections available in an LLC, where some oral understandings are not enforceable unless reduced to writing. See *Olson v. Halvorson*, 986 A.2d 1150 (Del. 2009) (statute of frauds applies to oral LLC agreements that cannot be performed in one year).

The doctrine of shareholder oppression protects the minority from the improper exercise of majority control. From which perspective is "oppression" measured—the conduct of the majority or the expectations of the minority? Some courts focus on whether the majority's actions have a legitimate business purpose (an echo of the business judgment rule), others on whether the majority's actions (whether justified or not) harm the interests of the minority. See Doug Moll, *Shareholder Oppression in Close Corporations: The Unanswered Question of Perspective*, 53 Vand. L. Rev. 749 (2000) (arguing that close corporation shareholders would likely bargain for a "minority perspective" that protects investment expectations of the minority, even at the expense of justifiable majority prerogatives).

Remedies for Oppression

Statistical evidence bears out the emerging judicial recognition of implicit dissolution rights in close corporations. Three studies of involuntary dissolution cases from 1960–1976, 1984–1985, and 1990–2000 show that the number of involuntary dissolution cases has increased in the last two decades and that courts are more willing to order relief, including buyout remedies:

	1960–1976	**1984–1985**	**1990–2000**
No relief	27 (50.0%)	4 (10.8%)	55 (36.9%)
Dissolution order	16 (29.6%)	10 (27.0%)	42 (28.2%)
Buyout order	3 (5.6%)	20 (54.1%)	42 (28.2%)
Other relief	8 (14.8%)	3 (8.1%)	10 (6.7%)
Total	54 (100%)	37 (100%)	149 (100%)
	3.4 cases/year	18.5 cases/year	13.5 cases/year

In recognition of the buyout remedy, the MBCA permits majority shareholders in a close corporation to avoid dissolution by electing to buy out at "fair value" the shares of a shareholder who petitions for involuntary dissolution. MBCA §14.34 (revised in 1991); Official Comment (provision gives majority a "call" option on minority's shares to prevent strategic abuse of dissolution procedure). Purchasing shareholders must give notice to the court within 90 days of the petition and then negotiate with the petitioning shareholder. If after 60 days the negotiations fail, the court may award the petitioner "fair value." If the petitioner had "probable grounds" for relief under the misconduct provisions of the involuntary dissolution statute, the award may include the petitioner's litigation costs (attorney and expert fees).

Valuation of Minority Shares

A significant issue in a buyout is the proper value for the minority shares to be bought. Normally, valuation involves determining the price that a willing buyer would pay a willing seller for the interest, assuming both parties are informed and neither party is under any compulsion to transact—the "fair market value." Under this approach, shares would be valued in three steps. First, a value is determined for a 100 percent interest in the company's business—looking at *asset value* (calculating the liquidation value of the business), *market value* (using information on the sale of similar businesses to estimate how much the whole business could fetch), or *income value* (such as by estimating the company's future net cash flows and discounting them to present value). See §37.2.2 (description of valuation methods in appraisal). Then the minority's proportional interest is calculated. Second, the minority shares are discounted to reflect their lack of control. That is, an outsider will pay more for shares that carry control (a "control premium") and proportionately less for shares that do not carry control. Third, the minority shares are further discounted to reflect their lack of liquidity. An investment is worth more if it can be readily resold, and less if it is illiquid.

But in a close corporation minority shares are, by nature, not traded or priced in any market. For this reason, most corporate statutes specify that the buyout should be calculated at "fair value." Most courts have decided that control and marketability discounts are not appropriate in valuing minority shares. In a buyout these discounts would force a minority shareholder to accept less for his shares than they are worth in the hands of the majority. To many this seems unfair, if not an invitation for majority opportunism. Generally, courts in close corporation cases look to the *undiscounted full value* of the selling shareholders' proportionate interest in the going business.

§27.2.2 Fiduciary Protection

In those states that do not have an "oppression" statute, minority shareholders have sought protection from majority opportunism under fiduciary principles. Reliance on fiduciary duties is also appropriate when the minority does not necessarily wants liquidity, but instead want such emoluments as employment or financial distributions from the corporation.

Business Purpose Rule

The fiduciary rules borrowed from public corporations offer frozen-out minority shareholders in close corporations little solace. Applying the traditional business judgment rule (see §21.2), courts have imposed the burden on the minority to show the majority's actions were motivated by fraud, pique, or self-interest—that is, "bad faith." Under this approach the majority is protected if it can advance some rational *business purpose* for the actions, thus negating a finding of bad faith. The focus is on the corporation's interests and not the parties' relationship.

Some courts have used the "business purpose" approach to deny relief to minority shareholders who challenged freezeouts, such as termination of employment or nonpayment of dividends. *Gottfried v. Gottfried*, 73 N.Y.S.2d 692 (App. Div. 1947) (no breach even though majority shareholder had said minority "would never get any dividends because the majority could freeze them out"); *Zidell v. Zidell*, 560 P.2d 1086 (Or. 1977) (no breach even though corporation had sufficient capital to pay dividends). If the majority can point to business justifications for its actions, such as expansion plans or personal incompatibility, these courts apply the business judgment rule and refuse to interfere.

Equal Opportunity Rule

The business purpose approach stands in marked contrast to the approach in a partnership where partners share in management and profits and owe each other duties of "utmost good faith and loyalty." *Meinhard v. Salmon*, 164 N.E. 545 (N.Y. 1928) (business opportunity case involving co-venturers). Absent a contrary agreement, partners are coagents of each other, have equal management rights, are entitled to an accounting of profits, and cannot be removed without payment of their partnership interest. See UPA §§9, 18, 22, 38; RUPA §§301, 401, 405, 701. The business justifications propounded by majority partners are irrelevant.

Some courts, recognizing the illiquidity problems for minority shareholders, have implied partnership-type fiduciary duties in close corporations. These courts (principally in Massachusetts) have fashioned a *direct* cause of action for minority shareholders, abandoning the thesis that corporate fiduciaries owe their duties to the corporation. Minority shareholders can sue (and recover from) controlling shareholders directly, without being subject to the usual impediments of a derivative suit. See §18.3.

A series of cases reflects this approach and identifies some of its doctrinal limitations:

- ***Donahue v. Rodd Electrotype Co.***, 328 N.E.2d 505 (Mass. 1975): The court stated close corporation shareholders, like partners in a partnership, have duties of "utmost good faith and loyalty." Concluding the majority must provide the minority an "equal opportunity" to participate in corporate benefits, the court compelled the majority to provide the minority plaintiffs an opportunity to redeem their stock on the same terms that had been made available to a controlling shareholder. As a remedy, the court allowed the plaintiffs to choose between rescinding the challenged redemption or participating on the same terms.

- **Wilkes v. Springside Nursing Home, Inc.,** 353 N.E.2d 657 (Mass. 1976): Soon after *Donahue* the Massachusetts court retreated from its broad equal-opportunity rule. The court concluded that in certain "legitimate spheres," such as employment matters, declaring dividends, mergers, and dismissing directors, the majority has discretion to manage the business, even at the expense of the minority. The court fashioned a balancing test. If the majority shows a "legitimate business purpose" for its action and the minority shows the objective could have been accomplished in a way less harmful to the minority's interest, then the court must balance the legitimate objective against the practicality of the alternative. In *Wilkes* the controlling shareholders were unable to justify taking the minority plaintiff off the payroll, and the court never reached the balancing test. The court remanded on the issue of the amount of lost wages.
- **Smith v. Atlantic Properties, Inc.,** 422 N.E.2d 798 (Mass. App. 1981): Close corporation opportunism can be a two-way street. A minority shareholder has fiduciary duties to exercise his management rights in good faith. The court held a 25 percent shareholder liable for unreasonably vetoing the payment of dividends, which resulted in the majority incurring tax penalties.
- **Merola v. Exergen Corp.,** 668 N.E.2d 351 (Mass. 1996): Just being a shareholder in a close corporation does not guarantee employment. When an at-will employee who purchased stock in the corporation was fired and sought to get his job back, the court held that stock ownerships does not entitle shareholders to continued employment.
- **Brodie v. Jordan,** 857 N.E.2d 1076 (Mass. 2006): The remedy in a corporate "freezeout" must match the reasonable expectations that have been frustrated. Thus, when a minority shareholder was removed from his position and the majority discontinued payment of salary or dividends, the court decided a buyout order was inappropriate. Instead, the remedy should have matched the harm—such as compelling the payment of dividends.

The "equal opportunity" rule is at odds with the premise that equity investments in the corporation are permanent and are not subject to easy withdrawal, as in a partnership. That is, parties often choose the corporate form because it assures the stability of corporate resources and operations. Shareholders can withdraw their investment only by selling to another investor; at-will employees can be fired, even though they also own shares. Based on this, some recent courts have refused to infer partnership-type duties in close corporations on the theory the parties could have contracted for them and, absent an agreement, corporate principles apply. See *Nixon v. Blackwell*, 626 A.2d 1366 (Del. 1993) (refusing to require company to repurchase stock held by nonemployee-shareholders, even though company had repurchased stock of employee-shareholders under employee stock ownership plan and key-man insurance policy).

EXAMPLES

Examples

1. Junior, Robert, and Clifton are in the oil business. Each owns 1,000 shares in Lambing Oil, an MBCA corporation. Since its incorporation 15 seasons ago, the three brothers have run the company on the understanding each would share equally in every aspect of the business. Although they never reduced their understanding to writing, each brother has sat on the board, drew the same salary, and vetoed any action with which he disagreed.
   a. One day Clifton wants out of the business. Can he withdraw and have the corporation dissolved?
   b. Clifton begins to veto all corporate action. He then claims that the board is deadlocked. Will a court order dissolution?

2. Things turn mean. At the next directors' meeting, Junior and Robert remove Clifton as officer and terminate his salary. They say Clifton is a liability because he has never been a cutthroat businessperson.
   a. Have the controlling shareholders breached a fiduciary duty under traditional fiduciary review? under a *Wilkes* test?
   b. If Junior and Robert breached a fiduciary duty, can the court order them to repurchase Clifton's shares?
   c. Is Clifton entitled to involuntary dissolution?

3. Things turn meaner. Robert and Junior issue to themselves 1,000 new shares at $2,000 per share, equal to an outside offer they had received (and turned down) to purchase one year before. Robert and Junior make the same offer to Clifton, who they know does not have $500,000—the purchase price. They know Clifton, with his poor credit, cannot borrow the money, either. After the issuance, Robert and Junior each become 40 percent shareholders, and Clifton 20 percent.
   a. Can Clifton challenge the new issue under a traditional fiduciary test?
   b. Can Clifton challenge the new issue under a *Donahue* approach?

EXPLANATIONS

Explanations

1. a. Probably not. Absent majority "bad faith" or a dissolution agreement, a minority shareholder has dissolution rights only through a petition to the court for involuntary dissolution. Under the MBCA Clifton would have to show board or shareholder deadlock, or misconduct by Junior and Robert. MBCA §14.30(2). There is no evidence of either. Even if a court were to interpret "oppression" as including frustration of reasonable expectations, there is no evidence that the parties expected they would be obligated to purchase the others' shares.

Clifton might argue that the parties' implicit understanding that he could deadlock the corporation entitles him to dissolution rights. But this argument may go beyond the MBCA, which favors an ongoing business and discourages easy dissolution.

b. Probably not. Clifton must show two things: (1) He has the power to deadlock the corporation; and (2) he did not violate his fiduciary duties by deadlocking it. It is unclear that Clifton has a veto power as the shareholders' agreement was never reduced to writing and signed by all the shareholders. Cf. MBCA §7.32(b). Even if a court finds that Clifton had "reasonable expectations" in a veto power, it is unclear that the majority's frustration of these expectations would amount to a fiduciary breach or "oppression." Minority shareholders have fiduciary duties not to abuse their control rights. See *Smith v. Atlantic Properties, Inc.*, 422 N.E.2d 798 (Mass. App. 1981) (see §27.2.2). Clifton's self-interested use of his veto undermines his arguments of majority overreaching.

   In a public corporation, Clifton's threat might have been perfectly acceptable—public shareholders are said to have the right to do with their shares and vote them as they please. But close corporation shareholders, both majority and minority, lack a market for their shares and have expectations that the other shareholders will not interfere with mutual advantage.

2. a. Not under the traditional business judgment rule; perhaps under *Wilkes* test. Junior and Robert seem to have legitimate business purposes for their freezeout, undercutting Clifton's claim of "bad faith." So long as they have some support for their doubts about Clifton's services, a court applying traditional fiduciary principles will not interfere in the majority's handling of business.

   The *Wilkes* approach—which refines (and narrows) the partnership-type approach of *Donahue*—balances the majority's expectations of control and the minority's expectations of equal treatment. See §27.2.2. Robert and Junior have the burden to show a business purpose for their action, such as pointing to particular business problems created by Clifton's lack of expertise. If the court finds the explanation credible and legitimate, Clifton must then show they could have accomplished their objective some other way—for example, by teaching Clifton the oil business and how to be cutthroat. The court would then balance the business purpose against the practicality of the alternative. The alternatives may not be practicable, and Clifton might be out of a job and salary under a *Wilkes* test.

b. Perhaps. Typically, the remedy for a self-dealing breach is rescission. Clifton would be restored to his position, with damages for back pay. But, in this case, rescission would only perpetuate the parties' animosity and invite further lawsuits or freezeout attempts. Forced redemption would disentangle the parties. Increasingly, courts take an activist role in adjusting the relationships of parties in close corporations.

c. Probably yes. A petition for involuntary dissolution on the ground of "oppression" is much like a *Wilkes* fiduciary challenge, except that the statutory remedy is dissolution—in effect, a forced buyout. If "oppression" turns on the minority's reasonable expectations, Clifton could point to the Lambing Oil history of coequal sharing and management to support his claim. From a "perspective" that seeks to vindicate the expectations of the minority, the majority's justifications for its actions would not be relevant to interpreting the original (and evolving) understandings among the parties.

3. a. No. If the corporation's business has not appreciated significantly in value, the self-dealing issuance of new stock seems to fall within a range of reasonableness. If the majority can proffer some business justification for the issue—raising new capital—the transaction would survive traditional loyalty review. See §13.3.2.

b. Perhaps. The *Donahue* "equal opportunity" approach, which applies to the majority's stock transaction, provides minority shareholders equal liquidity rights. The court reserved the question whether it also provides, in effect, preemptive rights. Even if it did, the majority shareholders in this case appear to have provided the minority an equal purchase opportunity.

Nonetheless, under the higher "utmost good faith and loyalty" fiduciary standard *Donahue* creates in close corporations, the majority may have to proffer legitimate business purposes for the issuance. Under the *Wilkes* balancing test, the court will scrutinize the justification and consider the minority's suggestion of less harmful means. Unless there are particularly good reasons for an infusion of equity capital, the majority shareholders are not saved by having "offered" the same deal to Clifton, who they knew could not afford it.

§27.3 DEADLOCKS

Sometimes the minority has an equity interest or board position sufficient to bring the corporation's business to a grinding halt—to deadlock the corporation. By *deadlock*, we and the corporate statutes do not mean the benign and common situation when the parties are evenly divided and unable to agree on a particular issue. Instead, deadlock is a symptom of fundamental disagreement among shareholders or directors that paralyzes the corporation's business.

§27.3.1 Environment for Deadlocks

The planner must be aware of how deadlock can occur: an even number of directors on the board, a "neutral director" who resigns or dies, equal division of stock, or the alignment of the parties into two equally powerful camps. See MBCA §14.30(2)(i), (iii); Cal. Corp. §1800; N.Y. BCL §1104. The problem of deadlock raises two questions:

- How should deadlock be handled once it happens?
- How can it be avoided by good planning?

§27.3.2 Judicial Deadlock Remedies

If the parties did not anticipate deadlocks, recourse is to the courts. The courts have a number of options:

- **Court-appointed custodians and provisional directors.** Many close corporation statutes authorize courts to appoint custodians and provisional directors. These court-appointed mediators are to continue the business *indefinitely* for the benefit of all the shareholders, both majority and minority, until their differences are resolved. Cal. Corp. §1802; Del. GCL §§352, 353.
- **Court-appointed receivers.** Some statutes authorize courts to appoint receivers on an *interim basis* for a deadlocked corporation that faces imminent dissolution. Cal. Corp. §1803.
- **Court supervision.** The court can retain jurisdiction to protect minority shareholders or order preliminary injunctive relief (such as salary reductions or an accounting) if there are allegations of misappropriation or other oppressive conduct. Cal. Corp. §§1804, 1806.
- **Court-ordered involuntary dissolution.** The ultimate step is for court-mandated disentanglement through an order of involuntary dissolution. (See the earlier discussion of the requirements for granting involuntary dissolution; see §27.1.2.)
- **Other court-ordered relief.** The court can order damages, a forced buyout, or require payment of salaries or dividends. Cal. Corp. §§1804, 1806.

§27.3.3 Planning for Deadlocks

Planners can provide methods to deal with deadlocks once they occur. Some we have already seen; others are new.

- **Mediation.** The deadlocked parties choose a person acceptable to both of them to help resolve their disagreement. The mediator has no power to compel a resolution.
- **Arbitration.** The deadlocked parties agree, in a pre-dispute or post-dispute contract, to allow an arbitrator to resolve their dispute in a binding decision. An example of a pre-dispute arbitration agreement is found in the *Ringling Bros.* case (see §26.1.2). The Federal Arbitration Act requires enforcement of arbitration clauses in any agreement affecting interstate commerce, and lately courts have shown less jealousy of their jurisdiction and greater respect for private solutions to their crowded dockets.
- **Deadlock-breaking director or shareholder.** The parties can create a structural tie-breaker. An example of a deadlock-breaking director is found in the *Lehrman v. Cohen* case (see §26.2.2). Whether the parties create a special class of stock or simply transfer a few shares to a mutually acceptable person, the result is a built-in arbitrator.
- **Voluntary dissolution.** The parties can agree to dissolution rights. Many statutes specifically allow the enforcement of preexisting agreements to dissolve. See MBCA §7.32(a)(7). Although it might seem drastic, dissolution may be the best solution for a paralyzed corporation. As we have seen, in most instances the corporation need not be liquidated or its business wound up when the parties agree to dissolve. Because of the business's value as an ongoing concern, one camp usually will buy out the other camp since liquidation and winding up would destroy an important component of the business's value.
- **Statutory buyout.** A growing number of statutes mandate corporate repurchase at a fair price as a remedy for deadlock and dissension. MBCA §14.34 (only in close corporations); Cal. Corp. §1804 (broad remedial powers to avoid involuntary dissolution); N.Y. BCL §1118 (remedy to avoid involuntary dissolution available only in close corporations).

Private deadlock remedies—many of which function as control devices to take management discretion away from the board—raise the same issues we saw before with restraints on directors' discretion. See §26.4. The problem is illustrated by *Vogel v. Lewis*, 268 N.Y.S.2d 237 (App. Div. 1966), *aff'd*, 224 N.E.2d 738 (N.Y. 1967), where two 50 percent shareholders had agreed to arbitration "in event of a dispute, or difference, arising between them."

When a warehouse lease expired and they could not agree on renewing it (because one had a side agreement with the warehouse's owners), the other shareholder sought arbitration. A majority of the court ordered that arbitration proceed, rejecting the obvious restraint-of-board argument. The dissenters, however, thought the arbitration clause was too broad and that either party could use it coercively to "destroy the business" by insisting on arbitration at the drop of a hat.

Examples

1. It turns out that Robert, Junior, and Clifton were not the only siblings who inherited Lambing Oil Corporation. A woman named Pamela appears and claims to be their long-lost sister. A probate court accepts her claim and makes her a 25 percent shareholder. With ownership divided equally among the four, Robert and Junior begin to worry that Pamela may join forces with Clifton and deadlock the business.
   a. How might deadlock occur?
   b. The Lambing Oil board has three directors—Robert, Junior, and Clifton. Can Robert and Junior prevent deadlock?

2. Pamela demands a seat on the board. Robert and Junior want to accommodate. But they also suggest the four decide on something to prevent deadlocks.
   a. Clifton suggests a shareholders' agreement under which each shareholder will vote his shares to assure that all four are elected to the board. Does this do the job?
   b. Clifton suggests a voting trust. The trustee will be Clay, the shareholders' stepfather. Does this do the job?
   c. Clifton persists and suggests a shareholders' agreement under which each party will be on the board. In case of a board deadlock, each shareholder will give Clay an irrevocable proxy to vote his or her shares. Clay can then elect a nondeadlocked board. Does this do the job?
   d. Clifton does not give up. He suggests that in case of a board deadlock, Clay will arbitrate any difference. He suggests a shareholders' agreement that would assure each shareholder a seat on the board and that allows for any director to "seek arbitration by Clay to resolve any dispute on the board." Does this do the job?
   e. Clifton is listening. He suggests the shareholders create five classes of stock, one for each shareholder. Each class will elect one director and receive approximately one-fourth of all corporate distributions. Clay will receive the fifth class of stock, which will elect the fifth director and receive 1/100 of all corporate distributions. Does this do the job?

Explanations

1. a. Deadlock can occur at either the shareholder or board level. At the shareholder level, if the Robert-Junior camp and the Clifton-Pamela camp are unable to agree, there will be no shareholder majority. The result will be that no shareholder action can be taken, and under a system of straight voting no directors can be elected.

   Board deadlock is not a necessary consequence of a 50-50 shareholder split. Deadlock among directors depends on the number of directors on the board and whether any directors have disproportionate voting (or veto) powers. If there were three directors—Robert, Junior, and Clifton—when Pamela acquired her 25 percent interest, there is little risk of board deadlock. Assuming that no special voting arrangements apply to the board, deadlock could occur only if one of the three directors were to resign or die and the remaining shareholders and directors were unable to fill the vacancy. Just because one director is always outvoted, or just because the board is occasionally unable to act, does not mean the board is deadlocked.

   b. Yes. They could prevent deadlock at the shareholder level by issuing new shares, assuming some are authorized. At the board level, there is little risk of board deadlock. Their presence and voting together at meetings assures that the board will not be deadlocked.

2. a. No. The shareholders' agreement avoids the risk of shareholder deadlock. If the shareholders abide by the agreement, they will always be able to elect directors. But a board with an even number of directors invites board deadlock.

   b. Not really. A voting trust eliminates the risk of both shareholder and board deadlock, but there is no assurance that the four shareholders will be represented on the board. Clay, for example, could decide to elect himself and the three brothers to the board, excluding Pamela.

   c. This seems no better than the voting trust. Each shareholder (or camp) risks that Clay will oust him or her from the board. Clay's authority extends beyond resolving the deadlocking issue or issues.

   In addition, the irrevocable proxy arrangement may not be valid (see §26.2.3). Some jurisdictions do not recognize the giving of an irrevocable proxy to a party who has no interest in the corporation or its shares. Cf. MBCA §7.22(d)(5) (valid in a shareholder agreement). Moreover, the granting of voting power to Clay has many of the attributes of a voting trust. If treated as a de facto voting trust, the arrangement must comply with the notice requirements and limits on duration to which voting trusts are statutorily subject.

   d. Clifton is getting warmer. If the management aspects of the agreement are valid, the agreement would help avoid deadlocks using a mechanism agreed to by the parties. The parties will be much more likely to go along with their "own" dispute resolution mechanism than one imposed by judicial fiat.

The validity of the agreement may depend on whether the relevant jurisdiction has a statute authorizing deviations from the traditional management model. See MBCA §7.32(a)(1) (authorizing agreement that "restricts the discretion . . . of the board"). Without statutory guidance, the agreement's validity is less than certain. By allowing Clay to arbitrate "any dispute" without any explicit limits on his authority, it is possible that even a modern court might hold that the mechanism violates public policy and sterilizes the board. As drafted, the mechanism runs a significant risk of abuse by contemplating arbitration whenever any director (perhaps when simply outvoted) considers there to be a dispute and wishes to have it arbitrated. Furthermore, there are no standards under which Clay is to conduct the arbitration, and there is little assurance that Clay's interests will be aligned with those of the corporation in general. He has no ownership interest, and this detachment is exacerbated since he will not necessarily be abreast of corporate developments when called on to arbitrate disputes.

e. Clifton seems to be there. The validity of the arrangement seems assured. See MBCA §6.01(c); *Lehrman v. Cohen* (see §26.2.2). This mechanism assures that Clay will be a permanent deadlock-breaking member of the board. As such, he will be abreast of corporate developments should disputes arise. Furthermore, by participating more than nominally in corporate distributions he will have an incentive to further the corporation's general interests in resolving those disputes. Perhaps the only problem with the arrangement is that it depends on Clay's continuing to be of sound mind and body. The parties should consider procedures for deciding on Clay's successor, should he die or become incapacitated. Without more, the parties might unwittingly make one of Clay's heirs (conceivably, one of themselves) the deadlock-breaker.

PART VII

Corporate Creditors

Rule of Limited Liability

Limited liability is a fundamental aspect of the corporation. It allows corporate participants to separate business assets from personal assets—leaving corporate creditors with recourse only against the assets of the corporation. It thus creates a nonrecourse relationship that externalizes the risk of business failure by moving it from insiders to outsiders.

Limited liability is not absolute, and corporate law gives corporate creditors a variety of protections against insider opportunism. Other chapters in this part describe these protections:

- liability of promoters during the incorporation process (Chapter 29)
- corporate liability based on the actions of corporate agents (Chapter 30)
- limitations on corporate distributions to shareholders (Chapter 31)
- protection of creditors under the judicial doctrine of "piercing the corporate veil," which disregards limited liability to impose personal liability on corporate shareholders and managers in special circumstances (Chapter 32)
- liability of corporate insiders under noncorporate regulatory schemes (Chapter 33)

This chapter explains limited liability (§28.1) and describes the history of corporate limited liability and its recent extension to other business organizations (§28.2).

§28.1 CORPORATE LIMITED LIABILITY

The modern corporation separates business assets from the personal assets of corporate participants. This means a corporate participant's liability for corporate obligations is limited to that person's investment in the corporation. By statute, a shareholder (equity investor) is not liable for corporate obligations beyond her investment. MBCA §6.22; Del. GCL §102(b)(6). The rule also applies to other corporate participants—such as lenders (debt investors), managers, and employees. In the normal course, none is liable for corporate obligations. Courts recognize limited liability even if it is the motivating reason for incorporation.

Limited liability is a default rule; it applies absent an agreement otherwise. Outsiders can demand that insiders assume contractual responsibility for corporate obligations. For example, bank lenders often require personal guarantees from shareholders before extending credit to closely held corporations. And suppliers sometimes insist on officers signing corporate contracts both in the corporate name and personally. But absent an assumption of personal liability, the rule is that corporate participants are not personally liable for corporate obligations. That is, outsiders are assumed to accept a *nonrecourse* relationship with corporate insiders.

Reasons for Limited Liability

Why the rule of limited liability? There are a number of explanations:

- **Capital formation.** The corporation, by limiting losses to the amount invested, allows investors to finance a business without risking their other assets. It reduces the need for investors to investigate and monitor whether the business will expose them to personal liability. Limited liability encourages investors to choose to invest in desirable, though risky, enterprises.
- **Management risk taking.** Without the promise of limited liability, shareholders might discourage and managers might be reluctant to undertake high-risk projects, even when the project promises net positive returns (expected gains exceed expected losses). Limited liability encourages desirable risk taking.
- **Investment diversification.** Limited liability permits investors to invest in many businesses—to diversify—without exposing their other assets to unlimited liability with each new investment. Diversification stimulates capital formation because it is often easier to raise capital through many small investments than from only a few large ones. Diversification spreads out investment risk, further reducing the need

for investors to investigate and monitor the business in which they invest. Limited liability thus reduces the costs of investing.

- **Trading on stock markets.** Stock markets are important for modern business. They make capital formation easier, reveal enterprise value through market prices, and provide a place to buy corporate control. How is limited liability related to stock trading? If limited liability did not exist, wealthy investors (with more to lose and more likely to be sued) would assign a lower value to identical securities than would poor investors (with less to lose and less likely to be sued). That is, the greater liability risk would reduce the securities' net value for the wealthy investors, but not poor investors. With limited liability, however, all corporate investors are shielded equally, and securities valuation does not depend on their individual willingness to risk other assets. That is, limited liability renders securities fungible regardless of who owns them and thus makes possible public stock trading.

Allocation of Risk

Why would those who voluntarily deal with the corporation, such as contract creditors, accept the rule that their only recourse is to the business assets? For voluntary creditors, such as lenders and trade creditors, the default rule of limited liability may well represent what these parties would have agreed to anyway. These outsiders (who extend credit to many businesses) generally are more diversified and better able to bear the risks of business failure. To reflect this risk, voluntary creditors often increase the cost of credit to incorporated businesses or demand contractual stipulations (such as debt limits or limits on distributions to insiders) to bolster the business's creditworthiness.

But remember that limited liability also allocates the risk of business failure to involuntary creditors—that is, outsiders who did not choose to become a creditor, such as tort creditors. Why should limited liability be the default rule for those who did not choose to bear the risk of the corporation's insolvency? For involuntary creditors, the case for limited liability is more tenuous. Many corporate creditors have no opportunity to demand higher returns to compensate for the risks they assume. Realistically, these creditors cannot protect themselves by negotiating contractual protections before dealing with the corporation. Are these outsiders better risk bearers than corporate insiders? Some commentators, who urge a dismantling of limited liability for involuntary creditors, say no. They point out that insiders, shielded by limited liability, do not internalize the costs of accidents or excessive risk taking. They assert insiders (acting for shareholders) are in a better position to have the corporation purchase insurance and avoid high-risk business strategies. See Hansmann & Kraakman, *Toward Unlimited Shareholder Liability for Corporate Torts*, 100 Yale L.J. 1879 (1991). Critics of this idea wonder whether a rule of pro rata vicarious liability in public corporations would be administrable or enforceable. Others imagine ways in which investors might avoid direct shareholder status, while still retaining a financial interest in the corporation's performance.

Despite this arguably inefficient and unfair allocation of risk, limited liability remains a centerpiece of the U.S. capitalist system that encourages entrepreneurialism and widespread public investment. That is, there appears to be a broad consensus that the benefits of limited liability outweigh its costs. In addition, there are also questions (particularly in public corporations) whether a scheme of shareholder liability would actually discourage untoward corporate risk taking. Without a clearly better alternative, limited liability remains the rule.

Choice of Law

Corporate limited liability, and its exceptions, are relatively uniform across U.S. jurisdictions. Nonetheless, the issue sometimes arises: What state law provides the rules that govern insiders' liability to outsiders? There is no clear consensus. Generally, courts assume that the rule of limited liability and statutory limitations on corporate distributions are internal affairs governed by the law of the state of incorporation. This logic has been extended to piercing cases, in which creditors seek to have the court disregard the rule of limited liability. See *Fletcher v. Atex*, 68 F.3d 1451 (2d Cir. 1995) (interpreting New York choice-of-law rule in case of parent-subsidiary piercing according to law of state of incorporation).

This approach, borrowed from the "internal affairs doctrine" for disputes among shareholders and managers (see §3.2.1), makes sense in contracts cases in which creditors dissatisfied with the incorporating state's default rules on limited liability can negotiate different terms. In tort cases, however, it can be argued that the state law with the most significant relationship to the parties and the occurrence should balance the policies of limited liability and tort compensation and deterrence. See *Yoder v. Honeywell, Inc.*, 104 F.3d 1215 (10th Cir. 1997) (interpreting New York choice-of-law rule in case of parent-subsidiary piercing under law of place of injury). Tort victims do not choose the corporation with which they deal, and the choice by shareholders and managers of a particular state of incorporation should not be binding on them.

§28.2 HISTORY OF LIMITED LIABILITY

Corporate limited liability is not inherent to the corporation. Originally, corporate law in the United States did not create limited liability for corporate shareholders. In the earliest U.S. corporations, shareholders were assumed to be liable for corporate obligations on the same basis as partners. But as shareholder investment became more widespread, judicial attitudes shifted and corporate statutes in the mid-1800s began to provide various limits on shareholder liability.

At first, the corporate form and limited liability were reserved for larger businesses that obtained special legislative charters. Limited liability encouraged investment by passive investors unwilling to bear the monitoring burden implicit in a full-liability partnership. But in early U.S. corporations limited liability was not always complete. Often shareholders remained liable for additional capital assessments (or calls) equal to a stated multiple of their original investment. For example, between the Civil War and the era of deposit insurance in the 1930s, bank shareholders were liable to pay up to the par value of their shares to satisfy outstanding claims if the bank failed. This regime of double liability assured bank depositors an additional capital cushion and led shareholders to insist that bank managers exercise prudent banking practices and quickly liquidate a troubled bank. Macey & Miller, *Double Liability of Bank Shareholders: History and Implications*, 27 Wake Forest L. Rev. 31 (1992) (finding that 50.8 percent of shareholder assessments ultimately were paid).

By the end of the nineteenth century, however, limited liability was the rule for nonfinancial companies incorporated under general incorporation statutes. Although California applied a rule of pro rata liability for shareholders during a period of dramatic state growth (from 1849 to 1931), complete limited liability for corporate shareholders was the norm for twentieth-century U.S. corporations. As a partial substitute for recourse against corporate shareholders, many corporate statutes imposed minimum capital requirements before a corporation could start business. But these minima were not significant ($500 to $1,000) and today have been abandoned.

Limited Liability Entities

Even more interesting has been the recent U.S. history of limited liability for noncorporate entities. As recently as the 1980s, U.S. business organizations fell into three categories:

- corporations for big businesses managed by professional executives and funded by public investors who enjoyed immunity from personal liability
- partnerships for small (often informal) businesses managed by partners who assumed personal liability for business obligations
- hybrid "incorporated partnerships" (such as closely held corporations and limited partnerships) that combined corporate-style limited liability and partnership-style management.

Limited liability was largely the province of the corporation. But in 1979 the Wyoming legislature approved a *limited liability company* statute. The LLC invention had been born of necessity. An oil and gas exploration venture, making plans to drill for oil in Wyoming, wanted an investment vehicle that combined (1) limited liability for venture participants, who included *active, foreign investors,* and (2) flow-through tax treatment. Neither a partnership nor a corporation worked. (Recall that a Subchapter S corporation cannot have non-U.S. investors—see §2.3.3.) The company had had earlier experience with projects organized as Panamanian "sociedades de responsabilidad limitada" (translated "companies of limited liability"), and its lawyers drafted a bill for the Wyoming legislature to accommodate the international investors. When in 1988 the IRS clarified that state LLC statutes following the Wyoming formula would be classified as flow-through partnerships, the LLC revolution exploded. Within eight years, every state offered an LLC choice.

Joining the LLC on the "alphabet soup" menu of state-offered business organizations has been a slew of other limited liability entities. Today, depending on the state, a business can be formed as a limited liability *partnership* (LLP), a limited liability *limited partnership* (LLLP), a limited *partnership association* (LPA), or a *professional* limited liability company (PLLP). In each case, the rights and duties of the participants (including their liability to outsiders) arise conceptually from their agreement. For some, this revolution has signaled the death of liability. See LoPucki, *The Death of Liability,* 106 Yale L.J. 1 (1996) (arguing that secured-debt and ownership structures have permitted businesses to avoid liability). Others have pointed out that today no well-structured business need risk exposing its participants to personal liability.

Nonetheless, limited liability is not complete. The limited liability statutes uniformly contain limitations on payments to owners, modeled on the corporate restrictions on dividends and other distributions to shareholders. See §31.2. Many statutes contemplate the possibility in appropriate cases that courts may "pierce the entity veil," a concept built on corporate law principles. See §32.1. And for entities intended for use by professionals—particularly, limited liability partnerships—many statutes retain rules of vicarious liability. For example, in Texas (the state that first enacted a limited liability partnership statute) partners are not liable for the firm's contractual or tort liability, unless a tort was committed by a person working under the "supervision or direction" of the partner and the partner (1) was directly involved in the wrongful activity or (2) knew of it and failed to prevent or cure it. Tex. Rev. Civ. Stat. Ann. art. 6132b §3.08. The statutes clarify, moreover, that the limited liability provisions do not affect the liability of a partner for his own misconduct.

As use of noncorporate limited liability entities has grown, courts have applied principles from agency and corporate law to determine the scope of limited liability. For example, LLC members are individually liable to third parties if they fail to disclose they are acting on behalf of an LLC. See *Water, Waste & Land v. Lanham*, 955 P.2d 997 (Colo. 1998) (citing "long-established" principles of agency and corporate law to find that initials on business card, without LLC designation, were insufficient to give notice to third party that he was dealing with LLC). And members of LLCs have been subject to piercing liability on the same basis as participants in a corporation. See *Kaycee Land & Livestock v. Flahive*, 46 P.3d 323 (Wy. 2002) (despite silence in LLC statute).

Liability during Incorporation Process

Incorporation creates a "no recourse" business structure, but does not make the business operational. For this to happen, capital must be obtained from investors and lenders; operating assets must be acquired; and contractual arrangements must be made with employees, suppliers, lessors, and customers. The people who perform these organizational functions earn the label "promoters," though they often continue to run the business after the initial set-up.

This chapter considers when corporate limited liability begins and the liability of promoters during the incorporation process. Promoters, unlike incorporators (see §3.1.2), have significant responsibilities in the formation of the business and can become liable to outside creditors for preincorporation contracts they sign before the business is incorporated (§29.1) and for contracts they sign in the corporate name for a corporation that was not properly incorporated (§29.2)

§29.1 PREINCORPORATION CONTRACTS

As we have seen, incorporation under modern corporation statutes is painless. Nonetheless, promoters sometimes enter into contractual arrangements for the to-be-incorporated business before the magic moment when the corporation comes into existence and, with it, limited liability for corporate actors. Who is liable on preincorporation contracts when both parties know there *is no corporation*—the promoter, the corporation once it is formed, neither of them, or both of them?

At the time of the transaction, the to-be-formed corporation does not yet exist and, under traditional contract and agency principles, cannot be a principal or a party to a contract. Some nineteenth-century cases, for example, held that under agency law a newly formed corporation could not ratify preincorporation contracts since no corporation existed when the contract was entered into. Although courts have abandoned this formalism, the question remains: who is liable?

Consider a well-known example. D. J. Geary bids to build a bridge for O'Rorke over the Allegheny River. Before Geary incorporates his Bridge Company to do the work, he signs a contract as follows: "D. J. Geary for a bridge company to be organized and incorporated." Since no corporation-principal exists, who is liable under the contract? The Restatement of Agency (Second), a source often used by modern courts, states that a purported agent acting for a nonexistent principal becomes a party to the contract—unless agreed otherwise. Parties can avoid this default rule by agreement, and Comment *b* to §326 describes some of the more common relationships Geary and O'Rorke might have agreed to:

- **Nonrecourse agent.** Geary is a mere messenger who carries O'Rorke's offer to Bridge Company. There is no contract unless Bridge Company is incorporated and adopts the contract. O'Rorke has no recourse against Geary even if for whatever reason Bridge Company never accepts the offer.
- **"Best efforts" agent.** Geary agrees to use his "best efforts" to bring Bridge Company into existence and have it accept O'Rorke's offer. There is no contract until Bridge Company is incorporated and it adopts the contract. Geary is liable only if he fails to use his best efforts to incorporate Bridge Company and have it accept the offer.
- **Interim contracting party.** Geary accepts liability to O'Rorke under the contract until Bridge Company is incorporated, adopts the contract, and is substituted in Geary's place. Upon such contractual substitution (novation), O'Rorke discharges Geary.
- **Additional contracting party.** Geary is liable under the contract, even if Bridge Company later adopts the contract. Under this arrangement, Geary is severally liable along with the corporation. His liability is "primary" if O'Rorke can look to him first, or "secondary" if O'Rorke must first exhaust recourse to Bridge Company.

Do promoters and third parties have the foresight to make clear which alternative they have chosen? Often no. See *O'Rorke v. Geary*, 56 A. 541 (Pa. 1903). Instead, courts must infer the parties' *intentions* from the circumstances.

Who becomes liable on a preincorporation contract? The following discussion looks at three permutations: (1) the third party sues the promoter; (2) the third party sues the newly formed corporation; and (3) the corporation or promoter sues the third party.

Note on LLC Pre-Organization Contracts

The liability of persons who contract on behalf of an LLC—prior to its formation or without disclosing they are acting as agents of the LLC—arises from the same agency principles as promoter liability in the corporate context. See *Water, Waste & Land, Inc. v. Lanham*, 955 P.2d 997 (Colo. 1998) (holding liable LLC members on agency theory when they contracted with engineering firm without informing firm they represented LLC).

§29.1.1 Promoter's Contractual Liability

The default rule adopted by the courts—and the one espoused by the Restatement (Second) of Agency §326 and the Restatement (Third) of Agency §6.04—is that the promoter is personally liable on a preincorporation contract absent a contrary intent. This common law rule essentially protects the understandings of the outside party.

Discerning Parties' Intentions

How can the promoter show the outside party agreed otherwise? Often the promoter will have signed the contract "for a corporation to be formed." This alone is not conclusive that the parties agreed to a "nonrecourse" status for the promoter since several liability is not precluded. Further evidence of the parties' intentions must be found in the contract document itself or in the surrounding circumstances. Consider some representative cases:

- **Negotiations.** The salesman for a supplier of nursery stock insisted on closing a supply contract with the "corporation" before the promoters had incorporated their business. The court held the promoters were not liable because the seller, by its agent's actions, had agreed to look only to the corporation for payment. *Quaker Hill, Inc. v. Parr,* 364 P.2d 1056 (Colo. 1961).
- **Postcontractual actions.** A hotel promoter entered into an architectural contract with an architect and, as contemplated, the architect partially performed before the promoter formed the planned corporation. Although the promoter signed as agent for "a corporation to be formed who will be the obligor," the court concluded the parties

intended the promoter would also be obligated if the corporation did not pay and held the promoter liable. *Stanley J. How & Associates, Inc. v. Boss*, 222 F. Supp. 936 (S.D. Iowa 1963).

- **Corporation's actions.** A movie theater promoter contracted to buy a movie theater on the understanding that before closing the promoter would form a corporation that would become liable under the contract. Even though the corporation was later formed, the court decided there was no novation since the corporation never adopted the contract. Discharging the promoter on mere incorporation could leave the seller with no party to hold accountable. The court held the promoter liable. *RKO-Stanley Warner Theaters, Inc. v. Graziano*, 355 A.2d 830 (Pa. 1976).

Often the issue will be whether the parties intended to discharge the promoter and substitute the corporation once the corporation was formed and adopted the contract—that is, a novation. The promoter and third party's intention that the corporation's adoption will act as a novation can be shown from the circumstances. For example, a novation intention might be inferred if the outsider deals first with the promoter and then, after incorporation, exclusively with the corporation. But just because the corporation performs under the contract does not necessarily establish a novation since such performance is also consistent with dual obligors. Furthermore, even if the parties intended a substitution, a novation requires corporate adoption, and courts have held that mere formation of the new corporation does not work a novation. There must be an affirmative act evidencing corporate consent (see below) before the corporation is bound and the promoter discharged.

Drafter's Role

As you can see, leaving questions of "party intention" to *ex post* clarification is fraught with uncertainty. The drafter of a contract for a corporation not yet formed can resolve this uncertainty *ex ante* with careful drafting. The drafter must resolve and make clear whether the promoter is liable initially on the contract, whether the corporation will become liable, and whether the promoter remains liable even after corporate adoption.

§29.1.2 Corporation's Contractual Liability

Outsiders often will want to hold the corporation liable on preincorporation contracts. A newly formed corporation, however, is not automatically liable for contracts made by promoters before incorporation. To protect new shareholders and other corporate participants from "surprise" corporate liability, the corporation must adopt the contract. (Some courts describe this as "ratification," but technically a corporation cannot ratify contracts that occurred before its existence.)

What constitutes a binding adoption? Although the clearest evidence would be a formal corporate resolution by the board of directors approving the contract (see §30.1), this is not necessary. Adoption can be implicit, for example, if corporate directors or officers with authority to bind the corporation knew of and acquiesced in the contract. See *McArthur v. Times Printing Co.*, 51 N.W. 216 (Minn. 1892) (inferring adoption of a preincorporation employment contract because all shareholders and officers knew about the contract and none sought to repudiate it). Later acts by the corporation consistent with or in furtherance of the contract—such as making payments under the contract or accepting its benefits—also provide evidence of adoption. See *Illinois Controls, Inc. v. Langham*, 639 N.E.2d 771 (Ohio 1994) (holding corporation and promoter jointly and severally liable under contract, after accepted benefits of contract, but did not formally adopt).

§29.1.3 Third Party's Liability on Contract

Promoter liability is a two-way street. If the promoter is liable under the contract to the third-party outsider, so too is the outsider to the promoter. Likewise, if the parties contemplated that the newly formed corporation could adopt the contract, this adoption binds the outsider. One way to test whether a promoter or corporation is liable on the contract is to ask whether the outsider is conversely bound.

§29.2 LIABILITY FOR DEFECTIVE INCORPORATION

In our discussion of a promoter's liability on preincorporation contracts, we assumed both the promoter and the outsider knew no corporation had yet been formed. What happens when the parties mistakenly believe a corporation already exists? One approach might be: "Tough luck! Valid incorporation is a statutory prerequisite for limited liability." This section considers when courts are willing to impute limited liability despite a defect in incorporation.

§29.2.1 De Facto Corporation and Corporation by Estoppel

Courts have generally viewed the "tough luck" approach as too harsh, particularly under earlier incorporation statutes rife with technicalities—such as notarization, filing in the county of the corporation's principal office, and complex filing fees. Imposing full liability on an unwitting investor or manager who in good faith thought he was shielded by corporate limited liability would not advance any rational corporate law purpose other than compliance with incorporation formalities. Imposing personal liability would be particularly harsh when the third party believed she was dealing with a "nonrecourse" agent for a corporation.

In response, courts developed the concepts of *de facto corporation* and *corporation by estoppel* to take the bite out of the harsh consequences of defective incorporation. Under these doctrines courts impute the attributes of corporate limited liability when the circumstances suggest the parties intended a "no recourse" relationship. Not surprisingly, the doctrines arise mostly in cases brought by contract creditors, rarely by tort victims.

- **De facto corporation.** The de facto corporation doctrine requires (1) some colorable, good-faith attempt to incorporate and (2) actual use of the corporate form, such as carrying on the business as a corporation or contracting in the corporate name. Although the state can challenge the existence of a de facto corporation, outside parties cannot. As to outsiders, a de facto corporation has all the attributes of a *de jure corporation*, including limited liability. (A de jure corporation has satisfied all or substantially all of the incorporation guidelines, and its existence cannot be attacked by anyone, including the state.)
- **Corporation by estoppel.** The corporation by estoppel theory arises when the parties have dealt with each other on the assumption a corporation existed, even though there has been no colorable attempt to incorporate. Outsiders who rely on representations or appearances that a corporation exists and act accordingly are *estopped* from denying corporate existence or limited liability. (This is an estoppel theory stood on its head; estoppel normally prevents *the person who makes a representation on which others rely* from denying the representation.)

Whether a modern court uses one of these common-law doctrines depends on two factors. First, does the state corporate statute permit judicial imputation of limited liability when there has been no incorporation? Second, if so, when do the circumstances justify a court imputing limited liability?

§29.2.2 Modern Abolition of the De Facto Corporation and Estoppel Doctrines?

Given the ease of incorporation under modern corporate statutes, forgiving an insider's failure to incorporate would seem overly permissive. For this reason, some courts have interpreted the modern easy-incorporation statutes to abolish the de facto corporation and corporation by estoppel doctrines. For example, in *Robertson v. Levy*, 197 A.2d 443 (D.C. App. 1964), the court concluded the D.C. corporate provisions modeled on the pre-1984 MBCA operated to create corporate limited liability only upon actual incorporation. (These provisions specified that corporate existence begins when the articles of incorporation are filed, and stated that persons "who assume to act as a corporation without authority" are personally liable.)

The case involved a somewhat typical chronology:

Dec 23	Levy agrees to purchase Robertson's business.
Dec 27	Levy submits articles of incorporation for a corporation that would be the buyer.
Jan 2	The articles are returned to Levy as defective.
Jan 8	Robertson transfers the business to Levy's "corporation," which gives a note in exchange.
Jan 17	Levy refiles the articles and is issued a certificate of incorporation.

The court held Levy personally liable on the note, even though Robertson assumed he was dealing with Levy on a "no-recourse" basis. Although the result seemed to give Robertson a windfall, Levy may have signed the notes knowing there was no incorporation. If so, the court's interpretation enforced the integrity of the incorporation process.

Despite the ease of modern incorporation, most courts have continued to use the judicial doctrines to impute limited liability. For example, in *Cantor v. Sunshine Greenery*, 398 A.2d 571 (N.J. Super. Ct. 1979), the court applied the de facto corporation doctrine to deny recovery in circumstances very similar to *Robertson*. Cantor agreed to lease commercial space to Brunetti, who had mailed articles to incorporate the new business 13 days before. Because of an administrative mix-up, the articles were actually filed two days after Brunetti signed the lease on behalf of the nonexistent corporation. When Brunetti's corporation later repudiated the lease, Cantor sought to recover from him personally. The court accepted a de facto corporation theory: Brunetti had made a colorable, good-faith attempt to incorporate and used the corporate form in his dealings with Cantor. To impose personal liability on Brunetti when the parties assumed a corporation, the court concluded, would be "unjust and inequitable." (Perhaps *Cantor* and *Robertson* are distinguishable. New Jersey's statute, unlike the D.C. statute in *Robertson*, did not specify personal liability for those assuming to act as a corporation. And it was unclear whether Brunetti knew of the incorporation defect when he signed the lease.)

In addition, some modern courts have used the estoppel doctrine if both parties believed there was a corporation even though there was no actual attempt to incorporate. For example, in *Cranson v. International Business Machines Corp.*, 200 A.2d 33 (Md. 1964), the court exonerated an attorney who inadvertently failed to file a certificate of incorporation. The attorney had falsely told investor Cranson that a corporation had been formed, and Cranson purchased eight IBM typewriters on credit as president of the nonexistent corporation. When the business stopped making payments, IBM sued Cranson personally. Although there could be no de facto corporation since there was no attempt to incorporate, the court accepted that there was a corporation by estoppel. IBM had extended credit on the basis that Cranson's business was incorporated.

Statutory Liability

The current MBCA (unlike the pre-1984 version) does not reject the judicial doctrines imputing limited liability, but takes a middle course. MBCA §2.04 states: "All persons purporting to act as or on behalf of a corporation, knowing there was no incorporation . . . are jointly and severally liable for all liabilities."

On the one hand, the section makes clear there is defective incorporation liability when insiders deceive outsiders about corporate status. On the other hand, the section implies that there is no liability if the insider purporting to act in her corporate capacity does not know of the incorporation defect. See Official Comment, MBCA §2.04 (no liability for those who "erroneously but in good faith" believe articles have been filed). To date, MBCA §2.04 has gotten scant judicial attention.

Notice that the MBCA's focus on the *insider's* knowledge differs from the judicial focus on the *outsider's* understandings. A comprehensive, statistical study of the defective incorporation cases suggests that *both* the insider's attempt to incorporate *and* the outsider's belief of incorporation may be critical in actual judicial decision making. See Fred S. McChesney, *Doctrinal Analysis and Statistical Modeling in Law: The Case of Defective Incorporation*, 71 Wash. U. L.Q. 493 (1993) (using multivariate statistical techniques to conclude that courts in defective incorporation cases are most likely to impute limited liability when there is both an attempt to incorporate and the outsider dealt with the firm as a corporation). That is, a court is likely to impute limited liability when there is an amalgam of the de facto and estoppel elements.

§29.2.3 Liability for Nonsignatory Participants

When there is an incorporation defect and the doctrines imputing limited liability are not available, courts impose liability on the luckless promoter who signed the contract on a variety of theories. Some courts resort to the statutory liability provisions. See MBCA §2.04 (liability for those who purport to act for corporation they know does not exist). Others impose liability on the theory the signing promoter breached a warranty, whether of his authority or of the existence and competency of the principal. See Restatement (Second) of Agency §329; Restatement (Third) of Agency §6.10 (liability for representation of nonexistent authority, unless disclaimer or knowledge of third party).

But defective incorporation does not necessarily impose liability on nonsignatory participants—that is, persons involved in the business as investors or managers, but who did not sign the contract on which liability is asserted. Courts are reluctant to impose partnership-type liability on participants who thought they had corporate limited liability, even though a defectively incorporated business bears all the hallmarks of a partnership. See RUPA §202(a) (defining partnership as "the association of two or more persons to carry on as co-owners a business for profit"). Many courts limit liability to active participants—that is, those who acted as directors, officers, or agents of the nonexistent corporation. Courts have not imposed liability on passive investors who did not act on behalf of the business. See *Frontier Refining Co. v. Kunkel's, Inc.*, 407 P.2d 880 (Wyo. 1965) (finding that outsider knew passive investors had invested on the assumption that the firm would be incorporated before conducting business).

§29.2.4 Administrative Dissolution

Corporate statutes provide for administrative dissolution if the corporation (though properly formed) fails to pay state franchise taxes and fees, to report a change in registered agent, or to file an annual report. See MBCA §14.20. Are corporate participants liable for activities carried out in the corporate name after administrative revocation of corporate status?

If the corporation is not reinstated, those who knowingly act on behalf of the nonexistent corporation become personally liable, even if creditors had not relied on personal assets. See MBCA §2.04 (imposing liability on those purporting to act as corporation knowing the corporation does not exist). This liability rule motivates corporate participants to comply with state requirements.

But if the corporation is reinstated, modern corporate statutes provide that the reinstatement relates back to the date of administrative dissolution as though the revocation of corporate status had never occurred. See MBCA §14.22 (requiring that reinstatement occur within two years of administrative dissolution). Even in states without reinstatement provisions, some courts have imposed liability only on those acting for a dissolved corporation with knowledge of the dissolution. See *Richmond Wholesale Meat Co. v. Hughes*,

625 F. Supp. 584 (N.D. Ill. 1985) (remanding for determination whether corporate actors knew, or should have known, of dissolution for failing to pay franchise taxes); compare *T-K Distributors, Inc. v. Soldevere*, 704 P.2d 280 (Ariz. 1985) (imposing personal liability on contract entered during four-month revocation even though insiders had no knowledge of revocation).

Examples

1. Bascomb plans a business offering moonlit carriage rides. He can buy ten antique carriages from Old Plantation, an antique dealer—if he hurries. Bascomb has not yet incorporated his business, but he plans to. He signs a contract with Old Plantation as "agent for Antebellum, Inc., a corporation to be formed, which will become party to this contract." The contract calls for installment payments over 12 months.
   a. Before Antebellum is incorporated, Bascomb takes delivery of the carriages. When the first installment comes due, is Bascomb liable on the contract?
   b. Assume Antebellum is incorporated, and it uses the carriages in the business. When Old Plantation is not paid, is Bascomb liable?
   c. Bascomb told Old Plantation's manager that he would wait to sign the contract until Antebellum's articles were filed. The manager had said, "Let's do the deal now. It's with the corporation, anyway." Does this affect Bascomb's liability?
   d. Before he stopped paying, Bascomb had paid the first four installments to Old Plantation with Antebellum checks. Does this affect Bascomb's liability?
   e. Bascomb sells his Antebellum shares to Carolyn, who repudiates the Old Plantation contract on behalf of Antebellum. She refuses to pay more installments and tries to return the carriages. Can Old Plantation hold Antebellum liable?
2. When Bascomb signed the Rebel Threads contract for nonexistent Antebellum, his sister Elizabeth had invested money and thought she was a shareholder of the corporation. She, however, had nothing to do with Bascomb's dealings with Rebel Threads. Is she liable to Rebel Threads on the contract?
3. The contract with Old Plantation specifies:

   > This contract is between Old Plantation and Antebellum, Inc., once the latter is formed. Bascomb is obligated only to use his best efforts to form a corporation that will duly accept the contract.

   a. Assume Bascomb does not incorporate Antebellum. Is he liable?
   b. Now assume Bascomb incorporates Antebellum, but it never acts on the contract. Instead, Bascomb accepts delivery of the carriages and uses them in the business. In light of the contract provision, is Antebellum or Bascomb liable?

4. The Old Plantation contract reads as follows:

   > It is understood by the parties hereto that it is the intention of the Purchaser to incorporate. Upon condition that such incorporation be completed by closing, all agreements, covenants, and warranties contained herein shall be construed to have been made between Seller and the resultant corporation and all documents shall reflect the same.

   a. Does this provision assure a novation once Antebellum is incorporated and adopts the contract?
   b. How should this provision be redrafted?
   c. Is there another way to avoid drafting a novation?

5. Assume Antebellum is incorporated, and Bascomb wants to make clear there is a novation. Old Plantation's manager agrees to tear up the original contract and sign a new one with Antebellum. Bascomb signs as follows:

   J S Bascomb

   J. S. Bascomb
   President, Antebellum, Inc.

   Does this signature accomplish Bascomb's purpose?

6. Bascomb enters into a contract with RebelThreads to purchase Confederate army uniforms for Antebellum's carriage drivers. He signs the contract as president of Antebellum, Inc. When Rebel Threads delivers the uniforms, Antebellum does not pay. Rebel Threads sues Bascomb on the contract.
   a. Assume Antebellum is not incorporated. Bascomb had mailed articles of incorporation for Antebellum to the secretary of state two weeks before signing the contract. But postal employees, now under indictment, threw away the mailing. How might Bascomb argue he is not liable under the contract?
   b. Assume again that Antebellum is not incorporated. Bascomb had asked his lawyer to create a corporation, Antebellum, Inc. But the lawyer forgot to file the articles. As Bascomb's new attorney, how would you argue Bascomb is not liable on the contract?

7. After signing the contract with Rebel Threads, Bascomb properly incorporates Antebellum, which adopts the contract and pays Rebel Threads. Several years later Bascomb contracts to buy additional uniforms from RebelThreads in the name of Antebellum. Before signing this contract and unknown to him, the state's corporate officials had revoked Antebellum's incorporation for failing to pay state franchise taxes. Later, after Bascomb learned of the revocation and he paid the back taxes, the state officials reinstated Antebellum's incorporation.
   a. Can Rebel Threads recover from Bascomb personally under the contract since Antebellum was not in existence when he signed it?

b. Can RebelThreads avoid the contract with Antebellum on the theory it could not have contracted with a nonexistent corporation?

Explanations

1. a. Most likely. As a general rule, a promoter is personally liable on any preincorporation contract unless a contrary intention is stated in the contract or can be shown from the circumstances. Because incorporation is so easy, the promoter's failure to incorporate suggests the parties were dealing with each other on a "full-recourse" basis.

   In this case Bascomb might argue that his signature as "agent for" the to-be-corporation indicates that the parties did not intend a contract until the corporation was formed and it adopted the contract. But Old Plantation's partial performance under the contract by delivering the carriages to Bascomb belies this argument. The phrasing of the signature line does not rule out the possibility of liability for both the promoter and the corporation.

   b. Most likely. If Bascomb was initially liable, his liability continues even after incorporation, unless there is a novation. There are two problems with a novation theory here. First, it is not clear that the parties intended a substitution of parties after the corporation was formed and adopted the contract. The statement in the signature line that Antebellum would "become party to this contract" is ambiguous; it is not unequivocal that the corporation would be the only party. Bascomb's picking up the carriages before incorporation is inconsistent with corporation-only liability. Second, even if the parties intended a novation, there is no indication that Antebellum adopted the contract—its incorporation is not enough.

   c. Probably. The events surrounding the contract's signing indicate Old Plantation intended to look only to the corporation; Bascomb was an agent of the corporation-to-be. Even if Old Plantation looks to Bascomb after Antebellum's adoption and breach, the parties' intentions and whether they entered into a "no-recourse" relationship must be gauged as of the initial transaction.

   d. Probably not. Bascomb's personal liability, suggested by his preincorporation acceptance of the carriages, continues until there is a novation. That Old Plantation accepted payments from Antebellum allows an inference of corporate adoption, but not necessarily novation. Bascomb would have to show some further evidence that the parties intended Antebellum's adoption would discharge Bascomb.

   e. Yes, but not on the contract. Antebellum's incorporation does not automatically result in an adoption of the contract, and Carolyn's repudiation made clear that Antebellum was not adopting it. Nonetheless, because the company kept the carriages, Antebellum may be liable on a quasi-contract theory.

2. Not necessarily. RebelThreads must establish a basis for holding Elizabeth liable. This would seem difficult where Elizabeth was a passive investor who did not act for the business or sign the contract. In the end, the outsider was not counting on her credit, and any personal liability would be a windfall. Consider the possible theories of liability:
   - **Warranty liability.** Liability based on warranty requires that the insider have given explicit or implicit assurances of corporate existence. Because Elizabeth did not deal with the outsider or sign the contract, a warranty theory seems unavailing.
   - **Statutory liability.** Statutory liability generally depends on the insider acting as or on behalf of the business, knowing it was not incorporated. See MBCA §2.04. As a passive investor, Elizabeth cannot be liable because she did not act for the business and did not know of the incorporation defect.
   - **Agent/partner liability.** Liability based on an agency or partnership relationship requires that the inadvertent principal or partner have authorized the acts by the other insider. There is no indication that Elizabeth had consented to Bascomb to act before incorporation as her agent. See Restatement (Second) of Agency §1; Restatement (Third) of Agency §1.01. Further, there is no indication Elizabeth and Bascomb agreed to carry on an *unincorporated* business as co-owners. See RUPA §202. She anticipated becoming only a shareholder. Moreover, even if Bascomb was her agent or partner, he lacked authority. He did not have *actual* authority to sign the contract until the business was incorporated. Any *apparent* authority would be negated if the outsider either knew of this limitation on Bascomb's authority or did not know of Elizabeth.

3. a. Perhaps, but not on the contract. The contract provision seems sufficient to establish the parties' intention that no contract was to exist until incorporation occurred and Antebellum adopted the contract. The transaction creates an option to Antebellum. But Bascomb promised to use his best efforts to incorporate Antebellum and to induce the corporation to accept the offer. If Bascomb shirked this duty, he could be liable on that promise.

   b. Antebellum is liable, but Bascomb is not. By its actions, Antebellum has adopted the contract. Adoption need not be formal and can be inferred from the acquiescence of those who would have power to accept the contract. The use of the carriages and the acquiescence by Antebellum's directors and officers constitutes implicit adoption. Bascomb is not liable because his only duty was to form a corporation and have it adopt the contract, which happened.

4. a. Maybe not. The provision is ambiguous. It fails to specify whether the promoter's liability ends with incorporation or whether the corporation simply becomes a co-obligor on the contract along with the promoter.

b. The provision should make clear that the third party will look only to the corporation after incorporation and adoption. Something along the following lines might work:

> The parties understand that Bascomb intends to organize a corporation that will, upon its adoption of this contract, become the sole obligor. Bascomb will be liable on this contract only until the corporation is organized and adopts the contract. Adoption by the corporation will operate as a novation, releasing Bascomb from all personal liability under this contract.

c. Besides incorporating and having the corporation sign the contract, another option would be for Bascomb to take an assignable option from Old Plantation on the carriages. Once the corporation is formed, Bascomb could assign the option to the corporation, which could exercise the option to purchase the carriages. Old Plantation, however, might not want to give an irrevocable option unless Bascomb were willing to pay for it.

5. No. Some courts have held that such a signature is ambiguous! It is not certain that Bascomb signed only in his corporate capacity. The signature can be interpreted to indicate that he is signing for himself and simply noting that he is also a corporate officer, or that he is signing both for himself and as agent for the corporation. To do it right, the signature should be *precisely* as follows (no less and no more):

   Antebellum, Inc.

   J S Bascomb

   By: J. S. Bascomb, President

   This makes clear the corporation is signing through its officer-agent, Bascomb. It insulates Bascomb from liability by making clear he is acting in his corporate capacity.

6. a. De facto corporation. Bascomb could argue he made a colorable, good-faith attempt to incorporate and contracted in the name of the corporation. The de facto corporation doctrine shields Bascomb from liability to outsiders to the same extent proper incorporation limits the liability of officers acting for the corporation.

   The MBCA, however, does not explicitly accept the de facto doctrine. In an MBCA jurisdiction, Bascomb escapes liability if he contracted not knowing of the defective incorporation. Official Comment to MBCA §2.04. That is, whether or not he attempted to incorporate, he must have used the corporate form believing there was proper incorporation. Whether a judge applying §2.04 would consider only Bascomb's knowledge, and not that of the outsider, is unclear. Judge-made law has been at the heart of the defective incorporation cases, even under modern corporate statutes. If past judicial attitudes are a guide to the future, Bascomb should also argue that the *outsider* anticipated a "no-recourse" relationship, evidenced by Bascomb's good-faith belief he was contracting on behalf of a properly incorporated business.

b. Corporation by estoppel. The lawyer's lapse eliminates any de facto corporation theory. Nonetheless, Bascomb could argue he believed there was a corporation and the outsider contracted on the assumption of a "no-recourse" relationship, thus estopping it from denying the existence of a corporation.

It is unclear whether the estoppel doctrine has survived easy-incorporation statutes. By forgiving promoters who make no colorable attempt to incorporate, the doctrine undermines the integrity of the incorporation process. Nonetheless, the MBCA accepts a modified estoppel theory. If Bascomb did not know of the lawyer's misfeasance, he would escape liability. Official Comment to MBCA §2.04. Nonetheless, it should be recognized that an important factor in defective incorporation cases has been the *outsider's* understandings. Bascomb should buttress his §2.04 argument by asserting that Rebel Threads also assumed it was dealing with a corporation.

7. a. Probably not. If Antebellum is incorporated in an MBCA jurisdiction and Bascomb reinstated the corporation within two years of the administrative dissolution, the reinstatement relates back so that it is as though the dissolution never happened. MBCA §14.22. This is the result whether or not Bascomb knew of the dissolution when he entered the contract. Any corporate disabilities would be extinguished, and corporate limited liability would insulate Bascomb from personal liability.

If Antebellum is not incorporated in an MBCA jurisdiction, Bascomb's liability depends on the judicial approach to a temporary defect in incorporation. In these cases courts have looked to the statutory provisions that impose liability on those who act for a corporation when none exists. See MBCA §2.04 (liability for those who purport to act with knowledge of the defect); pre-1984 MBCA §139 (liability for those who assume to act, whether or not the defect is known). Whether or not the statute contains a "knowledge" element, many courts have focused on the insider's knowledge and good faith. If the transaction is on a corporate basis and the insider knew (or had reason to know) of the dissolution, courts impose personal liability. But if the parties intend a corporate transaction and the insider did not know of the disability, as the example suggests for Bascomb, there is no personal liability. This approach makes sense since it avoids giving the outsider a windfall when both parties believed the contract was on a "no-recourse" basis and creates an incentive for insiders promptly to correct incorporation defects once they know of them.

b. No. Most courts have rejected this argument. Even in states that do not have a reinstatement provision, the third party remains bound if he thought he was dealing with a corporation. *Regal Package Liquor, Inc. v. J.R.D., Inc.*, 466 N.E.2d 409 (Ill. App. 1984) (estopping outsider from avoiding contract since the outsider assumed he was dealing with a corporation; incorporation defect during temporary revocation was a matter between state and corporation). To hold otherwise would give outsiders a windfall.

Authority to Bind the Corporation

The corporation can become liable to outsiders only through its agents. The authority to bind the corporation generally emanates from the board of directors—the traditional locus of corporate power.

Outsiders who deal with the corporation cannot be indifferent to corporate power. Board actions that do not comply with decision-making procedures mandated by corporate law are invalid; corporate agents who act without proper authority cannot bind the corporation. Although the emphasis in modern cases is on protecting outsiders' expectations, corporate interests in proper board deliberations and centralized decision making often trump outsider interests in commercial certainty.

This chapter considers when the corporation is bound to outsiders. It describes the procedures for valid board action (§30.1) and the authority of corporate agents (§30.2). Ultimately, the critical question is how much outsiders must inquire into the authority of corporate agents to confirm the corporation is bound. This chapter concludes by describing "respondeat superior" (§30.3).

§30.1 BOARD DECISION MAKING

In general, the board acts by majority vote as one body at a properly noticed directors' meeting at which a quorum is present. Unlike the rule for shareholders' meetings where once a quorum is present it cannot be broken by shareholders who leave the meeting, a director can break the quorum at a board meeting by walking out. When the transaction requires board approval, outsiders (or, more precisely, their legal counsel) must be sure these board procedures have been followed. (You should also keep in mind that the validity of board action is not only relevant to outsiders seeking to bind the corporation, but also to insiders who might question board actions.)

§30.1.1 Board Meetings — Notice and Quorum

Notice

As with shareholders, the board meets both at regular and specially called meetings. In general, the bylaws dictate whether, when, and how much notice must be given. MBCA §8.22(a) (no notice required for regular board meetings unless the articles or bylaws provide otherwise); MBCA §8.22(b) (two-day notice required for special meetings unless the bylaws or articles specify otherwise). (Board notice in Delaware corporations is not specified by statute, but instead left to the articles and bylaws.) Board action taken at a meeting at which all directors did not receive the required notice is invalid. Directors can waive notice in writing and are deemed to have waived notice by attending and not promptly objecting to the meeting. MBCA §8.23; Del. GCL §229.

Quorum

Generally, quorum requirements prevent a board minority from meeting and taking action that the majority would not have. A quorum exists when a majority of authorized directors are present at a meeting, unless the articles or bylaws specify a greater number. MBCA §8.24(a). Some statutes permit the articles or bylaws to specify a reduced quorum, but generally set a floor of one-third of the directors authorized. MBCA §8.24(b); Del. GCL §141(b). Many statutes require a quorum when the board votes, permitting directors to break a quorum and disable the board by not attending or walking out during a meeting. MBCA §8.24(c); Del. GCL §141(b).

The quorum requirements are relaxed when directors are filling vacancies. Under many statutes a majority of the directors *remaining in office*, though less than a quorum, constitute a quorum for filling director vacancies. MBCA §8.10(a)(3).

§30.1.2 Board Action — Majority Vote at a Meeting

Action by directors at a properly convened meeting at which a quorum is present is generally decided by *majority vote of those present* unless the articles or bylaws impose a supermajority requirement. MBCA §8.24(c); Del. GCL §141(b). Each director has one vote and cannot vote by proxy.

Meeting Rule

As a general rule, directors cannot vote separately, but must act together as a body at a properly convened meeting — the "meeting rule." This means that approval of a transaction by individual directors outside a meeting is not binding even if all of the directors consent. Unless there is an exception, failure to comply with the "meeting rule" invalidates any transaction approved by the directors. See *Fogel v. U.S. Energy Systems, Inc.*, 2007 WL 4438978 (Del. Ch. 2007) (vote by three independent directors to fire CEO had no validity because no formal meeting had been called).

The meeting rule, and its lesson for outsiders who deal with a corporation, is illustrated dramatically in *Baldwin v. Canfield*, 1 N.W. 261 (Minn. 1879). King was the sole shareholder of Minneapolis Agricultural & Machinist Association, Inc. (MAMA), whose sole asset was a fairground. King borrowed money from State National Bank and pledged all of his MAMA stock as collateral for the loan. King then agreed to have MAMA sell the fairground property to Canfield, who demanded that King first repay his bank loan and deliver to Canfield his MAMA stock. Without meeting, all of MAMA's directors individually and separately signed a deed of trust transferring the fairground to Canfield. His dirty business done, King skipped town with both the proceeds from the bank loan and the sale proceeds from Canfield. In a suit between the bank and Canfield over ownership of the fairground, the court held that Canfield's deed of trust was invalid because it had not been executed by the directors at a proper meeting.

What should Canfield have done? For one, Canfield should have insisted on receiving the MAMA stock as agreed; ownership of the corporation would have assured him title to the fairgrounds. Beyond that, Canfield also should have insisted on seeing the minutes of the meeting at which the deed was executed and a certificate from MAMA's corporate secretary of the minutes' authenticity and accuracy. The meeting rule assures shareholders (and other corporate constituents) that board decisions are made collegially where there can be group interaction and deliberation. As to complex matters of judgment, sociological studies confirm that group dynamics generally produce better decisions than those by the same individuals acting separately.

Exceptions to Meeting Rule

A strict meeting rule has drawbacks. To permit flexible and efficient board action, many statutes now allow boards to take action by the separate written and signed consent of the directors, provided the consent is unanimous. MBCA §8.21; Del. GCL §141(f) (also by electronic transmission). Moreover, many statutes also allow directors' meetings to occur over the telephone or by other means where all the directors can hear each other—the next best thing to being there. MBCA §8.20(b); Del. GCL §141(i). In some situations involving close corporations, courts have accepted that directors (even without a formal meeting) can ratify the act of a corporate officer or agent through their acquiescence. See *Hurley v. Ornsteen*, 42 N.E.2d 273 (Mass. 1942) (requiring knowledge and acquiescence of all directors).

§30.1.3 Delegating Board Functions to Committees

Statutes allow the board to delegate many of the board's functions to committees composed of some (though less than all) of the directors. MBCA §8.25; Del. GCL §141(c). Some statutes specify certain functions or powers that cannot be delegated to committees—such as authorizing distributions and share repurchases, issuing shares, approving mergers, amending the articles, amending the bylaws, and making other fundamental corporate changes. MBCA §8.25(e); Del. GCL §141(c) (for corporations incorporated after 1996, committee cannot approve corporate transactions requiring shareholder vote or changes to bylaws).

Board committees have assumed growing importance, particularly in public corporations. The *executive committee* acts on matters that come up between regular board meetings and often focuses on issues before presentation to the board; the full board in the usual course adopts or ratifies the committee's action. Other standing committees have particular functions: The *audit committee* reviews the company's financial position with the company's outside auditor; the *compensation committee* negotiates and sets executive compensation; the *nominating committee* selects directors to be nominated for election by the shareholders. Often these committees are composed largely of outside directors—directors who are not employees of the corporation—to provide an element of independence in matters involving potential conflicts between the interests of management (the corporation's top executives) and the interests of shareholders.

Under the Sarbanes-Oxley Act of 2002, all the members of the audit committee of publicly traded companies must be independent. Exchange Act §10A(m) (see §11.5.1). At least one member of the audit committee must be a "financial expert," and the committee must have complete authority to hire, fire, and supervise the company's outside accountants and auditors.

In a similar vein, the Dodd-Frank Act of 2010 requires that the compensation committee of publicly traded corporations be comprised solely of independent directors. Exchange Act §10C(a) (see §11.5.2). Moreover, the committee must be empowered to hire *independent* compensation experts for consultation, using SEC-formulated factors to ensure that the expert hired is independent. Exchange Act §10C(b).

In addition, specially appointed temporary committees have become more frequent to deal with particular transactions in which conflicts of interest are likely. Examples include special litigation committees to decide on the corporation's stance toward shareholder derivative litigation against management (see §18.5.4) and special takeover committees to decide on the corporation's response to takeover bids for the company (see §39.2).

§30.2 CORPORATE AUTHORITY

The sources of authority for corporate officers, like those for any agent, exist along a continuum. Corporate law borrows from the law of agency, treating the board as the corporate principal and the officers (and employees) as agents. Thus, whether the corporation is bound in a particular transaction raises the usual agency questions—actual, apparent, and inherent authority.

§30.2.1 Actual Authority—Internal Action

The clearest corporate authority—*express actual authority*—arises when the board, acting by the requisite majority at a proper meeting, expressly approves the actions of a corporate agent. As long as the corporate statute or the corporation's constitutive documents do not limit the board's authority, the board-approved action then binds the corporation.

Most corporate transactions, however, are not specifically approved by the board of directors. Rather, the board delegates categories of authority to corporate officers who act as the corporation's day-to-day agents on ordinary corporate matters such as employment agreements, supply and sales contracts, and credit arrangements. MBCA §8.41. Express actual authority for officers to bind the corporation can be found in a number of sources:

- the corporate statute (though now rare)
- articles of incorporation (but not often)
- bylaws (the most common source for broad descriptions of officers' functions and responsibilities)
- board resolutions (which authorize specific transactions or categories of transactions)

The board's delegation of authority to an officer constitutes corporate consent to the officer to bind the corporation. This authority exists whether or not the outsider knew about the officer's authority.

Often, even though an officer lacks express authority to act for the corporation, it can fairly be inferred that the board implicitly approved the action. In such situations, there is *implied actual authority*. There are two techniques for inferring this authority. First, consider the penumbra of the express actual authority delegated to the officer—such as when a corporate president is authorized to "manage the day-to-day affairs of the business." In such a case, it can be inferred that the board impliedly authorized the president broadly to do anything incidental to the open-ended grant of authority.

Second, look at the board's reaction to other similar actions by corporate agents as an indication that the action was already impliedly approved. In some of these cases implied authorization is easy to find, such as when the board knows of and acquiesces in an officer's longstanding course of conduct. When the officer engages in this conduct again, it can fairly be said that, considering the board's prior inaction, it has impliedly authorized the conduct. As in cases of express actual authority, the corporation is bound even if the outsider did not know about this implicit validation of corporate authority.

Ratification

Even when an officer's actions are not binding against the corporation when made, the board can create express actual authority retroactively by *ratifying* a prior act if the board has the power to authorize the act. Ratification creates the agency relationship and "relates back" so that the prior act, even if by a nonagent, is treated as authorized from the start.

Ratification can also be implied. The board's knowledge of and acquiescence in an officer's novel course of conduct, for which express and implied authority does not exist, may evidence implied ratification. The cases generally accept that informal acquiescence can bind the corporation, despite the rule that the board must act at a properly convened meeting. Some cases find implied ratification if all the directors knew about the transaction and did nothing—unanimous acquiescence. Other cases require only an acquiescent majority. In any event, courts seem inclined to infer ratification if the corporation derived a benefit from the transaction—to protect outsiders' expectations.

§30.2.2 Apparent Authority—External Appearances

What happens when there is no actual authorization, such as when the board has expressly denied authority to an officer? If the board induces an outsider to rely on an officer, even if the officer has no actual authority, the corporation may be bound on a theory of apparent authority.

The question of apparent authority often surfaces with respect to what is sometimes (confusingly) described as the "inherent" power of the president to bind the corporation. Early common law flew in the face of the popular assumption that a corporate president has broad "presidential" authority, and outsiders often discovered that the validity of their dealings with the corporation depended on internal corporate machinations and not outward appearances. To deal with this unfairness and the inefficiency of forcing outside parties to verify an officer's authority for every transaction, courts imposed liability if the board created the appearance that an officer was authorized to carry out a transaction.

How is the appearance of authority created? Much depends on the corporate officer's position in the corporation. The following describe the general areas of corporate officers' authority and the general assumptions that outsiders are entitled to make:

- **President or CEO.** The president (or often in modern usage the "chief executive officer") can bind the corporation as to matters in the usual course of business. (It is important to distinguish the president from the "chair of the board," who presides over board meetings but generally does not have administrative duties or the power to bind the corporation.)

  The president generally cannot bind the corporation as to *extraordinary matters,* such as entering into a merger agreement, bringing or settling litigation, offering lifetime employment contracts, and disposing of or mortgaging all of the corporation's assets. As to such matters, the outside party is on notice to demand proof of actual authority.
- **Vice president.** The vice president replaces the president when needed. With the modern proliferation of vice presidents in managerial positions, a vice president can only bind the corporation as to matters within her area.
- **Secretary.** The secretary normally does not bind the corporation but merely keeps and certifies corporate records.
- **Treasurer.** The treasurer normally does not bind the corporation but keeps the corporate books, receives payments, and makes other authorized payments.

Although this describes the general pattern, the authority given an officer in the bylaws or by virtue of the course of conduct of a particular company's officers may be enough to create the manifestations of authority that an outside party can rely on. Whether or not particular conduct is authorized, the corporation is estopped from denying the officers' apparent authority.

Often the question of apparent authority will turn on whether the transaction is ordinary or extraordinary. Courts assume the outside party is under a duty to verify authority if the transaction is extraordinary—that is, without apparent business justification or of such importance board approval would seem necessary. In the famous case of *Lee v. Jenkins Bros.*, 268 F.2d 357 (2d Cir. 1959), the court held that a president's promise to a new executive that the corporation would provide him a pension at age 60, which the court assumed became vested after he worked for a reasonable time, was not necessarily "extraordinary" because it neither implicated future managerial policy nor exposed the corporation to significant liabilities. On the other hand, other cases have found that a lifetime employment contract is "extraordinary," and absent actual board authorization the corporation is not bound. *Burke v. Bevona*, 931 F.2d 998 (2d Cir. 1991).

By the same token, the extent of the corporation's business interest in a transaction often determines whether it is ordinary or extraordinary. For example, a copper manufacturer was not bound on its treasurer's unusual and unauthorized guaranty of a loan to a construction company because the manufacturer had at best a tangential interest in the construction company. *General Overseas Films v. Robin Int'l, Inc.*, 542 F. Supp. 684 (S.D.N.Y. 1982). But a parent corporation was bound on its president's assertedly unauthorized guaranty of a subsidiary's contract for printing its catalogues because the parent stood to gain from the subsidiary's catalogue sales. See *Foote & Davies v. Arnold Craven, Inc.*, 324 S.E.2d 889 (N.C. App. 1985).

The theory of apparent authority focuses on protecting the reasonable beliefs of outside parties, and thus if the outsider actually *knows* the officer has no actual authority, there can be no apparent authority. Likewise, if the outsider does not know of a particular corporate course of conduct, the party cannot claim reliance and estoppel—that is, *unknown* manifestations of authority cannot create apparent authority. Further, when an officer expresses doubts about his authority, the outsider is put on notice and may be required to verify the officer's actual authority. In short, apparent authority only exists when the outsider reasonably believed the officer had the actual authority to bind the corporation.

Distinguish Implied and Apparent Authority

You should be careful to distinguish implied actual authority and apparent authority. The issue of implied authority turns on whether it can be inferred the board approved the officer's actions and is now trying to weasel. The outsider need not know about the relationship between the board and the officer. Apparent authority, although its proof sometimes overlaps with that of implied authority, focuses on the appearances of the officer's authority that the board has created for reasonably reliant outsiders.

§30.2.3 Inherent Authority

Some courts have also identified a third form of authority — *inherent authority* — that arises from the status of the corporate officer, particularly the corporate CEO or president. See *Menard, Inc. v. Dage-MTI, Inc.*, 726 N.E.2d 1206 (Ind. 2000) (president who operated with little board oversight and had purchased land in past held to have inherent authority to negotiate land purchase, despite lack of actual and apparent authority). Even though the board may not have authorized the agent to act or manifested the agent's authority to a third party, the agent's very position creates his authority. That is, inherent authority may exist even when there is no actual or apparent authority.

Inherent authority is said to derive "solely from the agency relation," and it protects third parties who are harmed by an agent acting generally in the corporation's interests. See Restatement (Second) of Agency §8A (Comment b); cf. Restatement (Third) of Agency (does not include inherent authority). The notion is that as between the corporation and an innocent outsider, the corporation receives the greater benefit from using agents and is in a better position to restrain renegade agents, and thus should bear the risk that an agent has acted beyond his authority. Under a theory of inherent authority, the corporation can become bound regardless of any actual or apparent authority as normally understood. If the officer's actions relate to transactions that he is generally authorized to conduct and the third party reasonably believes the officer is authorized and has no notice to the contrary, the corporation is bound. See Restatement (Second) of Agency §161.

This policy is particularly strong if, for example, the insider who allegedly bound the corporation is also a significant shareholder. See *In re Mathews Construction Co.*, 120 F. Supp. 818 (S.D. Cal. 1954) (holding corporation bound by the acquiescence of two sole shareholders even though board approval of transaction was invalid because third director received no notice of special board meeting). In such a case, allowing the corporation to disavow the contract for lack of internal formalities would shift the risk of loss to creditors while only marginally promoting the purposes of centralized corporate decision making.

§30.3 RESPONDEAT SUPERIOR — CORPORATE LIABILITY FOR EMPLOYEE TORTS

Corporate agents also can bind the corporation in noncontractual settings. If an officer or other employee commits a tort, even though the corporation has not actually or apparently authorized the employee to commit the tort, the corporation is nonetheless liable vicariously on a theory of *respondeat superior* if the employee was acting within the scope of his employment. Fundamental notions of responsibility and risk shifting, akin to those that drive the theory of inherent authority, place the burden on the entity for whom the employee was acting rather than on the victimized third party.

Examples

1. Swamp Acres, Inc. (SAI), incorporated in an MBCA jurisdiction, buys and drains swampland for resale. Its president, Flimm, signs a sales contract on behalf of SAI to sell Quagmire Estates to Priscilla. This is a major transaction for SAI.
   a. Flimm tells Priscilla that he has full authority to sell Quagmire. Should Priscilla press for more information?
   b. Three members of the five-person SAI board had signed a resolution that authorized Flimm to sell Quagmire Estates. Flimm had not shown Priscilla the resolution. Is the corporation bound?
   c. At a properly called meeting, only two directors had attended and a third was "present" through a conference phone call. The three authorized Flimm to sell Quagmire Estates. Flimm does not show Priscilla the minutes of the meeting. Is the corporation bound?
   d. One of the directors who had not attended the meeting now objects that none of the directors had received notice of the meeting. Does the lack of written notice undermine the validity of the Quagmire contract?

2. Flimm signs a contract on behalf of SAI to sell Bog Manor to Boyce. An SAI bylaw expressly states that all land sales require *prior* board approval. Although the five-person board has in the past ratified Flimm's unauthorized sales, the board disavows the transaction with Boyce.
   a. Boyce does not know about the bylaw or the company's past practice. He relied on Flimm's statement that as president he could sell Bog Manor. Is the corporation bound?
   b. At an SAI board meeting two weeks before the Bog Manor transaction, two of the three directors present approved the sale of Bog Manor. Is the corporation bound?
   c. Boyce reads the minutes more carefully. The director who had not voted for the sale had in fact walked out of the meeting before the vote was taken. Is the corporation bound?

3. Flimm signs a contract to sell Marsh Grounds to Naomi. He says SAI will accept an installment note from her. In the past, SAI has sold its properties under installment notes, and Naomi is aware of this.

a. Last week the SAI board voted to stop selling on credit. Flimm had nonetheless told Naomi that he was fully authorized to sign the contract. Is the corporation bound under the installment contract?
b. Naomi learns of the board's new policy and wants to make sure her contract will be honored. What should she do?

4. Flimm learns Naomi is worried the Marsh Grounds contract may not be valid. To allay her concerns, Flimm undertakes to have the SAI board ratify the installment contract. The board consists of five directors. Is SAI bound in the following situations?
   a. Flimm calls the three directors who are in town and asks them to attend an emergency board meeting. At the meeting the three directors unanimously approve a resolution ratifying the contract with Naomi. Flimm presents Naomi with a copy of this resolution certified by the company's secretary.
   b. Flimm notifies all five directors of the situation by e-mail. After exchanging a series of Internet instant messages, four directors send messages approving the contract. (The instant messages are all stored.)
   c. Flimm arranges for a six-way telephone conference call that includes him and all the directors. The directors receive no notice of the call, and there is a heated discussion about his authority to enter the installment contract. During the call, three directors vote to ratify the contract. The two dissenting directors then hang up in disgust.
   d. The board appoints a committee consisting of two directors and the company's outside lawyer to negotiate with Naomi. The committee is given full authority to bind the corporation. The committee and Naomi agree to a new contract.

5. Flimm wants to hire a sales assistant. He offers the job to Wiley, who demands that in addition to regular commissions she receive 2 percent for every sale over $1 million. Flimm, who owns a majority of SAI stock and controls the board, says it's a deal—but does not mention the deal to anyone.
   a. Wiley is hired and sells Sinkacre for $1.1 million. She demands her special bonus. Comparable bonuses are unheard of, and the SAI bylaws specifically state that employee bonuses must be approved by the board. Is the corporation bound?
   b. Flimm pays Wiley the bonus for Sinkacre and tells the board about their deal. A few months later, Wiley sells Sloughacre for $4 million and again demands her special bonus. Flimm and the board refuse. Is the corporation bound?

Explanations

1. a. Yes. Flimm, as an agent of the corporation, cannot create his own authority. Priscilla will want to have some assurance that the board approved the transaction and authorized Flimm to act for the corporation.

   In an important transaction with a corporation, third parties often will obtain a copy of the articles from state officials. The third party will also demand copies, certified by the corporation's secretary, of bylaws, relevant resolutions, and minutes of the meetings at which the resolutions were adopted. If an outside party does this, courts have held that they have done enough. Even if there was no actual authority, the corporation becomes bound under a theory of apparent authority. See *In re Drive-In Development Corp.*, 371 F.2d 215 (7th Cir. 1967). At some point, the actions of even renegade agents can bind the corporation.

   b. Perhaps. It depends on whether the resolution was approved and signed at a properly noticed board meeting. If not, under the "meeting rule," the directors have no power to act, and there is no actual authority. Although board action by consent is possible, the MBCA requires that it be unanimous. MBCA §8.21. This assures the opportunity for divergent views to be expressed and for collective decision making by the directors. Without having made inquiries, Priscilla cannot rely on Flimm's flat representations of authority. If the board met properly, however, there is actual authority. It does not matter whether Priscilla made any inquiries or what appearances Flimm created. The corporation is bound even though Priscilla neither knew of the authorizing resolution nor believed Flimm had authority.

   c. Yes. A majority of directors present at a properly called and convened board meeting authorized the sale. Unless the articles or bylaws preclude "presence" by means of audio communication, the director on the conference call is considered present at the meeting. MBCA §8.20(b). This "virtual presence" rule gives the board greater flexibility in handling emergency matters without the delay, trouble, and expense of a face-to-face meeting. The three directors constituted a quorum. MBCA §8.24. A majority of directors present at the meeting authorized the transaction. MBCA §8.24(c).

   That Priscilla was unaware of this board action is irrelevant to the existence of actual authority. But she takes a considerable risk in not investigating the board's authority. If, for example, the third director had given a proxy for another director to act in his place or had not been on a conference call in which the other directors could hear him, the action would not have been authorized.

   d. Yes. Although any notice defects are waived if the directors in attendance fail to object to them at the meeting, an absent director does not waive notice defects. MBCA §8.23. The notice requirements are meant to assure the representation of all views, and the failure of the absent director to waive the defect undermines the validity of actions taken at the meeting. Nonetheless, an absent director can waive notice in writing even after the meeting, if the notice is filed with the meeting's minutes.

2. a. Probably, under a few theories.

Implied actual authority. Under a theory of implied actual authority, the corporation can be bound by its past acquiescence in Flimm's practice of seeking after-the-fact board authorization. In effect, by its actions the board has implicitly revised the prior-approval bylaw. If Flimm had reasonably come to believe the board had given him authority, this understanding binds the corporation. But if his practice were not firmly established or if Flimm knew the board continued to consider the prior-approval bylaw to be binding, this internal understanding would be negated. In either event, implied actual authority is a matter of internal corporate delegation and does not depend on whether Boyce knew of Flimm's practice or the board's reaction to previous sales.

Apparent authority. Flimm's statements may also have created apparent authority. Boyce can argue that the board, by naming Flimm as president, created the appearance that he had authority to bind the corporation in the ordinary course of its business, including in selling corporate property. Under this theory, it is irrelevant that the bylaws had withdrawn actual authority for contracts not preapproved by the board. Apparent authority exists if contracts like the Bog Manor contract are ordinary for corporate presidents of comparable businesses or for Flimm.

If Boyce knew that it was common practice in comparable sales contracts for the corporate president to sign, the Bog Manor contract is ordinary and within Flimm's apparent authority. Even if there were no such practice, SAI is bound if the transaction was in its ordinary business — in the eyes of Boyce. This will depend on the nature of SAI's business, the uniqueness of Bog Manor, and the dollar size of the transaction. If Boyce knew that SAI was in the business of buying and reselling drained swampland, that property such as Bog Manor was easily found, and that the size of the transaction was not substantial for SAI, the contract would seem ordinary and Flimm's authority apparent. The absence of any of these factors, however, would compel Boyce to verify Flimm's authority.

Inherent authority. Flimm's position as president, if known to Boyce, might be enough to infer inherent authority. Although not all states recognize this theory and it has not been included in the Restatement (Third) of Agency, it provides a way of elevating third-party expectations over corporate centralized decision making. If Flimm were a major shareholder, requiring formal board approval would elevate form over substance, at the expense of the third party. Nonetheless, if Boyce had reason to doubt Flimm's authority because of the size of the transaction or Flimm's statements about the need for board approval, protection of Boyce's expectations would be less compelling.

b. Yes. The three directors constitute a quorum, and a majority vote of the directors present is sufficient for board action. See MBCA §8.24. Board action creates express actual authority, which does not depend on the outsider's knowledge or reliance.

c. No, not on a theory of express actual authority. According to the MBCA, a quorum must be present when the vote is taken. MBCA §8.24(c). Armed with the power to break a quorum, minority directors have additional hold-up powers in close votes. Some courts, however, have not allowed directors to challenge a vote if they absented themselves or left during a meeting to prevent a quorum.

3. a. Perhaps, under a theory of apparent authority or respondeat superior. As explained above, an outsider may rely on the appearances created by the corporate board. The corporation's practice of accepting installment contracts creates an expectation among outsiders, which the board must negate if it changes policies. Otherwise, outsiders' reliance binds the corporation.

In addition, Naomi can argue corporate liability on a respondeat superior theory. Flimm's intentional misstatements, if in the course of his employment, bind the corporation if Naomi relied on them to her loss. This theory might be difficult in an extraordinary corporate transaction, where the transaction is so unusual or large that a *reasonable* party would not rely on the agent's statements, but would demand verification of corporate authority. In such a case reasonable reliance—a necessary element of a deceit action—would be lacking. But if Naomi's reliance was reasonable, as seems to be the case in this example, the corporation would be liable for Flimm's tortious representation of authority—if it does not honor the contract.

b. She could seek board ratification. Although authority is measured at the time of the transaction, the board can create actual authority by ratifying the sales contract. Express ratification, in a board resolution, creates express actual authority retroactively—whatever the doubts about the agent's authority originally.

4. a. Not bound. Under the MBCA, all directors must receive at least two days' notice of a special meeting of the board. See MBCA §8.22(b). Although the resolution may indicate board action, Naomi will also want to see a copy of the minutes of the meeting that confirm that proper notice was given or waived by all directors. MBCA §8.23.

b. Perhaps bound. Without a meeting, the board action is not valid. Although board action by written consents is possible, the MBCA requires that it be unanimous. MBCA §8.21. In this example, even assuming e-mail constitutes a writing, not all directors gave their written consent. Nonetheless, it might be argued that their e-mail communications constituted a meeting, particularly if each member's e-mail comments were copied to the others. The MBCA requires that directors can participate in a meeting without being physically present if they "may simultaneously hear each other during the meeting." MBCA §8.20(b). Do persons "hear" each other in a series of Internet instant message exchanges? Arguably yes—so long as everyone sees the others' messages and can participate fully in the discussion.

c. Not bound. The meeting lacked the two-day notice required by statute. See MBCA §8.22(b). Although it might be argued that the directors (including those who abandoned the conference call) waived any objection to notice by participating in the meeting, the MBCA requires that such waiver be signed by directors entitled to notice and filed with the minutes of the meeting. MBCA §8.23. The corporation can act with some, but not complete, flexibility.

d. Perhaps bound. Although the board can delegate its functions to a committee, including negotiating and approving a contract, the committee must be composed of directors. MBCA §8.25. The appointment of a nondirector may render the committee's actions invalid. Nonetheless, it could be argued that the two directors appointed to the committee constituted a proper committee of two. Viewing the outside lawyer as an advisor to the two directors, the committee's action is perhaps binding.

5. a. Perhaps, on a theory of inherent authority. It would seem that there is neither actual authority (which requires board approval) nor apparent authority (because such a bonus is extraordinary). Nonetheless, as between SAI and Wiley, it can be argued that SAI should bear the risk of Flimm's usurpation of authority. Given Flimm's position and Wiley's reliance on him, the requirement of board approval—presumably to protect shareholders from the actions of rogue officers—is not terribly compelling. This is particularly so because Flimm is the majority shareholder. Allowing the corporation to avoid Flimm's promise would stand on its head the corporate authority rules, which are meant to protect the corporate principal (mainly shareholders) from renegade agents. That is, it would protect Flimm from himself.

b. Probably, on a theory of implied ratification. The board's acceptance of the special bonus in connection with the Sinkacre deal can be seen as an implicit ratification of the bonus contract. The effect of this ratification is as though Flimm had original authority to agree to the special bonus clause. The board cannot now disavow Flimm's exercise of authority.

Limitations on Corporate Distributions

Corporate distributions create potential conflicts between the corporation's shareholders and its creditors. Dividends and other distributions to shareholders deplete the cushion of corporate assets and cash flows that creditors count on for payment. Distributions allow junior claimants (equity shareholders) to jump ahead of senior claimants (bondholders and other creditors).

This chapter describes the methods by which the corporation can distribute money to shareholders (§31.1), the elaborate (often porous) legal apparatus meant to limit corporate distributions that put creditors at risk (§31.2), the contractual limitations sometimes placed on distributions (§31.3), and the liability of directors for authorizing illegal distributions (§31.4).

§31.1 DISTRIBUTIONS—TRANSFERRING ASSETS TO SHAREHOLDERS

The corporation can distribute its assets to shareholders through dividends, capital (or liquidating) distributions, and stock redemptions or repurchases by the corporation.

§31.1.1 Dividends and Distributions

Dividends

Dividends are periodic payments by the corporation to shareholders in proportion to their share ownership. Dividends are usually made in relation to past or current corporate earnings. Many corporations have *dividend policies* that call for dividend payments based on a percentage of earnings. In the United States, declaration of dividends—that is, the decision to pay them—generally is within the discretion of the board of directors and protected by the business judgment rule (see §12.2).

Dividends may be paid in cash or property. Once the board declares a *cash dividend,* shareholders obtain rights as creditors for the dividend amount as of the record date specified by the board. Once declared, the board has no discretion to rescind a cash dividend unless the dividend is not legally authorized or shareholders authorize the rescission. (Some early courts suggest rescission is acceptable when there is an intervening catastrophe, such as a fire at the manufacturing plant, that makes payment imprudent.)

Capital Distributions

A *capital distribution* is a payment to shareholders made in relation to capital, not earnings. Although some state statutes permit capital distributions in circumstances when dividends would not be permissible, the current MBCA does not distinguish between dividends and capital distributions. See Official Comment, MBCA §6.40.

Stock Dividends

A *stock dividend* is the pro rata distribution of additional shares of the corporation among existing shareholders. It does not distribute corporate assets to shareholders. Its effect is simply to divide ownership among a greater number of shares. Because no assets are transferred to shareholders, corporate statutes do not treat a stock dividend as a distribution. MBCA §1.40(6) (definition of "distribution" excludes transfers of corporation's own shares). Stock dividends can be made even when the corporation is insolvent. As with any issuance of new shares, however, there must be sufficient authorized but unissued shares.

Stock Splits

In a *stock split,* outstanding shares are converted into (and replaced by) additional new shares. For example, in a three-for-one stock split each outstanding share is extinguished and replaced by three new shares, which must be authorized. Most corporate statutes allow the board on its own initiative to authorize a stock split although some also require shareholder approval. From a financial standpoint, a stock split is identical to a stock dividend: Shareholders receive additional shares without paying any consideration to the corporation

§31.1.2 Redemption and Repurchase

The corporation can also distribute assets to shareholders by acquiring outstanding shares through redemption or repurchase—a corporate buyback. A *redemption* usually refers to a forced sale initiated by the corporation, in accordance with a contract or the articles of incorporation. A *repurchase* is a voluntary buy-sell transaction between the corporation and a shareholder.

Although buybacks were once a great conundrum of corporate law—''How can the corporation buy itself?''—all corporate statutes now recognize the power of the corporation to repurchase its own shares. MBCA §6.31. Share buybacks have become a preferred way for public corporations to distribute cash to shareholders, since each shareholder can choose whether to participate in selling shares back to the corporation and any resulting gain is treated as a capital gain, which sometimes has been taxed at lower rates than the receipt of dividends. In addition, stock repurchases (unlike cash dividends) do not decrease the stock price because after a repurchase there are fewer shares outstanding.

§31.2 LIMITATIONS ON DISTRIBUTIONS

A corporate distribution (whatever its form) transfers corporate assets to shareholders, thus jeopardizing creditor claims. Creditors are particularly vulnerable since the power to declare dividends resides with the board of directors—a body elected by and accountable to the shareholders. To protect creditors and sometimes preferred shareholders, corporate law specifies when distributions are legally authorized.

§31.2.1 "Equity Insolvency" Test

Corporate statutes uniformly forbid distributions that would render the corporation unable to pay its debts as they become due in the ordinary course of business. MBCA §6.40(c)(1). This common-sense *equity insolvency* test is concerned with liquidity—the ability of the corporation to meet its debt load. It does not depend on the relation of asset value to liabilities. (The test is called "equity" because it was used in equity courts to determine a debtor's solvency; it should be distinguished from the use of "equity" to refer to shareholders' ownership interests.)

In practice, the equity insolvency test reflects what primarily concerns creditors—namely, that the business will not have enough assets after a distribution to pay its debts. The test is similar to that of the Uniform Fraudulent Transfer Act, which deems any transaction without reasonably equivalent value (that is, where assets are transferred without fair consideration) to be fraudulent as to a debtor's creditors if it renders the debtor unable to pay its debts as they come due. UFTA §4(a)(2)(ii) (see §32.2).

§31.2.2 "Balance Sheet" Tests

In addition to the equity insolvency test, nearly all corporation statutes impose accounting tests to decide when distributions are legally authorized. The tests use accounting entries made on the corporation's balance sheet to evaluate whether specified accounts are sufficiently large for a particular distribution to be made.

Keep in mind that the *balance sheet* tests are unrelated to whether the corporation in fact has the cash or assets to make a distribution. Although courts, lawyers, and law professors often speak of whether dividends or other distributions can "come out" of surplus or some other account, this is only metaphorical. There is no bank vault into which money is deposited for each account. The balance sheet accounts are merely accounting entries. It is entirely possible that a corporation with a substantial "earned surplus" has no cash and cannot pay its debts as they come due.

Many balance sheet tests continue to use a conceptual framework based on par value to account for capital contributions and earnings of the corporation. See §4.2.1. These tests—intended to provide creditors a supposedly inviolable financial cushion known as "legal capital"—rely on highly conceptual and often meaningless accounting conventions that sometimes have nothing to do with the financial condition of the corporation. See Bayless Manning, *Legal Capital* 63-90 (3d ed. 1990) (scathing and highly readable criticism of legal capital regime). Many modern corporate statutes, including the MBCA, abandon legal capital concepts such as par value, stated capital, capital surplus, earned surplus, and treasury stock. But it is small comfort to today's law students that legal capital is on its deathbed. The concept of legal capital survives in some jurisdictions—most notably Delaware—and promises to torment at least one more generation of corporate lawyers. We first describe the accounting basics relevant to the balance sheet tests, and then look at the operation of the "legal capital" and other more modern balance sheet tests.

Balance Sheet and "Shareholders' Equity" Accounts

The balance sheet tests are essentially formulas into which you plug numbers derived from accounting entries on the corporation's balance sheet. Before discussing the tests, we provide a basic primer on balance sheet accounting and the three "Shareholders' Equity" accounts referred to by the legal capital regime.

A *balance sheet* is an accountant's snapshot of a corporation's financial status at a given moment.

Balance Sheet

Left Side of Ledger	Right Side of Ledger
Assets — nominal value of corporations assets (usually based on historical cost)	**Liabilities** — nominal value of corporation's short-term and long-term debts **Shareholders' Equity** — amount Assets exceed Liabilities — the corporation's net worth, sometimes referred to as "book value"

Whenever an item is changed on one side of the ledger, an equal amount must be entered on the other side — always a balanced sheet. The equation "Assets = Liabilities + Shareholders' Equity" always holds true. For example:

Corporation	Assets	=	Liabilities	+	Equity
• Issues new stock	Increases				Increases
• Borrows money	Increases		Increases		
• Makes money	Increases				Increases
• Loses money	Decreases				Decreases
• Repays a loan	Decreases		Decreases		

The legal capital regime (and the accounting profession) use Shareholders' Equity accounts to show capital contributions and corporate earnings.

- **Stated (or paid-in) capital.** Equity capital contributions are allocated to the *stated capital* (or *paid-in capital*) account. The amount in this account represents the aggregated par value of the corporation's outstanding equity securities. If there is no par, the board by resolution establishes a "stated value" for each share.

Illustration. Suppose immediately after its incorporation Corporation issues 2,000 common shares (par $100). According to the legal capital regime, Corporation has $200,000 in cash and $200,000 in its stated (or paid-in) capital account. This is represented by accounting entries on the balance sheet:

Assets		**Liabilities**		
Cash	200,000			0
		Shareholders' equity		
		Stated capital: $100 par common, 2,000 shares		200,000
Total	$200,000		Total	$200,000

- **Capital surplus (or paid-in surplus).** As we have seen, the corporation can issue low-par stock to avoid exposing shareholders to watered stock liability (see §4.2.1). If the corporation issues low-par stock, the amount paid for the stock in excess of its par value is reflected in the *capital surplus* (or *paid-in surplus*) account. (Modern accountants favor the term "capital contributed in excess of par.")

Illustration. Suppose Corporation issues 2,000 common shares, par $10, at a price of $100 per share. Because Assets increase by $200,000 and "stated capital" (the number of shares times par) is only $20,000, a "capital surplus" is created:

Assets		**Liabilities**		
Cash	200, 000			0
		Shareholders' equity		
		Stated capital: $10 par common, 2,000 shares		20,000
		Capital surplus		180,000
Total	$200,000		Total	$200,000

Illustration. If no-par stock is issued, the full issue price is allocated to stated capital, unless the board allocates some to capital surplus. Suppose Corporation issues 2,000 common shares, no-par, for $100 per share, with the board allocating $50,000 to stated capital and $150,000 to capital surplus:

Assets		**Liabilities**		
Cash	200, 000			0
		Shareholders' equity		
		Stated capital: no-par common, 2,000 shares		50,000
		Capital surplus		150,000
Total	$200,000		Total	$200,000

- **Earned surplus (or accumulated retained earnings).** After its initial capitalization, the corporation's financial affairs do not remain static. If all goes well, Assets will increase faster than Liabilities, and the business will show a profit; if not, Assets will fall faster than Liabilities, and the business will show a loss. In either event, adjustments will have to be made in the Shareholders' Equity accounts. *Earned surplus* (or, among accountants, *accumulated retained earnings*) represents accumulations of earnings (or losses) from earlier periods, less any dividends and other distributions paid in earlier years.

Illustration. Suppose the Corporation uses its capital to acquire working assets (inventory, plant, and so on), and after one year the Corporation's Assets exceed Liabilities by $230,000. Stated capital and capital surplus remain unchanged. The new surplus in Shareholders Equity is reflected as earned surplus:

Assets		**Liabilities**	
Cash	30, 000		0
Other assets	200,000	**Shareholders' equity**	
		Stated capital: no-par	50,000
		Capital surplus	150,000
		Earned surplus	30,000
Total	$230,000	Total	$230,000

- **Payment of dividend from surplus.** If the Corporation has a surplus, it may decide to pay a dividend—a transfer of Assets to shareholders. This will result in adjustments to the relevant Assets account (usually Cash) and the Shareholders' Equity accounts from which the dividend "is paid."

Illustration. Suppose the Corporation pays a dividend to shareholders of $30,000. The cash account is reduced as well as the earned surplus account. The stated capital and capital surplus accounts remain unchanged:

Assets		**Liabilities**	
Cash	0		0
Other assets	200,000	**Shareholders' equity**	
		Stated capital: no-par	50,000
		Capital surplus	150,000
		Earned surplus	0
Total	$200,000	Total	$200,000

"Legal Capital" Balance Sheet Tests

The legal capital tests limit corporate distributions according to the amounts in the Shareholders' Equity accounts. There is no one legal capital test; each depends on the language of the incorporating state's statute.

- **Surplus (capital impairment) test.** Many statutes allow distributions only "out of surplus," which Delaware defines as the amount by which "net assets [assets minus liabilities] exceed capital stock [stated capital]." Del. GCL §§154, 170 (dividends), 160 (repurchases). This "capital impairment" test is meant to keep the corporation's stated capital beyond the shareholders' reach on the simplistic assumption creditors will look to it as a measure of how much shareholders have paid into the corporate treasury since the corporation was formed.
- **Earned surplus test.** Some statutes employ a more demanding test and allow dividends (and corporate repurchases of shares) to come only from earned surplus. Pre-1980 MBCA §45(a) (dividends); pre-1980 MBCA §6 (repurchases).
- **Nimble dividends.** Some statutes allow dividends to come from current earnings, even when surplus (capital or earned) is unavailable. Pre-1980 MBCA §45(a) [alternative]. Such dividends are known as *nimble* dividends—current earnings are nimbly applied to dividends rather than to the deficit in the earned surplus account. Nimble dividends allow a corporation with large accumulated deficits and unpaid debts to attract new equity capital (on the promise of paying dividends if there are earnings), even though the corporation has no chance of taking on new debt. Thus, a deeply indebted corporation that earns a profit in the current year can distribute this profit to its shareholders before repaying its outstanding debts. Nimble dividend statutes offer little or no protection to creditors, and some statutes even allow nimble dividends from earnings of both the current and preceding year. Del. GCL §170(a).

Modern Balance Sheet Tests

A growing number of modern statutes, including the MBCA, do away with the legal capital concepts of stated capital, capital surplus, and earned surplus—rendering these accounts irrelevant for purposes of distributions. The MBCA balance sheet test requires only that, after a distribution, assets must exceed (1) liabilities plus (2) the total amount that would have to be paid on liquidation to any senior preferred shares. MBCA §6.40(c)(2). That is, the distribution may not be greater than Shareholders' Equity less any liquidation preferences. (This test is a strict interpretation of the historical "bankruptcy sense" of insolvency applied by law courts and is sometimes referred to as the "bankruptcy insolvency" test.)

California established the pattern for abolishing concepts of stated capital and surplus. The California statute, adopted in 1977, allows dividends if (1) total assets exceed 125 percent of total liabilities, (2) "current" assets exceed "current" liabilities, and (3) the payment does not endanger any liquidation preference. Cal. Corp. §§500(b), 502.

Effect on Balance Sheet

Normally, a distribution to shareholders reduces both Assets and Shareholders' Equity. Under the legal capital regime, a repurchase or redemption is reflected as *treasury stock*—technically issued, but no longer outstanding. Earned surplus is restricted until treasury stock is either resold, restored as authorized (but unissued), or canceled.

Illustration. Suppose Corporation issued 2,000 shares, par $100. After one year it has earnings of $25,000, and Corporation *repurchases* 100 shares for $200 per share. This $20,000 repurchase reduces the cash account in Assets and changes the Shareholders' Equity as follows:

Assets		**Liabilities**	
Cash	5, 000		0
Other assets	200,000	**Shareholders' equity**	
		Stated capital: $100 par common, 2,000 shares (100 shares in treasury)	200,000
		Earned surplus	
		Unrestricted 5,000	
		Restricted 20,000	25,000
		Less: 100 shares treasury stock	(20,000)
Total	$205,000	Total	$205,000

Under the legal capital regime, stock *redeemed* pursuant to the articles does not become treasury stock, but instead is automatically canceled or reverts to the status of authorized (but unissued) stock. The effect is to reduce stated capital by the par (or stated value) of the redeemed stock and to reduce the surplus account, if any, from which the redemption was made.

The MBCA does away with treasury stock and this elegant silliness—repurchased or redeemed stock reverts to authorized, but unissued, stock. Under the MBCA, the corporation can reacquire its stock so long as Assets exceed Liabilities (and any liquidation preferences). MBCA §6.40(c)(2). For example, if our Corporation has Shareholders' Equity of $205,000, it may repurchase up to $205,000 of its stock—regardless of stated capital, capital surplus, earned (restricted or unrestricted) surplus, current earnings, or treasury stock.

§31.2.3 Manipulating Balance Sheet to Increase Shareholders' Equity

Although the balance sheet tests have an air of plausibility, in practice they are porous. Based as they are on accounting entries, they recall the refrain that "figures never lie, but liars figure." By manipulating the amounts recorded as Assets, Liabilities, or Shareholders' Equity, it is possible to create legal capital on paper.

Whether and when this can be done raises a host of complex accounting issues, many beyond the scope of this book. For example:

Assets	Liabilities
• When should business expenditures be "expensed" and when should they be "capitalized" as an asset? • When should historical asset values be adjusted to reflect current market values? • When should losses be recognized and written off? • When can goodwill be capitalized and treated as an asset? • When can research and development expenses be capitalized?	• When should contingent liabilities be recognized and treated as liabilities? • How should long-term contingencies (such as pensions) be treated? • How should debts in foreign currencies be accounted for? **Shareholders' Equity** • How should stated capital change after a stock dividend? • What should be the treatment of stock that is not fully paid when issued? • How should convertible shares (such as $100 par preferred convertible into $1 par common) be treated? • What should be the effect of the corporation repurchasing its stock?

We consider only two (more common) methods by which boards can increase legal distributions to shareholders: "writing up" the value of appreciated assets and "writing down" stated capital.

Revaluation (or Reappraisal) Surplus

Because Assets must equal Liabilities plus Shareholders' Equity, any upward revaluation of Assets increases Shareholders' Equity. In general, the value assigned to Assets shown on the balance sheet is historical cost (less any depreciation), an amount often less than the assets' actual market value.

Some statutes and court decisions specifically allow good-faith revaluation of assets by the board. MBCA §6.40(d) ("fair valuation . . . reasonable under the circumstances"); Del. GCL §172; *Klang v. Smith's Food & Drug Center, Inc.*, 702 A.2d 150 (Del. 1997) (upholding repurchase of shares after board accepted revaluation of company's assets under "market multiple" approach). Some statutes expressly forbid it. If assets are revalued above historical cost, the legal capital regime refers to the surplus account that results as *revaluation surplus*.

Reduction Surplus

Under the legal capital regime, surplus can be created simply by reducing stated capital and making a corresponding increase in a new surplus account, often known as *reduction surplus*. (Some statutes do not have a separate label, but simply add this surplus to capital surplus. Pre-1980 MBCA §70.)

Reduction surplus can be created in a number of ways, including: (1) an amendment to the articles of incorporation approved by the shareholders reducing the par value (or stated value) and a board resolution transferring a specified amount from stated capital to reduction surplus [Del. GCL §242]; or (2) in the case of no-par stock, a board resolution approved by the shareholders transferring the amount from stated capital to reduction surplus. Some statutes also require the filing of a certificate disclosing such reductions. Del. GCL §§242, 244. Others, however, impose restrictions on using reduction surplus similar to those imposed on stated capital.

§31.2.4 Timing of Distributions

Under older statutes the distribution's legality is tested at the time the distribution is made, not when the board authorizes it. The MBCA measures the legality of a distribution on its authorization date unless the distribution is to be paid more than 120 days after authorization. MBCA §6.40(e). This reverses the older rule that a dividend declared when the corporation is solvent (and has a surplus) cannot be paid if the corporation becomes insolvent before payment.

Both rules create problems when the corporation makes a distribution by giving a promissory note that calls for installment payments to the shareholder. In this case, do the relevant distribution limits apply as each payment is made or only when the note was originally given? Many statutes treat the installment note as an ordinary debt of the corporation, provided full payment was legally authorized when the note was given. MBCA §6.40(f); Del. GCL §160; MBCA §45; see *Williams v. Nevelow*, 513 S.W.2d 535 (Tex. 1974). But some courts have held otherwise, subordinating the former shareholder's note to claims of other creditors.

§31.3 CONTRACTUAL LIMITATIONS ON DISTRIBUTIONS

Given the gaping holes in the legal capital regime, it should not surprise you that creditors and preferred shareholders rarely rely on legal capital rules when extending credit or investing their money. Instead, many long-term creditors (particularly bank lenders and bondholders) and preferred shareholders demand contractual limits on dividends and distributions, contained in a *trust indenture* (specifying the duties of a trustee who acts on behalf of bond holders) or sometimes incorporated into the articles of incorporation.

§31.4 LIABILITY OF DIRECTORS (AND SHAREHOLDERS) FOR ILLEGAL DISTRIBUTIONS

Corporate distributions represent a conflict-of-interest transaction as to creditors, and directors were once strictly liable for approving an illegal distribution. Modern statutes are not as exacting and impose liability on directors who assent to an illegal distribution only if they did not act in good faith. MBCA §8.33(a) (liability if director did not comply with §8.30(a)). Liability is to the corporation (or to creditors upon dissolution) and is joint and several. Some statutes allow directors held liable to seek contribution from other directors who assented to the illegal distribution and pro rata recoupment from shareholders who accepted the distribution knowing it was illegal. MBCA §8.33(b).

Under some statutes, shareholders who receive an illegal distribution may be liable to the corporation, along with directors, if the shareholders knew the distribution was illegal. Cal. Corp. §316. A distribution by an insolvent corporate debtor may also constitute a fraudulent conveyance, allowing creditors to recover directly from the shareholders who received the distribution. See UFTA §8(b) (if transfer voidable, creditor may recover value of asset transferred, subject to equitable adjustments, from first transferee).

Examples

1. Bacchanalia Banquets, incorporated in New Columbia, has one class of common stock, with 3,000 shares authorized and 1,500 shares issued and outstanding. The board of directors wants to declare a dividend of $1.50 per share.
   a. Bacchanalia's articles of incorporation require that a shareholder majority approve dividends in any year greater than $2,000. The New Columbia statute would otherwise permit the dividend. Can the board declare the dividend?
   b. Bacchanalia's shareholders approve the dividend. On September 15 the board fixes a record date of October 1 for payment. On October 1 Anna owns 500 shares of Bacchanalia stock, which she agrees to sell to Benny on October 10. The dividends are paid on October 31. Who is entitled to the dividends?
   c. A week after the record date of October 1, the directors learn the corporation's current earned surplus is smaller than they thought. The board rescinds the dividend. Can the board?

2. New Columbia has an old-fashioned legal capital regime that imposes a surplus (capital impairment) test. Bacchanalia's three shareholders—Anna, Benny, and Chris—each contributed $50,000 in cash and assets as the corporation's initial capitalization.
   a. Each shareholder received 500 shares, par $100. If there is no other corporate activity, can the board pay dividends? If so, how much?
   b. After the initial capitalization, a bank lends the corporation $90,000. What does the balance sheet look like now? Can the corporation repurchase shares? If so, how much can be paid?
   c. How might Anna, Benny, and Chris provide themselves greater access to the corporation's assets?

3. Suppose Bacchanalia's initial capitalization was $150,000 no-par common, and the board allocated $100,000 to capital surplus. Profits and losses are:

First year	losses of $100,000
Second year	profits of $10,000
Third year	profits of $55,000
Current year (to date)	profits of $20,000

There have been no distributions or other stock issues. As of the end of the most recent fiscal year, the corporation's assets and liabilities were as follows:

Balance Sheet
(after three years of operation)

Assets			**Liabilities**		
Cash		$10,000	Bank loan		$90,000
Accounts receivable		60,000	Accounts payable		44,000
Inventory		50,000		Total	$134,000
Warehouse		100,000			
Patents		29,000	**Shareholders' equity**		$115,000
	Total	$249,000		Total	$249,000

a. What are the Shareholders' Equity accounts?
b. Can the board distribute to the shareholders a pro rata amount of the corporation's accounts receivable? What if Bacchanalia were incorporated in Delaware?

4. Bacchanalia's fortunes continue to rise. Profits for the fourth year are $60,000.
   a. Using the Shareholders' Equity accounts in question 3a and assuming no distributions, what would the Shareholders' Equity accounts look like at the end of four years?
   b. Using this balance sheet, what is the maximum distribution the board can make under an earned surplus test that allows nimble dividends and capital distributions?
   c. Bacchanalia's shareholders want even more. Can they receive a further distribution from stated capital?
   d. Bacchanalia bought a warehouse for $100,000 four years ago. Because of increased land values, the warehouse today is worth $175,000. Does this increase in asset value increase the amount which the corporation can distribute?

5. Anna, one of Bacchanalia's founding shareholders, wants the corporation to repurchase her shares. An investment banker, using the earnings potential of the business, values the corporation at $600,000. Anna wants one-third, or $200,000.
   a. Using the statement of shareholders' equity in question 4d above, what is the book value of Anna's shares?
   b. Benny and Chris, the two other shareholders, are willing to have the corporation borrow $200,000 to fund the repurchase. Would the repurchase be legal under the MBCA?
   c. The corporation offers to repurchase Anna's stock with a note that would pay $50,000 a year for the next five years. Is the repurchase legal under the MBCA?

6. Two years after giving Anna a $250,000 note to buy her shares, Bacchanalia becomes insolvent. The bankruptcy trustee sells the corporation's warehouse for a mere $50,000 and sues Benny and Chris for the distribution to Anna, claiming their revaluation of the warehouse (writing up the $100,000 cost to $175,000) was improper. The court agrees the revaluation was unreasonable and the distribution illegal.
   a. Are Benny and Chris strictly liable for approving an illegal distribution?
   b. Benny and Chris assert they relied on an appraiser's report stating that commercial buildings in the area of the warehouse had increased in value by 80 percent since Bacchanalia's original purchase. Does this exonerate them under the MBCA?
   c. Benny and Chris are liable, how much are they liable for under the MBCA? (Remember that before revaluation, shareholders' equity was $175,000.)
   d. Anna liable? To whom, and for how much?

7. The bankruptcy trustee resuscitates Bacchanalia's business. New owners approach a bank for a loan. The bank, wary of porous legal capital protection, demands restrictions on corporate distributions to the new owners. Draft a contractual restriction for the bank.

EXPLANATIONS

Explanations

1. a. No. Even though the dividend is legally authorized by statute, additional restrictions can be imposed by contract or in the corporation's organic documents. MBCA §6.40 (distributions to shareholders subject to restrictions in articles of incorporation). The $1.50 dividend would result in total dividends of $2,250, requiring shareholder approval. In a closely held corporation, shareholders may not want dividends paid because of double taxation (see §2.3.1). It may be desirable for corporate profits to reach them as deductible salaries or other non-share payments.
   b. Anna is entitled to the dividends, as record owner on October 1. By setting a record date, the board simplifies the problem of identifying who is paid dividends (see §4.1.2). Because of this rule, sellers in stock sales agreements often will assign to the buyer any unpaid stock dividends.
   c. Probably, though it might depend on the statute. Although a declared dividend creates an obligation of the corporation to pay, it may be weaker than a fixed debt obligation. Courts have allowed corporations to rescind a dividend if the payment would be illegal or, according to some Depression-era cases, if circumstances change dramatically.

Under the MBCA, the dividend's legality would be determined when it was authorized, if paid (as here) within 120 days. MBCA §6.40(e)(3). Other statutes are not as precise and may permit the board to rescind a dividend that, though legal when declared, would be illegal when paid—as might happen if the corporation suddenly faced insolvency. Even if payment were not illegal, a court (whether or not in an MBCA jurisdiction) might well respect the board's good-faith determination to rescind the dividend for a valid business purpose. This is consistent with the rule that payment of dividends is within the board's discretion. Nonetheless, shareholders often rely on dividends when declared, and this expectation interest might force the board to have a compelling, not just rational, business reason for rescinding a dividend once declared.

2. a. No, under the relevant balance sheet test. The initial balance sheet is: Even though cash is available, legal capital is impaired because net assets less stated capital is zero—there is no surplus. Conceivably, non-cash assets could be revalued to create a surplus, but it would seem difficult since the board only recently valued them at $50,000 in connection with the initial capitalization. Stated capital is supposed to represent the long-term investment of shareholders. In theory, stated capital provides creditors the assurance that assets equal to shareholder investment are available to satisfy their claims.

Balance Sheet
(after initial capitalization)

Assets		**Liabilities**	
Cash	$100,000		$ 0
Other assets	50,000	**Shareholders' equity**	
		Stated capital:	
		$100 par common,	
		1,500 shares	$150,000
Total	$150,000	Total	$150,000

b. No repurchase is permitted. The new liability ($90,000 loan) will be balanced by new assets ($90,000 in cash):

Balance Sheet
(after bank loan)

Assets		**Liabilities**	
Cash	$190,000		$ 90,000
Other assets	50,000	**Shareholders' equity**	
		Stated capital:	
		$100 par common,	
		1,500 shares	$150,000
Total	$240,000	Total	$240,000

Even though the business is awash in cash, share repurchases are subject to the same legal capital limits as are dividends and other distributions. See MBCA §6; MBCA §1.40(6); Del. GCL §160. In this example, the corporation has no more "legal capital" to make a distribution than it did before the bank loan. Net assets (assets minus liabilities) less stated capital is still zero—there is no surplus.

c. The three should change their high-par shares to low-par or no-par shares. For example, if the three shareholders approved an amendment to the articles so that par is restated as $1, the shareholders' equity account would look like this:

Shareholders' Equity

Stated capital		$ 1,500
Capital surplus		148,500
	Total	$150,000

Under a surplus (capital impairment) test, the corporation could now pay *dividends* totaling $148,500. Moreover, even under an earned surplus statute, the corporation could make a *capital distribution* of $148,500, provided certain formalities were adhered to, though notably, notice to creditors is not among them. Creditors who naively relied on stated capital as an inviolable equity cushion might be surprised how easily shareholders can deplete the cushion. The only meaningful statutory protection for creditors is the equity insolvency test, which requires that after the distribution the corporation remain able to meet its debts (the bank loan) as they come due.

3. a. Shareholders' equity, as of the end of three years, would be as follows:

Shareholders' Equity

Stated capital		$ 50,000
Capital surplus		100,000
Earned surplus (deficit)		−35,000
	Total	$115,000

Most statutes respect the board's allocation of the no-par stock, $100,000 to capital surplus and $50,000 to stated capital. Earned surplus can be calculated: the sum of accumulated earnings for the prior years (a negative $35,000) less any distributions (none). Current earnings will show up once the end-of-year balance sheet is prepared. Notice that Assets [$249,000] = Liabilities [$134,000] + Shareholders' Equity [$115,000], as must always be the case.

b. Yes. Dividends can be in the form of cash or other property. MBCA §1.40(6) (distribution includes "transfer of cash or other property").

The accounts-receivable dividend must, however, meet the equity insolvency test and relevant balance sheet test.

Equity insolvency test. Whatever balance sheet test applies, corporate statutes uniformly require that the corporation be able to continue to pay its debts as they come due. MBCA §6.40(c)(1).

Balance sheet test. If the "equity insolvency" test is met, the legality of the dividend depends on which balance sheet test applies. Consider first the MBCA approach:

- **MBCA "bankruptcy insolvency" test.** The board can declare a $60,000 dividend because assets minus liabilities—that is, shareholders' equity—exceeds $60,000, provided the dividend does not endanger any liquidation preference. MBCA §6.40(c)(2). If, for example, preferred shareholders are entitled to receive $70,000 in liquidation, the board could not declare a $60,000 dividend because, after the dividend, assets would be less than the sum of (i) liabilities plus (ii) liquidation preferences ($189,000 is less than $134,000 + $70,000).

  Now consider the more convoluted Delaware approach:
- **Stated capital test.** There is sufficient surplus—capital surplus plus earned surplus totals $65,000. Del. GCL §170.
- **Earned surplus test.** Earned surplus is negative and therefore not a legal source for dividends. MBCA §45. Nonetheless, under some statutes, the board can declare a $60,000 dividend by calling it a capital distribution. Capital or paid-in surplus ($100,000) can be the source for such a distribution, if permitted in the articles or approved by the shareholders. MBCA §46.
- **Nimble dividends test.** Even though earned surplus is insufficient, the board might be able to declare "nimble dividends" using earnings from both the current year ($20,000) and the previous year ($55,000). Some statutes allow this, Del. GCL §170(a); others limit nimble dividends to the current year's earnings. MBCA §45 [alternative]. As you can see, the exceptions nearly engulf the earned surplus test.

4. a. The only change is an increase in earned surplus from a negative $35,000 to a positive $25,000:

Shareholders' Equity

Stated capital		$ 50,000
Capital surplus		100,000
Earned surplus (deficit)		25,000
	Total	$175,000

b. The maximum distribution: $125,000. Earned surplus can be a source for $25,000 and capital surplus can be a source for $100,000. Nimble dividends cannot be paid since there is earned surplus.

c. Yes. Under some statutes, the shareholders could approve a reduction of stated capital. Pre-1984 MBCA §69. If shareholders reduced stated capital from $50,000 to $1,000, the excess $49,000 would be added to capital surplus or become reduction surplus (depending on how the statute defined it):

Shareholders' Equity		
Stated capital		$ 1,000
Capital surplus		100,000
Reduction surplus (deficit)		49,000
Earned surplus (deficit)		25,000
	Total	$175,000

However described, this additional surplus could be used as a legal source for dividends under a surplus (capital impairment) test or earned surplus statutes that allowed capital distributions. The effect would be that $174,000 in assets could be distributed to shareholders.

In Delaware the same result could be accomplished if the board approved a corporate repurchase or redemption of shares and reduced capital by the amount represented by those shares. Del. GCL §244(a)(2).

d. Perhaps, by revaluing the warehouse on the balance sheet. The effect will be to increase shareholders' equity by $75,000, reflected in revaluation surplus:

Shareholders' Equity		
Stated capital		$ 1,000
Capital surplus		100,000
Reduction surplus		49,000
Revaluation surplus		75,000
Earned surplus (deficit)		25,000
	Total	$250,000

A number of jurisdictions permit use of revaluation surplus as a legal source for distributions. The MBCA requires that any revaluation be reasonable in the circumstances. MBCA §6.40(d). This may undermine the creditor-protection policy of the balance sheet tests and deviate from the accounting penchant to value assets at historical cost. But revaluation may more accurately reflect present value of the corporation's assets.

5. a. The book value of each share is Shareholders' Equity ($250,000) divided by the number of outstanding shares—or $166.67 per share. Anna's 500 shares have a book value of $83,333.33. It is frequently true that book value is less than appraised (or market) value. Book value represents the amount that would be realized if the business assets were liquidated at historic cost and all liabilities paid. In a going

concern, such as Bacchanalia's catering business, expected earnings provide a better guide to the value of an ownership interest than do current net assets.

b. Yes, assuming no liquidation preferences and no insolvency. Under MBCA §1.40(6), distributions include share repurchases. The repurchase satisfies the MBCA's bankruptcy insolvency test: Assets exceed liabilities by $250,000 (Shareholders' Equity). MBCA §6.40(c)(2).

c. Yes, since there is currently sufficient legal capital and assuming the corporation will be able to continue to pay its debts. The MBCA measures the validity of the repurchase when the corporation incurs the debt to Anna, not when each payment comes due. MBCA §6.40(f). If the business declines, Anna would be in the same position as any other unsecured creditor of the corporation. This means her sale of stock moved her residual equity claim ahead to that of a debt claim.

   In some jurisdictions, the validity of payments for the repurchase of shares is measured at the time of each payment. Thus, if the corporation lacked legal sources or would be rendered insolvent when it made any future payment, Anna's note might be subordinated to other creditors' claims against the corporation.

6. a. No, not under most modern statutes. Although some statutes prohibit revaluation surplus, most statutes make directors who approve an illegal distribution liable only if they did not act in good faith. Del. GCL §172 (directors "fully protected in relying in good faith" upon corporate records and professional or expert opinions); MBCA §§8.33(a). This suggests the presumptions of the business judgment rule apply, and Benny's and Chris's liability may well turn on whether they were personally interested, grossly negligent, or knew the revaluation was unjustified. See MBCA §8.30(a).

b. Perhaps. The report will undermine any argument that they were grossly uninformed. Nonetheless, they might still be liable if they stood to gain personally from the repurchase or if they knew the revaluation would seriously weaken creditor claims. It is telling that they did not seek to also sell their shares to the corporation and that the corporation did not become insolvent until two years after the repurchase.

c. The MBCA specifies that directors are liable only for the amount of the distribution that exceeds that which could have been distributed legally. MBCA §8.33(a). (Other statutes are not as clear.) Under the MBCA standard, a valuation of the warehouse of $100,000 (its historic cost, as opposed to its lower market value) would be consistent with usual "accounting practices and principles." Shareholders' equity (the excess of assets over liabilities) would then have been $175,000. This means $75,000 of the $250,000 distribution to Anna was not from a legal source. Benny and Chris would each be jointly and severally liable for this amount.

d. In many jurisdictions, Anna is liable if she *knew* the repurchase was illegal. MBCA §8.33(b)(2). This is an even more protective standard than applies to directors. Even if Anna sought to protect herself to the detriment of the firm's creditors—arguably not in good faith—Anna would be liable only if she knew that the revaluation was excessive.

Some statutes, such as Del. GCL §174(c) and MBCA §8.33(b), make shareholders liable in recoupment only to directors who are themselves liable for approving an unlawful distribution. Other statutes allow the corporation to recover directly from knowing shareholders. In either case, Anna would be liable in proportion to the amount she received. In our example, Anna would be liable for her share of the excess $75,000 (see previous answer).

7. A provision along the following lines could be inserted in an indenture agreement.

Section XX. Restrictions on Distributions

(a) The Corporation may not make any distribution in respect of Common Shares, unless the Corporation's annual income in the preceding fiscal year was at least $50,000. If so, distributions are permitted only as follows:
   1. $1.00 per share per fiscal quarter if income for the immediately preceding quarter was at least $10,000;
   2. $1.50 per share per fiscal quarter if income for the immediately preceding quarter was at least $20,000;
   3. $2.00 per share per fiscal quarter if income for the immediately preceding quarter was at least $30,000.

   Distributions in excess of $2.00 per share per fiscal quarter are permitted if authorized by the Bank in writing.

(b) For purposes of this section, a distribution is a direct or indirect transfer of money or other property (except the Corporation's own shares) or incurrence of indebtedness by the Corporation to or for the benefit of its shareholders in respect of Common shares. A distribution includes (i) a declaration or payment of a dividend, (ii) a purchase, redemption, or other acquisition of shares, and (iii) a distribution of indebtedness.

(c) The Corporation will cause its articles of incorporation to be amended to contain the restrictions of subsections (a) and (b) of this Section.

The indenture should specify that failing to abide by any of these restrictive covenants will be an event of default and that on default the lender may step in to protect its loan.

Piercing the Corporate Veil

Limited liability tempts insiders to exploit the corporation's creditors. Insiders can use their control to create a false appearance of corporate solvency, engage in self-dealing transactions, distribute corporate funds to themselves, or gamble on high-return corporate projects. In each case, insiders pass (externalize) risks to outsiders, with the gains accruing to the insiders and—because of limited liability—any losses falling on outside creditors.

As a protection against insider abuse, courts sometimes disregard the rule of limited liability and "pierce the corporate veil" to hold shareholders, directors, and officers personally liable for corporate obligations. Piercing is different from other protections afforded corporate creditors. In a piercing case

- the business has been properly incorporated (see promoter liability on preincorporation transactions, Chapter 29).
- the corporation is obligated to the creditor (see authority of corporate agents to bind the corporation, Chapter 30).
- any distributions to shareholders have been statutorily proper (see limitations on distributions to shareholders, Chapter 31).

When is piercing appropriate? This is one of the most perplexing and most litigated questions in corporate law. The cases are rich in metaphors—alter ego, dummy, instrumentality, sham—but often short on principled analysis. This chapter considers the factors courts have articulated in piercing cases (§32.1) and suggests a principled basis for weighing these factors (§32.2).

§32.1 TRADITIONAL PIERCING FACTORS

The piercing doctrine, an exception to limited liability, seeks to protect outsiders who deal with the corporation. When a court pierces the corporate veil, it places creditor expectations ahead of insiders' interests in limited liability. Courts do not take this step lightly. Disregarding limited liability chills capital formation and desirable risk taking. Furthermore, those who have voluntary dealings with the company can protect themselves by contract, and involuntary creditors (such as tort victims) often are protected by insurance or government regulation.

Courts have articulated different tests for piercing the corporate veil, such as the "instrumentality" doctrine or the "alter ego" test. These tests focus on the use of control or ownership to "commit fraud or perpetuate a dishonest act" or to "defeat justice and equity." But these tests provide little guidance, and results in particular cases do not seem to turn on which test a court employs.

Rather, particular piercing factors seem more relevant even though no one factor emerges as determinative. It is generally believed that courts are more likely to pierce in the following situations:

- the business is a closely held corporation
- the plaintiff is an involuntary (tort) creditor
- the defendant is a corporate (as opposed to an individual) shareholder
- insiders failed to follow corporate formalities
- insiders commingled business assets/affairs with their individual assets/affairs
- the business was not adequately capitalized
- the defendant actively participated in the business
- insiders deceived creditors

Although a few jurisdictions have attempted to codify the weight to be given some of these factors, piercing remains largely a judicial exercise. See Tex. BCA art. 2.21 (1997) (no piercing for failure "to observe any corporate formality" and in contract cases unless corporation used to perpetrate "actual fraud").

Note on Piercing in LLCs

Courts have applied similar factors to "pierce the LLC veil" and protect creditors of LLCs against insider abuse. The one difference, however, has been a judicial reluctance to use the failure of "company formalities" as a piercing factor given that LLCs typically

(continued)

do not have the organizational structure of a corporation with meetings of directors and shareholders. See ULLCA §303(b) (no piercing for limited liability company's failure to observe usual formalities).

§32.1.1 Closely Held Corporations

Courts pierce the corporate veil only in closely held corporations or corporate groups. No reported case of piercing has ever involved the shareholders of a publicly traded corporation. See Robert B. Thompson, *Piercing the Corporate Veil: An Empirical Study*, 76 Cornell L. Rev. 1036 (1991) (looking at all piercing cases on Westlaw through 1985). Shareholders in closely held corporations usually manage the business, choosing the risks the business takes and the asset coverage for those risks. Moreover, investment diversification and stock trading markets—two of the reasons for limited liability—are far less important to investors in a closely held business.

Just because a business is closely held, however, does not mean its shareholders or managers are subject to unlimited liability. Although courts in piercing cases often refer to shareholder "domination" or "absolute control" as factors, this is the usual state of affairs in most closely held corporations. Other factors must support piercing, because encouraging capital formation and rational risk taking remain valid reasons for limited liability in a closely held business.

§32.1.2 Involuntary Creditors

Courts often are less willing to pierce the corporate veil for creditors whose dealings with the corporation were voluntary—such as suppliers, employees, business customers, and lenders. So long as they are not deceived, voluntary creditors usually can anticipate the corporation's "no-recourse" structure and contract for personal guarantees, higher prices, or assurances on how the business will be conducted. For example, in *Brunswick Corp. v. Waxman*, 599 F.2d 34 (2d Cir. 1979), the court rejected a supplier's claim against shareholders who had set up a no-asset "straw" corporation solely to make payments under the supply contract. The court refused to pierce since the supplier, which knew the corporation had minimal capitalization and was incorporated to assure limited liability for its shareholders, was not misled and assumed the risk. Even when shareholders make vague assurances that they will "stand behind" the corporate obligations, courts have refused to pierce on behalf of sophisticated contract creditors who failed to insist on formal personal guarantees. See *Theberge v. Darbo, Inc.*, 684 A.2d 1298 (Me. 1996) (no piercing even though shareholder's actions described as "shrewd" and "sharp business tactics").

Involuntary creditors—such as tort victims and retail customers—cannot easily protect themselves contractually, nor do they knowingly assume the risk of dealing with a "no-recourse" business. But courts do not pierce simply because an involuntary creditor suffers a loss that exceeds corporate assets. The rule of limited liability shifts the risks of the business to outside creditors, whether voluntary or involuntary. To encourage corporations to buy liability insurance and to manage business risks better, some commentators have urged a rule of pro rata liability (liability assessed per share) in cases brought by tort creditors.

But in practice courts continue to pierce only when other factors are present. In fact, Thompson's study of reported piercing cases through 1985 found that piercing happens less frequently in tort cases (31 percent) compared to contract cases (42 percent). (Recent studies have found similar patterns for post-1985 cases.) Although this may simply reflect that tort victims are more likely to sue indiscriminately all available deep pockets, while contract creditors are more likely to sue only when they feel deceived or abused, the results demonstrate the respect that courts give limited liability.

§32.1.3 Enterprise Liability Doctrine

Courts sometimes use the *enterprise liability doctrine* to disregard multiple incorporations of the same business under common ownership. The doctrine pools together business assets to satisfy the liabilities of any part of the enterprise; the assets of individual owners or managers are not exposed. For example, the doctrine covers the situation where risky underinsured operations are placed in a manufacturing "subsidiary" while business profits flow to a marketing "parent" corporation. (A parent corporation is one that holds sufficient stock to exercise control over a subsidiary corporation.) Or the doctrine can be used when a business is split into a number of separate "brother-sister" corporations, each owned by the same investors, so that the assets of each "affiliate" corporation are isolated from the risks of the others. Enterprise liability is more likely when the managers who run the "asset" corporation also run the "risk" corporation.

Consider the famous case of *Walkovsky v. Carlton*, 223 N.E.2d 6 (N.Y. 1966). Carlton had set up ten wholly owned cab corporations in which he was the controlling and dominant shareholder. Following a common practice in New York City's taxi business, each corporation owned two cabs and employed its own taxi drivers. A taxi driver of one of the corporations ran over Walkovsky, who sued all of Carlton's corporations (the owner of the offending cab, the nine other cab corporations, and the owner of the central garage) and Carlton himself. As required by statute, each cab corporation carried insurance in the amount of $10,000, but no more. The cabs were heavily mortgaged and the only other assets of value (the licenses authorizing taxi operation in New York City) were judgment-proof by law.

Walkovsky sued on two theories: (1) Carlton's whole taxi enterprise was liable, making all the affiliated assets available on an enterprise liability theory, and (2) Carlton was liable in his personal capacity. The court accepted the enterprise liability theory since Carlton's corporations, held out to the public as a single enterprise, were artificially separated into different corporations. But the court rejected the argument that Carlton's use of multiple corporations or his minimal insurance coverage justified personal liability. The court remanded to allow the plaintiff to allege that Carlton had conducted the business in his "individual capacity" and suggested Carlton would be liable if he had "siphoned off" assets by taking wrongful dividends and distributions.

Parent-Subsidiary Piercing

When a subsidiary incurs liabilities, creditors will often look to the parent corporation's assets. Thus, it is possible for publicly held corporations to become liable for losses suffered by their controlled subsidiaries. But simply isolating business assets and risks in different corporations does not justify piercing. Instead, courts have required a showing that the parent dominated the subsidiary so that they acted as a "single economic entity" and recognizing corporate separateness would be unfair or unjust. See *Radaszewski v. Telecom Corp.*, 981 F.2d 305 (8th Cir. 1992) (refusing to pierce parent's corporate veil where subsidiary trucking company had purchased minimum insurance, even though insurance company was financially unsound and ultimately unable to pay claim). For example, a pharmaceutical company that had acquired a subsidiary that manufactured breast implants was held liable for the subsidiary's allegedly defective products since the parent controlled the subsidiary's board, annual budgets, financial arrangements, employment policies, regulatory compliance, manufacturing quality control, and public relations. In addition, the parent had failed to provide insurance to cover the subsidiary's potential exposure and had permitted the use of its name in the subsidiary's ads and packaging. *In re Silicone Gel Breast Implants Products Liability Litigation*, 887 F. Supp. 1447 (N.D. Ala. 1995).

Thompson's study indicates courts pierce to reach corporate defendants (37 percent) *less frequently* than individual defendants (43 percent). Although this result might seem surprising, it reflects the judicial value placed on limited liability as a tool in business planning. So long as creditor expectations are not abused or business risk taking is not excessive, the reasons for limited liability apply whether the investor is a corporation or an individual, and whether the assets to be protected are held by an individual or a business.

Successor Liability

Besides becoming liable for using different corporations to artificially separate "assets" from "risks" in the same business enterprise, business owners may become liable when they set up a series of corporations, ending one whenever liabilities mount and starting a new one to get a "fresh start." When this happens, courts will often treat the new corporation as a "successor corporation," fully responsible for its predecessor's liabilities. See §36.4.2.

§32.1.4 Failure to Observe Corporate Formalities

One of the most common, and most criticized, factors that courts mention in piercing the corporate veil is whether the corporate participants have observed corporate formalities, such as holding shareholders' and directors' meetings, issuance of stock, election of directors and officers, passing resolutions authorizing payments, and keeping corporate minutes. In deciding to pierce, courts sometimes refer to the failure to observe formalities on the theory shareholders have used the corporation as their "alter ego" or "conduit" for their own personal affairs.

The relevance of corporate formalities is hard to explain. Rarely do the unobserved formalities relate to the creditor's claim; their introduction at trial often seems little more than an afterthought. Nonetheless, the attention that courts give to corporate formalities can be explained at a few levels. First, it has been argued—perhaps simplistically—that anyone who disregards the corporate form should not be allowed to claim the privilege of limited liability. Second, it can be argued—more meaningfully—that the failure to observe formalities may indicate that creditors have been confused or misled about whom they were dealing with. Third, it can be argued—perhaps most meaningfully—that a lack of formalities suggests shareholders systematically disregard corporate obligations. That is, lack of formalities provides indirect evidence of shareholder commingling and siphoning of assets.

§32.1.5 Commingling Assets and Affairs

Courts also justify piercing when shareholders fail to keep corporate and personal assets separate. Using a *corporate* bank account to pay for *personal* expenses, for example, is a sure way to risk piercing. As with the emphasis on corporate formalities, the theory is that corporate creditors have a valid expectation that business assets will be available to meet their claims. The commingling of assets, often accomplished by corporate participants who "completely dominated" corporate affairs, allows an inference that the participants disregarded creditor interests.

In cases of enterprise liability, courts often cite confusion of a subsidiary's affairs with those of the parent corporation, or among subsidiaries, as a reason for disregarding separate incorporation. Creditors may be confused about which entity they are dealing with, whose credit is on the line, and which corporation is responsible for accidents. Mixing assets, failing to observe formalities, having officers who do not identify in which capacity they are acting, and using the same trade name or stationery are common indiscretions used to justify enterprise liability.

§32.1.6 Undercapitalization and Purposeful Insolvency

Courts state a willingness to pierce the corporate veil when a corporation is formed without capital adequate to meet expected business obligations. Courts sometimes justify piercing if there is nominal capitalization or a purposeful failure to insure. The courts, however, have not required that a business that was adequately capitalized at its formation be "topped off" with additional capital infusions when losses begin to accrue.

Simply organizing a business that has little or no capital, standing alone, is generally not sufficient to pierce the corporate veil. To require that corporations be formed with enough capital to meet all contingencies would add a significant burden to entrepreneurial activity—effectively swallowing the rule of limited liability. An exception proves the rule. In a largely discredited decision by the California Supreme Court, *Minton v. Cavaney*, 364 P.2d 473 (Cal. 1961), the piercing doctrine reached its zenith. The court suggested the undercapitalization of a corporation organized to run a swimming pool was sufficient to hold a director personally liable when a young girl drowned soon after the pool opened. Justice Traynor reasoned that piercing is proper when a corporation's capital is "trifling" compared to its business risks and the defendant actively participated in the conduct of corporate affairs. Courts in other jurisdictions, as well as more recent California courts, have rejected this broad undercapitalization rule. In fact, courts often decide not to pierce even after making explicit findings of undercapitalization. See *Baatz v. Arrow Bar*, 452 N.W.2d 138 (S.D. 1990) (refusing to pierce veil of bar that served alcoholic beverages to uninsured drunk driver, even though bar carried no insurance and was capitalized with borrowed money).

Sometimes undercapitalization is purposeful, as when the corporation is run to always be insolvent. In general, creditors expect that a business with which they deal will be run to be profitable with reserves set aside to meet corporate obligations as they become due and payable. Purposeful insolvency resulting from a shareholder's undisclosed siphoning of whatever corporate assets become available can justify piercing. For example, in *DeWitt Truck Brokers, Inc. v. W. Ray Flemming Fruit Co.*, 540 F.2d 681 (4th Cir. 1976), one Ray Flemming had set up a one-man corporation to run a fruit brokerage, selling growers' produce and arranging for its transportation to buyers. Flemming collected the sales price from buyers, taking out his selling commission plus an amount to cover transportation charges, and remitting the balance to the growers. Often, however, he paid himself a salary that included amounts he withheld as transportation charges. When one of the transporters sued for unpaid charges, Flemming claimed the company was insolvent and that his liability was limited. The court pierced the corporate veil and held Flemming personally liable. By pocketing transportation charges, he abused the transporters' extension of credit.

§32.1.7 Active Corporate Participation

Piercing the corporate veil does not imply a disregard of the corporate existence for all purposes. Often piercing—and hence personal liability—is appropriate for some corporate participants, but not others. See *Freeman v. Complex Computing Co.*, 119 F.3d 104 (2d Cir. 1997) (holding "consultant" liable for corporation's obligations where consultant received bulk of corporate revenues and, when corporation sold its assets, 60 percent of purchase price went to consultant). Shareholders who are not active in the business and have not acted to disadvantage creditors are less likely to be personally liable than those whose actions resulted in a depletion of assets. See MBCA §6.22 (shareholder "may become personally liable by reason of his own acts or conduct"); Del. GCL §102(b)(6) (same). Piercing, according to the Thompson study, is more likely in one-person corporations (49 percent) compared to corporations with three or more shareholders (35 percent).

One implication of this is procedural. A shareholder sued on a piercing theory has a due process right to litigate the underlying issue of corporate liability. Even if the corporation has been held liable, there is no res judicata or collateral estoppel effect if the shareholder was not a party to the suit against the corporation.

§32.1.8 Deception

Perhaps the most critical factor in piercing cases is the presence of a misrepresentation. In Thompson's exhaustive study of piercing cases, courts almost always pierced (92 percent) when there was a finding of misrepresentation, but rarely (2 percent) when the court explicitly stated there was no misrepresentation. That is, if a creditor is deceived into believing that the corporation is solvent or that the creditor is otherwise protected, piercing is a near certainty.

This makes sense. Corporate limited liability creates a default "no-recourse" rule that those who deal with the corporation will look only to business assets. Unless they obtain personal guarantees or take other protective steps, the personal assets of corporate participants are not available to satisfy corporate obligations. But when corporate participants falsely create the appearance of sufficient business assets or otherwise mislead creditors, courts understandably refuse to enforce the usual "no-recourse" understanding.

§32.1.9 Distinguishing Direct Personal Liability

Many cases that hold shareholders liable are not piercing cases at all. If a shareholder has personally obligated herself for debts of the corporation, liability arises not from disregarding the corporate entity but from the shareholder's *personal guarantee*. Some courts have extended this idea and have held that the statute of frauds is not an impediment to a creditor who extends credit to the corporation on the basis of a shareholder's oral guarantee. The creditor, induced to deal with the corporation by a false promise, can sue the shareholder personally. *Weisser v. Mursam Shoe Corp.*, 127 F.2d 344 (2d Cir. 1942). Other courts simply use the piercing doctrine as a safety valve to avoid the problems of enforcing an oral personal guarantee.

Likewise, if a shareholder or corporate manager commits a tort in the course of corporate business, she is liable under traditional tort and agency rules. For example, if a director approves business activities knowing that they will injure others, liability arises from the director's tortious act. See *Western Rock Co. v. Davis*, 432 S.W.2d 555 (Tex. App. 1968) (holding director liable for approving rock-blasting even after company, which was deteriorating financially, had been sued for previous blasting). Piercing the corporate veil is unnecessary to reach the tortfeasor's personal assets.

§32.1.10 Reverse Piercing

Some recent cases present a variation on the piercing theme and raise the question whether a creditor of a corporate shareholder can have access to the corporation's assets—a dicey issue if the corporation has other shareholders or creditors. Normally, a creditor that obtains a judgment against a corporate shareholder has access to any shares owned by the judgment debtor—but not the assets of the corporation, which is a separate entity. When the corporation is wholly owned by the judgment debtor, getting access is no problem: the creditor, once it becomes owner of the corporate shares, can dissolve the corporation and receive the corporation's net assets in a final distribution. See §35.2. But when the corporation has other shareholders, the creditor would be subject to regular corporate procedures to obtain access to the corporate assets. The relatively new doctrine of "reverse piercing," however, allows the creditor of a corporate shareholder to dispense with the procedures and—under some circumstances—collect its judgment from the corporation.

Courts have permitted reverse piercing when traditional piercing factors suggest that a dominant shareholder has treated the corporation as his "alter ego" to perpetuate a fraud or defeat a rightful claim. For example, when a 51-percent shareholder sought to have the corporation that he dominated sell its real estate holdings—with the proceeds to go to the shareholder's wife, who owned the other 49 percent—the court held that the transaction could be blocked and the shareholder's creditor could satisfy its judgment directly against the corporation. In re Phillips, 139 P.3d 639 (Colo. 2006). Because reverse piercing allows the creditor to circumvent normal judgment procedures and get full access to corporate assets, the court explained that reverse piercing was appropriate only when "equitable"—that is, when it would not prejudice innocent shareholders or creditors of the corporation.

A minority of courts, however, have not permitted reverse piercing on the theory that it gives creditors of shareholder-debtors a windfall, allowing the creditors to bypass normal judgment-collection procedures and attach corporate assets, rather than the judgment debtor's shares. *Cascade Energy & Metals Corp. v. Banks*, 896 F.2d 1557 (10th Cir. 1990).

Examples

EXAMPLES

1. Five years ago Don incorporated a clock repair business, Timend, Inc. The corporation rented a downtown storefront from Metro Realty under a ten-year lease. During the first few years, the business did modestly well. Don drew a salary that approximated net earnings (revenues less expenses). Although he kept meticulous records of receipts and payments, he did not observe any corporate formalities. He held no shareholders' or directors' meetings; he adopted no corporate resolutions when he paid himself a salary; he authorized no dividends. Last year the business began to struggle, and Don's salary began to shrinks.
   a. Don closes the shop. He tells Metro Realty that Timend can no longer make lease payments. Is Don personally liable under the lease?
   b. Can Metro Realty pierce the corporate veil to recover from Don personally?
   c. When Don signed the lease, he had told Metro Realty that he would stand behind it. Metro did not get Don's guarantee in writing. Does the statute of frauds prevent Metro from suing on the guarantee?

d. Last year Howard, a Timend employee, drove the company van over Petunia's prize flowers. Howard was acting within the scope of his employment, and Timend is liable to Petunia. Can Petunia recover from Don?

e. Last year Patrick brought his grandfather clock to Don's shop for repairs. Howard ruined it, and Timend's insurance does not cover the damage. Don admits he incorporated the business to shield himself from liability in these circumstances. Can Patrick recover from Don personally?

f. Suppose Don had set up a separate corporation, Heirloom Timepieces, to repair clocks valued at more than $5,000. Heirloom was wholly owned by Timend. Don used separate invoice forms for Heirloom, which subcontracted its work to Timend. If Patrick's repairs were on an Heirloom invoice, can he look to Timend's assets for recovery?

2. Rupert incorporates Exquisite Timepieces Ltd., a mail-order business that sells "designer" watches through TV infomercials. He capitalizes the business enough to buy TV time and an initial stock of watches. ETL gets off to a good start. Rupert receives a generous salary equal to 80 percent of gross receipts. He keeps meticulous records and observes corporate formalities to a tee. As new orders come in, he buys watches to fill prior orders. After a while, customer orders go unfilled. Soon there is a staggering backlog of unfilled orders.

   a. Rupert writes expectant customers, "ETL has experienced a cash flow crisis and cannot fill your order." Can the customers pierce the corporate veil?

   b. Paula, an ETL customer, says her watch has a corrosive backing that turned her skin purple. Assuming ETL would be liable in tort, is Rupert liable?

   c. Laura is Rupert's sister and a nominal ETL shareholder. She did not take a salary or participate in running the business. If the corporate veil is pierced because of Rupert's activities, is Laura also liable to the company's creditors?

   d. ETL was one of many mail-order businesses set up by Rupert—all separate subsidiaries of a holding company, Mail-Order Possibilities, Inc. Each subsidiary—one for watches, another for records, another for gold jewelry, another for vegematics—flowed through its profits to MOP. Are the assets of the MOP group available to cover ETL's debts?

   e. ETL declares bankruptcy, and a trustee is appointed to gather the remaining business assets and distribute the assets to creditors. The trustee wants to sue Ruptert for his "excessive" salary—under what theory?

Explanations

1. a. No, Don is not liable under the lease. Even though he signed it and stopped making payments, he acted on behalf of the corporation. The corporate form provides limited liability to managers who act for, and shareholders who invest in, the corporation. Unless Don obligated himself through a personal guarantee or a court uses the piercing doctrine to disregard corporate limited liability, Metro Realty can look only to corporate assets for repayment. This is the essence of limited liability.

   b. Probably not. The piercing factors are split:

For Piercing	Against Piercing
• Timend is closely held and Don dominated the business (factor 1) • Don did not observe corporate formalities (factor 4) • The business was operated on a no-profit basis and did not have sufficient capital to meet its ten-year lease commitment (factor 6) • Don was an active participant (factor 7)	• Metro Realty is a voluntary creditor that could have sought a personal guarantee (factor 2) • Don is an individual manager/ shareholder and imposing personal liability on him may discourage socially useful but risky businesses (factor 3) • Don kept corporate and personal assets separate and paid himself a salary only after covering expenses (factor 5) • Don did not deceive Metro Realty or give any personal guarantees (factor 8)

   The score is 4-4. As you might have suspected, the piercing factors alone do not provide a definitive answer for planning or in litigation.

   Nonetheless, Don's case is not a good piercing candidate. It seems little more than a case of a garden-variety failed business. If piercing applies here, it would apply to virtually every failed business, and limited liability would become an empty promise. Don never deceived or systematically avoided creditors. His failure to observe corporate formalities does not provide indirect evidence that he purposefully avoided creditor expectations. He paid himself after paying current expenses. By failing to get personal guarantees or security interests in particular business assets, Metro Realty assumed the risk of Timend's business failure. See *Consumer's Co-op v. Olsen*, 419 N.W.2d 211 (Wis. 1988) (refusing to pierce corporate veil of failed fuel wholesaler where there was no commingling of personal and corporate assets, and no improper withdrawals of capital).

   c. No. The statute of frauds is not a bar. Although Metro may not be able to hold Don contractually liable, Metro can hold Don personally liable on a piercing theory. Some courts have avoided the statute of frauds by piercing the corporate veil to protect creditor expectations. From the creditor's perspective, the transaction arguably was not on a no-recourse basis.

One important issue in this contract case will be whether Metro relied on Don's promise. Some courts have not permitted piercing when a sophisticated creditor could have insisted on personal guarantees or other protections. The case might turn on whether Metro was aware that an oral promise might not be enforceable.

d. Maybe. Don's liability in Petunia's tort case will depend on the same piercing factors discussed above in Metro Realty's contract case. The only significant differences are that Petunia, unlike Metro, is an involuntary creditor and the corporation did not carry sufficient insurance to cover her loss—both adding weight to a piercing argument. Nonetheless, courts remain reluctant to pierce in tort cases unless other factors support piercing. In fact, Thompson's study indicates that piercing occurs less frequently in tort cases compared to contract cases. The study, however, may reflect only that disappointed contract creditors, compared to injured tort victims, are more selective about the cases in which they assert piercing liability.

   Don't forget that Don may also be liable on other theories besides piercing. If he had hired Howard knowing that Howard had a miserable driving record or if he had told Howard to speed as he made deliveries, Don might be liable to Petunia in tort—regardless of piercing.

e. Probably not. Although the corporation is liable on a respondeat superior theory, piercing will depend on much the same factors discussed above with respect to Metro Realty. A significant question is whether Patrick should be treated as a voluntary or an involuntary creditor. In theory Patrick could have sought personal guarantees or demanded higher insurance coverage before he left his clock at the shop. But expecting retail customers to make such demands is unrealistic. Piercing may be a more efficient way of assuring responsibility to creditors. But piercing seems inappropriate if Don did not make any personal guarantees, mislead Patrick about insurance, or violate any minimum insurance requirements. That Don incorporated solely to avoid personal liability is not relevant. The promise of limited liability is meant to promote business in the corporate form.

f. Perhaps not. Piercing in a parent-subsidiary setting does not extend liability to an individual shareholder or manager, but instead redraws the boundaries of the enterprise's assets. Courts have accepted a theory of enterprise liability when a business artificially separates assets from risks to avoid claims by involuntary creditors. This is particularly so when, from the creditor's perspective, the business appeared to be more than a shell.

   In our case, enterprise liability may depend on whether Patrick was aware of the fragmentation. If Patrick did not know he was dealing with an assetless shell, a court might well aggregate the assets of the two corporations as though they were a single entity. The actual enterprise—as evidenced by its location, its subcontracted work, and the nature of its business—was essentially one. But if Patrick was aware of this separation, perhaps because of the separate invoice forms, he might be seen as a voluntary creditor who assumed the risk of dealing with a corporate shell.

2. a. Probably. Rupert is less deserving of limited liability. But, as in Don's failed business, the piercing factors are less than clear. Some indicate piercing is appropriate:

For Piercing	Against Piercing
• ETL is a closely held corporation (factor 1) • The mail-order customers were involuntary victims, hardly able to demand personal guarantees or contract protections (factor 2) • The business was operated so that eventually orders could not be filled (factor 6) • Rupert was an active participant (factor 7)	• Rupert is an individual manager/ shareholder (factor 3) • He observed corporate formalities (factor 4) • He kept corporate and personal assets separate (factor 5) • He never personally guaranteed that the orders would be filled (factor 8)

Again the score is 4-4. But unlike Don's business, Rupert's business constituted an abuse of creditor expectations. By taking a salary based on receipts, not after-expense earnings, Rupert put his interests ahead of the company's customers. Mail-order customers assumed their payments would be used to buy and ship their merchandise. Instead, they were used to construct a pyramid scheme. Piercing seems likely. Although he never expressly misrepresented the nature of the business, Rupert's case has a "sleaze factor" and smells of fraud. See *K.C. Roofing Center v. On Top Roofing, Inc.*, 807 S.W.2d 45 (Mo. Ct. App. 1991) (piercing corporate veil of roofing supply business where insiders took salaries and rent based on receipts and changed corporate names frequently).

b. Probably, on a few theories. Paula is an involuntary creditor, and the factors favoring piercing discussed in the previous answer also favor piercing in her case. The self-induced insolvency that resulted from the way Rupert ran the business, besides violating the expectations of contract creditors, also undermines tort deterrence and compensation goals. The business was run so that its risks were never internalized and so assets were unavailable to satisfy legitimate claims.

In addition, through his television ads, Rupert implicitly represented to customers that ETL would use customer payments to fill their orders, not line his pockets. From a customer perspective, the ads were misleading. Not only is this a powerful factor favoring piercing, it may also support an independent claim of deceit against Rupert. Even though customers purchased watches from the corporation, Rupert may be individually liable for intentionally misleading customers as to material facts on which they relied to their detriment—the tort of deceit. Privity is not necessary.

Finally, Rupert may be liable as a tortfeasor if his negligence caused Paula's injuries. If he had failed to exercise the care of a reasonable person in purchasing the business's merchandise—as suggested by the assumption ETL would be liable—he also is personally liable under negligence principles.

c. Probably not. The corporation does not cease to exist because some of its shareholders are subject to personal liability. Piercing the corporate veil—disregarding the rule of limited liability—happens shareholder by shareholder. Only those shareholders whose actions are related to the piercing factors, particularly those who "dominated" the business and abused creditor expectations, may be held personally liable for the corporation's obligations.

d. The question of disregarding corporate structures—whether "horizontal" (parent-subsidiary corporations), "vertical" (brother-sister corporations) or, as here, both—is a recurring piercing problem. Much will depend on the traditional piercing factors, including whether the plaintiff acceded to the no-recourse structure and whether there was confusion as to the separateness of the many corporations.

Beyond this, the principal reason for limited liability—promoting capital formation—provides a useful springboard for analysis. If the tiered corporate structure had encouraged desirable investment or business risk-taking, piercing (whether vertical or horizontal) may be inappropriate. Amassing all of the assets for the creditors of any one corporation would put businesses whose capital is provided by a holding company at a competitive disadvantage compared to those businesses whose capital is provided by individuals or widely dispersed investors. The holding company would be exposed to liability to which other limited liability investors are not; and the affiliates would be exposed to liability to which independent companies are not.

If MOP's mail-order subsidiaries operate separately, so that it can be said they represent separate investment decisions, the rule of limited liability teaches that a "no-recourse" structure deserves presumptive respect. The mail-order creditors would have to show more than the existence of related businesses.

e. The trustee has a number of options. Piercing the veil is not the only game in town to protect creditors when a business becomes insolvent. First, to the extent Rupert has any claims to unpaid salary, the trustee could seek to have these "unfair" claims **equitably subordinated**, so that any claim Rupert might have to corporate assets would be paid only after legitimate claims of other creditors were first satisfied. See §33.2. Second, the trustee could bring a fiduciary claim on behalf of the corporation against Rupert. The trustee, who would step into the shoes of the corporation, could argue the salary was unauthorized (see §14.2.2) or wasteful and in bad faith (see §14.2.4). Third, the trustee could seek to recoup the salary payments on the ground they were disguised distributions to shareholder Rupert and illegal either because they rendered the corporation insolvent or failed the relevant "balance sheet" test. See §31.2.

§32.2 DISTILLING A PRINCIPLE — SOLVING THE PIERCING CONUNDRUM

Is it possible on some *principled* basis to distinguish between Don's failed business and Rupert's mail-order fast shuffle? Counting and weighing factors is an unpredictable game with potentially high costs to efficient capital formation and business management. General principles of creditor protection — of which the piercing cases represent a subset — provide some useful insights into the piercing conundrum.

§32.2.1 Uniform Fraudulent Transfer Act

Limiting the discretion of debtors and protecting the expectations of creditors beyond the terms of their contract has a long history in the law. The notion that debtors cannot use sham transactions to hide their assets from creditors — whether or not the matter is addressed explicitly in the contract — is as old as Roman law and in England was codified in the Statute of Elizabeth (1571). Today it is embodied in the Uniform Fraudulent Transfer Act (UFTA). The UFTA helps explain many of the piercing factors, as well as when they are (or are not) relevant.

The UFTA, like its predecessor the Uniform Fraudulent Conveyance Act, is relatively straightforward. It defines certain debtor transactions as "fraudulent" and allows creditors with matured or maturing claims to void such transactions or to seize the property fraudulently conveyed. UFTA §7.

The UFTA defines three categories of "fraudulent" transfers:

- any transfer that the debtor made with the actual intent to hinder, delay, or defraud present or future creditors — particularly when the transfer is to an insider or relative of the debtor [UFTA §4(a)(1)]

- any transfer for which the debtor does not receive reasonably equivalent value and that leaves the debtor with unreasonably small assets in relation to her actual or anticipated needs [UFTA §4(a)(2)(i)]
- any transfer for which the debtor does not receive reasonably equivalent value and that the debtor knew or should have known would render him insolvent [UFTA §4(a)(2)(ii)].

In short, even when it cannot be shown the debtor is purposefully trying to avoid her creditors, transfers by the debtor are "constructively" fraudulent if they are for questionable value or threaten the debtor's ability to pay her other debts as they become due. For example, suppose Sam sold Patty a fancy sports car for $15,000 on her promise to pay over two years, but Sam foolishly failed to perfect a security interest in the car. If Patty stops making installment payments and sells the car to her brother Billy for $500, the UFTA permits Sam to have the transaction set aside as fraudulent and to attach the car.

§32.2.2 Applying UFTA to Piercing Conundrum

The UFTA, and its philosophy of protecting creditors from abusive debtors, is a useful starting point for considering the piercing conundrum. It helps explain the results in our two earlier piercing examples (see Examples and Explanations above):

- **Don's case — no fraudulent transfers.** Although Don continued to draw a salary, it was one that seemed related to the value of his services. The corporation's inability to meet its obligations under the lease was not because Don had siphoned away assets from the business for himself in transactions of questionable value. He had not misled creditors and had not acted to avoid the lease. Disregarding limited liability in the case of a failed business would dampen the incentive to invest and take rational business risks.
- **Rupert's case — fraudulent transfers.** Rupert's salary can be seen as lacking fair value. It was based on gross receipts, not the value of his services, and undermined the company's ability to fill customer orders. The salary left the company with unreasonably small assets in relation to its business and eventually rendered it insolvent. UFTA §4(a)(2). Moreover, these payments to an insider suggest an intent to hinder customers from receiving their goods as promised. UFTA §4(a)(1). Imposing personal liability does not discourage desirable risk-taking, but protects reasonable creditor expectations.

In this light, it is easier to see the relevance of corporate formalities and the intermingling of corporate and personal assets or affairs in deciding piercing cases. Disregarded formalities provide indirect evidence of "fraudulent transfers" and intermingling may provide direct evidence.

Both the UFTA and corporate veil-piercing doctrine create for corporate participants implicit duties (similar to fiduciary duties) to consider creditor expectations and place them ahead of their own interests. This is inherent in the corporate structure that makes creditor claims senior to shareholder residual claims.

§32.2.3 Limits of UFTA

Why haven't courts used fraudulent transfer law—whether the UFTA, the UFCA, or their common-law analogues—instead of the vague piercing doctrine? There are a number of difficulties with the fraudulent transfer approach, and creditor-plaintiffs have rarely invoked it. For one, fraudulent transfer law depends on identifying *specific transactions* lacking fair equivalent value. In a business where corporate records are sketchy or corporate formalities not followed, it may be difficult to identify all the transactions that operated to defraud creditors. Also, where a business is undercapitalized given its risks, there may be no identifiable transaction that leaves the business with "unreasonably small capital." The broader piercing doctrine avoids these problems of proof and thus has greater deterrent and compensatory force. It imposes unlimited liability, up to the full value of the creditor's claim, regardless of specific proof of unfair transactions.

Moreover, a fraudulent transfer analysis focuses on the "shady" actions of the corporate participant, rather than the understandings of the creditor. That is, the focus is on the insider's actions, not necessarily the outsider's expectations. Although most of the piercing factors (domination, siphoning, commingling, formalities) approach the question by looking at the actions of the corporate participant, the important deception factor looks at the problem from the perspective of the outside creditor. Even if there were no fraudulent transfers, but a creditor had been misled or confused about the corporation's solvency or the nature of its business, piercing nonetheless may be appropriate. That is, fraudulent transfer analysis may not catch some cases where the insider's deception led the outsider to deal with the corporation when full knowledge might have changed things.

Examples

1. Fenimore is the sole shareholder and president of Pent-Ultimate Inc., a high-rise construction company. The company, which Fenimore set up with only $1,000 in capital, leases all its equipment (scaffolding, machinery, cranes) at a high annual rent from Fenimore. Because of these heavy rentals, the corporation has rarely run a profit. Although Fenimore

generally does not follow corporate procedures, the rental arrangement between him and Pent-Ultimate was specifically approved by the company's three-person board.

a. Edifice Trust lent Pent-Ultimate money for the construction of a high-rise hotel. When construction costs run higher than expected, Pent-Ultimate defaults on the loan. Can Edifice Trust recover from Fenimore under the UFTA?
b. Patricia, a passerby at one of Pent-Ultimate's job sites, was badly hurt when a beam fell on her. The corporation has the minimum insurance required by law, but not enough to satisfy the judgment Patricia obtains against Pent-Ultimate. Can Patricia recover from Fenimore under the UFTA?

2. Should there be piercing liability:
   a. In Edifice Trust's case?
   b. In Patricia's case?

EXPLANATIONS

Explanations

1. a. Perhaps. If Edifice Trust can show the rental payments to Fenimore were "fraudulent transfers," it could recover the excess of the rental payments over market value from Fenimore as first transferee. UFTA §8(b)(1) (creditor may recover "value of the asset transferred, . . . subject to adjustment as the equities may require"). The rental payments would be fraudulent under the UFTA if Fenimore intentionally set them up to avoid creditors. Above-market transfers to insiders, especially when concealed, are badges of fraud. Comment, UFTA §4(b). In addition, the rental payments would be constructively fraudulent if: (1) they were not for "reasonably equivalent value" — that is, if they were significantly above market rates; (2) they left Pent-Ultimate with assets that were "unreasonably small" in relation to its business; or (3) Fenimore should have known Pent-Ultimate would incur debts (like the construction loan) beyond its "ability to pay as they became due." UFTA §4(b).

   A fraudulent transfer theory has some difficulties. It may be difficult to show that Fenimore intended to avoid creditors; he may have hoped the business would generate revenues to cover expenses. Presumably, the sophisticated Edifice Trust extended credit knowing of the rental arrangement and believing Pent-Ultimate had a sufficient margin for its business. And even though the rental payments were high, they may not have been unreasonable or clearly above market. Even if the rental payments were above market, they may not have been the reason for Pent-Ultimate's inability to pay the construction loan. The unexpected cost overruns may undermine the assertion that Pent-Ultimate was operating without sufficient assets.

b. Perhaps. Patricia, like any other creditor, would have to show the rental payments to Fenimore were "fraudulent transfers." UFTA §8(b)(1) (judgment against first transferee). The same analysis above would apply. If the rental arrangement was not above market, it may be hard to show Fenimore intended to avoid the company's creditors or that the company had not received "reasonably equivalent value." But operating a ultra-hazardous high-rise construction business with minimal reserves may suggest the company was run with "unreasonably small" capital. In this way, the particular risks of the business factor into the UFTA analysis.

If the rental arrangement was above market or left the business with insufficient assets to cover likely personal injury claims, Patricia might be able to recover from Fenimore to the extent the payments were unreasonable. Although Patricia became a creditor of Pent-Ultimate only when her claim against the company matured, the rental payments are fraudulent under the UFTA whether the creditor's claim arises before or after the transfer was made. UFTA §4(a).

2. a. Perhaps. The piercing analysis is similar to that under the UFTA. Applying the piercing factors, it will be relevant that Edifice Trust is a voluntary creditor that could have inquired, and presumably did, into Fenimore's rental arrangement. If Fenimore disclosed it, Edifice Trust could have protected itself against the corporation's insolvency by seeking personal guarantees or by demanding that Fenimore charge market-rate rentals. A principal reason for corporate limited liability—to encourage socially desirable risk taking—argues against piercing liability. The UFTA also recognizes this by not imposing liability if the above-market transfers did not undermine the business.

b. Perhaps. Piercing is more likely, though again the piercing analysis is similar to that under the UFTA. As the piercing factors suggest, Patricia (an involuntary creditor) was unable as a practical matter to protect herself against Fenimore's above-market rental arrangement. Fenimore's practice of effectively depleting the corporation of capital reserves was something that Patricia could not have prevented. The UFTA's prohibition against above-market transactions that leave the corporation with "unreasonably small" assets provides a framework for considering whether Fenimore owed a duty to Patricia (and other potential tort victims) not to siphon away assets.

On the one hand, the arrangement had been going on for quite a while without apparently hurting other creditors. Perhaps reserves were sufficient. The argument would be buttressed if the excess rental payments could have been properly paid to Fenimore as dividends or other distributions (see Chapter 31). Moreover, if Fenimore had complied with mandatory insurance requirements applicable to construction companies, state law would seem to favor corporations engaged in construction rather than the creation of reserves to satisfy potential tort claims.

On the other hand, Fenimore's rental arrangement created a "no-recourse" structure in which business assets were separated from business risks. If the company's ultra-hazardous activities could be expected to injure outsiders, its undercapitalization would likely factor into the court's analysis. If, as it appears, the rental arrangement was designed to leave an empty corporate shell, piercing is more likely. Passersby would expect that a big construction company has adequate financial reserves to back its responsibility to public safety.

CHAPTER 33

Statutory Recognition of Corporation

Modern regulation seeks to correct failures in private markets. The corporation, a private construct that allocates risks between insiders and outsiders, raises many regulatory issues. Is a loan to a corporation subject to usury laws when the same loan to an individual would be usurious? Can a business avoid hazardous waste liability by incorporating its environmental operations separately? This chapter considers the recognition of the corporation, particularly its personality and limited liability, under various regulatory schemes (§33.1). It also considers bankruptcy law's nonrecognition of certain transactions by corporate insiders (§33.2).

Statutory recognition of the corporation is sometimes confused with piercing the corporate veil (see Chapter 32). In piercing cases, courts decide whether to disregard corporate limited liability given outsiders' expectations under state contract and tort law. In statutory cases, courts and administrative agencies must interpret the regulatory scheme (federal or state) to decide whether it recognizes corporate attributes arising from state corporate law, such as corporate personality or limited liability. Not surprisingly, courts often give less weight to corporate attributes in defining the regulatory reach.

§33.1 STATUTORY RECOGNITION OF CORPORATION

§33.1.1 Corporation as Separate Entity

Most modern regulatory schemes explicitly place the same regulatory burdens and benefits on corporations as any other person or entity. Recognition of corporate personality, however, becomes an issue when a constitutional provision, statute, or regulation refers to a "person" without specifying whether corporations are included. As we have seen, corporations are treated as constitutional persons for most economic purposes, but receive only limited recognition in matters involving individual civil rights (see §1.3).

Corporate personality also is relevant when an individual attempts to use a corporation to create transactions with a "separate entity" to obtain government benefits. For example, many regulatory schemes provide benefits to individuals employed by another person—such as unemployment compensation and retirement benefits. Although most schemes recognize the legal personality of the corporation, interpretive issues arise where a corporation is used to create relationships (and benefits or immunities) that otherwise do not exist. In these cases the argument is that the corporate entity and individual should be treated as one—sometimes confusingly referred to as *reverse piercing*. See *Cargill, Inc. v. Hedge*, 375 N.W.2d 477 (Minn. 1985) (extending state homestead exemption to corporation that owned family farm).

Statutory recognition of corporate personality depends on the statute. For example, can a one-person corporation be used to create an employment relationship, entitling the person to government employment benefits? Different statutes produce different answers. In *Stark v. Flemming*, 283 F.2d 410 (9th Cir. 1960), an elderly woman otherwise not entitled to Social Security benefits set up a one-person corporation to hold real estate from which she derived rental income. To qualify her for Social Security benefits, the corporation "employed" her at a "salary" equal to the rental income. The court construed the Social Security law to respect the employment relationship, provided the salary was reasonable. Other courts, construing other statutes, have refused to respect similar uses of the corporate form. See *Baker v. Caravan Moving Corp.*, 561 F. Supp. 337 (N.D. Ill. 1983) (sham corporation cannot be used to escape obligations under the Employee Retirement Income Security Act).

§33.1.2 Corporate Limited Liability

In general, regulatory schemes respect corporate limited liability. For example, food and drug laws do not make individual shareholders liable to consumers for a corporation's unsafe products, and government contract rules do not bind corporate executives when their corporation contracts with the government.

Nonetheless, courts often interpret statutory schemes as superseding corporate limited liability to serve the overriding purposes of the statute. Federal discrimination laws, for example, impose liability on the parent corporation for claims by employees of an insolvent subsidiary if the parent is linked to the subsidiary's discriminatory policies. Federal intellectual property law makes officers and shareholders liable for the corporation's trademark and patent infringements if they "actively assisted" in the infringement.

Limited liability in statutory cases is thus a matter of statutory interpretation. Courts are called on to balance corporate limited liability and the statutory liability policies, recognizing the special weight these legislative policies carry. (This is different from the usual piercing case in which courts generally heed the legislative directive that corporate limited liability should outweigh state tort and contract principles.) Courts in statutory cases have been less willing to use the traditional piercing factors. In fact, courts in these cases refer to such traditional piercing factors as undercapitalization, failure to follow formalities, and misrepresentation only half as often as they do in contract cases. See Robert B. Thompson, *Piercing the Corporate Veil: An Empirical Study*, 76 Cornell L. Rev. 1036 (1991) (looking at all piercing cases on Westlaw through 1985).

Superfund Cases

An important and interesting juxtaposition of limited liability and regulatory policy is the Comprehensive Environmental Response, Compensation, and Liability Act (CERCLA) — the federal Superfund statute, which imposes liability on former and present "owners or operators" of hazardous waste sites. 42 U.S.C. §9607(a).

Since the statute's enactment in 1980, federal courts have taken different tacks in their attempt to reconcile state-based corporate separateness and federal environmental policy. For cases involving parent corporations with wholly owned subsidiaries that owned or operated waste sites, the Supreme Court resolved more than a decade of conflicting lower court views. *United States v. Bestfoods*, 524 U.S. 51 (1998). According to the Court, the parent corporation can be liable under CERCLA as follows:

- **No "owner" liability.** CERCLA does not abrogate the "ingrained" principle of corporate law that a parent corporation is a separate entity distinct from its subsidiaries. This means that a parent corporation, regardless of its degree of involvement in the subsidiary or its disposal activities, does not legally own the subsidiary's property and cannot be liable as an "owner."

- **Direct "operator" liability.** The parent corporation can be deemed an "operator" if it directs, manages, or conducts the affairs of a "facility"—that is, the subsidiary's hazardous waste site. If, for example, an executive of the parent (who is not also an official of the subsidiary) actively participates in and controls the subsidiary's environmental programs, the parent can become liable as an "operator."
- **Derivative piercing liability.** Even if the parent corporation does not incur "owner" or "operator" liability, it can be charged with "derivative CERCLA liability" when the subsidiary incurs CERCLA liability and the corporate veil may be pierced. The Court described piercing as a "fundamental principle of corporate law" that arises when the corporate form "would otherwise be misused to accomplish certain wrongful purposes" on the shareholders' behalf. The Court left open whether piercing factors would be borrowed from state law or would be a matter of federal common law.

The Supreme Court's approach rejects a view adopted by some circuits that CERCLA liability can arise if the parent held the power to control the subsidiary's disposal activities, even though it did not exercise the power. According to *Bestfoods*, control by the parent of the subsidiary's business is not in itself sufficient to create "operator" liability. Moreover, the Court's recognition of direct "operator" liability rejects the view that parent liability under CERCLA can arise only under traditional piercing rules.

In cases involving CERCLA liability of *individuals*, some lower courts have refused to look to traditional veil-piercing criteria—such as active participation and lack of corporate formalities—and have imposed liability on individual officers who "could have prevented" the hazardous discharge. The *Bestfoods* approach, however, raises doubts about this approach and suggests that direct individual liability under CERCLA, like corporate liability, depends on identifying actual managerial actions taken by the individual related to the company's hazardous waste activities. According to *Bestfoods*, CERCLA does not impose vicarious liability by virtue of corporate position.

Even though *direct* CERCLA liability requires showing more than corporate control, lower courts have used traditional piercing analysis to impose *derivative* CERCLA liability - that is, piercing liability on individuals for an insolvent corporation's CERCLA obligations. See *Carter-Jones Lumber Co. v. LTV Steel Co.*, 237 F.3d 745 (6th Cir. 2001) (applying Ohio piercing principles to uphold individual owner's liability for corporation's CERCLA cleanup obligations, when his control was "complete" and he caused the corporation to commit an illegal act).

§33.2 EQUITABLE SUBORDINATION DOCTRINE

The malleable corporate form permits insiders (particularly in close corporations) to undertake transactions that realign their relationship with outside creditors. Recognition of these transactions, particularly when undertaken on the eve of bankruptcy, may be inconsistent with the Bankruptcy Code. When insiders assert rights superior to those of outside creditors based on a corporate transaction, the Bankruptcy Code dictates whether the transaction should be respected, recharacterized, or disregarded to protect creditors. Bankruptcy Act of 1978, §510(c) (codifying "principles of equitable subordination").

Under the doctrine of *equitable subordination*, bankruptcy courts can subordinate claims by corporate insiders—that is, lower the normal priority of such claims—if the claim arose from a transaction that constituted a breach of a fiduciary duty (see §11.2). The doctrine, now codified in the Bankruptcy Code, was first articulated in *Taylor v. Standard Gas & Electric Co.*, 306 U.S. 307 (1939). There a parent corporation caused its subsidiary, Deep Rock, to enter into transactions with the parent and affiliated companies on terms highly disadvantageous to Deep Rock. Because these transactions violated the parent's fiduciary duties to the subsidiary, the Court subordinated the parent's claims to those of the subsidiary's preferred shareholders. This process of subordination came to be known as the "Deep Rock doctrine."

Pepper v. Litton

The most famous case of equitable subordination is *Pepper v. Litton*, 308 U.S. 295 (1939) (Douglas, J.). Dixie Splint Coal Company failed to pay Pepper royalties under a coal lease, so Pepper sued. Recognizing the suit would leave the company penniless, Litton (Dixie Splint's sole shareholder and dominant director) grabbed what he could. Litton said the company owed him back pay and had the company confess a judgment for this claim. Next, at the execution sale on his confessed judgment, Litton "purchased" the company's assets, paying with his confessed judgment. In effect, Litton acquired the company's assets in exchange for his back pay claims. Dixie Splint, now assetless, filed for voluntary bankruptcy.

Meanwhile, Pepper had obtained a judgment against Dixie Splint on his claim for unpaid royalties, but there was nothing left for him to collect. Could the bankruptcy trustee (on behalf of Pepper) disregard or subordinate Litton's salary claims and the company's confession of judgment? The effect would be to move Pepper ahead of Litton in the line of creditors. The Supreme Court agreed that Litton's back pay judgment was properly disallowed or subordinated to Pepper's judgment for unpaid royalties. Justice Douglas wrote that a one-person corporation could not be used to defraud creditors and that as a director Litton had a fiduciary obligation to the corporation and its creditors not to engage in unfair self-dealing (see §13.3).

Relationship to Piercing

This would all be simple enough except that bankruptcy courts often use piercing factors to justify subordination. Did the insider dominate the corporation without regard to corporate formalities? Did the insider commingle corporate and personal assets? Was paid-in capital nominal or was the corporation undercapitalized?

Two things should be kept in mind. First, equitable subordination is not as harsh as piercing. The insider is not held liable personally on corporate obligations but rather the insider's claims are disregarded or subordinated to those of other creditors. Second, the equitable subordination factors (as in the piercing cases) rest on broad equitable principles of creditor protection. Equitable subordination, like the Uniform Fraudulent Transfer Act (see §32.2.1), embodies the idea that debtors owe a duty not to prefer some creditors, especially themselves, at the expense of others.

EXAMPLES

Examples

1. Friendly Skies, Inc., is the holding company for a number of regional airline companies. One of its wholly owned subsidiaries, Orient Airlines, recently went bankrupt.
   a. Orient had a miserable workplace safety record and faces a number of workers' compensation claims. Always thinly capitalized by Friendly Skies, Orient does not have enough assets to satisfy all the claims against it. Friendly Skies, however, was diligent in making sure that Orient paid its workers' compensation taxes. Is Friendly Skies liable for these workers' compensation claims?
   b. Friendly Skies holds much of Orient's preferred stock. Before Orient's bankruptcy, the Friendly Skies executives on Orient's board authorized an exchange of preferred stock for debentures (unsecured debt obligations). The normal bankruptcy rule is that creditors (including unsecured creditors) have priority over preferred shareholders, but among unsecured creditors (including debenture holders) there is pro rata participation. Will Friendly Skies' debentures have the same bankruptcy priority as other unsecured debt?

2. Another Friendly Skies subsidiary, Friendly Maintenance, once operated a service center for airplanes in Friendly Skies' many regional fleets. Workers at the center regularly dumped spent fuel and cleaning residues in the lot behind the service hangars. Recently, the EPA included the site on its Superfund list and sought a court order to have Friendly Skies pay

for the cleanup. Friendly Maintenance was long ago sold to another airline company.

a. During the time of the dumping, executives of Friendly Skies sat on the board of Friendly Maintenance. But operational matters, including waste disposal decisions, were left to Maintenance executives. Friendly Skies could have requested information and stopped Maintenance's dumping practices, but did not. Is Friendly Skies liable under CERCLA?

b. Orient, the largest airline in the Friendly Skies family, had significant maintenance expertise. Its employees were frequently "lent" on a contract basis to Friendly Maintenance. They were the ones, it turns out, responsible for the dumping practices that led to the EPA suit. These employees never thought this dumping was harmful or hazardous. Is Orient liable?

Explanations

1. a. Perhaps. It depends on state workers' compensation law. Some traditional piercing factors—such as commingling of the companies' finances, undercapitalization, and perhaps the parent's direct participation in the operations of the subsidiary—suggest that Friendly Skies should be liable for its subsidiary's obligations. Nonetheless, the statutory scheme need not adhere to the usual piercing rules. Instead, under many workers' compensation schemes, the question is whether the parent was an "employer" of its subsidiary's employees. In similar circumstances, some courts have said the parent corporation can be treated as the employer, if its executives controlled the activities of the subsidiary's employees and the dangers to which they were exposed. See *Joyce v. Super Fresh Food Markets, Inc.*, 815 F.2d 943 (3d Cir. 1987). More information about Friendly Skies' relationship to Orient would be needed.

   b. Probably not. Friendly Skies' claims may be equitably subordinated to those of other unsecured creditors, if the preferred share-debenture exchange was a breach of the board's fiduciary duties. Because the transaction was a self-dealing transaction by a controlling shareholder, it will be subject to a "fairness" review (see §17.2). In particular, did the exchange approximate a transaction that would have occurred in an arm's-length transaction? Was the exchange one that made financial sense for the corporation under the circumstances? In this light, the exchange faces a difficult road. The value of the debentures cannot exceed the value of the preferred stock, and some corporate purpose for the exchange must have existed. Both are unlikely.

2. a. Perhaps. Again the question is whether the statutory liability scheme respects the usual rules of corporate limited liability. The Supreme Court has interpreted CERCLA to leave intact the corporate regime under which parent corporations are not liable for the activities of their subsidiaries, except when the parent manages or conducts the operations of the subsidiary's waste site (direct CERCLA "operator" liability) or when the parent misuses the corporate form so as to warrant piercing the corporate veil (indirect CERCLA "piercing" liability). See *United States v. Bestfoods*, 524 U.S. 51 (1998).

   Under this approach, Friendly Skies' mere presence on Friendly Maintenance's board and its power to control the subsidiary's operations are not sufficient grounds for direct CERLCA liability. Moreover, under traditional piercing rules, a parent corporation (even a 100 percent parent) is not liable for subsidiary liabilities even when there is complete control, unless there is also some accompanying fraud (such as deception about separate incorporation) or abuse of the corporate form (such as accepting the benefits of the subsidiary's business, while externalizing known harms). See §33.2.1 (*alter ego* test). More information about what Friendly Skies knew and did about the toxic dumping would be necessary.

   b. Perhaps, on a theory of direct liability. The issue of enterprise (or sister-company) liability is unusual in CERCLA cases, where the focus has been on parent liability for cleanup of subsidiaries' hazardous waste sites. Nonetheless, the Supreme Court's decision in *Bestfoods* creates an analytical framework. The analysis begins with an acceptance of corporate limited liability and corporate separateness, subject to relatively narrow theories of derivative or direct CERCLA liability. Derivative liability can arise under traditional enterprise liability or piercing theories; direct liability can arise if corporate actors can be said to have "operated" the hazardous site.

   In our example, it seems unlikely Orient would be liable under traditional piercing rules merely because it made its employees available on a contract basis to an affiliated company. More would have to be shown, such as the abusive or deceptive separation of assets and risks by the holding company parent.

   Nonetheless, CERCLA liability extends beyond traditional piercing liability. If Orient had managed or conducted the hazardous waste disposal practices through its own employees, Orient could well be liable as an "operator" under CERCLA. As the Supreme Court pointed out, "any person who operates a polluting facility is directly liable . . . whether that person is the facility's owner, the owner's parent corporation or business partner, or even a saboteur who sneaks into the facility at night." *Bestfoods*. But, in our example, the Orient employees were "lent" to Friendly Maintenance. If they made environmental decisions at the behest and under the control of Friendly Maintenance management, they would be like dual-capacity corporate officers. The Supreme Court made clear that an employee of the parent who also serves as officer or director for a polluting subsidiary does not necessarily create parent liability—on the theory that the dual-capacity official normally wears the subsidiary's "hat" when engaged in the subsidiary's business. Only if it could be said the "lent" employees were in fact working for the sister affiliate could there be direct liability.

PART VIII

Fundamental Corporate Changes

CHAPTER 34

Takeovers — An Introduction

Fundamental corporate changes alter the rights and powers that constitute the corporation. This part considers the mechanics of fundamental corporate changes and their treatment under state and federal law. Fundamental changes take various forms:

- internal realignments of the corporation's financial and governance structure—charter amendments, recapitalizations, and dissolution (Chapter 35)
- negotiated external changes affecting corporate control—mergers, sales of assets, and stock acquisitions (Chapter 36)
- nonnegotiated corporate takeovers—voting insurgencies and hostile tender offers (this chapter).

In a fundamental change, shareholders have rights that span the palatte of corporate law. State law gives shareholders voting rights, fiduciary protection, and liquidity rights through appraisal (Chapter 37). Federal law superimposes disclosure rights and substantive rules with respect to proxy voting (Chapter 9) and tender offers (Chapter 38). When management responds to an unsolicited control change, voting defenses (Chapter 8) and takeover defenses (Chapter 39) test the limits of corporate fiduciary law.

This chapter describes the takeover choices (§34.1) and tells the story of a corporate takeover (§34.2). Besides revealing the power of the shareholder right to sell and the centrality of director duties, it raises questions about the effect of takeovers on the economy and society (§34.3). Our treatment of the subject is by necessity an overview.

§34.1 HOSTILE CHOICES — PROXY CONTEST OR TENDER OFFER

Hostile takeovers are the exception. Most control changes occur in negotiated "friendly" acquisitions. The managements of two corporations bargain at arm's-length over terms, structure, and future management. After the boards approve the deal, it is submitted to shareholders of the acquired (and sometimes the acquiring) company for approval (see §35.2.2). If the two managements cannot agree, the matter usually ends.

But when the corporation is publicly held, a suitor can go over the heads of unwilling management and woo the shareholders directly. A suitor has three options:

- **Proxy contest.** The suitor can appeal to the shareholders' minds by soliciting their proxies to oust the incumbent board and install the suitor's slate of directors — a *proxy contest*. The suitor (or *insurgent*) must convince shareholders they will be better off under new management. If the insurgent fails, it will have little to show for the effort.
- **Tender offer.** The suitor can appeal to the shareholders' wallets by seeking to buy a controlling block of shares at above-market prices. To reach dispersed public shareholders quickly and minimize the risk of falling short, the suitor (or *bidder*) will publicly offer to buy shares at a premium above the market price on the condition that a sufficient number are submitted (tendered) within a specified period — a *tender offer*. A successful tender offer, unlike a proxy contest, gives the bidder a majority equity position and the assurance of control.
- **Combined proxy contest/tender offer.** The suitor can solicit proxies to replace the board, on the promise that it will make a tender offer after the new board removes any takeover impediments installed by the old board. This *two-step bid* is more costly than a straight tender offer, but may be the only way to acquire control in the face of an entrenched board.

In the 1980s most suitors chose a hostile tender offer over a proxy contest. A tender offer provided an element of surprise and a greater chance of success. And a bidder that failed to acquire control — often after another bidder or management offered a better price — could still profit by selling its low-price "toehold" position in the target's stock.

In the early 1990s hostile takeover activity fell off. There were many explanations: takeover financing dried up after many shaky deals in the late 1980s; there were fewer "good buys" to restructure profitably; state antitakeover laws passed in the late 1980s added significant expense and uncertainty to hostile bids; state courts gave incumbent boards significant latitude to resist outsiders, particularly with "poison pills."

Nonetheless, takeovers increased dramatically in the late 1990s and into the 2000s. Many have been negotiated deals—primarily in industries in flux, such as banking, medium-size manufacturing, telecommunications, and entertainment. The takeover activity of the 1980s was not an aberration.

§34.2 GARDEN-VARIETY TAKEOVER DRAMA

During the 1980s takeovers assumed nearly mythical proportions. They produced the largest private transactions in history, and they restructured the landscape and mentality of corporate America. Their disconcerting complexity, often played out in the news headlines, made the dramas seem surreal. Nonetheless, the actors in these dramas, their roles, the conventional scenes, the script devices, and the range of outcomes became standardized.

To acquaint you with the vocabulary and dynamics of a takeover, we present the story of a garden-variety takeover drama: the 1987 takeover battle for Burlington Industries, the nation's largest textile producer. The story had a surprising twist: Management ended up buying the company. It also has a sad ending: Fifteen years after the battle, the company declared bankruptcy and was sold.

Act I, Scene 1

Bidder Identifies Target

In 1987 Burlington was a publicly traded company listed on the New York Stock Exchange, with 27.3 million shares of common stock outstanding. At the beginning of the year, the stock was trading at around $40 a share; the company's aggregate market value was about $1.3 billion. Like most public corporations, Burlington was incorporated in Delaware. Its principal operations and corporate offices were in North Carolina.

A number of factors, discernible from publicly available information, suggested Burlington's attractiveness as a takeover target. The ratio of its stock price to book value was 1:1, its net sales (in a turbulent textile market) had fallen a modest 3.2 percent annually during the previous five years, its cash flow was running at 8 percent of sales, and its debt-to-equity ratio was about 4:5. In short, Burlington was a company with a strong asset base, relatively low debt, and strong cash flow. As with any potential target, there were a number of likely bidders for Burlington: companies in the textile business, conglomerates looking for diversification opportunities, and investment firms set up to find profitable takeover targets.

In Burlington's case, two likely bidders joined forces: Dominion Textiles (Canada's largest textile firm) and Asher Edelman (a financier who had made a fortune and reputation taking over companies). The two pooled their cash, raised money from outside sources, and agreed to take equal equity positions if the takeover succeeded. Like other raiders, they would become surrounded by a host of takeover professionals — lawyers, investment bankers, public relation experts — each of whom would garner handsome fees.

Usually bidders make do with available public information and rumors. But in the Burlington takeover bid, Dominion became interested in Burlington after receiving inside information from a former disgruntled Burlington executive. These contacts gave Dominion important confidential information about the value of Burlington's assets, which eventually would be the "smoking gun" that would be a "show stopper" for the Dominion-Edelman group. The pitfalls for a hostile bidder were (and remain) many.

Act I, Scene 2

Bidder Lines Up Money

In February 1987, Dominion's board formally began to explore the possibility of taking over Burlington. During the 1980s takeover binge, raising cash was not a serious obstacle. Dominion had many financing options, some of recent vintage. These financing techniques made it unnecessary for a bidder itself to have cash to buy the target. "Bootstrap" cash could come from the target — using *the assets and cash flow of the target* to finance the takeover by borrowing money that would be repaid once the takeover was successful and the bidder had gained access to the target's financial resources.

Two-tier buyout. During the early 1980s, many bidders began to structure their takeovers in two stages — a *two-tier buyout*. In the first stage, the bidder engaged in a "front end" tender offer for only enough shares to acquire voting control (51 percent of the stock). In the second stage, the bidder used a "back-end" squeeze-out merger to eliminate the remaining minority shareholders and gain full control of the target's assets (see §36.2.6). The minority shares remaining after the first stage typically were converted into high-risk, high-yield subordinated debt instruments — aptly called *junk bonds*. Front-end cash came from the bidder's own internally generated resources and sometimes bank financing; funds to repay the junk bonds came from the target's cash flow, once the takeover was completed. If cash flow was insufficient, the successful bidder could supplement it by selling parts of the target's business — a *bust-up takeover*.

Two-tier buyouts in which back-end shareholders received less attractive consideration than the front-end shareholders were structurally coercive. By announcing that the back-end would be worth less than the front-end, the hostile bidder pressured target shareholders into tendering to ensure themselves the front-end cash. Consequently, the bidder greatly increased its chances of acquiring a majority position. The front-end assured the success of the back-end, and vice versa. During the mid-1980s, this structural coercion was used to justify a variety of company-specific takeover defenses (see §39.2) and state antitakeover legislation (see §39.3). Today two-tier takeovers are common, but are almost always structured to offer the same consideration to shareholders in the front end as shareholders in the back end. This equal treatment eliminates a reason for the target board to oppose the bidder's overtures.

Any-and-all cash offers. By 1987 the two-tier bid had become obsolete. The success of takeovers generated huge investment pools, and most bidders could buy *all* of a target's stock in cash. This cash came from a variety of sources: (1) the bidder, (2) takeover cash pools held by investment bankers (financial institutions that assist in corporate mergers and acquisitions), (3) takeover firms (often referred to as "private equity" firms) and their cash pools, (4) private financiers (such as Asher Edelman), and (5) interim bridge loans from banks. Bridge loans, in particular, made it possible for the bidder to bid for all the stock in cash—an *any-and-all cash tender offer.* Once the bidder acquired control, any remaining shares could be cashed out in a back-end merger. The banks' bridge loans were then repaid from the proceeds of newly issued junk bonds and long-term, syndicated bank loans—both collateralized by the target's cash flow and assets. Insufficient cash flow was supplemented by selling off parts of the business.

Financing for the Edelman-Dominion bid came from Shearson Lehman Brothers (its takeover pool) and an international banking group headed by the First National Bank of Chicago and the Royal Bank of Canada. Together the three raised $2 billion in cash.

Act I, Scene 3

Bidder Quietly Buys a Toehold

At the same time that financing was being arranged, the Edelman-Dominion group began buying Burlington stock on the market. The group used various brokers and different account names to mask their purchases. Hostile bidders would acquire such a toehold for many reasons. Before the bid's announcement, market prices were lower than when the target came "into play." In addition, the toehold protected the bidder should management rebuff the hostile bid with a more lucrative offer. The bidder could sell into the management offer, thus compensating it for its effort.

On April 24, ten days after passing the 5 percent threshold and as required by federal securities law, the Edelman-Dominion group disclosed to the SEC (as well as the stock market and Burlington management) that it planned a takeover and had acquired 7.6 percent of Burlington's stock—an investment of about $100 million. As expected, the market price of the target's stock jumped from $54 on April 23 to $59 on April 27.

Act II, Scene 1

Bidder Puts Target in Play

Soon after revealing the toehold, Edelman proposed to meet with Frank Greenberg, Burlington's president and CEO, to discuss a negotiated transaction at $60 per share. A negotiated transaction, although sometimes more protracted and uncertain, would give the bidder more information about the target and avoid the risk of a successful defense. As often happened, Greenberg never responded to this uninvited "bear hug."

Then on May 6 the Dominion-Edelman group made a $67 cash tender offer to buy any and all of Burlington's shares, representing a total purchase price of $1.5 billion. Although the group needed only 43 percent more to gain control, open-market purchases were not a real option. Once a company has become a takeover target, shareholders generally hold out and wait for a higher price. A tender offer forced their hands with an above-market price — but only if the shareholders tendered within a specified period. Nor was a partial front-end loaded bid for 43 percent of the stock a wise option. Hostile bidders, by this time, had largely stopped using front-end loaded offers because of the takeover defenses these offers could invite.

In its tender offer filings, the Edelman group announced it would sell unspecified parts of Burlington's business if it gained control of the company. The Edelman group would later raise its bid to $72 and then to $77.

Act II, Scene 2

Arbs Take Center Stage

As rumors of a bid for Burlington began to circulate, later confirmed by the Edelman group's disclosure of its 7.6 percent toehold, the demographics of Burlington's shareholders began to change. Securities speculators known by the oxymoronic term "risk arbitrageurs" (or "arbs") were big purchasers. They bought stock hoping to make money on the difference between the trading price and the price for which the shares would eventually be sold — whether to the Edelman group, to another bidder, or even back to the company. With the announcement of the Edelman tender offer, the arbs' buying drove the market price toward the tender offer price.

Not surprisingly, individual and institutional shareholders — faced with the choice of selling at an attractive price or waiting for the tender offer to succeed — began to peel away. For some institutional shareholders, such as pension funds and bank trust departments, the decision to sell was compelled by their "prudent investor" duties to their beneficiaries.

The arbs, who often came to hold 60 to 70 percent of a target's stock, performed the important function of assuming the risk the tender offer might fail. They also were natural allies of the bidder, whose success they cheered. The arbs signaled the bid's strength. For example, if trading prices languished after a bid, it was a sign the arbs thought the bid would fail. If trading prices rose above the tender offer price (as sometimes happened), it showed the arbs thought the bid would be raised or bettered.

Act III, Scene 1

Management Defends

Immediately upon hearing of Edelman's stake, Burlington's Greenberg began to plan a defense strategy for "his" company. The Burlington board approved the hiring of two investment bankers and an outside law firm to advise it on antitakeover strategies.

During the 1980s, management's financial and legal advisors devised mind-boggling reactions and defenses to hostile bids. The defensive arsenal was extensive and its argot colorful:

- **Revise the corporate governance structure.** The board could be *staggered*, thus requiring an additional election cycle to vote in a new board majority. The charter could be amended to require *supermajority* approval of any mergers and other corporate combinations. The charter could be amended to include a *fair price* provision requiring a price at least equal to the tender offer price in any back-end transaction. These moves—sometimes known as *shark repellents*—often were taken in advance of a bid and required shareholder approval. They made control changes more drawn out and expensive.
- **Revise the capital structure.** The target could offer to repurchase its stock for cash or, as was often the case, a package of new equity and debt securities—an *issuer self-tender*. The target could buy its stock on the open market from arbs and others who accumulated blocks of stock in response to the takeover possibility—a *market sweep*. The board could give shareholders the right to buy the target's (or the bidder's) stock at sizeable discounts if the target were ever combined with the bidder—a *poison pill* (see §39.2.3). The board could issue new debt with *poison pill puts* that allowed debtholders to compel the target to redeem the debt at above-market prices in the case of a takeover. The board could issue debt securities with covenants restricting any new debt after a takeover or a combination with a hostile bidder. These changes to the capital structure, most of which could be effected without shareholder approval, threatened to distribute cash to shareholders or to create new debt (or both)—making the target less financially attractive.
- **Alter the shareholder mix.** An issuer self-tender could decrease the holdings of fickle shareholders and increase the proportion held by shareholders loyal to management. The target could sell stock (sometimes at favorable prices) to an investor friendly to management (a *white squire*) or to an *employee stock ownership plan* (ESOP) whose shares would be voted by trustees or employees sympathetic to management. The board could grant a stock lockup that promised stock to a favored bidder at bargain prices. These changes increased the proportion of shareholders sympathetic to (or controlled by) management.

- **Find a palatable buyer.** Management could induce a friendly bidder (*white knight*) to bid for or merge with the target on an understanding that management would not be replaced. The target could promise the white knight a *no-talk clause* that precluded the target from soliciting or giving information to other bidders — assuring the white knight it would not be a *stalking horse* for other bids. Or the target's management team could mount (alone or with investment partners) its own bid for the target, often financed with debt — a *management leveraged buyout* or *management LBO*. Each strategy increased the likelihood of management continuation.
- **Buy new businesses or sell existing ones.** The board could grant an *asset lockup* that gave a white knight the option to buy parts of the target's business at bargain prices. The board could sell or option a *crown jewel*, stripping the most desirable part of the target's business and undercutting the reason for the takeover. The target could buy new businesses or properties that would create antitrust or banking regulatory problems for the bidder, as well as diminish the target's debt capacity. These *scorched earth defenses*, none of which required shareholder approval, made the target less attractive from a business or regulatory standpoint.
- **Accelerate or increase management's employment benefits.** The board could grant senior executives *golden parachutes* that promised severance payments upon a takeover. (For tax reasons, these were usually set at three times salary.) The board could make pension and stock plans subject to contingent vesting if the takeover succeeded. These arrangements increased the costs of a takeover and softened the blow if one succeeded.
- **Buy out the bidder.** The target could pay *greenmail* by repurchasing the bidder's shares at a premium. Sometimes the target would require a greenmailer to enter into a *standstill agreement* obligating the greenmailer not to acquire more shares for a specified period. This, at least temporarily, ended the threat.
- **Attack the bidder.** The target could sue the bidder for violating antitrust merger guidelines, margin rules, securities tender offer rules, securities antifraud provisions, or state takeover legislation. The target could turn the tables and begin a tender offer for the bidder (the *Pacman defense*). These attacks added to the confusion and could undermine confidence in the bidder.

As was typical, Burlington's management chose a multipronged defense. On May 11 the board recommended that Burlington's shareholders reject the initial $67 offer as inadequate based on the advice of its investment bankers. It said it might seek control of Dominion — the involuted Pacman defense. The board also announced the *company* would commence an $80 issuer self-tender for up to 8 million (30 percent) of Burlington's shares and that it was considering a restructuring to benefit the remaining shares.

Meanwhile, management had begun a search for a white knight. On April 29 Greenberg had preliminary discussions with Morgan Stanley, an investment bank with its own access to takeover financing. They discussed a leveraged buyout (LBO) in which current management would be retained. The board approved giving Morgan Stanley confidential information, and on May 20 agreed to a merger. (As was often true in the 1980s, Morgan Stanley found that since the bidder group could line up financing, so could it.) On May 26 Morgan Stanley commenced an any-and-all tender offer for $76 in cash—a total bid of $2.4 billion. (The company's self-tender was made contingent on the Dominion-Edelman bid failing.) Morgan Stanley informally assured Burlington executives they would be equity participants in the new private company. Morgan Stanley later raised its offer to $78, which turned out to be the winning bid.

Burlington's board also authorized a lawsuit attacking the Dominion-Edelman group. The suit, brought in federal district court in North Carolina on April 29, claimed the group had improperly used inside information in making its bid—a violation of Rule 10b-5 (see §23.3). The suit also challenged a Dominion-Burlington combination as illegal under the merger guidelines of the federal antitrust laws.

The Edelman group responded with its own lawsuit, claiming Burlington had failed to disclose management's equity participation in Morgan Stanley's buyout. It also claimed the board violated its fiduciary duties by approving the merger agreement with Morgan Stanley without allowing the Edelman group a chance to participate in an auction for the company.

Act III, Scene 2

Management Turns to State Legislature

In the meantime, Burlington's management turned to the political process for help. Arguing that a Dominion-Edelman takeover would cost North Carolina jobs, taxes, and community support, management importuned the North Carolina legislature to pass laws that would make the hostile bid more difficult. The legislature acted promptly. On April 23 it passed a fair-price statute effectively requiring that any bid for Burlington satisfy a pricing formula. N.C. Gen. Stat. §§55-75 to 55-79. On May 13, it passed a control-share statute that limited the voting rights of any hostile bidder whose control acquisition had not been approved by the board or by the other shareholders. N.C. Gen. Stat. §§55-90 et seq. (These statutes, which purported to regulate corporations doing business and having investors and employees in North Carolina, even though incorporated outside the state, were of doubtful constitutionality after *CTS Corp. v. Dynamics Corp. of America*, 481 U.S. 69 (1987), which was decided by the Supreme Court on April 21, 1987. See §39.4.1.)

As it turned out in the Burlington takeover, these big guns were unnecessary. Nonetheless, the heavy artillery of state antitakeover legislation assumed great importance in the retrenchment of takeover activity in the 1990s. Delaware's 1988 takeover law, for example, fundamentally altered the bidding strategy for Delaware-incorporated firms. See §39.4.2.

Act III, Scene 3

Battle Unravels

In response to the Morgan Stanley offer, the Edelman group on May 28 raised its bid to $77 per share — for a total of $2.5 billion. But the group's resolve was beginning to fray. In late May it disclosed that it had reduced its holdings in Burlington from 13.4 percent to 12.3 percent.

On June 5 the federal district court in North Carolina enjoined the Dominion-Edelman group from continuing its bid on the ground it had misused inside information. Sensing victory, Morgan Stanley raised its bid on June 10 to $78 per share — $2.7 billion. On June 25 Morgan Stanley acquired control when nearly 80 percent of the shares were tendered to its $78 offer. Later in the summer Morgan Stanley bought out the remaining shareholders in a back-end merger. Burlington's management received a 17 percent interest in the new "private" company.

Perhaps the most salient feature of the Burlington takeover was that litigation proved to be both the wild card and the trump card. Although somewhat at a loss when faced with the titanic dimensions of takeover battles, courts have been pivotal in deciding the legality of bidding maneuvers and takeover defenses. Excellent lawyering has been at a premium.

Act IV, Scene 1

Aftermath

The 1987 battle for Burlington was remarkable in another significant respect: the hostile bidder lost. But its effect on Burlington was not insignificant. As things turned out, management restructured the company's businesses in much the same way that the Edelman group had planned. After the LBO, management cut worldwide jobs from 43,000 to 24,000, closed one-third of the company's plants, and embarked on a two-year corporate sell-off program to raise $900 million. The takeover battle had been over *who* would make Burlington leaner.

To reduce labor costs, the company in 1989 issued 35.5 percent of its shares to an ESOP, which took on a $112 million debt in exchange for the shares. The per-share purchase price of $38 was (after adjustments) four times greater than the price Morgan Stanley had paid for its stock two years before. Besides the munificent return on its $46 million investment, Morgan Stanley received a total of $87 million in fees for advising management in the LBO and then selling the junk bonds to finance the deal. It also collected an additional $33 million in fees to help Burlington divest some of its businesses and adjust its capital structure. In 1990 Morgan Stanley handed full control over to Burlington's management and the ESOP by exchanging all of its voting shares for nonvoting preferred stock.

Although by 1992 Burlington had reduced its debt to $1.8 billion, cash flows were insufficient to meet the company's debt load, and annual losses approached $100 million. To avoid bankruptcy, Burlington went "public" again by issuing 83 percent of its stock to public investors for $800 million. Within a year after this capital infusion, Burlington again became profitable. Burlington's management also fared well in the restructured company. Frank Greenberg, who stayed on as Burlington's CEO to oversee the company's restructuring, earned stock and other bonuses worth in excess of $8 million. In 1992 his salary of $1.8 million was the highest reported salary in the industry. In addition, he and other Burlington executives continued to hold a significant percentage of Burlington shares.

What happened to Asher Edelman? He was not discouraged by his defeat. In 1987, on the very day that Morgan Stanley completed its merger, Edelman announced his plans to buy Foster Wheeler for $888 million, and one month later he bid $965 million for Telex Corporation. Later that year Edelman created quite a stir when he proposed to teach a course at Columbia Business School titled "Corporate Raiding: The Art of War" in which the only assigned text was to be *The Art of War* by Sun Tzu and any student who identified a worthwhile takeover target would receive an "A" and $100,000.

Act IV, Scene 2

Denouement

Burlington was one of many U.S. textile companies to undertake an LBO or other restructuring in the 1980s. The resulting heavy debt loads forced textile companies to concentrate on their core businesses, often making significant investments to meet emerging competition from outside the United States. As the dust cleared after the turbulent 1980s, the U.S. textile industry in the early 1990s became more profitable than ever, and many believed the industry had emerged as one of the most efficient and technologically advanced of all U.S. industries.

The victory, however, was short-lived. When the economic slowdown of the early 2000s hit, the debt-heavy textile industry was not prepared to ride out the storm. In November 2001 Burlington filed for Chapter 11 bankruptcy protection. Management cited the company's excess debt load, along with liberalized U.S. import policies and the economic recession, as reasons for the filing. The company laid out a four-point business plan to emerge from bankruptcy: focus on its carpet business, expand its international sourcing, increase the use of its proprietary technology, and accelerate manufacturing improvements.

In 2003 Burlington emerged from bankruptcy and was bought by WL Ross Co. in a private buyout for $614 million. The buyout was part of

Wilbur Ross's strategy to revitalize bankrupt textile companies. Buying at deep discounts up to 50 percent of the debt of textile companies sliding toward bankruptcy, Ross would get himself elected as head of the creditors committee and then push out management and unsecured lenders. After the company emerged from bankruptcy, Ross would invest new equity capital and move the company's high-technology manufacturing to low-cost labor areas, such as Mexico and Vietnam.

The new International Textile Group set up by Ross (into which Burlington and other U.S. textile companies have been agglomerated) has built a global network that seeks to be "the cheapest, quickest, highest quality and most flexible clothmaker on the planet." Ross has looked to the developing world not only for cheap labor but, ultimately, as a source of new customers. In 2007 the company built a new plant in China; and in 2010, following the worldwide economic downturn in 2008 and 2009, the company expanded its operations in Vietnam, later withdrawing from the country because of political problems.

§34.3 EPILOGUE — IS THE TAKEOVER PHENOMENON HEALTHY?

One thing clear about the Burlington takeover, and most other takeovers in the 1980s, was that shareholders gained handsomely. According to estimates, takeovers in the 1980s increased net shareholder wealth by more than $200 billion. In the late 1990s premiums in negotiated takeover deals, often in the form of stock in the acquiring company, continued at an even larger and faster pace. And in the mid-2000s, driven by easy credit, negotiated takeovers flourished at prices that set record highs.

Why have bidders been willing to pay hefty premiums? There are a number of explanations, some focusing on the particular characteristics of the bidder and others on the nature of takeovers. Some of these explanations suggest that takeovers are beneficial:

- **Disciplining hypothesis.** The bidder, particularly one that borrows money against the target's cash flow, thinks a new management team will operate the business more profitably than incumbent management. Shareholders reap the unexploited value of their investment (or at least part of it) when the business is transferred to more efficient hands. Economists argue that this disciplining extends even to firms that are not taken over. In these firms, the takeover threat forces management to run the business in a way that keeps stock prices high and discourages takeover attention. Hostile takeovers in the 1980s often occurred in industries in decline in which managers had put resources to wasteful use (such as the broadcast and oil industries) and in industries in which managers failed to adjust quickly to rapid market, regulatory, or technological changes (such as the textile and airlines industries). The trend continued in the 1990s and 2000s when takeovers arose mostly in industries undergoing regulatory or technological change (telecommunications, entertainment, and finance).

- **Deconglomeration.** The target's business, particularly when diversified in many different industries, has more value broken into its individual pieces and sold than operated as a whole. This was the prevalent reason for corporate acquisitions in the 1980s, as takeover firms identified conglomerates that had been inefficiently assembled in the 1960s and 1970s.
- **Synergy hypothesis.** The target's business has unique synergistic value to the bidder. The value of the combined firm — such as a vertically integrated manufacturer and retailer — exceeds the sum of the two. In the 1990s and 2000s this has been a frequent explanation for "strategic" acquisitions of companies in related industries or in complementary markets in the same industry. The $9.8 billion acquisition in 1994 of Paramount by Viacom (telecommunications) offers a good illustration.

Other explanations suggest takeovers are bad:

- **Market myopia hypothesis.** The stock markets systematically undervalue the long-term prospects of firms. This undervaluation increases the possibility that the company will be put into play, causing managers to focus too much on the short term and creating general business uncertainty in the company. Although unsolicited bids put corporate control into higher-valuing hands, the problem is that the market systematically undervalues incumbent management.
- **Empire-building hypothesis.** The bidder (or more precisely its management) prefers to control more assets because executive prestige and compensation are often tied to company size, not necessarily to profitability. The phenomenon has been particularly noticeable in the banking and telecommunications industries. Shareholders of the target receive some of the spoils of this empire-building; shareholders of the bidder subsidize the frolic. Further, when the bidder enters an auction to acquire the target, bidders tend to overpay, unaware that in an auction for assets whose value is uncertain there usually is a "winner's curse."
- **Hubris hypothesis.** Related to the empire-building hypothesis is one that bidders tend to overpay for targets because the bidder's

management is overly confident about its ability to manage and find synergies in the combined firm. Proof comes from the typical decline in the stock price of bidders when they announce a takeover. Studies, however, indicate that over time corporate combinations tend to produce value (from synergies and selling off some of acquired assets) and that this value is shared about 60:40 between the bidder shareholders and the target shareholders.

- **Goring hypotheses.** Shareholder gains are at the expense of other stakeholders — employees, creditors, customers, and taxpayers. Streamlining the target sacrifices jobs and leads to lower wages, a violation of implicit promises of employment security. Increased leverage forces existing creditors (such as bondholders that have not negotiated antitakeover protections) to subsidize the takeover. Takeovers that combine competing businesses concentrate market power and force customers to pay higher, noncompetitive prices. Replacing equity with debt reduces the target's tax burden — because interest is deductible, while dividends are not — and forces taxpayers to pick up the slack. Cuts in long-term research and development after a takeover reduce American competitiveness and hurt everyone. Increased leverage puts firms in a precarious position, with little margin for error in an economic downturn.

So the hypotheses go. Empirical evidence tends to support an eclectic answer. Each hypothesis has some support, some more than others. Studies show that, on balance, leveraged buyouts and restructurings achieved efficiency gains by causing managers of debt-heavy companies to focus on the "bottom line" and redeploy assets to their most productive uses. Nonetheless, debt-heavy companies also became less able to ride out economic recessions or industry downturns.

In addition, many have questioned the stock market's ability to value firms, particularly since the collapse of the "irrationally exuberant" market of the late 1990s and the subprime-induced financial crisis of 2008. That is, a low-priced stock does not necessarily mean the company should be in better hands, and a high-priced stock does not mean the company is well-managed. Nonetheless, the markets do seem to take into account a firm's long-term prospects. Studies show that stock prices rise on announcements of increased R&D spending and that firms with high research and development expenditures are actually less vulnerable to takeovers. And institutional shareholders, dominant players in corporate takeovers, do not automatically accept premium bids, but often support management if it offers a better strategic alternative.

The loss of jobs (and lower wages) in some industries seems to be more the result of broad-based economic change than of takeovers. Studies show that layoffs are as frequent in companies that have not been taken over as in companies that have been. In addition, some studies show that on the whole existing bondholders are not worse off because of takeovers, though there are a number of individual exceptions.

One significant element that the takeover debate often disregards is the drain of transaction costs—whether the takeover is hostile or negotiated. Billions of dollars are paid in financing fees, investment advisory fees, and legal fees. Some have said that takeovers consume too much talent of America's best and brightest. As takeovers have continued into the 2000s, the talent drain continues. As proof, you have just finished reading this chapter.

CHAPTER 35

Internal Fundamental Changes

Charter amendments, recapitalizations, corporate combinations, and dissolutions—often referred to as *fundamental changes*—realign corporate rights and powers. Corporate law imposes a variety of protections, which we consider in the next three chapters:

- *internal* fundamental changes that affect only existing corporate participants (this chapter—charter amendments (§35.1) and dissolutions (§35.2))
- *external* fundamental changes in which two (or more) corporations are combined (Chapter 36)
- *appraisal remedy*—a protective procedure available in some fundamental changes that allows dissenting shareholders to obtain cash for their shares (Chapter 37)

Note on Revisions to MBCA

This chapter and those that follow refer to the 1999 revisions to the MBCA, which instituted sweeping changes for how fundamental changes are approved. In general, the 1999 MBCA revisions streamline (and equalize) the processes for restructuring the corporation. With respect to internal changes, obtaining shareholder approval of charter amendments is easier, and shareholders have fewer rights to dissent and seek appraisal. By contrast, the current Delaware statute and the pre-1999 MBCA impose more burdensome voting requirements for internal changes and, in the case of the pre-1999 MBCA (still used in most states), more opportunities for dissenting shareholders to seek appraisal.

§35.1 CHARTER AMENDMENTS

Modern corporate law's philosophy of majority rule extends to amendments to the articles of incorporation. Unlike partnerships, where the default rule is unanimous approval of any changes to the partnership agreement, corporate law adopts majority rule. Cf. RUPA §401(j). Individual shareholders have no vested rights in the corporate "contract." Absent contrary agreement, minority shareholders are powerless to block a charter amendment.

§35.1.1 Power to Amend Charter

Modern corporate statutes permit amendment of the articles of incorporation so long as the new provision (or deletion) could have been part of the articles as originally adopted. MBCA §10.01(a); Del. GCL §242(a).

No Vested Rights in Corporate "Contract"

State corporation statutes expressly authorize charter amendments, reserving to the majority the power to change the corporate "contract." Shareholders can have no expectations of immutability.

Corporate statutes also specifically reserve the *legislative power* to change the corporate statute. See MBCA §1.02; Del. GCL §394. This reservation has a constitutional dimension. In *Dartmouth College v. Woodward*, 17 U.S. (4 Wheat.) 518 (1819), the Supreme Court held that New Hampshire's legislature violated the Constitution's contract impairment clause when it sought to take control of Dartmouth College (a nonprofit corporation without shareholders) by amending its charter to change the name of the college, increase the number of trustees, and create a board of overseers appointed by the legislature. The amendment, the Court held, breached the vested rights arising under the "contract" between New Hampshire and Dartmouth College. In a concurring opinion, Justice Story suggested that states could avoid the problem by statutorily reserving the power to amend corporate charters—which they have done.

Limitations Set in Articles

The articles themselves can limit the corporation's amendatory powers. Supermajority provisions or special procedural requirements protect the interests of both shareholders and management. See §26.1 (close corporation supermajority voting).

§35.1.2 Mechanics for Approving Charter Amendments

Corporate law gives shareholders three layers of protection:

- the board must (generally) initiate the amendment
- a majority of the shareholders must then approve it
- dissenting shareholders, in some circumstances, may seek judicial appraisal to force the corporation to redeem their shares for cash

Board Approval

Most states require the board to propose any amendment to the articles; shareholders cannot initiate the amendment. MBCA §10.03 (b)(1); Del. GCL §242(b)(1). A few states, however, allow either the board or a specified percentage of shareholders to propose the amendment.

This first layer of protection gives the board a critical role in safeguarding the interests of shareholders and other corporate constituents. Board approval is subject to fiduciary review and can be invalidated for bad faith, illegality, self-interest, or gross negligence. See §12.3.

Shareholder Approval

The second layer of protection is approval by a shareholder majority. What majority? Many statutes require approval by a majority of all outstanding voting shares (absolute majority). Del. GCL §242(b)(1); pre-1999 MBCA §10.03(e) ("majority of votes entitled to be cast"). The MBCA, as revised in 1999, requires only approval by a majority of those present at the meeting (simple majority). MBCA §§7.25(c), 10.03(e). Thus, assuming a quorum is present at a meeting (a majority of shares entitled to vote), the amendment is approved when the votes for it exceed the votes against it—even though the shares voting for the amendment may be fewer than a majority of outstanding shares.

Who votes? Shares with voting rights (such as common stock) are entitled to vote on any amendment to the articles. Some statutes require *class voting*—separate approval by each class of shares (voting or nonvoting) substantially and adversely affected by the amendment. MBCA §10.04(a) (changes to preferential, redemption, seniority, preemptive, voting, distribution rights); Del. GCL §242(b)(2) (similar). For example, if the board proposed a new class of preferred shares with rights senior to all other shares, voting common and each class of existing preferred (voting or nonvoting) would have to approve.

The MBCA, as revised in 1999, constricts class voting. Under the pre-1999 MBCA, class voting arose when an amendment would change the number of shares of the class or create new classes of shares with "substantially equal" rights. Pre-1999 MBCA §10.04(a)(1), (a)(6), (a)(7). The revised MBCA, concerned about "hold up" power, does not require class voting when the corporation is increasing its capitalization and authorizing new shares that do not undermine the rights of existing classes. See Official Comment to MBCA §10.04.

In addition to these statutory voting rights, the board may condition any proposed amendment on a specified vote. For example, the board can require approval by a specified supermajority of voting shares or by a specific group of shareholders. MBCA §10.03(c); Del. GCL §242(b)(4) (any change to supermajority voting requirement must be approved by the same supermajority).

Appraisal Rights

Some state statutes allow dissenting shareholders to *opt out* of the charter amendment—in certain circumstances—by seeking appraisal to force the corporation to pay cash for the fair value of their shares. Pre-1999 MBCA §13.02(a)(4) (amendment "materially and adversely affects" rights of particular class of shareholders). The revised MBCA only permits appraisal when an amendment "squeezes out" shareholders by reducing the number of shares to a fraction, thus allowing the corporation to repurchase those fractional shares. MBCA §13.02(a)(4). Many states, particularly Delaware, do not create appraisal rights in the case of charter amendments. Del. GCL §262(a). Shareholders' only recourse is to vote against the proposed amendment or challenge it as a breach of the board's fiduciary duties.

§35.1.3 Recapitalizations

An important use of the amendment power is to alter the corporation's capital structure. Changes in the rights, privileges, powers, and immunities of corporate securities—such as a conversion of common stock into a package of cash and debt securities, or a conversion of preferred stock with dividend arrearages into common stock—provide financial flexibility. Recapitalizations are subject to abuse becausesince they change financial rights by majority action, and all the protections applicable to charter amendments are available.

A recapitalization also can be accomplished by merger (see §35.2): The corporation creates a shell subsidiary, the corporation then merges into the subsidiary, and shareholders receive a new package of securities in the surviving corporation. In *Bove v. Community Hotel Corp.*, 249 A.2d 89 (R.I. 1969), a preferred shareholder sought to enjoin a merger whose effect was to convert preferred stock (and its accrued, but unpaid, dividends) into common stock. The shareholder argued that if the recapitalization had been accomplished as an amendment to the articles, state law governing charter amendments would have required unanimous approval by the preferred shareholders. The statute, however, required that only two-thirds of the preferred shareholders approve the merger. Applying the doctrine of "independent legal significance"—namely, that corporate planners can choose whatever statutory technique they want to accomplish a result, even when another more-regulated technique also exists—the court accepted the board's choice of form and upheld the merger.

§35.2 DISSOLUTION

Dissolution is the ultimate fundamental change. Although dissolution results in the death of the corporation, it does not necessarily mean the death of the business. Because of its going-concern value, the business (its assets) usually will be sold intact. Dissolution simply redistributes the assets to an outside party (or shareholder faction). The shareholders then share pro rata in the proceeds of the sale.

§35.2.1 Dissolution Terminology

Dissolution terminology is often confusing.

- *Dissolution* is the formal extinguishment of the corporation's legal life.
- *Liquidation* is the process of reducing the corporation's assets to cash or liquid assets, after which the corporation becomes a holding shell.
- *Winding up* is the whole process of liquidating the assets, paying off creditors, and distributing what remains to shareholders.

§35.2.2 Process of Approval

Dissolution, like a charter amendment, is subject to majority rule. Typically, voluntary dissolution must be initiated by the board and followed by shareholder approval, though in some states all shareholders can consent to dissolve the corporation without board action. See Del. GCL §275(c). Absent oppression or deadlock, minority shareholders generally cannot dissolve the corporation. See §27.1.3 (involuntary dissolution). Likewise, minority shareholders cannot force the corporation's continuance.

Voluntary dissolution is subject to only two levels of protection: (1) initial approval by the board, and (2) subsequent approval by shareholders. MBCA §14.02(e) (simple shareholder majority); pre-1999 MBCA §14.02(e) (absolute shareholder majority); Del. GCL §275 (same). Board approval is subject to fiduciary review. See §12.3. State statutes provide no appraisal rights in a dissolution on the theory that all shareholders are being treated equally, and allowing some shareholders to demand cash would interfere with the winding-up process.

§35.2.3 Process of Winding Up

Corporate law protects creditors in a dissolution. In the winding-up process, the corporation must pay all known claims. The corporation must send notice to known claimants for them to submit their claims. MBCA §14.06 (minimum 120-days notice). Under some statutes, unknown claims (such as contingent tort claims) may be brought against the dissolved corporation. MBCA §14.07 (claims allowed for five years after notice of dissolution); Del. GCL §278 (claims allowed for three years after dissolution). If the corporation does not retain sufficient assets after the distribution, some statutes permit the claimant to seek satisfaction from former shareholders who received distributions in the dissolution. Under the MBCA, each shareholder (as a residual claimant who moved ahead in the priority line) is obligated to pay a pro rata share of the claim, up to the amount distributed to the shareholder in dissolution. MBCA §14.07(d)(2).

If creditors cannot satisfy their claims against the dissolved corporation or its former shareholders, they can assert their claims against the entity that acquired the business's assets under the successor liability doctrine (see §36.4.2). And if the board approves the distribution of assets to shareholders without the corporation first satisfying known claimants, the directors can be liable to the creditors, with recoupmentcontribution available from shareholders who knew the distribution was illegal. See MBCA §8.33 (see §31.4). To shield directors from liability, the corporation can apply to have a court determine how much security the corporation should set aside to satisfy anticipated claims. See MBCA §14.08.

Examples

1. Mega Motors is incorporated in a jurisdiction that has adopted the MBCA, as revised in 1999. Times have been tough in the auto industry, and the company has not paid dividends in the last two years, including those due on its nonvoting cumulative preferred stock. The Mega Revitalization

Committee (MRC), a group of common shareholders, proposes to amend the articles so that dividends on the preferred shares would be payable only in common stock (using a formula based on the common's market value when dividends are declared). In addition, existing preferred arrearages would be canceled by paying 1.37 common shares for each share of preferred. By eliminating the preferred arrearages and future cash drain, new financing becomes possible.

a. Can MRC do this?
b. The Mega board considers the MRC proposal and wonders whether preferred shareholders' rights can be changed this way. Is the amendment possible?
c. Mega has sufficient authorized common shares to pay arrearages under the plan. Which shareholders must approve the plan?
d. Some preferred shareholders object to having their rights to cash payments converted into noncash common stock. Can they prevent this conversion?

2. The Mega board proposes a charter amendment to authorize an additional 50 million shares of common stock to finance a major project to develop an electric car. There are 200 million shares of common outstanding.
   a. At the shareholders' meeting, 140 million shares are represented and 65 million vote for the amendment, 60 million vote against, and 15 million abstain. Has it passed?
   b. Mega's shareholders vote against the amendment, believing electric cars have no future. Management, convinced of the value of the project, creates a Mega subsidiary to develop an electric car. To finance the project, the subsidiary will issue 50 million shares. Is this permissible?

3. Five years ago Jerry, a compulsive tinkerer, designed an automotive "thermal ignition system" that replaces spark plugs in internal combustion engines. Jerry incorporates Tinker Corporation in an MBCA jurisdiction and sells common stock to his friends, keeping a majority of the stock himself. His technology is a major engineering breakthrough, and Tinker's business soars. Jerry now wants to get rid of his friends. He dissolves Tinker, and in the winding-up process sells the company's assets to JRS Combustion—a corporation wholly owned by Jerry. The minority Tinker shareholders receive $400 per share, based on a sales price of $1 million for the assets.
   a. Can Jerry's friends block his plan under the statutory dissolution procedures?
   b. Jerry's friends believe they have not received a fair price for their shares. Can they seek a judicial appraisal of their shares?
   c. Can Jerry's friends attack the transaction?

Explanations

1. a. No. Under the MBCA, as well as most other statutes, the board must initiate any charter amendment. MBCA §10.03(a) ("proposed amendment must be adopted by the board"). In theory, this assures that the board will look out for interests of all corporate constituencies, including minority shareholders and creditors. The board's action is subject to fiduciary review; a proposal by shareholders might not be. In a public corporation, the shareholder group could recommend that the board adopt their proposal under the shareholder proposal rule. See §9.4.2.

   b. Yes. The amendment calls for payment of stock dividends, which is permitted under the MBCA and could have been inserted in the articles originally. MBCA §6.23 (authorizing "share dividends") (see §4.1.2).

   c. Mega's common shareholders and preferred shareholders, each group voting separately. Under the MBCA, the amendment must be approved by both a voting common and the nonvoting preferred because, since it changes the dividend rights of the preferred. See MBCA §10.04(a)(3). The voting rights of common shareholders include the power to approve any amendment to the articles, whether or not their interests are adversely affected. Voting by the nonvoting preferred protects them against unilateral changes by common shareholders that frustrate their investment expectations.

   d. Probably not. Under most corporate statutes, including the MBCA, preferred shareholders are not assured payment of dividends and thus have no contractual or vested right to payment. See MBCA §6.40 ("board of directors may authorize . . . distributions"). (A few states, however, treat preferred dividends in much the same way as interest on debt, requiring their payment without any discretion in the board.) Under the MBCA, only if dividends have been declared do preferred shareholders have a right to payment. See MBCA §6.40(f) ("corporation's indebtedness to a shareholder incurred by reason of a distribution"). The failure of Mega's board to pay dividends, though giving preferred shareholders cumulative rights if dividends are ever declared, does not create a right to payment. But, as the previous answer indicates, any change that adversely affects preferred rights must be approved by a majority of the preferred.

2. a. Yes. Under the MBCA, as revised in 1999, more votes for (65 million) than against (60 million) at a meeting with a proper quorum (a majority of outstanding shares) is enough for passage. MBCA §§7.25(c), 10.03(e). This is substantially more facilitative than Delaware, which requires an absolute majority of the *outstanding* common shares (at least

100,000,001) be voted for any charter amendment. Del. GCL §242(b)(1). Mega's nonvoting preferred shareholders are not entitled to vote on this amendment because it does not adversely affect their legal interests. The new common shares will not have rights superior to the preferred shares.

b. Probably. The limitation in Mega's articles on issuing new shares does not apply to the subsidiary. As long as management satisfied its fiduciary duties in setting up the subsidiary—which the business judgment rule makes likely—there is nothing to keep the company from choosing one method of capitalization, even though another might trigger shareholder voting rights.

   A shareholder challenging the plan to capitalize the subsidiary might argue that the shareholders' rejection of the board's original plan implicitly blocks any financing for an electric car project. But in a public corporation, a shareholder veto of one plan does not prevent the board from choosing another course of action. Remember that the charter can be amended only through a formal board proposal and shareholder approval. If shareholder veto of a board initiative could create a de facto charter limitation, the board's role as initiator would be hampered. In a public corporation, the board has broad delegated authority. Implying such limits in a close corporation, however, may protect the participants' reasonable expectations (see §27.2.1).

3. a. No. Dissolution requires only a board proposal and approval by a majority of shareholders. MBCA §14.02. BecauseSince Jerry controls the board and has a majority of the shares, approval is inevitable. The minority shareholders have no vested right to retain an interest in the corporation.

   b. No. In a dissolution, shareholders have no appraisal rights. See MBCA §13.02(a). This prevents disgruntled shareholders from seeking a preferred position compared to other shareholders during the winding-up process. Furthermore, if dissenters could pursue an appraisal remedy, they would be entitled to a cash payment of fair value before the remaining shareholders received their pro rata distribution of the corporation's liquidated assets. In theory, the amount distributed in dissolution (based on the full going-concern value of the business) should be identical to the shares' fair value.

   c. Yes. The dissolution and the liquidation of Tinker's assets are self-dealing transactions. The board and Jerry (as controlling shareholder) have the burden to prove the transaction's fairness. If the sold assets were undervalued, the minority shareholders can have the transaction rescinded or have Jerry pay fair value (see §13.5).

CHAPTER 36

Corporate Combinations

Corporate law supplies various techniques for combining the businesses of two (or more) corporations under one management. Although these techniques can be made to produce functionally identical results, the choice of technique can affect (1) the protections available to shareholders, (2) the taxation of each corporation and its shareholders, and (3) the liabilities of the resulting entity. As in any complex legal system where different paths lead to the same result, clever lawyering is at a premium.

This chapter considers the state-based corporate "game rules" for structuring a corporate combination. It describes the combination choices (§36.1), the effects and mechanics of statutory mergers (§36.2) and sales of assets (§36.3), and the judicial doctrines used to equate the two techniques (§36.4).

We do not address the tax rules, though they are crucial to playing the game. Furthermore, this chapter makes only passing references to the disclosure and fiduciary protections that the various structures implicate. See Chapter 5 (federal disclosure rules applicable to the public issuance of stock in a merger or stock exchange); Chapter 38 (federal disclosure rules that apply to stock acquisitions and tender offers of publicly traded corporations); Chapters 6 to 10 (state rules defining shareholders' voting rights); and Chapters 11 to 18 (state-based fiduciary rules). No analysis of a corporate combination would be complete without considering these additional protections.

Note on Revisions to MBCA

This chapter refers to the 1999 revisions to the MBCA, which instituted sweeping changes to the rights of shareholders in fundamental changes. In general, the 1999

(continued)

MBCA revisions seek to provide the same shareholder rights regardless of the form of the combination—"substance over form." Generally, this means that voting and appraisal rights in corporate combinations (however structured) exist for shareholders of the acquired corporation, but only for shareholders of the acquiring corporation provided their rights are fundamentally affected. By contrast, the current Delaware statute and the pre-1999 MBCA provisions (which continue to apply in most MBCA jurisdictions) give corporate planners significant latitude to engineer shareholder voting and appraisal rights according to how the transaction is structured. Where relevant, we point out the differences between these three variants: revised MBCA, pre-1999 MBCA, and Delaware (see chart in §36.3.4).

§36.1 COMBINATION CHOICES—SOME BASICS

Suppose Alpha Corp. wants to buy closely held Sigma Inc. Everything is in order: Alpha has enough cash or authorized stock, and Sigma's management and shareholders are amenable. How might the transaction be structured?

- **Statutory merger.** Sigma could be merged into Alpha. In the merger, Sigma would be absorbed into Alpha and would disappear as a separate entity. Alpha would issue its shares or pay cash to the Sigma shareholders. (In the nomenclature of the Internal Revenue Code, this is an *A reorganization*.)
- **Asset acquisition.** Alpha could buy all the assets of Sigma. Alpha would issue stock or pay cash to Sigma for the assets; Sigma as an entity would remain unaffected by the sale. Normally, after the sale Sigma would be dissolved and Sigma's assets (the cash or stock paid by Alpha) would be distributed to its shareholders on a pro rata basis. (Under the IRC, this is a *C reorganization*.)
- **Stock acquisition.** Alpha could buy a controlling block of Sigma shares from Sigma itself (if there is sufficient authorized, but unissued, stock) or from some or all of the Sigma shareholders. Alpha would exchange its stock or pay cash for the shares, and Sigma would become a subsidiary of Alpha, though Sigma (as an entity) would be unaffected by the transaction. (Under the IRC, this is a *B reorganization*.)

In each case, the practical effect of the transaction is identical: Alpha pays consideration (directly or indirectly) to Sigma shareholders to acquire control of Sigma's business.

Note on Coverage

This chapter discusses the two combination techniques — statutory mergers and sales of assets — for which corporate law has traditionally afforded shareholders (and other corporate constituents) specific protections. Acquisition of control through stock purchases from shareholders, whether through open market transactions or by means of a tender offer, is subject to federal securities regulation (see Chapter 38) and state takeover law (see Chapter 39).

§36.2 MERGERS

In a *statutory merger*, the acquiring corporation absorbs the acquired corporation, the acquired corporation disappears, and the acquiring corporation becomes the surviving corporation. Below we diagram a stock-for-stock merger in which Sigma merges into Alpha, the shareholders of Alpha retain their shares, and Alpha issues its shares to Sigma's shareholders as consideration.

Sigma Merges into Alpha

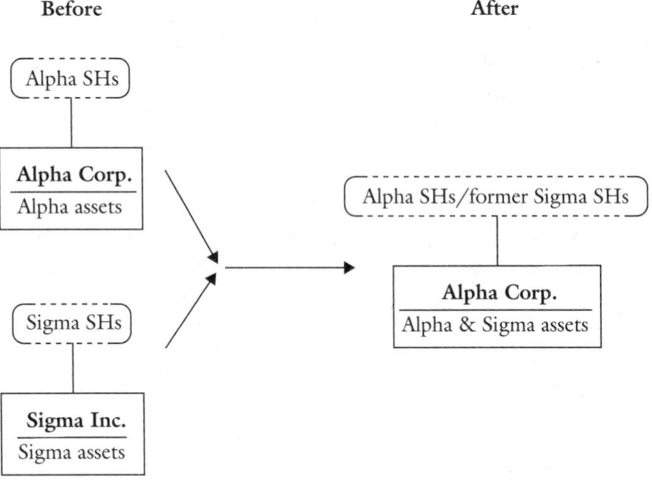

Consolidations

A *consolidation*, a close relative of the statutory merger, is of diminishing importance in corporate practice. In a consolidation, two or more existing corporations combine into a new corporation and the existing corporations disappear. (This new corporation is what distinguishes a consolidation from a merger.) The same rules that apply to mergers also apply to consolidations. Notice that a consolidation can also be accomplished using a statutory merger procedure:

(1) Alpha creates a shell subsidiary—let's say, Alphigma.
(2) Alpha, Sigma, and Alphigma enter into a tripartite merger agreement.
(3) In the merger Alpha and Sigma are absorbed into Alphigma, the new surviving corporation.
(4) The shares of Alpha and Sigma are converted into Alphigma shares.

For this reason, the MBCA and other modern statutes do not offer a separate consolidation procedure.

§36.2.1 Effect of Merger

In a merger the surviving corporation absorbs the acquired corporation when the required document is filed at the appropriate state office. MBCA §11.06 (articles of merger); Del. GCL §251(c) (certificate of merger). By operation of law, the surviving corporation becomes the owner of all the acquired corporation's assets, becomes subject to all its liabilities, and is substituted in all pending litigation. This complete absorption is a unique characteristic of a statutory merger compared to other corporate combination techniques.

Historically, this absorption concept also extended to the treatment of the acquired corporation's shareholders, whose shares had to be converted into shares of the acquiring-surviving corporation. Nearly all modern statutes do away with this requirement and allow consideration to be paid in the form of securities of the acquiring corporation (or any corporation), cash, property, or a combination of these. MBCA §11.02(c)(3); Del. GCL §251(b).

§36.2.2 Statutory Protections in Merger

A statutory merger carries three layers of protection: (1) board initiation and approval (implicating the board's fiduciary duties); (2) shareholder approval in some situations (creating disclosure rights under state fiduciary rules and federal securities law); and (3) appraisal remedies in certain mergers.

Board Adoption

The board of each constituent corporation must initiate the merger by adopting a document known as a *plan of merger*. The plan outlines the terms and conditions of the merger (including how shareholders will vote on it) and the consideration that shareholders of the acquired corporation will receive. MBCA §11.04(a); Del. GCL §251(b). Under some statutes, the merger plan may also amend the articles of the acquiring surviving corporation. MBCA §11.02(c)(4); Del. GCL §251(b).

Fiduciary duties and federal disclosure rules provide additional glosses to this first layer of protection:

- **Fiduciary duties.** In approving a merger, the directors are bound by their fiduciary duties of care and loyalty. See Chapters 11, 12, and 13. If the merger is with a controlling shareholder (parent corporation) or otherwise involves a conflict of interest, the merger is subject to review as a self-dealing transaction. See §17.3.
- **Disclosure duties.** The issuance of stock in a merger is a "sale" under the federal securities laws. See Rule 145, Securities Act of 1933. Shareholders who receive publicly traded shares for their stock are entitled to prospectus disclosure and receive antifraud protection under the federal securities laws. See Chapters 5 and 22.

Shareholder Approval

After board adoption, the plan of merger must generally be submitted to the shareholders of each corporation for their separate approval. MBCA §11.04(b); Del. GCL §251(c). This second layer of protection is supplemented by federal proxy rules for voting in a public corporation (see Chapter 9 and §10.2) and a "duty of disclosure" under state fiduciary law (§10.3).

At common law, shareholders' approval of a merger had to be unanimous, but modern statutes have done away with this vestige of the vested rights theory. Dissenting shareholders are bound by the will of the majority. Now most statutes require a majority of all outstanding voting shares—an absolute majority. Pre-1999 MBCA §11.03(e); Del. GCL §251(c). The 1999 revisions to the MBCA further relax the voting safeguard by requiring only that more votes be cast for the merger than against it at a meeting with a proper quorum—a simple majority. MBCA §§7.25(c), 11.04(e).

If a corporation has more than one class of voting shares outstanding, many statutes require separate approval by each voting class. MBCA §11.04(e). The merger is not approved if any voting class rejects it. Under many statutes, nonvoting shares also have a right to vote as a group on the merger if the shares are to be converted in the merger or would be adversely affected by the merger. MBCA §11.04(f)(1). Delaware, however, does not require class voting. Approval by a majority of *outstanding voting shares* is sufficient, even if nonvoting shares or separate voting classes might have rejected the merger. Del. GCL §251(c) (vote by "majority of outstanding stock . . .

entitled to vote thereon"). Any nonvoting shares have fiduciary protections and appraisal remedies.

Approval by shareholders of the *acquired* corporation is always required since their interests are fundamentally altered in a merger. MBCA §11.04(b). The story is different for the *acquiring* corporation's shareholders. When a big firm absorbs a smaller one, the effect on the *acquiring* corporation may be minimal, not justifying the expense and trouble of shareholder approval. Under the MBCA, as revised in 1999, the shareholders of the acquiring corporation do not have voting rights unless the corporation does not survive in the merger, its articles are changed, or its shareholders end up holding a different number of shares after the merger. MBCA §11.04(g). In addition, shareholders can vote if the acquiring corporation (whether publicly traded or closely held) issues new shares in the merger with voting power equal to 20 percent or more of the voting shares that existed prior to the merger. MBCA §§11.04(g)(4), 6.21(f). Delaware's statute is to the same effect. Del. GCL §251(f). In addition, stock exchange rules require a shareholder vote when a listed corporation issues more than 20 percent of its shares in a merger. See NYSE Listing Standard 312.03(c); NASDAQ Listing Rule 5635(a).

Appraisal Rights

Shareholders cannot opt out of a merger and retain their original investment. For this reason, all state statutes grant dissenting shareholders of the acquired corporation who are *entitled to vote on the merger* a right to receive the appraised, fair value of their shares in cash. MBCA §13.02(a)(1); Del. GCL §262. The story is different for shareholders of the acquiring corporation, even if they have voting rights. See MBCA §13.02(a)(1) (no appraisal for shareholders whose shares remain outstanding after the merger). This third layer of protection is discussed in Chapter 37.

§36.2.3 Short-Form Merger (Subsidiary into Parent)

When a parent corporation owns 90 percent or more of a subsidiary, many corporate statutes allow the subsidiary to be merged into the parent without approval by shareholders of either corporation. MBCA §11.05; Del. GCL §253. Only approval of the parent's board of directors is required.

The rationale for this streamlined, short-form procedure is that approval by the subsidiary's board and its shareholders is preordained, and the parent's shareholders will not be materially affected since the parent already holds at least a 90 percent interest in the subsidiary. The subsidiary's minority shareholders are protected at two levels:

- the fiduciary rules applicable to the parent as controlling shareholder in a squeeze-out transaction. See §17.3.
- appraisal remedies, which statutes automatically grant minority shareholders in a short-form merger. MBCA §13.02(a)(1)(ii).

§36.2.4 Merger of Corporations Incorporated in Different States

The merger of a domestic and a foreign corporation (see §3.2.2) presents a metaphorical problem: How can two "creatures" of different states' laws become a new "creature" of only one law? State statutes deal with this problem parochially. Nearly all statutes authorize the merger of a domestic and foreign corporation and allow the surviving corporation to be a domestic corporation. But the statutes maintain the purity of the "creature" metaphor: Each corporation is bound by the statutory merger requirements of its jurisdiction. MBCA §11.02(b); Del. GCL §252. That is, the corporate law of each corporation's state of incorporation defines shareholder protection for that corporation.

§36.2.5 Triangular Merger (and Compulsory Stock Exchange)

Absorption of the target into the acquiring corporation may not always be desired. In many instances, the acquiring corporation will want to keep the acquired firm's business incorporated separately—held as a wholly owned subsidiary. This may be necessary to comply with antidiversification requirements in regulated industries, such as banking or insurance. It may also be desirable to insulate the parent from the subsidiary's liabilities, to maintain separate business identities, or to keep the acquired business separate if the parent sells it in the future. Neither a statutory merger nor a sale of assets accomplishes this result.

Nonetheless, the statutory merger technique can fill the bill with a *triangular merger*. Consider the following series of transactions:

(1) Alpha sets up a new wholly owned subsidiary—let's say, Merger Sub. Alpha capitalizes Merger Sub with its shares or other assets (such as cash). In return, Merger Sub issues all its shares to Alpha.
(2) Merger Sub enters into a merger plan with Sigma under which Merger Sub will be the surviving corporation.
(3) Sigma merges into Merger Sub, and Sigma's shareholders receive as consideration the assets that Merger Sub received when Alpha capitalized it.

(4) After the merger, Alpha continues as the sole shareholder of the surviving Merger Sub, which typically adopts a new, more descriptive name like Alpha-Sigma, Inc. as part of the plan of merger.

Sketching out this series of transactions reveals the triangle namesake of this combination technique in which the new subsidiary merges into the acquired corporation, which survives in the merger—a "reverse triangular merger":

Sigma Merges into Merger Sub (and Becomes Subsidiary of Alpha)

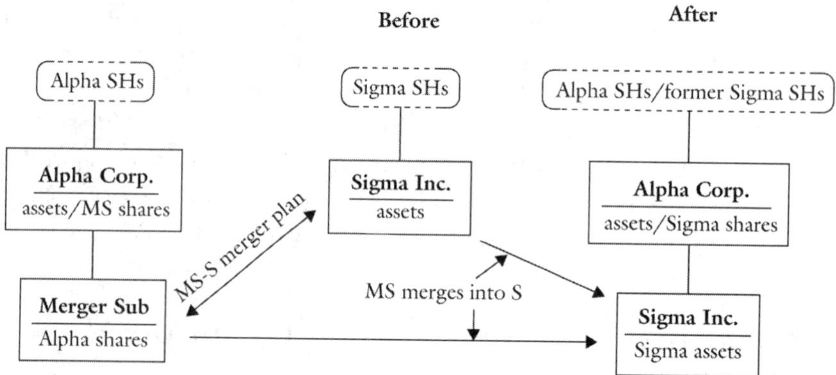

The triangular technique has many possibilities. It is also possible to extinguish the target's corporate existence and have the new subsidiary be the surviving corporation—a "forward triangular merger." A forward merger, compared to a reverse merger, has the disadvantage that the nonsurvival of the target corporation may potentially affect contracts or intellectual property that depend on the corporation's continuing existence. For example, federal patent licenses are generally not assignable unless expressly made so and thus could be lost in a forward merger.

Compulsory Share Exchange

Some statutes have adopted a more direct procedure for accomplishing the same result as a triangular merger. In a *compulsory share exchange*, the acquiring corporation can force the target's shareholders to exchange their shares for consideration offered by the acquirer. MBCA §11.03. Shareholders of the acquired corporation enjoy the same protections as they would in a triangular merger: The target's board must first approve the exchange, a majority of the target's shareholders must then approve it, and dissenters of the target have appraisal rights. If the exchange is approved, all the target's shareholders receive the consideration offered by the acquirer.

§36.2.6 Squeeze-Out Merger

As you can see, the statutory merger technique offers dizzying possibilities. One use, which has nothing to do with combining separate businesses, allows a controlling shareholder to rid itself of minority shareholders in what is known as a "squeeze-out merger." (This is sometimes less accurately referred to as a "freeze-out merger.") A squeeze-out merger is often the second step in a takeover once a bidder has successfully purchased a controlling interest in a front-end tender offer. See §34.1.

Assume that Alpha has acquired a majority of the voting shares of Sigma. In a squeeze-out merger, Alpha merges with Sigma. The plan of merger calls for disparate treatment of the Sigma shares held by Alpha and by the other shareholders. Alpha retains its Sigma shares while the other Sigma shareholders receive other consideration, such as cash or nonvoting debt securities. A squeeze-out merger in which the minority shareholders receive cash is referred to as a "cash-out merger":

Cash-Out of Sigma Shareholders
(Alpha Consolidates Control of Sigma)

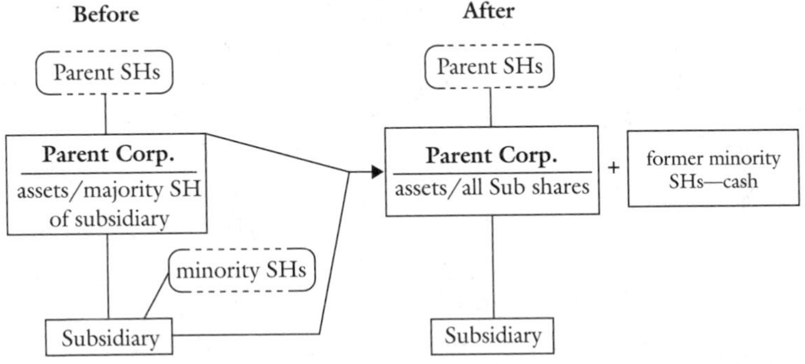

Squeeze-out mergers are subject to the three layers of protection that apply to every merger and, in particular, the self-dealing rules that apply to corporate transactions with controlling shareholders. See §17.3 (judicial review). In Delaware, for example, squeeze-out mergers are subject to review under an "entire fairness" test that requires fair dealing and fair price. *Weinberger v. UOP, Inc.*, 457 A.2d 701 (Del. 1983).

§36.3 SALES OF ASSETS

A corporation's business is no more than the sum of its tangible and intangible assets, and selling all of the corporation's assets effectively transfers control. Suppose Alpha buys all of Sigma's assets, giving Alpha stock as consideration:

Sigma Sells All Assets to Alpha

§36.3.1 Effect of a Sale of Assets

After selling all or "substantially all" of its assets, the corporation's existence does not automatically terminate. Instead, it becomes a shell or holding company whose only assets consist of the sales proceeds. The corporation can dissolve after paying its liabilities and distributing the remaining sales proceeds to the shareholders pro rata. See §35.2.

Unlike a merger, an asset acquisition does not automatically substitute the buying corporation for the selling corporation. Creditors, suppliers, lessors, employees, and others who deal with the selling corporation may have to consent to a substitution. But if consent is given, a sale of assets transaction (where all assets and liabilities pass to the purchasing corporation) can be structured to have much the same effect as a merger:

Alpha Acquires Sigma
(Sale of Assets Structured to Have Effect of Merger)

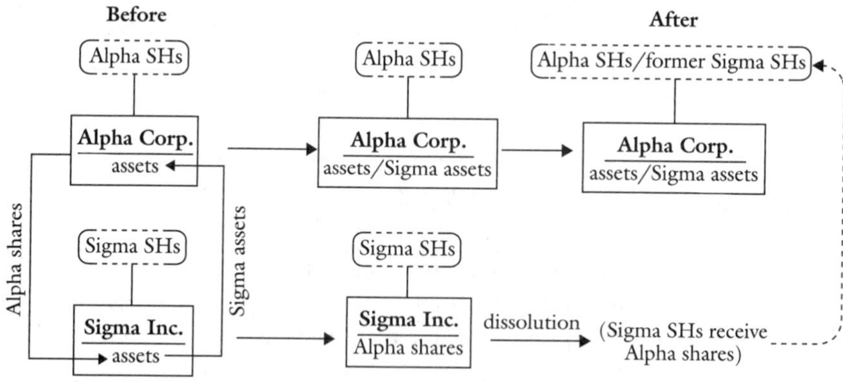

§36.3.2 Statutory Protections in Sale of Assets

Most state statutes treat the sale of all or substantially all of the corporate assets (not in the usual or regular course of business) as a fundamental change. For the shareholders of the selling corporation, the same protections apply to a sale of assets as apply to a merger: board approval, shareholder approval, and (in many instances) appraisal rights. MBCA §12.02; Del. GCL §271(a) (no appraisal rights).

For the shareholders of the purchasing corporation, however, the story is different. Under many statutes, including the pre-1999 MBCA, the shareholders of the purchasing corporation have neither voting rights nor dissenters' rights. The MBCA, as revised in 1999, changes this. If the purchasing corporation issues, as part of the transaction, new shares that have voting power equal to 20 percent or more of the corporation's voting shares that existed prior to the purchase, the shareholders of the purchasing corporation have voting rights. MBCA §6.21(f).

Sale in Regular Course

If substantially all of the assets are sold in the *regular course of business*—such as a real estate holding company that regularly sells all of its inventory—the transaction is treated like any other business transaction, and only board approval is required. MBCA §12.01(a).

§36.3.3 Conditions for Triggering Protections

Whether the shareholders of the selling corporation receive voting and appraisal rights depends on two questions: (1) Is the transaction a "sale"? (2) Does the sale involve "substantially all" of the assets?

"Sale" of Assets

Not all dispositions of assets trigger shareholder voting and appraisal rights. The MBCA specifies that a pledge, a mortgage, or a deed of trust to secure debt of the corporation—even if it covers all the corporation's assets—does not require shareholder approval. MBCA §12.01(2); Del. GCL §272. In addition, the transfer of a corporation's assets to a wholly owned subsidiary does not trigger shareholder voting rights. MBCA §12.01(3).

"Substantially All" Assets

When a corporation sells less than all of its assets outside the ordinary course of business, the three levels of protection apply only if "substantially all" were sold. Pre-1999 MBCA §12.02; Del. GCL §271 (no appraisal). The MBCA, as revised in 1999, articulates the test as whether the corporation is left without a "significant continuing business activity." MBCA §12.02(a). Under an MBCA "safe harbor," no shareholder voting or appraisal rights arise if the corporation retains a business activity that represents at least 25 percent of total assets *and* either 25 percent of after-tax operating income or 25 percent of revenues. MBCA §12.02(a) (measured at the end of the most recently completed fiscal year, on a consolidated basis).

The MBCA focuses on continuing business activities and its quantitative safe harbor addresses the difficulty courts have had construing "substantially all" under other statutes. In *Gimbel v. The Signal Companies, Inc.*, 316 A.2d 599 (Del. Ch.), *aff'd per curiam*, 316 A.2d 619 (Del. 1974), the Delaware Chancery Court adopted a disjunctive qualitative-quantitative test. Under the test, shareholder approval is required if the sale involves assets that are *either* quantitatively vital to the company's operations *or* qualitatively substantial to its existence and purpose. In the case, a parent corporation sold its energy subsidiary—which accounted for 41 percent of the total net worth, 26 percent of balance sheet assets, and 15 percent of the earnings of the conglomerate parent. The court concluded the subsidiary was neither *quantitatively* nor *qualitatively* substantial even though it had once been the bedrock of the parent's business. There was thus no requirement that the parent's shareholders approve its sale. Cf. *Katz v. Bergman*, 431 A.2d 1274 (Del. Ch. 1981) (shareholder approval required for sale of subsidiary that accounted for 45 percent of total net sales and 51 percent of parent's assets).

§36.3.4 Comparison of Merger, Triangular Merger, and Sale of Assets

Suppose Alpha acquires Sigma by using 25 percent of its shares (already authorized) as consideration in the transaction. What are the voting and appraisal rights of each corporation's shareholders—under the MBCA (as revised in 1999), the pre-1999 MBCA, and Delaware's statute? (For a more complete description of appraisal rights, see Chapter 37.)

Voting Rights	MBCA (revised) Alpha	MBCA (revised) Sigma	MBCA (pre-1999) Alpha	MBCA (pre-1999) Sigma	Delaware Alpha	Delaware Sigma
Merger	Yes	Yes	Yes	Yes	Yes	Yes
Triangular merger	Yes	Yes	No	Yes	No	Yes
Sale of assets	Yes	Yes	No	Yes	No	Yes

Appraisal Rights	MBCA (revised) Alpha	MBCA (revised) Sigma	MBCA (pre-1999) Alpha	MBCA (pre-1999) Sigma	Delaware Alpha	Delaware Sigma
Merger	No	Yes*	Yes	Yes	Yes**	Yes**
Triangular merger	No	Yes*	No	Yes	No	Yes**
Sale of assets	No	Yes*	No	Yes	No	No

*No, if market exception applies. See MBCA §13.02(b).
**No, if market-out exception applies. See Del. GCL §262(b).

Notice that the revised MBCA specifies consistent voting and appraisal rights regardless of how the acquisition is structured. Voting under the pre-1999 MBCA and Delaware's statute varies to some extent, and appraisal to a significant degree. These latter statutes invite gamesmanship.

§36.4 DE FACTO MERGER AND SUCCESSOR LIABILITY DOCTRINES

As you see, corporate combinations can be structured in many functionally identical ways—each affecting the protections available to shareholders and creditors. An asset acquisition, for example, can be structured under some statutes to have the effect of a merger and yet avoid shareholder approval and appraisal rights otherwise afforded shareholders. An asset sale can also be structured so that creditors' claims do not pass to the acquiring corporation.

§36.4.1 De Facto Merger Doctrine

Under the judicially created *de facto merger doctrine*, a handful of courts have interpreted the statutory merger provisions to give shareholders in functionally equivalent asset sales the same protections available in a statutory merger.

Under this doctrine, if the asset sale has the *effect of a merger*, shareholders receive merger-type voting and appraisal rights.

Farris v. Glen Alden Corp., 143 A.2d 25 (Pa. 1958), illustrates. Glen Alden acquired the assets of List in a stock-for-assets exchange approved by both companies' boards and the List shareholders, but not the Glen Alden shareholders. The transaction doubled the assets of Glen Alden, increased its debt sevenfold, and left its shareholders in a minority position. To protect the Glen Alden shareholders' expectation of "membership in the original corporation," the court recast the asset acquisition as a merger and enjoined the transaction for failing to give the Glen Alden shareholders the voting and appraisal rights they would have had in a statutory merger.

The use of the de facto merger doctrine to imply shareholder protection not explicitly provided by statute has been widely criticized. In the modern corporation, shareholders have no assurance the corporation's business, its capital structure, or share ownership will remain stable. In fact, modern shareholders purchase their shares with the expectation (and often the hope) of control transfers. Most courts have rejected the de facto merger doctrine and have refused to imply merger-type protection *for shareholders* when the statute does not provide it. *Hariton v. Arco Electronics, Inc.*, 182 A.2d 22 (Del. Ch. 1962), *aff'd*, 188 A.2d 123 (Del. 1963). In fact, in many states where courts have used a de facto merger analysis, the legislature has later abolished the doctrine by statute. See 15 Pa. CSA §1904.

In most jurisdictions, particularly Delaware, courts accept that corporate management can structure a combination under any technique it chooses. To maximize flexibility, form trumps substance. Each combination technique, including its particular protections, has its own legal significance—an "equal dignity" rule.

§36.4.2 Successor Liability Doctrine

In a statutory merger, all of the outstanding claims pass to the surviving corporation. In an asset acquisition, however, none of the liabilities are transferred unless the parties agree. This makes a sale of assets significantly more advantageous than a merger for the buying-successor corporation, if the seller retains some or all of the liabilities.

But the buying corporation cannot completely escape liabilities by agreement. Courts have fashioned a *successor liability doctrine* that imposes liability on the buying corporation (or another successor down the chain) when the claims were unknown or contingent at the time the assets were sold. (Known claims must be satisfied by the selling corporation when it is dissolved and wound up.) Courts use the doctrine to provide a source of compensation for tort claimants (particularly products liability victims) even though the buyer disclaimed liability for such claims.

Courts that impose successor liability often refer to the plaintiff's inability to seek relief against the original owner, the buying corporation's ability to assume a risk-spreading role (such as through insurance), and the continuity of the original business after the sale of assets. See *Turner v. Bituminous Casualty Co.*, 244 N.W.2d 873 (Mich. 1976); *Ray v. Alad Corp.*, 560 P.2d 3 (Cal. 1977) (successor liable when it continues to manufacture seller's product line).

Other courts have been less sympathetic to successor liability claims and have required that there be a continuity in the business, management, assets, and shareholders of the selling corporation, and that the selling corporation dissolve and liquidate after the buyer assumed known liabilities—in other words, a transaction with all the characteristics of a stock-for-stock merger. See *Niccum v. Hydra Tool Corp.*, 438 N.W.2d 96 (Minn. 1989).

Comparison of Successor Liability and De Facto Merger Doctrines

The successor liability doctrine is sometimes (confusingly) referred to as an aspect of the de facto merger doctrine, but the two are distinct. The successor liability doctrine protects involuntary creditors and the de facto merger doctrine protects shareholders. Some courts, while rejecting the de facto merger doctrine for shareholders, have accepted the possibility of successor liability on behalf of tort victimscreditors. *Heilbrunn v. Sun Chemical Corp.*, 150 A.2d 755 (Del. 1959).

EXAMPLES

Examples

1. JRS Combustion, incorporated in an MBCA jurisdiction that has adopted the 1999 revisions, holds method patents for a "thermal ignition system." The system is a technological breakthrough that promises to eliminate spark plugs and virtually eliminate auto pollution, while allowing vehicles to burn almost any fuel. Mega Motors, a public Delaware corporation, wants to acquire JRS.
   a. Mega proposes to pay JRS shareholders a package consisting of $600 in cash and ten shares of Mega common stock (with a market value of $400) for each JRS share. Can this be done by means of a statutory merger?
   b. Mega is most interested in the JRS patents. What documents will transfer the patents when Mega merges with JRS?
   c. Jerry (the company's founder, 25 percent shareholder, and dominant board member) has reservations about Mega's proposal. But the other JRS shareholders may be interested in a merger. Should Mega negotiate with them?

2. Mega overcomes Jerry's objections. The boards of Mega and JRS consider various merger plans:
   a. Plan #1: JRS shareholders will receive $1,000 cash. Shareholders holding 3,000 shares (of the 10,000 outstanding) say this will create a taxable transaction, and they will not go to the meeting. Shareholders holding 2,500 shares say they will attend and vote against the merger. The remaining shareholders will vote their 4,500 shares for the merger. Is the merger in trouble?
   b. Plan #2: JRS shareholders will receive a combination of cash and 2 million shares of Mega stock. The stock, which is already authorized, would increase the number of Mega's total outstanding shares to 22 million. Must Mega shareholders approve the merger?
   c. Plan #3: JRS shareholders will receive 5 million Mega shares. Mega must authorize additional shares and will amend its certificate of incorporation pursuant to the merger plan. If two-thirds of Mega's shares are represented at the shareholders' meeting on the merger and 60 percent of them at the meeting vote for the merger, is the merger approved?
   d. Plan #4: Mega will pay cash. To buttress its validity, the merger plan calls for the approval by at least 75 percent of the Mega shares represented at a shareholders' meeting on the merger. If 12 million of Mega's 20 million shares outstanding are represented at the meeting, how many must be voted for the merger?

3. For tax reasons, Mega wants to purchase all of JRS's assets instead of acquiring JRS in a negotiated merger. (This will give it a higher basis in JRS's assets, allowing it to deduct more depreciation.) In addition, Mega wants to hold the JRS assets in a separate subsidiary so it can easily resell the business in the future.
   a. Can a sale-of-assets transaction be structured to accomplish these purposes—that is, to have the effect of a triangular merger?
   b. JRS will sell all of its assets, but Mega does not want to assume any contingent liabilities. JRS will be dissolved after the sale, and its shareholders will receive pro rata consideration. After the transaction, if a patent infringement suit is brought against Mega for claims that arose when JRS operated the business, will Mega be liable?
   c. Mega will have a subsidiary purchase all of JRS's assets and assume all its liabilities in exchange for 4.5 million of already authorized Mega shares, more than 20 percent of Mega's outstanding shares. Is approval by Mega shareholders required?

4. In addition to its patents and its research facilities, JRS also owns a significant tract of prime commercial real estate on which the facilities sit. The land, deeded to the company by the founder, Jerry, has been used as collateral for loans to finance the thermal ignition research. Although

licensing of the thermal ignition patents accounts for nearly 90 percent of company revenues and earnings, the land represents approximately 50 percent of the value of the company's book assets.

a. Is shareholder approval required if the JRS board agrees to sell the thermal ignition assets, but not the land?
b. Would the result be different if JRS were incorporated in Delaware?

Explanations

1. a. Yes. The authority for the merger comes from both Delaware law and the MBCA. Delaware law authorizes Mega to merge with a foreign corporation and for it to be the surviving corporation. Del. GCL §252. The MBCA authorizes JRS to merge with a foreign corporation. MBCA §11.02(b). Under both statutes, consideration for the merger can include a combination of securities, cash, or other property—whatever is specified in the plan of merger. MBCA §11.02(c)(3); Del. GCL §251.

   b. In the normal case, the only necessary document is a plan of merger and the filing of merger documents with the respective states' secretaries of state. MBCA §11.05 (articles of merger); Del. GCL §252(c) (certificate of merger). As a result of the merger, Mega steps into JRS's shoes. Corporate law provides that Mega automatically acquires all of JRS's assets, including its patents. The complete substitution of the acquiring corporation for the acquired is a significant (and unique) characteristic of a statutory merger.

   For some regulatory and licensing purposes, however, a merger does not automatically transfer ownership of certain assets. In fact, federal patent law requires that patent assignments be explicit, even in the case of a statutory merger. A further written assignment would thus be necessary to transfer the patents from JRS to Mega.

   c. Not really. The boards of both corporations must approve the merger, before submitting it to their shareholders. The merger will go nowhere unless the JRS board is interested.

2. a. No. Under the MBCA, as revised in 1999, an absolute majority (5,001 shares) is not necessary. Cf. Pre-1999 MBCA §11.03(e) (requiring "a majority of all the votes entitled to be cast on the [merger] plan"). Instead, the revised MBCA requires only that more votes be cast for the merger (4,500 votes) than against it (2,500 votes) at a meeting with a quorum. MBCA §§7.25(c), 11.04(e). A quorum is present becausesince a majority of the votes entitled to be cast (7,000 or 10,000 votes) are represented at the meeting. MBCA §7.25(a). This means shares not at the meeting do not count as votes against the merger.

b. No. Delaware's statute, like those of most states, requires approval by shareholders of the acquiring corporation only if the merger is significant. Del. GCL §251(f). The statute uses certain factors to identify significance to the acquiring corporation. Satisfying any one factor triggers a requirement of shareholder approval. But in Mega's case, none applies:

- the merger plan does not amend Mega's charter
- the rights of Mega's outstanding shares will not be changed by the merger
- the number of shares of common stock outstanding after the merger (22 million) will not exceed by more than 20 percent the number of shares before it (20 million)

Del. GCL §251(f). Although the merger will dilute the equity and voting interests of Mega's common shareholders, the dilution will not be significant. The Delaware statute views shareholder approval in this case to be an unnecessary and costly bother becausesince the merger will be relatively inconsequential to Mega and its shareholders.

c. No. Mega's shareholders must approve the merger because the charter will be amended. In Delaware, this requires approval by a majority of Mega's outstanding stock entitled to vote—an absolute majority. Del. GCL §251(c). Even though a simple majority, the vote of 60 percent of two-thirds of the outstanding shares (40 percent of the outstanding shares) is not enough.

d. The answer is 9 million—three-fourths of the shares represented at the meeting. The problem is tricky. Although approval by a majority of the outstanding shares—10,000,001—generally sets a minimum for a merger plan, Mega is exempted in this case. See Del. GCL §251(c) (majority of outstanding voting shares); §251(f) (whale-minnow merger). The three-fourths approval condition, authorized by Del. GCL §252(b), supplies the relevant voting requirement.

This problem illustrates the possibility that approval by a simple supermajority (in this case three-fourths of the shares at a meeting) may not constitute approval by an absolute majority of the outstanding shares. For example, if 12 million of Mega's 20 million shares are represented at the meeting, approval by 9.5 million would be enough to satisfy the condition, but would not be a majority of the total outstanding shares.

3. a. Yes. The following steps will do it:

(1) Mega creates a wholly owned subsidiary (J-Sub) and capitalizes it with the consideration for acquiring the JRS assets.

(2) The JRS board and shareholders approve the sale of all the assets.

(3) J-Sub purchases all of the JRS assets, assumes all of its known and contingent liabilities, and is substituted in any pending litigation.

(4) J-Sub pays JRS with the consideration it received from Mega, which can be any consideration that would have been permitted in a merger.
(5) The JRS board and shareholders approve a plan of dissolution (which could happen at the same time they approve the sale of assets).
(6) JRS pays any creditors who did not accept a substitution.
(7) JRS is left with the consideration from J-Sub, which is distributed to its shareholders pro rata.

This structure, however, has some critical and unavoidable differences from a merger. Unlike a merger, the constituent corporations must obtain consent to the substitution from creditors, suppliers, lessors, employees, and others who deal with the corporation. The documentation will be very different. In a sale of assets, all the transferred assets and assumed liabilities must be identified. A bill of sale transfers personal property, and deeds must transfer any real property.

b. Probably not Mega. Remember that as a result of the transaction, Mega will hold a wholly owned subsidiary with the assets and liabilities of JRS. Even if the subsidiary is liable for contingent liabilities of JRS, Mega would be liable only if it assumed these liabilities by contract or on a piercing theory. See §32.1.3 (enterprise liability doctrine).

Can the subsidiary be liable for JRS's patent infringement? Assuming the subsidiary did not assume this liability contractually, a court might use the successor liability doctrine to treat the sale of assets as a statutory merger. The subsidiary would be deemed to have stepped into JRS's shoes and assumed its liabilities. Although the question of successor liability often comes up in products liability litigation, where plaintiffs are unlikely to have protected themselves from corporate liability shifting, Mega's acquisition of JRS may satisfy some of the factors courts have identified in finding a succession of interest: the continuity of JRS's business after the sale, the holding of Mega shares by former JRS shareholders, and the plaintiff's inability to seek relief against the original patent claimant or its shareholders. Other courts, however, have shown hostility to liability rules that discourage control transfers that put assets into higher-valuing hands. The successor liability doctrine seeks to balance the goals of protecting claimants and providing corporate-contractual certainty. For example, if the patent plaintiff had purposely desisted from suing until the asset sale, the goal of protecting the patent would seem less compelling than that of certainty.

It is important to remember that JRS's shareholders might also be held liable on the infringement claim. Under the MBCA, unknown claims (and known claims not properly discharged) may be asserted up to five years after dissolution and recovered from each shareholder to the extent of the shareholder's pro rata liquidating distribution. MBCA §14.07 (see §35.2.3).

c. Probably not. Even though the transaction would have required approval by Mega shareholders if structured as a merger—because the 4.5 million shares put it over the 20 percent threshold of Del. GCL §251(f)—no approval by the shareholders of the acquiring corporation is necessary when it purchases assets. Here the structure of the corporate combination will affect the degree of shareholder protection.

Some courts, however, have held that when an asset acquisition is functionally equivalent to a merger, statutory merger protections—shareholder voting and appraisal rights—are available under the de facto merger doctrine. This activist construction of the merger statutes has not found favor in Delaware, where Mega is incorporated. Delaware courts have adhered to the "equal dignity" rule and refused to imply additional protections not found in the combination technique chosen by the parties. (Notice that under the revised MBCA, approval by the acquiring corporation's shareholders is required becausesince voting shares issued in the transaction constitute more than 20 percent of the outstanding shares prior to transaction. MBCA §6.21(f). Approval would also be required if Mega were listed on the New York Stock Exchange, whose rules mirror those of the revised MBCA. NYSE Manual 312.03.)

4. a. Probably yes—under the revised MBCA. The revised MBCA looks at whether the corporation is left without a "significant continuing business activity." MBCA §12.02(a). Arguably, the corporation is not in the commercial real estate business and after selling its technology has no continuing business. Shareholder approval would seem to be required. Here the MBCA "safe harbor," which looks at assets *and* operating income/revenues, is not met. Although the real estate constitutes more than 25 percent of assets, it constitutes less than 25 percent of income and revenues. Cf. Official Comment to MBCA §12.02 (shareholder approval not required if company sells manufacturing assets but retains investment assets that meet the 25 percent test and that the company continues to actively manage).

This result would be different under the pre-1999 MBCA, which required shareholder approval if the corporation sold "substantially all" of its assets, which was meant to be synonymous with "nearly all." Official Comment, MBCA §12.01. The notion was that shareholder approval could not be avoided by holding back a few inconsequential assets. But otherwise, the *qualitative* productivity of the assets sold was not relevant. Even though the technology assets are the company's principal source of revenue and income (and thus value), the pre-1999 MBCA treated this as irrelevant. Shareholder approval would not be required becausesince retaining the land does not appear to be a pretext for avoiding a shareholder vote, and JRS is not selling "nearly all" its assets.

b. Probably the same. Under Delaware's disjunctive qualitative-quantitative test, shareholder approval would probably be required because the sale is *qualitatively* substantial to the corporation's existence and purpose. That is, shareholders should regard their investment as fundamentally changed when the high-tech JRS is converted into a real estate holding company. Under Delaware's approach, *quantitative* substantiality is not necessary if the sale is *qualitatively* substantial. The Delaware test thus gives shareholders greater protection than the pre-1999 MBCA's narrow quantitative test. See *Oberly v. Kirby*, 592 A.2d 445 (Del. 1991) (requiring shareholder vote where asset sale effected "radical transformation" of business, even though sold assets accounted for only 68 percent of total assets).

CHAPTER 37

Appraisal Remedy

Fundamental changes occur by majority rule. This gives the corporation the flexibility to adapt to new conditions, while avoiding minority intransigence. But it also risks majority opportunism. To protect the minority, corporate statutes universally provide an appraisal remedy that assures liquidity rights to certain dissenters who "opt out" of majority rule in specified fundamental transactions (§37.1). Under the procedure, these dissenting shareholders can insist after the transaction on being paid the "fair value" of their shares in cash (§37.2). Some statutes make this the exclusive remedy for shareholders challenging certain corporate transactions (§37.3).

Note on Revisions to MBCA

The MBCA, as revised in 1999, reflects a significant rethinking of shareholder rights in fundamental corporate changes. While increasing voting rights, the revised MBCA constricts appraisal. Appraisal is available only when a corporate transaction fundamentally affects share rights and there is substantial uncertainty about price fairness. It is not enough that shareholders had voting rights and dissented from the transaction. Reflecting this new approach, the revised MBCA changes the nomenclature from "dissenters' rights" to "appraisal rights." Although this chapter focuses on the revised MBCA, it references the pre-1999 MBCA (still prevalent in many MBCA jurisdictions) and Delaware's statute.

§37.1 APPRAISAL RIGHTS

§37.1.1 Transactions That Trigger Appraisal Rights

Appraisal is generally a matter of statutory right, though the board may specify nonstatutory appraisal rights to provide protection to shareholders in a transaction or to reassure them of the fairness of the transaction price. In addition, some corporate transactions are conditioned on a specified maximum of shares seeking appraisal—that is, an "escape clause" that rescinds the transaction if too many shares become subject to appraisal.

Corporate statutes specify appraisal in the following transactions. Corporate planners will sometimes structure a transaction—for example, choosing a sale of assets instead of a merger—to avoid appraisal rights. See §36.4.1.

Merger, Consolidation, or Compulsory Share Exchange

Generally, shareholders of the *acquired corporation* have appraisal rights, and shareholders of the *acquiring corporation* do not.

- **Revised MBCA.** Shareholders of the acquired corporation entitled to vote on a merger or compulsory share exchange have appraisal rights. MBCA §13.02(a)(1), (a)(2). Shareholders of the acquiring corporation do not, even if they have voting rights. See MBCA §13.02(a)(1) (no appraisal for shares that "remain outstanding" after the merger).
- **Pre-1999 MBCA.** Shareholders entitled to vote, whether of the acquired or acquiring corporation, can dissent and assert appraisal rights. MBCA §13.02(a)(1), (a)(2). This means shareholders of the acquiring corporation have no appraisal rights in a whale-minnow merger. Pre-1999 MBCA §11.03(g) (no voting rights when acquiring corporation does not issue more than 20 percent of its shares).
- **Delaware.** All record shareholders of the acquired corporation (both voting and nonvoting) in a merger or consolidation have appraisal rights. Del. GCL §262(a), (b). Shareholders of the acquiring corporation have appraisal rights, except when it is a "whale-minnow" merger or the shareholders have a "market out" (discussed below). Del. GCL §§251(g), 262(a), (b).

"Short Form" Merger

Under most statutes, shareholders squeezed out in a "short form" merger (parent merges with 90 percent-owned subsidiary) have appraisal rights, even though they do not vote. MBCA §13.02(a)(1)(i); pre-1999 MBCA §13.02(a)(2); Del. GCL §262(b). The shareholders of the parent corporation, which consolidates its control over the partially owned subsidiary, do not have appraisal rights.

Sale of Assets

There is significant variation in the statutes for sales of assets. The revised MBCA seeks to approximate the protections available in a merger, while other statutes generally provide less protection.

- **Revised MBCA.** Shareholders of the selling corporation entitled to vote on the sale have appraisal rights. MBCA §13.02(a)(3). Shareholders of the purchasing corporation have no appraisal rights, even if they vote on the issuance of shares in the transaction.
- **Pre-1999 MBCA.** Shareholders of the selling corporation entitled to vote on the sale can dissent and assert appraisal rights. MBCA §13.02(a)(3). But there are no appraisal rights if the sale is for cash, where the net proceeds of the sale will be substantially distributed within one year after the sale. Shareholders of the purchasing corporation have no appraisal rights.
- **Delaware.** Shareholders have no appraisal rights in a sale of assets, unless provided in the corporate charter. Del. GCL §262(c).

Charter Amendment

Again there is significant variation in the statutes.

- **Revised MBCA.** Shareholders have appraisal rights in an amendment to the articles of incorporation only if the amendment creates fractional shares that the corporation can repurchase—a forced redemption. MBCA §13.02(a)(4).
- **Pre-1999 MBCA.** Shareholders whose interests are "materially and adversely" affected by a charter amendment (such as in a recapitalization) can dissent and seek appraisal, even if the shareholders do not have voting rights. Pre-1999 MBCA §13.02(a)(4) (listing circumstances in which rights are deemed to be materially and adversely affected).
- **Delaware.** Shareholders do not have appraisal rights in a charter amendment. Del. GCL §262(c) (only if provided in charter).

Dissolution

Generally, dissolution does not trigger appraisal rights on the theory that all shareholders receive a pro rata distribution and appraisal claims would disrupt the winding-up process.

§37.1.2 Shares Subject to Appraisal

Shares

Generally, a shareholder must demand appraisal for all of the shares he owns. See Official Comment, MBCA §13.03 (to "prevent abuse" by shareholder who, though not opposed to fundamental transaction, may "speculate on the appraisal process" as to some of his shares).

Shareholders

Shares are often held of record by a nominee (such as a securities broker) on behalf of the beneficial owner. In this situation, who can assert appraisal rights? The revised MBCA, which tracks the pre-1999 MBCA, permits a record shareholder to seek appraisal on behalf of its beneficial owners, and beneficial owners can seek appraisal with the consent of the record owner. MBCA §13.03. To avoid any confusion, some statutes (notably Delaware) give appraisal rights only to record shareholders. Del. GCL §262(a); *Cede & Co. v. Technicolor, Inc.*, 542 A.2d 1182 (Del. 1988).

§37.1.3 Market Exception in Public Corporations

Revised MBCA

The revised MBCA, following the lead of Delaware's statute, excludes appraisal rights when target shareholders can sell their shares on a public trading market. The theory is that appraisal is unnecessary when a liquid, reliable market is available as a proxy for a fair price. No appraisal is available if the following two conditions are met:

- **Liquid market.** The traded shares are either (1) listed on the New York Stock Exchange, the American Stock Exchange, or the national market system of NASDAQ; or (2) held by at least 2,000 shareholders and the company must have a $20 million public float (market value of shares held by noninsiders). MBCA §13.02(b)(1). Not only must liquidity be available before the acquisition, shareholders must also receive either cash or marketable securities as consideration in the transaction. MBCA §13.02(b)(3).

- **Reliable price.** Even if there is liquid market, the price offered in the transaction is not be tainted by a conflict of interest. MBCA §13.02(b)(4). The market exception does not apply to a squeezeout by a controlling shareholder (20 percent or more of voting power, or power to elect at least one-fourth the board). Nor does the market exception apply to a management buyout in which directors or officers will receive a financial benefit in the acquisition not available to other shareholders.

In this way, assuming the transaction was arm's-length, target shareholders are assured a fair price for their shares (1) by being able to sell before or after the transaction in a public trading market, or (2) by being able to sell before the transaction or by receiving cash in the transaction.

Delaware

Delaware's statute also has a market-out exception that excludes appraisal in a stock-for-stock merger if *before* and *after* the merger the shares are traded on a national stock market or held by more than 2,000 shareholders of record. Del. GCL §262(b)(1), (b)(2). Unlike the revised MBCA, appraisal rights are available in a stock-for-cash merger when publicly traded shares are acquired wholly or partially for cash. Del. GCL §262(b)(2).

The theory for Delaware's "market out" exception is that a dissatisfied shareholder in a stock-for-stock merger who prefers cash can simply sell in a public trading market at a price the market has determined to be fair. Otherwise, such dissenters could interfere with fundamental changes by interjecting the additional (and unnecessary) expense of redeeming their shares for cash in an appraisal proceeding.

Pre-1999 MBCA

The pre-1999 MBCA rejects the notion that the market price is a good approximation of "fair value." Appraisal is available even if there is a trading market into which shareholders can sell, on the premise the market does not always reflect "true" value. The Official Comment explains that the market may be "demoralized"; some shareholders may hold "restricted securities" that cannot be sold publicly (see §5.2.2); some shareholders may hold large blocks that a thin market could not absorb; or the market may already reflect price depreciation in anticipation of the fundamental change. Official Comment, MBCA §13.01.

§37.1.4 Comparison of Merger and Sale of Assets

Suppose Alpha plans to acquire Sigma by using 25 percent of its shares (already authorized) as consideration in the transaction. What are the appraisal rights of each corporation's shareholders—under the MBCA (as revised in 1999), the pre-1999 MBCA, and Delaware's statute? (For a description of the various methods to accomplish a corporate acquisition and a chart on voting rights, see Chapter 36.)

	MBCA (revised)		MBCA (pre-1999)		Delaware	
Appraisal Rights	**Alpha**	**Sigma**	**Alpha**	**Sigma**	**Alpha**	**Sigma**
Merger	No	Yes*	Yes	Yes	Yes**	Yes**
Short-form merger	No	Yes*	No	Yes	No	Yes
Triangular merger	No	Yes*	No	Yes	No	Yes**
Sale of assets	No	Yes*	No	Yes	No	No

*No, if market exception applies. See MBCA §13.02(b).

**No, if market-out exception applies. See Del. GCL §262(b).

Notice that the revised MBCA specifies consistent appraisal rights regardless of how the acquisition is structured. Appraisal rights under the pre-1999 MBCA and Delaware's statute vary significantly depending on the transaction.

§37.2 APPRAISAL PROCEEDING

§37.2.1 Procedures

Appraisal procedures vary widely from state to state. Dissenting shareholders must strictly comply with complex procedures, often stacked against them. See Del. GCL §262.

Delaware Procedures

In Delaware appraisal procedures require the following:

- **Preserve right to appraisal.** Before the shareholders' meeting on the fundamental change, the corporation sends shareholders notice of their appraisal rights. The notice must contain sufficient information for the shareholder to make an informed choice on whether to seek appraisal or accept the consideration offered in the transaction. *Nagy v. Bistricer*, 770 A.2d 43 (Del. Ch. 2000). Shareholders who want to dissent must give the corporation written notice of their intent before the meeting. Shareholders must vote against, or at least not vote for, the proposed change.

- **Exercise right to appraisal.** After the effective date of the fundamental change, the corporation must notify shareholders of their appraisal rights. Within a specified number of days, dissenters must accept the terms of the change or tender their shares to the corporation and demand payment.
- **Bring appraisal action.** Dissenters must then bring an appraisal action in court and initially bear all their litigation expenses. Dissenters do not receive payment until finally ordered by the court. Dissenter's expenses (such as attorney and expert fees) can only be charged against the value of the appraised shares and cannot be recovered from the corporation.

Contested appraisal proceedings in Delaware are fraught with difficulties. The proceedings can drag on for years, leaving dissenting shareholders in a twilight zone. After tendering their shares, dissenters lose their status as shareholders, and the shares neither receive dividends nor appreciate in value during the pendency of the appraisal proceeding. Payment of fair value must await final court order, and an award of pre-judgment interest is discretionary. The dissenters cannot bring a class action and must bear the costs of litigation, including attorney fees.

MBCA Procedures

The MBCA attempts to make appraisal a more realistic option. If the dissenting shareholder preserves her appraisal rights, demands payment, and tenders her shares, the corporation *must* promptly pay the dissenter the corporation's estimate of fair value. MBCA §13.24. Then the corporation must attempt to settle any shortfall between the amount the dissenter seeks and the amount paid. MBCA §§13.26, 13.30(a). Judicial appraisal is a last resort only if the shareholder considers the corporation's payment to be inadequate and negotiations fail. If the dissenter's payment demand remains unsettled for 60 days, the *corporation* must commence a judicial appraisal proceeding and initially bear court and expert costs. The court may also order the corporation to pay the dissenting shareholder's attorney fees if it failed to act in good faith or to comply with the appraisal procedures.

§37.2.2 "Fair Value"

Shareholders seeking appraisal also face the risk that the court will undervalue the firm and its shares. Generally, valuation in an appraisal focuses on the going-concern value of the firm as a whole, followed by a computation of the proportional value of each share. The valuation is not supposed to take into account the effect of the fundamental change, and generally courts look to the shares' value immediately before the corporate action is taken. See MBCA §13.01(4)(i).

Traditional "Block Method"

Traditionally, courts determined fair value by weighting and then aggregating various indicators of value:

- **Earnings value.** Earnings value, or "investment value," seeks to measure the earning capacity of the corporation based on its past earnings record. Average annual earnings are computed and then capitalized by applying a multiplier, which is determined according to the business conditions and the type of business involved. *Beerly v. Dept. of Treasury*, 768 F.2d 942 (7th Cir. 1985) (fixing multiplier on basis of price-earnings ratios for sales of minority stock blocks in comparable companies).
- **Market price.** Market value is the price at which the corporation's shares were trading (if a market existed) or at which they could have been sold to a willing buyer. Less weight is given to the market price in the case of thinly traded shares, although unusual trading in a deep market before the transaction could justify discounting this factor.
- **Asset value.** Asset value can be determined using the firm's "book value"—that is, the excess of historical-valued assets over liabilities on the firm's accounting balance sheet. See §31.2.2. Book value does not reflect the ongoing earnings from the business. Asset value can also be determined using the firm's "liquidation value"—that is, the amount for which the firm's marketable assets could be sold for cash. It may fail to take into account the firm's value as an ongoing business.

In the past Delaware courts used an eclectic "block method" under which the appraiser assigned an arbitrary weight to these three values and then added them to get a weighted value. See *Tri-Continental Corp. v. Battye*, 74 A.2d 71 (Del. 1970). For example, a Delaware court valued a conglomerate in a depressed stock trading market by weighting assets 45 percent, average earnings 40 percent, and market price 15 percent. *Tannetics, Inc. v. A.I. Industries*

Inc., 5 Del. J. Corp. L. 337 (Del. Ch. 1979). The "block method" computation looked like this:

Type of Valuation	Appraisal	Weight Given		Amount
Asset value	$100	.45	=	$45.00
Earnings value	$120	.40	=	48.00
Market price	$ 75	.15	=	11.25
		Appraisal ("Fair Value")	=	$104.25

Modern Valuation — Discounted Cash Flows

Modern courts, following the lead of professional business valuators, look at "customary and current valuation concepts and techniques generally employed for similar businesses." MBCA §13.01(4)(ii). Courts have mostly abandoned the "block method," since it fails to recognize that shares, like any other investment, are valuable because they represent a promise of *future* income. In *Weinberger v. UOP, Inc.*, 457 A.2d 701 (Del. 1983) (see §17.3.3), the Delaware Supreme Court abandoned the "block method" and called on the appraiser to look to elements of future value, provided they are susceptible of proof.

The most widely used method of valuation in the financial community is *discounted cash flow*. Under this method, the present value of expected future cash flows is calculated using a discount rate to take into account the time value of money and the risks of those future flows. Consider the following simplified illustration. Suppose a firm's earnings prospects, based on past earnings and anticipated results, are $11 million per year. If we assume that annual earnings of $11 million will continue into the foreseeable future, it is possible to calculate the *present value* of this cash flow.

How can we calculate the present value of a stream of earnings? We need a discount rate, which takes into account the time value of money and the risk of the particular earnings stream. If the interest rate on no-risk, long-term U.S. government bonds is 5.0 percent and the additional risk premium associated with this particular firm is 7.5 percent, the annual cash flows of $11 million are discounted by 12.5 percent. Another way to put this: How much would you have to invest today to receive $11 million each year indefinitely, assuming an interest rate of 12.5 percent? The answer is $88 million. That is, an investor would be willing to pay $88 million today for the firm's earnings stream because the alternative—investing the same amount in a comparable-risk investment—would produce $11 million annually. Since a firm (like any other investment) has value depending on the return it provides investors over time, $88 million represents the present value of the firm.

In Delaware courts can take into account the firm's earnings potential after a merger, so long as this is not speculative—a limited sharing rule.

Weinberger ("elements of future value, known or susceptible of proof as of the date of merger and not the product of speculation, may be considered"). Thus, for example, a new business strategy implemented after a merger's approval, but before its effective date, could be used in valuing the dissenters' shares. See *Cede & Co. v. Technicolor, Inc. (Technicolor IV)*, 684 A.2d 289 (Del. 1996). Other statutes, however, exclude "appreciation . . . in anticipation of the merger"—a no-sharing rule. See Pre-1999 MBCA §13.01(3); *In re Valuation of Libby, McNeil & Libby*, 406 A.2d 54 (Me. 1979).

Valuation Discounts

A recurring issue in appraisal proceedings is whether valuation of minority shares should reflect their *lack of control*, which normally means they would trade at a discount compared to control shares. Most courts have not discounted minority shares for lack of control, on the theory that "fair value" is the value of the "proportionate interest in a going concern." See *Tri-Continental Corp. v. Battye*, 74 A.2d 71 (Del. 1950). The revised MBCA also adopts this approach. MBCA §13.01(4)(iii) ("without discounting for . . . minority status"). But when the appraisal is of shares in a conglomerate, where firm value is the sum of its many controlled subsidiaries, the valuation should reflect the value of selling control in each subsidiary. See *Rapid-American Corp. v. Harris*, 603 A.2d 796 (Del. 1992).

Another issue is whether shares in a closely held corporation, for which there is no trading market, should be valued to reflect this *lack of marketability*. Most courts refuse to discount for lack of marketability, on the theory that it would allow the majority to buy out the minority's financial interest without paying full value. See *Pueblo Bancorporation v. Lindoe, Inc.*, 63 P.3d 353 (Colo. 2003) (interpreting "fair value" to represent shareholder's proportionate interest in corporation, so marketability discount should not apply); *Royals v. Piedmont Electric Repair Co.*, 1999 NC BC 1 ("inequitable" to value minority shares at less than full value; to do otherwise would reward majority, who could acquire discounted minority shares and then resell at full value).

§37.3 EXCLUSIVITY OF APPRAISAL

A shareholder who dissents from a fundamental change has two legal remedies: (1) a court challenge seeking damages or rescission, and (2) an appraisal seeking payment of "fair value." Does the existence of an appraisal remedy foreclose a court challenge?

§37.3.1 Price or Process Fairness

Whether appraisal is exclusive turns on whether minority shareholders should be able to undermine majority will. On the one hand, if a dissenter considers the transaction to be financially unsound, an appraisal should fully protect her financial interest. But if there was abuse in the approval process (such as deception of shareholders or fiduciary overreaching), appraisal does not correct the abuse. Arguably, the appraisal option should not shield a tainted transaction.

States are divided on whether appraisal, when available, is the only remedy. Some statutes explicitly make appraisal exclusive, and courts have denied shareholders' attempts to challenge the transaction. In Delaware a shareholder may challenge a transaction, even if appraisal is available, if any of the following occurred:

- approval of the transaction was obtained fraudulently
- fiduciaries breached their duty of fair dealing
- the transaction did not comply with formal approval requirements

Weinberger v. UOP, Inc., 457 A.2d 701 (Del. 1983) (see §17.3.3). The MBCA, as revised in 1999, follows this approach, though it does not mention fiduciary breaches. MBCA §13.02(d) (appraisal is exclusive unless action was not effectuated properly or "was procured as a result of fraud or material misrepresentation").

§37.3.2 Nonappraisal Remedies

If a shareholder can challenge the process of approval of a fundamental change, what should be the remedy if the process is unfair? Arguably, the appropriate remedy is to undo the transaction because a damages award would be tantamount to an appraisal without the normal appraisal procedures. In many instances, however, rescission may impose a significant burden, particularly where the challenge is resolved long after the transaction closed. For this reason, some courts have accepted the possibility of rescissory damages—damages based on the value of the shares if the transaction had been originally rescinded—to compensate shareholders for unfair dealing or an inadequate price. *Weinberger v. UOP, Inc.* (see §17.3.3).

§37.3.3 Effect of Choice

Can a shareholder seek appraisal and then challenge the process of approval? Or can a shareholder who challenges the transaction then seek appraisal? The

Delaware Supreme Court has allowed shareholders in an appraisal proceeding who discover evidence of procedural unfairness to commence simultaneously a fairness challenge. *Cede & Co. v. Technicolor, Inc. (Technicolor I)*, 542 A.2d 1182 (Del. 1988). Suggesting that an *ignorant* shareholder should not be bound by her appraisal choice, the court permitted a shareholder who had first sought appraisal to bring a fraud action based on later-discovered evidence of board negligence. Both actions, the court said, could be consolidated—though the plaintiff would be limited to only one recovery.

Other courts have explicitly rejected that aggrieved shareholders must elect an exclusive remedy. Even after winning an appraisal award, dissenters may bring a damages action for fraud in the transaction triggering appraisal rights. *Popp Telcom v. American Sharecom, Inc.*, 210 F.3d 928 (8th Cir. 2000) (applying Minnesota law). To avoid double recovery, only consequential damages (the amount by which the shares would have appreciated absent the fraudulent transaction) are recoverable in the fraud action, not the fair value already awarded in the appraisal.

Examples

EXAMPLES

1. JRS Combustion, incorporated in a jurisdiction with the MBCA as revised in 1999, has agreed to merge into Mega Motors, a Delaware corporation. Both the JRS and Mega shareholders must approve the merger, and under the terms of the merger JRS shareholders will receive Mega common stock as consideration. Mega is traded on the New York Stock Exchange; JRS is held privately.
   a. Since announcement of the merger, Mega's stock price has fallen, apparently in reaction to the news. Many Mega employees hold restricted stock, which by contract they cannot sell on a trading market (see §5.2.2). Do Mega shareholders have appraisal rights?
   b. Many JRS shareholders are also executives of the company. Do these shareholders have appraisal rights?
   c. Mega wants to plan for the contingency of appraisal. When will Mega know how many shareholders are dissenting and how much they are seeking?
   d. Mega is worried about too many shareholders exercising their appraisal rights. How can it limit its exposure?

2. All JRS shares are represented at the shareholders' meeting on the merger. The shareholders approve the merger by a thin margin: 502 votes for, 498 votes against.
   a. Jessica, a JRS shareholder, has preserved her appraisal rights. She questions the validity of some JRS proxies cast for the merger. Should she challenge the merger or seek appraisal?

b. Mega promised Jerry (JRS's founder) a lucrative position with Mega after the merger. Dissenters claim that the JRS directors were dominated by Jerry and approved a lousy deal. They claim if the directors had fulfilled their fiduciary duties, shareholders would have received $25 million more for their shares. Can the dissenters challenge the merger price as unfair?

Explanations

EXPLANATIONS

1. a. No. Mega is subject to Delaware's appraisal statute, which withdraws appraisal rights in a stock-for-stock merger for all classes of shares of the surviving corporation that were traded on a national stock exchange before the merger. Del. GCL §262(b)(1), (b)(2). Delaware rejects the notion that a "demoralized market" might not reflect fair value and assumes that holders of restricted shares recognized their lack of both liquidity and appraisal rights. Mega shareholders who hold restricted shares have no choice but to accept the merger terms if approved by the majority, unless they can show a defect in the process of approval.

   b. Yes. The MBCA governs appraisal for JRS shareholders, which provides appraisal for shareholders of the nonsurviving corporation who are entitled to vote on the merger. MBCA §13.02(a)(1). There is no distinction between management and nonmanagement shareholders. Appraisal provides a "base floor" for the price of all shareholders.

   c. Mega acquires all of JRS's appraisal obligations after the merger. Before the shareholders' meeting on the merger, JRS shareholders must receive notice of their appraisal rights and must deliver before the vote a notice of their intent to demand payment for their shares. MBCA §13.21(a). This notice of intent, however, only provides information about the number of shareholders who *could* demand payment and appraisal.

   Under the MBCA, the corporation first learns the extent of its *potential* appraisal liability when dissenters demand payment after the merger. MBCA §13.23(a). This will happen within 40–60 days after shareholders receive notice of appraisal rights, which Mega must send at least ten days after the merger. MBCA §13.22(b). In effect, Mega will not know for two to three months after the merger how many shares are to be appraised. Even then, it may be possible that a court will value the shares for an amount greater than that sought by dissenting shareholders.

   d. Mega can make sure the merger is fair. One reason for appraisal is to induce corporations engaged in fundamental transactions to offer shareholders a fair price. A fair price in the merger will discourage dissenters who risk receiving an appraised value that is lower than the merger price.

In addition, Mega can condition the merger on approval by a supermajority of JRS shareholders, such as two-thirds or three-fourths. Shareholders who approve the merger cannot seek appraisal. Mega can also condition the merger on receiving less than a specified number of notices from shareholders perfecting their appraisal rights. See MBCA §13.23(a).

2. a. Jessica has a choice. She can challenge the merger for failing to comply with voting requirements—that is, the requisite majority did not approve the merger. MBCA §13.02(b). The appropriate remedy is rescission of the merger, not damages. If the challenge can be resolved quickly enough to undo the transaction without hardship to other shareholders or third parties, damages should not be available because of the speculative nature of valuing the lost voting rights.

   Even if Jessica only wants a better price, the voting challenge has some advantages and disadvantages. Challenging the transaction exposes Mega to a rescission remedy—easier for a close corporation than a public corporation—which could force Mega to pay a higher merger price to all shareholders. To avoid this, Mega may be more willing to settle on favorable terms with Jessica. Rescissory damages should reflect what her shares would be worth had the merger not been approved—that is, their current appreciated value!

   There is, however, a disadvantage to a voting challenge. Whether Jessica brings the action as a derivative or direct claim, she will not be entitled to payment of attorney and expert fees (if at all) until the end of the litigation. Under the MBCA appraisal procedures, the corporation must bear the ongoing expenses of court appraisal, and Jessica may ultimately be able to seek payment of her expenses under a more relaxed standard than would apply in a direct action.

   b. Probably not. The revised MBCA by its terms allows a dissenter to bypass appraisal and challenge the transaction only if the transaction was not effectuated properly or "procured as a result of fraud or material misrepresentation." MBCA §13.02(d). That is, only if Jerry's sweetheart deal and his domination of the board were not disclosed could shareholders challenge the process of the merger. The Official Comment explains that a minority dissenter should not be able to interfere with majority will because the minority "considers the change unwise or disadvantageous." The Official Comment explains that if shareholders disagree with the "financial consequences" of a corporate action they can vindicate their interests in a judicial appraisal proceeding.

   If the shareholders recast their price challenge as a process challenge, rescission of the merger (and perhaps a new, informed vote) would be the preferred remedy. If undoing the merger would be too difficult, courts have suggested that shareholders should receive the value of their shares as if the merger had not happened—rescissory damages. This may be advantageous if the JRS business has prospered since the merger, but disadvantageous if there have been post-merger losses.

One final point. What is the consequence that Mega may have bought Jerry's loyalty, and with him the JRS board? Although the MBCA assures appraisal rights when the acquiring corporation (directly or indirectly) controls one-fourth or more of the board, appraisal remains the exclusive remedy despite the existence of the conflict. See MBCA §13.02(b)(4)(i)(B). Instead, under the revised MBCA a fiduciary breach not involving fraud or misrepresentation cannot be challenged on price terms; appraisal is the exclusive remedy. Cf. Official Comment, pre-1999 MBCA (stating that appraisal not exclusive in the case of a transaction "in violation of a fiduciary duty").

CHAPTER 38

Federal Regulation of Tender Offers

Federal securities law adds informational rights to the mix of shareholder protections in fundamental corporate changes. The federal proxy rules mandate disclosure in any corporate combination (such as a merger) that requires approval by public shareholders. See Chapter 9. The federal prospectus disclosure rules apply to any exchange tender offer in which public shareholders receive securities for their shares. See Chapter 5. But until 1968 no federal disclosure rules applied to acquisition of a *control block for cash*, whether through open-market purchases or a tender offer.

To plug this regulatory gap, Congress in 1968 passed the Williams Act—a set of amendments to the Securities Exchange Act of 1934—to regulate stock purchases that affect corporate control. The Williams Act applies to public corporations whose securities are registered under §12 of the Exchange Act (see §9.2.1). This chapter describes how the Williams Act mandates disclosure for stock accumulations of more than 5 percent of a target's equity securities (§38.1), mandates disclosure by anyone who makes a tender offer for a target's equity securities, as well as the terms of such tender offers (§38.2), and provides for enforcement of its rules (§38.3).

Note on Effect of Williams Act

Despite protestations by the Williams Act drafters that the legislation was meant to be neutral—protecting shareholders without favoring management or bidders in takeover fights—some commentators have criticized the Act as having a pro-target bias. In fact,

(continued)

studies indicate that in the years immediately after the Act's passage in 1968 takeover premiums increased from 32 percent to 53 percent, while the frequency of takeovers declined. By imposing disclosure and timing impediments on bidders, without limiting the defensive arsenal of the target, some have argued the Act actually tilts the playing field in favor of target management. While a tender offer is pending, management can mount defenses whose substantive terms are not regulated by the Williams Act's principle of neutrality. See Chapter 39.

§38.1 DISCLOSURE OF FOOTHOLD POSITION

Any person (or group) that acquires *beneficial ownership* of more than 5 percent of a public corporation's equity securities must file a disclosure document with the SEC. Exchange Act §13(d). The disclosure alerts the stock market (and the target's management) of a possible change in control.

§38.1.1 Schedule 13D Disclosure

The filing, known as a Schedule 13D, must disclose

- the acquirer's (and any group member's) identity and background
- the source and the amount of funds for making the purchases
- the number of the target's shares held by the acquirer
- any arrangements that the acquirer has with others concerning shares of the target
- the acquirer's purposes for the acquisition and his intentions with respect to the target

A Schedule 13D must be filed within ten days after the 5 percent threshold is passed. This gives an acquirer a ten-day window during which to buy stock on the open market before having to signal that the company may be in play.

§38.1.2 Beneficial Ownership and Shareholder Groups

According to the SEC rules, beneficial ownership turns on whether the person (or group) has "voting power and/or investment power." Rule 13d-3(a). Thus, the shareholding of a father with the ability to control how his children vote their shares would be combined with the shareholdings of the children. Courts have looked at substance over form to determine whether there is a contract, arrangement, understanding, or relationship that suggests one person has voting or investment authority over another person's voting securities.

If persons who collectively hold more than 5 percent agree to act together for the purpose of affecting control, they (as a group) become subject to the §13(d) reporting requirement. Even if the group does not acquire more shares, their *agreement* triggers the reporting obligation. Rule 13d-5(b)(1); *GAF Corp. v. Milstein*, 453 F.2d 709 (2d Cir. 1971).

§38.2 FEDERAL TENDER OFFER RULES

Seeking control through open market purchases is problematic—rarely will enough shareholders be selling at market for a bidder to acquire a control block. A tender offer forces the question. The bidder greatly increases its chances by publicly offering to buy a specified number of tendered shares during a specified period at a premium over prevailing market prices. A tender offer operates much like a retailer's "Saturday night special at never-again prices."

Any tender offer for a public corporation's *equity securities* that would result in the bidder holding more than 5 percent of the target's equity securities is subject to both disclosure requirements and substantive rules governing the offer terms. Exchange Act §14(d). Federal tender offer regulation is meant to ensure that shareholders have sufficient information about the offer and adequate time to evaluate it, so they are not unfairly pressured into tendering their shares.

§38.2.1 Tender Offer Disclosure

The bidder must file a disclosure document with the SEC on the day it commences the tender offer. The document (Schedule TO) must include the same information as Schedule 13D, along with

- information about the tender offer
- past negotiations between the bidder and the target
- the bidder's financial statements (if material)
- any regulatory requirements that may be applicable to the bid
- any other material information

The target must cooperate in distributing the bidder's tender offer materials to shareholders, by either mailing them to shareholders (at bidder expense) or furnishing the bidder a current shareholders' list. Rule 14d-5.

Under rules promulgated by the SEC in 1999, a bidder can file a registration statement for securities to be issued in a stock-for-stock tender offer at the same time it files its Schedule TO and commences the offer. Securities Act Rel. No. 7760 (1999) (calling for expedited SEC review of exchange offers). This equalizes the treatment of exchange tender offers and cash tender offers. Before the new rules, securities issued in an exchange offer had to be registered with the SEC before the offer could be commenced; cash offers faced no such delay or uncertainty.

§38.2.2 Substantive Terms of Offer

Besides requiring disclosure, the Williams Act regulation prescribes how a third-party tender offer must be carried out—a departure from the general disclosure-only philosophy of federal securities regulation. SEC rules expand the minimum levels specified in the statute. The current rules require the following:

- **Minimum open period.** The tender offer must be left open a minimum of 20 business days. Rule 14e-1. If any change is made in the offered price or the percentage of shares being sought, the offer must be left open for an additional ten days after the change.
- **Withdrawal rights.** Shareholders can withdraw their shares (revoke their tenders) at any time while the tender offer is open. Rule 14d-7.
- **All holders.** The tender offer must be open to all shareholders of the same class and not exclude any shareholders from tendering. Rule 14d-10(a)(1).
- **Best price.** Each shareholder must be paid the best price paid to any other shareholder. Rule 14d-10(a)(2). If consideration alternatives are provided (such as a choice of cash or debentures), each shareholder can choose. Rule 14d-10(c)(1).
- **Pro rata purchases.** When the bidder seeks only a portion of all the shares (a partial tender offer) and shareholders tender more than the bidder seeks, the bidder must purchase the tendered shares on a pro rata basis. Exchange Act §14(d)(6). For example, assume the bidder seeks 50 percent of the target's stock and 75 percent is tendered. The bidder must purchase two-thirds (50/75) of each shareholder's tendered shares (disregarding fractions) and then return the unpurchased shares. Rule 14d-8.
- **No outside purchases.** The bidder cannot purchase outside the tender offer while it is pending. Rule 10b-13.

To make sure shareholders hear the other side of the story, target management must make a statement responding to the offer within ten business days after the tender offer commences. Rule 14e-2. The management statement (Schedule 14D-9) can either oppose or support the bid, take a neutral position, or take no position at all. Whatever its response, management must give its reasons.

§38.2.3 Regulation of Issuer Self-Tenders

Sometimes issuers defend against hostile tender offers by buying back their own stock. This increases the proportion of friendly shareholders or burdens the target with new debt, or both.

The Williams Act authorizes the SEC to promulgate rules regulating tender offers by targets—*issuer self-tenders*. Exchange Act §13(e). In general, the SEC rules regulate self-tenders much as third-party tender offers. Rule 13e-4. Self-tender regulation differs from third-party regulation in only two significant respects:

- **Outside purchases.** The issuer may purchase stock outside its self-tender. Open-market purchases, whether part of an ongoing corporate repurchase program or a defensive strategy, are not subject to the prohibition applicable to third-party tender offers. If made while another tender offer is pending, SEC rules require only disclosure. Rules 13e-1.
- **Cooling-off period.** For ten days after a self-tender terminates, the issuer is prohibited from making any purchases. Rule 13e-4(f)(6). This prevents an issuer from starting a tender offer, withdrawing it, and then purchasing stock in the resulting depressed market.

§38.2.4 Regulation of Deception (but Not Unfairness)

The Williams Act also contains a broadly worded antifraud provision. Section 14(e) prohibits any false or misleading statement—as well as any fraudulent, deceptive, or manipulative act—in connection with any tender offer or any solicitation for or against tenders. Although modeled on Rule 10b-5, §14(e) does not contain the 10b-5 "sale or purchase" language. This suggests that even those who did not enter into a securities transaction—namely, shareholders who did not tender and investors who did not purchase—may be protected by §14(e) even though they would lack standing under Rule 10b-5.

In *Schreiber v. Burlington Northern, Inc.*, 472 U.S. 1 (1985), the Supreme Court held that §14(e)'s prohibition against "manipulative acts" regulates only deception in connection with a tender offer and cannot be the basis to challenge a tender offer's substantive fairness. In the case, Burlington Northern withdrew a hostile tender offer and substituted a friendly offer with terms less favorable to shareholders. Target shareholders claimed target management had been bought off, making the second tender offer unfair and "manipulative." As it had with respect to Rule 10b-5 (*Santa Fe Industries v. Green*; see §9.3.1), the Court held that the sole objective of §14(e) is full disclosure, not regulation of corporate mismanagement.

Insider Trading during a Tender Offer

Using its §14(e) authority, the SEC has prohibited trading by those with inside information about a tender offer—whether the shares are publicly traded or not. Rule 14e-3 (see §23.3.3). The rule prohibits trading during the course of a tender offer by anybody (other than the bidder) who has material, nonpublic information about the offer that he knows (or has reason to know) was obtained from either the bidder or the target. There is no need under Rule 14e-3, unlike Rule 10b-5, to prove that a tipper breached a fiduciary duty for personal benefit.

Reminder: Rule 10b-5

Disclosure in connection with stock trading during a takeover is regulated under Rule 10b-5's broad antifraud prohibitions. See §22.2. In the takeover context, Rule 10b-5 has two significant effects. First, it regulates the issuer's disclosure of merger negotiations, such as when an unsolicited acquirer privately proposes a merger (a "bear hug") or during a target's discussions with a white knight or a management LBO group. See §34.2. Second, it regulates insider trading on the basis of material, nonpublic, confidential information about takeover plans, whether or not relating to a tender offer. See §23.3.

§38.2.5 Unorthodox Tender Offers

The term *tender offer* is not defined in the Williams Act or SEC rules. Usually, this is no problem. An orthodox tender offer is easy to recognize: A bidder publicly announces an offer to buy a specified number of shares at a premium within a specified period, subject to specified terms. But sometimes stock purchase programs, though not presented as a tender offer, involve the kinds of high-pressure tactics that led to the Williams Act. Are these programs *unorthodox tender offers?*

Consider a purchaser who announces a deadline to a select group of shareholders or a purchaser who publicly announces an open-market purchase program for a specified number of shares. If these purchase programs are tender offers, they are illegal. By their nature, they cannot comply with the SEC tender offer rules—such as the "all holders" rule and the minimum 20-day open period.

The cases have taken different tacks. Some courts have held that a tender offer occurs only when solicited shareholders lack information and are subjected to coercive pressure akin to that of an unregulated tender offer. In *Hanson Trust PLC v. SCM Corp.*, 774 F.2d 47 (2d Cir. 1985), on the same day a bidder terminated a public tender offer, the bidder purchased 25 percent of the target's stock in a series of five privately negotiated transactions and one open-market purchase. The Second Circuit, focusing (perhaps incompletely) on the negotiated purchases from institutional investors and arbitragers, held the purchases were not pursuant to a tender offer. The sellers had not been publicly solicited; they were securities professionals aware of the essential facts concerning the target; and they were not coerced to sell because the bidder bought at the market price without imposing any percentage contingency or time limits.

Other courts, and the SEC, have articulated an eight-factor "taste" test that describes the ingredients of an orthodox tender offer. Under the test, a "tender offer" exists if the offer to public shareholders is active and widespread, for a substantial percentage of the target's shares, at a premium price above market, firm and nonnegotiable, contingent on a fixed number of shares being tendered, and open for a limited time. As a result, offerees are subject to pressure to sell their shares, and there is a rapid, large accumulation of shares. *SEC v. Carter Hawley Hale Stores, Inc.*, 760 F.2d 945 (9th Cir. 1985).

Courts have been reluctant to subject open-market purchases to the tender offer rules, unless the purchaser publicizes its purchase plans or makes a general solicitation that coerces shareholders to sell. Even without such coercion, it is possible to buy a large block of stock after arbitragers have begun to acquire stock in reaction to a tender offer. Known as a "street sweep," this technique can be used to buy an effective control block (30 percent to 40 percent) virtually overnight. Although the SEC in 1987 proposed to prohibit unregulated purchases of 10 percent or more of a target's stock after a tender offer is made for the stock, the proposed rules proved unnecessary as state antitakeover statutes made it infeasible for a purchaser to acquire control in a street sweep. Delaware's statute, for example, imposes a three-year moratorium on any back-end transaction unless the acquirer buys 85 percent of the target's shares—a virtual impossibility in a street sweep. See §34.2.

§38.3 WILLIAMS ACT ENFORCEMENT

Although §21 of the Exchange Act explicitly authorizes the SEC to enforce the Williams Act in federal court, none of the Act's provisions expressly creates a private cause of action. Nonetheless, lower courts have inferred implied private actions under the Williams Act, although there have been two main sticking points: (1) Do bidders and targets have standing? (2) What remedies are appropriate—damages or injunctive relief?

§38.3.1 Standing to Represent Target Shareholders

Courts have held that target shareholders, for whom the Williams Act was passed, have standing to challenge violations of the Act. Commentators have pointed out that §14(e) does not mention "sale or purchase" and have suggested that standing extends to nontendering shareholders and non-purchasing investors, subject only to the usual requirement that they show materiality, reliance, causation, and damage. See §22.3.

The question of standing for the combatants—the bidder and the target—has been more difficult. Courts have been ambivalent about standing for bidders and targets because their interests will often be at odds with shareholder interests. Nonetheless, courts have accepted standing for bidders and targets to the extent they purport to represent shareholder interests.

§38.3.2 Remedies

Damages

Lower courts, buttressed by approving Supreme Court dictum, have awarded damages to shareholders injured by Williams Act violations. See *Osofsky v. Zipf*, 645 F.2d 107 (2d Cir. 1981) (approving shareholder recovery under a benefit-of-the-bargain theory). The Supreme Court, however, has held that a *frustrated bidder* cannot sue under §14(e) for damages arising from fraudulent statements made by the target in opposing the bidder's tender offer. *Piper v. Chris-Craft Industries, Inc.*, 430 U.S. 1 (1977).

Injunctive Relief

The Supreme Court has held that a target cannot sue to enjoin a bidder from exercising its voting rights, unless the traditional showing for injunctive relief—irreparable injury—has been made. *Rondeau v. Mosinee Paper Corp.*, 422 U.S. 49 (1975). Some lower courts have denied standing to targets seeking to disenfranchise bidders or to force them to divest their holdings. Most lower courts, however, have allowed bidders and targets to seek less burdensome relief, such as corrective disclosure and interim standstill injunctions.

Examples

1. Raider Partners is an investment firm engaged in the leveraged buyout of companies. Its dominant partner, Ernest Krass, has identified a target: Bullseye Industries, a consumer products manufacturer with widely respected brand names whose stock price has been in the doldrums at $40-$45. Bullseye has one class of common stock, which is traded on the New York Stock Exchange.
   a. Raider begins purchasing Bullseye stock surreptitiously on the NYSE through a number of brokers, without disclosing its identity or intentions. If Bullseye shareholders knew of Raider's plans, Krass acknowledges, they would not sell at prevailing prices. Must Raider disclose these purchases?
   b. After acquiring 4.9 percent of Bullseye, Krass tests the waters for a $65 takeover of Bullseye. He asks First Philly Investments (FPI), a leading investment banking firm, whether FPI would be willing to sell into a $65 tender offer for Bullseye. FPI's arbitrage department has been following Bullseye with great interest and already holds 2 percent of its stock. FPI says that $65 would be acceptable and FPI probably would sell. Does Raider have to report this contact?

2. Raider acquires 11 percent of Bullseye and discloses in its Schedule 13D that "Raider is considering its options, including gaining control of Bullseye." Soon after, trading in Bullseye stock increases dramatically and the price rises to $55. Arbitragers come to hold most of Bullseye's stock. Krass plans to push Raider's holdings above 50 percent. Here's his plan:
   - FPI (acting as broker for Raider) will have its reps call 30–40 arbs and institutional investors to ask if they would be willing to sell privately;
   - the reps will call on a Friday afternoon at 2:00 p.m. without revealing for whom they are calling, saying only they are soliciting others in the same way; and
   - the reps will ask each investor to sell at $60 per share and will require an answer by 5:00 p.m., after the NYSE closes.

   Is this market sweep legal?

3. Krass decides against a market sweep and instead considers a tender offer. He outlines his tender offer proposal and asks you to point out any problems:
   a. Any shareholder will be allowed to tender, though Raider will buy only 75 percent of Bullseye's stock (bringing its total holdings to 86 percent).
   b. The offer will be open on a first-tendered, first-purchased basis until the 75 percent threshold is reached.
   c. Consideration will be $65 cash or $70 in subordinated notes of Bullseye, at the option of each tendering shareholder, provided that no more than 50 percent of those tendering choose cash.

d. The offer will be open for 20 business days, and tendering shareholders can withdraw their shares during the first seven business days after the offer.
e. Raider will announce that its offer will be followed by a back-end squeeze-out merger (see §34.2) in which the remaining shares will be acquired for $65 in subordinated notes of Bullseye—less than that offered in the tender offer.
f. Raider will disclose its plans as follows: "If the offeror succeeds in gaining control of Bullseye, it will study Bullseye's business operations and prospects and after such examination may implement an alternative plan of operations."
g. Raider will disclose that both during and after the tender offer it may purchase shares on the open market, at prevailing prices.
h. Raider will condition its purchase of shares pursuant to the tender offer on the Bullseye board redeeming its poison pill and Raider obtaining a satisfactory commitment from an investment bank to sell junk (high-yield) bonds to finance the deal.

4. Raider makes a properly structured $65 tender offer for 40 percent of Bullseye's stock. Bullseye management thinks that the price is too low and that Raider is trying to coerce Bullseye to buy out Raider's interest at a premium (greenmail). Management proposes a restructuring in which the corporation will take on new debt and repurchase 50 percent of its shares for $75 cash per share. To frustrate Raider's greenmail plans, the issuer self-tender excludes Raider from tendering.
   a. Raider wants to have the issuer self-tender enjoined for violating the federal tender offer rules. Does the exclusionary tender offer violate the rules?
   b. Does Raider have standing to challenge the self-tender as a violation of the rules?

Explanations

EXPLANATIONS

1. a. No, as long as Raider's holdings do not exceed 5 percent of Bullseye's common stock. The Williams Act requires disclosure of open-market purchases only when a person (or group) acquires beneficial ownership of more than 5 percent of a class of registered equity securities. Exchange Act §13(d). Further, no disclosure is required under Rule 10b-5 because Raider has no fiduciary relationship with Bullseye or its shareholders and developed its purchase plan on its own. See §23.3.1.
   b. Perhaps. If Raider and FPI are members of a group for purposes of §13(d), their holdings must be aggregated. Under §13(d), as interpreted, a group arises even though its members make no additional

stock purchases. If Raider and FPI agreed to "hold, acquire, or dispose" of their Bullseye stock for purposes of affecting control in Bullseye, §13(d) would require them to report their identity, their holdings, their intentions, and their arrangement within ten days after their agreement.

Was FPI's statement that it probably would sell at $65 such an agreement? On the one hand, it could be argued that FPI did not commit to sell to Raider or to otherwise further Raider's takeover plans—there was no agreement to affect control. On the other hand, FPI's implicit commitment to sell its 2 percent into a $65 tender offer effectively meant that Krass could count on acquiring a total of 6.9 percent of Bullseye's stock—the 5 percent trigger had been reached and the Williams Act entitled Bullseye's shareholders to information about the possibility of a takeover. Much depends on how firm FPI's commitment was.

2. Perhaps not. If a tender offer, the purchasing program violates a number of the federal tender offer requirements—namely, the filing and distribution of a Schedule TO, the minimum 20-day open period, withdrawal rights for tendering shareholders, and equal treatment of all shareholders.

   At first blush, the plan seems to be an unorthodox tender offer. It contemplates stoking precisely the kind of "stampede mentality" that led to §14(d). The plan's goal is to coerce the investor-solicitees to sell quickly, without detailed information about the bid or about who is making it. They will be led to believe they must sell or lose any chance for a control premium. The solicitees will not have a 20-day period to evaluate the company, Raider's offer, and management's response. A very similar open-market pressure tactic was held to be a tender offer. See *Wellman v. Dickinson*, 475 F. Supp. 783 (S.D.N.Y. 1979).

   Other cases, however, suggest a different result. If sophisticated professional investors did not actually feel pressured to sell, Krass's plan might not be a tender offer. For example, perhaps they had evaluated Bullseye and believed the price would remain high even if Raider succeeded in buying a significant block. Applying the manipulable eight-factor test could lead to the same conclusion: (1) there was no public solicitation; (2) there was no premium over market; (3) the offer was not contingent on a specified tender; (4) the sophisticated offerees may not have been subjected to significant pressure. In the end, do the sophisticated investors solicited by Raider need the protection of the tender offer rules? There is some question whether the orthodoxy (and mandated egalitarianism) of a regulated tender offer should be imposed on all hostile takeovers.

3. a. No problem. Partial tender offers are possible under the tender offer rules. The "all holders" rule only requires that the tender offer be open to all shareholders. Exchange Act §14(d)(6); Rule 14d-8. If the offer is oversubscribed, the pro rata rules require the bidder to buy from each shareholder in proportion to the ratio of the number of shares sought and the number of shares tendered.

   b. Problem. The "pro rata" rule specifies how shares are to be purchased if the tender offer is oversubscribed. Buying shares on a first-come, first-served basis pressures shareholders to make ill-considered, rushed decisions—the main evil addressed by the tender offer rules. Although the open withdrawal rights provided for by the SEC rules ameliorate the problem of a first-come, first-served tender offer, the statute nonetheless requires pro rata purchases. Exchange Act §14(d)(6); Rule 14d-8.

   c. No problem. The bidder can offer alternative forms of consideration and condition the tender offer in any way that does not violate the tender offer rules. Rule 14d-10. The 50 percent cash condition does not create a "stampede" problem and acts much like a financing condition. If the tender offer will be too expensive, Raider need not accept the tendered shares.

   d. Problem. The withdrawal period must be as long as the tendering period—here the minimum 20 business days. To prevent fraudulent, deceptive, or manipulative tender offers, the SEC has required that the tendering period be at least 20 business days. Rule 14e-1. Although the statute contemplates that shareholders may withdraw tendered shares (in the normal case) only for the first seven business days of the offer, SEC rules expand withdrawal rights to extend through the entire period the offer is open.

   e. No problem. Even though a two-tier bid is coercive and "stampedes" shareholders into tendering, the Williams Act does not require that all the shares be acquired pursuant to a tender offer. In fact, there will always be some shareholders who will fail to tender into even the most generous tender offer because of stubbornness, lack of initiative, loyalty to management, or ignorance. If Raider acquires control (usually a condition of the tender offer) and wants 100 percent ownership (particularly if it contemplates self-dealing transactions to pay off the takeover debt), it can accomplish this in a back-end merger. As far as the federal tender offer rules are concerned, nontendered shares (as well as shares returned if the partial tender offer is oversubscribed) can be squeezed out in a merger for whatever consideration Raider decides to pay. The "best price" rule does not apply to the merger, nor does §14(e) require that the price or other terms of the merger be fair. The only Williams Act requirement is that the bidder not misrepresent its intentions, or say anything false or misleading about the merger during the tender offer. See Exchange Act §14(e). Stringent fiduciary rules under state law, however, apply to controlling shareholders in a squeeze-out merger—and a back-end merger in which the price were set below the front-end price would raise serious questions about the merger's "entire fairness." See §17.3.

f. No problem. If this is true and not misleading, the tender offer rules do not require full plans. In fact, recent courts have held that it is not even necessary for the bidder to have its financing for the offer lined up when it commences a tender offer as long as this is disclosed.

g. Problem. Third-party bidders cannot make purchases during the tender offer. Rule 13d-10. This keeps a bidder from starting a low-priced tender offer that artificially depresses the stock price and then buying at the manipulated price.

Under current rules, third-party bidders are not prohibited from making purchases after the tender offer ends. If this possibility was disclosed and the tender offer unequivocally withdrawn, post-bid purchases are not a continuation of the original tender offer. See *Hanson Trust PLC v. SCM Corp.*, 774 F.2d 47 (2d Cir. 1985). Unlike issuers that are subject to a ten-day cooling-off period after a self-tender, third-party bidders are required only to disclose the possibility of such purchases if they would be material to shareholders deciding whether to tender.

h. No problem. A tender offer, like any other contractual offer, can be conditioned on particular events occurring. So long as Raider does not make an illusory offer because (for example) it knows it cannot obtain financing, it may attach whatever conditions it chooses, subject to the federal tender offer rules. See *Gilbert v. El Paso Co.*, 575 F.2d 1131 (Del. 1990). The bidder does not breach its implied covenant of good faith under contract law unless it deliberately causes a condition precedent not to occur.

4. a. Technically, yes. Bullseye's exclusion of Raider violates the "all holders" rule, which requires that every tender offer (including a self-tender) be made to all shareholders. Rule 14d-10(a)(1); 13e-4(f)(8)(i). The SEC has justified the rule on two grounds. First, it comports with the equal treatment philosophy of §14(d), which assumes that equality means fairness. Second, without the rule, bidders could pressure the excluded group to sell to the included group, while avoiding the disclosure and substantive requirements of the tender offer rules. Excluded shareholders wishing to participate indirectly in the premium would not receive disclosure, would sell on a first-come, first-served basis, and would have no withdrawal rights.

These justifications for the rule, however, may not be as persuasive when the excluded shareholder group (Raider) is itself a bidder. The "all holders" rule effectively undercuts Bullseye's ability to respond to a perceived greenmailer with a self-tender. The rule would allow Raider to extract a premium at the expense of Bullseye's other shareholders, who would be forced to share their premium under the "pro rata" rules. Although excluding Raider may pressure it to give up the fight and sell to included shareholders, the Williams Act's pro-shareholder philosophy may not be concerned with the bidder's plight.

b. Perhaps not. Raider's exclusion benefits tendering shareholders, who need not share their self-tender premium with Raider. Because only Raider is excluded, it can be argued that Raider's challenge would not further the shareholder-protection purpose of the Williams Act. In *Piper v. Chris-Craft* (see §38.3.2), the Supreme Court held that a *bidder* could not recover damages for a violation of the tender offer rules. In the case, recovery to the bidder would have come indirectly at the expense of the shareholders who allegedly had been deceived.

   Nonetheless, Raider might assert standing in its capacity as a shareholder. If denied the ability to challenge the exclusionary self-tender, Raider could not recoup its bidding expenses by tendering its shares at a premium, thus removing one of the important cushions that soften the financial risk of launching a takeover bid. As a result, shareholders in general would be hurt if takeover bids became more expensive—a tilting of the playing field against bidders. The Williams Act regime, arguably, was intended to avoid such favoritism.

CHAPTER 39

Takeover Defenses

More than any other corporate device, a hostile takeover exposes management to shareholder control. It highlights the tension between management discretion and shareholder liquidity rights (and attached voting power). When shareholders receive a bid for their shares, what role should management have in assessing the bid?

This chapter discusses the many techniques management has used to blunt the force of a free-wheeling market in corporate control. In particular, the chapter describes the debate on the board's role (passive or active) when shareholders receive an unsolicited takeover bid (§39.1), judicial review of firm-specific takeover defenses (§39.2) and the power of the board to adopt such defenses (§39.3), and the history and legality of state antitakeover legislation (§39.4). For the mechanics and vocabulary of a takeover, you can review Chapter 34.

§39.1 DILEMMA OF TAKEOVER DEFENSES

Management of the corporation and control of the corporation's governance machinery reside with the board of directors. When shareholders are presented with a tender offer that management opposes, should the board be passive and not interfere, or should it be active and resist?

§39.1.1 Passive/Active Debate

Strong arguments can be made on both sides of the passive/active debate.

Passivity Thesis

A hostile bidder premises its bid on ousting incumbent management. There is an omnipresent specter of conflict of interest: Shareholders seek a premium price, while incumbent management has an ineluctable self-interest in opposing any hostile bid. The entrenchment motive—to perpetuate the lucre, power, and prestige of control—suggests the target board should not be allowed to use corporate resources to interpose obstacles. Empirical studies have indicated that targets that successfully repulse hostile bids do not recoup the bid's forgone value for their shareholders; target managers overestimate how good a job they can do. Although defensive tactics sometimes extract better bids, their possibility dissuades bidding and thus crimps the discipline of a robust market in corporate control. The board should be passive.

Activist Thesis

Despite the potential for conflicts of interest, the board is uniquely able to use corporate resources to further shareholder (and nonshareholder) interests. That is, the board can negotiate on behalf of dispersed public shareholders and represent otherwise voiceless nonshareholder constituents. Without a bargaining agent, shareholders could be pressured into accepting inadequate, ill-timed, or coercive bids. By serving the best interests of all corporate participants, the board fulfills a mediative role. Measured defensive tactics can drive away weak or destructive bids, induce better bids, buy time to find other bidders or company-sponsored alternatives (such as restructuring and stock repurchases), or otherwise assure fair treatment of corporate constituents. Empirical studies suggest that a bashful board—one that resists at first, but eventually capitulates—increases shareholder gains compared to a passive board. Moreover, the board can protect nonshareholder constituents—such as creditors, employees, customers, and communities—against bidders that may have no regard for them. The board should be active.

§39.1.2 Independence of Outside Directors

The passive/active debate turns in large measure on how we view the relationship of the corporation's senior executives and the board of directors.

See §11.4. The passivity thesis assumes that directors—whether because they also fear losing their positions or because of a built-in bias for management—will be closely aligned with senior executives. The activist thesis assumes independent directors, capable of putting aside their relationship with management and focusing on shareholder value. Today the boards of most public corporations are composed of a majority of nonemployee outside directors, who frequently own shares in the company.

§39.1.3 Board's Duties to Other Constituents

The passive/active dilemma also turns on whether we think the board should be responsible to constituents other than shareholders. If we conclude that the board's perspective in a takeover should be limited to shareholder wealth maximization, a passivity thesis may be more appropriate. But if we conclude that the board should (and would) consider a takeover's effect on nonshareholder constituents—such as employees, creditors, suppliers, customers, and communities—an activist role may be appropriate.

State "other constituents" statutes authorize the board to take into account nonshareholder constituencies in a takeover, as well as other corporate contexts. Pennsylvania's statute is typical: "In discharging [their] duties . . . directors of a business corporation may . . . consider . . . the effects of any action upon . . . shareholders, employees, suppliers, customers and creditors of the corporation, and upon communities in which offices or other establishments of the corporation are located." See Pa. BCL §1715. These statutes are meant to insulate a board's active defense against unwanted takeover bids. Significantly, Delaware does not have such a statute.

Although no constituency statute has to date been tested in court, some commentators view them as shifting the U.S. corporate paradigm of shareholder wealth maximization. These commentators have argued that the statutes should be read to permit nonshareholder constituents to enforce their extracontractual expectations in court, and to empower courts to reject the notion of shareholder primacy. Other commentators see the statutes as doing no more than restating current law, which permits the board to take into account nonshareholders if shareholders are not clearly adversely affected. Yet other commentators view the statutes as a cynical justification for management entrenchment.

§39.2 STATE FIDUCIARY REVIEW

State law determines the propriety of takeover defenses. The Supreme Court has made clear that current federal securities law requires only disclosure, not management fairness to shareholders. See *Santa Fe Industries, Inc. v. Green*, 430 U.S. 462 (1977) (Rule 10b-5 action challenging unfair merger, see §22.3.1); *Schreiber v. Burlington Northern, Inc.*, 472 U.S. 1 (1985) (§14(e) action challenging unfair tender offer, see §38.2.4).

Under state law, may the board consistent with its *fiduciary duties* to the corporation and the shareholders adopt takeover defenses? (On whether the board has the power to adopt the defense, see §39.3.) Corporate fiduciary law resolves the takeover dilemma rather clumsily. The traditional fiduciary model is dichotomous and points in opposite directions. On the one hand, defensive tactics involve an inherent conflict of interest. The traditional loyalty-fairness standards suggest strict judicial scrutiny. See Chapter 13. On the other hand, defensive tactics offer potentially unique value, and the board is in an ideal position to act on behalf of dispersed shareholders and other constituents. The traditional care standards (and the business judgment rule) suggest deferential review. See Chapter 12. It should not surprise you that judicial responses to the takeover dilemma have been ambivalent and inconstant.

§39.2.1 "Dominant-Motive" Review

Courts initially dealt with the takeover dilemma by a judicial sleight of hand. To ascertain whether an entrenchment motive lurked behind a takeover defense, courts adopted a process-oriented standard. The courts accepted defensive actions if the incumbent board could point to a "reasonable investigation" (preferably by outside directors) into a plausible business purpose for the defense—thus showing the *absence* of an entrenchment motive. Once this was done, the challenger bore the difficult burden to prove the board's dominant motive was entrenchment.

Using the dominant-motive analysis, courts readily accepted almost any business justification for defensive tactics. Specifically, the target board had only to identify a policy dispute between the bidder and management. In the case credited with originating the dominant-motive analysis, the target board paid greenmail to a large shareholder who had threatened to take control and undo the company's anachronistic direct-sales marketing. *Cheff v. Mathes*, 199 A.2d 548 (Del. 1964). The court upheld the defense because the board had investigated the threat that the acquirer posed to "the corporation in its current form" and because the buyout premium paid the greenmailer reflected a reasonable price for a control block.

The dominant-motive analysis met a storm of academic criticism during the early 1980s. Commentators decried its sophistry, which failed to account for management's obvious entrenchment motive and the board's structural bias favoring management. The dominant-motive test, which virtually absolved takeover defenses, insulated management incumbents from the discipline of the market in corporate control.

§39.2.2 Intermediate "Due Care" Review

One judicial response to the dominant-motive test was to impose heightened standards of deliberative care in takeover fights. Requiring directors to probe into the business and financial justifications for takeover defenses—thus putting teeth in the *reasonable* investigation standard—dissipates the misplaced business judgment presumption.

In *Hanson Trust PLC v. ML SCM Acquisition, Inc.*, 781 F.2d 264 (2d Cir. 1986), the Second Circuit applied New York law to invalidate two "crown jewel" lockup options conceded to a management LBO group by the target board during the final stages of a heated takeover fight. The options, giving the management group the right to buy two of the company's prime divisions at deep discounts if any other bidder acquired a control block, ended the bidding contest. The court concluded the outside directors' deliberations on granting the options revealed a predisposition toward management. The directors had failed to ask whether the lockup prices were fair, whether the management bid was in fact superior to the hostile bid, or how exercising the options would affect the company.

The heightened care standard has led target directors, on the advice of their lawyers, to carefully orchestrate procedural integrity. A common technique has been for the board to form a special takeover committee, composed of outside directors with no business affiliations to the target. The committee hires its own lawyer and investment banker, meets at length to carefully review documents and listen to advice, and sometimes sets up procedures for negotiating with management and other bidders. Throughout, the directors rely heavily on the orchestra conductor—the committee's lawyer.

§39.2.3 Intermediate "Proportionality" Review

Another judicial response to the takeover dilemma has been the adoption of intermediate *procedural* and *substantive* standards—between rational basis and intrinsic fairness. Seeking to find a middle ground, the Delaware Supreme Court formulated a "proportionality" test in *Unocal Corp. v. Mesa Petroleum Co.*, 493 A.2d 946 (Del. 1985). Under the two-prong *Unocal* test

- the board must reasonably perceive the bidder's action as a threat to corporate policy—a threshold procedural inquiry into the board's investigation, and
- any defensive measure the board adopts "must be reasonable in relation to the threat posed"—a substantive proportionality test.

If the defensive reaction fails either prong, the court invalidates the defensive tactic as a violation of the board's fiduciary duties.

Over the last two decades, the Delaware courts have shaped and reshaped the contours of the *Unocal* test. The decisions have not always been consistent. During the late 1980s, the Delaware courts showed doubts about board activism, permitting it only when the board articulated solid justifications tied to maximizing shareholder welfare—such as protecting shareholders from a coercive two-tier bid. Protecting other constituents was acceptable only if their interests coincided with maximizing shareholder interests. Otherwise, the Delaware courts seemed to view the board's proper role as mostly passive, including a duty to become an auctioneer when multiple bidders made a sale inevitable.

But during the 1990s the Delaware courts accepted greater board activism. The courts permitted defensive tactics aimed at preserving "corporate culture" or carrying out business strategies implemented by incumbent management. The board's role as auctioneer, the Delaware courts clarified, arose only when the board initiated a bidding contest or when a bust-up takeover was inevitable. Protecting shareholders from their own apathy and folly justified board intervention.

More recently, in the 2000s in response to Enron and other corporate scandals, the Delaware courts have shown a greater willingness to scrutinize the independence of outside directors and to impose substantive requirements on target boards, such as conditioning corporate sales on the ability to negotiate with other bidders—a so-called fiduciary out.

The following chronology of Delaware Supreme Court cases illustrates this judicial ebb and flow:

Year	Case	Delaware Supreme Court
1985	*Unocal Corp. v. Mesa Petroleum Co.*	Announces "proportionality" test that creates intermediate review for firm-specific defenses.
1985	*Moran v. Household International, Inc.*	Upholds "poison pill" that forces hostile bidders to negotiate with incumbent board, spawning a cottage industry in these plans.
1986	*Revlon v. MacAndrews & Forbes Holdings*	Requires board to conduct a fair and impartial auction when management-friendly bidder plans to bust up company.
1989	*Mills Acquisition Co. v. Macmillan, Inc.*	Scrutinizes preferences given a management-led buyout and sets high standards for conducting an impartial auction.

(continued)

Year	Case	Delaware Supreme Court
1990	*Paramount Communications, Inc. v. Time Inc. (Time-Warner)*	Permits a target board to sidestep an unsolicited (but attractive) cash bid to protect already negotiated deal.
1993	*Paramount Communications, Inc. v. QVC Network Inc.*	Prohibits a target board from preferring one all-cash offer over another without considering the alternative.
1995	*Unitrin, Inc. v. American General Corp.*	Defers to defensive tactics that weaken two-step proxy fight/tender offer bid on theory shareholders might be "ignorant."
2003	*Omnicare, Inc. v. NCS Healthcare, Inc.*	Requires board to include "fiduciary out" clause when negotiating lockups to protect a deal with a favored bidder.
2003	*MM Companies v. Liquid Audio*	Imposes heightened *Blasius* review, rather than *Unocal* review, when "board packing" would diminish influence of insurgent's nominees on board.
2009	*Ryan v. Lyondell Chem. Co.*	Allows board to adopt "wait and see" attitude when bidder acquires toehold position and then to negotiate merger over one-week period.
2010	*Versata Enterprises, Inc. v. Selectiva, Inc.*	Permits adoption of poison pill with 5-percent trigger to protect "corporate enterprise."
2011	*Air Products v. Airgas* (Del Ch.)	Does not require board to pull poison pill when independent directors determine bid is too low, thus keeping shareholders from considering bid.

Some have criticized Delaware's takeover jurisprudence as being too deferential to management. These critics assert that what began as careful judicial scrutiny of the justifications for particular defenses has ended in virtual abdication to management discretion, whether or not a bid is coercive or inadequate. Others defend Delaware's approach, which has provided significant latitude to independent directors to evaluate and respond to bids on behalf of shareholders and other corporate stakeholders.

Unocal (1985)

The court announced its heightened proportionality test, but applied it to uphold Unocal's decisive and brilliant defense against T. Boone Pickens of Mesa Petroleum. *Unocal Corp. v. Mesa Petroleum Co.*, 493 A.2d 946 (Del. 1985). The Unocal board responded to a Pickens front-end loaded 42 percent tender offer with its own self-tender (a debt-for-equity restructuring) that excluded Mesa's participation. Applying its two-step test, the court held the board (composed of a majority of outside directors) had sufficiently investigated the coercive nature of the Pickens bid by getting advice from outside investment bankers and lawyers. The court viewed the exclusionary feature of the self-tender as justified to dissuade greenmail and to proportionally increase share value for the remaining shareholders.

Household International (1985)

The court upheld a "poison pill" rights plan approved by a board in anticipation of the possibility of a takeover bid. *Moran v. Household Int'l, Inc.*, 500 A.2d 1346 (Del. 1985). Poison pills are designed to compel a bidder to negotiate with the board, ostensibly to assure shareholders and other corporate constituents fair treatment. Their operation is convoluted, resembling a corporate Rube Goldberg device.

The *Household* court held that the board, in adopting the plan, was properly concerned with the coercive nature of potential front-end loaded tender offers and the effect bust-up takeovers could have on company morale. The poison pill plan, the court concluded, was a reasonable response to these threats because it established the board's preeminent negotiating position. The court left for another day the question of how the board could use this ingenious tool in the midst of a takeover battle.

After *Household* the Chancery Court held the board had a fiduciary duty under *Unocal* to redeem poison pill rights in the face of a noncoercive, any-and-all cash tender offer. *City Capital Associates v. Interco*, 551 A.2d 787 (Del. Ch. 1988). The Delaware Supreme Court, however, later rejected these lower court decisions, and held the board has significant discretion to decide whether a bid poses a "threat to corporate policy and effectiveness." *Paramount Communications, Inc. v. Time Inc. (Time-Warner)*, 571 A.2d 1140 (Del. 1990).

Note on Poison Pills

How does a poison pill rights plan work? Consider the Household plan, which became a prototype for later plans.

Creation. The board issues one right for each common share outstanding. When issued, the rights are essentially worthless, entitling a shareholder to buy preferred stock at prices far in excess of current market value—that is, "out of the money."

First trigger. The real impact of the rights arises if any acquirer buys at least 20 percent (or makes a tender offer for at least 30 percent) of the company's shares. After this first trigger, the board has ten days to redeem the rights for a nominal amount (such as 10 cents per share). If the target fails to take this antidote, the rights become poison upon any further action by the acquirer.

Second trigger. Any back-end transaction with the tainted acquirer (such as a merger, sale of assets, or other self-dealing arrangement) activates a second trigger in which the target must swallow the plan's poison. The poison? Upon the second trigger, each right becomes exercisable, permitting the holder to purchase $200 worth of the acquirer's or the target's securities (depending on the structure of the back-end transaction) for $100. (A "flip-in" plan entitles the holder to buy discounted *target* securities and sensibly excludes the tainted acquirer from participating; a "flip-over" plan entitles the holder to buy discounted *acquirer* securities.)

Effect. The purpose of the plan is to force any bidder, before beginning a hostile takeover, to negotiate with the board—which holds the redemption antidote to the potentially devastating dilution if the rights are triggered and then exercised. Such plans, which have become a favorite among corporate defense tactics, have been adopted by a majority of large public companies.

Avoidance. One method to avoid a poison pill is for the bidder to seek first to replace the incumbent board in a voting contest, so the new board can then cancel the plan or redeem the rights and pave the way for the bidder's tender offer. Another, still uncertain, option is for the shareholders to adopt a bylaw amendment that prevents the board from adopting a poison pill without shareholder approval. See *International Bhd. of Teamsters General Fund v. Fleming Cos.*, 975 P.2d 907 (Okla. 1999) (ruling that Oklahoma law does not prevent shareholders from adopting resolutions or bylaws that require any rights plan to be submitted for a shareholder vote).

Revlon (1986)

The court invalidated preferential treatment given to a management-friendly bidder as a way of ending an auction with a hostile bidder. *Revlon, Inc. v. MacAndrews & Forbes Holdings*, 506 A.2d 173 (Del. 1986). The court ruled the board, in some circumstances, has a duty to sell the company in an impartial auction.

The case involved an asset lockup option conceded by Revlon's board to Forstmann Little, a white knight bidder. The board had granted the option to Forstmann to induce it to submit a higher bid in response to a hostile takeover bid by Pantry Pride. The option, which effectively killed a bidding contest for Revlon, would have allowed Forstmann to acquire two of Revlon's most desirable divisions at significant discounts from their appraised value if another bidder acquired more than 40 percent of Revlon's shares.

The board defended its preference for Forstmann because Pantry Pride proposed a bust-up takeover and the lockups were necessary to induce a higher Forstmann bid. The *Revlon* court did not focus on the board's deliberations concerning this perceived threat, but rather the reasonableness of the lockup response. Although the court said that a board could seek to frustrate a bust-up takeover, it held the board must assume the role of an auctioneer once such a takeover becomes inevitable. The board failed in this duty since the lockup option to Forstmann effectively ended the auction for "very little actual improvement in the final bid."

The *Revlon* court was also concerned that the directors had been coopted when Forstmann promised to support the market price of notes the board had issued during an earlier stage of the takeover fight. Noteholders angry about the falling price of their notes had threatened to sue the directors, and the Forstmann bid conveniently extricated the directors from their troubles. The court held the board could not prefer the noteholders, whose rights were fixed by contract, at the expense of shareholders.

Mills Acquisition (1989)

The court took a hard stance against preferences given a management-led buyout, setting high standards for conducting an impartial auction in such circumstances. *Mills Acquisition Co. v. Macmillan, Inc.*, 599 A.2d 261 (Del. 1989). The court invalidated a lockup agreement, granted during a purported auction of the target, to an LBO group led by Kohlberg, Kravis & Roberts (KKR) in which management had a 20 percent ownership stake.

The court held that when management has an interest in a bid and oversight by outside directors is lacking, the auction process must withstand rigorous scrutiny under the "intrinsic fairness" loyalty standard. The auction failed to meet this high standard on a number of counts: It had been conducted by management's hand-picked financial advisor (Wasserstein, Perella & Co.); Wasserstein rejected out of hand a substantially increased bid by the third-party bidder (Robert Maxwell); Wasserstein refused to negotiate with Maxwell; Wasserstein imposed unnecessarily short bidding deadlines and deliberately misled Maxwell. The court pointed out that nothing justified this hostility toward Maxwell, who had shown a willingness to operate the company as a going concern. The unfairness of the auction process was further compounded by a series of improper tips to KKR from both

Wasserstein and the target's CEO. The tips revealed the price and structure of Maxwell's first bid and suggested how KKR should improve its final bid. The court held that the board could not rely on Wasserstein's advice that KKR's bid justified conceding it a lockup agreement.

Time-Warner (1990)

The court sought to resolve when the *Revlon* auction duty is triggered and whether under *Unocal* a target can block an unsolicited (but attractive) cash bid. *Paramount Communications, Inc. v. Time, Inc.* (*Time-Warner*), 571 A.2d 1140 (Del. 1990). For many observers, the court's decision represents a significant retrenchment in the judicial scrutiny of takeover defenses.

In 1984 Time began exploring ways to expand from publishing and cable TV into entertainment production. Time identified Warner Communications (films, records, and Bugs Bunny) as a potential target, and in 1990 Time and Warner agreed to a stock-for-stock merger. Two weeks before the Time and Warner shareholders were to approve the merger, Paramount announced a $175 (and later a $200) cash offer for Time's shares, conditioned on the merger not happening. Convinced that the Time shareholders would turn down the merger to take Paramount's bid, Time and Warner agreed to restructure their deal so that Time would buy 51 percent of Warner's shares in a lucrative tender offer. Time would take on significant debt to finance the purchase, and Time's shareholders would be prevented from both voting on the restructured Time-Warner combination and taking the Paramount offer (which was conditioned on the nullification of the Time-Warner agreement).

The court rejected the argument that the Time-Warner combination constituted a change in control that triggered the *Revlon* auction duties. The court stated that *Revlon* duties are triggered generally when a target initiates an active bidding process or seeks a "breakup of the company" either unilaterally or in response to a hostile bid. Because the Time-Warner combination would not result in a breakup and ownership of the combined company would remain with public shareholders, no change of control occurred.

The court also held that Time's outside directors could decide, without violating *Unocal*'s proportionality standard, to restructure the Time-Warner combination to prevent shareholders from voting on it. The court accepted the directors' findings that Paramount's offer was inadequate and that Time shareholders might have been ignorant about the strategic benefit of combining with Warner or confused by the timing of the Paramount bid. These "threats" justified the board's taking the decision away from them. The court noted that in any event the combination was not final: Paramount or another bidder could still bid for the $30 billion combined entity. Thus, even in the face of a cash tender offer promising shareholders a significant premium, the court gave directors significant latitude to go forward with (and protect) an existing business plan.

Paramount II (1993)

After a hiatus, the court revisited the question of the board's duties in a takeover and outlined what seemed an invigorated judicial stance toward takeover defenses in control transactions. *Paramount Communications, Inc. v. QVC Network, Inc.*, 637 A.2d 34 (Del. 1993). In the case Paramount found the tables turned. After its unsuccessful bid for Time, Paramount had continued looking for other media/communications companies and in mid-1993 began discussions with Viacom, whose cable TV channels (MTV, Nickelodeon, and Showtime) offered a natural outlet for Paramount's entertainment assets. In September the two companies agreed to a merger in which Paramount shareholders would receive a combination of cash and Viacom stock—worth $69 per share. To facilitate and sweeten the deal, the Paramount board amended the company's poison pill to permit the Viacom merger and granted Viacom a stock lockup, a termination fee, and a no-shop promise.

Within days after the merger announcement, QVC (cable TV home-shopping network) proposed a competing two-step bid consisting of an $80 cash tender offer for 51 percent of Paramount's shares and a second-step merger with like-valued QVC stock. The offer was conditioned on invalidation of the stock lockup, which had become worth $200 million. Viacom countered by raising its offer to $85 per share, and QVC responded with a $90 bid. Showing remarkable disdain for the QVC interest, the Paramount board refused to modify the preferences for Viacom on the assumption that the QVC offer was "illusory."

QVC challenged the board's inaction as breach of fiduciary duty. On review, the Delaware court pointed out that in a control change the "fluid aggregation of unaffiliated shareholders" sell their voting control to a single buyer and give up forever their voting leverage. The court held that in these circumstances the board has a duty to evaluate the alternatives and seek "the best value reasonably available" for the public shareholders. This evaluation, the court stated, is subject to enhanced judicial scrutiny both of the decision-making process and of the "reasonableness" of the board's actions. Seeking to clarify *Revlon* and *Time-Warner*, the court said the duty to seek "best value"—the *Revlon* auction duty—arises not only when the company initiates a bidding process or when its breakup is inevitable, but also when there will be a change in control.

Applying this heightened standard of review, the court then had little difficulty concluding the Paramount board had failed its "best value" duties. The court faulted both the process and substance of the board's actions: the board approval of the potentially "draconian" provision of the Viacom stock lockup, its reluctance to modify the takeover defenses and negotiate with

QVC, its uninformed belief that the QVC bid was "illusory," and its stubborn commitment to a strategic alliance with Viacom.

In response to this decision, the Paramount board conducted an open auction for the company that Viacom eventually won when 90 percent of the Paramount shareholders tendered their shares in Viacom's winning bid, which consisted of $107 in cash for 50.1 percent of Paramount's stock. In a second-step merger, Paramount shareholders received Viacom stock guaranteed to reach a specified price level within three years of the merger.

Unitrin (1995)

The court again assumed a deferential attitude toward defensive tactics, even when shareholder voting rights were implicated in a two-step proxy fight/tender offer bid. *Unitrin v. American General Corp.*, 651 A.2d 1361 (Del. 1995). The court upheld Unitrin's repurchase program that responded to an unsolicited two-step bid by American General to replace the incumbent board in a proxy contest followed by a tender offer. AmGen claimed Unitrin's repurchase of approximately 10 percent of its shares, increasing management's holdings from 23 percent to 28 percent, chilled any outside bid for the company. AmGen argued that the buttressed management holdings, combined with a poison pill plan and supermajority "shark repellent" provision requiring 75 percent approval of any merger with any more-than-15-percent shareholder, made a proxy contest untenable. AmGen argued that if limited to 15 percent, it was unlikely to convince fellow shareholders of its intentions in a board election, and the poison pill precluded AmGen from proceeding with its tender offer.

The court reviewed the repurchase program under the *Unocal* proportionality test rather than the more demanding "compelling justifications" standard used in judging manipulation of the voting process. See §8.2. The court pointed out that the repurchase did not conclusively preclude a proxy contest. Outside directors, who held a substantial block of shares, might vote their shares against the bidder—if the price were right. As a 14.9 percent shareholder, the bidder could still win a proxy contest, particularly given that 42 percent of Unitrin's shares were owned by institutional shareholders. And, assuming a 90 percent turnout at a shareholders' meeting, AmGen as a 14.9 percent shareholder would need only 30.2 percent support from other shareholders to elect a new board, and 35.2 percent support to approve a merger.

The court concluded the repurchase program was a proportionate response to a low-price bid. It permitted the Unitrin repurchase as a means to buy out "short-term speculators" (arbitrageurs) whose actions may have been adverse to long-term shareholders and to give the board time to counteract the "ignorance or mistaken belief" among shareholders about the company's value. In effect, the court accepted the board could protect shareholders from their own impulsive folly.

Omnicare (2003)

The court reviewed a set of lockups granted by the target board after negotiating a merger with a bidder following a desultory auction of the company. *Omnicare, Inc. v. NCS Healthcare, Inc.*, 818 A.2d 914 (Del. 2003). The lockups (1) called on two of the target's major shareholders (whose Class B shares controlled 65 percent of voting power) to grant an irrevocable proxy to the bidder to vote their shares for the merger and (2) committed the board to not "shop" the company and to put the merger to a shareholder vote even if the board no longer recommended it. The combined effect of the lockups was to guarantee the merger, even if there were a higher outside bid. When such a bid materialized, the board said its hands were tied.

The court held that deal protections require "enhanced scrutiny" to protect the shareholders' "right to effectively vote" on the merger. In particular, the reviewing court must determine the deal protections are not "preclusive or coercive" before determining whether the protections fall within a "range of reasonableness." That is, heightened *Blasius*-type voting concerns come first (see §8.2) followed by a *Unocal*-type proportionality inquiry.

In the case, the court determined that the target board was duty-bound to have negotiated a "fiduciary out" clause. Whatever the bidder's contractual expectations, they had to yield to the supervening responsibility of the directors to discharge their fiduciary duties on a continuing basis. The court enjoined the merger and blocked implementation of the voting arrangement to the extent it interfered with the board's exercise of its fiduciary duties.

Liquid Audio (2003)

The court again looked at the board's duties in a two-step proxy fight/tender offer bid. *MM Companies, Inc v. Liquid Audio, Inc.*, 813 A.2d 1118 (Del. 2003). The court concluded that when the primary purpose of a defensive tactic is to impede or interfere with the shareholder franchise in a contested election of directors, review is under the more demanding *Blasius* standard rather than *Unocal*. Thus, *Blasius* (and its requirement that the board have "compelling justifications" before interfering with the shareholder franchise) is a condition precedent to the proportionality review under *Unocal*.

In the case, MM Companies made a bid for Liquid Audio, an Internet music company with a faltering business model but significant cash reserves from its still unspent IPO. When the Liquid Audio board rejected the offer, MM Companies proposed to nominate two directors to Liquid Audio's five-person board and increase the board size by four, filling the vacancies with its nominees. Liquid Audio responded by amending the bylaws to increase the board size to seven and then filled the two vacancies, thus making it more difficult for MM Companies to seat a board majority. (Notice that this was essentially the sequence of events in *Blasius*, see §8.2.3.)

Although the chancery court had concluded that the "board packing" by the incumbent board did not technically interfere with the voting rights of shareholders—who could still elect a majority of MM Companies' nominees to an expanded board—the supreme court reversed and held that the case presented a "paragon" of when *Blasius* applies. Even though the bidder-insurgent still could seat a board majority, the incumbents' board packing was for the primary purpose of diminishing the influence of the two MM Companies nominees by eliminating the possibility of a deadlock (if a director resigned) or their becoming a majority (if two directors resigned).

Lyondell (2009)

The court considered whether directors who in one week negotiated and finalized a merger violated their *Revlon* duties to maximize the sales price of the corporation. *Ryan v. Lyondell Chem. Co.*, 970 A.2d 235 (Del. 2009). Two months before the merger, the directors had been put on notice of an outside bidder's interest when it filed a Schedule 13D disclosing it held an 8.3 percent position in the company. The directors met to discuss the possibility of an acquisition by the bidder but opted for a "wait and see" approach—an "indifference" that the chancery court decided violated the directors' *Revlon* duties once the "company was in play." (The corporation had a §102(b)(7) exculpation provision, so the issue was one of loyalty (good faith), not care.)

The supreme court reversed and held that the directors did not have *Revlon* duties until they actually began negotiating the sale of the company, something that happened in the case over a one-week period during which the directors considered the bidder's eventual offer. During that week, according to the court, the directors did not act in bad faith, which would have required a showing that the directors "utterly failed to attempt to obtain the best sales price." Instead, the directors met several times to consider the bidder's premium offer, the CEO tried to negotiate better terms, they evaluated the company's value and the likelihood of obtaining a better price, and they solicited and followed advice of their financial and legal advisors. The court reiterated that when *Revlon* duties are triggered, the directors' decisions "must be reasonable, not perfect."

Selectiva (2010)

The court considered how low the trigger of a poison pill could be set, accepting that a target board could adopt a poison pill plan with 4.99-percent trigger meant to protect the company's net operating losses (NOLs) from being forfeited in an "ownership change" under the federal tax laws. *Versata Enterprises, Inc. v. Selectiva, Inc.*, 5 A.3d 586 (Del. 2010). Applying the first prong of the *Unocal* test, the court readily found the target board had acted reasonably, meeting over many hours with legal and investment banking advice, to consider the threat of the bidder triggering a forfeiture of the NOLs. Applying the second prong of *Unocal*, the court held the poison pill (combined with the target's staggered board) did not preclude a front-end proxy contest by a determined bidder to replace the incumbent board, citing instances when an insurgent with less than a 5-percent holding was able to place its nominees on the board. Just because defensive maneuvers make it "more difficult" to acquire control does not makes such measures "realistically unattainable [or] preclusive." The poison pill is alive and well in Delaware.

Air Products (2011)

The chancery court ended a year-long takeover battle between two determined companies, deciding that the target was not required to pull its poison pill when the board decided the bidder's offer was too low. *Air Products & Chemicals, Inc. v. Airgas, Inc.*, 16 A.3d 48 (Del. Ch. 2011). Air Products made a hostile bid to acquire Air Gas, which had both a poison pill and a staggered board. After Air Products undertook a proxy contest and successfully placed its candidates on the board, it followed with a $70 bid that the board (including the newly elected directors) rejected as too low. The board further refused to redeem the poison pill, which included a condition that the board could only be replaced at a special meeting with 67 percent shareholder vote.

Was the board independent and adequately informed under the first prong of *Unocal*? The court found that the Airgas board—which included the three directors nominated by Air Products—was composed of a majority of outside, independent directors, acting in good faith and with numerous outside advisors. After questioning the valuations themselves and seeking outside opinions, the board (including the Air Products nominees) had reason to conclude the $70 per share price was inadequate. "Air Products *got what it wanted*."

Was the board's refusal to rescind the poison pill "preclusive," making any takeover unattainable and thus unreasonable under *Unocal*? The court held that the combination of a poison pill and staggered board were not preclusive. Air Products, said the court, had viable options to continue to pursue Airgas by calling a special meeting to remove the entire board with a supermajority vote or waiting until the next annual meeting to nominate a new slate of directors. Thus, the board's defenses—even though they took away from the shareholders the question whether the Air Products bid was fair—were not preclusive.

§39.3 BOARD'S POWER TO ADOPT TAKEOVER DEFENSES

In most instances the power of the board to adopt a takeover defense is not an issue. The usual defensive tools—such as issuing stock, taking on debt, selling assets, repurchasing stock, or compensating management—unquestionably are all within the board's powers. But when the capital or governance structure is manipulated in novel ways—particularly with a poison pill—some courts have used the *ultra vires doctrine* (see §3.3) to invalidate the board's power to defend.

In response to early poison pill plans, federal courts interpreted state law to invalidate poison pills for violating the statutory requirement that all shares of a class have equal rights. (Remember that to ensure their dilutive effect, flip-in poison pills deny the hostile acquirer—but not other shareholders—the right to buy stock at a discount after a back-end transaction.) See *Asarco, Inc. v. Court*, 611 F. Supp. 468 (D.N.J. 1985) (applying New Jersey law); *Minstar Acquiring Corp. v. AMF, Inc.*, 644 F. Supp. 1252 (S.D.N.Y. 1985). Soon after, state legislatures rejected these decisions and specifically authorized exclusionary poison pills. N.J. BCA §14D:7-7(3); N.Y. BCL §4603(a)(2).

More recently, Delaware courts have invalidated poison pill plans that permit redemption or rescission only by incumbent directors or their chosen successors—called "dead hand" or "continuing director" plans. These plans seek to prevent a hostile acquirer from conducting a two-step takeover in which it first initiates a voting contest for control of the board and then, once its board is installed and terminates the plan or redeems any outstanding rights, undertakes a second-step acquisition. The courts have stated that restricting the powers of successor directors circumscribes the inherent, statutory authority of a properly elected board to manage the corporation's business and affairs, and thus is invalid under Del. GCL §141(a). *Quickturn Design Systems, Inc. v. Shapiro*, 721 A.2d 1281 (Del. 1998) (delayed redemption "dead hand" plan); *Carmody v. Toll Brothers, Inc.*, 723 A.2d 1180 (Del. Ch. 1998) ("dead hand" plan also invalidated as a breach of incumbent directors' fiduciary duties). But see *Invacare v. Healthdyne Technologies, Inc.*, 968 F. Supp. 1578 (N.D. Ga. 1997) (holding that since Georgia's "fair price" antitakeover statute includes continuing director provision, such provision can be incorporated into rights plan).

Examples

EXAMPLES

1. Alpha Corporation, a conglomerate with formidable cash reserves, has identified a takeover possibility: Marque Inc., a consumer goods company incorporated in Delaware. Alpha's CEO, Ernest Gahma, calls Marque's CEO Phess Makrel and offers to buy Marque in a negotiated transaction for $75 cash per share, threatening a hostile bid if Marque refuses. The

Marque board meets to consider the Gahma "bear hug." There are 11 directors on the board: three are management directors, two are outside directors whose firms have significant dealings with Marque (a bank and law firm), and six are nonaffiliated directors (CEOs of other companies and political types).

a. Can the board reject the bear hug and refuse to deal with Gahma—that is, neither meet with him nor ask for more information about his offer?
b. Marque's articles include an exculpation provision, absolving directors of personal liability unless they breach their duty of loyalty or act in bad faith. Can the directors be personally liable for shunning the Gahma overture?

2. The Marque board stonewalls the Gahma offer. Alpha then makes a cash tender offer at $80 per share for 51 percent of Marque's shares. Marque's investment banker, Trout Brothers, opines that the $80 price is "fair" but not "acceptable"—that is, it is within a market range, but it could be higher.
   a. The board adopts a poison pill, triggered by any acquisition of more than 20 percent of the company's shares. Can the board defend in this way?
   b. Alpha revises its tender offer to eliminate any coercion by making it an any-and-all $80 cash tender offer. Must the board remove the poison pill?
   c. The board justifies its action as consistent with the state's "other constituency" statute. Is this justification enough?
   d. Alpha begins a consent solicitation to replace the current board. In response, the board revises its poison pill so that only current directors or their "successors" can revise or redeem the poison pill rights. Is this valid?
   e. The board exercises the authority granted it under the corporate articles to stagger the board. Assuming that this is within the board's powers, is this action consistent with the board's fiduciary duties?

3. In the meantime, Marque management has been looking for a white knight. A leading consumer products company, Omega Corporation, is interested. Omega proposes an $85 cash buyout, to be financed in part by selling some of Marque's assets. Marque executives (including the management board members) would receive 10 percent of the new company's equity; and Marque would continue to be run by current management. Omega gives Marque three days to consider its offer.
   a. Marque's board forms a special takeover committee composed of outside directors, who consider the Omega offer at a day-long meeting. CEO Makrel explains that management had discussed bids for Marque

with ten other companies, but none (except Omega) had shown an interest in acquiring Marque. First Philly, Marque's long-time investment banking firm, opines that Omega's $85 price is fair and adequate. Must the committee notify Alpha of the Omega offer?

b. The committee asks Alpha and Omega to submit their best bids in a week. Omega bids $93 (a package of $50 cash and new Marque securities it values at $43) on the condition that Marque enter into a merger agreement and promise not to receive any further bids. Alpha's bid is for $90 in cash. Can the committee accept the Omega offer?

Explanations

1. a. Probably. *Time-Warner* makes clear that the board need not put the company in play or set up an auction in response to every takeover bid. See also *Ivanhoe Partners v. Newmont Mining Corp.*, 535 A.2d 1334 (Del. 1987) (upholding target board's declaration of special dividend that permitted white knight to gain 49.7 percent holding, thus protecting "independence" of target's board). Under *Unocal*, the board may refuse Alpha's bear hug, if the directors conduct a reasonable investigation and identify that the Gahma offer somehow threatens shareholder welfare. This investigation, under the due care standards articulated in *Smith v. Van Gorkom* (see §12.3.3), should delve into the $75 price, the timing of the offer, the effect of the offer on the company, regulatory issues, Gahma's intentions, Alpha's financing, and the ultimate price Alpha may be willing to offer. The board should seek the opinion of an investment banker concerning the fairness and adequacy of a $75 price, as well as the company's fair value. At this point, the board probably need not compose a special takeover committee since a majority of the board is composed of unaffiliated outside directors.

   b. Perhaps. The board cannot be predisposed to reject the unsolicited offer. Although the Delaware exculpation statute, Del. GCL §102(b)(7), was intended to absolve directors from liability for good-faith breaches of their duty of care—as in *Smith v. Van Gorkom*—the good-faith exception has been interpreted to mean the board "consciously disregards" its duties. See *Walt Disney Co. Deriv. Litig.*, 906 A.2d 27 (Del. 2006) (see §12.3.1). Thus, it could be argued that directors who blindly accede to management's entrenchment wishes do not act in good faith. In fact, the Delaware Supreme Court hinted that blind obeisance to management involved in an LBO could constitute a breach of a duty of loyalty. *Mills Acquisition Co. v. Macmillan, Inc.* Even though the corporation has adopted an exculpation clause, directors still face substantial liability exposure in takeover battle.

2. a. Yes. The tender offer is front-end loaded and is structurally coercive. To be sure to receive front-end cash and avoid the uncertainty in a back-end transaction after Alpha acquires control, a rational shareholder will tender. The Delaware courts, first in *Unocal* and confirmed in *Newmont Mining*, make clear that the board can assume a very active posture when the threat is a structurally coercive offer.

   b. Probably not. Even though the bid is not structurally coercive, its timing and price premium confront shareholders with the dilemma of tendering or waiting for a better price. *Time-Warner* and *Unitrin*—and especially *Selectiva* and *Air Products*—make clear the board has significant discretion to just say no, to protect shareholders from price "coercion." Although this is little different from the hold-sell dilemma that shareholders face daily with their investment, the Delaware courts allow the board to assume a role as negotiator—and price arbiter. A poison pill accomplishes this. The board must muster some price or continuing enterprise justification—a not too difficult task. So long as the poison pill does not completely preclude a two-step takeover, the board can institute (or choose not to redeem) a pill in response to a bid it determines is too low.

   c. Probably. In a jurisdiction with an "other constituency" statute that permits boards to consider nonshareholder interests—such as those of employees, creditors, suppliers, even communities where the business operates, see §11.1.2—the statute signals that the board has broad discretion to respond to takeover threats. In fact, recent studies indicate that courts in jurisdictions with antitakeover legislation are more likely to find that defensive maneuvers are consistent with the board's fiduciary duties.

   Although Delaware does not have an "other constituency" statute, the Delaware courts have permitted boards to protect the "corporate enterprise" and thus consider nonshareholder constituencies. See *Time-Warner* and *Selectiva*. It is enough that the board becomes informed about these other constituencies and articulates a threat posed to them by the bidder. In some ways, it is has been pointed out, this analysis represents a return to the "dominant purpose" test of *Cheff v. Mathes*.

   d. Probably not. There are limits to the board's role as negotiator. A poison pill that cannot be redeemed except by incumbent directors and their chosen successors insulates the company from unsolicited control changes. This undermines the authority of properly elected directors and is invalid under Del. GCL §141(a). See *Quickturn Design Systems, Inc. v. Shapiro*, 721 A.2d 1281 (Del. 1998). Moreover, a "dead hand" poison pill is contrary to fundamental notions of shareholder democracy.

   e. Probably. Antitakeover devices in the articles—and thus approved by shareholders—receive deferential review. On the theory that such provisions reflect that shareholders have ceded to the board the authority to pass on the fairness of outside bids, courts have reviewed staggered board provisions under the business judgment rule, not the more demanding *Unocal* standard. See *eBay Domestic Holdings v. Newmark*, 16 A.3d 1 (Del. Ch. 2010) (applying business judgment rule to staggered board provision). In fact, the Delaware courts have accepted the use of staggered boards, which combined with poison pills present (according to recent studies) an almost insurmountable obstacle to hostile bids.

Nonetheless, an argument might be made that sometimes during a takeover fight exercising the authority granted to the board in the articles is subject to special scrutiny. For example, when an incumbent board exercises its authority to amend the bylaws to expand the size of the board and fill the resulting vacancies with new directors, the Delaware courts have held that heightened *Blasius* review applies. See *Liquid Audio*. Thus, a board decision to institute a staggered board in the midst of a takeover fight may be viewed with more suspicion than a board decision to protect an existing staggered board structure.

The ambiguity in the standard of review that Delaware courts might employ highlights the indeterminism of Delaware corporate law, particularly in the area of takeovers. Some have criticized Delaware law for not being more coherent, while others see this as one of the strengths of the state's judicial system—namely, the ability to respond to political and economic situations as they arise.

3. a. Perhaps not. A board need not auction the company whenever presented with an outside bid. See *Lyondell*. Although Marque management's participation in the Omega bid makes the transaction a case of self-dealing, the Delaware courts have not automatically reviewed board responses to management-backed bids under a loyalty-fairness standard. See *Revlon; Mills Acquisition*.

   Nonetheless, the committee's refusal to negotiate with Alpha would fare poorly under the first prong of the *Unocal* test and the duty to consider other offers under the *Omnicare* analysis. Under *Unocal's* reasonable investigation test, the committee's reliance on First Philly is questionable. First Philly has an interest in maintaining its relationship with Marque management. The committee should have also (or instead) sought the advice of a nonaffiliated investment banker. Further, as *Omnicare* and other "deal protection" cases make clear, the committee must keep itself open to considering all viable options. See §39.2.3.

   b. Possibly. By setting up a bidding process, the committee is subject to the "fair auction" standards of *Revlon*. Which offer is better—from the shareholders' standpoint? Although Omega's offer is facially superior to Alpha's, it may not be valued that way by shareholders. The committee must investigate the value of the securities offered by Omega, principally by consulting with an outside investment banker.

According to *Revlon* and *Mills Acquisition*, if a board concludes one offer is better, it can agree to an auction-ending lockup only if no further bidding is likely. This means the committee cannot agree to the strict no-talk clause unless the directors conclude the Omega bid is superior and no further bidding by Alpha or any other bidder is likely. This seems improbable. The Delaware courts' process-oriented approach attaches much significance to directors not closing off possibilities. But when they do, it is enough that their decision was "reasonable." See *Lyondell*.

§39.4 STATE ANTITAKEOVER STATUTES

State antitakeover statutes complement firm-specific defenses and have assumed great importance in takeover contests. The statutes eliminate the uncertainty of firm-specific defenses and transform the validity of takeover defenses into a political and constitutional question rather than a common-law fiduciary one.

In 1987 the U.S. Supreme Court upheld the constitutionality of antitakeover statutes that restrict takeovers of companies incorporated in the regulating state. *CTS Corp. v. Dynamics Corp. of America*, 481 U.S. 69 (1987). Since then, state legislatures have accepted the Supreme Court's invitation to regulate the market in corporate control. Today most states, including Delaware, have enacted antitakeover legislation.

The political history of antitakeover legislation is interesting. Often the statutes were drafted by management or promanagement lobbies, rather than the bar committees that typically draft state corporate codes. The legislation responded to widely held fears that hostile takeovers hurt the local economy and tax base. Management entrenchment overlapped with legislative concern for jobs, political support, communities—in short, a concern for protecting the economic and political status quo. But to fit the statutes into the constitutional niche fashioned by the Supreme Court, the legislative rhetoric and substance revolved around protecting shareholders from coercion and the collective action problem.

§39.4.1 History—Three Generations

The history of state antitakeover statutes can be divided into three phases, each transition marked by a Supreme Court decision.

First Generation

After the passage of the "neutral" Williams Act in 1968, most states moved to regulate tender offers under their "blue sky" laws. These early antitakeover statutes applied broadly to public corporations either incorporated in the state or with significant contacts in the state. They generally imposed precommencement notice and state administrative hearing requirements that significantly impeded hostile tender offers.

In 1982 the Supreme Court held Illinois's first-generation antitakeover statute unconstitutional. *Edgar v. MITE Corp.*, 457 U.S. 624 (1982). The statute covered corporations incorporated in Illinois, as well as non-Illinois corporations that had their principal offices in Illinois or at least 10 percent of their capital "represented within" the state, provided at least 10 percent of the shares sought in the tender offer were held by Illinois residents. The statute imposed a 20-day preannouncement waiting period and allowed for potentially indefinite administrative review by state officials of the tender offer for fairness.

A 5-4 majority held the Illinois statute violated the "dormant" commerce clause because the statute's burden on out-of-state tender offers outweighed any state interest in disclosure and shareholder protection. A plurality in *MITE* concluded the delays allowed by the Illinois statute were preempted by the Williams Act's carefully balanced disclosure scheme.

Second Generation

After *MITE*, courts invalidated many of the first-generation statutes. States responded by enacting a second generation of statutes that purported to regulate corporate internal affairs, rather than impose securities regulation. These statutes, which were generally less burdensome, tended to apply only to domestic corporations (incorporated in the state) and imposed price or voting conditions that purported to address the evil of coercive tender offers. Many commentators, practitioners, and judges doubted their constitutionality.

But in 1987 the Supreme Court upheld the constitutionality of a second-generation Indiana statute. *CTS Corp. v. Dynamics Corp. of America*, 481 U.S. 69 (1987). The statute, which applied only to corporations incorporated in Indiana with significant Indiana shareholdings, required that disinterested shareholders (excluding the bidder and management) collectively vote to authorize voting rights for any bidder who sought to acquire a controlling interest in the corporation. That is, until the body of shareholders voted to enfranchise, the bidder's "control shares" would not carry voting rights. The Court held the statute's requirement of a shareholder vote was not inconsistent with the Williams Act as it did not interfere with the bidding process and comported with the traditional power of states to regulate the internal affairs of domestic corporations.

Third Generation

Encouraged by *CTS*, states have tightened their second-generation statutes or have adopted new variants. Some of these are modeled on the Indiana statute, while others go beyond it.

§39.4.2 Current Antitakeover Statutes

The third-generation statutes fall into a number of categories:

Control Share Statutes

An example of a control share statute is the Indiana statute upheld in *CTS*. These statutes allow the body of shareholders (but excluding the bidder and management) to vote on the bidder's fate. Under some statutes, the bidder can acquire "control shares" only if the other shareholders approve; under others, the bidder acquires voting rights only if the other shareholders approve. A bidder becomes subject to this rite of initiation when its total shareholdings exceed one of three specified "control" thresholds (usually 20 percent, 33 percent, and 50 percent). Under the statutes, the bidder must give notice and the board must set a date for a shareholders' meeting (usually no more than 50 days after the notice) to decide on the bidder's fate. Control share statutes are ostensibly meant to protect against coercive tender offers by mandating collective shareholder action.

Business Combination (or Moratorium) Statutes

A bidder who acquires a specified stock position (such as 15 percent) cannot enter into a back-end transaction (such as a squeeze-out merger) with the corporation for a moratorium period (such as three or five years). There are exceptions if (1) the board and a majority (or supermajority) of the other shareholders approve the transaction, or (2) the bidder acquired control in a tender offer for a significant majority of the stock (such as 85 percent), or (3) the original board of directors had approved the bidder's acquisition. The statutes are meant to give shareholders a greater chance to share in the control premium and the board enhanced negotiating leverage.

Delaware Statute

In 1988 Delaware passed a moratorium statute applicable to all public corporations incorporated in Delaware. Del. GCL §203. Under the statute, any person who acquires 15 percent or more of a Delaware corporation's stock (an "interested shareholder") is disabled for the next three years from effecting any merger or business combination, *unless* either

- the board of directors approved the business combination before the triggering 15 percent acquisition, or
- the interested shareholder crosses the 15 percent threshold in a transaction (tender offer) in which it acquires at least 85 percent of the company's stock, presumably at a highly favorable Price—the 85 percent excludes shares held by management and management-controlled ESOPs or
- the business combination is approved by the board and two-thirds of the shares held by other shareholders

The Delaware statute can be avoided in a number of ways. The statute itself specifies the bidder can (1) negotiate a deal with incumbent management, (2) make an attractive tender offer for 85 percent of the company's stock, (3) propose a back-end transaction that will gain two-thirds minority support, or (4) simply wait out the three-year moratorium. In addition, the bidder can mount a proxy contest for board control and, if successful, have the new board approve the bidder's proposed business combination. The Delaware statute is not mandatory, and a corporation can opt out of it in its original articles of incorporation or by amending its articles, subject to a one-year waiting period.

Fair Price Statutes

The fair price statutes, predecessors of the business combination statutes, prohibit back-end transactions after a bidder acquires control unless the bidder pays a fair price or the transaction is approved by one of the methods described above. Price fairness is usually defined by a formula that assures shareholders a price at least equal to that paid in the front-end acquisition of control. Fair price statutes are meant to prevent front-end-loaded tender offers and acquisition programs. New York adopted a moratorium-fair price statute in 1986. N.Y. BCL §§1600–1613.

§39.4.3 Constitutionality of Third-Generation Antitakeover Legislation

The Supreme Court's supremacy clause (Williams Act preemption) and dormant commerce clause analysis in *CTS* provides a blueprint for analyzing the constitutionality of the third generation of state antitakeover statutes.

Preemption

Absent an explicit congressional preemptive intent, federal law preempts a state statute only if compliance with both the federal and state regulatory schemes is physically impossible or if state law frustrates the purpose of federal law. In *CTS*, the Court pointed out that a bidder could comply with both regimes because the Indiana statute's mandate of a shareholder vote within 50 days after the triggering acquisition was consistent with the Williams Act rules, which require only that tender offers be open for at least 20 business days. See §38.2.2.

The Court then held that the Indiana statute did not frustrate, and in fact was consistent with, the purposes of the Williams Act regime. The Court understood the Williams Act's purposes to provide shareholders disclosure and an opportunity to make unhurried buy-sell decisions during a takeover. The Court held that the Indiana statute's procedure for a collective shareholder vote did not interfere with these purposes. Instead the Court stated that the statute's inhibition of coercive bids was consistent with the Act's shareholder-protection purpose. The Court cavalierly dismissed the argument that the Indiana scheme's 50-day waiting period impeded hostile bids, to management's advantage. The Court said that the Williams Act does not guarantee a perfectly level playing field and accepted the traditional power of states to authorize procedures, such as staggered boards and supermajority shark repellents, that protect management.

Commerce Clause

Even in the absence of congressional action, the Supreme Court has interpreted the Constitution's commerce clause as prohibiting state regulation that places a discriminatory, inconsistent, or excessive burden on interstate commerce. The *CTS* dormant commerce clause analysis, like the preemption analysis, assumed that the Indiana statute was meant to protect shareholder welfare. The Court did not address the political history of state antitakeover statutes to favor in-state management and protect political support, jobs, and the local tax base.

The Court rejected the argument that the Indiana statute discriminated against bidders, who usually are out-of-staters, because the statute on its face treated all bidders identically. The statute's application only to corporations incorporated in Indiana avoided any possible interstate burden created by inconsistent state regulations. As for whether the burden on the national market in corporate control exceeded Indiana's interests, the Court assumed that the statute was meant to protect shareholders from coercion. The statute's restrictions on the bidder's voting rights, the Court held, simply regulated the "internal affairs" of a domestic corporation, a power historically resting in state hands. The Court declined to involve itself or other federal courts in the debate on the costs and benefits of takeovers.

Examples

1. The state of Utopia has a Control Share Acquisition Act modeled on the Indiana control share statute upheld by the Supreme Court in *CTS Corp. v. Dynamics Corp. of America*. Even though Marque Inc. is incorporated in Delaware, the Utopia statute applies to Marque because (1) more than 50 percent of its fixed U.S. assets are in Utopia and more than 50 percent of its U.S. employees are residents of Utopia; (2) it has more than 500 shareholders, of whom more than 10 percent are Utopia residents; and (3) its principal office is in Utopia. Alpha is worried about the effect of the Utopia statute on its bid for Marque.
   a. What is the effect on Alpha if it must comply with the Utopia statute?
   b. Assuming the statute's validity, can Alpha avoid it?

2. Alpha cannot afford to make a bid for Marque under the Utopia statute. The statute will require that it keep its tender offer open beyond the minimum 20-day period required by federal law. Alpha makes an any-and-all tender offer and assures shareholders the same price in any back-end merger after the tender offer is completed. It then challenges the Utopia statute's constitutionality.
   a. How is the Utopia statute different from the Indiana statute upheld in *CTS*?
   b. Do these differences affect the Utopia statute's constitutionality under a preemption analysis?
   c. Do these differences affect the Utopia statute's constitutionality under a dormant commerce clause analysis?

Explanations

1. a. Once Alpha acquires a triggering percentage of Marque's shares (20 percent, 33 percent, or 50 percent), all shares that exceed the threshold (so-called control shares) are stripped of voting rights. The voting rights can be restored only if Marque's public shareholders approve the re-enfranchisement. Alpha can seek a special shareholders' vote on the question in a meeting that must occur no later than 50 calendar days after the bid. This is about three weeks after Alpha could have purchased the shares under the SEC tender offer rule that imposes a minimum open period of 20 business days (about four weeks). Exchange Act Rule 14e-2. See §23.3.3.

The effect is to chill hostile takeovers of corporations covered by the statute. The 50-day waiting period creates great uncertainty for bidders. Even if a majority of shareholders tender their shares, the bidder will not know whether it bought control until the shareholders' meeting. The additional delay imposes significant additional financing costs and risks that the deal may not be approved or may be blocked during the extended waiting period by some firm-specific defense. In the takeover game, time and risk are money.

b. Perhaps. Bidders can deflect some of the risks of the statutory 50-day waiting period and shareholder vote. The Supreme Court in *CTS* suggested a bidder could make its bid contingent on shareholders giving their consents or proxies when they tender. In addition, others have suggested that a bidder could purchase shares but retain an option to resell them if the results of the meeting were unfavorable, in effect making the tender offer contingent on the shareholders' vote. Others have suggested the bidder could use the statute to compel a shareholders' meeting at which it could replace the board, and the new board could then enter into a friendly negotiated deal.

2. a. The Utopia statute is different in one constitutionally significant way. It is extraterritorial-not only does it apply to domestic corporations, but also to foreign corporations having significant contacts with the state. Utopia cannot justify the statute to carry out its historic role of defining the attributes of corporations incorporated in the state.

b. Probably not. Utopia's statute does not interfere with the process by which tender offers are made. Compliance with the timing, disclosure, best price, and proration requirements of the Williams Act regime remains unaffected. Nonetheless, Alpha might argue the statute's extraterritoriality and its application to any-and-all bids frustrate the Williams Act purpose of shareholder protection in takeovers.

The statute's extraterritoriality arguably conflicts with the Williams Act because it exposes a bidder to potentially irreconcilable or overlapping *state* requirements, a burden that may offend the Williams Act's philosophy of an even playing field for bidders and target management. If the Utopia and Delaware antitakeover statutes both apply, Alpha may well have to make a tender offer for 85 percent of Marque's stock (to avoid the Delaware statute) and wait 50 days for voting rights (to gain control under the Utopia statute). Nonetheless, the Supreme Court in *CTS* did not seem concerned about the burden on the bidder, as long as the burden can be seen as furthering shareholder protection and not significantly undermining the bidding process. In this case, if Delaware's statute can be seen as preventing low-price or coercive bids, the additional burden of complying with it would not seem to be preempted under the deferential *CTS* analysis. In other words,

Utopia might well have passed a statute combining the elements of a control share and moratorium statute. Even though compliance might impose additional costs on Alpha, which would have to carry financing commitments for a longer time and on more shares, CTS did not seem concerned with regulatory costs unless they actually interfere with the bidding process.

Alpha's any-and-all bid assures all shareholders an equal price and is less coercive than the partial bid before the Court in CTS. According to the CTS Court, one of the principal justifications for the Indiana statute was that it protected shareholders against structurally coercive bids. It is unlikely, however, that the Court would probe the strength of the state's interest in regulating an any-and-all bid. For purposes of preemption analysis, it is enough that the Utopia statute does not undermine the bidding process and serves the ostensible purpose of reduce collective action problems that shareholders face in any bid. After CTS, the extent to which a state antitakeover statute favors management over bidders does not seem significant.

c. Probably. The "extraterritorial" Utopia statute creates the possibility of inconsistent state regulation and is probably unconstitutional under the dormant commerce clause.

   In CTS, the Supreme Court made much of the Indiana statute's regulation of the "internal affairs" of *domestic* corporations. The Utopia statute undercuts the well-established corporate law doctrine that the state of incorporation regulates corporate shareholder-manager relationships, which would include such matters as shareholder voting rights and business combinations involving controlling shareholders. The doctrine provides certainty and stability and is taken as a given in securities trading markets and markets in corporate control. A number of lower courts since CTS have struck down extraterritorial antitakeover statutes.

   Nonetheless, the Utopia statute applies to only those foreign corporations whose assets and employees are mostly in the state, minimizing the possibility of inconsistencies. Bidders will have to comply with, at most, two statutes. In this case, Alpha can comply with both the Delaware and Utopia antitakeover statutes by bidding for 85 percent of Marque's shares and waiting out the 50-day period. It might be argued that except in cases of actual or probable inconsistency—that is, where the bidder is unable physically to comply with both at the same time—the commerce clause should not be understood as interfering with state prerogatives to define corporate relationships. Nonetheless, this interpretation of the dormant commerce clause is at odds with the Supreme Court's apparent desire in CTS to avoid federal involvement in such fine questions of corporate governance. CTS preserves (if not constitutionalizes) the incorporation-based system of private ordering in the United States.

The Utopia statute's regulation of all bids, including noncoercive any-and-all bids, arguably burdens the interstate market in corporate control more than it benefits local interests. Nonetheless, the *CTS* Court made clear that it would not engage in such balancing. As long as the statute's regulation is related to some theory of shareholder protection, the deference to state corporate law is controlling. Although the statute may discourage efficient bids to protect the local status quo, its economic folly does not make it unconstitutional. See *CTS* (Justice Scalia, concurring).

Table of Cases

References are to section numbers and to end-of-chapter explanations. For example, "E&E 9-2a" refers to Explanation 2a in Chapter 9.

Index